A CENTURY OF NEWS

100 Years of Front Pages, Photos and Memories from the Press & Sun-Bulletin

Presented by

Press & Sun-Bulletin
pressconnects.com

 • ISBN: 1-932129-64-2

Published by Pediment Publishing, a division of The Pediment Group, Inc. www.pediment.com printed in Canada

Table of Contents

BINGHAMTON PRESS
SUBMARINE BOAT'S VICTIMS
Grewsome Find of Divers in Sunken Craft
Home Patriotism Prosperity
WHAT THE BINGHAMTON PRESS STANDS FOR
BRITISH TO EXPOSE THE LAMAS SECRETS
ODELL DENIES ATTACK ON LABOR UNIONS
THE EVENING PRESS
President Is Assassinated; Texas Governor Wounded
Suspect Is Held
Press & Sun-Bulletin
pressconnects.com
SADDAM 'CAUGHT LIKE A RAT'
'GOT HIM'
Former dictator found hiding in hole near hometown
Low-level aides helped U.S. troops discover hideout
Nor'easter deals region a snowy hand
Total accumulation may exceed a foot
For some Tier families, joy tinged with reality

MEET ME
FAIR

Acknowledgments

Loyal readers from around Greater Binghamton helped make this book possible, and to them we are very grateful.

Dozens of readers brought front pages, old snapshots, and life's ephemera to share with us. Some readers asked us to come to their houses and inspect their collections.

This book would not have been possible without our readers. It was their loyalty that allowed us to survive and prosper during the last 100 years. They stored our product in safe places for decades. Yet, when we asked, they were willing to share their material with us. We'd also like to give special thanks to our local Broome County Historical Society, which over the past three years has helped us create these books for you to enjoy.

Bernie Griffin
President and Publisher
Press & Sun-Bulletin

Foreword

People who work for newspapers usually are in love with their jobs. It's a seductive business. Whether you work in the newsroom, advertising, circulation or another department, you find the newspaper becomes part of you. It's fun. It's important. It's essential.

For some reason, it always surprises us that our readers feel the same way. Frankly, we were amazed when dozens of our readers turned out, some on very cold nights, to share their lives with us.

They brought historic front pages: Man On Moon and President Is Assassinated. But they also brought pages and photos that captured some element of their lives. All of it was intensely personal. Some readers had one or two pages. Others had extensive collections they had inherited from their parents.

We also owe a deep debt to the legions of newspaper men and women who worked for the many papers that came before the Press & Sun-Bulletin. While we are celebrating the 100th anniversary of the Binghamton Press, we have ties to many other papers. We've included a few front pages from those papers as well.

All of the contributions to this book touched us deeply. We hope you enjoy reading this book as much as we liked putting it together.

Damage from the tornado of 1905. *Courtesy Broome County Historical Society*

L. Frank Little, first postmaster of the Endicott Post Office, 1905. He was a direct descendent of General Burnside. *Courtesy James Little*

Brown & Whitney Blocks, Nanticoke St., Union, N. Y.

View of Brown and Whitney blocks, Nanticoke Street, Union, 1905.
Courtesy Richard Gillespie

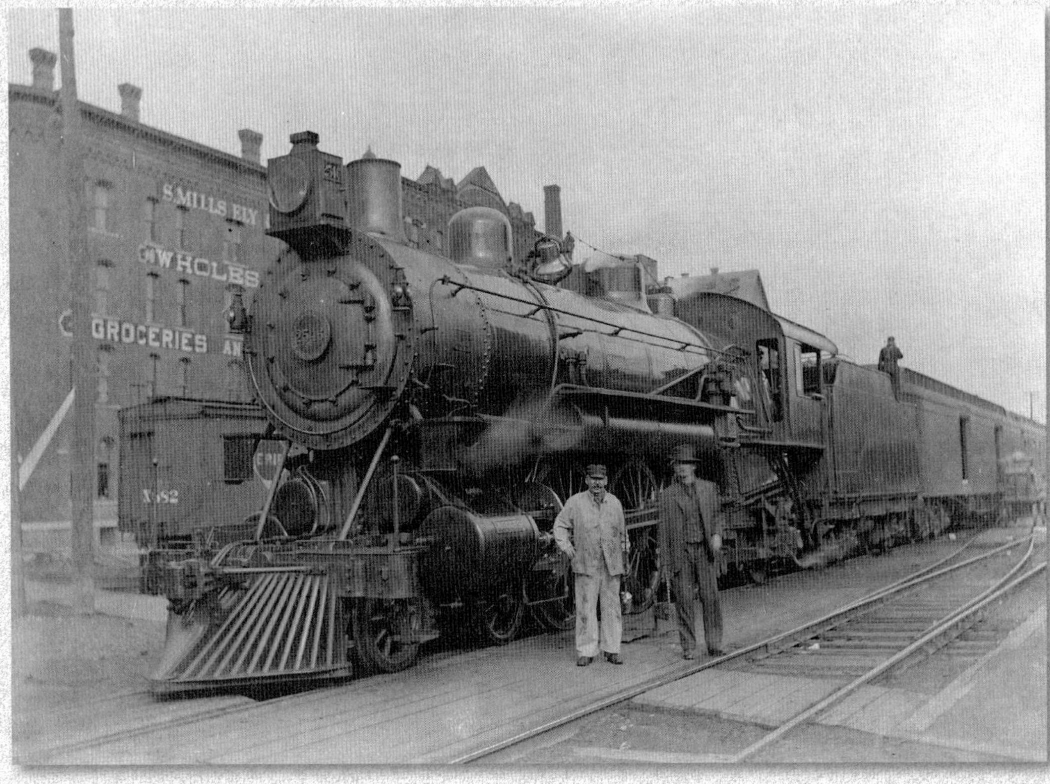
S.MILLS ELY
GROCERIES

Train parks in downtown Binghamton near the S. Mills Ely building, circa 1905. The building is now slated to become luxury housing in a plan to develop downtown Binghamton.
Courtesy Alan Jewell

1904 - 1909

The Binghamton Press is launched

PART ONE
Last Edition

BINGHAMTON PRESS

Weather
Cloudy tonight and Tuesday; occasional rains.

VOL. I. NO. 1 MONDAY EVENING, APRIL 11, 1904. FORTY-FOUR PAGES AND SOUVENIR MAP. PRICE ONE CENT

SUBMARINE BOAT'S VICTIMS

SECURITY MUTUAL BUILDING
MORE INDUSTRIES
GOOD CITIZENSHIP
GREATER BINGHAMTON
THE PRESS BUILDING
GOOD GOVERNMENT
CAPITAL
LABOR
COPYRIGHTED 1904 BY THE BINGHAMTON PRESS.
Home
Patriotism
Prosperity

WHAT THE BINGHAMTON PRESS STANDS FOR

Grewsome Find of Divers in Sunken Craft

Ten Bodies Discovered--Eleventh Supposed to Have Been Fired Out in the Torpedo Tube by His Doomed Comrades

Special Cable to the New York Journal and Binghamton Press.

LONDON, April 11.—Details of the grewsome find of the divers who succeeded in raising the sunken submarine boat A 1 reached here today in a dispatch of the Portsmouth correspondent of the Daily News.

The submarine craft was run down by the steamer Berwick Castle off the National lighiship.

There were eleven men in the submarnie boat at the time. The divers found only ten bodies. It is believed that the eleventh man was placed in the torpedo discharging tube and fired out, the object being to have him regain the surface with the view of getting aid to rescue his companions from the sunken vessel.

The divers stated that there had been no explosion. The awtertight doors had been closed, and the crews were enclosed in the secondary chambers.

It is surmised that it was impossible for them to work the apparatus and regai nthe surface. It is evident that water must have percolated into her inner compartment, as a small fish and crabs were found therein. The bodies were recognizable but had suffered from being eaten by crabs.

On the last visit of the diver it was ascertained that a message written on a sheet torn from a note book had been left by the crew. The wording of the message has not yet been made known.

BRITISH TO EXPOSE THE LAMAS SECRETS

Present Ruler of Tibet First in A Century to Escape Poisoning in His Youth

LONDON, April 11.—Strange developments are expected from the British expedition into Tibet. Irrespective of the success of Col. Younghusband, the English government is committed to a policy which must eventually end in breaking down Tibetan exclusiveness. More than this, it may bring about great changes in Asiatic religious matters.

The Dalai Lama, or Buddist Pope, has obtained much of his prestige through the mystery surrounding him. Much of this mystery must inevitably disappear with an open road to Lhasa. On the other hand, the Lama may take a more active part in ruling the affairs of the Buddhist church.

The present Lama is twenty-nine years old, and is the only Lama for the past hundred years who has reached this age. The Lamas are selected in their infancy and naturally during their infancy the church is governed by the priests of his entourage. In past times these have been so jealous of their power that they always poisoned the Lama as soon as he was old enough to show signs of wanting to rule himself.

For some reason which is not at all clear the present Lama was allowed to live, and is said to be a person of some force, who desires to shake off the shadowy rule of China, and govern the country entirely himself. At the present time the Chinese Amban, or resident minister, is waiting on the Chinese frontier of Tibet without daring to enter. He asked for a guard of 2,000 Chinese troops, but has not been able to get them and is afraid to complete the journey alone.

Very likely, if the Lama has his way, or if the British succeed in gaining the upper hand, the Amban will never come in. The chief thing the Tibetans would lose by cutting off the Chinese connected would be the Chinese annual subsidy, which consists of a vast quantity of tea for all of the monasteries and priestly establishments around Lhasa. Whether the gain of political independence would be considered adequate compensation for the loss of the tea is not known, but it is hardly likely that the spirit of the "Boston tea party" obtains the Lhasa.

Should the Lama continue his attitude of hostility to the British there is the possibility that the English will retaliate by supporting a rival Grand Lama, who resides at Tashe Lhumpo, in Northern India. Like his rival in Lhasa, he claims to be an incarnation of Buddha. In the rival claimants there is material for a great Buddhist schism.

KNIGHT FOR GOVERNOR

HIS BOOM GROWING

Ante - Republican Convention Talk for Mayor of Buffalo.

State Arranged for Delegates-at-Large to National Gathering at Chicago—Col. Dunn Dallies.

(Special to The Binghamton Press.)

NEW YORK, April 11.—The most important development prior to the Republican State convention, which meets to-morrow in Carnegie Hall, New York, is the sudden and apparently sincere boom for Erastus C. Knight, Mayor of Buffalo, for the nomination of Governor.

While Mr. Knight has been prominently mentioned at various times, it was the attitude of Gov. Odell yesterday that showed how strong his chances are.

Mr. Knight has been slated as one of the four electors at large to be voted on to-morrow, but yesterday, through the efforts of the Governor, he was made the alternate at large for the Governor himself.

List of Delegates.

The list as now definitely decided on for the delegates at large, with their alternates, is as follows:

Senator Thomas C. Platt, with Louis Stern, president of the Republican club in New York, as alternate.

Senator Chauncey M. Depew, with Charles R. Banks of Brooklyn, a wealthy tea merchant, as alternate.

Gov. B. B. Odell, Jr., with Erastus C. Knight of Buffalo as alternate.

Former Governor Frank S. Black,

(Continued on Page Three.)

ANOTHER HISTORICAL SUPPLEMENT COMING

Because of the great demand from advertisers for space in the first number of The Binghamton Press, it was necessary to divide the Souvenir Historical Supplement into two editions. Another supplement like Part III of this issue will be published next week in four colors, giving numerous illustrations and interesting descriptive matter concerning the leading cities and towns in the Press' parish not covered in today's section.

SUSPECT HELD IN MURDER CASE OF MABLE PAGE

Charles L. Tucker's Examination Continued Until April 21.

WALTHAM, Mass., April 11.—Charles L. Tucker, who was arrested Saturday night on the charge of having murdered Miss Mabel Page in her home in Weston, on March 31, was arraigned in court here this morning. Through his counsel he entered a plea of not guilty and upon the request of counsel for the government for a delay of ten days, the case was continued to April 21.

At the conclusion of the proceedings Tucker was remanded to the East Cambridge jail. He is held without bail.

The finding of a knife in his home, which was broken, and also a knife sheath found in a wagon in which Tucker rode to Weston on the day of the murder, are the strongest links of the chain of evidence against the prisoner. When the knife was shown to Tucker, he admitted that it was his.

After finding the knife the fact developed that the sheath which was found in the wagon fitted the knife. On the sheath were imprints of teeth as if some one held it in his mouth and forcibly sunk his incisors into it. A plaster cast of Tucker's teeth has been taken to compare them with the imprints on the sheath.

FELL FROM THE BRIDGE.

Section Hand Reports to Police a Probably Fatal Accident.

(Special to The Binghamton Press.)

Elmira, April 11.—"Joe" Suska, a section hand living in Lowmanville, has reported to the authorities that as he and John Giuam were walking from Elmira on the Lackawanna tracks last night Giuam fell off the Newton creek bridge, east of Elmira and he believes that he was drowned.

Captain Hartigan and four officers went to the spot where the accident was said to have occurred, but were unable to locate the body.

CHARGED WITH DESERTION.

Triangle Man Arraigned in Elmira Police Court.

Accused of desertion from the United States army and of being drunk, Ralph Graham of Triangle, this county, got a 20 days' sentence in the Elmira police court today. At the expiration of his sentence he will be turned over to the government.

THE CAT CAME BACK COVERING 337 MILES

Salt Lake Man Tries in Vain to Get Rid of Animal.

SALT LAKE CITY, April 11.—A cat owned by John M. West, of this city has broken all known records in the matter of finding its way home over a long distance.

To get rid of the cat, Mr. West placed the animal in a bag and concealed it under the seat of a coach on the San Pedro, Los Angeles and Salt Lake railroad. The cat was discovered and thrown off the train at Caloontes, Nev., 337 miles from its starting point.

Today it is home, having walked 337 miles across two mountain ranges, and many miles of desert. The cat will be permitted to stay.

MEMORIAL SERVICE HELD.

WASHINGTON, April 11.—The House of Representatives yesterday conducted memorial services in memory of the late Representatives Foerderer and Burke of Pennsylvania.

SUNDAY'S EXCISE ARRESTS.

BUFFALO, April 11.—Ninety-seven arrests were made here yesterday for alleged violations of the excise law.

BALTIC SQUADRON GOING EAST

Russian Fleets to Be Re-enforced by the End of August.

COMMANDER KULEZICKI REPORTS TO THE CZAR

Chee Foo Dispatch Says 2,000 Russian Artillery, With Sixty Guns, Has Reached New Chwang.

London, April 11.—A Paris despatch to the Times says that a telegram from St. Petersburg states that Commander Kulezicki handed a report to the Czar on Friday concerning the proposed voyage of the Baltic squadron to the Far East by way of the sea of Kara.

Commander Kulezicki says he will be able to get the squadron to its destination by the end of August.

A Chee Foo despatch to the Times says that about 2,000 Russian artillery and sixty guns arrived at New Chwang on Thursday.

GREEN CASE ADJOURNED.

Brooklyn Judge Sets Down Local Postoffice Case for June 30.

Adjournment was taken in the case of Senator George E. Green before Judge Thomas in Brooklyn on Saturday until June 30. The lawyers asked for three days to present their arguments and press of business in Judge Thomas's court would not permit of going on with it at that time.

ODELL DENIES ATTACK ON LABOR UNIONS

Explains His Treason Remark At Dinner of Sqadron A Saturday Night

NEW YORK, April 11.—Governor Odell declared to-day that he had not attacked labor unions, as wa intimated at the dinner of Squadron A on Saturday night. He said he had never mentioned labor unions in connection with the national guard.

"What I did say," said the Governor, "was that the national guard was a state organization and was part of the state government and that it was manifestly improper for that reason to stigmatize any one because of his membership in the national guard.

"Any organization that sought to do that or to ostracize those of their members who belonged to the national guard, I said, came dangerously near to treason. That was all I said which could have given rise to the reports of my speech."

SANTA FE STRIKE IS NOW THREATENED

WASHINGTON, April 11.—Indications point to an open rupture between the Atchison, Topeka & Santa Fe Railway Company and the International Association of Machinists, which will probably cause the declaration of a general strike in all the shops of the system within two days.

Previous to its adjournment Saturday the executive board of the association of delegated to President O'Connell authority to receive the election returns of the locals and take action conforming to the sentiment of the members of the association. All of the returns have not been received, but so far as can be determined now, the majority in favor of a strike is overwhelming.

President O'Connell will leave this city Thursday evening for Denver, Colo.

"No announcements can be made now," he said today, "because we have yet some locals to hear from. It looks though, as if a strike cannot be averted."

In case the men go out, Mr. O'Connell will make his headquarters in Denver from which place the general policy of the strike on the Santa Fe system will be handled. Some 15,000 machinists, emloyed in shops and round houses, extending from Chicago to Los Angeles will be involved.

The Binghamton Press sprang to life April 11, 1904, a very good time to start a newspaper.

Willis Sharpe Kilmer, armed with millions from his family's patent medicine business, launched the Press, partly in response to relentless criticism from the Binghamton Republican.

The new paper promised, as the Rev. John J. McDonald put it, to be "an honest, fearless and independent paper." The paper was an immediate hit and soon became the dominant news source in the valley.

The economy was ready to boom. Between 1900 and 1910, the population of Broome, Tioga and Chenango counties grew by 10 percent to 143,328 people. Endicott Johnson was about to start decades of rapid growth, and the forerunner of IBM was building its first offices in Endicott.

Local news occasionally made it to the front page. Editors put national and world news on the front page, serving readers who unlike today's readers had no radio, no television and no Internet. Those first editors and reporters established the sense of urgency that serves the paper even today.

April 11, 1904: The very first edition of the Binghamton Press. *Courtesy Broome County Historical Society*

"The Vacant Chair" Can not be filled, but that vacant room, house or office which you have for rent can easily be filled through the use of The Binghamton Press Classified Columns.

BINGHAMTON PRESS

The Weather
Snow tonight and Tuesday: warmer tonight.

VOL. 2, NO. 75. | LAST EDITION | MONDAY EVENING, JANUARY 9, 1905. | TWELVE PAGES | PRICE ONE CENT

BINGHAMTON POSTOFFICE ROBBERY!

YELLOW FEVER IN CANAL ZONE

EXISTENCE OF SCOURGE IS ADMITTED

Three Cases Were Reported Previous to Dec. 19, and Several Have Contracted the Disease Since.

MRS. JOHN SEAGER IS ONE OF THE VICTIMS

She Was the Wife of Chief Engineer Wallace's Secretary—Typhoid, Also, Is Feared.

Washington, Jan. 9.—Full official confirmation to the rumor that yellow fever had broken out at Panama is given in the report of the Public Health and Marine Hospital service.

It is shown that three cases had appeared as early as Dec. 19. Several additional cases have since appeared.

That the situation is serious is attested by the recent death from yellow fever of Mrs. John Seager of this city, wife of the secretary of Chief Engineer Wallace.

The Canal Commission has persisted in denying knowledge that fever existed at Panama. The report of the plague has excited the clerks and employes of the commission on the Isthmus. Many are anxious to get away. The reports will seriously hamper the canal work by keeping persons from enlisting in the work.

When the Isthmus Canal zone came officially under the jurisdiction of the United States on May 19, 1904, the eradication of yellow fever was one of the problems the government had to solve.

Governor Davis established his headquarters at Culebra, and issued a proclamation setting forth the articles of government. Climatic conditions and sanitation at once demanded the attention of those who had the interests of the new American residents to take into consideration.

What Barrett Said.

John Barrett, the American minister to Panama, less than four months ago said:

"The disagreeable and unhealthy features of the Panama climate have been ridiculously overstated. During July and August there was not a single uncomfortable night for sleeping. The average days were not hotter than those of New York and Washington.

"There has been hardly a single in-

(Continued on Page 5, Column 3.)

NEGRO DIES IN CHAIR AT SING SING

William Spencer, Who Murdered Charles F. McFarlane, Is Successfully Electrocuted This Morning.

DEATH RESULTS WITH THE FIRST CONTACT

Prisoner Is Accompanied to Death Chamber by Priests and Dies Praying for Mercy.

Ossining, Jan. 7.—Crucifix in hand and with a plea for mercy on his lips, William Spencer, colored, who shot and killed Charles F. McFarlane in New York city in June, 1903, was electrocuted at Sing-Sing prison at two minutes before 6 o'clock this morning.

"... [illegible] ...ion was one of the most successful I have ever seen," said Warden Johnson.

Spencer was dead after the first contact.

Little groups of witnesses gathered in the Warden's office at 5:45 o'clock this morning and five minutes later marched to the death house. State Electrician Davis and his assistants were in readiness to carry out the law's sentence. A lever was pushed down and the bank of incandescent lights across the arms of the chair sent up a flash of light which showed that the machinery was in perfect working order.

Shakes Hands With the Keeper.

A nod from the State electrician, and Principal Keeper Connaughton disappeared through the little door leading from the death chamber to the death house. "All ready," said the principal keeper, and as the condemned man stepped from his cell he grasped the officer by the hand and bade him good-by, an unusual proceeding since good-by's are ordinarily said before the hour of electrocution arrives.

With Spencer and the principal keeper walked Father Mahoney and his assistant, Father Martin, of St. Augustine's, Ossining, who were with the condemned man during his last hours, offering him spiritual consolation. Spencer became a convert to the Catholic faith eight months ago, and as he walked into the death

(Continued on Page 5, Column 2)

MONOPOLIES
SPECIAL PRIVILEGES
FAVORITISM
GREED
ILLEGAL TRUSTS
THE TARIFF
ROOSEVELT

Getting Ready for a Little Practical Work In Forestry

FLEET IS IN DANGER

Jap Squadron Said to Be After Baltic Ships

St. Petersburg, Jan. 9.—Grave fears have been created in St. Petersburg by the rumor that a strong Japanese squadron is en route at all possible speed for Madagascar to meet Admiral Rodjestvensky and take advantage of the Baltic vessels while they are undergoing repairs. If the Russian vessels try to escape, the Japanese will be able to overtake them, it is said, as Admiral Rodjestvensky's vessels have inferior speed to the Japanese.

FOCK AND SMIRNOFF WILL GO TO JAPAN

Headquarters Japanese Army at Port Arthur (via Fusan), Jan. 9.—Lieutenant Generals Fock and Smirnoff have decided to go to Japan as prisoners of war. Gen. Smirnoff was in command of the forts at Port Arthur and Gen. Fock commanded the fourth division of the army here. Gen. Fock says he will drill his men in Japan.

About one-half of the Russian officers will go to Japan and share with their men the fate of prisoners of war. There are five Russian Admirals at Port Arthur, one of whom will go to Japan. Among the Admirals is a Prince.

The transfer of prisoners at Port Arthur was completed at 4:30 p. m. yesterday. The total number of officers transferred was 878: men, 23,-491. It is understood that the Sanyo railway has been instructed to make preparations to transport 20,-000 Russian prisoners from Shimonoseki to Kure. It is probable that the prisoners will be quartered near Kure.

The most seriously sick and wounded will be left at Port Arthur in the field hospitals for the present. Those capable of being moved will be taken to Japan when arrangements for housing them have been completed.

EARL DE MONTALT DEAD.

Holyhead, Jan. 9.—The Earl de Montalt died suddenly here today while on his way to his home in Tipperary, Ireland.

The deceased had been a representative peer for Ireland since 1882. He was one of the speakers in the House of Lords in 1882.

ONE DEAD OF RAT POISON; 11 SICK

Italian Laborers Robbed in a Boarding House—Looking for Padrone.

Buffalo, Jan. 9.—In the town of Belvidere, near Olean, Guiseppe Rossi is dead, another is dying and 10 Italian railroad laborers are very sick at a boarding house. Somebody fed them rat poison on Friday night. Mrs. Minnie Middelano, wife of the padrone who kept the boarding house, was arrested for drunkenness on Friday night at Olean. She is now in jail at Mayville. The District Attorney of Allegheny county says he will hold her on suspicion when her sentence is over.

Pasquale Middelano, the padrone, is still at large. The police of all the towns hereabouts are looking for him. Sheriff's deputies are scouring the country, and the Buffalo police have been notified to watch the Italian colony.

Guiseppe Rossi, the murdered man, was robbed, the police say. He had quite a roll of bills on the day before he died, which is now missing. The others who were poisoned were robbed, too, the police think, though how much the total booty amounts to they are not sure.

AMERICANS ARE HONORED BY FRANCE

Four Are Decorated With the Badge of the Legion of Honor.

Paris, Jan. 9.—The list of those who had been decorated with the badge of the Legion of Honor, announced today, included the following Americans:

Mr. Kosminski, the general agent of the Compagne-Trans-Atlantic Company; Frederic Courtland Penfield, the New York journalist and magazine writer; Mr. Pintard, president of the French Society; Bien-Faisance of Philadelphia, and Charles H. Steinway, the piano manufacturer.

STEAMSHIP ARRIVAL.

New York, Jan. 9.—Arrived: Steamship Zeeland from Antwerp.

PEABODY SAYS HE WILL NOT CONTEST

He Is Bitter Over the Seating of Adams In Colorado

Denver, Jan. 9.—Governor Peabody says he will offer no contest. While Governor-elect Alva Adams prophesied a great tidal wave of prosperity for Colorado to follow the action of the Legislature in seating him as chief executive of the State, his defeated opponent was bitter in his denunciation of his supposed friend.

"I was defeated through treachery in my own camp," he said. "I am through with false friends. I wash my hands of them, and they shall not have opportunity to trouble me more."

The Governor added that he would do nothing further to save the State He added that, so far as he was concerned, Colorado might go "to the dogs."

"I shall not contest," said Peabody. "They want me to say I will contest so that they may have a threat to compel the confirmation of the two Supreme Court appointees. I do not care whether they are confirmed or whether Adams appoints others."

"I was confident all along," said Adams, "the manhood of Republican legislators would assert itself and that some of them at least would refuse to become a party to stealing my seat."

In other quarters it is declared Governor Peabody is sure to file a contest immediately after Governor Adams is inaugurated Tuesday. In any event, he has several days in which to change his mind.

Party leaders have been trying to explain to Peabody why the corporations deserted him so suddenly, but no explanations moved the Governor. He is extremely bitter over his defeat, which he attributes to the machinations of former Senator E. O. Wolcott. Officers of the Western Federation of Miners, who recently recalled their circular advising deported men to return to the district, have sent out a new one telling all former residents they are now at liberty to come back and guaranteeing they will not be molested.

AETNA VAULT CLOSED.

Hartford, Jan. 9.—Since Thursday the vault of the Aetna Life Insurance Company has remained closed owing to some trouble with the locks and though expert safe men have worked constantly on it since they have been unable to open it. It is thought the big door will have to be drilled.

SYRACUSE BEATS YALE.

Syracuse, Jan. 9.—In one of the hardest fought games ever seen in this city the Syracuse University basketball team Saturday night defeated the Yale five by the score of 19 to 15.

JAMES O. PEABODY,
Who Says That He Will Not Contest Adams' Claim to the Colorado Governorship.

PLAN DESTRUCTION OF CONSTANTINOPLE

Turkish Officials Alarmed by a Report Regarding the Bulgarians.

Constantinople, Jan. 9.—The Porte has been thrown into a state of alarm bordering on panic by a report that the Bulgarian revolutionists have planned the destruction of Constantinople. According to the report which has reached the Yildiz Kiosk, the Bulgarians have concealed a great quantity of explosives near Dedeaghatch, in the district of Salonika, which is at a railway junction, and is on the line which affords the most rapid transportation from Constantinople to the Turkish frontier.

The railway authorities have appealed to the Minister of War for protection. The Minister has met their appeal by ordering that reinforcements be placed along the line.

WOMAN BURNED TO DEATH.

Saratoga, Jan. 9.—Blazing sparks from a parlor match last evening communicated with the clothing of Mrs. Lydia M. Pulling, aged 70 years causing her death. She was temporarily alone in her cottage.

FOURNIER TO PRESIDE

French Member of the Dogger Bank Commission Is Elected as Its Permanent President.

BODY THEN RETIRES TO FORMUL[illegible]

Paris, Jan. 9.—The international commission, formed to investigate the Dogger Bank tragedy, reconvened this morning. The first order of business was the presentation of Admiral Spaun, of Austria, and Admiral Dubassoff, the new member for Russia. Admiral Spaun, as the oldest Admiral in the commission, called the body to order. He then proposed Admiral Fournier, the French member, as permanent president. In his nominating speech he said the honor should be conferred on Fournier not only as an act showing their appreciation of the hospitality of France, but also in pursuance of the common aim of the members to arrive at a prompt solution of the matter at issue.

Admiral Fournier was unanimously elected chairman. He addressed the commission, alluding to the example of wisdom and moderation given by King Edward and Czar Nicholas, in constituting the commission.

The body then retired for secret deliberation to agree on the regulations which shall govern the proceedings of the commission.

A second meeting has been announced for this afternoon. It is expected that today's program will be continued, and that two meetings will be held daily until the questions are settled.

SNOW STORMS IN MANCHURIA.

St. Petersburg, Jan. 9.—The newspaper Viestnik reports that heavy snow storms are raging in Manchuria. At the Nijnendinsk and Taischet stations on the Trans-Siberian railroad 70 locomotives have been held up by the storm, delaying the schedule of the military trains for three days. One hundred other trains are snow-bound on the Samaro-Slatoustovski line.

FIRE IN SPRINGFIELD.

Springfield, Mass., Jan. 9.—Fire which started on the third floor of the Springfield Door, Sash and Blind factory, 15 East Court street, early this morning, destroyed the top floor of the building causing a loss of $50,000.

CLERK A. F. GRAY IS ACCUSED OF STEALING LETTERS FROM MAIL

ARRESTED EARLY THIS MORNING

Eight Letters Supposed to Contain Money Said to Have Been Found in His Pockets.

MAIL ADDRESSED TO THE EDSON COMPANY

Complaint Made Some Days Ago and Investigated by Postal Authorities. Arrest Made by U. S. Marshal Black.

Arthur F. Gray, a distributor of city mail in the Binghamton postoffice was arrested at 6:35 o'clock this morning by United States Marshal S. F. Black, and lodged in jail. Up to a late hour this afternoon no formal charge had been made against him, but it is understood that he will be arraigned before United States Commissioner Hall tomorrow charged with stealing letters from the United States mail.

When arrested it is said that Gray had eight letters addressed to the American Advertising company of this city in his pocket. These letters have not been opened, but they are supposed to contain small sums of money. It is said that they were taken from the mail this morning by Gray while he was sorting.

The American Advertising Company, founded by Harris W. Edson, does a large mail order business. The company within the last 60 days has made several complaints to the Postoffice Department at Washington that mail addressed to the company had never been delivered. As a result of these complaints Postoffice Inspector Thomas H. Fuller was sent to Binghamton.

The Binghamton office was at once placed under surveillance and Postmaster Roberts was requested to detail a man to watch the distribution of mail. Assistant Postmaster A. K. Roberts reached the office shortly after 4 o'clock this morning, confident that in a few hours he would solve the mystery. Gray is employed as distributor of the city mail, sorting the leters arriving for distribution in this city from outside points.

He arrived at the office at 4:50 o'clock and, unaware of the presence of watchers, hung up his outer clothing and proceeded with his morn[illegible] duties. While sorting a bunch of [illegible], he was seen to slip his hand inside his vest, as though concealing a parcel.

A messenger was at once dispatched for United States Marshal Black and continuous watch was kept on the man. Other letters were secreted by him, it is charged. Marshal Black arrived at the office at 6 o'clock and Gray was taken into Postmaster Roberts' private office, where eight letters were found in the inside

(Continued on Page 4.)

ARTHUR F. GRAY,
Postoffice Clerk Arrested This Morning, With U. S. Mail in His Possession.

MOODY ON BEEF TRUST

He Pronounces Packers' Operations an "Unlawful Restraint of Commerce Among the States."

ATTORNEY GENERAL BEFORE SUPREME COURT

Washington, Jan. 9.—Attorney General Moody made the argument for the Government before the Supreme Court of the United States this afternoon in the "Beef Trust" case. He said in part:

"Let not the offense of these defendants be obscured by any refinement concerning the details of their product. Controlling 80 per cent of the fresh meat industry of the whole country, they sit down at their slaughtering and packing establishments, and with the aid of the telegraph their countless agents and attorneys spread throughout the country, clothing their transactions and sheltering their misconduct by ciphers and secret codes, lower or raise, and when thus lowered or raised, fix and maintain absolutely, as among themselves, the price of every pound of one of the great necessities of life, as it enters and follows the channels of interstate commerce.

"This is an unlawful restraint of commerce among the States, and was so declared in the Addison Pipe case, from which all the ingenuity of counsel cannot distinguish the case at bar."

MRS. ROGERS MUST HANG, SAYS BELL

Vermont's Governor Will Not Interfere in Her Behalf.

St. Johnsbury, Vt., Jan. 9.—Gov. Bell, being asked today what action he would take in the case of Mrs. Mary Rogers of Bennington, sentenced to be hanged Feb. 7 for the murder of her husband, replied that he should let the law take its course.

BISHHOP SPAULDING BETTER.

Peoria, Ill., Jan. 9.—Bishop Spaulding was reported at 8 o'clock this morning as still improving, and his physicians hold out hope of ultimate entire recovery. He passed a good night.

CONTENTS OF TODAY'S PRESS.

COMPANY FORMED TO BUILD TUNNELS

"Hudson Companies" Organized With a Capital Stock of $21,000,000.

Albany, Jan. 9.—The "Hudson Companies," formed to construct, equip, and prepare for operation tunnels, railroads, and tunnel railroads in the State of New York and New Jersey filed a certificate of incorporation with the Secretary of State today. The concern is also empowered to hold rights by lease or purchase of real estate and water, and to acquire or construct factories and mills.

The amount of capital stock is $21,000,000 of which $5,000,000 is common stock and $16,000,000 preferred. Two hundred ten thousand shares of stock are to be issued at a par value of $100.

SHAMEFUL ATTACK ON AN OLD WOMAN

Mrs. Ward Maltreated and Kept Captive for Over 24 Hours.

Petersham, Mass., Jan. 9.—Compelled at the point of a gun to submit to assault and to cook food for a young desperado, Mrs. Elsino O. Ward, 65 years of age, was kept a captive in her own home on a lonesome road, two miles from the center of Petersham, from about 5:30 Tuesday afternoon to 10 o'clock Wednesday night, when her assailant departed with threats that if the woman stuck her head out of the house he would blow it off with his shotgun.

January 9, 1905: This edition of the Binghamton Press featured coverage of the Binghamton post office robbery. *Microfilm archives*

QUICK SALES VIA THE BINGHAMTON PRESS WANT AD ROUTE

BINGHAMTON PRESS

The Weather
Thunderstorms tonight and Wednesday; cooler tonight.

VOL. 3, NO. 49 — LAST EDITION — TUESDAY EVENING, JUNE 6, 1905 — FOURTEEN PAGES — PRICE ONE CENT

TORNADO WORKS HAVOC ON SOUTH SIDE OF CITY

M. DELCASSE SUBMITS HIS RESIGNATION

French Foreign Minister Again Gives Up His Portfolio Owing to Complications in the Moroccan Situation.

PREMIER ROUVIER IS FILLING HIS OFFICE

It Is Regarded as Significant That German Chancellor Should Be Made a Prince the Same Day.

Paris, June 6.—It is officially announced that M. Delcasse, the French Minister of Foreign Affairs, has resigned. Premier Rouvier has assumed charge of the foreign office temporarily.

The action of M. Delcasse in resigning, it is understood, was prompted by the fresh crisis which has arisen in the Moroccan question, owing to the refusal of the Sultan to accept the French reform proposals.

His Former Resignation.

Several weeks ago, when the Moroccan question was occupying the attention of the Cabinet to the exclusion of almost every other subject, M. Delcasse offered his resignation, but was persuaded to continue in office. Ever since it has become known that the Sultan had declined to agree to the policy outlined by France, it has been rumored that unless the cabinet unanimously supported him in the policy he had pursued in the Moroccan affair that the Foreign Minister would surrender his portfolio. Some of the ministers, it is reported, have been inclined to question the wisdom of Delcasse's plans in regard to the Morocco policy, and it is said this led to the resignation as M. Delcasse did not relish this criticism on the part of the other ministers.

Significant Circumstances.

It is regarded as somewhat significant that the honor conferred upon Chancellor von Buelow by Kaiser William who has elevated his prime minister to the rank of Prince, should have been announced on the very day that M. Delcasse resigned.

The resignation of M. Delcasse was undoubtedly caused on account of the Moroccan question, and his retirement means that he failed in his policy toward that country. Von Buelow, who is the chancellor of the German Empire, conducted the German negotiations with the Sultan through the special embassies sent to Fez, which resulted in the rejection of the French plans for reforms in Morocco, is regarded by the Kaiser, his diplomatic victory [illegible] being openly celebrated.

M. DELCASSE.

SIX MEN HURT.

Harrisburg, Pa., June 6.—The mail express [illegible] on the Pennsylvania railroad last night, ran into a freight train at a switch near Newport, and six men [illegible] slightly injured. Four freight cars, two express cars and the engines of both trains were wrecked.

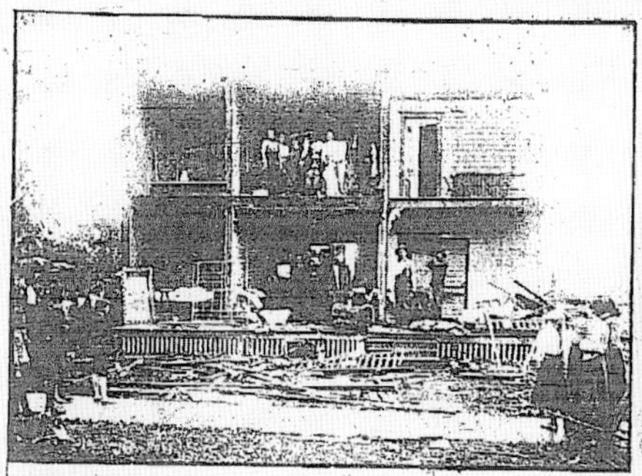

Photographs by The Binghamton Press Staff Photographer.

SOME SCENES WHERE THE TORNADO WAS AT ITS HEIGHT.

Top Row, Left—House in which Mr. and Mrs. George W. Thompson resided on the first floor and Mr. and Mrs. T. C. Young on the second floor at 20 Livingston street. Right—Barn belonging to J. W. Kinney of 239 Vestal avenue, which was completely turned over and in which two horses were imprisoned and freed by the firemen. Bottom Row, Left—The home of James Hartigan on Van Buren street. Mr. and Mrs. Hartigan were picked up in front of the house and their 6 year old boy was rescued from the debris under the gable at the left of the picture. Middle—Scene on New street, near the front of the New Street School. Right—House owned by A. D. Yeager at 6 and 6½ Gifford street, showing the bedroom in which Mrs. Yeager was sleeping and which she left a few seconds before the tornado struck the house.

GAYNOR AND GREENE ARE EXTRADITED

In a Lengthy Opinion Commissioner Lafontaine Decides Against the Two Men Wanted by United States.

THEY WILL BE GIVEN UP TO THIS COUNTRY

Commissioner Reviews the Evidence Against Them in Connection with Carter's Crime—Committed to Jail.

Montreal, June 6.—Extradition Commissioner Lafontaine delivered judgment in the extradition proceedings of the United States against Gaynor and Greene this morning. His judgment was the most lengthy ever delivered in extradition cases in Canada, occupying 150 pages of foolscap.

It was delivered in the presence of a large crowd of attorneys and is considered of marked importance in extradition matters. The following are the closing words of the judgment committing the prisoners for extradition:

"On the whole my conclusion is that the allegation of conspiracy to defraud the United States as being in existence between Carter and the accused on or about July 1, 1897, is proven, to wit: That Carter, a public officer and agent and trustee of the United States was convicted in the United States of fraud as declared by the Supreme Court of the United States in the case of Carter against McClaughey; that his offense of fraud and participation therein are punishable by laws of both Canada and the demanding country; that the accused have participated in the offense of fraud committed by Carter, for which he was so convicted; that fraud by an agent and trustee and participation therein are extraditable crimes.

"Second—That Carter was guilty in the United States and was convicted of embezzlement, which offense is known under our law by the term of theft, the difference in the name of the offense in the two countries being immaterial; that the accused have participated by their conspiracy with Carter in the embezzlement (theft) so committed by him; that such a participation is punishable by the laws of both countries and is an extradition crime.

"Third—That on July 6, 1897, the accused have fraudulently received from Carter the sum of $575,749.90, knowing then that the same had been embezzled (stolen) by him and that the offense of receiving stolen property is punishable under the laws of both countries and is by treaty section 3 an extradition crime. Consequently I determine that the accused must be committed to jail pending surrender."

ULTIMATUM TO RUSSIANS

Admiral Enquist Is Notified Either to Sail Within 24 Hours or to Dismantle Ships of His Squadron.

RUSSIAN COMMANDER AWAITS INSTRUCTIONS

Manila, June 6.—The ultimatum of Washington directing Admiral Enquist, commander of the Russian warships, which [illegible] harbor here, either to sail at [illegible] hours or dismantle his ships, was delivered to the Admiral this morning by Executive Secretary Ferguson, who boarded the flagship to deliver the message.

Admiral Enquist is waiting for instructions from St. Petersburg before making known his intentions. The repairs to the damaged ships have already commenced.

STEAMER CAN'T LAND.

Ogdensburg, June 6.—The Canadian Marine Department has refused to admit the American steamer Dorothy to the government drydock at Kingston, Ont., because she is laden with dynamite. In coming up the St. Lawrence, the Dorothy lost her propeller and she was towed to Kingston for repairs. She will probably go to Buffalo.

STEAMSHIP ARRIVALS.

New York, June 6.—Arrived: Ryndam from Rotterdam; Minneapolis from London; Finland from Antwerp.

SWEEPS PATHWAY OF DEVASTATION

Houses Are Wrecked, Trees Uprooted and Persons Blown from Their Beds—Several Are Injured, But There Are No Fatalities

MANY CURIOUS PRANKS ARE PLAYED BY THE BIG STORM

The worst cyclone that has ever visited this part of the country swept through the South Side of this city between the hours of 10 and 11 last night.

A half dozen houses were completely demolished, 100 others were badly damaged, big trees were torn and twisted like straws, and such havoc was wrought that the damage cannot yet be accurately estimated.

The strangest feature of the destructive storm was the absence of casualties. So far as has been learned only one person, Mrs. Thomas Thornton, living at Vestal avenue and Kress street, sustained any serious injury. Mrs. Thornton was struck in the head by flying debris.

On Upper Vestal avenue a gorgeous bed quilt hangs flapping from a tangle of telephone wires, high in the air. In other places branches of trees and pieces of tin roofs were caught in the wires and left dangling.

Whole plate glass windows in the stores along the east side of De Russey street were blown in and show cases upset. Part of the board walk on the west side of De Russey street was picked up and placed intact on the opposite side.

The path of the whirlwind seemed to be in a southeasterly direction. It broke first on the north bank of the Susquehanna, west of the city and at the junction of Front street and Riverside Drive it blew over a few trees into the water. Then it gathered force in crossing the ri-

(Continued on Page Two.)

MANAGERS FOR THE HOSPITAL

Messrs. McCormick, Mason and Bayless and Mrs. Ely of This City Among Those Appointed.

Albany, June 6.—Announcement was made at the executive chamber today of the appointment [illegible] Higgins of the members of the board of Managers of the State Hospitals for the Insane just prior to his departure for Duluth.

The managers for the Binghamton State Hospital are: Cornelius F. McCormick, editor of the Leader, Mrs. Kate M. Ely, William Mason, George C. Bayless, Binghamton; Henry D. Sill, Cooperstown; Jervis V. Langdon, Elmira; Miss Ellen T. Fish, Oneida.

JEWS ARE INDIGNANT.

St. Petersburg, June 6.—It is stated that the old time Russian custom of requiring all travelers to be furnished with passports will shortly be abolished except as it applies to convicts and Jews. The greatest indignation is expressed by Hebrews throughout the entire empire at the restriction which is placed upon them, and which really puts them in the same class with convicts.

OFFER MADE BY FRANCE

She Is Desirous of Playing the Part of Mediator Between Russia and Japan to End the War.

RUSSIA HAS AS YET GIVEN HER NO REPLY

Berlin, June 6.—The correspondent of the Publishers' Press is able to state authoritatively that the French Government has instructed the French Ambassador at St. Petersburg to inform the Russian Government that France is willing to act as mediator between Russia and Japan.

This communication was sent to the French Embassy immediately after the Russian naval defeat. Russia has given no reply as yet, because the Czar is undecided on the subject of whether the war is to be continued or not.

France is particularly anxious that her offer shall be accepted, as she desires to play the part of mediator and intends to prevent the United States from beating her and securing credit for ending the war. European diplomats are watching with interest the race between France and America to be the first with their offers of mediation and to secure the [illegible] of the Czar.

ROCHESTER GETS BIG TROY COLLAR FACTORY

As a Result of the [illegible], Cluett, Peabody & Co. Will Move There.

Troy, June 6.—Cluett, Peabody & Company announced today that they will establish a shirt and collar factory in Rochester, employing [illegible] persons.

CORPORATION PAPERS.

Albany, June 6.—[illegible] and Lancaster Light, Power & Conduit Company of [illegible] has filed with the secretary of State an increase of capital stock from $75,000 to $500,000.

The South Texas Developing Company, of Albany, capital $300,000, to lease or develop any lands within or without the State containing coal, iron or oil, was incorporated today.

SMITH MURDER TRIAL DRAGS ALONG SLOWLY

Much Trouble Is Found in Getting a Jury in Rochester Case.

Rochester, June 6.—With 10 jurors selected yesterday in the Ervin Smith murder case, early completion of the jury was looked for, but at the opening of court District Attorney Warren caused a stir by asking permission to further examine one of the jurors already selected and sworn. As the result of his re-examination Frederick T. Dias was excused.

Completion of the jury was more difficult than anticipated. The special panel of 150 talesmen was exhausted yesterday and another of 75 drawn. From this second panel it is expected the jury box will be filled.

The people will contend that the killing was done in a moment of ungovernable rage caused by the girl's importunities for him to marry her, that Smith had then concealed the body in the cistern near the packing house and the following night had removed it to the basement of the packing house and then fired the structure in an effort to destroy evidence of the murder.

GIRL COMMITS SUICIDE.

Albany, June 6.—While her employers were away enjoying wedding festivities [illegible] Winifred Keeler, the 22 year old domestic, overcome with despondency over the failure of her own love affair, took her life. The girl was found dead this morning by Mr. and Mrs. William Fleischmann, when they returned to the house, 277 Hudson street.

CONTENTS OF TODAY'S PRESS.

RUMOR THAT CZAR HAS BEEN ASSASSINATED

New York, June 6.—There were rumors in Wall street today that a sensational foreign event had occurred but the gossips could not say definitely what it was. Some had it that the Czar was assassinated and others that it was Kaiser Wilhelm that was killed.

Broker wires spread the news to other cities and many messages of inquiry were sent here.

Up to 10.30 this morning no confirmation of the startling rumors had come from London or the Continent.

It develops that the rumor that the Czar had been assassinated was current on the Bourse in Berlin this morning and was cabled to this country.

The Berlin Bourse rumor had it that the Mendelssohns, bankers of the Russian Government, had received a private telegram to that effect.

At the office of the Russian Consul here it was stated that there was no news of such a tragedy.

June 6, 1905: The tornado of 1905. *Microfilm archives*

Wreck on Erie Wed. Mar 7/06. Just above dry
bridge on Court Street.
No one killed.

Train wreck at Upper Court Street, Binghamton, March 7, 1906. *Courtesy Richard Gillespie*

Train wreck on Upper Court Street. *Courtesy Richard Gillespie*

ONLY EVENING NEWSPAPER IN BINGHAMTON A MEMBER OF THE ASSOCIATED PRESS

EXTRA

BINGHAMTON PRESS

AND LEADER

EXTRA

VOL. 28. NO. 279 • STATE EDITION WEDNESDAY EVENING, MARCH 7, 1906. TEN PAGES PRICE ONE CENT

ERIE TRAIN NO. 7 WRECKED; ENGINEER MAY DIE

MR. GREEN'S ATTORNEYS SUM UP FOR DEFENSE

Mr. Thurston Makes Address That Has Strong Impression on the Jury—Col. A. S. Worthington Makes Summing Up This Morning

ENGINE AND TENDER IN COURT STREET

Photographed for The Binghamton Press.

Detailed View of the Wreck as It Appeared from the North Side of Road

SIDE LIGHTS ON THE GREEN CASE

LIVE COALS SCATTERED, ENTIRE FIRE DEPARTMENT IS CALLED TO THE SCENE

Quick Work of Rescuers Saves Many From Death, Flames Speedily Extinguished and the Work of Clearing the Track Begun—All of the Passengers Shaken Up, but None Are Badly Hurt

Running 50 miles an hour, the second section of Erie train 7, west bound, consisting of three passenger coaches, two baggage cars and a postal car, with the engine and tender, left the tracks at Griswold street, at 4:15 o'clock this morning, the engine plunging down the embankment, turning over twice and landing on its trucks, nearly a total wreck. The tender followed, turning over once and a half, while, the postal, baggage and express cars landed in a slanting manner on the embankment, the postal car catching fire.

Engineer Samuel L. Mason of Owego had several ribs broken, received several severe internal injuries and general bruises and contusions. His condition is desperate and he may die at any moment.

Fireman Leslie Jackson of Hornellsville had an arm broken, his back injured, received severe scalp wounds and general contusions. His condition is serious.

The responsibility for the accident lies with the switch near the corner of Court and Griswold streets. There is located at this point what is known as a "D" switch, operated from the signal tower. When a Delaware, Lackawanna & Western train is passing the Erie tracks at the "cross-over" above the tower, the switch is opened and the track blocked by signal. Then an Erie train running by the block signal strikes the "D" switch and is thrown from the rails to prevent a collision. A third, or guard, rail runs for a distance of 100 feet westward from the "D" switch, and to this is due the fact that the entire train did not plunge down the embankment.

According to the story of the switchmen on duty in the Erie yard when the accident occurred, the yard employes in that vicinity were in the switch shanty at 4:15 when they heard No. 7 approaching from the east. They state that the train was running fully 50 miles an hour and they heard the engineer shut off his steam when he struck the "D" switch. This was almost instantly followed by a thundering crash, resembling the sound of an explosion.

When the engine left the track it plowed along the ties for more than 100 feet, being held to the roadbed by the third rail. At a point half way between the dry bridge that spans Court street and Griswold street, the huge, groaning, swaying machine left the track and went diagonally down the embankment, turning over twice and landing in an upright position across the street car tracks. Fortunately the fireman and engineer escaped by jumping and were thrown free from the machine. Otherwise they inevitably would have been crushed to a shapeless mass. The engine struck a telegraph pole in its descent, snapping the huge timber like a match, but this checked the speed of the locomotive. The engine tender which followed turned over once and a half, landing bottom upward next to the engine.

The postal car was first in the train and followed the tender down the embankment, landing cornerwise against the engine tender. As the engine rolled over it threw live coals from the firebox onto the car, setting it on fire.

There were in the car at the time, Chief Postal Clerk E. L. Jones, W. F. Barlow, B. L. Gray and E. A. Cramph. The men were hard at work sorting mail when Mr. Jones, who was in the forward portion of the car felt the car leave the tracks, the trucks, grating along the rails. He started towards the rear when there was a sensation of falling and the car struck with a force that burst open the doors and scattered mail matter in the mud along the embankment.

WRECK CATCHES FIRE.

Almost instantly the car was ablaze on the outside as the result of hot coals from the engine.

An alarm of fire was turned in from box 231, near the Waterworks, to which the companies of the fire department quickly responded and several lines were laid. Quick work by the firemen resulted in saving the contents of the wrecked car and prevented the remainder of the cars from burning.

None of the mail matter was burned, but a considerable amount was badly damaged by being strewn along the roadbed in the mud. The postal clerks were all more or less bruised and suffering from nervous shock, but bravely began rescuing the many bags of mail matter that were in danger, piling them beside the track and standing guard until the arrival of train 25 at 8:15 this morning, when the mail matter was transferred to the postal car. The men in the postal car say the train was running at a high rate of speed.

EXPRESS MESSENGER'S EXPERIENCE.

W. S. Seton, the express messenger on train 7 had a thrilling experience. Mr. Seton was in the second car from the engine and went down the embankment when the train left the track. Packages and parcels flew about his head and when the postal car took fire, threatening the train, he found himself imprisoned among the many boxes, but reached the door on the side of the car toward Court street and made his escape by kicking a hole through the panels, and crawling through the aperture. The damage done to packages in the express car cannot be determined until all are carefully examined. Bert E. Coon, local manager of the Wells-Fargo Express Company, was early on hand to look after the company's interest and stood guard until the contents of the car could be properly cared for.

The employes on the baggage car, though badly shaken up, escaped serious injury from flying trunks.

NO PASSENGERS HURT.

In the passenger coaches the only damage done was by the sudden application of the air brakes, which brought the train, running at a high rate of speed, to a sudden halt. One of the Pullman porters was thrown the length of the car and considerably bruised and many of the passengers considerably frightened.

Within half an hour after the accident an extra No. 7 had been made up and two car loads of passengers were on their way West.

Conductor C. Lord of Port Jervis was in charge of the train, but neither he or the brakemen were injured.

The wrecking crews from Susquehanna and this city were summoned at once and the work of clearing the west bound track was begun. During the blockade trains were run through this city over the east bound track, thereby preventing any tie-up on the road.

ERIE TRAIN KILLS TWO

Second Section of No. 8 Strikes Wagon Near Corning—Purse and Glasses Are Found on Engine

Special to The Binghamton Press.

Corning, March 7.—The second section of train 8, an east bound passenger train on the Erie railroad, in charge of Engineer Broadwick and Conductor Chase, both of Hornellsville struck a covered rig at the Centerville crossing one and a quarter miles west of this city late last night. The occupants, a man and woman, were thrown out, but the horse was uninjured. The train was stopped and the people brought to this city. The man was dead, but the woman lived two hours, although never regaining consciousness. The bodies were later identified as that of John Wood, who was employed at the livery stables of Armstrong & Morrow in this city. He was a stepson of John Westbrook of Troy, Pa., who formerly resided at Mosey Glen, town of Corning.

The woman was Miss Rose Maddock, a domestic employed at the residence of Hon. S. T. Hayt, on East First street this city. The accident is supposed to have been caused by the driver being unable to see the fast approaching train owing to the carriage top being up. A train had just gone west and the noise of that train probably drowned that of the on coming train.

A special dispatch to The Binghamton Press from Susquehanna says that a woman's purse containing $23, and a pair of glasses were found on the pilot of the engine of train No. 8 this morning.

BERTHE CLAICHE HAS PLEADED GUILTY

By Associated Press.

New York, March 7.—The trial of Berthe Claiche for the murder of Emil Gerdron came to a sudden termination yesterday when the young French woman pleaded guilty, on advice of her counsel to manslaughter in the first degree. That this, however, is not the end of the case and that an attempt will be made to continue it as an investigation of a certain class of policemen with Berthe Claiche as State's evidence was made plain by statements both of the Judge, before whom the trial was conducted, and by the defendant's own counsel.

Supreme Court Justice Davis in remanding the young woman for sentence until March 29, and in discharging the jury, said:

"There are many features of the case which induced the Court to accept and the defendant to offer the plea of manslaughter in the first degree, and I think when final results shall have been reached, the sentence imposed, the Court will see that the interests of justice will be served."

COMMISSION TO INVESTIGATE BANKS

By Associated Press.

Albany, March 7.—The Senate Finance Committee by a vote of 7 to 5 yesterday afternoon decided to report a bill providing for a commission to inquire into the operation of the banking law, and to investigate any charges against the Superintendent of Banks which may be referred to it by the Governor. Two former chief justices of the Court of Appeals, Alton Brooks Parker, Democrat, of Esopus, and Charles Andrews, Republican, of Syracuse, are named in the bill to constitute the commission.

GRIGGS CHAIRMAN OF THE COMMITTEE

By Associated Press.

Washington, March 7.—Representative J. M. Griggs of Georgia was unanimously chosen chairman of the Democratic Congressional committee last night, at a meeting in the capitol attended by 31 members of the committee. Representatives Bowers of Mississippi nominated Mr. Griggs. There were no other nominations and the secretary was instructed to cast the entire vote for Mr. Griggs.

PASSENGER RATE WAR IS BEGUN

By Associated Press.

Chicago, March 7.—The eastern passenger war which has been threatening for some time owing to the differential trouble, was precipitated yesterday by the Grand Trunk whose officials wired to Washington a notice of reduced schedules to take effect next Saturday. The new rates will affect the eastern points wherever differential fares now apply. The new rates make the first class fare from Chicago to New York $16 and second class $15. Chicago to Boston $15 and $15 and a like reduction to all intermediate points east of Buffalo.

March 7, 1906: The wreck of Erie Train No. 7 tops this Press front page. *Microfilm archives*

ONLY EVENING NEWSPAPER IN BINGHAMTON A MEMBER OF THE ASSOCIATED PRESS

EXTRA

BINGHAMTON PRESS

AND LEADER

EXTRA

VOL. 29. NO. 7 • STATE EDITION WEDNESDAY EVENING, APRIL 18, 1906. TWELVE PAGES PRICE ONE CENT

EARTHQUAKE IN 'FRISCO

FLAMES ARE RAGING, CITY PARTLY RUINED

BIG BUILDINGS DEMOLISHED

Dead and Injured Are Being Taken Out as Rapidly as Possible—No Water to Fight Flames—Mains Broken by Tremors

ONLY ONE TELEGRAPH WIRE IS WORKING

(By Associated Press.)

San Francisco, April 18.—San Francisco was practically wrecked by an earthquake at 5:10 this morning. The shock lasted three minutes. Thousands of buildings were damaged or destroyed. The loss of life is reported great. There is no water and fires are breaking out all over the City. All the wires with the exception of one are gone. The City Hall, costing $7,000,000, is in ruins. Modern buildings suffered less than those of brick and frame.

Terror and excitement are indescribable. Most of the people were asleep and rushed into the streets undressed. The buildings swayed and crashed, burying many occupants. Panic reigns in the down town hotels. The Lick House is badly damaged, but no loss of life there is reported.

A disastrous fire has broken out on the south side of Market street and is now within one block of the Palace Hotel. The water mains have burst and the fire department is practically helpless. The utmost confusion exists. All business is suspended. At this moment there is only one wire out of San Francisco, a Postal wire. The Postal Building is badly damaged. The operating room is a wreck. The power of every kind is gone, and there are no lights, either gas or electric. Neither the Palace Hotel nor the St. Francis are gone, that is, as far as the outside goes, but the inside plastering, etc., is greatly damaged. Between the postoffice and the water front there has been great damage by fire, which is burning fiercely, and there is little or no water.

The fire is burning both on the east and south side of the Postal Telegraph Building.

A telegram from Sacramento to the Western Union Telegraph Company reports that three miles of railroad sank out of sight as a result of the earthquake between Suisun and Benicia and all wires were taken with it. At Pleasanton there were several cars burned on the tracks.

The Palace and St. Francisco hotels stood the shock. People flocked to the telegraph offices to send messages to friends and were frantic because there were no wires. The greatest damage was done to buildings south of Market street, where mostly they are frame and tenement houses. Fires occurred in every block in that district.

The business section of the city from Main street to Mission street and from the bay back has been almost completely wrecked. The Call and Examiner buildings are destroyed. Many buildings along Market and Mission streets, including the department stores collapsed. Hundreds of people in the cheap tenement district are reported killed. Fires are raging and owing to the scarcity of water are practically beyond control.

Business is practically suspended. The offices of the Postal Telegraph Company in the Hobart building are wrecked, as is the Associated Press building at 303 Montgomery street. The residence portion is but slightly damaged, although nearly every house has been more or less injured.

New York, April 18.—A severe earthquake wrecked many buildings and caused a loss of life in San Francisco this morning. The shock was felt at 5:13, San Francisco time. Following the wrecking of buildings numerous fires broke out. The Postal Telegraph office was wrecked and communication was lost at 8:50 New York time.

At about 9:40 o'clock the Postal Telegraph Company had communication with its San Francisco Office, but lost the connection again almost immediately. In the brief period that the wire was working the San Francisco office reported that a number of buildings had collapsed and that the dead and injured were being taken from the ruins as rapidly as possible. At the time this message came through the principal danger was from the fires, a number of which had started and were making great headway, owing to the lack of water.

The Postal Telegraph Company has received information that the greatest damage from the earthquake was done to property in the following streets: Drumm, Davis, Front, Battery, Sansom, Montgomery, Kearney, Spear, Main, Beale and Fremont.

Chicago, April 18.—The telegraph companies here are entirely without wires to San Francisco.

The Sacramento office of the Western Union reports a very heavy earthquake west. Los Angles reports having lost all wires at 5:13 a. m.

Considerable damage from earthquake is reported as having occurred in the city of Sacramento, as in San Francisco.

Kansas City, Mo., April 18.—At 8:35 this morning the Postal Telegraph Company here states that the only information obtainable from the West was that their operators at San Francisco had left their building in that city and reported that many buildings were collapsing and many fires breaking out, with no water available to fight the flames. People were fleeing from the affected district.

New York, April 18.—The Western Union Telegraph office at Fresno says that it is the most severe shock ever known. They have no further details.

NEW GREEN TRIAL?

DIST. ATTY. BAKER'S MOVE

Asks That Supreme Court of the District of Columbia Grant a Severance of Doremus Indictments

WILL ASK FOR NEW TRIAL NEXT MONTH

By Associated Press.

Washington, April 18.—District Attorney Baker has filed a motion in the Supreme Court of the District of Columbia, to grant a severance in the several indictments against George W.

DIST. ATTY. D. W. BAKER, Who Announces That He Will Move for a New Trial in Green-Doremus Cases

Beavers George E. Green and Willard D. Doremus, alleging conspiracy and bribery in connection with the sale to the Postoffice Department of the Doremus stamp cancelling machines. It is the purpose of the District Attorney to consolidate the cases against Green and Doremus, and he has given notice that on Friday next he will request the court to set a day for their trial some time in May.

FRANKLIN'S PICTURE NOW IN AMERICA

Interesting Relic, Returned by Earl Grey, Arrives in Philadelphia

Philadelphia, Pa., April 18.—The portrait of Benjamin Franklin, which was taken by Major Andre during the revolution, has arrived here and has been placed in the Pennsylvania Academy of Fine Arts. The picture was in the possession of Sir Charles Grey and one of his descendants, Earl Grey, Governor General of Canada, returned it to this country.

$100,000 FIRE AT NEW PALTZ NORMAL

School Completely Wrecked, but 300 Scholars Are Away on Vacation

By Associated Press.

Poughkeepsie, April 18.—Fire early this morning destroyed the New Paltz Normal School. The students to the number of about 300 are away on their Easter vacations. Several firemen were somewhat injured by falling walls. The loss is estimated at $100,000, on which there is an insurance of about $65,000.

HUGHES TO INVESTIGATE COAL TRADE

He Has Been Retained by the U. S. Government to Act as Special Counsel to Probe the Trust

STRONG STATEMENT BY ATT'Y GENERAL MOODY

Plan Has Long Been Considered by the Administration—Henkel Decision a Factor in Determining Case

Washington, April 18.—The government has employed as special counsel for the proposed investigation into the interstate transportation and sale of coal Charles E. Hughes, who was chief counsel for the Armstrong Insurance Investigating Committee. Mr. Hughes has agreed to undertake the work. Alexander Simpson, Jr., will be associated with Mr. Hughes. The announcement was made in the following statement of Attorney General Moody:

"Charles E. Hughes, Esq., of the New York bar and Alexander Simpson, Jr., of the Pennsylvania bar have been retained by the Department of Justice to take under consideration all the facts now known or which can be ascertained relating to the transportation and sale of coal in interstate commerce, to advise what, if any, legal proceedings should be begun, and to conduct, under the direction of the Attorney General, such suits or prosecutions, if any, as may be warranted by the evidence in hand and forthcoming.

"The general subject for some time has been under consideration by the Department. It is believed that sufficient evidence has been developed in the investigations of the Interstate Commerce Commission and otherwise to warrant the employment of counsel under the provisions of the appropriation act of Feb. 25, 1903, authorizing the employment of special counsel and agents in proceedings of this nature.

"An important element in arriving at this conclusion is the recent decision of the Supreme Court in Hale against Henkel, holding that the Federal government has the right, under legal proceedings, to examine the books and records of corporations engaged in interstate commerce."

SHARE TAX IS VALID

Justice Vann Answers Objections of Bill's Opponents

Albany, April 17.—The Court of Appeals, in a unanimous decision, upholds the constitutionality, in every feature, of the law of this State taxing the transfer of shares of capital stock. The opinion of the court was written by Justice Vann and overturns all of the contentions made by those who sought to overthrow the act.

As to the argument that the bill should have been on the desks of the members of the Legislature in its final form in each house for at least three calendar days, the court holds that the intention of the constitution was that the bills should be on the desks of the members for three days and not for six, as the Legislature means the whole body, and not each separate house. In answer to the objection that the classification made by selecting one kind of property and taxing the transfer of that only, the court says:

"All taxation is arbitrary, for it compels the citizen to give up a part of his property; it is generally discriminating, for otherwise everything would be taxed, which has never yet been done, and there would be no exemption on account of education, charity or religion, and frequently it is unreasonable, but that does not make it unconstitutional even if the result is double taxation."

CHARLES E. HUGHES, Selected by Government to Investigate Coal Trust

INSTITUTE FOR THE TEACHERS

Today's Program an Interesting One, Embracing Lectures and Discussions of Value to Those Attending

Special to The Binghamton Press.

Windsor, April 18. The village High School has been crowded so far this week with teachers and prominent educators who are here to attend the sessions of the Teachers' Institute for the first commissioner district of Broome county. Commissioner E. Edward Hurlburt is a very busy man, as on his shoulders has fallen much of the responsibility for carrying out the details of the various programs. Over 100 teachers have registered and the meetings are proving very helpful to all who attend. Owing to illness in his family, Irving B. Smith is unable to act as conductor. Jeremiah H. Thompson has taken his place.

This evening there will be an entertainment in the Windsor Lyceum course. Thursday the prize speaking contest will occur.

In connection with the institute the following announcements are made concerning examinations: Aug. 9-10, Binghamton, Nov. 8-9, Deposit; regents, June 11-15; grade, June 12-13, Dec. 18-19; Cornell scholarship, June 2, at Binghamton. State certificate, Aug. 20-24, at Binghamton.

An interesting educational exhibit has added much interest to the sessions of the institute.

The following are the officers of the institute for this year: Conductor, Irving B. Smith, A. M., Warsaw; instructors, J. Richard Street, Ph.D., Syracuse University, Jeremiah H. Thompson, Ph.D., State Educational Department; Myra Ingalsbe, school commissioner, Harford, Conn.; Mark M. Maycock, M. P., Normal School, Buffalo, J. S. Kingsley, AM. M., Newark Valley, reporters, Principal James P. Culhane, Principal Mary F. Donaldson, Inez Livingston; secretaries, E. W. Neff, Katherine Dailey, Millicent Potter, music committee, Principal A. B. Voorhes, M. Francis Dailey; committee [illegible] Carson, Florence Newton, [illegible] Chamberlain, Mary A. Weed, Nettie M. Barta; committee on resolutions, William F. Lange, E. J. Heath, E. F. Eaton; committee on entertainment, Board of Education and Faculty of Windsor High School; C. A. Mider, chairman, J. Edward Hurlburt, commissioner.

COURT OF INQUIRY HAS BEEN NAMED

Will Investigate the Cause of the Kearsarge Explosion

By Associated Press.

Washington, April 18.—Rear Admiral Evans, commanding the Atlantic fleet, has arrived at Guantanamo, Cuba, on his flagship Maine and has cabled the Navy Department that he has appointed a court of inquiry, consisting of Rear Admiral Brownson, commanding the armored cruiser division of the fleet, Captain Ingersoll of the cruiser Maryland, and Lieutenant Commander Bradshaw of the Kentucky to investigate the accident of the Kearsarge last Friday. Lieutenant Commander Harrison, the inspector of rifle practice, will act as judge advocate of the court.

LONG CABLE IS COMPLETE AT LAST

President and Empress of China Exchange Messages Over It

By Associated Press.

Washington, April 18.—Messages of congratulation have been exchanged between President Roosevelt and the Dowager Empress and Emperor of China in commemoration of the opening of the last link of the Postal Telegraph and Cable Company's cable, connecting the United States and China.

OPERATORS REFUSE TO COMPROMISE

They Tell the Miners That They Will Not Concede the Concessions Asked by Scale Committees

BRIEF REVIEW OF WHOLE SITUATION

The Opposing Industrial Forces Are Now Deadlocked and the Miners Must Make Next Move

New York, April 18.—The formal answer of the anthracite operators' committee of seven to the last proposition of the committee of the anthracite mine workers has been sent by the operators to John Mitchell. It is an unqualified rejection of all the propositions of the miners.

While the letter does not say specifically that the operators' last offer still holds good, it was declared last evening that it holds good until a break comes, as does also the alternative offer to continue the agreement under the award of the anthracite strike commission for three years longer.

The operators feel that they are under no pledge to refrain from attempting to resume work as the suspension is to all intents and purposes looked on as a strike. Preparations are being made by the operators for strike emergencies and the starting up of the washeries is the entering wedge in breaking the deadlock.

The letter of the operators reviews briefly the situation and then points out that the offer for an agreement with the committee as "representatives of the anthracite mine workers" instead of with the United Mine Workers direct, is merely a matter of form, inasmuch as the miners' committee represents the United Mine Workers and Mitchell's last proposition provides in several instances for action by "the officers" and "the district officers."

The letter continues:

This proposition (that of the miners) restricts production by strictly limiting hours of labor and providing that no miner can work in more than one chamber, or have more than two laborers; it seeks to equalize wages with reference merely to the name of the employe's position, and not at all to his capacity or the work which he actually does. It provides that no new veins or collieries can be opened without an arbitration as to wages, and that no contract of employment can be terminated without an arbitration; it makes the employers the agents of the union to aid it in levying upon the wages of the employes the dues fixed by the union, it provides for increase in wages and rates of payment which would approximate 21.6 per cent, and would increase the cost of the domestic sizes of coal about $1.20 per ton, and it suggests diluting the present conciliation board into three boards having coordinate powers. It provides still further that the arrangement proposed [illegible] look merely for one [illegible]

FR. MARTIN IS DEAD

"Black Pope" Victim of Cancer in Rome This Morning

By Associated Press.

Rome, April 18.—Father Louis Martin, general of the Jesuits known

FATHER MARTIN, "Black Pope," Who Died in Rome Today

as the "Black Pope," died shortly before noon today. He had been suffering from a cancer in the chest.

DR. E. F. HALLENBECK, Elected Moderator of Binghamton District at Waverly

ADJOURNMENT OF PRESBYTERY

Dr. E. F. Hallenbeck Is Elected Moderator for Ensuing Term; Special Meeting at Bainbridge, May 15

Special to The Binghamton Press.

Waverly, April 18.—The Spring meeting of the Binghamton Presbytery adjourned here yesterday afternoon, after several highly interesting sessions in the First Presbyterian Church. It was resolved to adjourn to May 15, when a special meeting will be held at Bainbridge to consider several important matters necessarily left over from this meeting.

An important feature of the present session is that the Presbytery of Binghamton will, in all probability, be entitled to send two delegates, instead of one, to the General Assembly this year. The delegates have until now numbered 35, but an addition of one delegate to the Presbytery allows another representative at the General Assembly, to be held this year in Des Moines, Ia., in May. The prominent candidates were Rev. Dr. Clements of Cortland and Rev. R. B. Pedine of Binghamton. Dr. Clements was chosen unanimously.

The sermon of the retiring moderator, Rev. A. M. Brown of McGraw, was a masterful effort, and was closely listened to by the large congregation. The Rev. Dr. E. F. Hallenbeck was elected moderator for the ensuing term, and reports read from the various permanent committees revealed that the Presbytery is in a most prosperous condition.

[illegible]UGHING MAN" IS NOW FREE AGAIN

Ex-Confederate Who Fooled Many People Released from Prison

By Associated Press.

Chicago, April 18.—A dispatch to the Tribune from Michigan City, Ind., says: "The man with a cough," Colonel A. B. Ward, one time Confederate army officer and daring spy, one of the men sent north to burn New York City during the Civil war, was released from State prison here yesterday. Ward is one of the last of the old time confidence men. Born near Indianapolis of wealthy parents, 73 years ago, he was cast off by his family because of too high living. Later in Washington, D. C., he killed an army officer and fled South where at the outbreak of the rebellion he enlisted in the Confederate army.

The second year of the war he was sent North to burn New York City and was arrested while applying the torch to the Astor House. Sentenced to be hanged, he devoted himself to the care of Confederate prisoner soldiers while in prison, so that President Lincoln pardoned him. After the war Ward ran a packet on the Mississippi river, which was fitted up lavishly, and numbered among its patrons the biggest gamblers in the United States. He later went to New York, and on one occasion broke Phil Daly's gambling house, winning over $10,000 in one night. Ward's wealth gradually slipped away, and he took to forging checks, and he served many terms in prison during the last 40 years. He got the title, "the man with a cough" several years ago when he secured a pardon from a Southern prison by coughing and regarded his cough as his principal stock in trade.

JAPAN OPENS PORTS.

Tokio, April 18.—It is semi-officially announced that Antung and Tatungkay (both near the mouth of the Yalu river) will be opened to trade and travel May 1. Mukden will be opened June 1 and other places soon after that date.

BIG CAVE FOUND IN WEST VIRGINIA

By Associated Press.

Chicago, April 18.—A dispatch to the Record-Herald from Charleston, W. Va., says:

The city of Charleston was thrown into excitement yesterday by the discovery of a gigantic cave directly beneath the town. The cave contains a large lake.

Men blasting rock made this discovery of the lake and cavern when the discharge caused the earth to crumble and fall in, leaving a great hole. Workmen ventured into the cavern, exploring it for a considerable distance. They discovered the lake and returning to the surface procured a small boat, in which they rowed around for several hundred yards. There are limestone formations in the cavern similar to those in the noted Luray caves.

The water of the lake is remarkably pure and is cold and sweet to the taste. A systematic exploration of the cavern will be begun today.

April 18, 1906: This Binghamton Press Extra announces the disastrous earthquake in San Francisco. *Microfilm archives*

ONLY EVENING NEWSPAPER IN BINGHAMTON A MEMBER OF THE ASSOCIATED PRESS

EXTRA **BINGHAMTON PRESS** EXTRA

AND LEADER

VOL. 29. NO. 9 • STATE EDITION FRIDAY EVENING, APRIL 20, 1906. TWELVE PAGES PRICE ONE CENT

LITTLE LEFT OF 'FRISCO, THOUSANDS HOMELESS

PARKS ARE FULL OF THE SUFFERERS

Flames Raced Unchecked All Night; Pinch of Hunger Is Already Felt by Survivors

REGULARS BEHAVE NOBLY

San Francisco, Cal., April 20.—The people of San Francisco, homeless and starving, are facing the calamity which has overtaken them and practically swept out of existence [a] great city of which all were so proud. There are no evidences of weakness to be seen among the crowds of stricken people moving back reluctantly upon each advance of the destroying flames, which continue to sweep toward the ocean. Appalled for the moment, but undaunted, the bravery exhibited by men, women and children in face of overwhelming disaster, is that of a race destined to arise stronger than ever out of the ruins which now surround them.

There is little left today of the city by the Golden Gate. There seems little hope now of saving the choicest residence district lying west and north of Van Ness avenue. The men of the fire department, who have throughout the entire conflagration done such splendid work, are still making strenuous efforts to check the all devouring flames, but without avail. Water is in better supply, but it is of little use, apparently, against the headway now gained by the fire. Owing to the intense heat the buildings for some distance from the fire are as dry as tinder and seem to disappear like a flash the minute the flames reach them.

San Francisco, April 20.—This morning San Francisco sits in the waste of her ruins awaiting the time when the flames that have already taken out her vitals shall have worn themselves out through the very lack of that fuel. Hope has gone. The whole city seems doomed.

With black ruin covering more than seven square miles in its very heart, the city now waits in a stupor the inevitable reign of starvation and possible anarchy that must crowd close upon the disaster. Early this morning the flames were eating out the central residence portion about the Western Addition and fashionable Pacific Heights.

After sucking dry even the sewers, the fire engines have either been abandoned or moved to the outlying districts in the vain hope that the water mains broken by the earthquake may be repaired in time to permit of a final stand being made against the whirlwind march of the flames.

"No more dynamite! No more dynamite!" a fireman ran shrieking up Ellis street past the doomed Flood building late yesterday afternoon and as he ran tears sprang from his smoke smirched eyes. "No more dynamite!" moaned the crowd that stood in the glare of approaching flames. "No more dynamite and we are lost!"

So, with the explosive exhausted and not a dozen streams of water being thrown in the entire fire zone, the stunned fire fighters and the stupid people sat still to watch the remnant of the city burn.

Hope Gone.

There is no help. Water gone, powder gone, hope even now a fiction, the fair city of the Golden Gate is doomed.

The stricken people, who wander through the streets in pathetic hopelessness and sit upon their scattered belongings, have reached the stage of dumb, uncaring despair. A city dissolving before their eyes has no significance longer.

Marius sitting among the ruins of Carthage saw not such a sight as presents itself in the dim haze of the smoke pall across the bay. Ruins, stark naked, yawning at fearful angles and pinnacled into a thousand fearsome shapes, mark the site of what was three-fourths of the total area of the city.

Desolation Everywhere.

There is no business quarter—it is gone. There is no longer a hotel district, a theater, a place where night beckoned to pleasure. Everything gone. Only a part of the residence domain of the city remains, and the jaws of the disaster are closing down on that with relentless determination.

All of the city south of Market street even down to Islais Creek and out as far as Valencia street, is now a smouldering ruin.

Into the western addition and the Pacific avenue heights three broad fingers of red are feeling their way with a speed that foretells the destruction of a major part of the palaces of the city before morning. There is no longer a downtown district. A blot of black spreads from East street to Oakland and is bounded on the south and north by Broadway and Washington streets and Islais Creek, respectively.

No Banks; No Exchanges.

Not a bank stands. There are no longer any exchanges, insurance offices, real estate offices, all that once represented the financial heart of the city and its industrial strength. Up Market street from the Ferry building to Valencia street and nothing but the black fingers of jagged ruins point to the smoke blanket that presses low overhead. Visit what was once California, Sansome and Montgomery streets and you must ask a panting fireman to direct you out of the labyrinth of grim, blackened walls.

Chinatown is no more. Union Square is a barren district. The Call building stands proudly erect, lifting its whited head above the ruin like some staring eyes that look upon nothing but a wilderness. The great Flood building is a hollow shell. The St. Francis Hotel, one time place of luxury, is naught but a box of stone and steel.

Yet the flames leap on exultantly. They dance, they roar in bacchanalian glee. They leap chasms like a waterfall taking a precipice. Now they are here, now there, always passing on, on to the west and through to the end of the city.

Washington, April 20.—The following Western Union dispatch was received at the War Department today: "San Francisco, April 20—5:19 a. m.—The fire, which heretofore had crept around the base of Telegraph Hill and left the few houses standing, there, has crept back from the west and is now in full possession of the houses on the Hill and will no doubt take everything down to the water front on VanNess avenue. The main fire has reached Octavia street and is going at a fast rate. There is no one in from the fire since midnight. At that time it had started afresh on the south end of the line of fire and was burning fast.

"The ferry buildings present a fearful scene. Men, women and children are crowded there with the few articles they have tried to save. They will leave the city by the first boat they can get away on.

"The roads leading from the ferry north and around the shore of the bay as far as Fort Mason are strewn with all sorts of vehicles that have broken down. Baby carriages, wheelbarrows, etc., that would not stand the loads over the rough way, have ben abandoned, and in some cases with their loads.

"The fire came ver yclose to Fort Mason last night and the big Fontama warehouse and nearby canneries will no doubt go today. I think the fire will make a clean sweep of everything as far as Golden Gate Park. Would not be surprised to see it take the great tres that line the park and burn the shrubury clear to the ocean beach."

Oakland, Cal., April 20.—San Francisco is apparently gone. To the west, across the bay, there is nothing but a great cloud of smoke, shot this morning with streams of fire and shaken now and then with the dynamite explosions by which the firemen are trying to check the flames. The fire is now everywhere.

Every refugee who makes his way here through the smoke cloud brings news of a new region burning and gone. As nearly as can be learned it has run all the way down the Mission Valley, taking the little houses of the working people, leaped up the California street hill, taking Chinatown in its path, and swept away the mansions which have crowned the city and is breaking out sporadically in the western addition, where live the prosperous people.

Little Spared.

So it has spared nothing, for the business district is already gone, and the fire is reaching further and further every hour into the tenement district to the south. It has taken all the thickly crowded parts of the tenement district and is reaching toward the thinly scattered parts on the Potrero. How much will be left when the fires finally burn down and go out we cannot dare to guess. If there is anything left, it will be the hills of the western addition. It is hard to see how anything else, absolutely anything, can escape.

Without sleep, without food, people watched all night, all day, looking off toward that veil of fire and smoke which hides from them the city which has become a hell. Back of that sheet of fire and retreating backward every hour must be most of the people of the city, forced toward the Pacific by the gradual advance of the flames.

Green Havens of Refuge.

Thank heaven for the open space of the Presidio and for Golden Gate park! The great park, largest in any American city, runs on its western extent past a thinly populated district. The flames cannot leap across that; it will shelter the inhabitants on their last stand. The Presidio, wide spreading and with only a few houses, is also safe, provided that the forests which form part of its area do not catch on fire. There is at least an escape; but half the people whom the fires have cut off from the waterfront and an escape from the peninsula are homeless.

Late yesterday afternoon a launch ventured out from the Oakland water front and made the run as far as the Gate. The bay was overhung with smoke, but a change of the wind blew a rift as they passed the Western Addition, which stands on the hills skirting the bay. Through this rift the passengers could see sporadic fires in a dozen places and the little black forms of men fighting the flames without water. This part of the city may be saved—probably will be—but it will owe it to the scattered buildings in that part of the city and to the character of California redwood, which smolders rather than burns.

O for a rain! The time of heavy rains is over; but often at this season of the year there comes a gentle and soaking Spring rain. The heavens cannot be seen on account of the smoke, but the feel of the air is dry, and even that mercy seems to be denied.

Flames Spread All Night.

At intervals news comes from the refugees of what is doing behind the smoke cloud. It appears that the area of the flames spread all night. People who had decided that their houses were outside of the dangerous area and had decided to pass the night, even after the terrible experience of the shake up, under their roofs, hourly gave it up and struggled to the parks. There they lay in blankets, their choicest valuables by their sides, and the soldiers kept watch and order.

Terrible Tales.

There came out, too, tales of [illegible] heroism and crime. The firemen have been at it for 36 hours under such conditions as firemen never faced before, and they are practically out of it. They attempted to do little more than give directions, while the volunteers, thousands of young Western men, who have remained to see it through, do the work. The troops have all that they can do to handle the crowds in the streets and prevent panics. The work of dynamiting, tearing down and rescuing is in the hands of the volunteers.

Yesterday morning an eddy of flame from the edge of the burning wholesale district ran up the slope of Russian Hill, the highest eminence in the city. All along the edge of that hill and up the slopes are little frame houses which hold Italians and Mexicans. A corps of volunteer aides ran along the edge of the fire, warning people out of the houses. But the flames ran too fast and two women were caught in the upper story of an old frame house. A young man tore a rail from a fence, managed to climb it, and reached the window. He bundled one woman out and slid her down the rail, then the roof caught fire. He seized another woman and managed to drop her on the rail, down which she slid without hurting herself a great deal. But the roof fell while he was struggling with another woman and they fell together into the flames. There must have been hundreds of such heroisms and dozens of such catastrophes. The people are so drunken and dulled by horror that they take such stories calmly now.

More Large Buildings Go.

What can be said in detail of the disaster except that the whole town not already burned must go? The business district, including all the big structures which escaped the fire of the first day, is gone. The flames have taken the Merchants' Exchange building, brand new and 10 stories tall, and Mechanics' Pavilion, which, after housing prize fights, conventions and great balls, found its last use as an emergency hospital. When it was seen that it could not last, every vehicle in sight was impressed by the troops, and the wounded, some of them frightfully mangled, were taken to the Presidio, where they will be out of danger and find comfort in tents. The physicians are working on, without sleep and almost without food. There is food, however, for the injured—the soldiers have seen to that. Even the soldiers are flagging and are keeping guard in relays, while the relieved men sleep on the ground where they have dropped.

Big Clubs and Churches Go.

Early in the day the fire struck Union Square, the prettiest park in the city, where stands the St. Francis Hotel. The tourists were gone from there long ago and the fire found only an empty building, which it gutted. On the way it burned up the houses of the Bohemian, Pacific Union and Family clubs and the big retail shops along Post street. The separate fire in the residence district took St. Luke's, the biggest Episcopal Church. There is no wor dof the fate of the First Presbyterian, which stands only a block away, but this must have gone with St. Luke's. All along that street are old mansions, built of wood, after the fashion of the '70s and these too must have gone.

When day broke the fire was running into the Mission district. This is a low country which runs from the terminus of Market street to the suburbs. In a general way it is the habitation of the aristocracy of the working class, although it is sprinkled with old time residences, notably the house of James D. Phelan, former Mayor of San Francisco. This went, too. Everything that is attacked goes. The dynamite only checks it. Nothing but rain can save the remnants of the [illegible]

MAP OF THE DESOLATE CITY AND ITS ENVIRONS

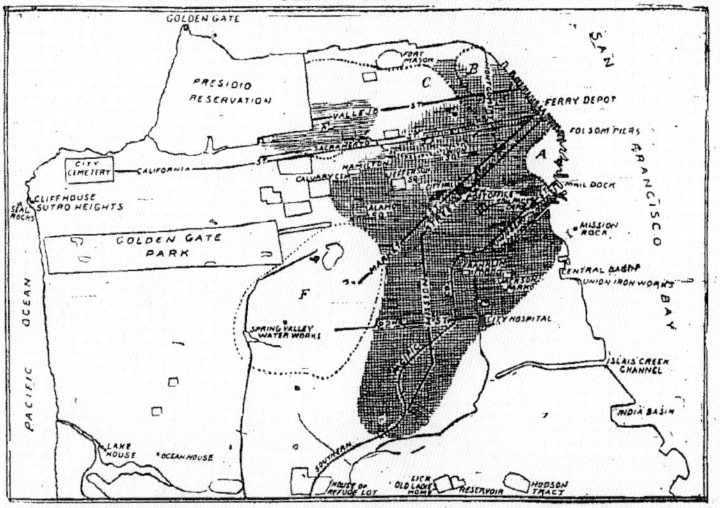
GOLDEN GATE
PRESIDIO RESERVATION
FORT MASON
FERRY DEPOT
FOLSOM PIERS
CITY CEMETERY
CALIFORNIA
CLIFF HOUSE
SUTRO HEIGHTS
SEAL ROCKS
GOLDEN GATE PARK
MAIL DOCK
MISSION ROCK
CENTRAL BASIN
UNION IRON WORKS
CITY HOSPITAL
SPRING VALLEY WATER WORKS
ISLAIS CREEK CHANNEL
INDIA BASIN
LAKE HOUSE
OCEAN HOUSE
HOUSE OF REFUGE LOT
LICK OLD LADIES HOME
RESERVOIR
HUDSON TRACT
SOUTHERN
PACIFIC OCEAN
SAN FRANCISCO BAY
A
B
C
F

A—Rincoon Hill; B—Telegraph Hill; C—Russian Hill; D—Nob Hill; E—Pacific Heights; F—High Land. The Shaded Part Marked by Squares Is Destroyed or Burning. The Spot at "E" Marked by Straight Lines Is Burning in Spots, but There Is No News of the Presidio and the Region About Sutro Heights, Which Was Probably the Refuge of Most of the People of San Francisco Last Night and Today.

TRYING TO GET THE FIRST TRAIN THROUGH

Chicago, April 20.—The Southern Pacific Company, which has the largest transportation interests in San Francisco, has been endeavoring to establish both rail and wire communication with San Francisco for 29 hours, without success. Rail communication on the north is cut off at Santa Rosa, which is 60 miles above San Francisco. On the south trains cannot run north of Fresno. On the east the railroads are gone west of the Utah line. It is believed tha a train can get from Sacramento to Oakland or San Francisco via the "long route," through Stockton, and an attempt to get this train is now being made. E. H. Harriman, chief owner and president of the Southern Pacific, has issued orders to establish rail and wire communication with San Francisco without regard to cost and every possible effort is being made simultaneously on the three lines of the Southern Pacific from the North, South and East to restore communication, but so far without result.

BRAWLEY WAS NOT SERIOUSLY DAMAGED

Los Angeles, Cal., April 20.—Late reports last night show that Brawley, Cal., suffered less by Wednesday's earthquake than originally stated. About 100 buildings in Brawley and the surrounding valley were damaged, but none destroyed. There were no fatalities. Brawley was the only settlement in Southern California affected on Wednesday.

WESTERN UNION WILL SEND NEWS FREE

New York, April 20.—President Clowry of the Western Union Telegraph Company made the following announcement today: "The Western Union Telegraph Company will transmit free domestic messages relating to the relief of sufferers at San Francisco when offered by duly constituted relief organizations or public officers in their official capacity."

SURVIVORS TELL THEIR STORIES

By Associated Press.

Los Angeles, Cal., April 20.—Albert H. Gould of Chicago has arrived here from San Francisco.

"I was asleep on the seventh floor of the Palace Hotel," he said, "at the time of the first quake and was thrown out of bed and half way across the room.

"Fearing that the building was about to collapse I made my way down six flights of stairs and into the main corridor. Clerks and hotel employes were running about like madmen. Other guests soon appeared. Most all wore night clothing only.

"I remained in San Francisco until 8 o'clock and then went to the Oakland ferry station. People by the thousands were at the ferryhouse. They clawed at the iron gates like so many maniacs. They sought to break the bars and failing in that turned on each other. After a maddening delay we got aboard the boat and crossed the bay."

J. R. Ritter of Houston, Tex., said: "I was in the Golden West Hotel when the first shock came. When I awoke, the hotel was rocking like a cradle. [illegible] was dressing, the rear wall of the hotel fell into the dining room. I was dressed by the time the second shock came and was going to rush out of the building, but the appeals of the women on the same floor stopped me. With some of the other men guests on the fourth floor, we got the women out. Most of the women were hysterical.

"Many naked and half dressed persons were in the streets, running about crying, screeching, wild with fear, while buildings toppled over and choked up the streets.

R. A. Cole, a horseman, was at the Palace Hotel when the quake came.

"I never saw anything like it," said Cole. "I was in the St. Louis cyclone and the Baltimore fire. They were nothing. I saw all San Francisco staggering and rocking and then in flames."

Mrs. Agnes Zink said: "I was staying at 35 Fifth street, San Francisco. The rear of the house collapsed and the landlady and about 20 roomers were killed. I escaped by the roof as the stairway had collapsed in the rear. Out in the street it was impossible to find a clear pathway. I saw another lodging house near ours colapse. I think it was at 39 Fifth street, and all the inmates were killed. In a few moments the entire block was in flames."

LATE NEWS FROM GREAT UNIVERSITY

By Associated Press.

Sacramento, Cal., April 20.—The following signed statement furnished to the Associated Press by President Jordan of Leland Stanford, Jr., University was received today: "The earthquake did great damage to the buildings of Stanford University. Only two lives were lost, one a student named J. A. Hanna of Bradford, Pa., and a fireman, Hans Stroh. Eight students were injured, none seriously. The buildings wrecked are the Memorial Church, the new library, the gymnasium, the memorial arch and the power house. Many buildings of the outer quadrangle were seriously damaged as well as some of the shops. The chemistry building, Encina Hall and the inner quadrangle, are practically uninjured. The damage will approximate \$4,000,000. The books, collections and apparatus are not greatly damaged. This message, together with 400 private messages from university community, are sent from Sacramento, as all telegraph communication at Palo Alto and all around the bay is out of commission."

BERKELEY CARING FOR MANY REFUGEES

Berekeley, Cal., April 20.—This town is caring for over a thousand refugees, who have been brought across the bay to escape the terrors of the San Francisco fire. The homeless and hungry were fed last night at the station from long benches provided by the citizens' relief committee. The women students and professors of the University of California are doing great work for the sufferers. The university gymnasium has been turned into a lodging house where hundreds have been installed, while many have been provided with blankets in the open air under the university oaks. Women and children are lodged in private houses.

MAYOR SCHMITZ'S PATHETIC APPEAL

San Francisco, April 20.—The following appeal for aid has been sent out by Mayor Schmitz to Governor Pardee and shows the destitute condition of the people and their dire need of food and shelter: "Send all supplies and tents possible to Golden Gate Park. Have bakeries in small towns bake all the bread they can. We want bedding, food and tents."

ODELL WINS A BIG FIGHT IN NEW YORK

Parsons' Reapportionment Plan Is Completely Turned Down by Republican County Committee

BITTER SPEECHES AND MUCH DISORDER

~~L. E.~~ Quigg and William Halpin Outgeneral the "Reformers" Chiefs in a Warm Executive Session

..New York, April 20.—In one of the stormiest meetings it has ever held, the Republican county committee, dominated by Lemuel E. Quigg and William Halpin, representatives of Benjamin B. Odell, Jr., last night defeated Herbert Parsons, president of the committee, by sidetracking the Senate reapportionment plan devised by Mr. Parsons' sub-committee and approving the plan prepared by followers of Mr. Odell.

This action was preceded and followed by bitter speeches and by scenes which several times threatened to become riotous. It was evident throughout the meeting that Mr. Parsons is not the leader of the committee, nor has he control of the executive committee, but he declared at the finish that he has no intention or resigning. He will make a determined fight to undo what was done by the executive committee last night and to carry the reapportionment fight to the Legislature.

At a Climax.

Affairs reached a climax when Lemuel E. Quigg, to force the absolute defeat of Mr. Parsons, moved that a committee of five, with Chairman Parsons, be named to submit the approved plan to the Legislature and urge its passage. Mr. Parsons declared he preferred not to serve on the committee.

"I do not believe this plan adopted tonight the best one that can be prepared," he said, "and shall not urge its passage. On the contrary, I shall urge the adoption of the one I think is the best."

While his enemies were demanding a vote, a committeeman moved as an amendment that the name of Mr. Quigg be submitted for Mr. Parsons. This created consternation in the Quigg camp, but before there was time to plan, the motion in the amendment was put and carried. At this excited period a motion to adjourn was made, followed by an amendment by Mr. Halpin that a roll call be taken to ascertain if a majority of the members wanted a motion to adjourn to be entertained.

While scores of committeemen were striving to be heard and motions were being made a dozen a minute, and while angry words were being exchange across the floor, a suggestion to the solution of the difficulty was made. It provided that neither Mr. Quigg nor Mr. Parsons be on the committee.

ROBBED OF $500,000

Thieves Get a Big Haul in Montgomery, Alabama

Montgomery, Ala., April 20.—J. D. Hand, a prominent saw mill operator of Bay Minett, Ala., was robbed in Montgomery last night of securities approximately estimated at $500,000 in value. The stocks and bonds were in a satchel and were taken from the hall of the residence of W. A. Collier, an attorney.

VETERAN YARDMAN KILLED BY CARS

Corning, April 20.—James C. Dowd, yardmaster here for the New York Cenatral Railroad Company, was run over by the cars in the lower yard last night, crushing his right leg from the effects of which he died at 1 o'clock this morning. Dowd had ben employed for over 36 years in various capacities b ythe old Fall Brook Railway, continuing with the New York Central when that company absorbed the Fall Brook. He succeeded the late W. H. Cleveland as night yardmaster about seven years ago. Dowd was 52 years of age and one of the best yardmen in this section of the State. He was widely known and well liked and is survived by a wife and four children.

THE WEATHER

Fair tonight and Saturday.

April 20, 1906: More details emerge on the devastation in San Francisco. *Microfilm archives*

Canoe race on the Susquehanna, July 4, 1907. *Courtesy Alan Jewell*

ENDICOTT

Men all dressed up pose with a cider wagon that says Endicott, circa 1907. *Courtesy Richard Gillespie*

MEET ME
FAIR

People and animals helped advertise the upcoming fair in Binghamton, 1908. *Courtesy Richard Gillespie*

Front Street in Owego is all decked out for a Firemen's Convention in 1908. *Courtesy Richard Gillespie*

Ely's tower in Binghamton, 1908. The base was 134.5 feet above sea level and 500 feet above Binghamton. The tower was 134 feet high, 10 stories and 152 steps. The viewing tower was an attraction at Ely Park. Ely's tower blew down during a spring wind storm, April 11, 1909. *Courtesy Alan Jewell*

The boathouse and surrounding area was a popular summer place for playing and relaxing in Binghamton. Photo taken July 4, 1909. *Courtesy Richard Gillespie*

Employee at work in the Bundy Mfg. Plant in Endicott, 1909.
Courtesy Alan Jewell

SWAMP ROOT

John Henry Thayne, an employee of Dr. Kilmer's Swamp Root Factory in Binghamton, is pictured at far left with a hammer in his hand, 1909. Notice the box says "Dr. Kilmer's Swamp Root. A Kidney, Liver, and Bladder Conditioner."
Courtesy John Telfer

Chenango Bridge being swept away during the 1910 flooding. *Courtesy Alan Jewell*

Ice pressed against the Chenango Bridge during the flood of 1910.
Courtesy Alan Jewell

Flood waters continue to rise in Binghamton, 1910. *Courtesy Alan Jewell*

Flood waters rise in Binghamton and surrounding areas on March 2, 1910.
Courtesy Richard Gillespie

1910 - 1919

Decade begins with devastating flood

ONLY EVENING NEWSPAPER IN BINGHAMTON A MEMBER OF THE ASSOCIATED PRESS

No matter what you have to dispose of or what you wish to buy, try a Press Want Ad. You will be surprised at the results it will accomplish for you.

BINGHAMTON PRESS AND LEADER

THE WEATHER. Fair weather, partly cloudy sky tonight and Thursday; not much change in temperature.

VOL. 32. NO. 273. LAST EDITION WEDNESDAY EVENING, MARCH 2, 1910. TWELVE PAGES PRICE ONE CENT

60 SWEPT TO DEATH IN AVALANCHE

SEN. HINMAN, WITNESS AND JUROR, TAKES STAND TODAY

Proceeding Proper, Chairman Rules—Republicans Postpone Selection of Sen. Allds' Successor as Leader

FLOOD SCENES AT CHENANGO BRIDGE

TWO STORMBOUND TRAINS ARE HURLED INTO CANYON

Great Northern Limited and Fast Mail Carried Over Ledge at Wellington, Wash., Landing in Mass of Wreckage

SECRETARY WILSON TAKES ISSUE WITH MR. PINCHOT

WILDLY ENTHUSIASTIC RECEPTION FOR PARTY

INTRODUCE BILLS IN STATE LEGISLATURE

FLOODS INUNDATE VILLAGES; CARRY ON TRAFFIC BY BOAT

Farms Flooded, Public Services Crippled, Families Compelled to Leave Homes and Heavy Losses Result

NO SIGN OF SETTLEMENT OF TROUBLE

Transit Company Does Not Respond to Efforts to Effect Agreement

THOUSANDS MOURN AVALANCHE VICTIMS

GENERAL STRIKE ON FRENCH STATE ROAD

FARMER CLEARED OF CHARGE OF MURDER

ORR IS RENOMINATED FOR PENSION AGENT

MICHIGAN GOVERNOR TELLS OF PRIMARIES

SEVEN INJURED IN TROLLEY COLLISION

MOB LYNCHES NEGRO ASSAILANT IN SOUTH

LATE BULLETINS

(Continued on Page Two.)

(Continued on Page Five.)

March 2, 1910: Story of flood damage is told on this front page. *Microfilm archives*

Philip Graham, the former publisher of the Washington Post, once described newspapers as the "first rough draft of history." Our front pages, particularly ones dominated by important breaking news stories, show the truth of that observation.

The sinking of the Titanic dominated front pages for days in 1912. The powerful story of the wreck of the unsinkable ship and the deaths of so many of its passengers, many of them wealthy, made for a story that fascinates readers even today. Front pages from April 15 and 16, 1912, change tone as the scope of the disaster become better known.

Editors put out an extra on July 12, 1913, so readers could get the latest news about the terrible fire at the Binghamton Clothing Co. Eventually, 33 people died from injuries caused by the fire.

The paper has a tradition of showing world and national events as they relate to people living locally. It showed how the local Armenian population was reacting to the many deaths in its homeland. Local troops took part in the effort to secure the national border with Mexico.

Several forces helped shape the Greater Binghamton region. The flow of immigrants to jobs at Endicott Johnson started in earnest, driving the population in Broome from 79,000 people to almost 114,000, an increase of 44 percent.

Thomas Watson Sr. took over at International Time Recorder. EJ and ITR adopted the eight-hour workday.

As the nation was recovering from the effort to win the War to End All Wars, the anti-liquor forces were gaining steam. In 1918, Binghamton became the largest municipality in New York to ban the sale of alcohol, and the rest of the nation went dry a year later.

AVERAGE DAILY CIRCULATION LAST WEEK, 25,957—A PRESS IN EVERY HOME.

BINGHAMTON PRESS

AND LEADER

If you want *what* you want *when* you want it, use the Press Want page and *get* it

THE WEATHER

Overcast, unsettled weather, with probably showers tonight or Tuesday.

VOL. 35. NO. 4. LAST EDITION MONDAY EVENING, APRIL 15, 1912 FOURTEEN PAGES PRICE ONE CENT

TITANIC SMASHES ICE BERG; 1,470 SAVED

WIRELESS BRINGS AID; PASSENGERS TRANSFERRED AT SEA

Liners Rush to Assistance of White Star Leviathan Reported Sinking; Vessel Still Afloat and Under Control

SEA IS SMOOTH AND WEATHER FAVORABLE

FACTS ABOUT THE TITANIC.

[illegible] cost $10,000,000. Was launched last May at Belfast. [illegible] steamship ever built is 882½ feet long, has tonnage of [illegible]. Bigger than two Delaware Dreadnaughts. [illegible] furnished with nine decks. From keel to funnel top is 175 feet.

[illegible] accommodates 5,000 passengers, and is a floating city in itself. [illegible] are Captain E. J. Smith, commander; surgeon, W. F. N. [illegible]; assistant surgeon, J. E. Simpson; purser, H. W. McElroy; [illegible] purser, R. L. Brocker; chief steward, A. Latimer.

Wireless dispatches up to noon today showed that the passengers of the monster White Star liner Titanic, which struck an iceberg off the Newfoundland coast last night, were being transferred aboard the steamer Carpathia, a Cunarder which left New York April 13 for Naples.

Already 20 boat loads of the Titanic's passengers have been transferred aboard the Carpathia, and allowing 40 to 60 people as the capacity of each lifeboat, some 800 or 1,200 people have already been transferred from the damaged liner to the Carpathia.

Another liner, the Parisian, of the Allan Company, which sailed from Glasgow for Halifax on April 6, is already close at hand and assisting in the work of rescue.

The Baltic and Virginian are also near the scene, and the Olympic is apparently near at hand, as the wireless information concerning the transfer comes from Captain Haddock of the Olympic.

The latest reports indicate that the transference of passengers is being carried on successfully and safely. The sea is smooth and the weather calm. It is probable that all of the passengers of the Titanic are safe.

While badly damaged, the Titanic is still afloat and is reported to be making her way toward Halifax under her own steam.

Views on Titanic and Some of Her Notable Passengers on Maiden Trip

ALFRED GWYNNE VANDERBILT.

C. M. HAYS.

Upper photograph, main dining saloon; lower, restaurant-reception room.

J. BRUCE ISMAY.

MRS. JOHN JACOB ASTOR.

JOHN JACOB ASTOR.

TRIP IS EVENTFUL FROM VERY START

TOWN FUNDS TIED UP IN BANK SMASH

Teachers in Many School Districts Also Unable to Get Money

MERCHANTS ARE AFFECTED

National Examiners Work Day and Night on New Berlin Defalcation

Utica, April 15. Two more examiners have joined the force under Chief E. F. Rorebeck and they put in several busy hours yesterday examining the accounts of the First National Bank of New Berlin. The men work day and night in the hope that the tangled affairs will soon be known. Mr. Rorebeck said today the final figures of Cashier Arnold's defalcation would be given out by the Treasury Department at Washington. He will not be permitted to make them public.

The bank examiners have discovered that many towns in Chenango county had their deposits in the bank. They are tied up and the towns cannot secure funds. Many school districts are affected and the teachers in them are without funds. Hundreds of fraternal organizations are also affected and are unable to pay sick or death benefits. Several merchants in the Unadilla Valley have returned their Spring stock of goods owing to lack of funds and some New Berlin business men have been obliged to telephone to out-of-town friends for funds to carry them along. A number of the banks in nearby places have offered to assist the business men here.

Wilfred F. Porter of Syracuse, a representative of the American Security Company of New York, was here Saturday. This company is on bonds of the towns of Columbus and New Berlin to the extent of $25,000 and stands to lose some.

It developed today that Arnold used his aged mother to spread the story a dozen years ago that he had been given an annuity of $12,000 a year from the estate of his wife's father. In after years when his mode of living changed and his extravagance increased, it was she who made it known that the amount had been increased to $25,000 a year. These stories were circulated when some of the directors became suspicious and intimated that their cashier had gone wrong. The bank directors now believe that Arnold even deceived his mother.

Bernard Rix of Buffalo, who is engaged to marry Miss Elizabeth Wright the favorite niece of Arnold, was a guest at the Arnold mansion yesterday.

MEXICANS MUST STOP MURDERS

Warning Couched in Strong Language Is Sent to Federals and Rebels

Washington, April 15. The murder of American citizens in Mexico, even those taken as prisoners of war, must stop. Warning, couched in strong diplomatic language and equivalent to an ultimatum, was served yesterday upon Mexico that the government and people of that country will be held responsible strictly for the protection of American life and property.

This applies both to the Mexican Government and the revolutionary forces under General Pascual Orozco. Both sides are warned that the execution of Americans taken prisoner is regarded by the United States Government as "practical murder," and that retaliation by the Mexican Government upon Americans captured from the rebel ranks will not be tolerated.

This warning, the strongest yet given to the Mexican Government and the rebel leaders, was sent at [illegible] o'clock yesterday afternoon in the form of a lengthy telegram to the American Ambassador at the City of Mexico, and in a separate despatch to the American consul at Ciudad Juarez with instructions to forward it [illegible] to Marion Letcher, the American Consul at Chihuahua.

PENNSYLVANIA IS FOR ROOSEVELT

T. R. Gets 70 Delegates to Chicago to 6 for President Taft

Philadelphia, April 15. — President Taft will have only six of the Pennsylvania delegates to Chicago to 70 for Theodore Roosevelt. It may be that the entire 76 will be swung for the former President. The figures given are based on fairly complete returns from Saturday's primaries.

Politicians look upon the triumph of Colonel Roosevelt with astonishment. The supporters of the former President were without a State organization and without an organization in many of the 32 Congressional districts.

The vote polled was light. In some districts it did not go much over 50 per cent of the total vote cast at the last general election. Col. Roosevelt received his heartiest vote from the reform element of the State represented by the Keystone party, which since its organization about two years ago, has opposed the regular Republicans at every election and succeeded in electing a reform Mayor in Philadelphia last year.

The supporters of President Taft carried only one district west of Philadelphia, that comprising Lancaster County, where Mayor McClain has a strong organization. In Philadelphia the Taft supporters carried the First, Second and Third districts, and elected one delegate in the Fifth district.

NOVEL STORAGE BATTERY INVENTED BY HANNOVER

Danish Professor Increases Power of Accumulator Five Times.

Copenhagen, April 15. Prof. Hannover, president of the Polytechnic Academy, has invented an electrical accumulator which he says will revolutionize the question of storage.

It has five times the capacity of the accumulators now in existence without any increase over them in size or weight. He uses porous lead alloy sheets, the capacity of which is increased by perforating them with millions of microscopic holes.

Prof. Hanover's accumulator, while it is likely to be more expensive, will be most valuable for aeroplanes and submarine boats and in lighting railroad trains.

April 15, 1912: Titanic disaster hits the front page of the Binghamton Press. *Microfilm archives*

AVERAGE DAILY CIRCULATION LAST WEEK, 25,957—A PRESS IN EVERY HOME

¶If you want *what* you want *when* you want it, use the Press Want page and *get* it

BINGHAMTON PRESS
AND LEADER

THE WEATHER: Fair and some cloudiness night and Wednesday. Cold tonight with lowest temperature about 35 degrees.

VOL. 35. NO. 5. LAST EDITION TUESDAY EVENING, APRIL 16, 1912. FOURTEEN PAGES PRICE ONE CENT

ONLY 868 ESCAPE

1,350 SOULS GO TO BOTTOM WITH HUGE LEVIATHAN TITANIC

Except for Those on Board Carpathia All Hope of Other Survivors Is Abandoned When Liners Report They Have No Castaways Aboard

WHOLE WORLD PLUNGED IN DEEPEST GLOOM

The appalling magnitude of the wreck of the giant liner Titanic has been but little mitigated by the fragmentary information which has filtered in today.

The rescuing steamer Carpathia has 868 survivors on board, according to the latest news received at the offices of the White Star Line in this city. This increases the list of saved by about 200 from the number first reported. But except for this, the favorable details are insignificant compared with the supreme fact that the Titanic is at the bottom of the Atlantic and that the shattered wreck took with her about 1,350 victims to their death.

The first reports giving the total survivors at 675 were varied by more favorable news early today, first from Captain Rostron of the Carpathia, who gave the number at about 800, and later by the positive announcement of the White Star Line that there are 868 survivors of the Titanic on board the Carpathia.

But with these revised figures there remain 1,341 persons who were aboard the Titanic, passengers and crew, who are today unaccounted for and apparently lost.

St. Johns, N. F., April 16.—All hope that any of the passengers or members of the crew of the Titanic, other than those on the Carpathia, are alive was abandoned this afternoon. All of the steamers which have been cruising in the vicinity of the disaster have continued on their voyages.

[illegible]

Continued on Page Two.

Notables on Wrecked Ship and Place Whence News of Their Fate Came

LADY DUFF GORDON, "CECILLE." Thought Lost

MRS. JOHN JACOB ASTOR. Young Rescued.

COL. JOHN JACOB ASTOR.

MAJOR ARCHIE BUTT, President's Aid, Thought Lost

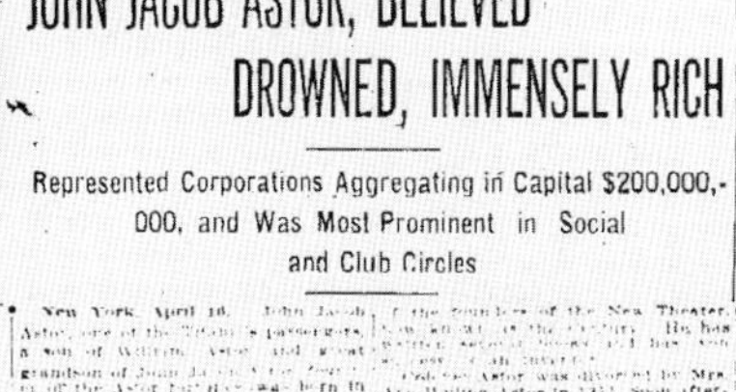

WILLIAM T. STEAD.

BENJAMIN GUGGENHEIM, Believed Drowned.

JOHN JACOB ASTOR, BELIEVED DROWNED, IMMENSELY RICH

Represented Corporations Aggregating in Capital $200,000,000, and Was Most Prominent in Social and Club Circles

New York, April 16.—John Jacob Astor, one of the Titanic's passengers, [illegible]

'NOT GUILTY' IS VERDICT

Charles W. Davis Freed on Charge of Burning South Gibson Store

Montrose, April 16.—[illegible]

SON OF RAILROAD MAN.

Los Angeles, April 16.—[illegible]

STEAMER ARRIVALS.

New York, April 16.—[illegible]

13 PARISHES IN LOUISIANA FACE DELUGE

Many Small Towns Are Wiped Out of Crest of Mississippi Flood

WATER 6 TO 20 FEET DEEP

At Least 50,000 Are Made Homeless in Parts of Two States

New Orleans, La., April 16.—Parts of 13 parishes in northeastern Louisiana are facing a deluge unparalleled in the history of disastrous floods of the lower Mississippi Valley.

Many small towns in East Carroll and Madison parishes already have been wiped out, vast stretches of valley lands are covered by from six to 20 feet of water, and a wall of the devastating waters 20 feet high and more than a mile in width is rushing through the great Dog Tail crevasse near Alsatia, La.

Already thousands are homeless and destitute. What will be the toll when the waters from the Panther Forest and Red Fork crevasses in Arkansas join with the water pouring through the Dog Tail breach no one can say. Parts of 13 Louisiana parishes and two Arkansas counties will be under water, and a conservative estimate is that the homeless in that territory will total at least 50,000. A large portion of a territory 180 miles in length and from eight to sixty miles in breath will be inundated.

To add to the alarming situation a veritable cloudburst in the Tensas Basin of North Louisiana yesterday resulted in from four to six inches of rainfall in 10 hours. High winds accompanied the rain and made more difficult the work of rescue in the overflowed districts.

Relief work is centered at Vicksburg, Miss., where already hundreds of homeless and destitute persons from the flooded Louisiana territory are quartered. Governor Brewer of Mississippi has sent tents and supplies there for the unfortunates and yesterday Governor Sanders of Louisiana ordered tents and bedding sent there. Large supplies of tents also are en route to Vicksburg from the federal authorities at St. Louis.

Although a number of negroes are reported missing, no verified reports of loss of life had been received. The live stock loss is enormous and the property damage in the territory under water and that yet in the path of the torrents will amount to several million dollars.

FLOOD AS FAR AS EYE CAN REACH

Tallulah, April 16.—As far as the eye can reach north, east and west from the highest point in this town nothing but water can be seen.

[illegible]

PRESIDENT ASKS FOR $768,000.

Washington, D. C., April 16.—President Taft yesterday sent to Congress a special message urging the immediate appropriation of amounts aggregating nearly $768,000 for use in combating the floods of the Mississippi river and to aid flood sufferers. [illegible]

GOVERNOR SIGNS 74 BILLS TODAY

Includes Measures for Protection of Factory Employes and for Canal Work

Albany, April 16.—Among 74 bills signed by Governor Dix today were eight measures recommended by the New York State Factory Investigating Commission [illegible]

LIGHTSHIP IS STRUCK BY PASSING STEAMER

Cornfield Point Boat Has Bow Stove in by Unknown Vessel

Saybrook, Conn., April 16.—The Cornfield Point lightship [illegible]

CUSTOMS REGULATIONS SUSPEND FOR CARPATHIA

New York, April 16.—[illegible]

RESOLUTION OF SYMPATHY IS ADOPTED IN CONGRESS

Washington, April 16.—The House of Representatives unanimously adopted a resolution today extending sympathy to the relatives of those who met their death in the disaster of the Titanic.

BATTLESHIP UTAH IN COLLISION WITH CONDOR

Big Fighting Craft Puts Into Navy Yard for Repairs

New York, April 16.—The battleship Utah steamed into the Brooklyn Navy Yard today for repairs because of slight injuries sustained in a collision yesterday with the Merchant's Line steamer Condor, between Green Point and Gravesend Bay. The Utah's injuries are so slight that it was at first thought no repairs would be necessary. The Condor was also slightly damaged.

April 16, 1912: News of the Titanic disaster gets worse as more details become available. *Microfilm archives*

ENGINE
MONOGRAM
OIL
8000 MILES
MONOGRAM
OIL
SAN FRANCISCO
AS USUAL

During an Excelsior promotion, riders stop in Binghamton before they continue their trek to San Francisco in 1910. *Courtesy Alan Jewell*

Burt Jewell, a well-known participant in the motorcycle races at the fairgrounds, poses on his Excelsior in Binghamton, circa 1910. *Courtesy Alan Jewell*

FIRST
NATIONAL
BANK

Riders line up for a race at the Phelps Bank building at Court and Chenango streets in Binghamton, 1910. Fourth and fifth from left are Karl Wright and Johnny Braico. *Courtesy Alan Jewell*

Binghamton clothing factory fire, July 22, 1913. *Courtesy Richard Gillespie*

Ruins And Burned
Post Office

Ruins of the Binghamton clothing factory on July 22, 1913. The post office suffered fire damage as well. *Courtesy Richard Gillespie*

AVERAGE DAILY CIRCULATION LAST WEEK, 26,650—A PRESS IN EVERY HOME

EXTRA **BINGHAMTON PRESS** EXTRA

AND LEADER

VOL. 36. NO. 86. TUESDAY EVENING, JULY 22, 1913. PRICE ONE CENT

OVER 25 ARE KILLED

TERRIFIED WOMEN LEAP FROM BUILDING

OVER 50 WOMEN INJURED IN MOST DISASTROUS FIRE OF BINGHAMTON'S HISTORY

At least 25 dead and 50 injured is the record of the worst fire in the history of Binghamton, which destroyed the four-story brick and timber building of the Binghamton Clothing Company on Wall street, next to the Postoffice, this afternoon.

The flames were discovered under the front stairway just before 3 o'clock. Mrs. Reed B. Freeman, wife of the president of the company tried with both telephone systems to reach Central Fire Station. The companies were absent on another alarm, and she could get no response. The first alarm was sounded from the box at Chenango and Warren streets, many blocks from the fire.

While the companies were responding to the alarm, the flames were licking up human lives in the doomed building.

At first the women, most of whom were employed on the upper floor, paid little attention to the alarm, thinking that there was a fire drill. They rose leisurely from their machines and prepared to walk out, when suddenly, the entire building was enveloped in dense black smoke.

Then, "Hell let loose for breakfast," said E. J. Lawrence, bookkeeper for the firm. The women rushed to the fire escapes at the east and south sides of the building.

Scores jumped from the windows. There were 134 persons in the building, according to the statement of Fire Chief Hogg at 4:15 o'clock. Of these he had been able to locate but 17, who were at the hospitals. It is known, however, that many women who were in the building escaped in safety, and either fled from the scene in horror, or lost themselves in the crowds that gathered in an instant.

It is conservatively estimated that the dead will number 25, and that at least 50 were hurt, many of whom will not recover. At 4:30 o'clock, 15 bodies had been taken from the ruins, and one woman had died at the Terrace Hospital.

The fire spread to the Postoffice, where the roof was burned off, and to the buildings of the McKallor Drug Company, Simon O'Neil, and the Binghamton Motor Car Company garage on Water street. The total damage will exceed $100,000. Christ Church also was scorched.

The Overall Company building had fire escapes and an automatic fire alarm. The fire alarm began ringing at 2:30 o'clock this afternoon and Mrs. Reed B. Freeman, who was in the office remarked, "That is another false alarm," referring to a number of fire drills that had been held in the factory.

Sees Flames in Stairway.

Stepping to the side door she saw flames creeping up the stairway leading to the upper floors from the street. Running to the telephone she tried to call the Central Fire Station first on one phone then on the other, without result, for an alarm had just come in calling the companies to the box on the corner of Chenango and Warren streets.

In a few seconds the flames and smoke were sweeping up the stairway and through the halls and work rooms.

The floors were covered with lint scraps of cloth cotton and other inflammable material through which the fire ran with inconceivable rapidity.

The employes in the cutters' room ran for the fire escapes as soon as the alarm sounded, and all are thought to have escaped.

The third floor employes were not so lucky. Here the first intimation was a smell of smoke, followed almost instantly by the [illegible] of the fire gong.

Many of the girls employed are of foreign nationality and at once became highly excited. Some of these ran to the stairway to be met by a cloud of smoke and flame, only to rush back to the windows from which the smoke was pouring. Shrieking and fainting the girls clung to fire escapes and made their way to the ground.

Many Jump from Windows.

[illegible] jumped from the windows and were picked up bruised and [illegible] and carried to the Knickerbocker garage.

[illegible] on the top floor was almost indescribable. Here the [illegible] were placed closer together, and the litter on the floor was [illegible].

The fire creeping rapidly up the stairway found its way to the [illegible] shaft and shot to the top floor, making this a living furnace [illegible] the space of a few minutes.

What happened here may never be known. Some of the girls [illegible] scrambling down the fire escapes, others recall jumping and [illegible] finding themselves assisted to places of safety, but what happened to a majority of those on the upper floor is only a matter of [illegible].

[illegible] of the girls crowded onto a fire escape in the rear of the building and were seen to cling there as a burst of smoke and flame [illegible] outward from the rear, then nothing more was seen of them.

Before the fire companies, which had been called to Warren street, got fairly at work every window in the overall factory was a sheet of flame. The roof had fallen in and the intense heat drove the workers back until it was almost impossible to strike the building with [illegible].

The flames were swept eastward by a strong breeze, and in a few minutes the Mitchell & Church factory was on fire. The building occupied by the Automatic Music Company had caught; the Postoffice windows were shattered by the heat and the window cases were burning.

These Snapshots Were Taken by The Binghamton Press Staff Photographer Thirty Minutes After the Fire Broke Out in the Binghamton Clothing Company's Four-Story Brick Building on Wall Street. The Picture on the Left Shows the Front View and the One on the Right the Rear View. The Heat from the Blaze at This Time Was Terrific, the Firemen Were Fighting Heroically in Face of the Scorching Funeral Pyre and Trying to Get as Near the Building as the Safety of the Apparatus and Their Own Lives Would Permit.

Second and third alarms were turned in and every available piece of apparatus in the city set at work. [illegible]

Advance of Flames Checked.

[illegible]

Mr. Freeman's Statement.

Reed B. Freeman, proprietor of the Binghamton Clothing Company, said: [illegible]

Fireman Rescue Body.

[illegible]

Postoffice on Fire.

[illegible]

12 GIRLS TAKEN TO CITY HOSPITAL

[illegible]

Mrs. Hotaling Tells Story.

Mrs. Ida Hotaling, as she lay upon [illegible] broken limbs [illegible] story of the fire.

"I was on the fourth floor and the first we knew was when we saw the fire coming up the elevator shaft. Then we heard the screams of the people on the first floor and I dashed among the first, heading down the stairway.

"Dozens and dozens of men and women crowded behind me on the stairs. When I reached the second floor, I plunged headlong through a window, which is all I remember.

"There must have been scores and scores of girls left on the fourth floor and caught in the stairway."

WOMEN MADE NO EFFORT TO HURRY

E. J. Lawrence, bookkeeper of the company, said that he was working in the office posting when the first alarm sounded. The flames were under the front stairway. There also was a rear stairway, and fire escapes at the south side of the building.

Most of the women were employed in the machine operating room on the fourth floor. They made no attempt to hurry from the building at first, thinking that the alarm was for a fire drill.

Messengers rushed through the building to drive the women out.

"Just then," said Lawrence, "the whole building burst into flames. It was a factory construction, with timber supports and brick walls. But it went up as though it had been powder. When the flames rushed up the front stairway, it was hell let loose for breakfast. The women were in a panic in an instant.

"The women might have been saved, I believe, but for the panic. They rushed to the fire escapes, and many of them leaped from the windows.

"I had 125 names on my pay rolls, and some of the employes were gone on vacation. The lists were all in the safe and are burned up, so that it is impossible to call the roll and get a line on those who are missing."

Binghamton's Beautiful Postoffice, Which Cost $80,000, Erected Under the Administration of President Cleveland and Which Was Damaged by the Fire.

SEES FIVE HANG TO FIRE ESCAPES

John M. Davidge of Davidge & Worden, heard the cry of fire while he was in the office of the firm's Water street garage and reached the immediate vicinity of the conflagration just in time to see several girl employes making frantic efforts to get out of the building.

No less than five of these employes were burned beyond recognition and disappeared from sight in the [illegible] mass of flames that swept through the interior of the building.

Others appeared at the windows and a half-dozen or more jumped from the fourth floor openings in efforts to escape being burned up.

"I never saw such a sight before in my life," said Mr. Davidge. "The cries of the girls for help were heart-rending. I helped pick up and carry to autos and other vehicles which were used to convey them to the hospitals no less than six badly burned and injured employes.

"I believe that there are fully 50 charred bodies in the ruins of the building, and perhaps the list will be increased to larger proportions when it is fully determined how many of the employes in the building at the time of the fire are missing.

RELATIVES ARE TAKEN TO SCENE

Several touring cars carried relatives of those employed in the factory to the scene of the fire and to the various hospitals. Mothers and sisters wrung their hands and children wept in an agony of suspense as they rushed from hospital to hospital and back to the burning building in a vain effort to locate their dying or dead.

SEES 4 WOMEN BURN TO DEATH

George Dearie, an employe of C. E. Hall's bottling establishment, was at the side of the bottling works at Division and Wall streets when he first noticed the smoke coming from the first floor of the building.

"There was no explosion," he said. "But the flames began to pour from the upper floor windows almost before I could sense what was happening. I rushed around to the front of the building. Three women plunged from a window and one of them landed on the sidewalk. The awning caught the others. At the south side of the burning building, I saw a woman come to a window near the middle and lean out. She burned to death before my eyes. I saw some come to the fire escape and three of them burned to death before they could reach the ground." The flames licked out of all of the windows and wiped them off the fire escape.

REED B. FREEMAN,
President of the Binghamton Clothing Company.

FIVE OTHER FIRES DURING 24 HOURS

Continued drought has rendered outbuildings exceedingly susceptible to sparks and the result has kept the fire department busy the past few days. Within the past 24 hours there were five other alarms.

The first alarm came in from the box at the corner of Exchange and Susquehanna streets shortly before 5 o'clock yesterday afternoon and was caused by children playing with matches. They ignited a box of refuse on the rear porch of the six-family apartment house at 23 Kenwood avenue but the flames had been extinguished without loss when the department arrived.

The second alarm was at a few minutes past [illegible] o'clock last evening, when flames were discovered in a shed in the rear of the residence at 42 Water street, owned by the B. S. Curran estate, and occupied by Joseph Bradley. The fire originated in some refuse in the shed corner. Two small boys were sent to sound the alarm from the box on Weed's Tannery, but they waited for a street car to approach and requested the conductor, who saw the blaze, to pull the box.

Three water lines were laid and these concentrated on the burning shed quickly subdued the fire, while a chemical line inside the house kept the flames from finding their way through upper windows. The damage, which is estimated at $600, is covered by insurance.

The third fire came at 11:15 o'clock this morning, when an alarm was rung in from box 424 at the corner of Clinton and Holland streets. The fire was in the two-story frame house at 246 Clinton street owned by George Ferner and occupied by Lewis A. Leet. The fire started from an oil stove on a back porch. The firemen used a garden hose to good advantage, extinguishing the flames just as they had burned a small hole into the attic of the residence. The loss will not exceed $50 and is covered by insurance.

Two still alarms just before and just after noon called the department to the Wolfe block on DeRussey street and to Kenwood avenue. The former was of small consequence and the latter was in some garbage and rubbish.

FOREIGNERS THINK CALL FIRE DRILL

Women Refuse to Respond to Alarm Because of Recent False Alarms

NEWS SPREADS RAPIDLY

Old Men and Women Search Frantically Among Ruins for Relatives

News of the tragedy spread through the city with incredible swiftness. Crowds of curious onlookers gathered, but curiosity gave way to practical efforts at rescue and relief as the full extent of the horror became evident.

Automobiles were pressed into service and the physicians who had responded to the summons for help used these, with the ambulance, to carry the injured to the hospitals.

The scene at the height of the fire was beyond adequate description. With flames crackling above their heads, the firemen worked with a desperation born of the terrible need. As the crushed and burned bodies were borne away, white-faced men and women pressed about in an effort to identify relatives or friends.

Old men and women from the Clinton street district were there looking for daughters who were known to have been in the doomed building. Brothers and sisters of the employes crowded about, or struggled through the crowds to gain a look at the faces of those who were carried out.

Yet many of those who perished had no relatives here. The news of their death will bring sorrow to humble homes far off in Europe.

Through all the confusion the firemen, the physicians and the volunteer helpers worked with a swiftness and precision that could not have been surpassed. Everything that could be done was done to save life.

The building where the fire originated was formerly the tobacco factory of Kendal & Clock. In the rear of the factory the barns of the Cotton livery stable stood until the fire which destroyed them about a month ago. The walls of the stables had been torn down. If these stables had been standing, nothing could have kept the flames from sweeping through them, and in all probability the entire block wolud have been destroyed.

One pitiful fact stands forth, above all others. Many lives—perhaps every life in the building—might have been saved if the girls and women on the fourth floor had heeded the first alarm.

Some of them did. But many of them, when the gong sounded, merely shook their heads and went on with their work. They had heard it often before. They did not believe there was danger. They were tired of being called from their work. So that the very signal which ought to have been their salvation went unheeded.

Some perhaps did not understand the meaning of the alarm. The result was that only a few on the upper floor responded while there was yet time to escape.

When messengers darted up the stairs to warn them it was too late. There was a rush for the stairway. A few of the foremost got down in safety. But behind these there was a jam, some fell, and those behind crowded down over them.

It is believed that among the dead are some of those who fell on the stairway.

But among those who reached the lower floors many were trapped by the flames and smoke. They dashed to the fire escapes, sprang to the windows, and some, in a frenzy of fear, leaped blindly to the ground.

A few of these escaped without serious injury. But high above them on the top floor of the building, while the flames roared and crackled beneath them, others wer cut off from the stairs and forced to seek the fire escape.

A crowd of these frenzied girls gained the fire escapes at the rear of the building. They climebde out of the windows and clung there, over a score of them, terror stricken and helpless. Then, while the onlookers held their breath in horror, the flames leaped out of the windows lower down and swept over the clinging figures, the smoke enveloped them, and they vanished from sight. But through the smoke clouds one and then another leaped, their bodies whirling over and over and striking with a force that mangled and crushed them.

July 22, 1913: News of the Binghamton Clothing Co. fire dominates this front page. *Microfilm archives*

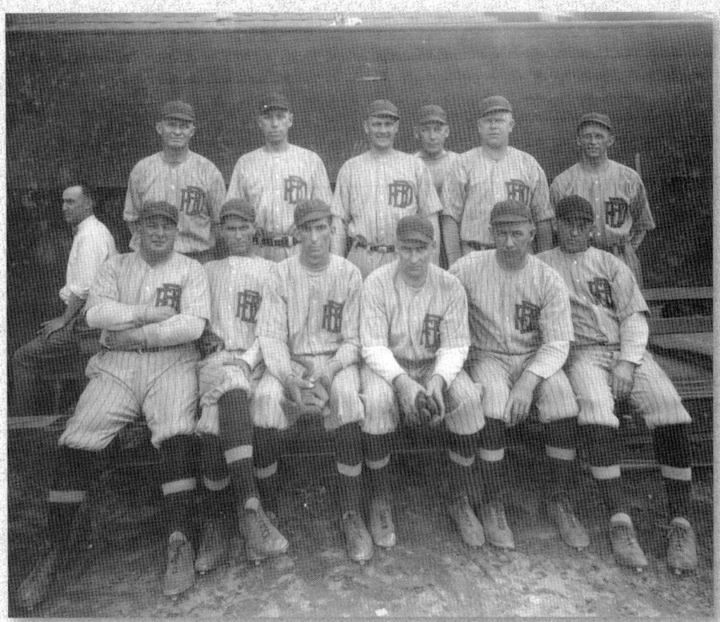

Binghamton Fire Department baseball team. Captain Jeremiah A. Foley is standing in the second row, far left. *Courtesy James P. Foley*

Elna Dodge, owner and driver of the car, takes her friend on a ride in Binghamton. The Broome County Courthouse can be seen in the distance. The house is believed to be the home of a public official. *Courtesy Marilyn Masters*

Binghamton Bridge Co.'s large 110-foot derrick at work on Binghamton High School, circa 1914. *Courtesy Richard Gillespie*

Binghamton High School Debate Team, circa 1914. C. Addison Keeler, Robert O. Brink, Julius Greengard and William A. Miller Jr. *Courtesy Broome County Historical Society*

THOMPSON'S
HOTCHKIN
REAL ESTATE

Hotchkin Real Estate and Thompson's Department Store fire at 71-75 Court Street, Binghamton, circa 1915. *Courtesy Richard Gillespie*

Interior of Hull, Grummond & Co. Cigar Factory at Wall and Henry streets, Binghamton, circa 1916. *Press & Sun-Bulletin archives*

Fifth Grade A

The fifth grade at Laurel Avenue School, Binghamton, circa 1916. The school later became Horace Mann Elementary School. Recreation Park is at right. *Courtesy Richard Gillespie*

"A. B. C."
The Binghamton Press and Leader is a member of the Audit Bureau of Circulations, 130 Railway Exchange Building, Chicago.

AVERAGE CIRCULATION LAST WEEK (*Net Paid*) 28,700—A PRESS IN EVERY HOME

BINGHAMTON PRESS
AND LEADER

THE WEATHER
Cloudy tonight and Saturday, with probably rain; much colder Saturday.

Vol. 39. No. 163. LAST EDITION FRIDAY EVENING, OCTOBER 20, 1916. TWENTY-FOUR PAGES PRICE ONE CENT

8-HOUR DAY, NEW ADDITION, AT I. T. R.

MAN CARRYING KNIFE TRIES TO CLIMB ON WILSON'S CAR

Prisoner, Knocked Down by Secret Service Man, Admits He Is Not Satisfied with President

HAS BOTTLE WITH LIQUID

Bryan and President Meet in Pittsburgh for First Time in Months and Have Auto Ride

Pittsburgh, Pa., Oct. 20.—While President and Mrs. Wilson were being driven about the city parks in an automobile here today, a man, apparently ... with a bag of tools ... on the running board of the ... but was knocked off by a secret service man.

...

BRYAN IS WORKING HARD FOR WILSON

...

NEW YORK CENTRAL TO RAISE $25,000,000

New York, Oct. 20.—Directors of the New York Central R. R. Company today authorized an issue of $25,000,000 new stock to be offered to stockholders at par on the basis of 10 per cent. of their present holdings. It is understood that the new stock will be issued early in the coming year. The proceeds will be devoted to general corporate purposes of the company, these probably including additional construction and improvements.

KING RECEIVES U. S. ATTACHES.
London, Oct. 20.—King George received yesterday in farewell audience Commander Powers Symington, the retiring American naval attache, and received his successor, Captain W. D. MacDougall.

BINGHAMTON REFUGEES FROM STRICKEN ARMENIA

At left, Essender Vardanasin, his sister, Mrs. Vosge Kalenian and her baby ... Brook avenue ... At right, Mrs. Bogoslan ... her sons, daughter-in-law and grandchild. Her husband was slain ... Turks ... Mardeos Gertmenian, formerly of this city, who is missing in Armenia.

LYONS WILL SEE NOLAN CASE PROBE THROUGH TO END

District Attorney Asks Commissioner Green to Furnish Additional Information

CONFERENCE IS HELD

...

BATTERY C DUE HOME OCT. 27

McAllen, Texas, Oct. 20.—Battery C probably will arrive in Binghamton on Friday, Oct. 27 ...

...

HOLLAND TAUNTS U. S. ON U-BOATS

...

SEABURY ATTACKS WHITMAN FINANCES

...

MANY LOCAL ARMENIANS MOURN FOR RELATIVES

G. A. Gertmenian Seeks in Vain to Get Information About His Brother, Formerly of This City

...

DOGS HELP SPREAD OF PARALYSIS, MONTREAL OFFICIALS BELIEVE

...

PASTEURIZATION IS CALLED NEEDLESS

...

MASTER PLUMBERS WILL HAVE REORGANIZATION

Changes Will Be Made to Suit Government Regulations

Washington, Oct. 20.—The Department of Justice has been advised that the directors of the National Association of Master Plumbers, which has been under attack as in violation of the Sherman law, have passed a resolution by which the entire plan of operation and by-laws of the organization are to be revised to meet the government's criticism.

FOOTBALL IS CALLED MOST SPIRITUAL GAME

...

G. W. FAIRCHILD'S ENDICOTT PLANT ANNOUNCES PLANS

Change in Hours Will Be Effective Nov. 1, to Accommodate Train Schedule

'GREATER THINGS' COMING

...

CONGRESSMAN FAIRCHILD.

...

KING DEPOSED, GREECE IS NOW NEAR ANARCHY; SOLDIERS RIOT

Constantine Tells British Minister Allies Had Better Address All Proposals to Former Premier Venizelos

TO START CENSORSHIP

Reservists in Athens Assemble in Groups and Take Law in Their Own Hands; Authorities Are Inactive

London, Oct. 20.—King Constantine of Greece, in an interview with the British Minister to Athens, complained bitterly of the action of the Allies in recognizing the provisional government at Saloniki, according to an Athens dispatch to the Daily Mail. The King told the Minister, according to the dispatch, that as the Allies had deprived him of all power they had better address their proposals to Venizelos.

...

HERALDS VENIZELOS AS WASHINGTON OF GREECE

...

SERBIANS MAKE GAIN AT MONASTIR

...

October 20, 1916: International Time Recorder, a predecessor to IBM, joined the push to an eight-hour workday. *Microfilm archives*

"A. B. C."
The Binghamton Press and Leader is a member of the Audit Bureau of Circulations, 330 Railway Exchange Building, Chicago.

AVERAGE CIRCULATION LAST WEEK (*Net Paid*) 29,000—A PRESS IN EVERY HOME

BINGHAMTON PRESS
AND LEADER

THE WEATHER
Fair tonight and Friday; cooler tonight.

VOL. 39. NO. 168. LAST EDITION THURSDAY EVENING, OCTOBER 26, 1916. TWENTY PAGES PRICE ONE CENT

BATTERY C IS GREETED BY CHEERING THRONG

PRESSURE OF TEUTON ARMY IN DOBRUDJA IS WEAKENED

Rumanian Troops Arrest Progress of Superior Austro-German Forces on Transylvania Front, Is Report

FRENCH TAKE 2 VILLAGES

Russians in Wooded Carpathians Successfully Withstand Assaults Made by Central Powers

PETROGRAD (VIA LONDON), OCT. 26.—The pressure of Field Marshal Von Mackensen's army in Dobrudja against the Russian and Rumanian forces has weakened somewhat, the War Office announced today.

On the Transylvanian front, the statement says, Rumanian troops arrested the progress of superior Austro-German forces.

PETROGRAD (VIA LONDON), OCT 26—Russian troops in the wooded Carpathians are successfully withstanding Teutonic assaults, the War Office announced today. It reports the repulse of an attack on the height northwest of Capul Mountain in that region.

PARIS, OCT. 26.—French cavalry on the Macedonian front, supported by infantry, occupied two villages southwest of Lake Doiran yesterday, the War Office announced today. The Serbians threw back German and Bulgarian forces in the region of the Cerna River.

PARIS, OCT. 26.—German artillery shelled positions captured by the French in the region of Vaux and Douaumont, on the Verdun front last night, says today's official report. The Germans undertook no infantry attacks.

RUMANIAN SITUATION IS REPORTED CRITICAL

Berlin, (By Wireless to Sayville), Oct. 26. "The capture of Tchernavoda by Field Marshal von Mackensen's army has definitely turned the military situation in Dobrudja in our favor," writes the military critic of the Overseas News Agency.

"The right wing of the combined Bulgarian, German and Turkish force marched on after the taking of Constanza and in a powerful push advanced 20 kilometres (about 12 miles) beyond that place. From that moment the capture of Medjidie was only a question of a few hours, as the town was threatened on the flank. The Russo-Rumanian position thus being rolled up from the east, the western point of support on the Danube, the town of Rasova also had to be given up.

"With this situation brought about, the attacking Teutonic Allies stood before the strong Danube bridgehead of Tchernavoda, which then had to serve as a cover for the hasty retreat of the defeated Russians and Rumanians. Today the railroad line from Constanza to Tchernavoda is completely in the hands of the victorious Allies constituting with the valuable material in locomotives and railroad cars taken with it, a first class base for strategic operations. All this material was abandoned by the fleeing Russians and Rumanians.

"The defeated army was separated into two parts. Those who did not remain on the battlefield or were not taken prisoner saved themselves by fleeing across the Tchernavoda bridge over the Danube, or to the northward in Dobrudja.

"After the capture of Tchernavoda the famous Danube bridge was dominated by Von Mackensen's guns. The bridge is the largest in all Europe and the swampy and frequently impassable terrain traversed between 17 kilometres. It was completed in 1896.

"With the loss of the Constanza-Tchernavoda line by Rumania the transport of provisions from Russia will have to be conducted over two minor and less efficiently equipped railway lines in Moldavia or by way of the Danube ports of Galatza and Ibraila which are by no means comparable to Constanza. At the same time the most important route for artillery transportation, by way of the railway from Constanza to Bucharest, is virtually eliminated. All shipments must go by way of Ibraila and Ploesci.

"The military situation for the Rumanians during the past two days has become much more critical, especially as the Germans and Austro-Hungarians already have partially conquered the Carpathian passes."

FRENCH FOLLOW UP ADVANTAGES AT VERDUN

Paris, Oct. 26.—The French troops at Verdun are following up as fast as

(Continued on page nine.)

SCENES ATTENDING RETURN OF BATTERY C TO BINGHAMTON

Above, at left, is picture of the Batterymen as they left Lackawanna station for march to State Armory; at right is picture showing crowd about station as train pulled in. Below shows Battery as it swung into Court street from Chenango during parade.

MISSIONARIES TO HOLD ELECTION

War and Work In Turkey Is Subject Discussed at Morning Session

Toledo, O., Oct. 26.—Addresses by missionaries, a business session with election of officers and miscellaneous business will occupy the third day of the convention of the American Board of Commissioners for Foreign Missions here today. More than 300 delegates are in attendance.

During the afternoon there will be a separate meeting for women. Miss Ellen Stone and other women missionaries will speak.

War and the work in Turkey will be discussed at the morning session by four men, Rev. C. T. Riggs of Constantinople, who was born of missionary parents at Marsovan; Dr. A. R. Hoover, ten years a medical missionary at Talas; Dr. C. E. Clark of Sivas, and Rev. W. N. Chambers of Adana, who has been 27 years in Turkey. "Bulgaria's Future" will be discussed by Rev. T. T. Holway of Sofia. Missionaries from the heart of Africa will also speak.

Tonight the president's annual address will be given by Dr. E. C. Moore of Cambridge. Four mission converts, one each from Africa, Peking, Madura and Turkey, will tell what the American Board has done for their people. Five student volunteers also will give brief addresses and will be consecrated to their work in the foreign field.

The meeting will close on Friday morning with addresses about conditions under the Russian flag by Dr. Clarence Ussher, who has just passed through the typhus epidemic and siege at Van, Turkey, and Rev. Robert Stapleton, at Erzerum, who went to Turkey in 1897.

TRACTION CAR HITS AUTO; 6 ARE DEAD

South Bend, Ind., Oct. 26.—Six persons were killed yesterday when an automobile in which they were riding was struck by a Northern Indiana traction car at the Indiana-Michigan line. Five were instantly killed and the sixth, a baby, died a few minutes later. All of the bodies were hurled over the Michigan line and Michigan authorities are investigating the accident. Curtains on the machine are supposed to have prevented Frank Brown, who was driving, from seeing the traction car.

MRS. BOISSEVAIN GIVES UP EUROPEAN TOUR

Los Angeles, Oct. 26.—Mrs. Inez Milholland Boissevain of New York has been compelled to cancel her transcontinental tour in support of a Federal amendment for woman suffrage.

Mrs. Boissevain collapsed after her address in this city on Monday. Tonsilitis developed yesterday, her physician announced.

SUPERDREADNAUGHTS START OUT FOR PACIFIC

Norfolk, Va., Oct. 26.—The superdreadnaughts Pennsylvania and Nevada, after being stormbound for several days, put to sea last night to complete their Fall target practice. The big 14-inch guns will be tested out completely at short and intermediate ranges, firing at moving targets.

Villa and Zapata Plan to Act With Felix Diaz

U. S. OFFICERS GET PROOF OF CAMPAIGN TO OUST CARRANZA

Southern Leader Sends 1,000 Men to Help Bandit; Washington Is Puzzled Over Gathering in United States of Non-combatant Mexicans

San Antonio, Oct. 26.—Army intelligence [illegible] obtained possession of [illegible] it is reported, give in detail a plan for the overthrow of Carranza, in which Villa and Zapata are to join forces with Felix Diaz in the campaign which military authorities believe is now well under way.

A statement made to Army Headquarters here by a representative of Zapata confirms a report through military channels that plans under way for many months for a joint campaign by Villa and Zapata are now being put in operation. An exchange of messages between Villa and Zapata, this report says, resulted in Zapata starting more than 1,000 troops northward to join a Villa command, about 30 miles west of Chihuahua City, as well as the shipment of a large supply of ammunition for these and additional troops.

VILLA IS MASSING FORCE NEAR YSABEL AND YSIDRO

El Paso, Oct. 26.—Gen. Gonzales last night announced the receipt of a message from Gen. Trevino at Chihuahua City stating that all was quiet there and authorizing him to deny "in vigorous terms" the report that the city had fallen before an attack by Villa.

Skirmishing with a Villa force continues near Chihuahua, but the panic in the city has been allayed by the concentration there of 8,000 troops, embracing practically all the de facto forces in the States of Coahuila, Tamaulipas, Nuevo Leon and Zacatecas, to reinforce the Chihuahua troops.

Villa is reported to be gathering his men in considerable numbers between San Ysidro and Santa Ysabel. The skirmishing that is going on is believed to be a sort of rear guard action to safeguard the withdrawal of the force with the eleven trains captured from Gen. Osuna.

A decree issued by Carranza ordering that all taxes be paid in gold has been received at Chihuahua City.

Gen. Trevino received yesterday a wireless message from Carranza, announcing that the First Chief is a candidate [illegible] stating that [illegible] many changes in his [illegible]. Pablo Gonzales, it stated, is to give up his command of the First Military Division to accept a special confidential commission.

GUARDS SHOULD BE KEPT AT BORDER, IS BELIEF

Washington, Oct. 26.—Villistas' activity near Chihuahua yesterday had the effect today of convincing officials here that no thought should be given soon to removal of guardsmen from border patrol duty or withdrawal of General Pershing's column from Mexico. Fear was felt that if Villa should succeed in his apparent movement to capture Chihuahua, he might find it easy to get control later of nearly all northern Mexico. The entire Mexican situation was regarded as more serious than for many months.

Conditions at Chihuahua were the subject of greatly conflicting reports. Mexican Ambassador Arredondo received from Consul Garcia at El Paso a denial of General Trevino that he was short of ammunition or intended to evacuate Chihuahua. Carranza losses in the fight with Villistas at Santa Ysabel had been slight, he said, and 8,000 troops had arrived to reinforce the garrison. War Department reports, however, were that Villa was encamped five miles from Chihuahua with a considerable force, after having defeated Carranza troops severely and that Trevino was ready to abandon the city.

Officials Are Puzzled.

Official reports received here showing that members of the Carranza, Obregon, Trevino, Huerta and Madera families are now in San Antonio, Tex., have puzzled observers seeking an explanation of the gathering in the United States of non-combatant Mexicans.

Some officials believe economic and social conditions generally in Mexico are such as to make Mexicans of the wealthy class anxious to get their women folks out of the country for the present. The dispatches indicate that most of the women have come recently from Mexico.

The State Department has not received, so far as known any official reports bearing out the charges of General Carranza's political enemies that his grip is relaxing and that he is preparing to leave Mexico.

Situation Highly Uncertain.

It is agreed in official circles that the military situation in Chihuahua State has been made highly uncertain by renewed bandit activities. Despite reports that Villa is personally leading his men against the Carranza garrison at Chihuahua City, neither the State nor War Departments has receiving convincing reports that he is alive.

Military experts are frankly pessimistic of the results of the Carranza campaign against these bandits because they have no transport trains and supply systems which would permit them to chase the outlaws into the barren hill country. It is known that this weakness of the Mexican forces has been strongly presented to the American-Mexican commissioners. To the minds of American army officers, it represents a serious obstacle to the present restoration of order in northern Mexico.

ROB TICKET AGENT; $1,040 IS TAKEN

South Bend, Ind., Oct. 26.—A. M. Trost, night ticket agent at the Lake Shore depot, was robbed of $1,040 shortly after midnight. He was on his way to the express office with the money when he was attacked from behind.

NAME INVESTIGATOR TO PROBE ELECTION FRAUDS

New Impetus Is Given to Federal Inquiry.

Washington, Oct. 26.—New impetus to the federal inquiry into election frauds was given here today with the appointment of Frank C. Dailey as special assistant to the Attorney-general of charge of investigation and prosecutions of election law violations in Indiana, Ohio and Illinois.

Assistant Attorney-general Graham will have charge of the Washington end of the investigation.

EPISCOPALIANS TO HAVE NEWSPAPER

Pastoral Letter to Review World Conditions And European War

St. Louis, Oct. 26.—Publication of a weekly periodical "based upon newspaper rather than on magazine lines" will be started by the Protestant Episcopal Church, Jan. 1, it was announced at today's session of the church convention here. This, it was announced, will be the first step in an attempt to preach the Gospel through the press.

The pastoral letter of the general convention of the church will deal with world conditions and will review the European war in its effect upon the other nations of the world and upon the United States in particular, according to another announcement made today.

The letter being prepared by the Right Rev. Charles H. Brent, bishop of the Philippines, the Right Rev. William Lawrence, bishop of Massachusetts and the Right Rev. Charles P. Anderson, bishop of Chicago, is the message of the general convention to the communicants of the church and will be presented at the final joint session tomorrow. Subsequently it will be read in every Episcopal church in the United States. Today the House of Deputies planned to attempt the completion of the division report of the joint commission on the revision and enrichment of the book of common prayer.

It was announced that the lower house would meet in executive session late today to consider the selection of the House of Bishops of the Rev. Frank Touret of Colorado Springs for the missionary bishopric of western Colorado and the Rev. Hugh L. Burleson of New York for the missionary episcopate of South Dakota.

BRITISH STEAMER SINKS; CREW LANDS

London, Oct. 26.—The British steamship Sidmouth has been sunk and her crew has been safely landed, reports Lloyds' Shipping Agency.

The Sidmouth hailed from Cardiff, was built in 1903, of 4,045 tons gross, and belonged to Anning Brothers of Stockton. She was last reported as arriving at Spezia, Italy from Cardiff, on Sept. 11.

YONKERS CARS RUN UNDER POLICE GUARD

Mayor Warns People to Keep Off Streets.

Yonkers, Oct. 26.—With four policemen on each car and with citizens warned by a proclamation by Mayor Lennon to keep off the streets trolley service was resumed by the Yonkers Railway Company today after an interruption which had continued longer than a month.

The trips of the first cars which started out were not attended by violence. Citizens refused to ride, apparently fearing trouble. Automobiles carrying police moved in front of and behind each car.

QUICKER PAY FOR CARRIERS.

Washington, Oct. 26—Mail messengers and postal screen wagon contractors will receive their pay through postmasters instead of the Department at Washington, beginning Nov. 1. Under this system the carriers will receive their pay 20 days earlier than under the old method.

HUNDREDS WELCOME RETURNING SOLDIERS

Last of City's Militia Organizations Comes Back from Border Service Amid Great Demonstration by Citizens

TANNED, HALE, HAPPY

Artillerymen Given Opportunity to Greet Relatives After Parade, but Will Remain Under Federal Orders for Time

A rousing reception was given to Battery C on its arrival from the border at 12:30 o'clock this afternoon.

Hundreds of people surrounding the Lackawanna passenger station, lining the viaduct railings and wherever a good view could be obtained of the boys in khaki on board the special, cheered madly, waved small flags, blew horns and uncorked enthusiasm of the sort to let the artillerymen know that the entire city is glad all have safely returned from four months of Federal service.

The Battery special was hauled into Binghamton by engine 1010, one of the fast passenger type of the Lackawanna system. Arriving in Elmira over the Northern Central at 6:30 o'clock this morning the train was delivered to the Lackawanna road shortly after 10 o'clock. During the interval of stopping in Elmira the horses on the train, 37 in all, occupying two cars, were exercised, watered and fed.

Leave Elmira at 10:48.

The special left Elmira at 10:48 o'clock and should have reached Binghamton at 12:15 o'clock, but was held up by three freight trains ahead of it. Throngs of people congregated at the station hours in advance of the arrival of the Battery. As the hour for arrival drew near the crowd steadily increased in numbers until it was with difficulty that passage ways could be cleared for people having business with the railroad to move freely through the crowds.

"Uncle Sam," riding a white horse, and George Washington Lee with his drum arrived early, attracting much attention. The local units of the National Guard marched from the State Armory, to the station shortly after noon and were stationed on Lewis street as the Battery train pulled in. When the engine hove in sight pandemonium reigned. The huge throng let loose their pent-up feelings and pushed and shoved their way to positions as near as possible to the tracks, so that they could extend gladsome greetings to the boys from the border.

Behind the engine were seven flat cars, on which were caissons, supply and escort wagons, a motor truck—the gift of George F. Johnson to the company during its stay on the border—four guns and limbers.

Next in line were two box cars, containing 37 horses, five of which were private mounts.

Soldiers in Pullmans.

The four Pullmans bringing up in the rear of the long train held the soldiers. The windows of the cars were open, and tanned and hardened faces appeared with smiles overspreading countenances as they recognized mothers, sisters, brothers, sweethearts and friends among the people crushing in about the cars with upturned faces reflecting the gladness of their hearts over the return of the artillerymen.

It was a welcome the boys in khaki will not soon forget. No person in the crowd could stand and witness the scene of open-armed welcome without being thrilled with the patriotism and feeling the emotion that comes when soldiers move by.

A detailed of patrolmen tried to keep the crowd back, but failed, for there was no denying the relatives and friends a place where they could grasp the hands of the boys and tell them how delighted they were over the homecoming.

Parade is Formed.

The artillerymen filed from the forward Pullman and formed in two long lines on the platform to the east of the station. Brisk orders were given to keep in line. When all were out of the cars the order "forward march" was given and Batterymen marched west on the platform and to the street directly east of the viaduct. The head of the line was halted near the intersection of Lewis street. The procession was formed on Chenango street. "Uncle Sam" on his white horse was in the lead. Directly following was the headquarters staff officers of the First Infantry Regiment, N. Y. N. G.

(Continued on Page Twelve).

October 26, 1916: Binghamton's militia service returns from Mexican border service. *Microfilm archives*

"A. B. C."
The Binghamton Press and Leader is a member of the Audit Bureau of Circulations, 11E Railway Exchange Building, Chicago

AVERAGE CIRCULATION LAST WEEK (*Net Paid*) 28,880—A PRESS IN EVERY HOME

BINGHAMTON PRESS
AND LEADER

THE WEATHER
Fair, partly cloudy tonight and Thursday; cooler tonight.

VOL. 39. NO. 173. | LAST EDITION | WEDNESDAY EVENING, NOVEMBER 1, 1916 | EIGHTEEN PAGES | PRICE ONE CENT

13,000 PEOPLE GREET PRESIDENT HERE

DEUTSCHLAND ARRIVES HERE ON SECOND TRIP ACROSS OCEAN

German Submarine Freighter Ties Up at Berth in New London, Conn., Harbor at 2:35 o'Clock This Morning

HER COMING IS SURPRISE

Brings Cargo of Medicines and Chemicals: Is Screened from Sight by Pontoon Carrying High Board Fence

PRESIDENT SHAKES HANDS WITH HUNDREDS HERE

General view of great crowd which greeted President Wilson when his train stopped at Johnson City this morning. In the circle the President is shown shaking hands over the railing of the rear platform of his car with people in the crowd at Johnson City.

WILSON IS OBJECT OF OVATION BY 2 CROWDS

Throngs in Binghamton and Johnson City Ignore Politics in Paying Tribute to Chief Executive of Nation

HE EXPRESSES PLEASURE

George F. Johnson Joins Party and Is Cheered While Country's Highest Official Congratulates E.-J. Employes

Binghamton and Johnson City gave the President of the United States a greeting this morning which should remain long in his memory as one of the most enthusiastic of his career.

Between 12,000 and 13,000 people cheered him, not as a politician but as the head of the Nation.

It was also the occasion of another ovation for George F. Johnson, who joined the President in this city and continued as his guest on the train bearing the President to Buffalo, where he speaks this afternoon and evening.

President Wilson's private car was attached to the second section of Lackawanna train 15 and reached this city shortly after 8 o'clock. The President made no effort to address the crowd in this city confining his acknowledgment of the greeting to handshaking. The crowd which greeted him in Johnson City was more fortunate as he made a short address there.

A crowd estimated at 10,000 persons greeted the President at Johnson City this morning and rent the air with cheers when his train stoped at the Arch street station.

Men and boys were packed closely upon sheds, the roofs of factories, in the windows, clinging to telegraph poles like flies on a stick of candy; crowded standing and sitting on top of a string of freight cars ...

FIVE AMERICANS DROWN WHEN MARINA IS SUNK

Affidavits Secured by Consul at Queenstown Agree That Boat Was Torpedoed Without Warning: Boat Goes Down in Six Minutes

TWO SUBMARINES WERE PRESENT, SAILOR SAYS

RUMANIAN AND TEUTON ARMIES GAIN SUCCESSES

Russian Attacks on Approaches to Lemberg Are Repulsed, Berlin Says

HUGHES WILL MAINTAIN ALL RIGHTS OF AMERICANS, HE SAYS

Would Not Put Embargo on Munitions or Warn Citizens Off Ships, He Declares in Response to Heckler in Indiana

(Continued on page 4, column 3)
(Continued on page eight)
(Continued on page 4, column 1)

November 1, 1916: President Woodrow Wilson visits the Southern Tier. *Microfilm archives*

A National Guard unit poses for this photograph in front of the old armory in Binghamton in 1916. *Press & Sun-Bulletin archives*

Troops march through Binghamton at a gathering before they head off to combat in 1917. *Press & Sun-Bulletin archives*

B-100.000

Bond drive in Courthouse Square in Binghamton, 1916. *Press & Sun-Bulletin archives*

"A. B. C." The Binghamton Press and Leader is a member of the Audit Bureau of Circulation, 330 Railway Exchange Building, Chicago.

BINGHAMTON PRESS AND LEADER

THE WEATHER: Snow or rain tonight; colder; Saturday, probably fair.

VOL. 39. NO. 304. LAST EDITION FRIDAY EVENING, APRIL 6, 1917. TWENTY-FOUR PAGES PRICE TWO CENTS

PRESIDENT SIGNS DECLARATION OF WAR; U-BOATS READY TO ATTACK OUR SHORES

WILSON ISSUES PROCLAMATION DIRECTING ARMY AND NAVY TO BE PUT ON BATTLE FOOTING

Affixes Signature to Resolution Passed by Congress Declaring State of Conflict to Exist with Germany

APPEALS TO CITIZENS OF U. S. TO BE LOYAL

WASHINGTON, APRIL 6.—President Wilson today signed the resolution of Congress declaring a state of war between the United States and Germany.

All the naval militia and naval reserves were called to the colors with the President's signing of the war resolution.

The war resolution was signed by the President at 1:11 o'clock.

The President also signed a proclamation formally declaring a state of war between the United States and Germany. In the proclamation he called upon American citizens to give support to all measures of the government.

CO. H WILL BE MUSTERED INTO FEDERAL DUTY

Detail Probably Will Be Left at Peekskill to Guard Prisoners

PLAN DETENTION CAMP

Local Militiamen Are Given Target Practice After Record Hike

UNITED STATES SEIZES GERMAN SHIPS INTERNED IN MANY PORTS

Collectors at Various Harbors Act Early Today on Instructions Received from Treasury Department

BOSTON FIRST TO ACT

91 Vessels, Which Have Been Laid Up Since European Conflict Began, Are Placed Under American Guards

$5,000 WILL BE ASKED FOR 200 SPECIAL POLICE

Auxiliary Force Will Assist in Guarding City for Duration of War

TO SERVE WITHOUT PAY

Council Tonight Also Will Consider Charter and Paving Problems

TEUTON SUBMARINES IN GULF OF MEXICO, BELIEF IN CAPITAL

Hitherto Unconfirmed Report Is Supported by Word Received from Neutral Country Contiguous to Germany

ARE SUPPLIED FROM MEXICAN BASE

Washington, April 6.—Persistent but hitherto unconfirmed reports of German submarines waiting in the Gulf of Mexico for the opening of hostilities of the United States were further supported today by advices to the government from Europe.

The report was received from one of the neutrals contiguous to Germany, which has served as a clearing house for German information since the severance of diplomatic relations.

It was reported that more than a score of German submarines were already in Mexican waters.

GERMANS, INDICTED IN NEW YORK, SENTENCED

GERMANS ENDEAVOR TO INCITE NEGROES

GERMAN PAPERS HEAP ABUSE UPON WILSON

MOVIE TAX BILL TO BE INTRODUCED

WILSON WILL HAVE $100,000,000 FUND

NEW YORK COLLEGES TO OFFER ALL RESOURCES FOR WAR TO GOVERNOR

Meeting Will Be Held in Albany April 11

NEARLY 100 GERMAN VESSELS ARE SEIZED

CANADIAN DRAFT DENOUNCED.

(Continued on page eight)

(Continued on Page Twenty-two)

April 6, 1917: The United States enters World War I. *Microfilm archives*

"A. B. C."
The Binghamton Press and Leader is a member of the Audit Bureau of Circulation, 330 Railway Exchange Building, Chicago

BINGHAMTON PRESS
AND LEADER

THE WEATHER
Fair and colder tonight and Friday; lowest temperature 35 degrees.

VOL. 40. NO. 2. | LAST EDITION | THURSDAY EVENING, APRIL 12, 1917. | EIGHTEEN PAGES | PRICE TWO CENTS

U. S. WILL LAUNCH COLOSSAL CAMPAIGN TO BREAK DOWN SUBMARINE BLOCKADE

BRITISH TAKE TWO POSITIONS FROM GERMANS AT VIMY RIDGE

English Troops Now Astride River Souchez and More Prisoners Are Captured, Official Announcement Says

FRENCH CONTINUE GAINS

Teutons Are Driven Back to Southwestern Edge of Upper Coucy Forest; Enemy Suffers Losses on Woevre

London, April 12.—The British captured early this morning two important positions in the enemy's lines north of Vimy Ridge and are now astride of the River Souchez, according to an official statement issued by the War Office. A number of prisoners were taken. The statement says the weather is stormy."

Two German counter attacks on Vimy Ridge were broken up last night with heavy losses to the attackers. The statement follows:

"The weather continues wet and stormy. Early this morning we attacked and captured two important positions in the enemy's lines north of Vimy Ridge, astride the River Souchez. A number of prisoners were taken by us.

"During the night two hostile attacks upon our new positions on the northern end of Vimy Ridge were driven off by our machine gun fire with heavy German losses. Some progress has been made south of the River Scarpe."

FRENCH DRIVE GERMANS BACK; TAKE TRENCHES

Paris, April 12.—In an attack last night on the new front below St. Quentin, between Coucy and Quincy-Basse, the French drove back the Germans to the southwestern edge of the upper Coucy forest, capturing several important positions, the war office announces. In the Champagne the Germans were ejected from trenches east of Sapigneul. The statement follows:

"Between the Somme and the Oise artillery fighting continued with violence during the night, especially in the region of Urvillers.

"South of the Oise our troops after artillery preparation attacked the German positions east of the line from Coucy La Ville to Quincy-Basse. After a spirited engagement we forced back the enemy as far as the southwestern edge of the upper Coucy forest. Several important points of support fell into our hands notwithstanding the resistance of the enemy, who left a number of dead on the ground and prisoners in our hands.

"Northeast of Soissons there were patrol encounters and active artillery fighting, especially in the sector of Laffaux. North of the Aisne our reconnoitering parties penetrated the German lines at several points and brought back 40 prisoners, including an officer.

"East of Sapigneul a sharp attack enabled us to expel the enemy from certain portions of trenches which he had held since April 4, and our line was re-established intact. Two surprise attacks by the Germans in the Champagne, in the sectors of Ville-Sur-Tourbe and Butte-Du-Mesnil, were broken up by our fire, which inflicted losses on the enemy.

"In the course of an incursion into the German lines in the Woevre, northeast of Remenauville, we inflicted appreciable losses on the enemy. Patrol encounters occurred southwest of Leintrey."

GERMANS MINIMIZE VICTORIES OF ALLIES

Copenhagen, (via London), April 12.—The battle of Arras, in the opinion of the German press, is an event of only local importance, lamentable it is true but already brought to a standstill and not affecting in any degree the strategic situation. It is interpreted by general consent as part of the plan of the Anglo-French command, foiled in its intentions of delivering a shattering blow on the Somme front, to roll up the new Hindenburg line by assault on both flanks, at Soissons and Arras. Both attempts are already described as failures, despite regrettable losses in men and probably guns. The British official reports are given scanty notice and are printed in inconspicuous type without headlines. The censorship authorities are evidently assured that the reading public generally accept the German version and that confidence in Field Marshal von Hindenburg is unimpaired.

An interview between the Field Marshal and a Spanish correspondent is given prominence by the German

(Continued on Page 8, Column 5).

LOCAL UNITS OF FIRST REGIMENT RETURN HOME AFTER 9 WEEKS OF SERVICE

MAYOR FIXES MONDAY EVENING FOR RECEPTION TO WELCOME FIRST REGIMENT BACK HOME

OUR soldiers of the First Regiment have come home after a long period of service which has been peculiarly monotonous and trying. They have guarded the water supply of New York City, patrolling a bleak, desolate country, much of the time during bitter Winter weather.

They have experienced actual hardships, cheerfully, and are now awaiting further calls to serve their country.

It is due our soldiers to show them that the city they represent appreciates the service that they have rendered, honors them for the soldierly spirit in which it has been rendered, and is grateful for the distinction which the city has achieved through their disciplined patriotism.

Therefore, in the name of the City of Binghamton, I ask that our people gather at the State Armory in Washington street Monday evening, April 16, to welcome our soldiers at an informal reception and to thank them as individuals for what they have done.

FRANK H. TRUITT, Mayor.

Believed That Infantrymen Will Be Called to Federal Duty in Next Week or 10 Days

MEDALS ARE PRESENTED TO MARKSMEN

The Binghamton infantry units of the First Regiment—Company H, Headquarters Company and Mounted Detachment—returned to the home station this morning, arriving in the city over the Delaware & Hudson Railroad in a special train at 4 o'clock.

Few residents of the city knew the time of the arrival of the militiamen, and consequently the welcome to the boys in khaki after nine weeks' absence from home was not what the city would have given had the guardsmen detrained and marched to the State Armory later in the day. For this reason plans are being made for a rousing welcome home next Monday evening.

After marching to the drill hall at the State Armory and placing kits and rolls, the men were dismissed by Second Lieutenant Floyd D. McLean, the acting commander of the Company, with orders to report for assembly at 2 o'clock this afternoon. A similar ceremony was followed by the dismissal of the other units.

Many relatives and friends of the soldiers were in the galleries when the commands lined up in the drill hall at 2 o'clock. The assembly was marked by the presentation of badges by Second Lieutenant McLean to the following men.

Expert riflemen—Sergeant Elwood, Private Stever.

Sharpshooters—Corporals Jenkins, St. John, Cornelius D. Wolcott, Privates Goodenough, Keeler, Kline and Raymond.

Marksmen—Corporal Cunningham, Musician Whitcomb and Privates Benjamin, Page, Hall, Taylor, Ballantine, Bass, Collins and Hathaway.

The men were dismissed following the ceremony and ordered to assemble at 9 o'clock tomorrow morning in citizens' clothes.

The company quarters have been alive with rumors for many days as to the ultimate destination of the First New York Regiment and not until the actual work of packing up did

(Continued on Page 9, Column 1).

U. S. OFFICIALS PLAN FOR WAR COUNCILS

Delegations from England and France Are Expected in Washington

Washington, April 12.—The government today began to prepare for important war councils to be held here soon with commissions from England and France. The State Department announced it expects the arrival within 10 days of a British delegation, headed by Foreign Minister Arthur J. Balfour, and including Admiral De Chair, representing the Navy; General Bridges, representing the Army, and the Governor of the Bank of England. It was learned authoritatively also that a French commission, headed by M. Viviani, Minister of Justice, and former Premier, will arrive about the same time.

The conference will take up such questions as the steady supply of munitions and food to the Entente Allies, the proposed $3,000,000,000 loan, naval co-operation, military participation of the United States, readjustment of diplomatic relations between the United States and the entente nations, relations with the remaining neutrals and future peace terms.

Although as a result of the conferences a concert of action to effect the most thorough military and naval co-operation is certain, it is felt that the discussions will not change the United States' traditional policy of not entering into European alliances.

CAN SUPPLY CLERKS.

Washington, April 12.—The Civil Service Commission has assured Secretary Baker of its ability to supply the big increase in the clerical force required by the War Department as an incident to enlargement of the army, from its rolls of eligibles.

COMMITTEE OF 7 TO RULE RAILROADS

National Transportation Facilities Will Be Merged Voluntarily

Washington, April 12.—National transportation facilities of the principal railroads in the United States during the war will be merged voluntarily and operated under the general direction of a central executive committee of seven, co-operating closely with the Government in handling troops, military supplies and general commodities.

The central committee will decide all matters of general railroad policy and will operate through the American Railroad Association's special committee on defense, whose membership will be increased to 28 and divided into six sub-committees to work with the six military departments. This system is expected to produce co-operation not only among the railroads but between them and the Government.

RUSSIAN GOVERNMENT SEIZES RESERVE FOOD

All Corn and Cereals Fit for Fodder Are Taken

London, April 12.—A Petrograd dispatch to Reuters says that the provisional government has ordered all reserves of the 1916 harvest of corn and cereals, which are fit for fodder, to be placed at the disposal of the State.

The entire reserves of 1917 harvest, except what is required for seed and the needs of the families of the peasants, has also been expropriated.

RAINS PREVENT RUIN OF GRAIN FROM DROUGHT IN MIDDLE WEST

Oklahoma Wheat Crop Will Be from 20,000,000 to 23,000,000 Bushels If Soaking of Ground Continues

IS LESS THAN LAST YEAR

Oat Fields in Kansas Are Expected to Benefit Particularly from Downpour; Bankers Furnish Seed for Replanting

Kansas City, April 12.—Rains that soaked the wheat and grain belts in Oklahoma and Kansas yesterday, saved thousands of acres that would have been ruined had the drought continued a few days more, according to the opinions expressed today by expert agriculturists. Reports received here today indicated that at various points in Kansas and Eastern Oklahoma the rain is continuing.

Frank M. Gault, president of the State Board of Agriculture of Oklahoma, declared last night that if the rain continued today the wheat crop in that State would be from 20,000,000 to 23,000,000 bushels as compared with last year's crop of 27,000,000.

The situation in Kansas was summed up by J. C. Mohler, the secretary of the State Board of Agriculture, with a statement that the general rain would save much of the grain and that it had been of untold value to the Winter wheat.

The oats crop in Kansas was expected to benefit particularly from the downpour which amounted to more than an inch yesterday in the western parts of the State.

The largest oats acreage in the history of the State is being sown this Spring, it is said, and the ground is in excellent condition now for the planting of corn.

In Oklahoma arrangements have been made by the Oklahoma Bankers' Association to furnish seed where replanting of wheat becomes necessary.

MARRIAGE LICENSE RUSH CONTINUES IN CHICAGO DESPITE CALLS FOR MEN

Ministers Will Refuse to Marry 'Slackers'

Chicago, April 12.—While the Army, Navy and Marine Corps recruiting officers in Chicago clamored for men, the rush for marriage licenses continued today. Numbers of [illegible] were waiting before the bureau opened for the day's business. Recruiting details were stationed [illegible] license office to attempt to dissuade those seeking matrimony to escape war duty.

Meanwhile a number of ministers announced that they would not perform a wedding ceremony for a "slacker." Yesterday 591 licenses were issued, and several hundred applicants were in line when the office closed.

One applicant admitted that he had proposed to a dozen girls since the declaration of a state of war with Germany before he found one to marry him. Another, who remarked that it was "up to the men with money to do the fighting," was promptly decorated with a streamer of yellow ribbon by a private detailed from the National Guard for recruiting duty.

GOVERNMENT TO BUILD PLANTS AT CHARLESTON

Congress Appropriates $12,700,000 for Work

Washington, April 12.—Construction of the Government's armorplate and projectile plants at Charleston, W. Va., will be started immediately, Secretary Daniels said today, following his announcement of the selection of a site there for the proposed factories.

Congress appropriated $11,000,000 for the armorplate plant and $1,700,000 for the projectile plant.

TWINS NAMED FOR WILSON.

Huntington, April 12.—Mr. and Mrs. Clarence J. Hamilton, colored, of this village, yesterday named their twin sons Woodrow and Wilson.

Lloyds Bets 10 to 1 War Ends in Ninety Days

New York, April 12.—Lloyds, London, is wagering 10 to 1 that the war will be over in 90 days according to a report in leading Wall street brokerage houses.

Early in March some local interests cabled Lloyds, London, as to what they would ask on a policy covering the end of the war by September, and they replied that it was a 50-to-1 shot.

Local insurance underwriters who would know as to whether Lloyds were willing to write policies that the war would end in 90 days at 10 to 1 yesterday asserted that they were not aware of the fact. They were extremely interested in the report. One of the underwriters immediately cabled London and hopes to receive a reply today.

ACCIDENTAL BLAST KILLS 1, INJURES 1

Government Arsenal at Frankford, Near Philadelphia, Has Explosion

Philadelphia, April 12.—An accidental explosion of powder in the detonating department of the Government Arsenal at Frankford, a suburb, where ammunition is being manufactured in great quantities, killed Philip McNally and fatally injured Joseph Miller. The two men were the only occupants of the small structure in which they were working. McNally was instantly killed. Miller was blown through a window and terribly injured.

In buildings nearby 1,500 women and girls were at work making ammunition and soldiers' clothing. They were in no danger.

Colonel Montgomery, commandant at the arsenal, said the explosion was purely accidental.

EDDYSTONE DISASTER IS BLAMED ON PLOTTERS

Chester, Pa., April 12.—After extended investigation company officials today reaffirmed their belief that an ingenious plan, conceived in the brains of enemy plotters, was the cause of the disastrous explosion on Tuesday at the plant of the Eddystone ammunition corporation near here. They asserted their conviction that the disaster was deliberately perpetrated as part of a campaign of terrorism.

Opposed to this view is the statement of G. Chalport, State fire marshal, who declared there is no evidence of a plot. He advanced two theories as to the cause. One is that an accidental "flare up" of black powder in the east end of "F" building caused a general explosion. The other is that an accidental ignition of loose black powder in one of the four troughs on the base loading tables set that portion of the plant afire, and caused the shrapnel shells to explode.

In support of the plot theory, Captain W. Wilhelm, general manager of [illegible] factory, points out the [illegible] of three accidental explosions occurring within a few seconds of each other.

SUMMER RESORT MEN WONDER ABOUT LIGHTS

Refuse to Sign Leases Until Matter Is Settled

New York, April 12.—On behalf of the Summer resorts along the Atlantic Coast, Congressman Caldwell has been asked to ascertain whether the war department intends to prohibit brilliant illuminations at these places during the war.

The question has been raised by the local authorities at Rockaway Beach, where concessioners have declined to take out leases until it is settled.

HOLD CONGRESSIONAL ELECTION IN NEW YORK

To Fill Vacancy Caused by Death of Representative Conry.

New York, April 12.—A special election was held in the Fifteenth Congressional district today to fill the vacancy caused by the death of Representative Michael F. Conry, a Democrat.

Thomas F. Smith, secretary of Tammany Hall and one of the best known Tammany men in the city, is the Democratic candidate. His opponents are John N. Boyle, Republican, and Joseph D. Cannon, Socialist.

THOUSANDS OF SHIPS WILL BE BUILT TO TAKE FOOD ABROAD

Three 2,000-ton Wooden Vessels Will Be Constructed Daily to Carry War Supplies to Allies

GOETHALS WILL SUPERVISE THE WORK

Washington, April 12.—A campaign of colossal proportions to break down the German submarine blockade and keep the Entente plentifully supplied with food, clothing and munitions has been determined upon by President Wilson and his advisers as America's first physical stroke against her enemy.

Unable now to send an army into the trenches, the President believes the United States can do even greater service in the common cause against Germany by providing a great armada of merchantmen to invalidate the undersea campaign about which have been rallied the fading hopes of Prussian conquest.

For weeks officials have been at work on such a plan, but not until today was it revealed on how great a scale the task had been projected. Virtually every detail has now been completed and by Fall the campaign itself will be in full swing.

Quickly built, light wooden ships of 2,000 tons and upward are to make up the fleet of merchantmen, and to insure maximum construction the shipping board has enlisted the country's entire shipbuilding facilities, now the greatest in the world. Upwards of 100 private plants on all the coasts will help, giving the board's orders precedence over every other class of work except the most urgent naval construction. Once under way the production is expected to reach an average of three ships a day.

Materials Are Promised.

Already lumber interests have given assurances of an adequate supply of timber at reasonable prices. Engine manufacturers have pledged their co-operation, too, and all the necessary machinery for the vessels can be assembled as fast as they can be turned out at the yards.

The question of labor, however, is giving officials some concern, and a call may be issued appealing for patriotic co-operation by labor to insure that the campaign against the submarine begin at the earliest possible moment. The shipping board estimates that 150,000 men will be needed to work all the plants to capacity.

The total is nearly 10 times the number of laborers now employed in building merchant craft throughout the country.

Volunteers for this class of public service, it is pointed out, need not be experienced in ship building, as comparatively little expert labor will be required for the type of wooden vessels to be built. Within a few days the board will establish a labor bureau to enlist such volunteers. The American Federation of Labor already is co-operating.

Goethals for Supervisor.

Major General George W. Goethals, builder of the Panama Canal, has been selected to supervise the construction program, which is expected to involve within the next year a total tonnage of three million tons, or more than now is building in all the shipyards of the world.

Built for the most part of pine and fir, the ships will range from 2,000 to 3,500 tons. Most of them probably will be equipped with standardized oil burning engines, and all will carry wireless and be armed.

An average cost of about $300,000 per ship is counted on by the board. Each will carry a crew of about 25 men.

The first of the vessels are to be ready in about six months, and during the year following the number afloat is expected to pass 1,000.

In their calculations the President and the shipping board have had the advice of allied naval authorities and have computed carefully the ability of the German U-boats to cope with large numbers of merchantmen.

To Exhaust German Resources.

They are convinced that by building ships of only 2,000 or 3,000 tons, and forcing Germany to pay with a torpedo for each one sent to the bottom, the United States soon can exhaust the resources of the submarine fleet for operating far from its base.

If the blockade running campaign does not actually end the war by destroying Germany's faith in the U-boat, to which her reliance was transferred after hope of decisive victory on land apparently had been abandoned, the administration is confident it at least will thwart the German threat of forcing an early peace on the Allies through a starvation blockade. Officials are alive to the dangers to this country which might follow such a peace, and have been fully advised of the Allies' need of supplies. Although the blockade is considered far from successful, it is felt that an effective stroke at the campaign of ruthlessness is sure to have a telling effect and to furnish the best means of translating quickly into deeds the nation's great potentialities.

ACTION OF U. S. SHOWS KIND OF WAR—PREMIER

London, April 12.—Addressing the American Luncheon Club today, Premier Lloyd George said that the advent of the United States into the war had given the final stamp and seal to the character of the conflict, which was a struggle against military autocracy.

The premier said he was not surprised that America had taken time to make up her mind as to the character of the struggle, having regard to the fact that most of the great wars in Europe in the past had been waged for dynasty aggrandizement and conquest.

Early in the war, Mr. Lloyd George continued, the United States did not comprehend what had been endured in Europe for years from the military caste in Prussia. Saying that Prussia was not a democracy but that Emperor William had promised it would be after the war, he added:

"I think the Kaiser is right."

The luncheon, held to celebrate the entrance of the United States into the war, brought together the most distinguished gathering in the history of the club. The guests included Chancellor Bonar Law, Col. Winston Spencer Churchill, Lord Reading, Gen. Smuts, Lord Derby, Lord Bryce, Walter Hume Long, the Italian Ambassador, Marquis Imperiali Di Francavilla; the Cuban minister, Garcia y Velez, and Herbert C. Hoover, chairman of the American Commission for Relief in Belgium.

Premier Lloyd George, the guest of honor, delivered the principal speech after a brief introduction by Ambassador Page. The Premier received a tremendous ovation when he entered the room. Toasts were drunk to President Wilson and King George.

U. S. GOLF ASSOCIATION APPROVES PLAN TO TILL UNUSED PARTS OF LINKS

New York, April 12.—The movement to till unused portions of golf links to increase the country's food supplies reached national proportions yesterday with the announced approval of the plan by the United States Golf Association. The idea was started by the Dunwoodie Country Club of Yonkers. It is proposed to use the profits from golf links agriculture for purposes of national defense.

PROHIBITION BILL ADVANCED.

Concord, N. H., April 12.—A bill to prohibit the sale of intoxicating liquors for beverage purposes was passed yesterday by the State Senate, 14 to 9. If approved by the Governor it will become effective May 1, 1918.

April 12, 1917: World War I news dominates this front page. *Microfilm archives*

TOTAL DISARMAMENT OF GERMANY ASSURED BY ARMISTICE SIGNED IN PARIS EARLY TODAY

EXTRA **BINGHAMTON PRESS** EXTRA

AND LEADER

VOL. 41. NO. 181. MONDAY EVENING, NOVEMBER 11, 1918. TWELVE PAGES PRICE THREE CENTS

PEACE! GREATEST OF WARS ENDS! CITY JOINS NATION IN BIG HOLIDAY

PEOPLE OF CITY WILD WITH JOY

Crowds Gather Quickly When Bells and Whistles Announce Glad Tidings That Armistice Is Signed

STREETS ARE BEDLAM

Factories and Business Places Are Closed When Employes Join in Big Celebration Instead of Going to Work

Let Flags Fly on Every Building in Binghamton

Hang out your flags! The United States has helped largely in the winning of the greatest war the world has ever known.

It is only fitting that every home and business place in the nation should display Old Glory to attest the joy which is felt at the coming of Peace.

Citizens of Binghamton, show your colors.

Binghamton today had its second big celebration within a week.

The difference was that today's was a real celebration of an accomplished fact and was much larger in volume than the one of last Thursday when the fake announcement of the signing of the armistice was given out.

Today the armistice had really been signed, peace had come to the world once more and the citizens of the city made the most of it.

The celebration started at 3 o'clock this morning. The news of the signing of the armistice was flashed over the wires of the Associated Press at 2:52 o'clock and in accordance with previous arrangements it was at once telephoned to the ministers of the city churches and to the owners of large manufacturing plants.

Within five minutes church bells were ringing throughout the city and factory whistles were blowing. The first bell to ring was that of the First Presbyterian Church. Christ Church bells began next, the Rev. Dr. John J. Lawrence and the Rev. Theodore J. Dewees having risen from their beds, dressed and rushed to their churches to sound the first strokes in person. Other bells quickly took up the sounding of the glad tidings and whistles throughout the city and its suburbs soon were ringing.

Thousands of persons awakened by the noise rushed from their homes and joined in processions that marched to the central part of the city, where the real celebration began. The tolling of the bells and the blowing of the whistles continued until long after daylight and the crowds in the streets grew rapidly and the noise was terrific most of the times. Automobiles rushed about the streets blowing their klaxons and dragging old pails, cans and other metallic articles which would make a noise, attached to them by ropes. Truck loads of factory workers went here, there and everywhere. Nobody in the factories and the mercantile establishments reported for work, only the newspaper offices attempting to render the usual week-day service to the public. At 9 o'clock the acting Mayor, Leroy E. Barnes, issued a proclamation declaring a holiday and then the celebration went forward with new vigor.

CHURCH SERVICES STARTS CELEBRATION

With the first blast of the victory whistles and the first clang of the bells

(Continued on Page Ten.)

"When Freedom from her mountain height
Unfurled her standard to the air,
She tore the azure robe of night,
And set the stars of glory there."

The President Issues Peace Proclamation

Washington, Nov. 11.—President Wilson issued a formal proclamation at 10 o'clock this morning, that the armistice with Germany had been signed.

The proclamation follows:

"My Fellow Countrymen: The armistice was signed this morning. Everything for which America fought has been accomplished. It will now be our fortunate duty to assist by example, by sober friendly council and by material aid in the establishment of just democracy throughout the world.

"WOODROW WILSON."

Acting Mayor Calls Upon All People in City to Celebrate

To the People of Binghamton:

This is a day of universal rejoicing and thanksgiving!
Let our people give full vent to their long-pent-up feeling!
Let the welkin ring and joy be unconfined!
The God of Justice, Mercy and Love hastriumphed!
"Let us have peace!"

The sweetest words on earth, immortal words, uttered in the long ago of another civil strife, have again been uttered.

It is due to our people that we in common with the rest of the United States and the whole world should fittingly observe this greatest of all great occasions.

By virtue of the power in me vested, I order and declare this to be a public holiday to be known as World Peace Day.

Let all our schools and public offices be closed and all public business be suspended for the day.

LEROY E. BARNES,
Acting Mayor.

German Garrison Along Dutch Frontier in Revolt

AMSTERDAM, Nov. 11 (By the Associated Press.)—German garrisons along the Dutch frontier are reported in revolt. Officers are being disarmed and are being treated roughly in some instances.

ARMISTICE IS SIGNED AT 5 A. M., PARIS TIME; WAR ENDS AT 11 A. M.

Red Revolution Grasps German Empire, Whose Navy Is Scattered in Disjointed Units—Berlin, Leipzic, Stuttgart, Cologne, Hamburg, Frankfort and Dresden in Hands of Rebels

WORLD-WAR HAS LASTED 1,567 DAYS

Washington, Nov. 11.—The World War ended at 6 o'clock this morning, Washington time, with red revolution in Germ[illegible] with William Hohenzollern, for-[illegible]

Anno[illegible] the armist[illegible] imposed by the Allied [illegible] American governments had been signed by the German envoys at midnight last night, 5 o'clock Paris time, and that hostilities would cease six hours later, was made at the State Department at 2:45 o'clock this morning.

Terms of the surrender of Germany were not made public coincident with this announcement, but they were to be given out later in the day. The momentous news of the ending of the war was given to newspaper correspondents verbally by an official of the State Department. He said:

"The armistice has been signed. It was signed at 5 o'clock a. m. Paris time and hostilities will cease at 11 o'clock this morning Paris time."

Information that the armistice had been signed was transmitted to the White House after it was received by the government and President Wilson was expected to issue a statement to the American people today.

Lloyd George Makes Official Announcement in England

LONDON, Nov. 11.—It is officially announced that the armistice between the Allies and Germany has been signed. The announcement was made by Premier Lloyd George, who said:

"The armistice was signed at 5 o'clock this morning and hostilities are to cease on all fronts at 11 o'clock today."

PARIS, Nov. 11.—Announcement is made that the German delegates signed the armistice terms at 6 o'clock (French time) Monday morning.

News of the signing of the armistice soon became known to those persons in the center of the city as flags were immediately flown to the breeze, and the issuance of evening newspapers, for which there was a great rush, at 11 o'clock. The first official celebration came when the old air raid signals were fired from all police and fire stations.

Hostilities will en[illegible] 11 o'clock this morning.

The official announcement from Washington early today said that the armistice terms were signed at 5 o'clock, French time. The London announcement fixed the same hour of signing.

Evacuation of Left Bank of Rhine Is Extended 24 Hours

LONDON, Nov. 11.—The period given for the evacuation of the left bank of the Rhine by the German forces has been extended by twenty-four hours, according to a French wireless dispatch received here.

Mons C[illegible]red by Canadians U[illegible] Gen. Horne Early Today

LONDON, [illegible]—Mons, the Belgian town near where British troops engage[illegible] fighting with the Germans at the beginning of the war, w[illegible] this morning by Canadian troops under General H[illegible] Field Marshal Haig's announcement today.

Wurttemburg, Schleswig-Holstein and Hesse-Darmstadt Proclaim Independent Republics; Poland Annexes Itself to Crownland of Galicia; Soldiers and Workmen Control Berlin

CROWDS IN BERLIN SING "MARSEILLAISE"

(BY THE ASSOCIATD PRESS.)

After 1,567 days the greatest war in history ended this morning at[illegible] of the tremendous event w[illegible] is made at the State Department at the Capital at 2:45 [illegible] this morning, and in a few seconds was flashed throughout the continent by the Associated Press.

At 5 o'clock, Paris time, the signatures of Germany's delegates were affixed to the document which blasted forever the dreams which embroiled the world in a struggle which has cost, at the very lowest estimate, 10,000,000 lives.

When the war began the Teutonic Alliance was headed by two of the proudest houses in history—the Hohenzollerns and the Hapsburgs.

Today William II. of Germany is a fugitive in Holland and Charles I. of Austria, while he may be still in his country, has been stripped of power and has seen his empire shattered into pieces.

Ferdinand of Bulgaria, another of the rulers in the Teutonic combination, has fled from his country, and Mohammed V. of Turkey, who also joined in the attempt of Germany to dominate the world, is dead; slain, it is said, by the hand of an assassin.

While the curtain was rolling down on the most stupendous tragedy in mankind's history, events were moving with terrible swiftness in Germany.

Berlin, Leipzic, Stuttgart, Cologne, Hamburg and Frankfort are in the hands of the revolutionists, who last week raised the red flag at Kiel.

Germany's navy is apparently scattered into disjointed units, each seeking sanctuary in Danish ports or waiting in German harbors for the latest turn of events.

Crowds singing the "Marseillaise" are marching through the streets of Berlin and a Soldiers' and Workmen's Council has taken over the government of the empire.

Wurttemburg, Schleswig-Holstein and Hesse-Darmstadt have declared themselves independent republics, following the action taken by Bavaria last Friday. Wilhelm II. of Wurttemburg is reported to have abdicated. Saxony is said to be near a like declaration and the revolutionists are said to be in control at Dresden.

The republic of Poland has served official notice on Austria that Poland has annexed the crownland of Galicia.

As the last hours of the mighty combat drew near, French, British, Belgian and American forces were rapidly pushing the last German troops from France and Belgium.

General Pershing's men attacked yesterday over a front of seventy-one miles from the Meuse southeastward into Lorraine. This drive, probably the last to be recorded in the war, gained an average of two or three miles and approached within ten miles of the fortress of Metz.

It is suggested that William Hohenzollern is not safe from the consequence of his deed, even though he has fled to Holland. After the sinking of the Lusitania and during the early days of aerial raids on London, he was indicted in England three times for murder. Under international law requisition for his extradition may be made by England.

With the granting of the armistice to the beaten German armies by Marshal Foch, the next step will be the arrangements for the meeting of the peace conference, which will endeavor to reach a permanent settlement of the vast issues arising from the great world war.

Beginning in August, 1914, as the direct result of the assassination of the heir to the Austro-Hungarian throne, the Archduke Francis, and his consort, at Sarajevo, Bosnia, by a Serbian student more

(Continued on Page Three).

November 11, 1918: This Extra edition of the Binghamton Press announces the end of World War I. *Courtesy Carolyn Fitzgerald*

Extra BINGHAMTON REPUBLICAN-HERALD Extra

96TH YEAR, No. 291 | MONDAY MORNING, NOVEMBER 11, 1918 | PRICE—THREE CENTS

WORLD WAR ENDS AT 6; ARMISTICE SIGNED; REVOLT IN GERMANY

WASHINGTON, Nov. 11.—The World War will end this morning at 6 o'clock, Washington time, 11 o'clock Paris time. The armistice was signed by the German representatives at midnight. This announcement was made by the State Department at 2:50 o'clock this morning.

WASHINGTON Nov. 11 (By A. P.) Armistice terms have been signed by Germany the State Department announced at 2:45 o'clock this morning.

The Department's announcement simply said "the armistice has been signed".

GERMAN EMPIRE IN STATE OF REVOLT; REDS HOLD BERLIN

LONDON, Nov. 10.—Severe fighting took place in Berlin between 6 and 8 o'clock last night and a violent cannonade was heard from the heart of the city.

The revolution is in full swing in Berlin and the Red forces occupy the greater part of the German capital, according to a Copenhagen dispatch to the Exchange Telegraph Company, quoting Berlin advices sent from there at 3 o'clock this morning.

The Crown Prince's palace was seized by the revolutionists. The people shouted "Long Live the Republic" and sung "The Marseillaise."

(Continued on Page Eleven)

WASHINGTON, Nov. 11.—The announcement was made verbally by an official of the State Department in this form:

"The armistice has been signed. It was signed at 5 o'clock a. m. Paris time, and hostilities will cease at 11 o'clock this morning, Paris time."

The terms of the armistice, it was announced, will not be made public until later. Military men here, regard it as certain that they include:

Immediate retirement of the German military forces from France, Belgium and Alsace-Lorraine.

Disarming and demobilization of the German armies.

Occupation by the Allied and American forces of such strategic points in Germany as will make impossible a renewal of hostilities. Delivery of the German high seas fleet and a certain number of submarines to the Allied and American naval forces.

Occupation of the principal German naval bases by sea forces of the victorious nations.

Release of Allied and American soldiers, sailors and civilians held prisoners in Germany without such reciprocal action by the associated governments.

PEOPLES' GOVTS. HAVE BEEN ESTABLISHED THROUGHOUT KINGDOM AND EMPIRE

Friedrich Ebert, Socialist Leader, Appointed Imperial Chancellor and Has Issued a Proc'amation Saying That It Is His Purpose to Bring About a Speedy Peace

ARMISTICE TERMS REACH GERMAN GRAND HEADQUARTERS

(By the Associated Press)

William Hohenzollern, the abdicated German Emperor and King of Prussia, and his eldest son, Frederick William, who hoped some day to rule the German people, are reported to have fled to Holland.

The revolution which is in progress throughout Germany, although it seemingly is a peaceful one, probably threw fear into the hearts of the former Kaiser and Crown Prince and caused them to take asylum in a neutral state.

William II., reigning King of the monarchy of Wurttemberg, is declared to have abdicated Friday night, and reports have it that the Grand Duke of Hesse, ruler of the Grand Duchy of Hesse, has decreed the formation of a Council of State to take over the government there. Every dynasty in Germany is to be suppressed and all the Princes exiled, according to Swiss advices.

Peoples' governments have been established in the greater part of Berlin and in other cities of the kingdom and empire. Leipzig, Stuttgart, Cologne, Essen and Frankfort have joined the revolution. In Berlin there has been some fighting between the revolutionists and reactionaries in which several persons were killed or wounded. The palace of the Crown Prince has been taken over by the revolutionists. "Long live the Republic" and the singing of "The Marseillaise" have been heard in the streets of Berlin.

William Hohenzollern and Party Arrive at Eysden

Practically Whole German General Staff Accompanies Former Emperor—Ten Automobiles Required to Carry Fugitives

BELIEVE VON HINDENBURG TO BE ALONG

November 11, 1918: Extra edition of the Binghamton Republican-Herald announces the end of World War I. *Courtesy Amy Toner*

SHOES
Downtown Binghamton, circa 1920. *Press & Sun-Bulletin archives*

BUTLERS
Downtown Binghamton in the 1920s. *Courtesy Broome County Historical Society*

The Carlton Hotel bar room, Binghamton, circa 1920. *Courtesy Broome County Historical Society*

The Endicott Johnson Public Market in Endicott, circa 1922. *Courtesy Broome County Historical Society*

1920 - 1929

Region booms during the Roaring Twenties

The Binghamton Press has the largest circulation of any daily newspaper in the United States which is published in a city of the size of Binghamton.

BINGHAMTON PRESS AND LEADER

THE WEATHER

VOL. 43. NO. 109. CITY EDITION WEDNESDAY EVENING, AUGUST 18, 1920. EIGHTEEN PAGES PRICE THREE CENTS

SUFFRAGE AMENDMENT IS RATIFIED

POLISH COUNTER ATTACK WINS ON ENTIRE WARSAW FRONT

THOMPSON SETS NEW RECORD IN HURDLE EVENT

Dartmouth Star, Representing Canada, Clips 1-5 Second from World's Record in 110-Metre Event, Nosing Out Two Americans

ITALY TAKES WALK

THOMPSON BREAKS WORLD HURDLE RECORD

Dry Law Agent Is Thirsting for Swig of Tickle Cocktail

Wall Street May Have Gold Mine Right at Home

Engineer Finds Some Yellow Particles Which He Hopes Will Prove Real Stuff

FRENCH MUNITIONS BARRED AT DANZIG

Allied High Commissioner Forbids Landing Supplies Intended for Poland

RECEIVER FOR PONZI MAY BE NAMED BY U. S. JUDGE TODAY

BRITISH PREMIER ON WAY TO SWITZERLAND

DANZIG CORRIDOR IS ALSO SWEPT FREE OF REDS BY POLISH ARMY

Bolshevik Recoil from Polish Counter-attack Has Assumed Almost the Proportions of a Rout, with Red Army Separated from Its Base of Supplies

IN PEACE CONFERENCE AT MINSK REDS SUBMIT TERMS TO POLISH DELEGATES

Retreat of Reds Before Counter Attack of Poles Is Nearly Stampede

MORALE OF POLISH TROOPS EXCELLENT

POLISH DELEGATES GET PEACE TERMS

SOVIET PEACE TERMS MAY BE MODIFIED

RED ARMY LOSES TOUCH WITH SUPPLIES

GERMAN ADVICES TELL OF VICTORY OF POLES

To Run Campaign for Cox in West

FRANK DORREMUS

CLOUDBURST IN SULLIVAN COUNTY FLOODS LIBERTY

Crest of Waves Reach Second Floors of Business Places

DAMAGE IS VERY LARGE

ALCOHOLIC CASES IN BELLEVUE EQUAL TO PRE-PROHIBITION DAYS

RIVER PIRATES FAIL IN RAID TO STEAL WHISKEY FROM PIER

TENNESSEE WRITES ANTHONY PROPOSAL INTO CONSTITUTION

Wild Scenes Feature Second Day of Debate in Tennessee House, Which Twice Refuses to Table Resolution and Finally Passes It by Vote of 50 to 46.

AMENDMENT BECOMES LAW OF LAND WITH FORMAL RATIFICATION BY THE 36th STATE

POLISH CITIZENS CALL ON WILSON TO HELP POLAND

America Is Already Working to Create Favorable Situation Officials Say

CAN GIVE TANGIBLE AID

NORTH CAROLINA SENATE REFUSES TO RATIFY NOW

(Continued on Page Two)

August 18, 1920: Suffrage amendment leads the news for this edition. *Microfilm archives*

The decade ended with the Binghamton Press celebrating its 25th anniversary, a milestone noted by government leaders in Albany and Washington.

In a way, the entire decade was one big party. Women celebrated getting the vote, and almost everybody looked for ways around Prohibition.

Henry B. Endicott died in 1920, leaving control of the great shoe company to George F. Johnson and his family. EJ workers erected arches over Main Street, celebrating the home of the Square Deal.

Thomas Watson changed his company's name to International Business Machines in 1924. Johnson and Watson helped build Ideal Hospital. Johnson donated money for parks, a golf course and a church.

When the decade started, 40 percent of Binghamton's residents were immigrants or first-generation Americans. Immigrants kept flowing into the new Endicott Johnson factories. Population in Broome County grew to 147,022, up 29 percent from a decade earlier.

The Ku Klux Klan got a foothold here. Binghamton became the state headquarters of the racist, anti-foreigner organization. It held marches through Endicott.

While bigots tried to fight the tide of immigration, others were focused on innovation. The year the stock market crashed was the same year Ed Link invented his pilot trainer, starting a brand-new industry.

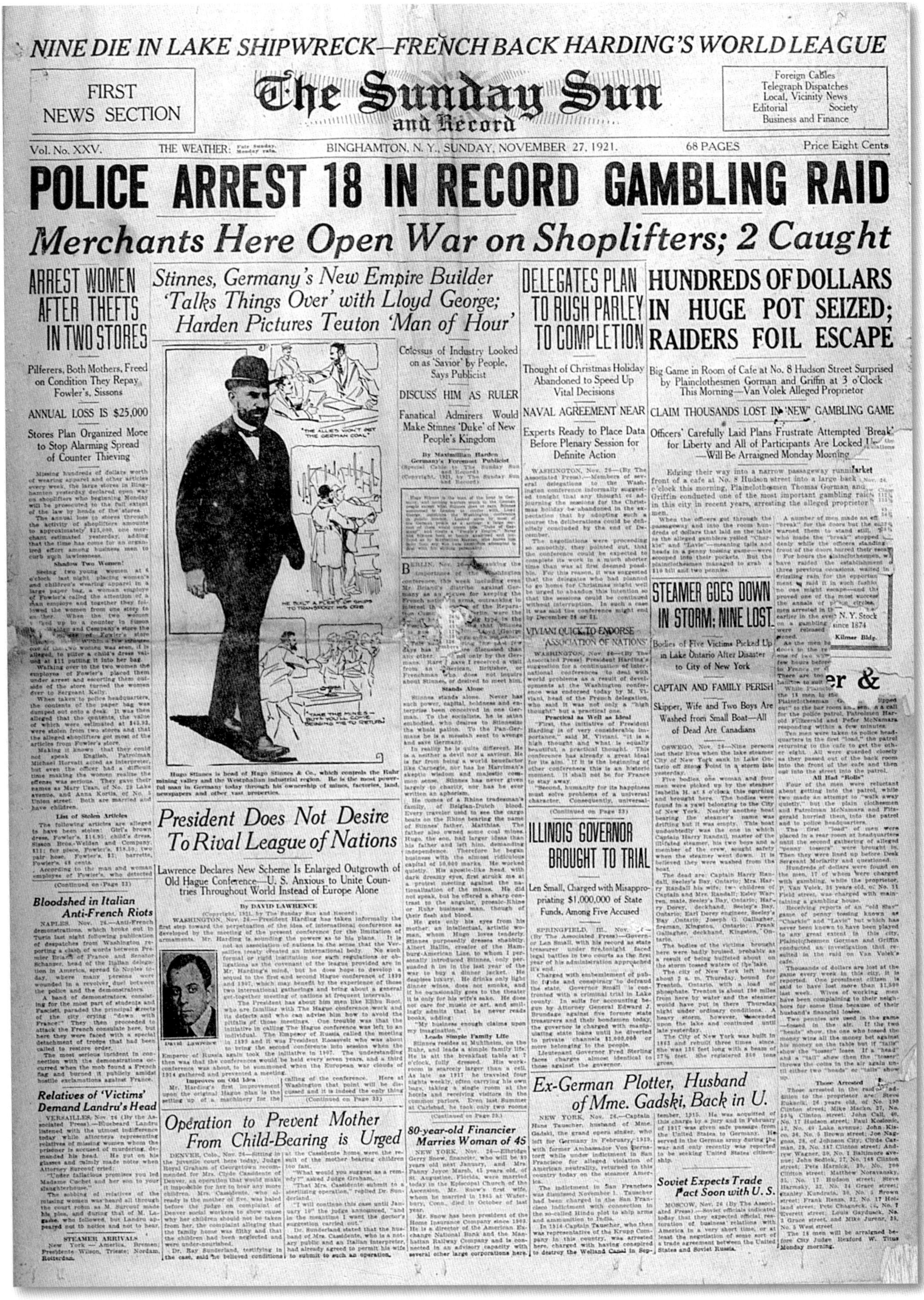
NINE DIE IN LAKE SHIPWRECK—FRENCH BACK HARDING'S WORLD LEAGUE

FIRST NEWS SECTION

The Sunday Sun and Record

Foreign Cables
Telegraph Dispatches
Local, Vicinity News
Editorial Society
Business and Finance

Vol. No. XXV. THE WEATHER: Fair Sunday, Monday rain. BINGHAMTON, N. Y., SUNDAY, NOVEMBER 27, 1921. 68 PAGES Price Eight Cents

POLICE ARREST 18 IN RECORD GAMBLING RAID

Merchants Here Open War on Shoplifters; 2 Caught

ARREST WOMEN AFTER THEFTS IN TWO STORES

Pilferers, Both Mothers, Freed on Condition They Repay Fowler's, Sissons

ANNUAL LOSS IS $25,000

Stores Plan Organized Move to Stop Alarming Spread of Counter Thieving

Stinnes, Germany's New Empire Builder 'Talks Things Over' with Lloyd George; Harden Pictures Teuton 'Man of Hour'

Colossus of Industry Looked on as 'Savior' by People, Says Publicist

DISCUSS HIM AS RULER

Fanatical Admirers Would Make Stinnes 'Duke' of New People's Kingdom

By Maximilian Harden, Germany's Foremost Publicist

Hugo Stinnes is head of Hugo Stinnes & Co., which controls the Ruhr mining valley and the Westphalian industrial region. He is the most powerful man in Germany today through his ownership of mines, factories, land, newspapers and other vast properties.

DELEGATES PLAN TO RUSH PARLEY TO COMPLETION

Thought of Christmas Holiday Abandoned to Speed Up Vital Decisions

NAVAL AGREEMENT NEAR

Experts Ready to Place Data Before Plenary Session for Definite Action

VIVIANI QUICK TO ENDORSE 'ASSOCIATION OF NATIONS'

HUNDREDS OF DOLLARS IN HUGE POT SEIZED; RAIDERS FOIL ESCAPE

Big Game in Room of Cafe at No. 8 Hudson Street Surprised by Plainclothesmen Gorman and Griffin at 3 o'Clock This Morning—Van Volek Alleged Proprietor

CLAIM THOUSANDS LOST IN 'NEW' GAMBLING GAME

Officers' Carefully Laid Plans Frustrate Attempted 'Break' for Liberty and All of Participants Are Locked Up—Will Be Arraigned Monday Morning

STEAMER GOES DOWN IN STORM; NINE LOST

Bodies of Five Victims Picked Up in Lake Ontario After Disaster to City of New York

CAPTAIN AND FAMILY PERISH

Skipper, Wife and Two Boys Are Washed from Small Boat—All of Dead Are Canadians

President Does Not Desire To Rival League of Nations

Lawrence Declares New Scheme Is Enlarged Outgrowth of Old Hague Conference—U. S. Anxious to Unite Countries Throughout World Instead of Europe Alone

By DAVID LAWRENCE

David Lawrence

ILLINOIS GOVERNOR BROUGHT TO TRIAL

Len Small, Charged with Misappropriating $1,000,000 of State Funds, Among Five Accused

Bloodshed in Italian Anti-French Riots

Relatives of 'Victims' Demand Landru's Head

Operation to Prevent Mother From Child-Bearing is Urged

80-year-old Financier Marries Woman of 45

Ex-German Plotter, Husband of Mme. Gadski, Back in U.

Soviet Expects Trade Pact Soon with U. S.

November 27, 1921: The Sunday Sun and Record reports on a major gambling raid. *Courtesy Carolyn Fitzgerald*

The Binghamton Press Has the largest circulation of any daily newspaper in the United States which is published in a city the size of Binghamton.

BINGHAMTON PRESS
AND LEADER

THE WEATHER
Partly cloudy, little change in temperature, fair tonight and Saturday.

Vol. 45, No. 97. | CITY EDITION | FRIDAY EVENING, AUGUST 3, 1923. | THIRTY-SIX PAGES | PRICE THREE CENTS

COOLIDGE TAKES HELM OF U. S. WHEN HARDING DIES SUDDENLY

VICE PRESIDENT TAKES OATH AS CHIEF EXECUTIVE

Man, Who Succeeds to Highest Office in Land, Pledges His Fealty to Constitution and People in Vermont Farmhouse

FATHER HOLDS BIBLE

Plymouth, Vt., Aug. 3 — (United Press)—Calvin Coolidge became president of the United States at 2:47 a. m. today.

The oath of office was taken in private in the old farmhouse of his father here.

Coolidge's father, John C. Coolidge, who is a notary public, administered the oath.

Coolidge was formally notified of President Harding's death in a joint telegram from Attorney General Daugherty, Secretary of the Interior Work, Secretary of Agriculture Wallace and Secretary of Commerce Hoover.

It was a few minutes after receipt of this formal notification that the vice president quietly retired to his father's home and took the oath that made him the nation's chief executive.

Oath on Old Family Bible.

The extraordinary ceremony was ...

Takes Oath as President Before His Aged Father in Vermont Village

CALVIN COOLIDGE

American People Bow Their Heads in Grief

Nation Mourns the Passing of Its Leader to Whom Death Came Suddenly as Faithful Wife Kept Lonely Vigil

WASHINGTON SLOW TO REALIZE GREAT LOSS OF NATION

Suddenness of Blow Strikes with Numbing Force to Official Employes Who Knew Friend in Their Chief

KINDLY FACE GONE

Washington, Aug. 3—(Associated Press)—From its highest official to its humblest citizen, Washington awoke today to slow realization that President Warren G. Harding lay dead in far away San Francisco.

The suddenness of the blow struck last night with numbing force. Not until the morning papers bore the news over the city was it fully credited.

And among the common folk everywhere realization of the truth carried with it a sense of personal loss. The big, kindly man, who for two years had lived at the White House, had come to be looked upon with very friendly eyes as he moved about the city. There was that in his face that won friendship for him from thousands who saw him only as chance brought him into the streets or public places.

To the very few in high official life who were in Washington when the wires brought the ill tidings over the country, the shock came with trebled force. They knew him best, and after many hours of anxiety and eager scanning of the bulletins from his bedside, they had been lulled into confidence that he was soon to be among them again, the calm, kindly leader with whom they have toiled shoulder to shoulder.

It was to a strangely scattered official family that word of their leader's death was flashed. Of all the cabinet, only Postmaster General New was actually within the limits of the national capital. Secretary Hughes, the only other cabinet officer within more than a day's journey, was at his summer residence in Maryland, a score of miles away.

Hughes Hastens to Duties.

Official word of Mr. Harding's death came in a message from Attorney General Daugherty in San Francisco to Secretary Hughes. The telegram stated merely that President Harding had died of cerebral hemorrhage. This message the secretary promptly relayed to all members of the cabinet.

Mr. Hughes received the first news of what had happened, however, from the press wires relayed to him at his summer home. He came immediately to his office at the state department ...

Latest Picture of Harding Shows Plainly How Heavy Burdens of State Had Aged Him

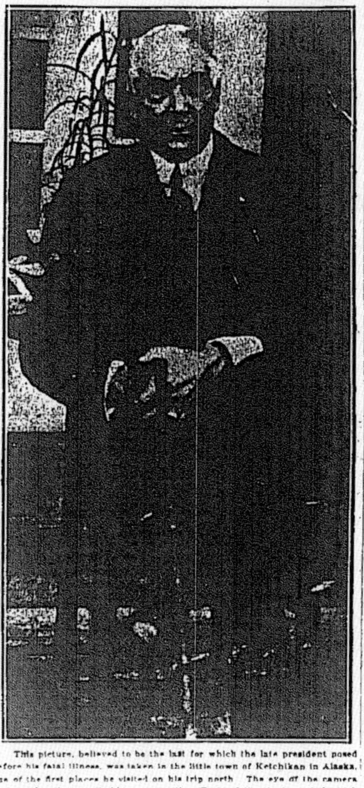

This picture, believed to be the last for which the late president posed before his fatal illness, was taken in the little town of Ketchikan in Alaska, one of the first places he visited on his trip north. The eye of the camera registered with remarkable accuracy the effects of the strain under which Mr. Harding had been since his inauguration nearly two and one-half years ago and which had helped to break down his health.

Photo by International.

Overwork and Strain of Trip Weaken System

President Seen by Physicians as Victim to High Duty in Trip to Alaska Following Attack of Influenza

San Francisco, Aug. 3—(United Press)—President Warren G. Harding died ... of apoplexy or a rupture of a blood vessel in the area of the brain near the respiratory center, his five physicians said in a formal statement issued at midnight. The statement said: ...

APOPLEXY KILLS PRESIDENT WITHOUT ANY WARNING AS WIFE READS TO HIM

Nation's Chief Passes Away as Last Rays of California's Golden Sunshine Were Pouring Into Room; Patient Was Apparently Resting Comfortably When, with Slight Shudder of His Weakened Body, the Tide of Life Ebbs

SPECIAL TRAIN LEAVING TONIGHT WILL TAKE BODY BACK TO WASHINGTON

By LAWRENCE MARTIN
(United Press Staff Correspondent.)

Palace Hotel, San Francisco, Aug. 3—(United Press)—The president is dead.

Death, apparently balked by medical science, struck suddenly and with no warning at 7:30 o'clock last night.

The president was definitely on the road to recovery from ptomaine poisoning, acute indigestion and a pneumonic infection which followed them.

But death found a way through the armor—it struck into the brain with apoplexy, and without struggle or word, and only a shudder of his weakened frame, and the raising of one hand, the nation's head passed beyond.

Tonight they will take Warren Gamaliel Harding's body home—back to the White House where he lived and worked as the chief magistrate of the people, who today, shocked beyond expression by his death, mourn for him and with his wife.

After the simplest private funeral service in the presidential suite at the Palace Hotel, where he took to his bed on Sunday morning, the president's body will be placed aboard a special train, which will leave San Francisco at 7 p. m. for Washington.

He will be laid to rest in his old home town, Marion, O.—the country village which he raised from rural obscurity into national prominence. Before the final obsequies there which will mark his burial, the president's body probably will lie in state in Washington.

Calvin Coolidge of Massachusetts, the vice-president, today wore upon his shoulders the mantle of authority and tremendous responsibility which slipped last night from Mr. Harding, when he passed beyond the ken and power of mortal things.

The president passed with the sunset. The last rays of California's golden sunshine were pouring into his room, where Mrs. Harding, the wife who has been by his side since he was stricken seriously last Saturday, sat reading to him from a magazine. Brigadier General C. E. Sawyer, his old friend and personal physician, sat at the bedside.

SEEMED TO BE RESTING COMFORTABLY

The president was lying very still, listening to Mrs. Harding read. He seemed to be resting quite comfortably. ...

SOUGHT TO WARD OFF DEATH'S BLOW

...

(Continued on Page Nine)
(Continued on Page Three)
(Continued on Page Nine)
(Continued on Page Three)
(Continued from Page Three)

August 3, 1923: Front-page announcement of President Harding's death in office. *Microfilm archives*

BIBLE SCHOOL PARK N Y

Students congregate at the Bible School, Binghamton, 1922. *Courtesy Richard Gillespie*

CENTRAL FIRE STATION

Central Fire Station, 76 Carroll Street, 1922. *Courtesy Broome County Historical Society*

Broome County Sheriff Charles E. Watson and deputies, 1926.
Courtesy Broome County Historical Society

Helen Woughter Wickham, 9, cradles the doll she was given as a prize stemming from a circulation promotion with the newspaper; Binghamton, 1925. The doll is still in the Wickhams' possession and remains in good condition.
Courtesy Helen Woughter Wickham

SECOND SECTION

BINGHAMTON PRESS

AND LEADER

SECOND SECTION

TWENTY-FOUR PAGES — MONDAY EVENING, JANUARY 5, 1925. — PAGES 13 TO 24

BINGHAMTON CLUB ELECTS OFFICERS FOR COMING YEAR

Frederic W. Jenkins Heads Club and Jesse Truitt Is Chosen Vice

YEAR WAS SUCCESSFUL

No Opposition to Men Placed Before Club for Balloting

72 Auto License Plates Issued in 20 Minutes

CITIZENS PLEASED WITH NEW LIGHTS ON MAIN STREET

But Petition Must Be Filed with Council if They Remain

ARE ONLY TEMPORARY

Sample Display Competely Eliminates Dark Accident Traps on Road

GIRL SCOUTS TO BE INSTRUCTED

Educational Work Will Begin This Week with Classes in Dramatics and Tests

TAX COLLECTOR READY TO RECEIVE PAYMENT

OUR WEATHER BOY

Little Mothers at Party Given in Their Honor at Binghamton Theater Saturday Afternoon

Children Enjoy Party as Doll Lady's Guests

Theater Filled with New Mothers of Wonderful Dollies That Speak and Act Like Real Babies and Gladden New Year

BY THE DOLL LADY

BETTY WATSON, 27 Dennison Avenue

ELIZABETH M. LAWLOR, 13 Helen Street, Johnson City

JANE ELLEN MINSKY, 53 Park Street

AUTOMOBILE CLUB TO HOLD MID-WINTER MEETING ON JAN. 30

SEARCH FOR MISSING GIRL ENDS ON RETURN

ANNUAL ICE HARVEST BEGINS ON RIVER ABOVE ROCKBOTTOM DAM

Girls! Have Pretty Eyes

KNIGHTS TEMPLAR WILL GIVE BALL

Arrangements Under Way for Social Function in Temple Last of Month

Mild Weather Here for Visit This Week

Sky Will Remain Overcast but the Mercury Will Not Sink to Usual Low Levels for Time at Least

CITY OFFICIALS BEGIN FORMATION OF PAVING PROGRAM

BARELY MISSES WOMAN, PAYS $2 TRAFFIC FINE

LOCAL MOTION PICTURE FILM STARTS THURSDAY

'Who's Who' Is Title of Scenes to Be Exhibited at Binghamton

PRIZES ARE OFFERED

Later Reels Will Show Completed Views and Reveal the Winners

New Discovery Ends Need of Rupture Truss

January 5, 1925: This second-section front page featured photos and articles on "Little Mothers" and their dolls. *Microfilm archives*

The Binghamton Press has the largest circulation of any daily newspaper in the United States which is published in a city the size of Binghamton.

BINGHAMTON PRESS
AND LEADER

THE WEATHER
Partly overcast, fair. Moderate temperature tonight and Thursday.

Vol. 46, No. 227. CITY EDITION WEDNESDAY EVENING, JANUARY 7, 1925. THIRTY-SIX PAGES PRICE THREE CENTS

SMITH DENOUNCES G. O. P. MOVE FOR NEW DRY LAW

EARTH TREMORS HIT BAY STATE ON NORTH SHORE

Gloucester, Marblehead, Salem and Other Cities and Towns Near Boston Report Shocks Lasting 20 to 30 Seconds

ROAR ACCOMPANIES

M'CLINTOCK DEATH DRAMA IS RAISED AGAIN BY JUDGE

Claims His Brother Died Shortly After Shepherds Had Visited Him

WANTS BODY EXHUMED

CLEAN BOOK BILL DROPPED IN HOPPER

Overnight Features in News of World

Woman Solon Has First Taste of Legislation

Mrs. Rhoda Fox Graves Likes Experience She Declares

PAULINE FREDERICK IS GRANTED DIVORCE

Airplane and Truck Crash, Killing Two, at Dayton Grounds

Accident First of Kind on Record to Result in Fatality

AVIATORS MISS DEATH

Motor Car in Which Field Employes Were Riding Is Demolished

SCORE INJURED IN RAIL WRECK

Two Coaches, Baggage Cars and Engine Plunge Over Embankment

CHEMUNG ROUSED BY SUNDAY DANCE

Baptist Clergyman Calls for Volunteers to Close up Den to Fantastic Devotees

RAID ON DANCE HALL YIELDS 100 MEN AND WOMEN IN NEW YORK

GREATEST CHRISTMAS IN POSTOFFICE HISTORY

CRACK TRAIN HITS LOCAL AS BOTH RACE FOR CROSSING

Only Four Persons Injured in Crash and Small Station Destroyed

SCORES ESCAPE DEATH

DANCING TEAM IN LOVE TANGLE

'Peggy and Cortez' New York Favorites Defendants in Divorce Action

STORK FLUTTERING ABOUT CHAPLIN HOME, DUE IN SUMMER

POLICE USE BAYONETS TO PUT DOWN RIOT

KNIGHT WINS LEADERSHIP IN STATE SENATE

Wyoming County Solon Captures Honors from George R. Fearon of Syracuse in Republican Caucus at Capital

McGINNIES SPEAKER

STRIKER KILLED IN OLD FORGE

Youth Shot Down as He Stands in Front of Store Near Scranton

FUNSTON INVITES FEDERAL AGENTS TO RAID IN SCHENECTADY

Congress Today

U. S. DELEGATES BAR DISCUSSION OF ALLIED DEBTS

Three American Diplomats in Conference Opening in Paris

SEEK GERMAN PAYMENT

STUDENT TEACHER FATALLY INJURED

Minnesota Man Kills Self After Shooting Woman at Madison, Wis.

COMMITTEE PARING 14 MILLION FROM RIVERS, HARBORS BILL

MESSAGE OF GOVERNOR ATTACKS HYPOCRISY IN STATE WET ENFORCEMENT

Declares Whole Question Is Imbedded in Insincerity; Suffering from Too Many Statesmen Who Talk Dry and Act Wet, He Says; Have Enough Law but Lack Enforcement, He Adds; Favors Child Labor Amendment and Reduction in Taxes

NOTES DEFEAT OF DEMOCRATIC TICKET, ASKS COOPERATION OF LEGISLATURE

Albany, Jan. 7—(United Press)—Continuation of the 25 per cent. reduction in the income tax and on real property taxes; submission of the proposal to amend the federal constitution to abolish child labor to an "advisory" referendum; practical abandonment of the "pay as you go policy"; of the state, and no prohibition legislation by the state were the outstanding points in the message of Governor Alfred E. Smith to the legislature today.

January 7, 1925: Liquor law leads this edition's news. *Microfilm archives*

Anniversary Section

BINGHAMTON PRESS

AND LEADER

Anniversary Section

THIRD SECTION — SATURDAY EVENING, SEPTEMBER 5, 1925. — THIRD SECTION

Memorial Bridge, Its Beautiful Approaches and Dedicatory Tablets

Riverside Drive Plaza

Washington Street Plaza

BINGHAMTON TO OBSERVE 125TH ANNIVERSARY

City Plans for Biggest Celebration in Its History at Dedication of Memorial Bridge Over Susquehanna River

PAGEANT TO FEATURE

Facts About the Memorial Bridge

Cost of bridge structure, $400,000.

Cost of land for approaches paid to date, $159,596.

Approximate cost of land for approaches, still to be paid, $31,000.

Length of river span, 500 feet.

Length of west approach, 300 feet.

Length of east approach, 300 feet.

Width of roadway, 36 feet.

Tons of sand and gravel used, 15,000, exclusive of sidewalks and pavement.

Amount of cement used, 20,000 barrels.

Tons of reinforcing steel used, 350.

Number of boulevard lighting fixtures, 41.

Amount of water-proofing fabric used, 32,000 square feet.

Amount of asphalt used, exclusive of pavement, 11,000 square feet.

Square yards of pavement, 8,300.

Lineal feet of granite curbing, 3,500.

Amount of excavation, 7,000 cubic yards.

Amount of "fill," 12,000 cubic yards.

ERECTED BY
THE CITY OF BINGHAMTON
1925
AS A MEMORIAL TO THOSE CITIZENS
OF BROOME COUNTY WHOSE
UNSELFISH SERVICE
IN OUR AMERICAN WARS
EXPRESSES MAN'S HIGHEST IDEAL
OF PATRIOTIC DEVOTION

MEN OF BROOME
WHO SERVED FOR US
TO YOUR NAME THIS BRIDGE WE GIVE
THAT YOUR LAURELS MAY GROW GREEN
THAT YOUR MEMORY MAY LIVE
FLOWING STREAM AND WOODED HILLS
SPANNED BY ARCH OF CLASSIC GRACE
HERE WE SPEAK OUR GRATITUDE
HERE WE HOLD YOUR DEATHLESS PLACE

Two bronze tablets, which will be unveiled during the dedicatory ceremonies on Monday. The sentiments expressed are from the pen of Mary Brecht Pulver

Time Schedule for Celebration Events

10 a. m.—Baseball game between "Triplets" and Elmira teams at Johnson Field.

12 m.—Reserve officers' association luncheon in honor of Col. Peter E. Traub, U. S. A., at the Arlington Hotel.

1:15 p. m.—All organizations to be at assigned places for the parade.

2:00 p. m.—Parade moves.

3:30 p. m.—Memorial bridge dedication ceremonies at Memorial Circle, foot of Washington and Water streets.

4:30 p. m.—Drills by various uniformed organizations at Stow park upon arrival of units at the park following the dedication ceremonies at Memorial Circle.

[illegible]

CELEBRATION MARKS GREAT CITY ADVANCE

125 Years of Life of Municipality Will Be Depicted in Elaborate Pageant in Labor Day Parade

THOUSANDS COMING

[illegible]

(Continued on Page Two)

September 5, 1925: Coverage of the new Memorial Bridge makes the front page of the Binghamton Press second section. *Microfilm archives*

The Binghamton Press has the largest circulation of any daily newspaper in the United States which is published in a city the size of Binghamton.

BINGHAMTON PRESS
AND LEADER

THE WEATHER: Partly cloudy tonight; Sunday increasing cloudiness; showers afternoon or night; slightly warmer Sunday.

Vol. 47, No. 125. CITY EDITION SATURDAY EVENING, SEPTEMBER 5, 1925. SIXTY PAGES PRICE THREE CENTS

MURDERERS GAG AND BURN GUNMAN TO DEATH IN AUTO

BIG DIRIGIBLE DROPPED 2,100 FEET TO DOOM

Missing Baragraph Which Recorded Shenandoah's Death Flight Discovered Near Where Control Cabin of Craft Fell

PROBE IS CONTINUED

FINAL INQUIRY BOARD WILL PROBE DISASTER

BODY OF CULLINAN SENT TO BINGHAMTON

(Continued on Page Two)

INVESTIGATE DEATH OF AUTO VICTIM

The Binghamton Press Will Observe Labor Day on Monday

Agreeable to custom The Binghamton Press will observe the Labor Day and Anniversary Holiday on Monday and no editions of this paper will be issued during the day.

Tin Plate King's Grandaughter Is Now Plain Nancy

Helen Marie Leeds Will Be Forever an American, Says Royal Mother

'WAITING GAME' IN MINE STRIKE

Both Sides Delay Until Pinch of Shortage Will Bring Mediation

PREHISTORIC STAG OF HORNLESS SPECIES FOUND IN SAXONY

First Photographs of Shenandoah Disaster Received Here

The Binghamton Press today received the first photographs of the Shenandoah disaster. The upper photo shows the wreckage of the big dirigible near Ava, O. Below is a close up of the wreckage and at the bottom is all that is left of the control cabin, out of which Pilot James Cullinan of this city was hurled to his death.—Photos by International News Reel.

JERSEY POSSES FIND NO TRACE OF KIDNAPER

Hunt Continues for Murderer Who Killed Chauffeur and Fled with 6-Year-Old White Child After Shooting Pursuer

DESCRIPTIONS VARY

(Continued on Page 22)

1,000 HOMELESS IN CONFLAGRATION AT SHREVEPORT

Property Loss of More Than Half Million Dollars Caused by Fire in Louisiana Which Destroy Nine City Blocks

250 HOMES BURN

Coolidge's Political Manager Will Beard Lion of Insurgency

Chairman Butler Will Start on Tour of Northwest in September—Stand by President to Be Slogan in Congressional Elections

By MARK SULLIVAN.

(Continued on Page Two)

HANDS TIED BEHIND HIS BACK, BODY DISCOVERED IN CAR'S SMOKING RUINS

Imprisoned in Oil-Saturated Automobile, Gunman Meets Horrible Death in New York City's East Side; License Plates Removed from Vehicle Before It Is Set on Fire

FEATURES BURNED BEYOND RECOGNITION; SLIGHT CLUE LEADS TO HIS IDENTITY

TAMMANY HALL ACTS TO SPIKE GUNS OF HYLAN

Municipal Assembly Called by Leaders to Pass Bill Which Provides Five Cent Fare Cannot Be Increased Unless by People

MAYOR LOSES ISSUE

ANCIENT PEACE PIPE OF CREE INDIANS FOUND

FRANCE TO TAX 'IDLE WEALTH'

Returns It Is Expected Will Bring in Hundred Million Francs

CONVICT MAKES GETAWAY.

September 5, 1925: Violence in New York City and the crash of the dirigible *Shenandoah* top this front page. *Courtesy Carolyn Fitzgerald*

THE WEATHER

BINGHAMTON PRESS

AND LEADER

City Edition

Vol. 49, No. 37. THIRTY PAGES MONDAY EVENING, MAY 23, 1927. PRICE THREE CENTS

CAPT. LINDBERGH'S OWN STORY

Flyer Tells How He Fought Gale Over Ocean All Night; Tempted to Turn Back, but Keeps on, Flying Low in Storm

Acadians Torn from Homes by New Torrents

Boats Hurry to Rescue 200 Trapped as Eight-Inch Rain Raises Flood; Deluge at Evangeline Oak; More Villages Cut Off

15,500 REACH CAMP

Fall Indicated Above New Orleans and Planters Prepare to Seed Soon as Waters Recede--Oil Fields and Salt Mines Covered

Lindbergh's Rainbow End Turns to Million-Dollar Pot of Gold as Dazzling Offers Assail Him

Quake Feared Cataclysm in Distant Clime

Earth Jars Indicated as 7,500 Miles from Washington

TEMBLOR LASTS HOURS

Italian Braves Atlantic Flying Toward Home

1,600 Miles of Ocean Ahead Until De Pinedo Hits Azores Islands

THREE RIDE IN PLANE

Four-Continent Flyer Expects to Cross Sea in Twelve Hours

France Hails and Decorates 'Slim' as Hero

President Doumergue Pins Cross of the Legion of Honor on Lindbergh's Breast, Sweeps Flyer Into Arms and Kisses Him

BIRDMAN DEEPLY MOVED

Lindbergh's Day Made More Glorious by Discovery He Now Holds Long Distance Non-Stop Record of 3,647 Miles

Novelist Cline Pleads Not Guilty to Murder During Drinking Bout

U. S. Destroyer Replies to Raking Chinese Fire; Standard Tank Ablaze

Dynamite Wrecks Home of Ohio Dry Officer

Rogers Bids Lindbergh to Oklahoma Kiwanis Club

President Will Review Great U. S. Fleet June 1

BANKER BEEBE DIES

'AM I ON ROAD TO IRELAND?' LINDBERGH ASKS FISHING BOAT

Called 'Lucky' but Says Luck Isn't All—Modestly Shares Credit with Plane and Builders of Motor, Adding: 'I Hope I Made Good Use of What I Had'

IRISH COAST 'A BEAUTIFUL SIGHT' TO HIM

After Erin, It Was Easy, Except the Landing—Won't Repeat Hazardous Trip, but Expects to Have a Good Time and Do a Little Flying While in Europe

By CAPTAIN CHARLES A. LINDBERGH.

Copyright, 1927, in the United States, Canada, Mexico, Cuba, South America, Europe and the British Empire by the New York Times Company. All Rights Reserved.

Special cable to the New York Times and The Binghamton Press.

Paris, May 23 — Well, here I am in the hands of American Ambassador Herrick. From what I have seen of it, I am sure I am going to like Paris.

It isn't part of my plans to fly my plane back to the United States, although that doesn't mean I have finished my flying career. If I thought that was going to be the result of my flight across the Atlantic, you may be sure I would never have undertaken it. Indeed, I hope that I will be able to do some flying [illegible] of my plane last night.

Incidentally, that reception I got was the most dangerous part of the whole flight. If wind and storm had handled me as vigorously as that Reception Committee of Fifty Thousand I would never have reached Paris and wouldn't be eating a 3-o'clock-in-the-afternoon breakfast here in Uncle Sam's Embassy.

There's one thing I wish to get straight about this flight. They call me "Lucky," but luck isn't enough. As a matter of fact, I had what I regarded and still regard as the best existing plane to make the flight from New York to Paris. I had what I regard as the best engine, and I was equipped with what were in the circumstances the best possible instruments for making such efforts. I hope I made good use of what I had.

That I landed with considerable gasoline left means that I had recalled the fact that so many flights had failed because of lack of fuel, and that was one mistake I tried to avoid.

Weather Almost Made Him Turn Back.

All in all, I couldn't complain of the weather. It wasn't what was predicted. It was worse in some places and better in others. In fact, it was so bad once that for a moment there came over me the temptation to turn back. But then I figured it was probably just as bad behind me as in front of me, so I kept on toward Paris.

As you know, we (that's my ship and I) took off rather suddenly. We had a report somewhere around 4 o'clock in the afternoon before that the weather would be fine, so we thought we would try it.

We had been told we might expect good weather mostly during the whole of the way. But we struck fog and rain over the coast not far from the start. Actually, it was comparatively easy to get to Newfoundland, but real bad weather began just about dark, after leaving Newfoundland, and continued until about four hours after daybreak. We hadn't expected that at all, and it sort of took us by surprise, morally and physically. That was when I began to think about turning back.

In Serious Danger From a Sleet Storm.

Then sleet began, and, as all aviators know, in a sleet storm one may be forced down in a very few minutes. It got worse and worse. There, above and below me, and on both sides, was that driving storm. I made several detours trying to get out of it, but in vain. I flew as low as 10 feet above the water and then mounted up to 10,000 feet. Along toward morning the storm eased off, and I came down to a comparatively low level.

I had seen one ship just before losing sight of Newfoundland, and I saw the glow of several others afterward through the mist and storm. During the day I saw no ships until near Ireland.

I had, as I said, no trouble before I hit the storm I referred to. We had taken off at 7:55 in the morning. The field was slightly damp and soft, so the take-off was longer than it would have been otherwise. I had no trouble getting over the houses and trees. I kept out of the way of every obstacle and was careful not to take any unnecessary chances. As soon as I cleared everything, the motor was throttled down to three-fourths and kept there during the whole flight, except when I tried to climb over the storm.

Checked His Course at Newfoundland.

Soon after starting I was out of sight of land for 300 miles, from Cape Cod over the sea to Nova Scotia. The motor was acting perfectly and was carrying well the huge load of 451 gallons of gasoline and 20 gallons of oil, which gave my ship the greatest cruising radius of any plane of its type.

I passed over St. John's, N. F., purposely going out of my way a few miles to check up. I went right through the narrow pass, going down so low that it could be definitely established where I was at that hour. That was the last place I saw before taking to the open sea.

I had made preparations before I started for a forced landing if it became necessary, but after I started I never thought much about the possibility of such a landing. I was ready for it, but I saw no use thinking about it, inasmuch as one place would have been about as good or as bad as another.

Despite the talk about my periscope, I had no trouble in regard to visibility. The view I had on both sides was quite good enough for navigating the ocean, and the purpose of the periscope was only to enable me to see any obstacle directly in front of me. The periscope was useful in starting from New York and landing in Paris. Other than that I used it very little. I kept a map in front of me and an instrument showing practically where I was all of the time.

Flew Over an Iceberg Zone.

Shortly after leaving Newfoundland I began to see icebergs. There was a low fog and even through it I could make out bergs clearly. It began to get very cold, but I was well prepared for cold. I had on ordinary flying clothing, but I was down in the cockpit, which protected me, and I never suffered from the weather.

Within an hour after leaving the coast it became dark. Then I struck clouds and decided to try to get over them. For a while I succeeded, at a height of 10,000 feet. I flew at this height until early morning. The engine was working beautifully and I was not sleepy at all. I felt just as if I was driving a motorcar over a smooth road, only it was easier.

Then it began to get light and the clouds got higher. I went under some and over others. There was sleet in all of those clouds and the sleet began to cling to the plane. That worried me a great deal and I debated whether I should keep on or go back. I decided I must not think any more about going back. I realized that it was henceforth only a question of getting there. It was too far to turn back.

Thought of the Air Mail Flyers Back Home.

The engine was working perfectly and that cheered me. I was going along at 100 miles an hour and I knew that if the motor kept on turning I would get there. After that I thought only about navigating, and then I thought that I wasn't so badly off after all.

It was true that the flight was 34 hours long, and that at almost any moment in it a forced landing might be what you might call "rather interesting," but I remembered that the flying boys I knew back home spent some hours almost every week in bad flying when a forced landing would have been just as bad for them as a forced landing would have been for me. Those boys don't get credit for it, that's all, and without doubt in a few years many people will be taking just as many chances as I took.

The only real danger I had was at night. In the daytime

(Continued on Page Eight.)

The Man Who Did It and Mother

Captain Charles Lindbergh and his mother, Mrs. Evangeline L. Lindbergh, photographed together as he said goodbye to her before making his epochal flight. Mrs. Lindbergh is an instructor in chemistry in the Cass Technical High school, Detroit. She went to Curtiss Field, Long Island to bid her boy God-speed, then she went back to her classes and waited and prayed. Mrs. Lindbergh is a widow.

May 23, 1927: Lindbergh's flight is detailed in this edition of the Binghamton Press. *Courtesy Carolyn Fitzgerald*

SPORTS SECTION---ANNIVERSARY EDITION

Third Section

BINGHAMTON PRESS

Third Section

TWENTY-FIFTH ANNIVERSARY EDITION

WILLIS SHARPE KILMER BRINGS WORLD-WIDE FAME TO CITY WITH $5,000,000 BREEDING HARAS AND GREAT TURF FEATS

Breeding Farm Here Proves Thoroughbreds Can Be Raised in State

Story of How Sun Briar Court Was Established as Breeding Center—Sun Briar Was City's First Turf Champion—Word Pictures of Court Manor, Remlik Hall and Sky Lake

Carry Name of Sun Briar Court to International Fame

Champion Sun Briar is pictured, above, winning the Great American Handicap at Aqueduct in July, 1917. He is the center horse. Lucullite, which was second, is on the outside, and Tracksend, third, is hidden at the rail. Right, Reigh Count, by Sunreigh-Contessina, being crowned winner of the Kentucky Derby in 1928. Inset is head of Sally's Alley.

Champion Sun Briar and Other Horses Have Won Almost Every Important American Stake Race

Leading Sire Established American Mile Record—79 of His Get Have Earned $803,287 in Seven Years, Mark Equaled by No Other U. S. Breeder

MR. KILMER'S EXTERMINATOR GREATEST CUP HORSE IN HISTORY; STABLE'S OUTLOOK ROSY

Boots and saddle for Sun Briar Court!

Within the short time of the last 12 years, Willis Sharpe Kilmer of Binghamton has built up a $5,000,000 thoroughbred horse breeding haras, centered here on his native heath, very largely through the preeminence of one great horse—Sun Briar—which cost $6,000.

Meantime, as the result of Mr. Kilmer's sagacious selection of thoroughbred mares for mating with illustrious Sun Briar, the beautiful and extensive court which so proudly flourishes under the title of the fastest racer of his day, has become a byword that is synonymous with Binghamton over all the world.

61 Matrons at Court Manor Called "Million-Dollar Mares"

Elks Won Title at Trapshooting

Captured National Crown; State Shoot Held Here in '24; Mack Breaks 100 Twice

Jonas M. Kilmer Gained Fame as Owner of Trotters Which Were Factors in Grand Circuit

Pomeroy Still Checker King of the World

Binghamtonian Undefeated Since Winning Title from Jordan

April 11, 1929: The Binghamton Press celebrated its 25 years by printing a large paper. This section's front page was devoted to Willis Sharpe Kilmer's racing interests. *Courtesy Carolyn Fitzgerald*

NATION, STATE SEND CONGRATULATIONS

THE WEATHER
Cloudy and fair tonight. Friday showers; lowest temperature tonight 38.

BINGHAMTON PRESS
TWENTY-FIFTH ANNIVERSARY NUMBER
City Edition

Vol. 51, No. 1. ONE HUNDRED FORTY-EIGHT PAGES THURSDAY EVENING, APRIL 11, 1929. PRICE THREE CENTS

TORNADO KILLS 46; SCORES HURT

U. S. Troops Mobilize as Mexican Battles Near

Messages Pour in as Press Has 25th Birthday

Southern Tier's Leading Newspaper Marks a Generation of Service

ALL U. S. SENDS PRAISE

From North, South, East and West Tributes Come to Willis Sharpe Kilmer

Trout Caught by Clarke in Stuart Lake Grace President Hoover's Table

Major Clashes at Sonora and Naco Impend

1,500 Troops Ordered to Proceed to Arizona and New Mexico Points

PLANES PATROL LINE

Will Shoot Mexican Craft Over U. S. Down; Gas Warning Issued

Godspeed from Washington and Albany

Others Missing; Entire Village Is Blown Away

Rain and Debris Choked Roads Hamper Efforts of Rescue Workers

MANY CHILDREN DIE

Twister Rips Through North Central Arkansas; Fear Deaths Will Mount

Gov. Roosevelt Draws Wrath of Both Parties

Republicans Angered by Charges of Politics, Democrats by Lack of Patronage

Ban on Alien Canadians Makes Natives Subject to $8 Head Tax, $10 Visa Fee

Four Men Are Killed in Airplane Collision

Rebel Plot to Blow up Calles' Train Frustrated

Mrs. Hoover Turns from First Lady Role to Be "One of Girls" at Alumnae Meet

Texas Guinan Says She Never Had Drink in Her Life; Got Half Profits

Valley Forge Site Given U. of P. for Auxiliary

Germans Wait for Allies to Meet Figures

Their Statement as to What Reich Can Pay Is Submitted as Final

Lindbergh Drops Out of Sight Again; Gave Warning This Time

Six Injured in Explosion Aboard President Roosevelt

Cuban's Rum for Mexican Leader Poured in N. Y. Bay

Table of Contents 25th Anniversary Number

One Hundred Forty-eight Pages

10 U. S. Liners to Resume Sale of Rum at Sea

Leviathan Sails Wet, Ready to Open Stores Beyond 12-Mile Limit

Grand Jury Refuses to Indict Under Jones Law on One Agent's Word

April 11, 1929: The Binghamton Press, now having dropped "And Leader" from its flag, received congratulations on its first 25 years from Gov. Roosevelt, Vice President Curtis and other leading federal officials. *Courtesy Frances Zigmont*

THE BINGHAMTON SUN, FRIDAY, AUGUST 23, 1929 — 17

CORRECTED PROGRAMS OF LEADING STATIONS

Radio Features and Home Interest Page

DAILY FASHIONS AND AIDS FOR HOMEMAKERS

Jack Lynch and His Rhythm Boys at Sun Studio Tonight

WELL KNOWN DANCE BAND TO BE HEARD

Program Over WNBF Assured of Large Radio Audience When Popular Organization Holds Forth

PUBLIC INTERESTED IN 'BETTER MUSIC'

Monday and Friday Night Broadcasts Already Have Brought Pleasing Response From Triple Cities Listeners

Tonight's offering over WNBF from the new studio of The Binghamton Sun will be Jack Lynch and his Rhythm Boys. This program will go on the air from 9 to 10 o'clock this evening and will offer a number of novelties and special features in addition to a well rounded program of dance music.

Jack Lynch and his company of artists, all of whom are soloists, will be assured of a large audience of listeners tonight since they are well known to lovers of the dance throughout the Southern Tier. The organization is especially popular and has been booked for numerous appearances throughout the state.

The artists are:

Matthew Danek, violinist and leader.
Jack Lynch, banjo and owner.
John Dorin, drummer.
Jack Smiley, bass.
Bernie Dailey, first saxophone.
James Lynch, second saxophone.
William Danek, pianist.
George Litell, first trumpet.
Louis Mahoney, trombone.

The program: "My Sin," "Louisana Bobo," "I've Got a Feeling I'm Falling," "Do Something," "Pagan Love Song," (waltz); "Kansas City Kitty," "Love Me or Leave Me," "Jericho," "Some Sweet Day," "Medley of waltzes, "Marie," "Where Is the Song of Songs for Me," "Coquette"; "Sunrise to Sunset," "Dream Mother," "Lover Come Back to Me," "I Get the Blues When It Rains," "Sweetheart of Sigma Chi," (waltz); "Heigh Ho, Everybody! Heigh Ho!"

The Rhythm Boys are featured every Saturday night at the George F. Pavilion, where they are favorites. Bernie Dailey, first saxophone, does all of the singing for the band and will be heard tonight in two or three numbers. All of the "Rhythm Boys" have personality and pep which they put into their music. The organization is known as the dance band with "it."

Jack Lynch himself is the youngest orchestra owner in town and has made rapid progress in getting to the top. His popularity is due largely to his willingness to play request numbers. The band plays every kind of dance tempos including waltzes, blues, fox-trots and stomps.

Popularity of the "Sundown Hour" from the Sun Studio was illustrated Monday night when telephone calls congratulating the artists and P. Joe Congdon, program director, clogged the switchboards at The Sun office and at the main studio of WNBF at the Arlington. The number of requests and expressions from listeners indicated that the programs broadcast each Monday and Friday night are appreciated.

The Sun is attempting through these programs not only to bring the best in music to the local listening public but to demonstrate that local musical organizations are equal to any now being heard over the larger broadcasting stations. Comparison of the programs already presented and those to come, with some of the popular groups being heard over the national chains is invited.

Numerous good features have been booked for the remainder of the Summer and early Fall for appearances at The Sun studio, including a number of artists and groups of musicians who have never before consented to appear before the microphone. Announcement of these programs will be made at an early date.

Paula Hemminghaus, contralto, and Theodore Webb, baritone, featured artists of several NBC programs, will be heard in the "Evening Stars" broadcast this morning at 10:30 o'clock. These stars are heard during the Winter in the programs broadcast over the NBC System by the National Grand Opera Company. They also sing major roles in the Gilbert and Sullivan opera series, which is a current NBC presentation each Wednesday night. Ludwig Laurier will direct the orchestral program. This broadcast is dedicated to KSD, St. Louis, an associate station of the NBC System. (WEAF)

Varied moods, inspired by the dance, the carnival and the rousing strains of battle, are revived for listeners in the concert program of the Pacific Little Symphony, which will be broadcast from the NBC System San Francisco studios over a coast-to-coast network this afternoon at 3 o'clock. The old masters are represented by Rossini's overture to "William Tell," an opera now seldom heard. Representative works of the moderns, Borodin, Debussy and Bizet, are included, and the concert reaches its musical climax in two bright numbers by Leo Delibes.

Guiding Your Child

By MRS. AGNES LYNE

WASTEFULNESS

Children are naturally wasteful, and unless they are trained to be otherwise they grow up wasteful of food, clothing, money and materials.

A child's eyes are always bigger than his stomach. He takes more food on his plate than he can possibly eat. He is careless of his clothing. A sweater left on the baseball field, a pair of shoes forgotten on the lake shore, mean nothing to him. If he is using wood, cloth or paper he invariably cuts wastefully and never thinks about saving the scraps.

Wastefulness is an unserviceable trait for which there is no excuse. It requires only proper early training to teach children a decent thriftiness and a wholesome respect for things which have cose work and money.

Begin early to train your child. Put only as much food on his plate as you are sure he can eat. Make it a rule that he must empty his dinner plate before he may have dessert.

If, through sheer carelessness, he loses some article of clothing, don't replace it at once. Let him feel the want of it before you do.

When you give him material to use, provide only so much as necessary for his purpose. Show him how to avoid waste.

If he is extravagant with money, make sure that he has a reasonable allowance and then permit no appeal from its limitations. The money spent on an inconsequential trifle is gone and an empty purse teaches its lesson much better than a dozen lectures on economy.

Give him opportunities to earn money, so that, having experienced the effort required to get a little of it, he will be more thoughtful in spending it.

Helping the Homemaker

By LOUISE BENNETT WEAVER

TURMERIC PICKLES ADD FLAVOR

MENU FOR DINNER
Molded Rice and Salmon Sauce
Tumeric Pickles
Bread — Grape Jam
Head Lettuce and Russian Dressing
Watermelon — Coffee

MOLDED RICE

2 cups cooked rice.
½ teaspoon salt.
¼ teaspoon pepper.
¼ teaspoon celery salt.
2 eggs.
½ cup milk.
3 tablespoons butter, melted.

Mix the ingredients and pour into a greased pan. Set in a pan of water and bake in a moderate oven for 25 minutes. Carefully unmold and surround with the Salmon Sauce.

SALMON SAUCE

4 tablespoons butter.
4 tablespoons flour.
2 cups milk.
½ teaspoon salt.
¼ teaspoon paprika.
1 cup salmon, flaked.

Melt the butter and add the flour. Blend and add the milk. Cook until a creamy sauce forms. Add the rest of the ingredients and cook slowly for 2 minutes. Pour around the rice mold. Garnish with parsley.

TURMERIC PICKLES

24 four inch cucumbers.
1 cup sliced onions.
¼ cup salt.
2 cups vinegar.
½ teaspoon pepper.
2 tablespoons mustard seed.
1 tablespoon celery seed.
½ teaspoon turmeric powder.
2 cups brown sugar.

Mix the cucumbers, onions and salt. Let stand for 4 hours. Drain well. Boil the rest of the ingredients for 10 minutes. Pour into sterilized jars and seal.

After boiling rice, rinse it thoroughly in warm water and it will never be "sticky."

A KITCHEN SUGGESTION

Have you ever thought of using the little closet built in the outside wall of your kitchen for a cupboard instead of as a garbage pail container?

Keep this compartment absolutely clean and lined with fresh papers and it makes an excellent cold cupboard to keep foods like cheese, etc., that spread an undesirable flavor to other foods.

Cheese, for instance, should be kept in a cool place but not in the refrigerator with other foods unless tightly covered.

During the Winter this cold closet will take quite a strain from the refrigerator and lower the ice bill.

Another handy place for the covered garbage pail may readily be found.

Leo O'Rourke, tenor, will be the soloist in an elaborate program of musical gems when the Cities Service Concert is broadcast over the NBC System tonight, at 7 o'clock. The Cavaliers, a male quartet, will have a group of typical selections, including "Let Me Call You Sweetheart" and "Old Uncle Ned." Another highlight will be a piano solo by Milton Rettenberg, "Sweet Nothings." Rosario Bourdon directs the concert orchestra. (WEAF).

Masters of Rhythm Broadcast Tonight

Jack Lynch and his group of artists who will be heard over Station WNBF, Binghamton, through the new studio of The Binghamton Sun this evening from 9 to 10.

IN THE AIR TODAY

(By The Associated Press)

Programs in Eastern Standard time. All time is p. m. unless otherwise indicated. Wavelengths on left of call letters, kilocycles on right.

348.6—WABC, New York—860
6:30—Fashion Plates; also WCAU, WNAC, WEAN, WFBL, WJAS.

454.3—WEAF, New York—660
5:00—Black and Gold Room Orchestra; Scores, WEAF.
5:30—Twins; also WJAR, WTAG, WCSH, WRC, WGY, WTAM, WWJ.
6:00—Rapid Tranis Sketches; also WRC, WSM, WJAR, WTAG.
6:30—Dark Town Wanderers; also WCAE, WGR.
7:00—Concert Orchestra and Cavaliers; also WEEI, WTIC, WLIT, WRC, WGR, WCAE, WTAM, KYW, WWJ.
8:00—"Whispering Tables"; also WGY, WEEI, WJAR, WTAG, WRC, WGR, WCAE, WWJ, WSAI.
8:30—Gus and Louie with the Town Band; also WTIC, WJAR, WTAG, WCSH, WLIT, WGY, WGR, WCAE, WWJ, WRC, WEEI, WSAI, WFJC.
9:00—Summer Melodies; also WTIC, WTAG, WRC, WCAE, WWJ, WSAI, WSM.
9:30—Family Goes Abroad; also WTAG, WRC, WGY, WCAE, WWJ, WTIC.
10:00—Dance Orchestra Hour; also WTIC, WWJ, WSAI, WFJC.
11:00—Ben Pollack's Dance Orchestra (one hour); also WRC.

394.5—WJZ, New York—760
5:00—Hotel Dance Orchestra, WJZ; Scores, WJZ.
6:00—In the Good Old Summer Time; also KDKA, WBAL.
6:30—Uncle Bob Sherwood, stories of the Circus and Novelty Band—also WBZ, WBAL, KDKA, WLW, WJR, KYW, WHAS, WSM, WSB, WBT.
7:00—Mildred Hunt and Orch.; also WBZ, KDKA, WHAM, WJR, WLW.
7:30—Adventures of Nivk Carter, WJZ and stations.
8:00—Phil Cook and Vic Fleming; also WBZ, WHAM, KDKA, KYW, WHAS, WSM, WSB, WBT, WJAX, WRVA, WAPI, WIOD, WLW.
8:30—Memories; also WBZ, WHAM, KDKA, WLW, WJR, KYW.
9:00—Quaker Girl; also WBZ, KDKA, WHAM, WLW, KYW.
9:30—Orchestra and Chorus; also WBZ, WHAM, KDKA, WJR, WLW, KYW, WBT, WJAX, WHAS, WSM, WSB, WAPI, WRVA.
10:00—Amos 'n' Andy (from WMAQ); also WBZ, WHAM, KDKA, WJR, WLW, KYW.
10:15—Slumber Music; also KDKA, WIOD, WRC, WSM.

[illegible]—WOR, Newark—710
7:00—Hawaiian Shadows; also WNAC, WEAN, WFBL, WKBW, WCAO, WJAS, WLBW, WMAL, WADC.
7:30—The Rollickers; also WNAC, WEAN, WMBL, WKBW, WCAO, WADC, WGHP, WMAQ, WLBW, WMAL.
8:00—Story Hour; also WCAU, WNAC, WEAN, WGRC, WFBL, WMAK, WCAO, WJAS, WADC, WGHP, WMAQ, WSPD, WHK, WLBW, WMAL.
9:00—Radio Time; also WCAU, WNAC, WEAN, WFBL, WMAK, WCAO, WJAS, WADC, WKRC, WGHP, WMAQ, WSPD, WHK, WLBW, WMAL.
9:30—Russian Music; also WCAU, WNAC, WEAN, WFBL, WCAO, WJAS, WGHP, WSPD, WHK, WMAL, WKRC, WLBW, WMAK, WMAQ.

199.9—WNBF, Binghamton—1500
10:50 a. m.—Morning Melodies.
11:00—Sara Lane.
11:30—Studio Program.
11:50—Washington News.
12:00—Weeks & Dickinson Hour.
1:00 p. m.—Time. Weather forecast. Stevencraft Hour.
1:30—Musical Session.
5:30—Baseball Scores.
5:40—Washington News.
5:50—Where to Go.
6:15—Walter Stanzel
6:30—Local News Items.
6:45—Chimes.
7:00—Shopping Service.
8:00—Organ.
8:30—Spaulding Baker Family.
9:00—"Sundown Hour," Jack Lynch and his Rhythm Boys from The Sun studio.
10:00—Correct Time.

379.5—WGY, Schenectady—790
5:45-7.00 a. m.—Setting-up exercises.
7:00 a. m.—Larry Brier's orchestra.
7:15 a. m.—Federation Morning Devotions.
7:30 a. m.—"Cheerio."
7:50 a. m.—Correct Time.
8:52 a. m.—Aviation Weather Report.
9:00 a. m.—National Home Hour.
10:00—Musical program.
10:15-10:30 a. m.—Radio Household Institute.
10:30-11:00 a. m.—Evening Stars.
11:55 a. m.—Time signals.
12:00 m.—Weather forecast.
12:02—Produce market report.
12:10—Farm flashes.
12:30—Correct Time.
12:30—New York stock reports.
12:45—Weather forecast.
12:55—Aviation Weather Report.
1:00—Orchestra, Albany.
4:59—Correct time.
5:00—Stock reports, produce market report. News items and Saratoga Race results.
5:25—Baseball scores.
5:30—Correct time.
5:30—Program from New York.
6:00—Literary Cameos.
6:20—Health talk.
6:25—Baseball scores.
6:30—Program from Rochester.
6:45—Program from Rochester.
7:00—General Electric Orchestra.
8:00—Whispering Tables.
8:30—Schradertown Brass Band.
9:00—General Electric Orchestra.
9:30—Family goes abroad
10:00-11:00—Dornberger's Orchestra, Saratoga Springs.

348.6—WABC, New York—860
5:00—Odds and Ends.
5:30—Orchestra; Entertainers.
6:30—Chain Key Station.
7:00—Entertainers; Orchestra.
8:00—In Old Vienna; Play.
8:30—Sea Senior; Choral Singers.
9:30—Negro Achievement program.
10:00—Dance Music Hour.

422.3—WOR, Newark—710
5:30—Concert Ensemble.
6:00—Hotel Orchestra.
6:30—Fiesta.
7:00—Chain Key Station (3 hrs.)
10:00—News; Dance Hour.

305.9—KDKA, Pittsburgh—950
5:00—Band Concert; Scores.
6:00—Same as WJZ (4¼ hrs.)
10:15—Bestor's Orchestra; Scores.

428.3—WLW, Cincinnati—700
6:00—Memory Tunes; Sports; Scores.
6:30—Same as WJZ (3½ hrs.)
10:00—WJZ; Gene, Ford and Glenn.
10:30—Radioet Presentation.
11:00—Chime Reveries.
12:00—Dance Music.
12:30a—Sweet and Lown Down.
1:00a—Gene, Ford and Glenn.

When Dinosaur Wagged It's Tail 15-Foot Radius Was Endangered

WASHINGTON (AP). — When a dinosaur wagged its tail, the surrounding territory was in for some damage.

A 15-foot tail belonging to one of the giant reptiles before it was transformed into rock millions of years ago, has been uncovered by a Smithsonian expedition in the San Juan basin in New Mexico.

It was complete, with all joints intact, but there was no trace of the rest of the beast which browsed on plants or animals before the ice sheet blanketed a part of the world.

Parts of a skull of a horned dinosaur, never before found in fauna of the same formation, were unearthed and a collection was made of more than 20 turtles, all practically complete. The turtles, some measuring three feet in length, represented both land and water types.

The desert sands, pierced by sagebrush and scanty vegetation and now the home of Navajo Indians peacefully tending herds of sheep, was rich with surface indications of the ancient reptiles.

The ground, according to Dr. Charles W. Gilmore, curator of vertebrate paleontology of the National museum and head of the expedition, was literally covered with fragments of dinosaur bones.

The region, heretofore worked only by geologists and not before by paleontologists, was covered with wind-blown sand. When the giant reptiles roamed the land millions of years ago, the era was one of swamp land.

The bones uncovered were petrified or agatized. From a study of them, since some have never been found to occur before under the same circumstances with other distinct fauna, the scientists may unravel further the story of the pre-ice age giants.

Besides Doctor Gilmore, the expedition included N. H. Boss of the Smithsonian institution; George F. Sternberg of Hays, Kas., and Charles Sternberg of Chicago. In all, more than a ton and a half of bones were shipped from the field.

Jack Himself

Popular banjoist and owner of favorite dance band.

Styles by ANNETTE Paris—New York

551

DISTINCTIVE LINES

A printed crepe de chine that will prove a smart addition to your Summer wardrobe. Tucks at left hip create a charming swathed movement to slenderize the figure. The skirt has grouped plaits at left side to flare the hem. Neckline also tapers to left side in diagonal treatment, which all combine to carry out a vertical line to lengthen the silhouette. The bow at neckline with long scarf ends is youthful. Style No. 551 is designed in sizes 16, 18, 20 years, 36, 38, 40 and 42 inches bust. Printed voile in gingham check in blue and white will make up lovely, and will prove an economical choice for warm days. Shantung, silk broadcloth, silk pique, printed rajah, polka-dotted dimity, georgette crepe, and shantung also fashionable.

For each pattern send 12 cents in coin, which includes 2 cents for postage, to The Binghamton Sun, Pattern Department. If your order is for more than one, enclose 2 cents additional postage for each pattern. Enclose 10 cents additional if you wish a copy of our large new Fashion magazine containing all the new styles for Spring.

These patterns are mailed direct to our subscribers from New York City. Upon receipts of complaint of non-delivery of patterns, same is immediately re-ordered.

BROKEN WINGS by Barbara Webb

You'll enjoy this tale of clashing wills, of high romance and thrilling adventure.

(Copyright, 1929)

SYNOPSIS

She lay asleep in a bed hollowed out of sand, with an old sheet and a sheepskin jacket for a cover. Across the fire slept the man she hated, even though he had prepared her bed and given her all the available covering. Her name was Katherine Boyd. She was the daughter of a multimillionaire and she had never been thwarted in her life. His name was Bill Daly and he was the pilot of the Falcon which lay a mass of tangled wreckage not far from their campfire. They had attempted to fly to Australia from California and had been swept far from their course by a storm. Now they were marooned on a tiny island, the only human beings alive on its shores. Bill wanted to make an adventure of it, having Katherine share the work necessary to keep them alive until help could come. But Katherine was filled with rage and resentment and had made up her mind to do nothing whatever to help. Her father and mother and her fiance were searching for them, but they were many hundreds of miles away, and Bill realized that help might be weeks in reaching them. However bravely he might face the situation, Katherine was resolved to sulk and shirk. The second morning of their stay on the island dawned.

CHAPTER 7

Vain Regrets

"Very well," Katherine's voice was icy again. No matter what she wanted, what she suggested, it was wrong. She brooded over her helplessness, chafed at its unfairness. Not once did she feel a sense of thankfulness for the miracle of their escape, unharmed, from the wreck. Nor did she give a thought to the skill, functioning automatically, that had lifted them over the rock, saved their lives. She grew more and more morose. Sleep did not come.

Bill for his part now regretted not having given her the brandy. It might have soothed her on this first trying night. He peered at her. Apparently she was asleep now. He hoped she was. His own bones ached from weariness. He threw another log, a big one that he had been saving for this time, on the coals. Then stretched full length on the [illegible] he fell into deep and dreamless slumber.

When Katherine was sure he slept she raised herself on one elbow, and across the coals regarded him long and earnestly. He would expect her to work. He would ask her to share the making of the hut he had spoken of. She knew that. Well, she wasn't going to do it. She hated him. She hadn't really wanted that brandy, but she did want her own way. She had always had her own way. She was going to do it. She hated him. Tears of self-pity filled her eyes. She was alone on a desert island, with the one human being whom she loathed and hated with all the force of her being.

Never had Jackson 3d seemed so desirable, so safe, so comforting. "If only I had married him instad of making this crazy flight," she moaned to herself, and she fell asleep finally, dreaming of their wedding.

Rebellion

Katherine had lain awake so long nursing her grievance that she slept late the next morning. In the hour before she fell asleep she had concentrated all her misery on Bill. There was no justice in her feeling of resentment against him. She simply felt, down to the marrow of her bones, that he was responsible for her present plight. And she soothed that resentment with the resolve to do nothing to further his plans. He would have to work alone.

When she woke she found that he had dragged some boards from the Falcon, propped them in the sand, covered them with green branches, and thus formed a cool spot for her to slumber in. She felt no gratitude. She simply accepted this as proof that he realized that she was the one to be sheltered and protected. She stretched lazily and winced at the sand that ran down her neck when she turned.

"I need a bath," she thought. "I'll have a swim somewhere today. It will make me feel bettr and do something to pass the time. Surely it won't be long before father gets here in the Seahawk."

Bill was working around the Falcon when she stepped from her sandy bed. He waved to her and called. "There's a swell place to bathe, just around the curve of the beach, if you feel sandy. I've had mine and when you finish we'll have some breakfast."

He was not a prepossessing sight. Three days' growth of beard made an unpleasant stubble on his face. He had discarded all clothing save his khaki trousers, and these were rolled to his knees, leaving his legs and feet bare.

Katherine said good morning distantly as she passed him. She felt unreasonably that he might have worn more clothes, might have made some attempt to shave, though she did not stop to remember that he had brought nothing with him, having planned to buy necessaries in Honolulu and later in Sydney. Jackson would never, never let himself look like that.

"Wait a minute," he called. "I found some stuff of yours in the Falcon when I examined her innards this morning. Maybe you'll want them for your bath."

He indicated a small case which Katherine remembered now had been fitted with her own special brand of bath soap, cold cream, perfume and powder, just before she left San Diego.

"Thanks," she said, picking them up and tucking them under her arm.

"Go easy on the soap," Bill advised her. "It may be a long time before we have any more, and if you're wise you'll cut your clothes down to next to nothing. It's going to be one hot day and we have work to do."

Katherine went on toward the bathing place he had indicated without answering.

"Gosh," Bill said to himself, "I hope she gets over that grouch soon."

Katherine found a small pool in the curve of the beach. The water [illegible] and shallow and she stripped off her clothes and stepped into its grateful depths. After dawdling around she tried using the soap and found that it made very little lather, even when she rubbed it vigorously over her body. "It's the salt water," she decided. "He'll have to find some place where I can bathe in fresh water. This stuff will ruin my hair when it needs washing, too."

She felt refreshed when she stepped out and was annoyed at having no towel. There was none to be had, of course. While she was hesitating she found that the sun had dried her thoroughly, and that a dusting with her talcum powder, fragrant with lavender, took the sticky feeling away. It was hot. Too hot for the clothes she had been wearing. She had come away in a tweed suit, disdaining any sensational togs. Now she discarded the coat and matching sweater and put on only the skirt and tailored silk shirt. She hesitated over the stockings and then, as they were the only pair she had, decided to save them for the grand day of her rescue. But the shoes were uncomfortable without stockings, so she finally walked back to the Falcon in her bare feet.

Bill had made a fire and was cooking more clams over it. He looked up to smile at her. "Feel better? I see you've given up shoes. I have, too, except when we go to the woods, when we'll have to wear them. Ready for ham and eggs?"

Katherine looked discontentedly at the shellfish and with distaste at the cup of cocoanut milk he proffered her. She started to refuse, and then realized that she was really hungry and would have to eat what there was to eat.

"Can't you find anything else except this stuff?" she asked when she had finished the cocoanut milk.

"Sure, but it will take a little time. I have an idea we can find nests with eggs in them, and there ma[y be] fruit growing back on the is[land]. I've got a plan for catching fish, a[nd] I think I can set traps and catch some birds. There may [be] other small animals in the woods, too. Oh, we'll live high when we get on to the ways of this place. But first thing we must do is rig up a signal of some kind, and then we must get some huts made.

"I've been looking around and I think we can make two, one for you and one for me on either side of that big rock. We'll pile branches down for a floor, cut the small limbs and leaves off, and lay leaves and all at an angle to form sides. Now, after breakfast, when we get our dishes washed," he waved the solitary thermos cup at her, "we'll get the huts built. I've cut a big pile of branches up at the edge of the woods there, and you can bring as many down as you can carry. About three trips and we'll have enough for the floors."

Katherine interrupted him. "Don't count on my help," she said in a final tone of voice.

"Do you mean that you are going to continue refusing to be of any help in digging ourselves in comfortably here until we are rescued?" Bill asked evenly.

"You may interpret it in that way if you choose."

"Suppose I order you to do your share?"

"Ordering is one thing, getting me to take orders is another."

"I see."

(To be continued)

His quiet tone angered Katherine. "I won't be ordered about! I won't do a single thing unless I choose"

August 23, 1929: This "Radio Features and Home Interest Page" features an article on Jack Lynch and his band, opposite page. *Courtesy Mary Giblin*

Fire Dept. Hook & Ladder Truck

Bingham Fire Department hook and ladder truck, circa 1928. *Courtesy Richard Gillespie*

JACK LYNCH
&
HIS
RHYTHM BOYS
BINGHAMTON, N.Y.

Jack Lynch and his Rhythm Boys band was a local group that performed at the Fountains Pavilion, playing swing music. Lynch was born in 1906 and died in 1976. *Courtesy Mary Giblin*

THE WEATHER

Increasing cloudiness and colder tonight; lowest temperature 26 to 30. Tuesday cloudy, followed by rain.

BINGHAMTON PRESS

City Edition

Vol. 51, No. 169. TWENTY-SIX PAGES MONDAY EVENING, OCTOBER 28, 1929. PRICE THREE CENTS

BANKERS FIGHTING STOCK CRASH

Bingham Rips Accusers; Senate Censure Asked

'Slimy Politics' in Lobby Probe, Senator Cries

Committee "Framed," Connecticut Legislator Shouts, Answering Caraway

NORRIS ASKS REBUKE

Nebraskan Declares He Will Offer Resolution in View of Charges

Washington, Oct. 28—(Associated Press)—Presentation of a resolution of censure of Senator Bingham, Republican, Connecticut, was forecast in the Senate today at the close of two hours of savage, personal exchanges between the Connecticut senator and members of the lobby committee, who condemned his relations with the Connecticut Manufacturers' association.

Chairman Norris of the judiciary committee, who appointed the lobby committee, announced he intended to offer a resolution shortly.

Later he explained that in view of the attack made by Bingham upon the committee and in view of the committee's condemnation of Bingham, he felt the Senate should place itself on record.

(Continued on Page Eight)

Chicago Lovers Still Can Laugh at Locksmiths but Holdup Men Are Different

Chicago, Oct. 28 — (United Press) — Love may laugh at locksmiths, but it shows a wholesome respect for Chicago holdup men.

Lloyd Bryer and his fiancee of a day, Miss Bernice Hansen, were whispering sweet nothings in the former's automobile when four youthful bandits robbed them of $30 and the engagement ring.

Salvatore Tamosa was bidding farewell to his sweetheart, Maria Rosak, in front of the girl's home, when the same gang appeared, and took from them $12, a $300 watch and her ring.

Tariff Death Inevitable Now, Leaders Think

Senate to End Session Nov. 15, Capital Hears; Reed Gives up Hope

(Continued on Page Eight)

Snook, Sentenced to Die Nov. 29 for Murder of Hix Girl, Files Error Writ

Mexican Army and Church Pledge Strict Neutrality in November Presidential Vote

Pacific Council Opens in Japan; U. S. Sends 43

Delegates Unofficially to Settle Problems of Moment in the Orient

CHINESE QUESTION UP

Mechanization of the East One of Issues Experts to Consider

Heart in Wrong Place, but Woman Owes Life to "Botch" by Nature

Kirksville, Mo., Oct. 28—(United Press)—Mrs. William W. Wilson's heart is not in the right place. She owes her life to that fact.

Mrs. Wilson was in an automobile which police commandeered to follow two fleeing thieves. A gun battle occurred. Mrs. Wilson was shot through the spot where her heart was presumed to be. But she lived.

At a hospital an X-ray picture disclosed that her heart was on the right side of her body. She probably will recover.

Socialists Hold Key to French Cabinet Crisis

New Premier's Success Depends on Leftist Support; Briand Takes Post

UNION LEADER HURT WHEN BOMB LETS GO AS HE STARTS AUTO

Staggers in House After Being Hurled Through Roof of Garage; Then Topples Unconscious

Addison Man Killed Instantly by Automobile

MacDonald Attends Church Services on Ship; Studies Problems Waiting at Home

8 Chinese Held on Drug Charges at Rochester; Young Girls Involved

TWO SMUGGLERS EXECUTED

German Prince Von Buelow Is Dead in Italy

"Second Bismarck" Rebuked the Kaiser for His Militarism

TRIED TO AVERT WAR

Failure to Hold Rome to Triple Alliance Resulted in His Downfall

Deflation of Stocks Sought by U. S. to Stabilize Trade; Wildest Readjustment in History

Thousands Impoverished by Crash in 6 Weeks of Structure 5 Years in Building

Firm Business Policy Is Pushed by Hoover to End Speculation

By Carter Field

(Continued on Page Eight)

Naming Kahn as Treasurer Upsets Party

Moses Stands by Appointment of Banker to Senate Committee

Jury Convicts Pantages; Term 1 to 50 Years

7 Women and 5 Men Out 53 Hours Before They Reach Verdict

College Student Shot Fatally When Detected Stealing Gas in Garage

SUCCESSOR IS CALLED AS CATT COUNTERFEIT CASE GOES TO JURY

Boy Found Dead in Mine Shaft Believed Victim of Starvation by Kidnaper

Buffalo Youth Kills Girl While Displaying Gun at Sister's Party

Pittsburgh Man Dies After Living a Month With Bullet in Heart

Texas Judge on Trial for Murder in Killing of His Daughter's Lover

Market Saved as Pool's Cash Is Dumped In

Billions of Dollars in Values Thrown Overboard in Today's Upset

"BLUE CHIPS" CRACKING

"Little Fellow," Already Out of Market, Now Big Boys Are Hit

New York, Oct. 28—(Associated Press) — Another violent break on the Stock Exchange today wiped out $3,000,000,000 in market value of various issues before the banking pool, with billions at its command, could control the situation and restore calm. Selling attained such proportions that the whole financial section became alarmed.

(Continued on Page Eight)

200 Firemen Receive Canary "Razzberry," Go Home Licked

Chicago Murder Suspect Is Arrested in New York

'Pussyfoot's' Chauffeur Jailed for Intoxication; Goes on Tear

Houses of Future Will Be of Glass, Professor Says

BYRD HONORARY "CO-ED"

New Cancer Treatment Method Found by Medical Experiment

October 28, 1929: The day before the legendary stock crash that ushered in the Great Depression, the market was already unnerved. The story says the market lost $3 billion on Monday. *Microfilm archives*

Second Section

BINGHAMTON PRESS

Second Section

THIRTY-TWO PAGES — WEDNESDAY EVENING, OCTOBER 30, 1929. — PAGES 17 TO 32

American Business Sound, Notwithstanding Stock Crash, I. B. M. Head Says Here

Market Upturn Is Greeted Here With Optimism

Local Investors Buy Heavily as Leaders Jump Ahead 5 to 30 Points

FEW ARE SUSPICIOUS

"Sell, Sell" Cry Subsides; Some, Cleaned Out, Watch in Daze

With the stock market rounding upward from the lowest "bottom" in history, floors of local brokerage offices today became less like funeral parlors.

[illegible]

Sixty Boys Form 10 Teams for Central Y. M. C. A. Drive to Enroll 500 Members

[illegible]

Agfa Ansco Employe Faces Larceny Charge

[illegible]

BE CAREFUL IN USING HALLOWEEN LIGHTS, FIRE CHIEF CAUTIONS

Brown Threatens Prosecution of Any Who Turn in False Alarms of Fire

Halloween celebrators should be careful in use of Japanese lanterns, candles, jack-o'-lanterns and various bare lights in connection with their fun, Chief Engineer Elmer J. Brown of the Bureau of Fire, warned today. He issued a warning that police will be on the alert to detect anyone sending in false alarms and that children or grownups who cause the firemen useless runs will be taken into custody.

Flimsy decorations should be protected from open flames, he said.

Two Religious Holidays Will Be Observed

Episcopal, Catholic Churches to Mark All Saints' and All Souls' Days

[illegible]

Members of Italian Organizations to Join Night of Fun Parade

[illegible]

Nursery School Patrons Will Meet Thursday

[illegible]

Banquet Given by I. B. M. in Honor of A. Ward Ford

Jury Awards $350 for Car Lost in Fire

Verdict Given for Plaintiff in Action Against Garage Proprietor

[illegible]

Driver Jumps From Cab of Truck as Train Hits It on Cortland Crossing

[illegible]

Work Starts on Addition to Port Dickinson School; All Contracts Awarded

[illegible]

Girl Under Age, $5,000 Action Is Thrown Out

Mrs. Beatrus Conklin Must Get Guardian to Push False Arrest Action

[illegible]

More Than 100 Attend Resnick's Masquerade Dance at Boathouse

[illegible]

RETURNS FROM JAMESTOWN

[illegible]

More Than 600 Attend Dinner Honoring I. T. R. Vice President

Testimonial Tendered A. Ward Ford, Marking 40 Years' Service With Company, Largest Affair of Kind Ever Held in Binghamton

[illegible]

(Continued on Page Twenty-four)

Miss Eva Kinney Bride of David Wadsworth at Cortland Ceremony

[illegible]

St. Catherine's to Be Opened Here on Dec. 8

All Priests of Binghamton Deanery Are Expected to Attend Dedication

[illegible]

Moose Hold Smoker Here at Clubhouse

[illegible]

Decline Is Due to Speculation, Watson States

No Danger of Panic, He Declares; Intrinsic Value of Stocks Unaffected

QUOTES PROFIT TABLES

I. B. M. Gains 28 Per Cent Over 1928; to Expand Endicott Plant

"American business is fundamentally sound and the public should not be deluded by recent fluctuations in the stock market," declared Thomas J. Watson, president of the International Business Machines Corp., who presided at a testimonial dinner in the Arlington hotel Tuesday night in honor of A. Ward Ford, vice president of the International Time Recorder Co.

"While quotations of many stocks have dropped radically during the last two weeks, their intrinsic value is exactly the same as it was before the recent flurry in the market," President Watson continued. "This flurry, which has brought large 'paper' or actual losses to many persons, has seemingly left a large portion of the public in a more or less befuddled state of mind, and perhaps in some instances has resulted in a loss of confidence in the stability of American business.

"I see absolutely no reason why the public should feel alarmed over the situation nor get the idea that a money or business panic might be impending. Our Federal Reserve System has probably banished panics for all time. The decline in stock values is, in my opinion, due chiefly to speculation on borrowed money—and mostly by persons who could ill afford such speculation.

"This seems to be a good time to point out the fallacy of judging values by reference to stock market quotations. One must judge business values, if one wishes to obtain the facts, by reference to the earnings and balance statements of the concerns under consideration.

"Probably no better indication of the general prosperity of the country as a whole can be obtained than the United States Steel Corporation's statement for the first nine months of the year. This showed profits of about [illegible], as against about [illegible] for the corresponding period of 1928. I feel that this statement can be taken as a barometer of the entire nation's industrial status.

"So far as I. B. M. is concerned we have had an excellent year so far with our profits about 28 per cent over those of the corresponding period of last year. We are planning an expansion of our plant in Endicott, as announced last spring, to meet the production needs of our business. We are badly crowded right now, and unable to keep pace with the demands of the business except by working overtime."

Children's Story Hour Begins at Library Friday

[illegible]

MEETS WITH SCHERER

[illegible]

Our Weather Man

For Binghamton and Vicinity: Fair tonight and Thursday.

[illegible]

Temperatures in Other Cities

[illegible]

October 30, 1929: The day after the crash, IBM leader Thomas Watson was trying to assure the world that the market would recover. He insisted on going forward with a huge banquet the day Wall Street melted down. *Microfilm archives*

Friends and family gather in 1931 for a picnic north of Greene on the Chenango River. Left to right: Steve Bystrak, Mrs. Jurik, Mrs. Kachany, Judith Bystrak, Mary Hurbanis and Rudy Bystrak (the young boy) are pictured with a 1928 Studebaker. *Courtesy Rudy Bystrak*

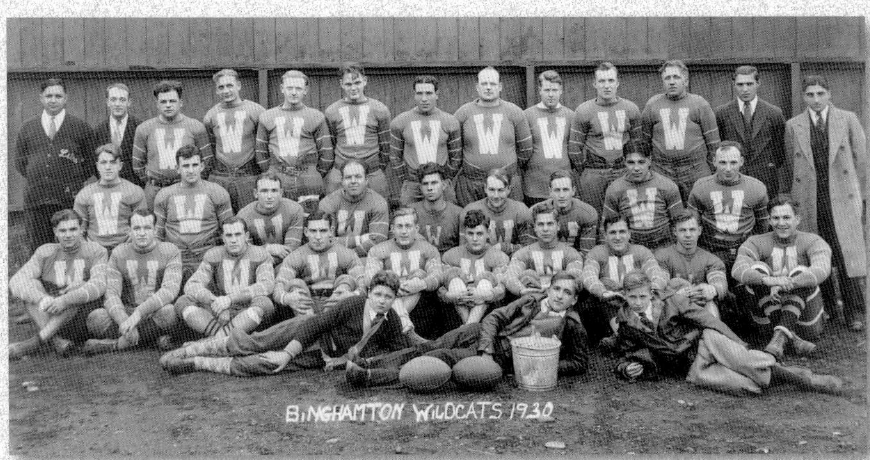
BINGHAMTON WILDCATS 1930

Binghamton Wildcats football team, 1930. *Courtesy Ann Smith*

Bystrak brothers at a birthday party on May Street in Binghamton, circa 1930. The three brothers are all wearing sweaters. Paul (left), John (right, back, with headband), and Rudy (in front of John) pose for the camera. The brothers would later join the war. *Courtesy Rudy Bystrak*

The Fair Play Caramel Team, Johnson City, 1930. *Courtesy Broome County Historical Society*

The George F. Johnson parade celebrating the 50th anniversary of his coming to town, Binghamton, August 1931. *Courtesy Broome County Historical Society*

1930 - 1939

EJ, IBM soften blow of Depression

THE BINGHAMTON PRESS, WEDNESDAY EVENING, AUGUST 26, 1931.

125 Floats in Line As Geo. F. Johnson Reviews Awe-Inspiring Parade

Score of Bands Play as 40,000 Pass in Streets

Procession One of Greatest Seen in This Section of United States

THRONGS LINE CURBS

Every Member of Police Bureau Drafted to Preserve Order

Section of Jubilee Parade Passing Reviewing Stand

A bird's eye view of a section of the parade as it passed the reviewing stand in front of the Courthouse. The procession—the largest in the history of the city—took four hours to pass in review. Mr. Johnson, standing in the front row with distinguished guests, is acknowledging the cheers of the marchers.

GEORGE F. JOHNSON DIDN'T KNOW WHAT TO MAKE OF IT ALL

"Overwhelmed and Touched by Emotion," He Says Words Fail to Tell His Feelings

Geo. F. Stands as Thousands Roar Tribute

Remains on Feet to Wave Greetings to Hundreds Marching By

CHOKES WITH EMOTION

Doak, Wagner, Thatcher and Other Notables View Parade

Jubilee Gems

Geo. F. Starts Day Prosaically, but It Soon Becomes Lively One

He Arises Early, Has Quiet Breakfast With Judge Landis as Guest—Then He Starts for Jubilee Fete Marking Milestone in History

City Churches Mark Jubilee With Services

Catholic Parishes Hold High Masses for George F. Johnson

150,000 Persons Out for Jubilee, Largest Crowd in City's History

Even While Binghamton Was Awakening Loaded Autos Were Headed Here From all Directions to Honor Geo. F.

Geo. F. Jubilee Reduces Attendance at Meeting of Exchange Club Today

THREE PERSONS FAINT; GIRL HIT BY AUTO DURING BIG PARADE

All Four Are Treated at City Hospital, Discharged in Short Time

Alleged Speeder Arrested After Wreck, Forfeits $8 Bail at Cortland

August 26, 1931: Coverage of parade and festivities honoring George F. Johnson. *Microfilm archives*

News of the killing of the Lindbergh baby, the outrages of brazen criminals like Dillinger and the abdication of the king of England dominated the front pages. The gathering storms in Europe and Japan began showing up in news reports.

Contemporary newspaper reports about George F. Johnson reflect a landscape incomprehensibly different from modern times.

In Binghamton, on August 25, 1931, there was a huge party to celebrate the 50th anniversary of George F. Johnson's arrival in town. There is no contemporary business leader in America who could draw the kind of adulation demonstrated that day.

People flocked to a parade in his honor from all over the state. One story puts the crowd at 150,000 people, more than the entire population of Broome County. One headline: "Even while Binghamton was awakening, loaded autos were headed here from all directions to honor George F." The entire Binghamton Police Bureau was called out to preserve order.

During the Depression, EJ and IBM kept most of their work forces on the payroll. The companies shortened hours, but resisted the severe cutbacks that affected most of the nation. EJ started giving free meals to all in the community at its company diners. It served more than a quarter of a million free meals in 1930 and 1931.

LINDBERGH BABY DEAD

Stock Market All of Today's Transactions of the New York Stock Exchange by Associated Press Wires Direct from Wall Street on Page 26

THE WEATHER

BINGHAMTON PRESS

EXTRA

Vol. 54, No. 28. THIRTY-TWO PAGES THURSDAY EVENING, MAY 12, 1932. PRICE THREE CENTS

Charles Lindbergh Jr.--Dead

CHILD FOUND BY NEIGHBORS NEAR LINDBERGH HOME, SAYS STATEMENT BY GOV. MOORE

The Lindbergh baby has been found—dead.

The body of Charles Augustus Lindbergh, Jr., was found near his parents' Hopewell home this afternoon, according to Governor A. Harry Moore of New Jersey.

The Governor told the Associated Press he had been informed by the New Jersey state police that the baby had been found by neighbors near the Lindbergh home.

International search for the child, who was snatched from his crib on the night of March 1, focused the attention of the entire civilized world on the misfortune of the world-famed flier and came to an end today.

The abrupt and dramatic ending came after the greatest manhunt in history with more than 100,000 official participants and millions of volunteer civilians running down every clue in an effort to recover Charles Jr.

Betty Gow, the Lindbergh nurse, put the baby to bed at 7:30 o'clock, March 1. At 10 o'clock she ran screaming to Col. and Mrs. Lindbergh that the baby was gone. Kidnapers had stolen the child from the second floor nursery of the Lindbergh's Sourland Mountain home near Hopewell, N. J.

The ensuing chapters of the most sensational news story since the Armistice began to unfold with the questioning of the Gow girl and the discovery of a postcard and letter at Hartford, Conn. The printing on these corresponded with that on the first postcard received by the Lindberghs the day after the kidnaping.

Henry "Red" Johnson, sailor sweetheart of Betty Gow, was arrested at East Hartford, held on his own statement, and put through a series of grueling interrogations.

The entire country was kept at fever heat for two weeks with all night broadcasts and streaming headlines in newspapers telling of latest developments. Hundreds of newspapermen were rushed to the rustic town of Hopewell. Police throughout the nation for many days were on 24-hour duty, stopping suspicious looking motorists and patrolling all highways.

Then came an appeal to the underworld. Salvatore Spitale and Irving Bitz, leaders of New York's gangdom, entered the case as appointed intermediaries of Col. Lindbergh.

With the advent of the Norfolk negotiators, the underworld activity in the search apparently died. Col. Lindbergh was reported as holding unimportant the original belief of the Virginians that the kidnaped child was in a yacht off Norfolk in Chesapeake Bay.

Gradually the importance attached to the Norfolk negotiators became greater. They were in daily contact with Col. Lindbergh. They made numerous secret trips. They gave out little information.

Two plane trips were made to Martha's Vineyard off Cape Cod, Mass. They made several other trips to points along the Atlantic coast, ostensibly to visit boats.

New Jersey police in the meantime continued active participation. Major Charles H. Schoeffel was sent abroad. He conferred with officials of Scotland Yard and visited the home of Betty Gow's mother in Scotland.

Secrecy in movements was the watchword of the Lindberghs and other officials throughout the last weeks of the search. None, but carefully worded statements, were given out to the press, officials fearing that publicity would thwart any made plans.

CONGRESSIONAL, FINANCIAL LEADERS AND HOOVER AGREE ON FEDERAL RELIEF PLANS

Washington, May 12 — (Associated Press) — The compromise Federal relief plan discussed today between President Hoover, Congressional and Federal financial leaders involves an increase in the borrowing power of the Reconstruction corporation by $1,500,000,000.

Under the proposal, the corporation would be authorized to make loans exclusively to states up to a total of $300,000,000. This money would be limited in use exclusively for relief purposes.

The remaining moneys would be employed to make secured loans to assist private and public construction on condition that the construction concerned is reproductive in nature.

GASTON MEANS REARRESTED ON A DISORDERLY CHARGE

LOSS OF GAS BY DIRIGIBLE CAUSES CUTTING OF CREW TO LIGHTEN CRAFT FOR HOP

GOV. LONG FOR ROOSEVELT, ASSURING CHIEF 20 DELEGATES

3 BANKERS TESTIFY HASTINGS NEVER REPAID $382,500 LOANS

—Latest News Bulletins—

SENATE COMMITTEE VOTES APPROVAL OF WORLD COURT

Dublin Docks Deserted as Free State Puts 43 New Tariffs in Effect

Siam off Gold Standard as Price of Rice Slumps

WATCH FOR SECOND EXTRA OF THE BINGHAMTON PRESS

May 12, 1932: The Press published an extra announcing the death of Charles Lindbergh's son, missing since March 1. *Courtesy Arlene Pewterbaugh*

SECOND EXTRA

Stock All of Today's Transactions of the New York Stock Exchange by Associated Press Wires Direct from Wall Street on Page 26

SECOND EXTRA

BINGHAMTON PRESS

Vol. 54, No. 28. THURSDAY EVENING, MAY 12, 1932. PRICE THREE CENTS

BABY LINDBERGH FOUND DEAD BY NEIGHBORS NEAR HIS HOME

Charles A. Lindbergh Jr.--Dead

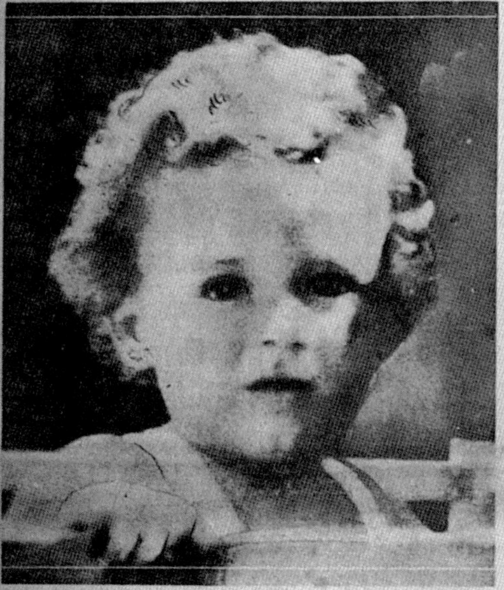

Negro Finds Skeleton in Woods Near Sourlands; Identified by Flannel Shirt; Attempt to Bury Indicated; There Since Night of Kidnaping

Hopewell, N. J., May 12—(Associated Press)—Formal announcement that the body of a baby, identified through clothing and other means as the missing son of Colonel and Mrs. Charles A. Lindbergh, has been found was made late today at the Lindbergh estate.

The Lindbergh baby has been found, dead, in the brush 75 feet back from a little-traveled crossroad leading from Hopewell to Princeton, N. J.

From the condition of the body, described by the negro who found it and by officials as "a skeleton," it is indicated that it may have been there since the night the child was stolen from his crib in the nursery of the Colonel Lindbergh estate, Tuesday, March 1.

The spot where the body was found is four miles, as the crow flies, directly across the heavily wooded Sourland mountains from the Lindbergh home. It is five miles southeast by road from the Lindbergh estate.

BUTLER CONFIRMS FINDING OF BABY

Englewood, N. Y.—May 12 (UP)—The Butler at the Dwight W. Morrow estate here told a United Press Correspondent late today that the Lindberg baby had been found dead near the Lindberg home on Sourland Mountain. Asked whether such a report were true, the butler said: "Yes, that is true." Advise quickest what if any further protection desired.

Trenton, May 12—(Associated Press)—Governor A. Harry Moore of New Jersey late today said he had been informed by Colonel H. Norman Schwarzkopf of the state police that the kidnaped Lindbergh baby was found dead near the famous flier's estate at Hopewell, N. J.

Governor Moore spoke from his office in the state house here. Communication with the Lindbergh home, where the state police have maintained headquarters, was disrupted immediately after he spoke to Colonel Schwarzkopf.

Every available motor vehicle for hire in Trenton was pressed into service to transport persons to the Lindbergh home.

Today's developments answered a question that had puzzled the nation since Tuesday night, March 1—"Is the Lindbergh baby alive or dead?"

A brisk wind whistled through the clear night outside the Sourland mountain estate of the famous flier as Mrs. Lindbergh, assisted by Betty Gow, the nursemaid, put her 20-month-old son to bed at 7:30 o'clock.

The abrupt and dramatic ending came after the greatest manhunt in history with more than 100,000 official participants and millions of volunteer civilians running down every clue in an effort ot recover Charles Jr.

Betty Gow, the Lindbergh nurse, put the baby to bed at 7:30 o'clock, March 1. At 10 o'clock she ran screaming to Colonel and Mrs. Lindbergh that the baby was gone. Kidnapers had stolen the child from the second floor nursery of the Lindbergh's Sourland Mountain home near Hopewell, N. J.

The ensuing chapters of the most sensational news story since the Armistice began to unfold with the questioning of the Gow girl and the discovery of a postcard and letter at Hartford, Conn. The printing on these corresponded with that on the first postcard received by the Lindberghs the day after the kidnaping.

Henry "Red" Johnson, sailor sweetheart of Betty Gow, was arrested at East Hartford, held on his own statement, and put through a series of grueling interrogations.

The entire country was kept at fever heat for two weeks with all night broadcasts and streaming headlines in newspapers telling of latest developments. Hundreds of newspapermen were rushed to the rustic town of Hopewell. Police throughout the nation for many days were on 24-hour duty, stopping suspicious looking motorists and patrolling all highways.

Then came an appeal to the underworld. Salvatore Spitale and Irving Bitz, leaders of New York's gangdom, entered the case as appointed intermediaries of Col. Lindbergh.

With the advent of the Norfolk negotiators, the underworld activity in the search apparently died. Col. Lindbergh was reported as holding unimportant the original belief of the Virginians that the kidnaped child was in a yacht off Norfolk in Chesapeake Bay.

Gradually the importance attached to the Norfolk negotiators became greater. They were in daily contact with Col. Lindbergh. They made numerous secret trips. They gave out little information.

Two plane trips were made to Martha's Vineyard off Cape Cod, Mass. They made several other trips to points along the Atlantic coast, ostensibly to visit boats.

Official Statement

The formal police statement:

"We have to announce apparently the body of the Lindbergh baby was found at 3:15 p. m. William Allen, a negro, was riding from Mount Rose, N. J., to Hopewell with Orville Wilson on a truckload of timber. They stopped the truck near a woods. He, Allen, went into the woods on the Mount Rose hill in Mount Rose, N. J. Going under the bush he lowered his head and as he raised a branch he saw a skeleton on the ground, and a person's foot.

"He called back to Mr. Wilson. Mr. Wilson ran into the woods, saw what it was and decided to go to Hopewell to get police. They notified Chief Wolf of the Hopewell police, who notified these headquarters. Inspector Walsh of Jersey City, Sergeant Moffett of the Newark police, Lieutenant Keaton of the New Jersey state police and a number of other detectives immediately went to the scene.

"They reported finding the body of a child estimated to be between 1½ and 2 years old in a bad state of decomposition, having blonde hair and wearing what appeared to be an undershirt and a flannel band around the body.

"Not satisfied with this as identification the men sent back to Hopewell to the Lindbergh estate to get samples of the undershirt the baby wore and of the flannel shirt the baby had on the night of the kidnaping (March 1). This flannel shirt had an embroidered collar on it. Three articles were taken back to the scene and were compared with the clothing found on the body and were matched closely enough to afford an identification of the body as that of the Lindbergh baby.

"The statement of William Allen and Orville Wilson says that the body was pretty well concealed by leaves, dirt and brush.

"The skull had a hole in it about the size of a 25 cent piece above the forehead. There apparently had been an attempt to bury the body face downward. It was in a bad state of decomposition. Mercer county coroner and the county physician were immediately called. The physician is Dr. Charles H. Mitchell. The coroner is Walter Swayze, both of Trenton.

"The body was found about 75 yards off the road in the woods."

The statement was read to reporters by Colonel H. Norman Schwarzkopf.

New Jersey police in the meantime continued active participation. Major Charles H. Schoeffel was sent abroad. He conferred with officials of Scotland Yard and visited the home of Betty Gow's mother in Scotland.

Col. Lindbergh was not in evidence as the statement was read to reporters. Neither was Mrs. Lindbergh nor her mother, Mrs. Dwight Morrow, but both were understood to be in the residence.

Col. Schwarzkopf, state police head, made his announcement from a long table in the Lindbergh garage where his headquarters has been since the child was kidnaped.

Col. Schwarzkopf promised a further amplification of his statement later tonight at Trenton, N. J., but for the time being he withheld any information as to the Lindbergh family or the disposition of the body.

Reporters were directed to the Lindbergh garage immediately upon arriving and told to take seats at the long headquarters table. The first to arrive were those quartered in the village of Hopewell proper and they were told that they must wait for the newspapermen from Trenton. The latter were escorted to the estate by state police.

THE BINGHAMTON PRESS FIRST NEWS PAPER IN STATE TO REACH STREET WITH EXTRAS

The first. The Binghamton Press extra carrying the news that the Lindbergh baby had been found was rushed to the street at 5:58, 20 minutes after the story was flashed over the wires—the first newspaper in the state to tell the story.

Walter Horsky was the first newsie to hit the street. But the crowds in front of The Press building watching the presses spin off the extras could not wait, rushed into the annex alley to snatch up the papers from the newsies, their arms filled with extras hot off the press.

The news that the baby had been found spread like wildfire through the city. Newspaper offices were deluged with phone calls. The Peach edition of The Press had rolled off the presses only a short time before the news was flashed by the Associated Press in New York.

In less than 15 minutes the entire staff was reassembled and the presses were spinning.

Word of the tragedy was sent crackling through the air by radio stations in New York city.

Crowds returning home at the end of the day were electrified by the news.

MRS. DWIGHT MORROW TOLD ABOUT FINDING OF BODY

Englewood, N. J., May 12—(Associated Press)—The home of Mrs. Dwight Morrow said they had been informed the kidnaped infant of Colonel and Mrs. Charles A. Lindbergh had been found dead near the Lindbergh home outside of Hopewell.

Both the Lindberghs and Mrs. Morrow are at the Lindbergh home, it was stated.

Dramatis Personae of Case

By the Associated Press

The dramatis personae of the kidnaping of the Lindbergh baby:

The baby, Charles Augustus Lindbergh, Jr., curly-locked, 20 months'-old when abducted.

His father, Colonel Charles Augustus Lindbergh, imperturbable, hair, as usual, was mussed.

His mother, Anne Morrow Lindbergh, daughter of late Senator Dwight W. Morrow, calm, hid from the world her anguish.

The nurse, Betty Gow, young native of Scotland, who discovered the kidnaping.

The butler, Ollie Wheatley, taciturn, correct.

His wife, cook in the Lindbergh home at Hopewell.

The baby's grandmothers, Mrs. Elizabeth Morrow, of Englewood, and Mrs. Evangeline Lindbergh, of Detroit.

Colonel H. Norman Schwarzkopf, West Point trained commandant of state police, in charge of investigation.

Major Charles H. Scheoffel, of state police, who made mysterious trip of investigation to Europe.

Colonel Henry Breckinridge, attorney, friend and adviser of Colonel Lindbergh, who worked unceasingly for child's recovery.

His wife, who with Mrs. Morrow sustained the baby's mother during the ordeal of waiting.

Governor A. Harry Moore, of New Jesrey, who put every resource at the state at the disposal of investigators, and this afternoon announced the body had been found.

Henry "Red" Johnson, red-headed Norwegian sailor, friend of Betty Gow, held on suspicion but later released.

Fred Johnson, his brother, also questioned.

Johansen Junge, who helped "Red" Johnson establish his alibi.

"Salvy" Spitale and Irving Bitz, New York underworld leaders, authorized by Colonel Lindbergh to negotiate for baby's return.

Morris Rosner, thin, black-haired "man of mystery," reputed former undercover investigator for Department of Justice, who assumed duties of go-between with little apparent success.

The Rev. H. Dobson-Peacock, Protestant Episcopal clergyman of Norfolk, Va., who announced he was in touch with the kidnapers.

John Hughes Curtis, shipbuilder of Norfolk, who made a similar announcement.

LINDBERGH PICTURES AND HISTORY OF CASE---PAGES 3, 4 AND 5

May 12, 1932: By the second extra, the paper took care to notify readers we were the first in the state to report the tragedy. *Courtesy Arlene Pewterbaugh*

Newspaper carriers Walter Malinich (13-14 years old) and William Malinich (8-10 years old) pose for a photograph in the early 1930s. *Courtesy William Malinich*

Joe Banovic, known as "Bingo Joe," was a local boxer who was widely known among sports personalities. He started boxing in 1926 under the tutelage of Jersey Jones and went on to box in 77 professional fights. Some of his opponents included Max "Slapsy Maxie" Rosenbloom, Bob Olin and Juan "Kid" Herrera. There is a sports arena in Kingston, Jamaica, named after Banovic. *Courtesy Ann Smith*

Kindergarten or first-grade class, Fairview School on the East Side of Binghamton, 1931.
Courtesy Virginia Hibbard

DESCRIPTIONS OF LINDBERGH PLOTTERS BARED; COAST GUARDS ENCIRCLING BOAT

Stock Market All of Today's Transactions of the New York Stock Exchange by Associated Press Wires Direct from Wall Street on Page 14

THE WEATHER
Fair and warmer tonight and Sunday.

BINGHAMTON PRESS

THE PEACH FINAL
Closing Stocks, Bond and Curb Prices. Latest Baseball Scores Today.

Vol. 54, No. 30. TWENTY PAGES SATURDAY EVENING, MAY 14, 1932. PRICE THREE CENTS

KRESS HAS 'BEER PARADE,' ARRESTS 3

Give Clues in Killer Hunt

One of the first moves of the law in its effort to find the slayers of the Lindbergh baby was to question Dr. John F. Condon, left, author of the "Jafsie" advertisements, and John H. Curtis, right, Norfolk boat manufacturer, in an attempt to obtain some clew to the identity of the kidnapers.

Tick On Is Favorite in Preakness

ODDS SWING TO MRS. KAUFMAN'S THOROUGHBRED AS 40,000 START JAMMING IN PARK

Pimlico Racetrack, Baltimore, Md., May 14—(Associated Press)—A decided swing to Mrs. Louis G. Kaufman's Tick On was evident in the wagering as the advance guard of the expected crowd of 40,000 began pouring through the gates of Pimlico for the forty-second renewal of the Preakness today.

(Continued on Page Three)

Sheriff Carts Bar, Equipment From the 'Stag'

He Arrests Paul Corrigan and Furman by His Old Trick

(Continued on Page Three)

CURTIS IDENTIFIES PLOTTERS AND THEIR BOAT, COAST GUARD SLOWLY CLOSING IN ON CRAFT

Hopewell, N. J., May 14—(Associated Press)—The nicknames and descriptions of five men with whom he negotiated on behalf of Col. Charles A. Lindbergh for the return of the kidnaped baby were furnished to New Jersey state police by John Hughes Curtis, Norfolk, Va., boat builder, Col. H. Norman Schwarzkopf, state police head, announced today.

Mr. Curtis also described to police a boat which he said the alleged kidnapers were using and through Federal agencies, cooperating with the New Jersey state police, the Coast Guard was requested to make a search for the vessel. Colonel Schwarzkopf said that as yet no report had been received concerning the results of the search.

Kidnaping of Col. Lindbergh Plotted, His Yacht Armed

Norfolk, Va., May 14—(United Press)—Capt. Frank H. Lackmann of the yacht Marcon, used by Norfolk negotiators in an attempt to contact kidnapers...

—Latest Baseball Scores—

NATIONAL LEAGUE	Innings	R	H	E
Brooklyn	0 1 0 0 0 2			
Cincinnati	0 0 1 2 0 0			

Brooklyn—Clark and Lopez; Cincinnati—Carroll and Lombardi.

Boston	2 0 0 3			
Chicago	1 2 0 0			

Boston—Brown and Hargrave; Chicago—Grimes and Hartnett.

Philadelphia				
St. Louis				

Only Games Played

AMERICAN LEAGUE	Innings	R	H	E
Chicago	0 0 0 0 0 0 0 0 0	0	4	1
New York	1 0 0 0 0 0 4 1 x	6	9	1

Chicago—Jones and Grube; New York—Pipgras and Dickey.

Cleveland	0 0 3 3 0 0 0 0 0	6	11	0
Boston	0 0 0 0 0 0 0 0 0	0	4	1

Cleveland—Brown and Sewell; Boston—MacFayden and Tate.

Detroit	1 0 2 0 1 0			
Washington	1 0 1 0 0 0			

Detroit—Uhle and Ruel; Washington—Brown and Berg.

St. Louis	0 0 0 0 0 0 0 0 0	0	4	0
Philadelphia	1 0 1 0 0 1 0 0 x	3	7	0

St. Louis—Hadley and Ferrell; Philadelphia—Grove and Cochrane.

NEW YORK-PENNSYLVANIA LEAGUE	Innings	R	H	E
First Game				
Triple Cities	0 0 0 0 0 0 0 0 0	0	8	0
York	0 0 2 0 0 0 0 1 x	3	8	0

Triple Cities—Lehr and Shatzer; York—Kirsch and Gogarine.

Second Game				
Triple Cities	0 0 0			
York	0 1 3			
First Game				
Elmira	0 0 1 0 0 0 0 0 2	3	8	2
Harrisburg	0 2 0 3 4 0 0 1 x	10	10	1
Second Game				
Elmira	0 0 0			
Harrisburg	1 0 2			
Wilkes Barre	0 0 0			
Hazleton	4 0 0			

Wilkes Barre—Wertz and Urmann; Hazleton—Hockett and Hill.

First Game				
Scranton	0 0 0 2 0 1 0 0 0	3	8	0
Williamsport	2 0 0 1 0 0 0 5 x	8	10	0

Scranton—Reitz and Quinlan; Williamsport—Brown and Ernst.

TRIPLETS DROP FIRST GAME TO YORK, 3-0, AFTER WINNING 6 IN ROW; KIRSCH IS HERO

York, Pa., May 14—The Triple Cities team of the New York-Pennsylvania League suffered its first setback of the season when it dropped the first game of a doubleheader to the White Roses here this afternoon. The score was 3 to 0.

MONT. VOTE FOR ROOSEVELT IS URGED BY SENATOR WALSH

(Continued on Page Two)

—Latest News Bulletins—

BOY INJURED WHEN HIT BY CAR

M'KELLAR COLLAPSES

Hoover Talk Hurts Nation, Garner Says

(Continued on Page Two)

KATHLEEN NORRIS URGES WOMEN TO BUILD MONUMENT OF KINDNESS TO UNFORTUNATE FOR BABY LINDY

By Kathleen Norris

(Continued on Page Nine)

$150,000 Blaze Destroys Six Buildings in Heart of Kerhonkson Business Area

75 U. S. Ships Closing In On Craft; Believed Circled

(Continued on Page Nine)

"Alice," off for England, Bids Cordial Farewell to American Friends

May 14, 1932: Lindbergh news continued to fascinate the nation. The "Peach Final" allowed editors to get complete stock listings and late ball scores to afternoon customers. *Courtesy Carolyn Fitzgerald*

Binghamton Centennial Parade, October 9, 1934. *Press & Sun-Bulletin Archives*

New York National Guard marches in the Binghamton Centennial Parade, October 9, 1934. *Press & Sun-Bulletin Archives*

THE WEATHER
Fair tonight and Tuesday. Continued cool tonight. Slightly warmer Tuesday.

BINGHAMTON PRESS

City Edition

Vol. 56, No. 87. TWENTY-SIX PAGES MONDAY EVENING, JULY 23, 1934. PRICE THREE CENTS

U. S. STRIKES AT SLAIN DILLINGER'S MOB

McGinnies Opens Fight to Stay in Power

Dunmore Aids Chief in Battle Against Macy

Assembly Leaders Lash Back at Chairman in Statements

BOTH TO RUN AGAIN

Elect Legislature Before Quarreling Over Speakership, They Advise

Albany, July 23—(Associated Press) — Although Speaker Joseph A. McGinnies and Majority Leader Russell G. Dunmore have refrained from commenting on the move to overthrow their leadership, their friends declare they are ready to fight to the finish to maintain control of the Assembly.

They have both announced their candidacies for reelection to the Legislature, but they say the question of the speakership should not be made an issue until after the election.

Republican State Chairman W. Kingsland Macy, on the other hand, is now openly at war with the two "old guard" Assembly leaders. He has indicated he will use every means at his disposal to replace them with leaders more in sympathy with the liberal and progressive ideas that dominate the rank and file of the party.

Over the week-end, while the state chairman held conferences with Republican leaders in the heart of the "old guard" upstate territory, Mr. Dunmore announced he would seek re-election and Mr. McGinnies made it clear that Mr. Macy's opposition would not change his plans to return to Albany.

Assemblyman Dunmore said he thought it would be an excellent idea for those seeking to depose the speaker to make certain of electing a Republican Assembly before determining who is to have the speakership.

(Continued on Page Eight)

Even the Town Clock Is Hit by Curfew Law

Butler, Pa., July 23—(Associated Press)—Not even the town clock is going to disturb the slumber of Butler residents, the county commissioners have decided. They passed a law forbidding striking of the clock between 10 p.m. and ...

"Good Girl"

I was at a dance that Cassy Logan spoke to Kent Starles for the first time. She had seen him often on ... years of inspection through ... cotton mill his mother ... and where she worked, ... that was the first time her ... had made any impression on him.

Read what happens when a girl falls in love with a man her "friends" think is too good for her. It's told by Peggy Gaddis.

"Good Girl" begins in The Binghamton Press today on page 16.

End of a Happy Outing

Charred remains of bus that plunged off viaduct near Ossining railroad station Sunday and took fire, killing at least 16 persons and injuring a score of others. Flames destroyed a lumber yard with loss estimated at $225,000.

Bus Crash Laid to Negligence; Death Toll 16

More Than Score Hurt in Ossining Tragedy; Inquiry Opens

(Continued on Page Eight)

Relief Party Unable to Get to Byrd's Hut

Grave Concern Is Felt for Admiral's Safety in Antarctic

Little America, Antarctica, July 23 — (Associated Press) — Grave concern for the safety of Rear Admiral Richard E. Byrd was felt today. The trail leading to his lonely weather observation outpost was lost.

Connor Baby Regains Most of Lost Weight

Girl Killed as Auto Goes Through Railing

Early Action Pledged on Air Corps Reforms

Baker's Aviation Report Calls for Additional Fighting Force

6 RECOMMENDATIONS

Administration Expected to Endorse Findings to House Group

Washington, July 23 — (United Press) — Early official action on the recommendation of the Baker board, which investigated army aviation and urged extensive reforms in the Air Corps, was promised at the White House today after publication of the board's report.

The report by a board headed by Newton D. Baker, secretary of war under President Wilson, recommended:

(Continued on Page Eight)

MacDONALD VISITS NEARLY FORGOTTEN ACADIAN VILLAGE

New Edinburgh Built Century Ago by Scottish Pioneers Almost Deserted

A Marriage Too Many Causes Lot of Trouble

Will Finds 'Frisco Teeming With Alibis on Recent Strike

To the Editor of The Binghamton Press

S. S. Malolo, San Francisco, Calif., July 23 — Just steaming out of the beautiful San Francisco bay. They are putting a bridge across it. They will build a bridge to Honolulu if the government don't run out of credit.

WILL ROGERS.

Deaths by Heat in Nation Rise to Total of 275

Thousands of Cattle Perish and More Are Given up at Forced Sales

By the Associated Press

Dannemora Prisoner Is Critically Stabbed

Mulrooney Boosts N. Y. Liquor Laws on Birthday

Roosevelt's Ship Due to Dock at Hawaiian Port Tuesday

Aboard the U. S. S. New Orleans, with President Roosevelt at Sea, July 23—(By Radio to the United Press)—The U. S. cruiser Houston, carrying President Roosevelt over smooth seas in the Hawaiian islands, drew close to its mid-Pacific destination today.

Agents Score Big Victory in War on Crime

Department of Justice Is Elated Over Death of Arch Outlaw

LONG SEARCH ENDED

Washington Always in Close Touch With Progress of Case

Washington, July 23 — (Associated Press) — The government today hailed John Dillinger's end as one of the most smashing blows ever delivered at crime in the United States.

(Continued on Page Two)

DOOLING AVERTS PARTY FIGHT OVER MAHON AS LEADER

New Tammany Chief Achieves Victory in Uniting N. Y. County Democrats

Ontario Man Kills Brother by Blows With Bottle

Steel Output Is Down to 27.7 Per Cent Level

Grierson at Reykjavik on Flight to Ottawa

Shot to Death

JOHN DILLINGER

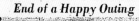

Woman, Shot in Leg, 'Glad They Got Him'

Stray Bullet Victim Tells of Seeing Dillinger Meet Death

By Mrs. Etta Natalski

(As Told to the United Press)

Chicago, July 23—(United Press)

Army Board of Inquiry to Probe Pond Tragedy

Farley Says Roosevelt Is Leading Nation Ahead

23 Persons Are Injured When Street Cars Crash

Woman Friend May Have Set Killer's Trap

Leader of Marksmen Who Shot Gangster Won't Name Slayer

BRIEF INQUEST HELD

Thousands Gather at Scene Where Bullets Cut Down Fugitive

Chicago, July 23 — (United Press) — Federal agents whose bullets killed John Dillinger in a quick, dramatic encounter outside a Chicago theatre last night followed the backward trail of the outlaw today in a dogged drive to close their books on America's most vicious criminal gang.

Like many other criminals, Dillinger apparently lost his battle with the law because of a woman.

(Continued on Page Two)

In Spite of Its Age, Clock Acts Childishly

Philadelphia, July 23—(Associated Press)—The stately old clock in Independence Square's historic State House has lapped out the hours since the nation was born—but it isn't too old to play pranks.

July 23, 1934: Notorious criminal John Dillinger was killed on a Sunday night, and the Binghamton Press had to wait until Monday afternoon to report the police success. *Microfilm archives*

THE WEATHER

BINGHAMTON PRESS

City Edition

Vol. 57, No. 74. TWENTY-SIX PAGES MONDAY EVENING, JULY 8, 1935. PRICE THREE CENTS

12 DEAD, PROPERTY LOSS IS MILLIONS IN WORST FLOOD IN TIER'S HISTORY

Morgenthau Submits Wealth Tax Schedules

Higher Income Levies Urged to Slash Debt

New Imposts Won't Produce Undesirable Social Consequences, He Says

START FROM $100,000

Inheritances as Small as $50,000 Would Be Included in Plans

Will Rogers Is Proud of Both the Helens; Gameness Impresses

Port Crane Flood Area From Airplane

Scores Homeless After Cloudbursts Hit Southern Tier

The Ferry street bridge washed out at 2:25 o'clock this afternoon.

All bridges of the city were ordered closed to all traffic by police order immediately following the washout.

The most disastrous flood in the history of the Southern Tier today had caused damage estimated at several millions of dollars and a possible death toll of 12. Full extent of the loss will not be determined for several days.

Scores of buildings were swept away, an undetermined number of bridges were reduced to tangled wreckage, hundreds of acres of farm crops were destroyed, traffic was at a standstill and hundreds were engaged in rescue work and in giving temporary aid to the homeless.

Five men were facing momentary death near Chenango Bridge while rescue forces were [illegible] boat and attempts [illegible] tempts to save them. Because of [illegible] [illegible] reported in Broome county.

They are:

MRS. HAZEL BARROWS of Lisle, drowned when her home was swept away. The body was brought to Whitney Point by state troopers this afternoon.

MRS. RALPH SMITH of Lisle.

Six persons were missing and two were in the City hospital.

The missing are:

ROBERT BRONSON HARTFIELD of 71 Bennett avenue, pathologist for the Endicott Johnson Corporation at Wilson Memorial hospital, whose car plunged into the old Chenango canal between Brisben and Greene Sunday night.

HAROLD AND BEVERLY CHASE, son and daughter of Mr. and Mrs. Harold Chase, believed drowned in Ross creek south of Greene. Mr. and Mrs. Chase are in the Binghamton City hospital.

ARRIL BROWN and his two-year-old son, William, who left Binghamton Sunday night by automobile for their home in Cincinnatus and who have not been heard from.

Destruction of 19 bridges had been reported to the Binghamton office of the State Department of Public Works up to noon and additional reports of bridges being swept away are expected this afternoon as efforts to get in touch with the officials in many sections of the afflicted counties failed this morning.

Long sections of pavement also were ruined by the flood waters, officials said. Estimates of the damage will not be available for several days. Funds for temporary repairs must be obtained at once, however.

Binghamton escaped lightly in comparison to other sections of the area.

The Chenango river, however, jumped from 13.5 feet at 8 o'clock this morning to 20.66 feet at 1:30 o'clock and flood warning was issued by the Weather Bureau.

City Manager C. A. Harrell ordered the Ferry street bridge closed to traffic at 11 o'clock when the water had risen to within two feet of the floor. Debris was piling up against the DeForest street bridge and City Engineer John A. Giles reported the structure was in danger.

Whitney Point, Newark Valley, Richford, Chenango Forks, Walton and Delhi were among the communities that suffered the heaviest damage.

Four buildings in the business district of Newark Valley were swept away or crushed, a large portion of Whitney Point was under several feet of water and more than 100 persons were rescued from their homes at Chenango Bridge.

Scores of communities throughout the area were isolated and in many cases even telephone communication was impossible. Water supplies were cut off, electric service was disrupted and railroad transportation was halted or delayed.

Several hundred CCC camp recruits aided in the rescue work. Hundreds of other workers were being pressed into service to rescue marooned persons, to save remaining bridges and to repair railroad tracks and highways.

Showers were predicted by the Weather Bureau for tonight and probably Tuesday.

With flooded rivers rising and rain still falling at 11 o'clock this morning Captain Daniel E. Fox commanding state police in the heavily flooded areas of the Southern Tier put out the following warning and request:

"It is respectfully suggested that for the good of all concerned as few persons as possible leave their homes or use telephones until the flood crisis has passed.

"We have no way of telling exactly what roads or bridges are safe and because of the emergency it is necessary that lines of communication be kept open as far as possible. Please refrain from un-

(Continued on Page Five)

Long Controls Army, Ballot in New Coup

Louisiana Legislature Gives Kingfish All Remaining Power of State

Pennsylvania Group Upsets G.O.P. Parley

Six-State Conference of 'Crusaders' Develops Committee Fight

Italy Speeds up Mobilizing for Invasion of Ethiopia

War Predicted Before End of Rainy Season in September as Nation Rallies to Duce's 'Won't Turn Back' Challenge

8 Known Dead Millions Loss in State Flood

Red Cross, Gov. Lehman Survey Damage, Ready to Speed Aid

ROOSEVELT PLANS WEST COAST TRIP AS CONGRESS ENDS

Tentatively Arranges for Stop-off at Milwaukee Aug. 23

Rabbit Disguises Self but That Isn't Enough

Condemned Slayer Tries Suicide in Death Row

Pa. Inspection of Cars Set for Aug. 1 to Oct. 21

6 Saved When Schooner Burns off Long Island

Farmer Decides 'Chute Jumpers Are Nuisances

50 Million-Year-Old Egg Sought by Doctor

4,000,000 on U. S. Relief Rolls Must Stay There Until Nov. 1

Pirates Raid Gambling Barge, Escape With $32,000 in Loot

Schultz Case Witness Fights for His Freedom

Crowing About the Climate?

July 8, 1935: The Binghamton Press reports on a devastating flood. The Ferry Street Bridge is where the Clinton Street Bridge now stands.

Courtesy Paul S. Kucera

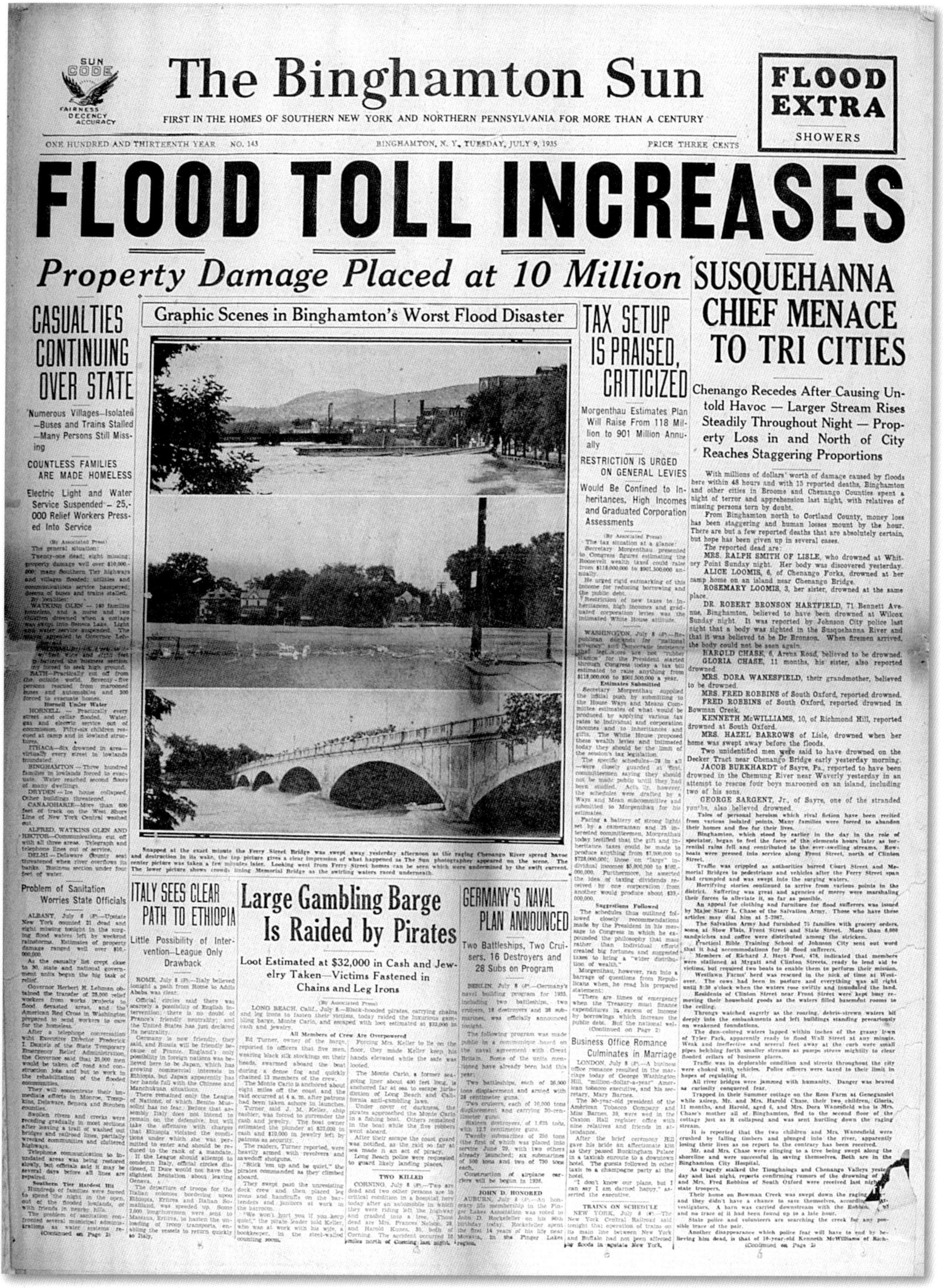

SUN CODE — FAIRNESS DECENCY ACCURACY

The Binghamton Sun

FIRST IN THE HOMES OF SOUTHERN NEW YORK AND NORTHERN PENNSYLVANIA FOR MORE THAN A CENTURY

FLOOD EXTRA

SHOWERS

ONE HUNDRED AND THIRTEENTH YEAR NO. 143 — BINGHAMTON, N. Y., TUESDAY, JULY 9, 1935 — PRICE THREE CENTS

FLOOD TOLL INCREASES

Property Damage Placed at 10 Million

CASUALTIES CONTINUING OVER STATE

Numerous Villages—Isolated—Buses and Trains Stalled—Many Persons Still Missing

COUNTLESS FAMILIES ARE MADE HOMELESS

Electric Light and Water Service Suspended—25,000 Relief Workers Pressed Into Service

(By Associated Press)

The general situation:

Twenty-one dead; eight missing; property damage well over $10,000,000; many Southern Tier highways and villages flooded; utilities and communications service hampered; dozens of buses and trains stalled.

By localities:

WATKINS GLEN — 140 families homeless, and a nurse and two children drowned when a cottage was swept into Seneca Lake. Light and water service suspended. The Mayor appealed to Governor Lehman for aid.

[illegible] feet wide and eight feet deep battered the business section. Many forced to seek high ground.

BATH—Practically cut off from the outside world. Seventy-five persons rescued from marooned buses and automobiles and 300 forced to evacuate homes.

Hornell Under Water

HORNELL — Practically every street and cellar flooded. Water, gas and electric service out of commission. Fifty-six children rescued at camp and in lowland structures.

ITHACA—Six drowned in area—virtually every street in lowlands inundated.

BINGHAMTON—Three hundred families in lowlands forced to evacuate. Water reached second floors of many dwellings.

DRYDEN—Ice house collapsed. Other buildings threatened.

CANAJOHARIE—More than 600 feet of track on the West Shore Line of New York Central washed out.

ALFRED, WATKINS GLEN AND HECTOR—Communications cut off with all three areas. Telegraph and telephone lines out of service.

DELHI—Delaware County seat threatened when river overflows its banks. Business section under four feet of water.

Problem of Sanitation Worries State Officials

ALBANY, July 8 (AP)—Upstate New York counted 21 dead and eight missing tonight in the surging flood waters left by weekend rainstorms. Estimates of property damage ranged well over $10,000,000.

As the casualty list crept close to 30, state and national government units began the big task of relief.

Governor Herbert H. Lehman obtained the transfer of 25,000 relief workers from works projects to flood devastated areas, and the American Red Cross in Washington prepared to send workers to care for the homeless.

After a telephone conversation with Executive Director Frederick I. Daniels of the State Temporary Emergency Relief Administration, the Governor said that 25,000 men would be taken off road and construction jobs and put to work in the rehabilitation of the flooded communities.

They will concentrate their immediate efforts in Monroe, Tompkins, Delaware, Seneca and Steuben counties.

Swollen rivers and creeks were receding gradually in most sections after leaving a trail of washed out bridges and railroad lines, partially wrecked communities and cluttered highways.

Telephone communication to inundated areas was being restored slowly, but officials said it may be several days before all lines are repaired.

Southern Tier Hardest Hit

Hundreds of families were forced to spend the night in the open, out of the flooded lowlands, or with friends in nearby hills.

The problem of sanitation confronted several municipal administrations as water systems re-

(Continued on Page 2)

Graphic Scenes in Binghamton's Worst Flood Disaster

Snapped at the exact minute the Ferry Street Bridge was swept away yesterday afternoon as the raging Chenango River spread havoc and destruction in its wake, the top picture gives a clear impression of what happened as The Sun photographer appeared on the scene. The center picture was taken a few minutes later. Looking west from Ferry Street homes can be seen which were undermined by the swift current. The lower picture shows crowds lining Memorial Bridge as the swirling waters raced underneath.

TAX SETUP IS PRAISED, CRITICIZED

Morgenthau Estimates Plan Will Raise From 118 Million to 901 Million Annually

RESTRICTION IS URGED ON GENERAL LEVIES

Would Be Confined to Inheritances, High Incomes and Graduated Corporation Assessments

(By Associated Press)

The tax situation at a glance:

Secretary Morgenthau presented to Congress figures estimating the Roosevelt wealth taxes could raise from $118,000,000 to $901,500,000 annually.

He urged rigid earmarking of this income for reducing borrowing and the public debt.

Restriction of new taxes to inheritances, high incomes and graduated corporation levies was the intimated White House attitude.

WASHINGTON, July 8 (AP)—Republican demands for "national solvency" and Democratic insistence that legislators are not "rubber stamps" for the President started through Congress today a tax bill estimated to raise anything from $118,000,000 to $901,500,000 a year.

Estimates Submitted

Secretary Morgenthau supplied the initial push by submitting to the House Ways and Means Committee estimates of what would be produced by applying various tax rates to individual and corporation incomes and to inheritances and gifts. The White House proposed these wealth levies and intimated today they should be the limit of the session's tax legislation.

The specific schedules—78 in all—were closely guarded at first, committeemen saying they should not be made public until they had been studied. Actually, however, the schedules were drafted by a Ways and Mean subcommittee and submitted to Morgenthau for his estimates.

Facing a battery of strong lights set by a cameraman and 25 interested committeemen, Morgenthau today testified that the gift and inheritance taxes could be made to produce anything from $7,000,000 to $728,000,000; those on "large" individual incomes $5,000,000 to $102,000,000. Furthermore, he asserted the idea of taxing dividends received by one corporation from another would produce about $33,000,000.

Suggestions Followed

The schedules thus outlined followed closely recommendations made by the President in his message to Congress in which he expounded the philosophy that mass rather than individual efforts created big fortunes and suggested taxes to bring a "wider distribution of wealth."

Morgenthau, however, ran into a barrage of questions from Republicans when he read his prepared statement:

"There are times of emergency when the Treasury must finance expenditures in excess of income by borrowings which increase the public debt. But the national wel-

(Continued on Page 2)

SUSQUEHANNA CHIEF MENACE TO TRI CITIES

Chenango Recedes After Causing Untold Havoc — Larger Stream Rises Steadily Throughout Night — Property Loss in and North of City Reaches Staggering Proportions

With millions of dollars' worth of damage caused by floods here within 48 hours and with 15 reported deaths, Binghamton and other cities in Broome and Chenango Counties spent a night of terror and apprehension last night, with relatives of missing persons torn by doubt.

From Binghamton north to Cortland County, money loss has been staggering and human losses mount by the hour. There are but a few reported deaths that are absolutely certain, but hope has been given up in several cases.

The reported dead are:

MRS. RALPH SMITH OF LISLE, who drowned at Whitney Point Sunday night. Her body was discovered yesterday.

ALICE LOOMIS, 6, of Chenango Forks, drowned at her camp home on an island near Chenango Bridge.

ROSEMARY LOOMIS, 3, her sister, drowned at the same place.

DR. ROBERT BRONSON HARTFIELD, 71 Bennett Avenue, Binghamton, believed to have been drowned at Wilcox Sunday night. It was reported by Johnson City police last night that a body was sighted in the Susquehanna River and that it was believed to be Dr Bronson. When firemen arrived, the body could not be seen again.

HAROLD CHASE, 6, Arena Road, believed to be drowned.

GLORIA CHASE, 11 months, his sister, also reported drowned.

MRS. DORA WANESFIELD, their grandmother, believed to be drowned.

MRS. FRED ROBBINS of South Oxford, reported drowned.

FRED ROBBINS of South Oxford, reported drowned in Bowman Creek.

KENNETH McWILLIAMS, 10, of Richmond Hill, reported drowned at South Oxford.

MRS. HAZEL BARROWS of Lisle, drowned when her home was swept away before the floods.

Two unidentified men were said to have drowned on the Decker Tract near Chenango Bridge early yesterday morning.

JACOB BURKHARDT of Sayre, Pa., reported to have been drowned in the Chemung River near Waverly yesterday in an attempt to rescue four boys marooned on an island, including two of his sons.

GEORGE SARGENT, Jr., of Sayre, one of the stranded youths, also believed drowned.

Tales of personal heroism which rival fiction have been recited from various isolated points. Many families were forced to abandon their homes and flee for their lives.

Binghamton, which stood by earlier in the day in the role of spectator, began to feel the force of the elements hours later as torrential rains fell and contributed to the ever-swelling streams. Rowboats were pressed into service along Front Street, north of Clinton Street.

Traffic was crippled as authorities barred Court Street and Memorial Bridges to pedestrians and vehicles after the Ferry Street span had crumpled and was swept into the surging waters.

Horrifying stories continued to arrive from various points in the district. Suffering was great and agencies of mercy were marshaling their forces to alleviate it, so far as possible.

An appeal for clothing and furniture for flood sufferers was issued by Major Starr L. Chase of the Salvation Army. Those who have these articles may dial him at 2-2987.

The Salvation Army had furnished 75 families with grocery orders, some at Stow Flats, Front Street and State Street. More than 4,000 sandwiches and coffee were distributed among the stricken.

Practical Bible Training School of Johnson City sent out word that it had accommodations for 50 flood sufferers.

Members of Richard J. Hoyt Post, 478, indicated that members were stationed at Mygatt and Clinton Streets, ready to lend aid to victims, but required two boats to enable them to perform their mission.

Westlawn Farms' herd was rescued in the nick of time at Westover. The cows had been in pasture and everything was all right until 3:30 o'clock when the waters rose swiftly and inundated the land.

Residents of Clinton Street near Front Street were kept busy removing their household goods as the waters filled basement rooms to the ceiling.

Throngs watched eagerly as the roaring, debris-strewn waters bit deeply into the embankments and left buildings standing precariously on weakened foundations.

The dun-colored waters lapped within inches of the grassy lawn of Tyler Park, apparently ready to flood Wall Street at any minute. Weak and ineffective and several feet away at the curb were small pipes belching forth smaller streams as pumps strove mightily to clear flooded cellars of business places.

Traffic was in deplorable condition and streets throughout the city were choked with vehicles. Police officers were taxed to their limit in hopes of regulating it.

All river bridges were jammed with humanity. Danger was braved as curiosity conquered fear.

Trapped in their Summer cottage on the Ross Farm at Genegantslet while asleep, Mr. and Mrs. Harold Chase, their two children, Gloria, 11 months, and Harold, aged 6, and Mrs. Dora Wanesfield who is Mrs. Chase's mother all of Binghamton, fled to the second floor of the cottage just as it collapsed and was sent hurtling down the raging stream.

It is reported that the two children and Mrs. Wanesfield were crushed by falling timbers and plunged into the river, apparently losing their lives as no report to the contrary has been received.

Mr. and Mrs. Chase were clinging to a tree being swept along the shoreline and were successful in saving themselves. Both are in the Binghamton City Hospital.

As tragedy stalked the Tioughnioga and Chenango Valleys yesterday and last night, reports confirming rumors of the drowning of [illegible] and Mrs. Fred Robbins of South Oxford were received last night [illegible] state troopers.

Their home on Bowman Creek was swept down the raging [illegible] and they didn't have a chance to save themselves, according [illegible] vestigators. A barn was carried downstream with the Robbins [illegible] and no trace of it had been found up to a late hour.

State police and volunteers are searching the creek for any possible trace of the pair.

Another disappearance which police fear will have to end by believing him dead, is that of 10-year-old Kenneth McWilliams of Rich-

(Continued on Page 2)

ITALY SEES CLEAR PATH TO ETHIOPIA

Little Possibility of Intervention—League Only Drawback

ROME, July 8 (AP)—Italy believed tonight a path from Rome to Addis Ababa was clear.

Official circles said there was scarcely a possibility of English intervention; there is no doubt of France's friendly neutrality; and the United States has just declared its neutrality.

Germany is now friendly, they said, and Russia will be friendly because of France. England's only possibility in foreign nations was believed here to be Japan, which has growing commercial interests in Ethiopia, but Japan apparently has her hands full with the Chinese and Manchukuan situations.

There remained only the League of Nations, of which Benito Mussolini has no fear. Before that assembly Italy does not intend to remain on the defensive, but will take the offensive with charges that Ethiopia violated the conditions under which she was permitted to enter and should be reduced to the rank of a mandate.

If the League should attempt to condemn Italy, official circles disclosed, Il Duce would not have the slightest hesitation about leaving Geneva.

The departure of troops for the Italian colonies bordering upon Ethiopia, Eritrea and Italian Somaliland, was speeded up. Some 2,000 longshoremen were sent to Massaua, Eritrea, to hasten the unloading of troop transports, enabling the vessels to return quickly to Italy.

Large Gambling Barge Is Raided by Pirates

Loot Estimated at $32,000 in Cash and Jewelry Taken—Victims Fastened in Chains and Leg Irons

(By Associated Press)

LONG BEACH, Calif., July 8—Black-hooded pirates, carrying chains and leg irons to fasten their victims, today raided the luxurious gambling barge, Monte Carlo, and escaped with loot estimated at $32,000 in cash and jewelry.

All Members of Crew Are Overpowered

Ed Turner, owner of the barge, reported to officers that five men, wearing black silk stockings on their heads, swarmed aboard the boat during a dense fog and quickly chained 13 members of the crew.

The Monte Carlo is anchored about eight miles off the coast and the raid occurred at 4 a. m. after patrons had been taken ashore in launches.

Turner said J. M. Keller, ship cashier, was forced to surrender the cash and jewelry. The boat owner estimated the plunder at $22,000 in cash and $10,000 in jewelry left by patrons as security.

The raiders, Turner reported, were heavily armed with revolvers and sawedoff shotguns.

"Stick 'em up and be quiet," the pirates commanded as they climbed aboard.

They swept past the unresisting deck crew and then placed leg irons and handcuffs on the bartenders and janitors at work in the barroom.

"We won't hurt you if you keep quiet," the pirate leader told Keller, who was at work with his wife, a bookkeeper, in the steel-walled counting room.

Forcing Mrs. Keller to lie on the floor, they made Keller keep his hands elevated while the safe was looted.

The Monte Carlo, a former seagoing liner about 400 feet long, is anchored far at sea to escape jurisdiction of Long Beach and California anti-gambling laws.

Under cover of darkness, the pirates approached the Monte Carlo in a fishing boat. Others remained in the boat while the five robbers went aboard.

After their escape the coast guard was notified, as the raid so far at sea made it an act of piracy.

Long Beach police were requested to guard likely landing places.

TWO KILLED

CORNING, July 8 (AP)—Two are dead and two other persons are in critical condition in a hospital here today after an automobile in which they were riding left the highway and crashed into a tree. Those dead are Mrs. Frances Nelson, 28, and Harold Kunes, 30, both of Corning. The accident occurred 10 miles north of Corning last night.

GERMANY'S NAVAL PLAN ANNOUNCED

Two Battleships, Two Cruisers, 16 Destroyers and 28 Subs on Program

BERLIN, July 8 (AP)—Germany's naval building program for 1935, including two battleships, two cruisers, 16 destroyers and 28 submarines, was officially announced tonight.

The following program was made public in a communique based on the naval agreement with Great Britain. Some of the units mentioned have already been laid this year:

Two battleships, each of 26,000 tons displacement and armed with 28 centimeter guns.

Two cruisers, each of 10,000 tons displacement and carrying 20-centimeter guns.

Sixteen destroyers, of 1,625 tons, with 12.7 centimeter guns.

Twenty submarines of 250 tons (the first of which was placed into service June 29, with two others already launched; six submarines of 500 tons and two of 750 tons each.

Construction of airplane carriers will be begun in 1936.

JOHN D. HONORED

AUBURN, July 8 (AP)—An honorary life membership in the Finger Lakes Association was voted to John D. Rockefeller on his 96th birthday today. Rockefeller spent the first 14 years of his life near Moravia, in the Finger Lakes region.

Business Office Romance Culminates in Marriage

LONDON, July 8 (AP)—A business office romance resulted in the marriage today of George Washington Hill, "million-dollar-a-year" American tobacco executive, and his secretary, Mary Barnes.

The 50-year-old president of the American Tobacco Company and Miss Barnes, 39, were wed in the Caxton Hall register office with nine relatives and friends in attendance.

After the brief ceremony Hill gave his bride an affectionate kiss as they passed Buckingham Palace in a taxicab enroute to a downtown hotel. The guests followed in other taxis to a champagne party at the hotel.

"I don't know our plans, but I can say I am darned happy," asserted the executive.

TRAINS ON SCHEDULE

NEW YORK, July 8 (AP)—The New York Central Railroad said tonight that operation of trains on its main line between New York and Buffalo had not been affected by floods in upstate New York.

July 9, 1935: The Binghamton Sun, always a fierce competitor to the Press, put out an extra edition with the latest flood news. *Courtesy Paul S. Kucera*

SUN CODE
FAIRNESS DECENCY ACCURACY

The Binghamton Sun

FIRST IN THE HOMES OF SOUTHERN NEW YORK AND NORTHERN PENNSYLVANIA FOR MORE THAN A CENTURY

TRIPLE CITIES EDITION

FAIR
Temperature unchanged

ONE HUNDRED AND THIRTEENTH YEAR NO. 144 BINGHAMTON, N. Y., WEDNESDAY, JULY 10, 1935 PRICE THREE CENTS

FLOOD CRISIS BELIEVED OVER

Death Toll Reaches 40 in Flood Area

Life and Property Given Little Chance by Raging Elements

—Photos by Capron.

AID RUSHED BY FEDERAL GOVERNMENT

All Relief Agencies Pressed Into Service—3,000 Persons Temporarily Homeless

PRECAUTIONS ARE TAKEN FOR PROTECTING HEALTH

Hornell Badly Hit—Fires Add to Damage—2 Bridges Are Washed Out in Vicinity of Oneonta

(By Associated Press)

The general flood situation:

Forty dead, five missing, nearly 2,000 temporarily homeless, damage estimates remain around $10,000,000, fire and disease threaten isolated sections of flood zone, waters slowly receding into Northern Pennsylvania.

Receding River Waters Provide Ray of Hope—Survivors Tell Stories

Susquehanna Still Menacing—Flood-Stricken Sections Being Policed — Work of Rehabilitation Starts With Government Agencies Participating — Eye-Witness Accounts Presented for First Time

Facing the nearly impossible task of estimating the staggering loss of life and money wrought by the worst flood in the history of New York State, Binghamton and other cities and villages in Southern and Central New York will look upon a new world of receding waters today containing ruin and discouragement.

Word from all sides that the rivers and overflow in cities is lowering is the one encouraging note of the day, carrying with it the thought that safety and confidence will once more return to the valleys.

Both the Chenango and Susquehanna Rivers were reported going down early this morning and despite reports of rising waters in a few outlying spots, the general condition is good. Additional reports of drownings and missing persons as the raging waters back away trickle in from far-flung sources and the magnitude of the holocaust, is just being realized.

Smithville Flats Section in Ruins

RIVERS ON RAMPAGE IN PENNSYLVANIA

Bridges and Highways Torn Out—Industries Crippled, Crops Ruined

Utility Lobby Inquiry Brings Shout of 'Liar'

Probers Hear of Threatened Reprisals in Connection With Vote on Recent Holding Company 'Death Sentence'

(By Associated Press)

Atmosphere Is Electrified at Times

Southwestern Plains Area Experiencing Heat Wave

Mary Nolan Enters Suit Against Hollywood Man

TAX BILL CLEARS MAJOR OBSTACLE

Preliminary Effort to Broaden Limits Meets With Failure

Goodrich Denies Slaying, Plea Coming as Surprise

RAY LONG DEAD

Bradford County Sections Swept by Flood Waters

Steps Taken to Guard Against Epidemic Danger

Heavy Rains Again Sweep Over Dansville Section

Bible Clutched in Hand

Calls Go Unheard

Parsonage Battered

(Continued on Page Two)

(Continued on Page 10)

July 10, 1935: The Binghamton Sun starts chronicling the cleanup after one of the region's worst floods. *Courtesy Paul S. Kucera*

Aftermath of the July 1935 flood in Binghamton. *Press & Sun-Bulletin archives*

Site of the Ferry Street Bridge during the flood in 1935.
Press & Sun-Bulletin archives

Workers rebuild the south approach to the railroad bridge over the Chenango River after the 1935 flood.
Press & Sun-Bulletin archives

Chenango River recedes after the 1935 floods. *Press & Sun-Bulletin archives*

Seetoo Quon (father), Lew Tain You (mother) and Fai Mai (baby) pose for this photograph in 1937. This was the first Asian family to settle in Endicott in March 1936 and opened the first Chinese hand laundry that serviced IBM customers who wore white starched shirts. *Courtesy George Quon*

1934-35

Slavic Lutheran Church of the Ascension championship basketball team, 1935. First row, left to right: Matey, Micha, Yuricek, Pavlovik, Sinek. Second row: Mitach, Sukup, Sukup, Hores, Pavlovik. *Courtesy Rudy Bystrak*

Pisani
271

Home of Seetoo Quon and Lew Tain You, the first Asian family to settle in Endicott in the 1930s. The house was located at 1309 Monroe Street, Endicott. *Courtesy George Quon*

BINGHAMTON
GAS WORKS
No 36

George Funnell, left, and Charlie Jenks pose by the gas works truck in Binghamton, 1935. Jenks was a fireman for the City of Binghamton for 27 years before retiring. *Courtesy Charlie Jenks*

THE WEATHER

Fair tonight with lowest temperature 62 to 65 degrees. Saturday probably unsettled.

BINGHAMTON PRESS

City Edition

Vol. 57, No. 108. THIRTY PAGES FRIDAY EVENING, AUGUST 16, 1935. PRICE THREE CENTS

POST AND ROGERS KILLED AS PLANE FALLS 50 FEET INTO ALASKAN RIVER

Tax Bill Passes; U. S. Securities Included

Further Exempt Issues Banned by Amendment

$250,000,000 Measure Is Sent to Conference, Where Clause May Die

VOTE IS 57 TO 22

Passage Paves Way for Adjournment by End of Next Week

Washington, Aug. 16—(United Press) — Adjournment of Congress neared today with the record breaking, two-day passage of the tax-the-rich bill by the Senate. The eight-months session marked by much disputed legislation, probably will end next week.

With the President's $250,000,000 tax-the-rich bill safely in the hands of friendly conferees, major obstacles to adjournment were half a dozen bills yet to be reported out of ...

House Fight Seen on Free and Open Silver

Food for Ambitious Men

Daughter Rehearsing in an Air Crash Drama When the News Came

Lakewood, Me., Aug. 16 — (United Press) — Will Rogers wife and pretty 19-year-old actress-daughter, Mary, bore up bravely here today as they listened to the news of his death in an Alaskan airplane crash.

Ironically, Mary has been playing the feminine lead in the Lakewood Players' presentation of the Broadway success, "Ceiling Zero," a thrilling aviation drama.

A feature of the play is an off-stage plane crash in which a pilot is killed.

Mr. Rogers son James, had planned to come here next Monday.

Ponca City, Okla., Aug. 16—(United Press)—Mrs. Wiley Post who originally intended to make the Alaskan aerial tour with her husband and Will Rogers, was grief stricken today at reports of the death of the two Oklahomans.

She was unable to discuss the tragedy. She left her husband at Seattle and returned here, where she has been visiting at the home of I. E. Gray.

"We can't let her talk to anyone, at least not now," Mrs. Gray said. "She is unable to talk."

Gray is a flier who has been a friend of Mr. Post for years. Mrs. Post came here when she decided not to accompany her husband and Mr. Rogers on the hunting and sight-seeing trip in the Far North.

Hopson Hotly Defends Cost of Lobby Fight

Charges Wheeler-Rayburn Bill Would Kill $6,000,000,000

Will Rogers Even Spoke Humorously About Death

Nation's Shock Is Voiced in F. D. R. Tribute

Post and Rogers Were Outstanding Americans, Says President

WASHINGTON GRIEVES

Loved Humorist as Few Others; Byrns Tells of Premonition

Hyde Park, Aug. 16—(Associated Press)—President Roosevelt expressed the shock of the nation today upon learning of the death of Will Rogers and Wiley Post, who he said were "outstanding Americans and will be greatly missed."

... "Both were outstanding Americans and will be greatly missed."

Crash 'Terrible Shock' to Him, Hoover Says

Death Was the Stowaway

Will Rogers and Wiley Post just before they climbed into their plane at Renton airport, Washington state, to take off on their vacation jaunt to Alaska, where they crashed to their deaths.

Last Words That Will Rogers Wrote for Binghamton Press

Fairbanks, Alaska, Aug. 16— ...

Rogers Flew Across U. S. to Save Friend's Show

Rogers-Post Plane Licensed Only Aug. 8

Col. Lindbergh May Fly After Crash Victims

Coast Guard Cutter Also Is Sent Back to Point Barrow

Farm Bankruptcy, Rail Pension Bills Planned

Engine Goes Bad at Takeoff After They Asked Way

(Copyright, 1935, by Associated Press)

Seattle, Aug. 16—(Associated Press)—Will Rogers, cowboy philosopher, actor and air travel enthusiast, and Wiley Post, who circled the earth alone in a plane, were killed last night when their plane crashed 15 miles south of Point Barrow in northernmost Alaska.

The word of their death came today to the United States Army Signal Corps headquarters here from their Point Barrow station.

The first terse message said:

"Post and Rogers crashed 15 miles south of here (Point Barrow) at 8 o'clock (11 p. m., Binghamton time) last night. Have recovered bodies and placed them in care of Dr. Greist (in charge of a small Point Barrow hospital). Standing by on Anchorage (Alaska) hourly."

The message was signed by Staff Sergeant Morgan, the only Army man on duty at the small Point Barrow settlement.

Later, he wirelessed the plane crashed from only 50 feet in the air after taking off from a small river:

"Native runner reported plane crashed 15 miles south of Barrow.

"Immediately hired fast launch, proceeded to scene, found plane complete wreck, partially submerged two feet water.

"Recovered body of Rogers, then necessary tear plane apart extract body of Post from water.

"Brought bodies to Barrow, turned over to Dr. Greist, also salvaged personal effects, which I am holding.

"Advise relatives and instruct this station fully as to procedure.

"Natives camping small river 15 miles south here claim Post and Rogers landed, asked way to Barrow.

"Taking off engine misfired on right bank while only 50 feet over water.

"Plane out of control, crashed, tearing right wing off and topping over forced engine back through body of plane.

"Both apparently killed instantly.

"Both bodies bruised.

"Post's wrist watch broken, stopped 8:18 p. m."

Dr. Henry W. Greist operates the Presbyterian hospital at Point Barrow which is maintained primarily for the care of Eskimos.

Mr. Post and Mr. Rogers were on an aerial vacation, which Mr. Post had planned would take him to Moscow, but Mr. Rogers had not decided whether he would accompany him further than Nome, where Wiley planned to establish a base for his projected flight across Siberia.

Early plans for the flight included arrangements for Mrs. Post, the flier's wife, to accompany them. At the last moment Mrs. Post withdrew and Mr. Post and Mr. Rogers flew into the north country alone.

...

Post was an excellent bad weather flier. ...

(Continued on Page Eight)

Other stories on Will Rogers and Wiley Post on Pages 8, 12 and 25.

Home for Birthday of Son, F. D. R. Pushes Utilities Bill

(Continued on Page Thirteen)

Rogers' Home Town and Movie Colony Stunned by Tragedy

Hollywood, Calif., Aug. 16—(Associated Press)—The movie capital was stunned by the news from Alaska of the sudden airplane death of Will Rogers and Wiley Post.

August 16, 1935: Famous entertainer Will Rogers once was a contributor to the Binghamton Press. *Microfilm archives*

Second Section

BINGHAMTON PRESS

Second Section

THIRTY-SIX PAGES — WEDNESDAY EVENING, NOVEMBER 27, 1935. — PAGES 19 TO 36

Bishop Duffy Dedicates Lourdes Hospital Addition With Solemn Mass

Bishop Lauds Hospital Board in His Sermon

Stresses Value of Lourdes as Healing Center in Southern Tier

CITES EARLY HISTORY

Calls Institution a Gift of the Late Bishop Curley

Preaching the dedication sermon at the solemn pontifical mass in the new chapel of the new addition to Our Lady of Lourdes hospital today, Bishop John A. Duffy reviewed the healing ministry of Jesus Christ during His earthly ministry. He also paid tribute to the work of the building committee, headed by John A. McDonald, chairman, and other friends of the hospital. He stressed, too, the value of the enlarged institution as a center of healing to the entire Southern Tier.

Bishop Duffy took as his text the following quotation from the Gospel of St. Matthew: "Jesus went through all their cities and villages teaching in their synagogues and preaching the Gospel of the Kingdom, and healing every sickness and every disease among the people."

"There is no need," the bishop said, "to stress the importance of the occasion that has brought us together this morning. The moment is one filled with the deepest emotion, the fulfillment of an ardent hope and desire in the hearts of the priests and people of the Southern Tier. The occasion in fullest reality is a dream come true.

"The words of the text carry us back over 19 centuries to Jesus of Nazareth, going about teaching in the synagogues and healing the sick. The marvelous works of mercy and charity illustrated in the Savior's life will continue through agencies, such as Our Lady of Lourdes hospital, newly opened today. Teaching and healing were the characteristic features of our Savior's life. They are the characteristic notes of this hospital dedicated today to Christ's poor. As the major number of the Savior's extraordinary acts were works of mercy done for the poor and neglected, this hospital, like Him, will devote itself to mercy and charity for the poor and afflicted. Christ, however, works in these latter days through secondary human instruments. The ideals and purposes of Christ are carried out by human hearts and hands and this hospital is a particular example of human generosity given in the spirit of Christ.

"The first human agencies who caught the spirit of this movement and supported it were the priests and sisters of this area. From the very beginning when the object was first broached, our priests and sisters gave up their time and energy and their means that the work might go forward. This is a day of joy and gratitude for others. It is a day of triumph for the sisters and priests of this diocese. Closely aligned with them is the committee under whose auspices the means for the erection of this building were first collected and who have supervised its progress with earnest zeal. So [illegible] has been their agency and generous their aid that their names deserve a lasting memory. It is a matter of pleasure for me to list the committee of Our Lady of Lourdes hospital and to offer them the slight homage of my praise: Benjamin F. Welden, chairman, John A. McDonald, Peter McManus, Edwin Tierney, Harry Rubin and Sister Angelica. [illegible] man, however, stands out with particular prominence in this [illegible]. His generosity from the

(Continued on Page Twenty)

Colorful Assemblages in Solemn Rites of Dedication at New Hospital

Dedicating the cornerstone to the new addition to Our Lady of Lourdes hospital this morning: the Most Rev. John A. Duffy, the Rev. D. F. Cunningham, the Rev. Florian Billy, the Rev. Ambrose M. Dwyer, the Rev. Dennis C. Flynn, the Rev. Joseph Wilmes and the Rev. William H. Purcell.

Sisters, priests and nurses watching the dedication ceremonies of the new $350,000 addition to Our Lady of Lourdes hospital in Riverside Drive this morning, marking the culmination of three years work in raising funds and a year of actual construction work.

The Most Rev. John A. Duffy, bishop of Syracuse, assisted by his secretary, the Rev. D. F. Cunningham, marking the sign of the cross on the cornerstone.

The Rev. John W. Lynch and the Rev. D. F. Cunningham assisting the Most Rev. John A. Duffy as he sprinkled the walls of the new chapel with holy water.

Cornerstone Laid, Chapel Walls Blessed

Priests, Deacons, Acolytes Take Part in Impressive Ceremonies

SCENE IS COLORFUL

Bishop Will Speak at Thanksgiving Eve Dinner Tonight

Blessing the outside walls of the chapel and laying the cornerstone of the new $350,000 addition to Our Lady of Lourdes hospital, the Most Rev. John A. Duffy, bishop of Syracuse, today dedicated with a solemn pontifical mass the culmination of three years of devoted work.

"This is the morning we have been waiting for, for a long time," a member of the building committee remarked to one of the sisters as the low Latin chant of the celebrants rose from the chapel and Bishop Duffy, preceded by deacons and acolytes, sprinkled the walls with holy water.

The richly embroidered gold robes and lace vestments of the officiating ecclesiastical dignitaries were framed against the brick walls of the new addition as Bishop Duffy sprinkled the cornerstone with holy water, marked the sign of the cross with a trowel, and placed the box of records inside. A circle of visiting priests, sisters in their wide starched hats and flowing robes and nurses wearing dark capes over their white uniforms watched the workmen seal the box and shove it into place.

Leaving the hospital grounds in a procession, the guests and priests reentered the main building to conduct the pontifical solemn high mass marking the completion of the new addition, a year from the day the foundations were dedicated.

Bishop Duffy and party are dining at the hospital this afternoon with the medical and surgical staffs and he will close the day with an address at the Thanksgiving Eve dinner-dance in the Arlington hotel tonight under the auspices of the Lourdes Hospital Guild.

Colorful scenes were presented about the hospital buildings and grounds all the morning. Slowly-moving processions of high ecclesiastics from all parts of the diocese escorted Bishop Duffy inside and out of the building, and there were guards of honor of the Fourth Degree Knights of Columbus and of the Broome County Federation of the Holy Name societies.

Priests were attired in vari-colored robes and vestments and there were choirs of altar and choir boys, and adults, too, singing and chanting, sometimes accompanied by deep-toned music from the organ in the new chapel.

Holy ritual was recited, in tones now soft and low, and now high and triumphant, and there was waving of incense burners at the special pontifical mass that filled the little chapel.

Following the mass Bishop Duffy was accompanied in processional to the south end of the main corridor on the ground floor, and there he dedicated a beautiful painting of the late Bishop Joseph Curley, who preceded Bishop Duffy in this diocese. The painting, by a Syracuse painter, Lee S. Trimm, is a gift by the bishop to the hospital.

The exercises started at 9 o'clock, when the bishop blessed the new chapel, now completed and ready for hospital service, made possible by the gift of $10,000 received for that purpose from Binghamton court, Catholic Daughters of Amer-

(Continued on Page Twenty)

CCC Leaders Perfect Film Project Plan

Three Circuits to Be Used in District; 12 to Get Jobs

Aims and scope of the visual education program to be undertaken by the recreation division of District Five, Civilian Conservation Corps, were discussed at a conference of state district and camp leaders at the headquarters in Hillcrest Tuesday.

Andrew Rougvie, TERA recreational supervisor for New York state, and Mrs. Marion Beaufait, supervisor of visual education in CCC camps of the state, met with Joel E. Nystrom, district educational adviser and recreational directors of 12 of the 27 camps of the district, to perfect plans for the program, which will be carried out with 35 and 16 millimeter cameras and projection equipment.

Results of the conference were twofold:

One—Decision was made to employ 12 persons—with some degree of general education and a knowledge of electricity—as visual education instructors.

Two—Assurance was given that recreational instructors who have been employed during the TERA program will be absorbed under the new visual education program. These instructors would otherwise have lost their positions, it was said.

Three motion picture circuits—a circuit to comprise five or six camps—will be formed in district five within the next two weeks. Seventeen camps will be affected by the three circuits, with Binghamton, Deposit and Elmira as circuit headquarters.

The 12 newly created posts in the CCC organization, Mr. Nystrom explained today, will be filled from the ranks of unemployed who were certified for relief before Nov. 1—a WPA requirement. Persons seeking the posts should apply at the Binghamton welfare office at 221 Washington street where they should contact Jess Huffman.

First Civil Suit for November Term Opened

Judge T. A. MacClary Hears $3,000 Action for Damages

The first civil action on the Broome County Court calendar for November opened before Judge Thomas A. MacClary and a jury today with Martin J. Franey of Seminary avenue seeking $3,000 from the Triple Cities Traction Corporation as the result of a collision Jan. 22.

A. E. Gold and John R. Normile, trial counsel for Mr. Franey, told the jury in opening the suit that the accident happened as a result of negligence on the part of the bus driver, whose machine crashed into the Franey car at Oak and Main streets.

The plaintiff, they claimed, was driving west on Main street and attempted to make a south turn into Oak street when the bus struck the rear end of the car, throwing him against the side of the machine and inflicting severe injuries.

Edward F. Ronan, attorney for the traction corporation, made a general denial of the negligence claim and charged that the crash resulted from Mr. Franey stepping on the brakes of his car suddenly and skidding the machine in front of the bus.

The suit in which Mr. Franey is asking $2,900 for personal injuries and $100 for damages to his car, was expected to close late Friday.

RUMMAGE SALE

Hope Chapter will conduct a rummage sale at 103 Court street, Friday and Saturday.

If you don't know where to find what you want at the price you want to pay—use the Classified section.

OUR WEATHER MAN

[illegible] Binghamton and Vicinity: Rain [illegible] and Thursday; warmer tonight; [illegible] Thursday night; lowest temperature tonight 39° to 45° and highest [illegible] 49° to 55°.

[illegible] The western storm area has [illegible] considerable energy and [illegible] northeastward to the upper [illegible] valley (Des Moines, 29.32 [illegible]). It is producing general rains [illegible] to Ohio and the upper Lake [illegible] and southward to the west Gulf [illegible] with snows in Minnesota and the [illegible]. Areas of high pressure overlie [illegible] Atlantic and Pacific states (Atlantic [illegible] 30.30, and Portland, Oregon, 30.32 [illegible]). Temperatures are higher generally east of the Plains states.

[illegible] temperature at 8 a. m. today ... 36
[illegible] temperature at midnight ... 39
[illegible] temperature at 5 p. m. yesterday ... 40
[illegible] temperature yesterday ... 41
[illegible] temperature last night ... 35
[illegible] Press thermometer at [illegible] today ... 47
[illegible] year ago today it was ... 42
[illegible] years ago today it was ... 28
[illegible] years ago today it was ... 20
[illegible] for last 24 hours to [illegible] today ... Trace
[illegible] Pressure — Station elevation [illegible]: 8 p. m., Tuesday, 29.20 in.; [illegible] today, 29.32 in.; 8 a. m., today, 29.33 in. (reduced to sea level, [illegible] in.); noon today, 29.27 in.

Temperatures in Other Cities

	High	Low		High	Low
[illegible] Tex.	[illegible]	[illegible]	Jacksonville	66	56
[illegible] Mass.	[illegible]	[illegible]	Los Angeles	66	46
[illegible] N. Y.	[illegible]	[illegible]	Miami, Fla.	[illegible]	[illegible]
[illegible] Alb.	[illegible]	[illegible]	Montreal, Que.	[illegible]	32
[illegible]	[illegible]	[illegible]	New Orleans	[illegible]	[illegible]
[illegible]	[illegible]	[illegible]	New York	[illegible]	[illegible]
[illegible], O.	[illegible]	[illegible]	Philadelphia	[illegible]	[illegible]
[illegible] Colo.	[illegible]	[illegible]	Phoenix, Ariz.	[illegible]	[illegible]
Des Moines	[illegible]	[illegible]	Portland, Ore.	[illegible]	[illegible]
[illegible] Mich.	[illegible]	[illegible]	Raleigh, N. C.	[illegible]	[illegible]
[illegible] Minn.	[illegible]	[illegible]	Salt Lake City	[illegible]	[illegible]
[illegible] Pa.	[illegible]	[illegible]	San Francisco	[illegible]	[illegible]
[illegible] N. C.	[illegible]	[illegible]	Scranton, Pa.	[illegible]	[illegible]
[illegible] Mont.	[illegible]	[illegible]	Shreveport, La.	[illegible]	[illegible]
[illegible] S. D.	[illegible]	[illegible]	Washington	[illegible]	[illegible]

Parent-Teacher Notes

An Armenian program was given by the Henry W. Longfellow Parent-Teacher association at the school Tuesday night. Mrs. Ruby Shahinian, who had charge of the music, gave several vocal selections, singing some in Armenian and some in English. Piano solos were played by Annette Basmajian, Albert Shahinian, Louise Kakusian and Marian Hekminian. Vahe Garbedian entertained with his guitar, and Elizabeth Bodinian with her piano accordion. Armenian dainties were served by the committee headed by Mrs. Meg Basmajian.

Mrs. Jerry Carroll, vice president, presided at the business meeting. Mrs. J. R. Price spoke briefly concerning the work of the membership committee. Mrs. Charles Miller announced that the parental education meeting will be held Dec. 19 in the school clinic room.

The third grade mothers are in charge of the Christmas luncheon which will be given Dec. 10 at 1 p. m. in the school. Mrs. Floyd Mottram and Mrs. Herbert Nichols are attending to the Christmas tree and gifts.

Mrs. Harold Morss, chairman of the membership committee of the Theodore Roosevelt Parent-Teacher association, has announced the completion of the membership drive with a total of 356 members of whom 54 are fathers. Grade 3B taught by Mrs. Ruth Fairbanks, was awarded a ball for the largest membership of 133 per cent. Other honor grades are: 1-A, taught by Mrs. Bertram Mapes, 111 per cent; grade 3-B, taught by Miss Doris Van Buskirk, 107 per cent; 1-B, taught by Mrs. Stanley Heslop, 103 per cent; grade 5-B, taught by Mrs. Dorothea Sperling, 100 per cent; and grade 7-B, taught by Miss Julia Zall, 100 per cent.

Four Criminal Case Appeals Before Court

Judge MacClary to Hear Arguments Slated for Dec. 3

Four appeals from convictions of criminal charges in police court and justices of the peace courts were scheduled by Judge Thomas A. McClary today for argument in Broome County Court Dec. 3.

The case of Gordon S. Bitner of Elmira, who was sentenced to pay a fine of $50 and given a suspended term of 30 days in Broome county jail for driving while intoxicated, was the first appeal listed.

Bitner, who is represented by George L. Andrews, was arrested in Endicott Sept 24 and pleaded guilty to the charge when he was arranged in justice of the peace court. Despite the plea, however, he contends through counsel that he misunderstood the charge.

Michael Makrosky of Lester avenue, Johnson City, who was found guilty Sept. 25 of selling beer to a minor, will appeal his conviction in police justice court in the town of Union. Makrosky was sentenced to pay a $100 fine and to serve 30 days in the county jail.

James F. Hickey of Binghamton will appeal his conviction in police court Sept. 16 of operating a dance without a license in violation of a city ordinance. He will be represented by John J. Cucci.

Gerald Dalrymple of Conklin, who was convicted Sept. 7 of non-support, in peace justice court in the town of Conklin, will appeal through his attorney, Wayne Bullock.

PETER T. CAMPON SPEAKS

Peter T. Campon, past grand knight of Binghamton Council, Knights of Columbus, was guest speaker at the meeting of the Geneva Kiwanis club in that city Tuesday.

"Americans and Americanism" provided Mr. Campon's topic. Tuesday night Mr. Campon spoke at the annual observance of Italian night of the Geneva Knights of Columbus. He discussed "Italian Gifts to America."

Bishop Duffy to Address 800 at Lourdes Guild Banquet

Annual Thanksgiving Eve Dinner-Dance Scheduled for Tonight at Arlington Hotel—John B. Curran, President, Also to Speak

The Very Rev. John A. Duffy, bishop of the Catholic diocese of Syracuse, will be the principal speaker at the annual Lourdes Hospital Guild Thanksgiving Eve dinner-dance tonight in the Arlington hotel.

More than 800 are expected to attend the affair which gets under way at 6.15 p. m., according to John B. Curran, president of the Guild.

Mr. Curran will introduce Bishop Duffy at 8.15 p. m.

David F. McManus, head of the committee on arrangements, will be toastmaster and there will be special music by the Sacks trio.

The program will open with a march, "The Guild Theme Song," words of which were written by John H. McMahon of Johnson City, and sung to the tune of "Notre Dame Victory Song."

Among those at the speakers' table will be Bishop Duffy, Catholic pastors of the Triple Cities, the Rev. David F. Cunningham, secretary to Bishop Duffy; the Rev. James J. Bannon, director of charities of the diocese; Mayor James T. Ivory, Mayor-elect Thomas W. Behan, Toastmaster McManus, John A. McDonald, chairman, and members of the building committee, and Mr. Curran.

The Lourdes Hospital Guild dates from three years ago when Miss Anne O'Donnell of St. Patrick's and Mrs. Margaret Plunkett of St. Mary's, while calling on the Sisters of Lourdes, suggested the formation of a Guild to assist the Sisters in obtaining necessities for the charity patients of the hospital.

The two women began making contacts and telephone calls that resulted in informal meetings throughout the community.

Mrs. John A. McNicol was chosen to solicit the aid of clergy, Miss O'Donnell was made temporary treasurer and Mrs. Plunkett was made temporary secretary.

The following officers then were chosen to head the Guild for its initial year:

President, Mrs. John A. McNicol; vice president, Mrs. George Phelan; second vice president, Francis J. O'Connor; third vice president, Michael L. Sullivan, secretary, Mrs. Margaret Plunkett; treasurer, Miss Anne O'Donnell; directors, three years, David McManus, chairman, Edwin M. Tierney, Mrs. Louis J. Hennessey, Jr., Mrs. William J. Doyle, Mrs. James F. Loughlin, Mrs. Julius D. Hodskin, directors, two years, Mrs. James F. Woolfe, John A. McDonald, Michael Foley, Mrs. Fred Gillen, Mrs. H. J. Toomey, and Mrs. Robert J. Rice, directors, one year, Mrs. William J. Fitzgerald, Mrs. J. R. Casey, Miss Helen Crowe, George Loughlin, Mrs. James Mack, and M. J. Cullen; nominating committee, Miss May Ryan, Mrs. Margaret Toomey, Mrs. John D. Bowen, and Mrs. Margaret Plunkett.

David F. McManus was elected chairman of the board of directors.

The Guild officers and directors elected for 1934, the second year, were:

President, Michael H. Sweeney; vice presidents, Mrs. Margaret Plunkett, John B. Curran, and W. J. Conlon, secretary, Miss Mary Connor; treasurer, Miss Anne O'Donnell; directors, three years, Milton Duffy, George Loughlin, Margaret Phalen, Cecelia McNicol, M. J. Cullan, and Francis O'Connor.

Officers and directors elected for 1935 were:

President, John B. Curran, vice presidents, Mrs. J. D. Hodskin, Mrs. Mary Lincoln, Mrs. N. C. Ward; secretary, Miss Mary Connor, treasurer, Miss Anne O'Donnell; directors, three years, Michael Sweeney, Joseph Crowe, John A. McDonald, Robert McCabe, Mrs. John Southee and Mrs. Helen Mugan.

The Guild now has a membership of about 2,500.

There's no place like home, and there's no place like The Press Classified Section to find one.

Major Share of Flood Data Almost Ready

Army Engineers' Survey to Include All Damages in Tier

By a Binghamton Press Staff Writer

Elmira, Nov. 27 — One hundred engineers, statisticians and clerks engaged in compiling data assembled on ravages of the July flood in Central and Southern New York, will complete the major share of their work before January according to Donald L. Bower, associate engineer in charge of this phase of the $200,000 army engineers' survey.

This compilation will include all details relative to losses suffered in the flood, Mr. Bower explains. The data is being broken down into more than a score of subdivisions to be used by the New York district engineer's office in preparing the report of the survey.

The primary breakdown is to be a classification of damage in cities, towns and villages with description of each unit as to population area, assessed valuation, highways, railroads and streams.

Each unit in the primary breakdown will be further detailed by a report of the residential, commercial and industrial losses in urban private property and general losses in rural private property.

Semi-public and community property damages in each primary unit also will be listed.

Utility damage suffered in each unit is to be reported with two classifications—railroad and other than railroad. Highways and bridges damaged will be classified in four groups, those constructed with Federal aid, those built with state funds and county and town highways and bridges.

Damage to municipal village and county streets, sewage and water supply facilities and buildings will be described.

The report is to contain an explanation of the damage per square mile, the damage per capita and the damage per dollar of assessed valuation. It also will detail information on estimated indirect damage.

November 27, 1935: The dedication of a new addition to Lourdes Hospital merited extensive coverage inside the paper. *Microfilm archives*

Second Section

BINGHAMTON PRESS

Second Section

THIRTY PAGES — MONDAY EVENING, MARCH 16, 1936. — PAGES 15 TO 30

E J to Build New Rubber Factory; Will Employ 400 More Workers

Press Cooking School to Open on March 24

Miss Laura Kennedy to Conduct Sessions at High School

FOUR ARE TO BE HELD

All Lectures in Course to Be Given Evenings at 8 o'Clock

Miss Laura Kennedy will conduct The Binghamton Press Free Cooking school in Binghamton Central High school auditorium next week.

Regardless of how long a woman has been running a home, she will find interest in the cooking school.

Sessions Tuesday, Wednesday, Thursday and Friday nights of next week at Binghamton Central High school auditorium will be free and no tickets will be required.

The far-reaching benefits of the course of lectures by so widely known an authority as Miss Kennedy make the cooking school an especially worthwhile event. Miss Kennedy has had many years of experience, with a nation-wide reputation for bringing timely hints on the world's oldest and most important calling, that of coping with the responsibilities of a home, such as marketing, budgeting, child feeding, diet for fat and lean, menu planning, time and labor saving appliances, and also that equally important angle of modern housekeeping — charm and beauty in the home.

The cooking school will be a constructive conference on housework and not a social or theoretical entertainment. Housekeepers are entitled to receive practical information from a lecturer of mature experience. That is just what Miss Kennedy at The Binghamton Press cooking school proposes to give to Binghamton.

Miss Kennedy finds problems of housekeeping pretty much the same the country over. ...

To Offer New Recipes

MISS LAURA KENNEDY

Market Roads Drive Renewal Planned Here

First Result of Conference of Agricultural Leaders of Broome Saturday

IMPROVEMENTS URGED

Supervisor Brewer Proposes Reduction in Dirt Highway Mileage

A renewed campaign for the construction of farm to market roads throughout Broome county may be the first result of a conference of agricultural leaders Saturday in the Courthouse to discuss possibility of mapping a long time agricultural program for the county.

Reports presented at the conference show that 44.1 per cent of the roads in Broome county are dirt as compared to an average of 32 per cent for the entire state.

Belief that efforts should be made to reduce the mileage of dirt roads in the county through a farm to market road construction program was voiced by Supervisor Eugene W. Brewer of Triangle.

Mr. Brewer pointed out that it probably would be worth while to construct some of these roads even in areas of the county where the land classification survey has revealed that conditions probably will result in the abandonment of additional farms.

"Gravel roads to these areas would enable residents of the city to drive out into the wilder areas of the county," he said.

Other dirt roads which should be improved are located in areas that will remain permanently in agriculture, and should be improved to give the farmers a road that will be open at all periods of the year, it was pointed out.

A further meeting of the agricultural leaders is planned after Dr. M. C. Bond of the State College of Agriculture drafts a report on the probable trend in agriculture in the county during the next few years.

This report will be based on the trend during the last half century and on opinions expressed by those present at the conference Saturday.

Agricultural Leaders in Conference Here

Agriculture leaders at a meeting in the Court house Saturday discussed the possibility of drafting a long time program for agriculture in Broome county. Seated, left to right, W. J. Golan of Binghamton, Maurice Mallory of Windsor, M. P. Green of West Chenango and George Burrows of Harpursville. Standing, County Attorney Clarence L. Chamberlain, Karl Keisler of Binghamton, Christopher Ayres of Conklin, Eugene Brewer of Triangle, Clifford L. Robinson of Fenton, William Moore, Farm Bureau agent, and Dr. M. C. Bond of the State College of Agriculture.

50,000 Square Feet of Floor Space Planned

Five-Story Building Will Be Between South End, Sunrise Plants

TO TAKE SIX MONTHS

Another Half-Year Will Be Required to Train Personnel

Because of a big demand for rubber footwear, the Endicott Johnson Corporation has decided to construct a five-story factory in Johnson City this spring.

Work on the new structure, which will be built between the Sunrise and South Side factories, connecting the two buildings, will start as soon as weather permits, according to an announcement released today by officials of the shoe corporation.

The building will measure 125 by 80 feet and provide 50,000 square feet of floor space. It is expected that six months will be required to construct the new unit while another six months will be required to teach new workers and build up production.

Employment for about 400 additional workers will be provided in the new building, the announcement says. It will add materially to existing payrolls and give a proportionate boost to business throughout the Southern Tier, in the opinion of business leaders.

Heads of the corporation pointed out today that because of the time required to build the factory, install the equipment and get it in actual operation the management stresses the fact that no applications for employment will be received at this time.

Based on the shoe concern's average weekly payroll of $26 per worker, the new unit, when in full operation, will boost the total payroll by approximately $540,000 per year. E J today has a daily payroll of about $100,000 and employs 19,000 workers.

Business leaders throughout the Triple Cities today welcomed the announcement as indicative of better business. "It's simply another indication that this is the bright spot in the nation and we all know why—because we have stabilized industries in our Valley of Opportunity," declared Benjamin F. Sisson, of the Sisson Bros.-Welden Co. of Binghamton.

"I am greatly pleased to hear the announcement," said Mayor ...

School Board to Study Plans for North High

Similar Action Scheduled for City Council Session Today

Income Tax Returns — Must All Be Filed by Midnight Tonight

P. S. C. Probe of Gas Works Resumes Soon

Neal Brewster to Hold Hearing at Courthouse March 27

Housekeeper Claims $2,465 From Her Former Employer

Miss Lucinda Dougale Says She Worked for Seven and a Half Years for M. A. Youngs of Port Crane Without Wages

2 Insurgents Draw Bottom Ballot Places

Names of Whalen and Casey to Be Below Those of 'Regulars'

Board Praises City Hospital Nursing Unit

Secretary of Examiners Says School Here Is Found 'Noteworthy'

Glasses Case Clue to Identity of Train Victim

Binghamton Optician's Name on Carton Found on Body

Lions Club Speaker to Tell About Ireland

Irish Folk Lore List Ready at Library Here

Deposit Farmer, Wife File Bankruptcy Petitions

Our Weather Man

Parent-Teacher Notes

Ithaca City Engineer to Be Speaker Here

Harpursville Pupils Will Get Health Test

Mother of Syracuse Priest Succumbs at 56

Firemen Extinguish Three Blazes, Damage Is Slight

Foreign War Veterans Seek New Quarters

Z. B. Phelps, Jr., Speaks at LaFayette Wednesday

Eatons and Flaesches Dine Together in California

Francis J. O'Connor to Speak on Music

WPA District Pay Office Is Established Here

Apalachin Water System Proposals to Be Asked

Miss Harriet G. Yates Speaks at Church Meet

Auxiliary Will Fete 1898 War Veterans

Chenango Bridge Man Gets Warship Berth

Robert F. Adams of Chenango Bridge who enlisted in the U. S. Navy about four months ago, has completed his preliminary training at the naval station at Newport, R. I., and has been assigned to the U. S. S. West Virginia, flagship of the Pacific fleet, with base at San Pedro, Cal., according to information received at the Navy recruiting station in the Federal building today.

March 16, 1936: In the midst of the Great Depression, EJ's announcement it would build a new factory and hire 400 workers was second-section news. *Microfilm archives*

THE WEATHER
Cloudy, probably occasional rain today and Thursday. Colder tonight.

BINGHAMTON PRESS

City Edition

Vol. 57, No. 288. THIRTY PAGES WEDNESDAY EVENING, MARCH 18, 1936. PRICE THREE CENTS

WATERWORKS SHUTDOWN, 6 BRIDGES CLOSED, RIVERS HIGHEST IN HISTORY

U. S. Flood Control Action Demanded at Once

Board Hears Tier Plea As Streams Rage

Army Engineers Told That Congress Must Act Immediately

HEARING IS TENSE

New Yorkers Spurred by Hourly Reports From Rampage Here

BINGHAMTON PRESS BUREAU
WASHINGTON, D. C., MARCH 18

While flood waters rolled over the Eastern United States today raging through the valleys of the Southern Tier, full force and weight of the State of New York, as represented by the New York State Flood Control Commission and the 16 counties smashed by the floods of last July were thrown behind a demand that the United States Army Board of Engineers for Rivers and Harbors recommend to Congress full and immediate protection for the areas devastated by the 1935 flood.

The demand was made of the board sitting in open session in the ... commonplace board room ... Munitions building ... Constitution avenue.

... the first public showdown ... the United States government ... going to do about flood ... Central and Southern New York and Northern Pennsylvania ... while the crowd of ... was being reenacted in ...

(Continued on Page Two)

National Guard Ordered to Prepare for Flood Aid

Harrisburg, Pa., March 18— (Associated Press)—Governor George ... ordered National Guard ... of Pennsylvania ... to enter the Johnstown ... Harrisburg airport ...

(Continued on Page Thirty)

False Alarms Are Very Dangerous

...

City Waterworks Pumps Disabled by Flood

Pumping units at the city water works disabled as the Susquehanna river poured over the Court street flood wall, swept across the thoroughfare and into the plant. City's water situation was critical with only a 24-hour storage supply in reservoirs.

Above, members of the city force which was defeated in the all-night and early morning fight to keep flood waters from reaching the plant boiler room. In raincoat, knee-deep in water, John L. O'Brien, chief clerk of water bureau.

Italy Against Sanctions for Reich Action

Grandi Tells League His Country Won't Invoke Penalties

London, March 18 ...

(Continued on Page Thirty)

Corinth and Lake George Schools Reopen Monday

Corinth, March 18—(Associated Press)— ...

AUTO DERAILS TRAIN

Lake Charles, La., March 18— (Associated Press)— ...

Engineers' Flood Control Plans Call for 41 Dry Dam Reservoirs at Ultimate $34,000,000 Cost

17 Dention Type Bowls Suggested in the Initial Proposal Costing $15,410,000 — Institution of Methods Against Erosion Seen Needed

BINGHAMTON PRESS BUREAU
WASHINGTON ...

General details of the Army Engineers' $34,000,000 program for flood control in the counties of central and southern New York and northern Pennsylvania became available ...

(Continued on Page Seventeen)

6 Reported Drowned in Lock Haven District

Lock Haven, Pa., March 18— ...

CCC Worker Receives $250,000 Wage Check

Visalia, Cal., March 18—(Associated Press)— ...

Water 18 Feet in Johnstown, Threat Passes

Water Still Raging but Officials Note Rivers Are Receding

Johnstown, Pa., March 18 — ...

(Continued on Page Two)

All Passenger Plane Flights in Pa. Cancelled

Newark, N. J., March 18— ...

Children Whimper as Flood Waters Creep Nearer Doors

...

F.D.R. Orders Help Sent to Stricken Area

Federal Agencies Mobilized to Meet Immediate Flood Needs

AID TO BE RUSHED

WPA Administrators Told to Give Assistance Upon Request

Washington, March 18—(Associated Press)—President Roosevelt today mobilized Federal agencies to advance immediate aid to flooded areas.

He appointed a committee headed by Secretary Dern to give whatever aid is necessary to prevent loss of life and destruction of property. The use of any government equipment required was authorized.

Other members of the emergency flood committee included Secretary Morgenthau, the acting secretary of the Navy, Rear Admiral Adolphus Andrews; Harry Hopkins, works progress administrator, and Robert Fechner, director of the civilian conservation corps.

The committee was directed to cooperate with the American Red Cross. The President put army planes at the service of the Red Cross to fly that agency's officers to the Johnstown, Pa., area.

The President issued the following memorandum to the emergency flood committee:

"I request that you act as a committee to determine and to carry out such plans as may be necessary on the part of the Federal government to prevent loss of life, destruction of property and distress arising from spring floods ..."

Families Fleeing Homes; Workers Build Barricades

City Has Only 24-Hour Supply of Water—No Relief in Sight—All Schools Closed—Health Warning Issued

Disaster swept over the Triple Cities today on the crest of a flood unequalled in the history of the area.

Striking at all sections of the city, raging torrents of water mocked efforts of hundreds of workers who were waging a battle against almost insurmountable odds to protect the city from further damage.

With both the Susquehanna and Chenango rivers at the highest levels in history, a survey of the damage already registered revealed:

The city waterworks flooded, disabling all pumping equipment and leaving the city with water to last only one day.

A sand bag barricade at McDonald avenue swept away, pouring torrents of water into Front street, Gaines street, Vality street, Franklin street and Winding Way, flooding scores of homes.

The entire First Ward threatened with a worst disaster than that of last July if workers fighting to hold back the Chenango river with a sandbag barricade at Prospect street are unsuccessful in their fight.

A further rise in the rivers is predicted. Breaking of the barricade at McDonald avenue was expected to halt the rise in the water level of the Chenango river temporarily, but a further increase was expected this afternoon.

All seven bridges of the city are closed except the Memorial bridge, with the South Side completely isolated.

The Court street bridge is reported in danger of being swept away.

Hundreds of families are evacuating homes throughout flooded districts of Binghamton, Endicott and Johnson City.

The waterworks at the Binghamton State hospital is out of commission and hundreds of patients are being supplied from a reservoir containing approximately one day's supply.

The Endicott waterworks is about to be closed with only one day's supply available in reservoirs.

All highways leading into Binghamton closed to traffic.

Residents of the Triple Cities warned to boil all drinking water.

Three National Guard companies mobilized to assist police if their services are needed.

Factories of the Endicott Johnson corporation and the International Business Machines corporation closed.

With the breaking of the sand bag barricade in MacDonald avenue scores of residents began a frantic exodus from their homes, carrying children, pets and household goods.

Officials pointed out that this break in the flood barrier threatened the Endicott Johnson power plant at C. F. J. Park if the water pushes through the First Ward into Johnson City.

With the disablement of the water works, Fire Chief Elmer J. Brown stressed the fire hazard that results and urged that watchmen be stationed in every store and other establishment throughout the city tonight.

Water reached so high a level in the engine and pump rooms of the Waterworks that it was necessary to shut down the plant at about 12:05 p.m. ...

It was stated by officials at the plant that five and a half million gallons of water were in the reservoirs. This, they said, was only enough to last the city a day at ordinary rate of consumption but would do for two or three days if the people are careful not to use more than is absolutely necessary and no bad fires break out.

At 1 o'clock the water pouring over the upper Court street retaining wall had pushed up within two feet of the Tompkins street bridge.

Five small gas tanks in the rear of the larger ones of the Binghamton Gas Works had been partly tipped over by the force of the overflow and was leaking from them ...

...

H. W. Green, in charge of 48 men manning the sand bag dike ... Front street at Prospect street, ... stated that if it is possible to prevent the water from breaking through this barricade it ... save thousands of dollars of damage in the First Ward.

He announced that it was necessary to reinforce the barricade with four thicknesses of sand bags to meet the increasing pressure of the river. The barricade also was extended back of the Romp ... filling station as the flood waters continued to rise.

City Engineer John A. Giles, who was called back from Washington because of the emergency here, this afternoon was attempting to obtain an army plane from the War Department to make the trip.

T. E. Reed, U. S. meteorologist, of Binghamton, also was ordered to return home at once.

Throughout the morning scores of workers racing against time to throw up sand bag barricades were reinforced by hundreds of additional workers recruited from various city departments and the WPA.

At 2 o'clock the question of whether the sand bag barricades in Front street would hold still was in doubt as the rivers con-

(Continued on Page Three)

Chaplin and Leading Lady in Singapore, Are Silent

Singapore, Straits Settlements, March 18—(Associated Press)—Charles Chaplin and his leading lady, Paulette Goddard, arrived here today from Shanghai, as close-mouthed as mummies about what the actor insisted was "our private affairs."

Both talked freely about their Far Eastern holiday, but neither would confirm or deny reports that they planned to marry here after disembarking from the steamer Suwa Maru.

March 18, 1936: The worst flood yet left Binghamton with only a 24-hour supply of water. *Microfilm archives*

Stella School students, 1936-37. The school was on Route 17 Interchange and Airport Road in Binghamton. *Courtesy Rudy Bystrak*

Horse Traders' Convention held in the Village of Kirkwood, circa 1937. In front of the barn, owned by Elta Benjamin, is the area where the convention was held. Those known: Elta Benjamin, at far left, Theodore Beagell, fourth from right. *Courtesy Dorothy Diffendorf*

"NATWOL"
MARTZ BUS
The Binghamton Sun
STATE PARK-PORT CRANE-CHENANGO BRIDGE-BINGHAMTON
Old Gold

Carriers for The Binghamton Sun take a moment for a photo before leaving on a Blue Mountain Coach Line bus for Rocky Glen, 1937. *Courtesy Alan Jewell*

West End Victory Cutting Room
100% for Red Cross + E J A A

Endicott Johnson Red Cross drive at the west-end shoe factory.
Courtesy Rudy Bystrak

U.-E. DEFEATS CURTIS, 7 TO 0

THE WEATHER

Fair and cooler tonight and Sunday. Lowest tonight 40.

BINGHAMTON PRESS

GRIDIRON NEWS

Today's scores in the nation's football games, with special picture stories--printed FIRST for fans who want to know today's results today.

THE FOOTBALL

Vol. 59, No. 171. TWENTY-FOUR PAGES SATURDAY EVENING, OCTOBER 30, 1937. PRICE THREE CENTS

Norwich Whips North, 41-0; J.C. Wins, 20-0; Cornell Beats Lions, 14-0; Syracuse Victor

Mirabito Stars but Indians Put up Real Battle

Chenango Team Retains Its Unscored on Record With Ease

NORWICH High school's powerful undefeated and unscored upon eleven crushed the little Scarlet Indians of Binghamton North High 41-0 at Binghamton Central High school stadium this afternoon.

Despite the size of the score, Coach Bob Redman's gridders played surprisingly well. Several times [illegible] Indians halted the Chenango county invaders when it looked as though the Purple would boost the total. [illegible]

[illegible] At that time, Norwich's second team was in the game and the Indians battled them on almost even terms.

Dick Watson, left halfback for North, was the outstanding player for the losers. Right end Lindsey and right tackle Marco Mastrogiacomo starred for North on the line.

Norwich scored in the first seven minutes of play, when "Toots" Mirabito, burly fullback, knifed his way through left tackle for 48 yards.

Diminutive Red Morris, substitute Norwich halfback, raced 31 yards around right end for the invaders third touchdown in the second quarter.

FIRST PERIOD

Norwich won the toss and chose to receive, defending the south goal. Lindsey of North kicked off to Palmatier who ran the ball back 18 yards to his own 34. On the first play he skirted left end for 11 and a first down. E. Robertson took a reverse from Palmatier and drove to North's 33 yard line. Toots Mirabito fumbled and North recovered on its own 31. Watson and Thomas gained only two yards for the Indians in two plays and [illegible]

(Continued on Page Seventeen)

He Scores and Scores---That Boy They Call 'Toots'

Mirabito, powerful Norwich fullback, fights his way to a touchdown from North High school's one-yard line in the second period of the game between the Chenango county gridders and North school at B. C. H. S. Stadium this afternoon.

MARTINAK SCORES FOR TORNADO JUST BEFORE GAME ENDS

Thompson Stadium, Stapleton, Oct. 30

SMASHING through to a touchdown from her highly-touted opponents' nine-yard line, with only three minutes to play of game remaining, Union Endicott's Orange Tornado defeated the Curtis high of Staten Island, New York City, 7 to 0 here this afternoon.

Blocking of Bill Wiley's punt by Mitchell Olenski paved the way for Endicott touchdown. The ball sailed out of bounds on the nine yard stripe. Line bucks and an offside penalty put it on the one, whence Rudy Martinak carried it over for six points. Charles Ketchuk's placement added a point.

About 5,000 people saw Coach Ty Cobb's eleven conquer the 1936 mythical eastern secondary school champions in perfect weather, except for a strong crosswind that hurt passing and punting.

The schools, it was learned today, have agreed to a return game at Endicott next fall at a date to be set later.

The Orange and Black received splendid support from the section of about 200 Endicott rooters, urged on by the school's cheer leaders.

FIRST PERIOD

Ketchuk of U.-E. kicked off to Bergendale, who came back 18 to his 32. [illegible]

(Continued on Page Sixteen)

Yonkoski Goes Over 3 Times, Beats Walton

Johnson City's Wildcats bounced back from their 12-0 defeat suffered at the hands of U.-E. last week and trounced Walton High 20 to 0 in a bitterly-fought contest on Johnson Field this afternoon.

The game, witnessed by more than 1,500 fans, was marked by spectacular passing and numerous fumbles by both teams. Johnson City scored one touchdown in the second period and two in the final period. Walton's gridders came to Johnson City with only 12 points scored against them this season but bowed under the Wildcats' heavy aerial attack.

Roe, Walton fullback, was easily the outstanding player for the visitors while Hales, who went in for Coddington at quarterback, played stellar ball for the Wildcats.

Yonkoski scored all three touchdowns, the first on a reverse, the second on a pass from Hales and the third on a reverse.

FIRST PERIOD

Walton kicked off to Labakis who ran it back to his own 30 where he fumbled, Silvanic recovering for Johnson City. Labakis fumbled again in the 29 when tackled on a left end run by Belmont. The visitors recovered. Roe's 15-yard pass to McNaught placed the ball on Johnson City's 16.

Belmont lost two yards at right end. Two passes by Roe were incomplete and Johnson City took the ball on downs. Muska cracked right tackle for six yards. Coddington went to the 18 through the same hole. Johnson City failed to gain on the next play and Kurst kicked outside on his own 25 but Walton was offside and the penal-

(Continued on Page Sixteen)

PECK AND EICHLER SCORE AGAINST COLUMBIA FOR BIG RED TEAM IN THIRD

By the Associated Press

Ithaca, Oct. 30

TWO TOUCHDOWNS in the third period, both via the air gave Cornell its first victory since 1931 over Columbia, 14-0, on Schoellkopf field today. Twelve thousand spectators saw Peck score on a 27-yard pass play and Eichler on a 60-yard run after a pass interception. Rose converted both points.

FIRST PERIOD

Columbia halted Cornell's opening 40-yard overland drive on its own 40 on downs, then opened up with Luckman's running and his pass to Radvilas to reach Cornell's 30, where Taylor's fumble was recovered by Moulton. Baker got away for a first down on the Red 45, but Columbia pushed Cornell back in a kicking duel.

Baker and Moulton picked up another first down, but Columbia halted the Cornell running attack. Luckman again outkicked Hooper, one of the Cornell guard's punts dripping short on Columbia's 44. Luckman's return punt went out on Cornell's 7 as the period ended.

SECOND PERIOD

Taylor's second fumble, recovered by Holland, gave Cornell the ball on Columbia's 27 and Baker passed to Holland on Columbia's 23. Columbia batted down two more passes and took the ball when Holland just failed to gain first down on the Blue 11. Cornell pushed the Lions back to the 8, and Luckman's punt reached only to the Blue 31.

[illegible]

THIRD PERIOD

Columbia again halted Cornell on the two yard mark after Van Baker intercepted Luckman's pass and returned it 15 yards to the [illegible]

(Continued on Page Sixteen)

YALE AND DARTMOUTH WIND UP BITTER FIGHT IN 9-9 TIE

New Haven, Oct. 30—(Associated Press)—Yale and Dartmouth played a bitter tussle to 9-9 tie this afternoon after Yale scored in a last minute rally.

FIRST PERIOD

The official attendance was set at 78,000 as Dartmouth's Gibson kicked off to Yale's 20. The Eli's converted early kicking "breaks" to brief advantage. They gained possession at midfield after an exchange between Hutchinson and Colwell. Captain Clint Frank twice picked up the yardage needed for first down but the Blue stalled on the Green's 43-yard line and Colwell booted into the end zone. Neither running attack showed much until Dartmouth, following a poor kick by Colwell which [illegible]

caromed out on the Green's 38, seized its first chance to open up. Hollingsworth completed a pass to Giles for first down on the Green's 42. Then Bob MacLeod broke around his own right end to cross midfield and reach Yale's 47. The speedy Bill Hutchinson combined with MacLeod to make it four first downs in succession as the Indians slashed to the Eli 21. Dartmouth's drive ended just short of Yale's 20-yard stripe as the period ended. Hollingsworth passed once into the end zone, over the heads of all [illegible]

(Continued on Page Seventeen)

Today's Football Scores

	First Period	Second Period	Third Period	Fourth Period	Final Score
NORWICH	7	20	0	14	41
NORTH HIGH	0	0	0	0	0
WALTON	0	0	0	0	0
JOHNSON CITY	0	7	0	13	20
UNION-ENDICOTT	0	0	0	7	7
CURTIS H. N. Y. C.	0	0	0	0	0
KANSAS	0	0	0	0	0
MICHIGAN STATE	0	0	0	16	16
TEMPLE	0	0	0	0	0
HOLY CROSS	0	0	0	0	0
TUFTS	0	0	0	0	0
BROWN	6	0	6	7	19
HARVARD	13	7	0	14	34
PRINCETON	0	6	0	0	6
V. M. I.	0	0	0	0	0
ARMY	6	0	7	7	20
LEHIGH	0	0	0	0	0
RUTGERS	6	7	7	14	34
NORTH CAR. STATE	0	6	0	6	12
BOSTON COLLEGE	7	0	0	0	7
COLUMBIA	0	0	0	0	0
CORNELL	0	0	14	0	14
NAVY	0	0	7	0	7
PENNSYLVANIA	0	14	0	0	14
FRANKLIN & MAR.	0	0	0	0	0
LAFAYETTE	0	0	0	14	14
OHIO STATE	0	14			
CHICAGO	0	0			
VILLANOVA	7	0	0		
DETROIT	0	0	0		
CARNEGIE TECH	0	7	0	7	14
PITTSBURGH	6	3	9	7	25
COLGATE	0	0	7	0	7
NEW YORK U.	7	0	0	7	14
DARTMOUTH	0	0	0	9	9
YALE	0	2	0	7	9
NOTRE DAME	7	0	0	0	
MINNESOTA	0	6	0		
FORDHAM	7	0	7		
NORTH CAROLINA	0	0	0		

(Continued on Page Sixteen)

Orange Stages Comeback for 19-13 Victory

Syracuse, Oct. 30 — (Associated Press) — Under clear skies Syracuse and Penn State elevens lined up today in a rivalry that dates back to 1922. Syracuse won, 19 to 13.

FIRST PERIOD

A punting duel rapidly developed after both teams found an alert and swift charging opposition line too much for a ground attack.

Penn State got the first break when Halfback Jack Hinkle fumbled on the Orange 25-yard mark and the Lions recovered. Wear, tiny Penn State halfback, made it a first down on the Syracuse ten. Syracuse stiffened but on the fourth play the officials ruled interference on a goal line pass and State was given a first down on the one-foot line. On the next play Skemp, reserve back, bucked for the score. Substitute Pollack's try for point failed as the period ended with the score Penn State, 6; Syracuse, 0.

SECOND PERIOD

Penn State got another break as the second period began when De Marino, State tackle, blocked Marvil's punt on the Orange 15-yard line and Toretti recovered for State. Wear promptly ran 25 yards on a wide sweep around right end to score after completely fooling the Syracuse defense. Pollack's try for point was good.

Penn State threatened to score again a short time later after a scintillating march from midfield but Syracuse finally stiffened and stopped the drive. Rabbit Wear again did most of the work but

(Continued on Page Sixteen)

Army Defeats V. M. I., 20 to 7 Before 27,000

West Point, Oct. 30—(Associated Press)—Army worked a hard driving attack by land and air today to rout Virginia Military Institute, 20 to 7, in their intersectional football battle before a capacity crowd of 27,000 spectators today. Held to six points the first half, the Cadets found the scoring range and were unstoppable by the red-shirted invaders.

Penn Crushes Navy, 14-7, in Surprise Win

Philadelphia, Oct. 30—(Associated Press)—Pennsylvania beat Navy, 14-7, today in the twenty-second game of their football series dating back to 1888 before a near-capacity crowd of 63,000.

Navy was trying for a comeback after its defeat by Notre Dame last Saturday.

FIRST PERIOD

Navy staged three consistent marches, ending on Penn's 7-, 16- and 19-yard lines but could not muster the drive to push over a score. Penn, aided by Daly's 14-yard drive through center, moved along to Navy's 24 before losing the

(Continued on Page Seventeen)

HARVARD CRUSHES TIGERS, 34-6, BEFORE 50,000 FANS

Princeton, N. J., Oct. 30—(Associated Press)—In the sixtieth renewal of their "Big Three" gridiron rivalry today, Harvard scored its first victory over Princeton since 1923. The score was 34 to 6.

A near-capacity crowd of 50,000 sat in on the proceedings in Palmer Stadium, shedding their overcoats as an Indian-summer sun beat down on the arena. Each team had been beaten once this year, the Tigers by Cornell, Harvard by Dartmouth.

FIRST PERIOD

Starting off with Mountain's 32-yard runback of Struck's kickoff, Princeton rolled to two first downs and the Harvard 45 on line plays and sweeps before Mountain kicked out of bounds on the Crimson 13. When MacDonald's punt went almost straight up, the Tigers had first down on the invaders' 43.

Princeton couldn't gain, kicked, and Harvard got its first break as the Tigers were penalized 15 yards for interfering with MacDonald when the Harvard right half signalled for a fair catch. With Struck carrying the ball on three plays, Harvard's reverses and fake reverses worked out three straight first downs to the Tigers' 29. Struck, spinning over his own guard, went 16 to the Princeton 7 for another first down. With fourth and one, MacDonald plowed over his own left tackle for the touchdown. Boston's kick was good.

Princeton was given an advantage when Struck's kickoff went [illegible]

(Continued on Page Seventeen)

October 30, 1937: On Saturday evenings, the Press devoted a special front page to football news. *Courtesy Paul S. Kucera*

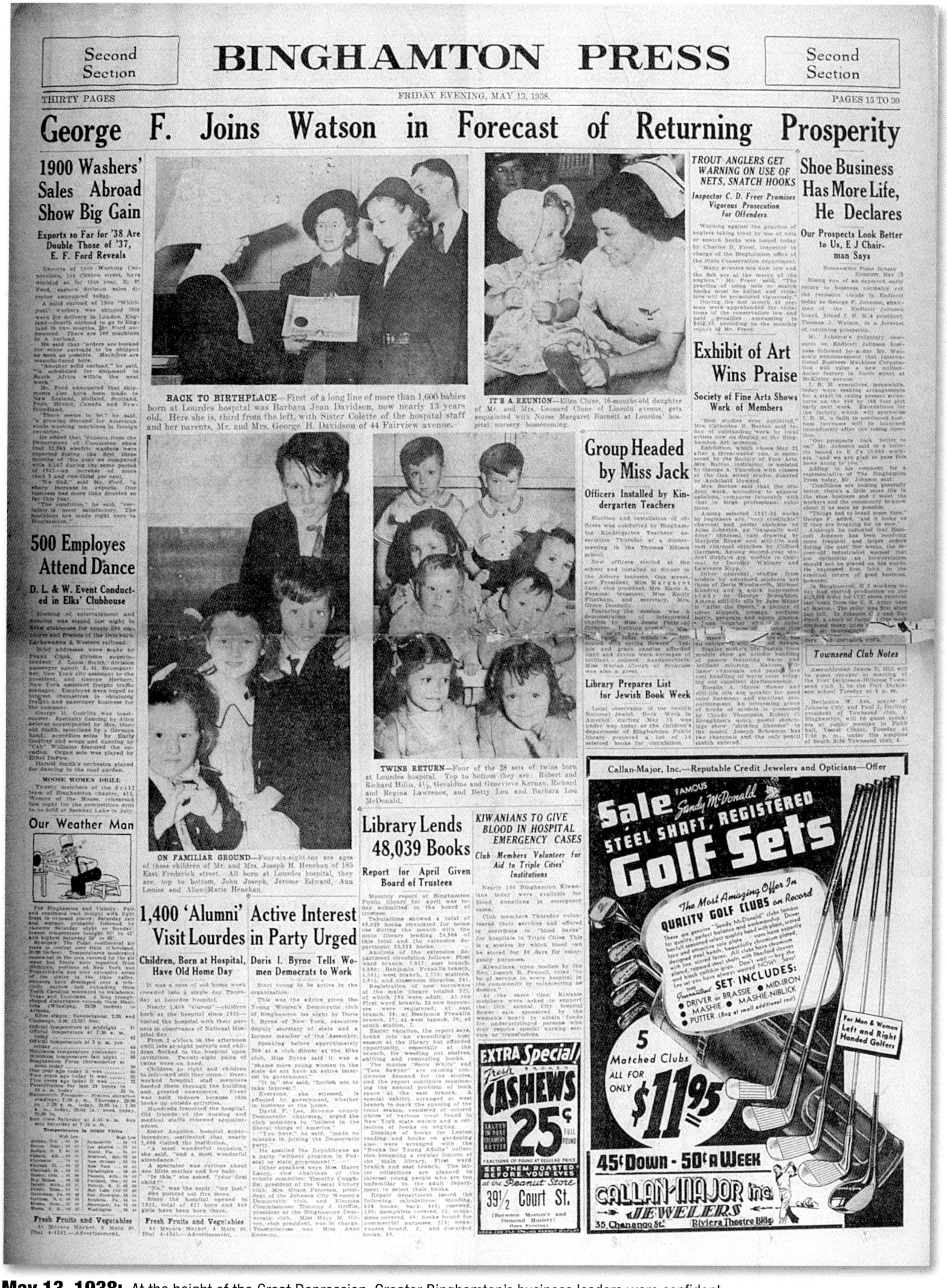
Second Section

BINGHAMTON PRESS

Second Section

THIRTY PAGES — FRIDAY EVENING, MAY 13, 1938. — PAGES 15 TO 30

George F. Joins Watson in Forecast of Returning Prosperity

1900 Washers' Sales Abroad Show Big Gain

Exports so Far for '38 Are Double Those of '37, E. F. Ford Reveals

BACK TO BIRTHPLACE—First of a long line of more than 1,600 babies born at Lourdes hospital was Barbara Jean Davidson, now nearly 13 years old. Here she is, third from the left, with Sister Colette of the hospital staff and her parents, Mr. and Mrs. George H. Davidson of 44 Fairview avenue.

IT'S A REUNION—Ellen Clune, 16-months-old daughter of Mr. and Mrs. Leonard Clune of Lincoln avenue, gets acquainted with Nurse Margaret Burnett at Lourdes' hospital nursery homecoming.

TROUT ANGLERS GET WARNING ON USE OF NETS, SNATCH HOOKS

Inspector C. D. Freer Promises Vigorous Prosecution for Offenders

Shoe Business Has More Life, He Declares

Our Prospects Look Better to Us, E J Chairman Says

Exhibit of Art Wins Praise

Society of Fine Arts Shows Work of Members

500 Employes Attend Dance

D. L. & W. Event Conducted in Elks' Clubhouse

Group Headed by Miss Jack

Officers Installed by Kindergarten Teachers

Library Prepares List for Jewish Book Week

Townsend Club Notes

MOOSE WOMEN DRILL

ON FAMILIAR GROUND—Four-six-eight-ten are ages of these children of Mr. and Mrs. Joseph H. Heneham of 185 East Frederick street. All born at Lourdes hospital, they are, top to bottom, John Joseph, Jerome Edward, Ann Louise and Alice Marie Heneham.

TWINS RETURN—Four of the 28 sets of twins born at Lourdes hospital. Top to bottom they are: Robert and Richard Hillis, 4½, Geraldine and Genevieve Kernan, Richard and Regina Lawrence, and Betty Lou and Barbara Lou McDonald.

Our Weather Man

Library Lends 48,039 Books

Report for April Given Board of Trustees

KIWANIANS TO GIVE BLOOD IN HOSPITAL EMERGENCY CASES

Club Members Volunteer for Aid to Triple Cities' Institutions

1,400 'Alumni' Visit Lourdes

Children, Born at Hospital, Have Old Home Day

Active Interest in Party Urged

Doris I. Byrne Tells Women Democrats to Work

Fresh Fruits and Vegetables

Fresh Fruits and Vegetables

EXTRA Special!
Fresh CASHEWS
25¢
SEE THEM ROASTED BEFORE YOUR EYES
at the Peanut Store
39½ Court St.
Callan-Major, Inc.—Reputable Credit Jewelers and Opticians—Offer
Sale
FAMOUS Sandy McDonald
STEEL SHAFT, REGISTERED
Golf Sets
The Most Amazing Offer In QUALITY GOLF CLUBS on Record
SET INCLUDES:
DRIVER or BRASSIE
MID-IRON
MASHIE
MASHIE-NIBLICK
PUTTER
For Men & Women Left and Right Handed Golfers
5 Matched Clubs
ALL FOR ONLY
$11.95
45¢ Down - 50¢ A Week
CALLAN-MAJOR Inc
JEWELERS
35 Chenango St.
Riviera Theatre Bldg

May 13, 1938: At the height of the Great Depression, Greater Binghamton's business leaders were confident. *Courtesy Paul S. Kucera*

Coca-Cola
DANCELAND
DINNERS 25¢
HERB'S PLACE
BEER
GREGORY'S

Kirkwood Speedway was run by Elta Benjamin around 1938. It was located where Kirkwood Veterans' (Memorial) Park is now. *Courtesy Dorothy Diffendorf*

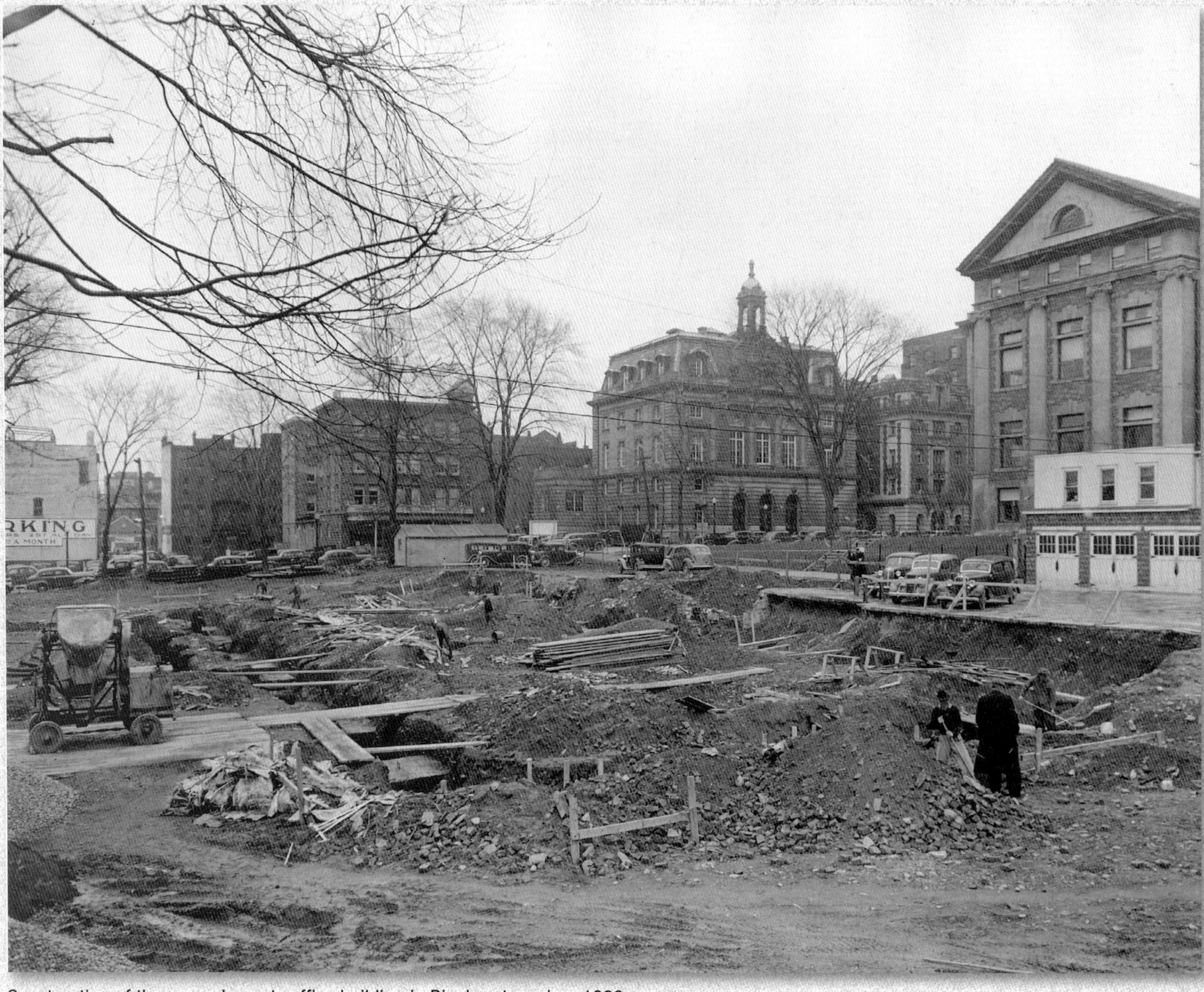
RKING

Construction of the second county office building in Binghamton, circa 1939. *Courtesy Alan Jewell*

THE WEATHER

Probably showers tonight. Tuesday possibly fair. Slightly cooler tonight.

BINGHAMTON PRESS

City Edition

Vol. 60, No. 83. TWENTY-TWO PAGES MONDAY EVENING, JULY 18, 1938. PRICE THREE CENTS

CORRIGAN, IN PATCHED UP $900 PLANE, FLIES SOLO TO IRELAND IN 28 HOURS

Queen Marie of Rumania Is Dead at 62

Dies Two Days After Return From Dresden

Suffers Relapse When Physicians Hope For Recovery

ILL ALMOST A YEAR

Burial Will Be Beside Her Husband; Nation in Mourning

By the Associated Press

Bucharest, July 18—Dowager Queen Marie of Rumania, who helped shape the destiny of her country for a generation, died today in her sixty-third year.

The Queen Mother, famed for her beauty, died at her palace at Sinaia, the royal summer residence, at 6:25 p. m. (11:25 a. m., E. S. T.).

Prime Minister Miron Cristea, who also is patriarch of the Rumanian Orthodox church, celebrated mass in the palace immediately after her passing. Previously he had administered extreme unction as death neared.

In Bucharest all public buildings immediately displayed flags at half staff.

King Carol, her son, and Crown Prince Mihai and Princess Elizabeth of Greece were at the queen's bedside. Her last illness found her in the same bed in which her husband, King Ferdinand died in 1927.

The queen had been dangerously ill for most of the past year. However, only Saturday she had returned to Rumania from Dresden after a month in a sanatorium and had been welcomed home ceremoniously.

There was a serious relapse yes-

(Continued on Page Twenty-two)

JOURNEY'S END—Dowager Queen Marie of Rumania who died today after a long illness. (Other pictures, life story on Page 22.)

More Victims Added in Jew, Arab Conflict

Bomb Throwing Continues in Haifa; Jerusalem Tension Heightened

Jerusalem, July 18 (AP)—A fresh wave of disorders swept Palestine today, adding more victims to the toll of the bitter Arab-Jew conflict.

One Jew was killed and three wounded while working in the fields at an isolated Jewish settlement in the Beisan valley near Tiberias. First reports said they were ambushed by an Arab band. One of the attackers was killed.

An Arab who appeared on the streets of Safad in defiance of the curfew law was shot and killed by soldiers.

(Before today's clashes the toll of the renewed conflict, dating from July 3, had reached 79 Arabs and 31 Jews killed, 139 Arabs and 162 Jews wounded.)

Bomb-throwing continued unchecked in Haifa. Two bombs exploded in the city, but no casualties were reported.

Tension in Jerusalem was heightened today by reports that a mysterious leader was mobilizing a large terrorist force on the outskirts of the city.

There was and could be no confirmation of the story at once, but among the rumors was one that the supposed new organizer had entered the country only a few days ago.

Fear of reprisals might have been one reason for silence among those who knew definitely—officials here saw an indication of such fear in the fact that not one informer claimed any part of $175,-000 in rewards for tipping the government to hiding places of terrorist gangs.

The violence continued, and there were several instances yesterday of attacks at twilight upon persons walking or riding at the edges of towns.

Sunday's scattered incidents brought death to five Arabs and three Jews. One Arab, two Jews and one British policeman were wounded.

Snipers concealed in an orange grove at Ramatgan, near Telaviv, shot dead a Jewish wagon driver. Near Hadera, on the plain of Sharon, an Arab quietly drew his revolver and killed a Jewish policeman after chatting with him for half an hour.

A gang raided a military post near Jaffa and seized a trench mortar. Three Arabs were killed near Telaviv and Jaffa.

West Is 'at Sea' With President on Third Term

Many, Including Some in Immediate Party, Are Wondering

STILL DRAWING CARD

Crowds Turning Out to See Him, Shows He Still Is Popular

San Diego, Cal., July 18 (INS)—President Roosevelt headed southward into the blue Pacific today, leaving a great many people in this western country, including some members of his own immediate party, wondering whether he plans to be a candidate for a third term.

Certainly, Mr. Roosevelt neither saw nor experienced anything on his 16-day crossing of the continent to discourage the idea—if such an idea is lurking in his mind.

As on his previous trips into the great west which lies beyond the Mississippi river, Mr. Roosevelt met with continuous enthusiastic welcomes which might better be described as ovations.

Whether it was a major stop or a brief appearance on the rear platform for a wave and a few words at some desert spot it was always the same — enthusiasm, cheers and, occasionally, a shout from the crowd "how about 1940?"

Mr. Roosevelt took it all in his stride, good humored and laughing. Neither by expression nor demeanor did he indicate his attitude toward 1940. Nor did he show any signs of having heard the

(Continued on Page Eighteen)

—Wide World Photo.

HE 'DID IT' IN $900 PLANE—The world was amazed this morning when Douglas Corrigan, 31, brought his nine-year-old $900 plane down on the Baldonnel Airport, near Dublin, Ireland, after a 28-hour flight from Floyd Bennett Airport, New York. Mr. Corrigan made a non-stop 2,700-mile hop from California to New York, July 9. An admirer of Colonel Charles A. Lindbergh, he helped build Lindy's 'Spirit of St. Louis' in 1927. (Other pictures and stories on Page 2.)

Crossed Sea 'by Mistake,' Says Aviator

Tells Amazed Irish Officials He Thought He Was Flying to California

HAS NO AIR PERMIT

Puts His 9-Year-Old Ship Down Near Dublin; Had No Radio

By International News Service

Dublin, July 18 — With the astounding explanation he had flown the Atlantic ocean "by mistake," Douglas P. Corrigan set his nine-year-old $900 aerial "jalopy" down at Baldonnel airport today after a flight as courageous and unique as the immortal achievement of Colonel Charles A. Lindbergh.

Unheralded and unexpected, he landed at Baldonnel at 2:30 p. m. (9:30 a. m., E. D. T.), just 28 hours and 13 minutes after taking off from Floyd Bennett airport, New York.

He ran straight into the arms of the Irish customs authorities, who for some time after his arrival held him up on the grounds he had no right to land on Irish soil without official permission.

"When I took off from Floyd Bennett airport," he said, "I headed out toward the ocean to escape the New York aeronautical authorities.

"I thought I turned back west but found out later I had crossed the ocean by mistake.

"I went up high and was over the clouds for the entire trip. When I thought the proper time had elapsed, I descended expecting to see Los Angeles beneath me.

"Instead it was Ireland."

Without passport, landing permit or other credentials of the sort, Mr. Corrigan went straight to a telephone and called the United States legation.

"I told them who I was and what I had done," he said. "They never heard of me. I guess they thought it was some one trying to play a joke. They hung up the phone."

Incredible as it may seem, Mr. Corrigan's amazing description of his epic flight had bore some touch of logic. When he flew nonstop from California to New York a week ago, the 2,700-mile flight took him just 10 minutes under 28 hours.

He has been in the air only a little more than this time when, as he said, he ducked down from above the clouds to get his bearings and learned—to his undying amazement, he soberly declared—that he had entered aviation's hall of fame with a solo flight across the Atlantic.

When he landed at Baldonnel, Mr. Corrigan had but 75 gallons left of the 320 gallons of gasoline he had loaded aboard his ancient "crate" for the takeoff.

Early reports said Mr. Corrigan planned to continue on to Croydon Aerodrome, near London, but it later appeared he would spend the

(Continued on Page Two)

German-American Camp 'Bombed' With Leaflets

Yaphank, July 18 (AP) — Camp Siegfried, a resort maintained by the German-American Settlement League, an affiliate of the German-American Bund, was "bombed" yesterday by 25,000 red, white and blue leaflets dropped from a plane chartered by the Non-sectarian Anti-Nazi League.

The leaflets, which fell among 1,500 German-American residents eating picnic lunches at the camp, listed the qualities of a "real American" and stressed the "obvious advantages of living in a country governed by the people and not by dictators."

The camp has been assailed by American Legion officials as a "center of Nazi propaganda."

Retired U. S. Financier Renounces Citizenship

New York, July 18 (AP)—William M. Greve, 54-year-old former financier and yachtsman, has renounced his American citizenship to become a subject of Liechtenstein, a tiny tax-free principality in the Swiss Alps.

A certificate of admission, listing him as an alien when he arrived in this country to visit his daughter, disclosed his transfer of allegiance.

Mr. Greve was born in New York. He retired from business in 1926.

Remember 'Way Back When

Men looked like they were poured into their trousers and button shoes were all the rage. Old Dobbin was actually a means of transportation and not just an exercise or sport. Ladies hats resembled a cross between a flower or vegetable garden and a bird's nest.

Lillian Russell was the toast of the American stage and the Floradora girls were the popular sextette.

Binghamton Press Want Ads have been the popular result producers for the public of the Triple Cities for years. And they're still going strong. No matter what you have for sale, rent or trade you'll find them both effective and economical.

Just Dial 2-2411 or call Endicott 141 (no toll) and ask for an ad-taker.

Truck Drivers Vote to End Strike in New Orleans

New Orleans, July 18 (AP)—Paul Heide, organizer for the Committee for Industrial Organization, said today that C. I. O.-affiliated truck drivers had voted to end a strike against eleven drayage firms called June 22.

He said the United Transport Workers, Local Industrial Union No. 501, unanimously voted to call off the strike "in order to consolidate the union on the job and prepare for the hearing set by the National Labor Relations Board."

New Blast Rips Oil Refinery at Wellsville; Loss Is 5 Million

100 Weary Firemen Avert Another Explosion by Snuffing Out Blaze in 50,000-Barrel Storage Tank—3 Spectators Killed; 75 Hurt

Wellsville, July 18 (AP)—A spectacular explosion early today spread new havoc in the $15,000,000 Sinclair Oil Co. refinery where three men were killed and 75 injured in a chaos of fire and explosions last night, but firemen finally appeared to be bringing the fire under control.

A storage tank containing 2,100 barrels of naphtha exploded shortly before daybreak with a deafening roar and a cloud-sweeping flash of fire. No one was reported injured, but a similar tank, exploding last night, skyrocketed clear across the nearby Genesee river and killed three spectators on the opposite bank.

Chief Hollis Johnston of the company's fire department said damage, including business as well as stock and equipment, would amount to about $5,000,000.

Emergency calls for oil fire fighting chemicals were broadcast through western New York and Pennsylvania after the new explosion today. Soon afterward, a 50,000 barrel tank of highly inflammable naphtha caught fire, but a crew of 100 tired firemen took their lives in their hands and approached close enough to snuff out the fire with chemicals.

Other explosions, less intense, jarred the refinery during the forenoon but there were no further injuries and each hour found firemen more hopeful that the fire might be extinguished by night.

One explosion burst open an 80,000 gallon "chilling tower" filled with naphtha. This was one of several gaunt towers which stood above

(Continued on Page Seventeen)

Plane 800 Ft. in Air Turned Over by Blast

Wellsville, July 18 (UP)—Eyewitnesses today gave these accounts of the explosions and fire sweeping the 75-acre Sinclair Oil Refinery just south of here:

B. HARRIS, Wellsville aviator—I was flying about 800 feet above the fire when the naphtha tank blew yesterday. The explosion was so terrific that it turned my plane completely over in the air. I never saw anything like it. I thought it was a tornado.

DICK THOMAS, student—I was standing down on the flats when the tank went. The cover that killed those people missed me by about ten feet. I was running to get off the flats when I heard the explosion. I stumbled and fell. I thought I was a goner then. I suffered burns from the heat.

MRS. JOHN BRYSON, Wellsville housewife—I saw the naphtha tank explosion yesterday afternoon. There was a rumble like an earthquake. A ball of fire seemed to shoot over the plant buildings. I was standing in the cemetery at the time. The flaming tank top landed in the gully below the cemetery. It was an awful sight.

Nazi Secret Police Seize Wulle, Who Aided Hitler

Berlin, July 18 (AP) — Reinhold Wulle, publicist and nationalist who hid Adolf Hitler for weeks in 1923, has been arrested with his wife and several members of his publication staff, it was disclosed today.

Herr Wulle and his wife were seized by the Gestapo (secret police) between 6 a. m. and 7 a. m. on July 14. Several of his coworkers were taken at 9 a. m. as they reported for work. The Gestapo refused to give any reasons.

Herr Wulle, 55, ran a little publishing house known as National Book Service.

Japanese Fire Chinese Planes With Matches

Land at Inland Airport in Most Daring Attack of the War

Shanghai, July 18 (UP)—A Japanese navy communique today said a squadron of Japanese airplanes had landed early this morning at Nanchang airport, in the heart of Chinese territory, set fire to Chinese planes with matches, and escaped.

The raid was described as "the most daring attack in the annals of the war" and the communique said all but one of the Japanese planes engaged in the raid had returned safely to their bases.

According to the Japanese reports, the crews of the bombers vaulted from the planes the instant they came to a stop on the Nanchang landing field, ran to the hangars where Chinese planes were stored and touched off the fires with matches.

They also chased a gasoline truck driver, who tried to escape from the field, into a nearby rice field, the report said.

Two machine guns were seized from the Chinese planes and the raiders also prowled through vacant hangars, but found nothing worth taking.

The communique said a total of 78 Chinese planes were destroyed, including eight "fighters" shot down in a dog-fight near Nanchang, just before the raiding squadron landed.

Seven planes were bombed from the air as the raiding planes swept over the airfield, and then the Japanese landed and set fire to five remaining planes.

King and Queen Pack Trunks for Paris Trip; Leave Tomorrow

London, July 18 (AP)—One hundred heavy trunks were trundled out of Buckingham Palace this morning, the equipage of King George and his Queen on their state visit to France.

The trunks were sent to Dover, where the royal couple are to start their journey tomorrow aboard the British admiralty yacht, Enchantress.

A flotilla of nine destroyers arrived at Dover today from Portsmouth to escort the Enchantress, and 12 naval planes also will be on hand when the yacht sails.

The King, recovered from the attack of gastric influenza which sent him to bed a week ago, rested in the palace for the trip which will put a heavy burden on his slender frame.

Queen Elizabeth supervised the final details of packing. They had motored to London from Windsor House last night.

There was a big weekend rush of Britishers to Paris, anxious to see the monarch in the gigantic parades and fanfare France is staging to show the world the two great European democracies still are firm friends.

Englishmen on this side of the channel won't see anything akin to the pageantry Paris has planned—King George and his party will drive "privately" to Victoria Station and board a rose-garlanded royal train for Dover.

Ninety minutes later they are to be aboard the Enchantress.

Paris, July 18 (UP)—Thousands of regular troops and reserve officers were ordered on duty today as France made final preparations for the arrival tomorrow of King George VI and Queen Elizabeth of Great Britain for a four-day state visit regarded as one of the great political events of the year.

Corrigan Tells How He Flew Ocean in 9-Year-Old 'Jalopy'

'Came Down Out of Clouds After 25 Hours to Find a Country I Didn't Recognize,' He Says—Declares Compass Was Set Wrong

(EDITOR'S NOTE: One of the strangest stories ever told—that of a flight across the turbulent Atlantic "by mistake"—was narrated today to International News Service by Douglas P. Corrigan, 31-year-old Los Angeles flier who crossed from New York to Dublin in a $900 plane.)

By Douglas P. Corrigan

AS TOLD EXCLUSIVELY TO INTERNATIONAL NEWS SERVICE.

(Copyright 1938 by International News Service. Reproduction in whole or part strictly prohibited.)

Baldonnel Airport, Dublin, July 18 (INS)—I took off from New York early Sunday morning with the intention of flying back to Los Angeles without a stop.

It was a hurried take-off. I was anxious to get away from the Floyd Bennett authorities, who didn't want me to leave. They had held me up on a night takeoff which I had planned.

Shortly after taking off, I headed into the clouds and had to depend upon my compass. I set my course by what I thought was to the west.

I flew all the way by compass. I couldn't see anything at all because of the clouds and I had to depend upon that instrument.

It was about 25 hours after the start that I decided I had better come down out of the clouds and have a look around. I came down expecting to see Los Angeles. Instead I saw the hills of a countryside that I knew could not possibly be California.

There was no brush below me as there would be on the California coast. I saw a few small fishing boats and these as well as everything else beneath me were unfamiliar in their aspect.

Then I began to get suspicious of myself and check up on my compass. I found I had been flying eastward instead of west.

That was about noon today. Then I headed on still further east and later found myself some miles north of what turned out to be Baldonnel.

By that time I was begining to realize I must be over Ireland and

(Continued on Page Two)

Shure--and Columbus Made Error

Dublin, July 18 (INS)—Said the little Irishman to the big Irishman today:

"But how did Corrigan wind up in Dublin if he started for Los Angeles?"

Said the big Irishman to the little Irishman:

"And what of that? Sure Columbus started for India and wound up in America!"

'Very Remarkable' Says Hughes, Accents 'Very'

Roosevelt Field, July 18 (UP)—Howard Hughes said today that Douglas Corrigan's flight was "very remarkable."

The Texas millionaire, who flew around the world in little more than three times the number of hours it took Mr. Corrigan to pilot his nine-year-old "crate" to Ireland, learned of the Californian's feat when he came here to inspect an airplane.

The flier, dressed in his shirt sleeves, plucked off the now famous brown hat which accompanied him around the world, scratched his head and gazed at the sky for almost half a minute before commenting.

"It's very remarkable," he said, speaking slowly and accenting the "very."

Uncle Worried, Sure Douglas Has No Money

Los Angeles, July 18 (UP)—The clergyman uncle who taught Douglas Corrigan about navigation that led him true to his course to Ireland began worrying today about how to get money to his adventurous nephew.

"The Lord be blessed," exclaimed the Rev. S. Fraser Langford, at news of Mr. Corrigan's successful

(Continued on Page Two)

Nationwide Rail Strike Threatened With Pay Cut

Chicago, July 18 (INS)—Confronted with prospects of a protracted deadlock, railway executives and labor chieftains started negotiations today on a proposed $250,-000,000 wage cut for the nation's 900,000 union railroad workers.

Little hope for immediate settlement was held with both sides firmly voicing determination to stick by their demands. Speaking for the vast army of workers, union chieftains have bluntly told the industry that it must choose between a nation-wide strike or withdrawal of its proposed 15 per cent wage slash.

Railway executives insist that pay cuts must be made as the financial condition of the various roads is so precarious that only immediate remedial action can stave off [illegible].

Labor Vs. Industry

The American public knows the trouble this country is having in labor disputes. But across the sea Sweden and Great Britain have hit upon a formula to settle industrial strife. Webb Miller has made a survey of conditions and has written a series of articles for

The Binghamton Press

He gives a clear cut picture of methods employed to minimize the trouble between capital and labor. The first article appears today.

Turn to Page 22

July 18, 1938: Coverage of "Wrong-Way" Corrigan's famous flight across the Atlantic. *Courtesy Carolyn Fitzgerald*

THE WEATHER
Rain and slightly warmer tonight. Saturday light snow and colder.

BINGHAMTON PRESS

City Edition

Vol. 60, No. 257. THIRTY-TWO PAGES FRIDAY EVENING, FEBRUARY 10, 1939. PRICE THREE CENTS

CARDINALS CALLED TO ELECT NEW POPE AS WORLD MOURNS DEATH OF PIUS XI

Franco Aides Predict Peace in Few Days

Insurgents Assert Miaja Plans to Surrender Madrid Zone

LENIENCY IS PROMISED

Loyalist Premier Flies to Central Zone to Keep up Resistance

By the Associated Press

Perpignan, France, Feb. 10—Peace in Spain within a few days was foreseen today by supporters of Insurgent General Franco.

After the Insurgents' double victory yesterday in reaching France's eastern Pyrenees frontier and taking the Mediterranean island of Minorca, the surrender of the Madrid-Valencia zone — the last territory left to the Spanish government — was confidently predicted.

General Franco's minister of the interior, Ramon Serrano Suner, said in Barcelona "I hope we shall not be long in announcing new and definite successes which will cause joy for all."

Despite denials from the government side and spirited protests of determination to carry on the war, Insurgent sources said General Jose Miaja, dictator of the Madrid-Valencia zone, already was negotiating with General Franco for a peace agreement.

The date of Feb. 14, when the civil war will be just 31 months old, has been suggested for the surrender of the central zone. The terms appeared to be those demanded by Franco—unconditional surrender.

General Franco has long held that this was the only way to end the war. Britain and France seeking to speed peace, were understood, however, to have been assured by the Insurgents that ...

(Continued on Page Twenty-eight)

—Associated Press Photo.
CARDINAL MUNDELEIN

—Associated Press Photo.
CARDINAL DOUGHERTY

—Associated Press Photo.
CARDINAL O'CONNELL

ON WAY TO ROME—Three American cardinals who will sail for Italy to take part in the election of a new pope.

Three Prelates From U. S. Will Travel to Rome

Cardinals O'Connell, Mundelein and Dougherty to Take Part in Elections

ALL ON WAY TO N. Y.

Hope to Sail on Rex, Leaving Tomorrow; Hull Expresses Regrets

Washington, Feb. 10 (U.P.)—Three United States cardinals arranged today to hurry to Rome to take part in the election of a successor to Pope Pius XI and represent this nation's 21,451,460 Catholics in the ensuing, history-making affairs of the church.

At the same time, Secretary of State Hull extended the condolences of the United States on the death of the Pope.

George Cardinal Mundelein, archbishop of Chicago, on a vacation at Hobe Sound, Fla.; Dennis Cardinal Dougherty, archbishop of Philadelphia, and William Cardinal O'Connell, who has been vacationing at Nassau, Bahamas, will attempt to reach the Vatican City before the College of Cardinals convenes on Feb. 25, church dignitaries said.

William Cardinal O'Connell, archbishop of Boston and ranking priest in the sacred college, has been in failing health and was in seclusion at "The Hermitage," Nassau, Bahamas, when the Pope died.

He is flying from the Bahamas on his way to New York. On the deaths of the two previous pontiffs, Pius X and Benedict XV, Cardinal O'Connell speeded to Rome, each time arriving a few hours after a new Pope had been elected. His protest against the college's failure to await the arrival of American cardinals before electing Pope Pius XI caused that Pontiff to promise that upon his death, the election of a successor would be delayed 15 to 18 days, instead of the former 10 days.

Only rarely before have American cardinals been able to participate in papal elections. Catholic officials recalled only two previous instances. In 1903 the late James Cardinal Gibbons voted in the election of Pius X and in 1914 the late Cardinal Farley participated in election of Pope Benedict XV.

Three liners sailing for Europe today and tomorrow would be available to the three cardinals. They are the Italian liner Rex, sailing at noon Saturday and due at Naples Feb. 18; the French liner Paris, sailing at 11:30 a.m. Saturday and due at Havre Feb. 18; and the Cunard White Star liner Queen Mary, sailing at 3:30 p.m. today and due at Southampton Feb. 15. The Italian government was reported to have placed the Rex at the service of American cardinals who decide to make the trip.

Cardinal Mundelein's secretary made plans for him to go to New York where it is hoped the Rex will be held until he arrives.

Cardinal Dougherty, at Philadelphia, is preparing to leave for New York as soon as possible.

Cardinal O'Connell, dean of the United States hierarchy, is 79. Cardinal Dougherty is 73, and Cardinal Mundelein is 66. There were four American cardinals prior to the death of Patrick Cardinal Hayes, archbishop of New York last Sept. 4. Although the three survivors all rank among the first 10 of the 62 cardinal priests in the sacred college, the ranking being based on priority of their creation as cardinals, Cardinal O'Connell has been ...

(Continued on Page Twenty-eight)

Japan Awaits Protests Over Taking Hainan

Chinese Island Seized in Defiance of Great Britain, France

Tokio, Feb. 10 (U.P.)—The government calmly awaited protests from France and Great Britain today over the Japanese seizure of the strategic Chinese island of Hainan, commanding the east coast of French Indo-China and vital British trade routes between Hong Kong and Singapore.

In defiance of warnings from both Great Britain and France, Japanese soldiers and sailors landed on the island at dawn ...

Hainan is only 200 miles from the Philippines ...

Albany Blamed by Dewey for Hines Trial 'Leak'

New York, Feb. 10 ...

—Wide World Photo.

WORLD MOURNS HIS DEATH—Pope Pius XI, shown here at prayer, died last night at 11:31 E. S. T. at the Vatican in his 82nd year.

Cardinals to Meet on 15th Night, Ballot Next Day on New Pontiff

Two-thirds' Vote Necessary for Choice—Italians Are in Majority—Time Extended to Allow American Prelates to Participate

Vatican City, Feb. 10 (U.P.)—Election of the 262d bishop of Rome, successor to Pope Pius XI, will begin in 15 days instead of the hitherto traditional 10, an extension granted by the late pontiff after his election so that American cardinals may participate in the voting.

Whether the American cardinals go to Rome is a matter of their own choice, to be determined by considerations of health and duties in the United States.

Every Pope since 1591 has been an Italian. Usually, as at present, there are more Italian cardinals than those of all other nationalities combined. There are now 37 Italian cardinals and 29 of other nationalities. Only members of the sacred college of cardinals may vote for a Pope. A two-thirds vote is necessary for election.

The conclave for election of a new Pope is called for the 15th night after the pontiff's death and the first ballot is taken on the morning of the 16th day. Two votes are taken daily, one in the morning and one in the afternoon.

The ballots are burned after each vote and Italians, gathered in great numbers to learn the result, believe that this can be determined by the color of the ...

(Continued on Page Twenty-nine)

Unique Rites Mark Pope's Death, Choice

Centuries of Tradition Are Behind Every Act in Vatican

Vatican City, Feb. 10 (P)—There is no person whose death could inaugurate such a chain of picturesque rites as that running its course for Achille Ratti — Pope Pius XI.

From the moment the Holy Father died today until his body ...

(Continued on Page Twenty-Nine)

Getting Back to Horse, Buggy Days

Buffalo, Feb. 10 (U.P.)—A horse was victor over an automobile yesterday in a "battle" near the business section of the city.

The horse, running away with a bakery wagon, reared on its hind legs and rammed a wicked right hoof through the windshield of an automobile which suddenly appeared in front of the animal.

Climbing all over its "opponent" the horse dented the hood of the car and smashed the headlights. Then, cut and bleeding it galloped a short distance away and halted.

The driver of the automobile was uninjured.

Good Deed Is Made Legal

Evansville, Ind., Feb. 10 (P)—When Mrs. Fred Guth died Dec. 21, 1937, her will was accidentally destroyed. Attorney H. L. Taylor thought he had kept a copy but couldn't find it, nor could he recall its contents.

A burglar solved the problem. He broke into Mr. Taylor's office, ransacked it and strewed papers all over the floor.

Among the scattered documents was the missing copy of Mrs. Guth's will.

F. D. R. Sends Vatican 'Profound Condolences'

Washington, Feb. 10 ...

Palace Has Non-Lighting Lights, No-Water Bathtubs

New York, Feb. 10 (P)—A palace of 200 rooms, each with a bathtub but no running water—and with electric lighting fixtures throughout but no electricity ...

Roosevelt Confined to His Bed With Slight Attack of Grippe

Washington, Feb. 10 (U.P.)—President Roosevelt was suffering from a slight attack of grippe today and all White House engagements were cancelled.

Dr. Ross T. McIntire, White House physician, said Mr. Roosevelt's temperature was 99—one degree of fever. He instructed the Chief Executive to remain in bed today.

White House Secretary Stephen T. Early said Mr. Roosevelt likely would be confined to bed over the weekend. All engagements, including the usual Friday morning press conference, were cancelled.

"He has a light touch of grippe," Mr. Early said.

The President's indisposition set in yesterday when he was confined to his room by a slight head cold but saw several callers.

'Peace' Last Word of Pontiff; Pacelli Temporary Head

Papal Secretary of State Summons Prelates to Election Feb. 25—Thousands in St. Peter's Square Kneel in Prayer

By the United Press

Vatican City, Feb. 10—The body of Pope Pius XI, who died at dawn today with a faint whisper of "Peace" as his last message to a troubled world, was transferred this afternoon with all the pomp of the Catholic church to the Sistine chapel of the Vatican.

The mournful procession from the Pope's private apartments to the chapel was headed by the Swiss guards in their medieval uniforms, and included the entire diplomatic corps to the Holy See, all the cardinals now in Rome, the Palatine guards, the staff officers of the various armed corps of the papal state, and ecclesiastical and lay dignitaries.

The Pope lay in state in semi-private surroundings in the Sistine chapel tonight, but tomorrow the body will be removed to St. Peter's and the public will be permitted to file past the bier.

It was the first time since the death of Leo XIII in 1903 that the body of a Pope had been placed in the Sistine chapel—in which are the famous Raphael frescoes—before the formal lying-in-state at St. Peter's. It had been customary in recent years to remove the body to the throne room.

This afternoon only the Roman aristocracy, members of the diplomatic corps and officials of Vatican state were permitted to file past the body, which was clad in pontifical white robe with a red-hooded cape which hung loosely over the head and shoulders and revealed a serene expression on the face of the dead Pontiff.

A silver crucifix was pressed into the white-gloved hands of the Pope and four noble guards with drawn swords pointed at the floor stood as a death guard around the bier.

The transfer of the body to the Sistine chapel followed the taking of a death mask by the official Vatican engraver and sculptor, Aurelio Mistruzzi, and a formal act of identification of the body by Cardinal Pacelli and members of the apostolic chamber.

There were several changes in the ages-old ritual which accompanies the death of a Pope. Cardinal Pacelli did not carry out all of the ritual in connection with formal declaration that the Pope had died. Instead, he solemnly looked down upon the Pope and said:

"The Pope is truly dead."

The custom, five centuries old, of striking the Pope thrice on the forehead with a silver hammer and repeating his Christian name—Achille—with each blow, was omitted.

The only other change of importance in the ceremony was the selection of the Sistine chapel instead of the throne room for the repose of the body until the formal lying-in-state in St. Peter's.

As his quiet voice broke the stillness beside the bed, the penitentiaries of St. Peter, the cardinals and high officials of the Vatican who were present fell to their knees and recited "De Profundis."

The ring of St. Peter the Fisherman, then was removed from the Pope's lifeless finger and given to Cardinal Pacelli to keep as a symbol of authority until the concord elects a new pope.

The procession from the private apartments of the Pope to the Sistine chapel lasted about 10 minutes.

Eugenio Cardinal Pacelli assumed active leadership of the Roman Catholic church ...

(Continued on Page Twenty)

INDEX ON PICTURES, STORIES ABOUT POPE

Index to Features

February 10, 1939: Months before Germany and the Soviet Union invaded Poland, a dying pope called for peace. *Microfilm archives*

JOHN HIZA
RICHFIELD

John Hiza Sr., stand operator, shows off his meat products at the Endicott Johnson Public Market in the late 1930s. *Courtesy John G. Hiza*

RICHFIELD

Bill Nash and his father, Earle, owner and operator of Richfield gas station, in the 1930s. The station was located at 26 Collier Street at the present government complex site. *Courtesy Bill Nash*

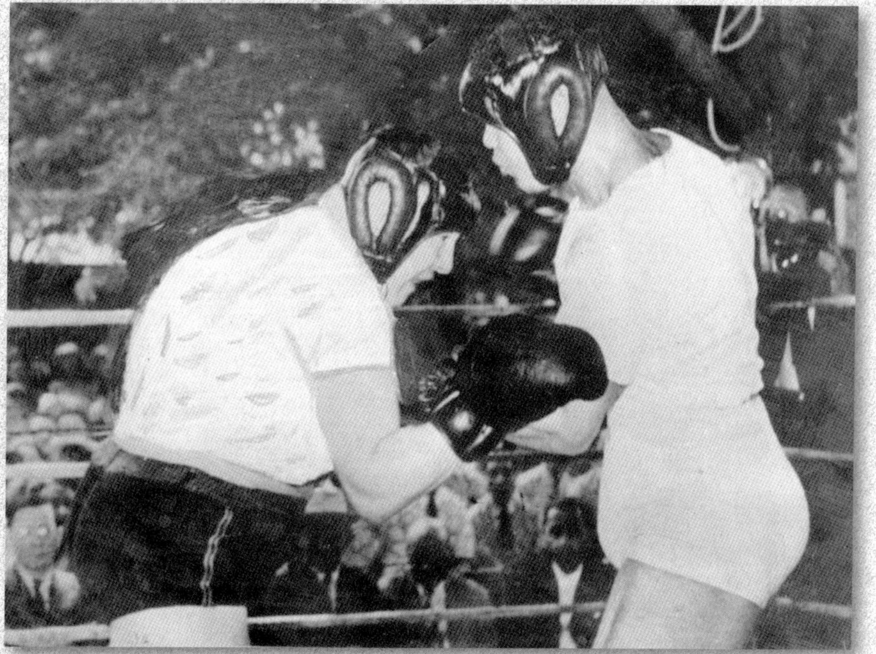

Joe Banovic, known as "Bingo Joe," spars with Joe Louis in 1939. Banovic started boxing in 1926 under the tutelage of Jersey Jones and went on to box in 77 professional fights. *Courtesy Ann Smith*

MUSKA'S TAVERN

Muska's Tavern (now Delgado's Café) at 119 Harry L Drive, Johnson City, early 1940s. This tavern was visited by the Budweiser four-team hitch. In the photo, left to right, Steve Muska, George Muska, (tavern owner), and John Muska Sr. *Courtesy Judith Muska Hiza*

Edith Schoonmaker Hibbard poses in front of a friend's car in Binghamton, July 4, 1941.
Courtesy Virginia Hibbard

Russian Club convention at St. Mary's Russian Orthodox Church, Binghamton, early 1940s. *Courtesy Marlene Yacos*

1940 - 1949

The war years

THE WEATHER

BINGHAMTON PRESS

City Edition

Vol. 63, No. 203. THIRTY-TWO PAGES MONDAY EVENING, DECEMBER 8, 1941. PRICE THREE CENTS

3,000 U. S. CASUALTIES; FLEETS BATTLING; MANILA IS BLASTED

CONGRESS VOTES WAR IN 43 MINS.

Senate Unanimous, House for It 388-1 After F. D. R. Plea

Washington, Dec. 8 (INS)—The United States today entered the second war when Congress formally declared a state of war has existed with Japan since early Sunday when Nippon launched a blitzkrieg attack on America's pacific outposts.

The House and Senate passed the war resolution within 43 minutes after President Roosevelt asked a joint session of Congress to smash Japanese treachery" in the pacific and pledged the United States to an "inevitable triumph—so help us god." The Senate vote was 82 to 0.

There was a half second of uncertainty in the House when Representative Jeannette Rankin (R., Mont.) objected to unanimous consent for immediate consideration of the war resolution.

Speaker Sam Rayburn brushed the objection aside. It was she who in the small hours of April 6, 1917, faltered, wept and finally voted "no" against a similar resolution aimed at Germany.

Attack on Hawaii Continued; Thais Quit; Latin American Nations Join up as Our Allies

New York, Dec. 8 (AP)—Manila is under bombardment by Japanese planes, an NBC correspondent reported late today (Tuesday morning, Manila time), with the raiders smashing at Fort William McKinley, Nichols airfield and the Radio Corporation of America short wave transmitter.

"The fire is simply raging out there," said Bert Silen, the radio reporter.

(By the Associated Press)

The White House acknowledged today a bloody toll of 3,000 killed and wounded in the Japanese attack on Honolulu—about half of them fatalities—as the battle of Hawaii continued and imperial Tokio headquarters claimed smashing naval and air victories over United States. A great air-sea battle was reported raging off the Philippines.

Great Britain formally declared war on Japan, an American war declaration was passed by Congress, and mighty forces of the U. S. fleet were reported combing the waters of the Pacific for Japanese warships.

The Message

Japs Force Us in, Churchill Tells Britain

No Need to Wait for U. S. to Declare War, He Says in Commons

Nazis Give up Winter War Upon Moscow

High Command Says City's Capture Is No Longer Expected This Year

Latest Bulletins

NAVY TO KEEP ALL FOR DURATION

COLOMBIA TO GIVE U. S. BASES

THAILAND BEING OCCUPIED

TWO AIR RAIDS ON HONGKONG

R. A. F. BOMBS JAP TRANSPORTS

BRITISH-JAPS BATTLE IN NORTH MALAYA

First U. S. Casualties of the War

Index to Features

Mrs. Roosevelt Going to West Coast Tonight

Fight With Everything, Hoover Advises Nation

Comment on Jap Attack Refused by Lindbergh

INSIDE GERMANY TODAY

Turn to Page 14

December 8, 1941: Attack on Pearl Harbor plunges U.S. into WWII. *Microfilm archives*

World War II shaped everything. The war effort touched everyone in America, including more than 20,000 men and women from Broome County who served in the armed forces. An estimated 625 of those died.

These are staggering numbers. Almost all of those in the armed forces were men. Approximately one of every five males served in uniform. The proportion would be higher if you looked at just draft-age men.

War Department telegrams flowed into Broome, telling mothers and wives of the deaths or captures of their loved ones. Throughout the hostilities, the Binghamton Press and its sister papers produced extra after extra, keeping readers informed of the latest developments.

Among the most emotion-laden photos in our files are those of the celebrations at the end of the war. The joy in those pictures lifts the spirit almost 60 years after they were taken.

Two of the most important businessmen in the community died during the 1940s. Willis Sharpe Kilmer died in 1940, and three years later his Binghamton Press was sold to Frank E. Gannett.

In 1948, George F. Johnson died. In the 1960s, his family would lose control of the company that so dominated Greater Binghamton.

Public Market, operated by Endicott Johnson for the benefit of its employees, early 1940s. *Press & Sun-Bulletin archives*

Bystrak brothers, Rudy, Paul and John, in uniform, 1942. *Courtesy Rudy Bystrak*

Binghamton and Chemung county draftees at the train depot in Binghamton in 1942. *Press & Sun-Bulletin archives*

IBM banquet believed to be a thank-you for the management team, Binghamton, 1941. *Courtesy Dan Murray*

C. Fred Johnson Middle School January graduation classes in 1942. *Courtesy Rudy Bystrak*

C. Fred Johnson Middle School June graduation classes in 1942. *Courtesy Rudy Bystrak*

I.B.M.
40

THE WEATHER

BINGHAMTON PRESS

City Edition

Vol. 63, No. 206. FORTY-EIGHT PAGES THURSDAY EVENING, DECEMBER 11, 1941. PRICE THREE CENTS

U. S., NAZIS AT WAR

We Sink Giant Japanese Battleship; Draft May Cover Men From 18 to 45

U. S. TROOPS CRUSH JAP FORCES TRYING TO INVADE LUZON

By the Associated Press

Washington, Dec. 11—The sinking of the 29,000-ton Japanese battleship Haruna by army bombers off the northern coast of Luzon in the Philippines was announced today by Secretary of War Stimson.

At his press conference, Mr. Stimson said the Navy Department had confirmed the sinking, previously reported by the army as a battleship of the Haruna class.

Determined resistance by American forces, Mr. Stimson reported, have confined Japanese landings on Luzon to the vicinity of Aparri at the extreme northern tip of the island.

(From Manila, however, came reports that Japanese parachutists had seized an airport six miles from Ilgan in eastern Luzon.)

The war secretary said there were continued attacks by Japanese aircraft in the vicinity of Manila yesterday, particularly on the air fields at Cavite and Nichols Field.

Mr. Stimson said that losses of planes in the attack on Hawaii Sunday, although heavy, already were being replaced.

The communique—No. 3 of the war—follows:

"Philippine theatre:

"The commanding general, Far Eastern command, confirms the sinking of a 29,000-ton Japanese battleship yesterday by the American Army Air forces north of Luzon. This battleship is believed to be the 29,000-ton Haruna, or a vessel of the Haruna class.

"Continued attempts by strong Japanese forces to establish themselves along the northern coast of Luzon, were reported. Determined resistance has confined this action to the attack in the vicinity of Aparri at the extreme northern tip of Luzon, where the Japanese attempted to establish a beach-head yesterday. Air activity continued in the vicinity of Manila with intermittent attacks on air fields at Cavite and Nichols Field throughout the day."

By the Associated Press

American battle forces early today crushed the first waves of sea-borne Japanese troops landed on the Luzon coast of the Philippines and were mopping up the few enemy troops still in action, a U. S. Army spokesman announced. Japan threw more parachute troops into its invasion attempt, however, and the seizure of a Luzon airport was reported in Manila.

Giant Army of 4,000,000 Is New Goal

Registration up to Age of 65 Considered by Washington

PRESENT LIMIT IS 28

Many With Dependents Likely to Be Taken Into Forces

CONGRESS ACTS AS HITLER, DUCE PUT US INTO CONFLICT

By the Associated Press

The Congress of the United States without dissent voted war against both Germany and Italy today, swiftly countering Axis declarations of war against this country.

Not a single "No" vote was registered in either Senate or House. The Senate voted 88-0 for war against Germany, 90-0 for war against Italy. The House vote for war with Germany was 393 to 0 and for war with Italy 399 to 0. But in each instance one member voted present.

Montana's Republican woman Representative Jeanette Rankin, who cast the lone vote against war with Japan and who voted against the war with Germany in 1917, was recorded as "present."

Congress' lightning speed in passing both resolutions—even more rapidly than in voting war against Japan—came after a message from President Roosevelt urging a "rapid and united effort" for victory "over the forces of savagery and barbarism."

"The long-known and long-expected has taken place," Mr. Roosevelt said, in a noon message to Congress.

"The forces endeavoring to enslave the entire world now are moving toward this Hemisphere. Never before has there been a greater challenge to life, liberty and civilization. . .

"I therefore request the Congress to recognize a state of war between the United States and Germany, and between the United States and Italy."

Only a few hours earlier the Axis dictators had invoked war against the United States, with Premier Mussolini exhorting crowds in Rome that "it is an honor to fight together with the Japanese."

JAPS RUN INTO REAL TROUBLE

Japan Attacked by U. S.--Hitler

Italy Goose-Steps Into New Lineup

One for All, All for One, Say Japs

Russians Tell of New Gains in 3 Sectors

Claim Nazis Thrown Back in Ukraine, Before Moscow, at Leningrad

Victory Sure, but Not Quick, Says Churchill

Naval Losses Great, He Admits; Lauds Reds; Cites Hitler Blunder

"It may well be," he declared in a sweeping review of the broadened war, "that we shall have to suffer considerable punishment, but we

(Continued on Page Fifteen)

11 Residents of Brest Executed by Nazis

Vichy, Unoccupied France, Dec. 11 (AP)—Eleven residents of the port of Brest were shot today for possession of arms and explosives, premeditated violence against the German army and espionage, German authorities announced in the Paris press.

Reports from the occupied zone said police made mass arrests in Southern France and ear-marked hundreds of Jews and Communists for concentration camps.

British Bombers Strike at Nazi Tanker, Rail Head

White House Measured for Blackout Curtains

Survivors of Collision at Sea Brought to Port

Quezon, Gen. MacArthur Lauded by Roosevelt

Manila, Dec. 11 (AP) — President Manuel Quezon of the Philippines and Lieut.-Gen. Douglas MacArthur, commander of United States Far Eastern forces, today received messages of commendation and encouragement from President Roosevelt.

24-HOUR RECRUITING

Philadelphia, Dec. 11 (AP) — The Navy tossed away the key to its recruiting office here today and went on a 24-hour day basis. "We have tossed away the key for the duration," said Lieut. Comm. H. E. Curlee in reporting that 7,489 had volunteered for service since Monday.

Index to Features

WAR NEEDS MONEY!

It will cost money to defeat Japan, Germany and Italy. Your government calls on you to help now.

Buy defense bonds or stamps today. Buy them every day, if you can. But buy them on a regular basis.

Your Binghamton Press

carriers will bring stamps to you once a week.

Bonds cost as little as $18.75, stamps come as low as 10 cents. Defense bonds and stamps also can be bought at all banks and post offices and retail stores.

The Binghamton Press urges all Americans to support your government with your dollars.

Latest Bulletins

EL SALVADIR TO TRAIN ALL MEN

San Salvador, Dec. 11 (AP)—The government of El Salvador today ordered universal military training for all male citizens from 15 to 50 years.

SENATE VOTES DRAFT EXTENSION

Washington, Dec. 11 (UP)—The Senate today unanimously passed a bill authorizing the use of National Guard and drafted troops outside the West Hemisphere and extending their terms of service for the duration of the war.

JAP AIR BASE IS BOMBED

Batavia, Java, Dec. 11 (AP)—A Netherlands East Indies Army communique declared today that Australian bombers based in the Nei raided a Japanese air base on the little island of Pobra between the Celebes and the Japanese-mandated Palau islands southeast of the Philippines.

BRITISH FLEET GETS NEW COMMANDER

Singapore, Dec. 11 (AP)—Vice Admiral Sir Geoffrey Layton took over temporary command of Britain's Far Eastern battle-fleet today in the place of Admiral Sir Tom Phillips, reported missing after the sinking of his flagship, the battleship Prince of Wales.

December 11, 1941: The Press announces the European war has engulfed the U.S. *Courtesy Carolyn Fitzgerald*

Local Youth Killed in Africa; Vestal Boy Wounded

Your Newspaper—A Bulwark of Liberty

ENDICOTT DAILY BULLETIN

Today's Weather
Rain and Cooler

PRICE, FOUR CENTS | TWELVE PAGES | ENDICOTT, N. Y., WEDNESDAY, MAY 12, 1943 | VOLUME FIFTY-NINE, NO. 25

FDR, CHURCHILL MAP ATTACK ON NIPS AS AFRICAN WAR NEARS END

British Troops Encircle Enemy; Occupy Cap Bon

● **Allied Headquarters in North Africa, INS**—Allied air forces ran out of targets on Cap Bon peninsula today as the Tunisian campaign neared a close and troops of the British First army threw a ring around the entire thumb of land after accupying Cap Bon itself.

The crack troops of Lt. Gen. Kenneth A. N. Anderson's veteran Dunkirk army transformed themselves into battle-grimed M. P.'s as their job turned from fighting into the far more pleasant task of herding Axis prisoners by the thousands into prison camps.

Allied aerial activity over the peninsula came to an end at least when no more Axis targets worthy of attack were to be found. The only battleground in all Tunisia was an area 80 miles square west of Bou Ficha and north of Enfidaville, where the British Eighth army, First army troops and French units still holding their ground.

Famed Empire troops which at present are not able to be identified are holding the northwestern part of the Allied ring some 10 miles east of Zaghouan, where the village of Marie Du Zit and its important airport have been occupied.

Massed Allied air formations participated in assaults against the Nazi "island of resistance" in the Bou Ficha-Enfidaville region to facilitate a new and final drive by Gen. Sir Bernard L. Montgomery's long-stalled Eighth army.

Complete collapse of Nazi troops on the peninsula enabled undivided attention to be given to this last enemy pocket. The last time the air force was needed on Cap Bon peninsula was when the Axis made a futile attempt to evacuate some of its troops in JU-52 transports.

A few of these were intercepted by night-flying Hurricanes and one of them was shot down into the sea.

The high command of the Northwest African tactical air force found suddenly that the British advance in the Cap Bon area was so swift that bombing had to cease lest Allied troops became endangered. The German air force was out of the air and enemy supply dumps themselves had been set afire by the retreating Axis. So the Allied air arm turned back to the west and went to work on the Nazis north of Enfidaville.

There followed a systematic bombing and strafing of Axis troops trapped around St. Marie du Zit, Grombalia and north of Enfidaville as well as in the Zaghouan sector of the Atlas mountains. Reconnaissance flights reported many fires raging, indicating the enemy was burning its own vehicles in preparation for surrender.

As the sun rose on Cap Bon's silenced battlefield, the Union Jack was raised above military garrisons and prison camps all the way to the tip of the peninsula itself.

Some 100,000 Axis prisoners now have been taken. These included two more companies of the crack Hermann Goering regiment which, after having been isolated in almost impregnable deep-dug positions at Djebel Achkel for the last week, hauled down the swastika and sent the white flag across the lines.

This ended the last island of resistance in the United States Army Second corps area.

Bou Ficha now has fallen to the British and tattered Axis remnants are being held in a crushing grip in a tiny pocket extending from the Gulf of Hammamet. Liquidation of this pocket is proceeding apace.

First crack-up of this Axis group came five miles south of Zaghouan when the so-called "Pfeiffer" German army group—80 per cent of whom were Italians—gave in and surrendered unconditionally.

These Axis forces capitulated to French General Mathint, who acting for General Jacques LeClerc, had brought his fighting French force northward all the way from Lake Chad.

With regard to the last German holdouts, a spokesman said:

"The enemy has little possibility left for organized resistance, and is accepting the situation."

On the whole, it is all over but the shouting. There is stray shooting and an occasional spurt of activity, but come what may, there is nothing Hitler or Mussolini can do to whitewash their defeat.

The American Second Army corps which took Bizerte had rounded up a total of 37,998 captured Germans and Italians.

Rear Admiral Dies

● **Washington, INS**—The death of Rear Admiral James Morgan Minter, of the Navy Medical corps at his U. S. Naval hospital, Bethesda, Md., was announced today by the Navy.

Italy Begins To Evacuate Coast Areas

● **London, INS**—Reports of mass Italian evacuations from endangered coastal areas flowed into London today as feverish activity in every area of the Nazi-occupied continent betrayed grim fears of an early Allied invasion.

The German propaganda agency DNB, for reasons of its own, broadcast reports on the whereabouts and activities of Adolf Hitler. One of them said the fuehrer has transferred his headquarters at least temporarily from the Russian front to the west.

Reporting from "an unspecified place in the west," DNB said that Hitler had received from Albert Speer, the fortications expert who succeeded the late Fritz Todt, builder of the Siegfried Line, a full report on "construction of the Atlantic wall."

The inference was that Hitler had inspected the fortications. Whether or not he came away satisfied was not mentioned in the broadcast.

Simultaneously, Axis-inspired reports from Cairo said that Field Marshal Erwin Rommel, now revealed to have pulled out of Tunisia two months ago, had been given the task of preparing the defenses of Greece, Crete and the Dodecanese islands against invasion.

Benes, Czech Leader, Here

● **Washington, INS**—The White House announced today that Eduard Benes, president of Czechoslovakia, would arrive in Washington late this afternoon.

Presidential Secretary Stephen T. Early said that Benes already has arrived safely in this country from London.

President Roosevelt, Vice President Wallace, Secretary of State Hull and high ranking government officials will greet Benes on his arrival here. He will be honored at a dinner at the White House tonight and remain an overnight guest at the executive mansion.

He was expected to meet Prime Minister Churchill of England who also is a White House guest, but Churchill will not be present at the dinner tonight. He will dine with English diplomatic officials at the British Embassy.

Jury Convicts Stephan Aide

● **Detroit, INS**—A Federal court jury today convicted Theodore Donay, former German soldier and Detroit importer, of misprision of treason in the Max Stephan case.

The jury of nine men and three women balloted twice and returned a verdict in 37 minutes.

Killed in Action

Pvt. John Vassalakos

Endicott Greek Dies in Desert

● **Pvt. John Vassalakos**, 24, nephew of Mr. and Mrs. Nick Vassos (Vassalakos), 132 Washington Ave., today was reported "killed in action March 29 in the North African area," according to a War department telegram sent to his uncle, Mr. Vassos, with whom the soldier had resided.

Private Vassalakos worked with his uncle in a Washington Avenue shoe shine shop before his induction in the Army Feb. 27, 1942. Last letter received from the youth was seven weeks ago, written in North Africa.

After his induction, the soldier received training in a Tennessee Army camp, later being transferred to Camp Edwards, Mass. He was stationed at Fort Bragg, N. C., prior to being sent overseas with an infantry group.

Born in Stamford, Conn., he had resided with his uncle and aunt for six years. He has a brother, James Vassalakos, stationed with the Navy in Norfolk, Va.

The soldier held membership in the Sons of Pericles lodge, junior organization of the Endicott Chapter of the Greek Order of Ahepa, and recently was given honorary membership in the Ahepa lodge.

His parents, who returned to their native Greece several years ago, have not been heard from since the German invasion.

Lewis Arrives In Washington

● **Washington, INS** — John L. Lewis, president of the United Mine Workers' union, arrived in Washington from New York today to raise the possibility that he may confer with Coal Czar Harold L. Ickes over the miners' new threat to strike next week. The UMW chieftain earlier had refused to attend the WLB meetings, and his presence in Washington also caused speculation as to whether he might rescind his stand and finally appear before the board.

Lewis went directly to his office after he arrived in the capital and would not comment on his trip to Washington. He was expected to return to New York late today or tomorrow.

● **Washington, INS**—House passage of its new, "super" anti-strike bill within a week was forecast today as friends of labor sought to stem a tide admittedly precipitated by the coal strike.

Chairman May (D) Ky., of the Military Affairs committee said he has "every reason to believe that the bill will pass the House by a considerable majority."

"I am going to seek immediate consideration," he added.

As drafted by the House committee, the measure contains substantially the same provisions as a drastic bill, authored by Rep. Smith (D) W. Va., which passed the House in December, 1941, by a 252 to 136 vote.

Hitler Appoints Grave Designer

● **New York, INS**—With Nazi casualties mounting as the months roll by, Adolf Hitler has named an architect as official designer of all German military cemeteries and war monuments, the British radio said today.

The broadcast was heard by the government's foreign broadcast intelligence service.

Reds Forge Ahead Near Novorossisk

● **Moscow, INS**—Red army tank and infantry forces, after overrunning a center of German resistance on the lower reaches of the Kuban river, today forged forward in the West Caucasus toward the Black Sea naval base of Novorossisk.

Big batteries of Soviet artillery, along with Russian Stormovik dive-bombers, smashed repeatedly at Nazi fortifications in advance of the on-rushing troops and knocked out numerous enemy firing points.

"Northeast of Novorossisk," said the noon communique of the high command, "artillery destroyed 12 firing points and a blockhouse."

One Soviet unit dislodged a force of Germans from a wood and killed 130 of them in the engagement. Considerable booty was captured.

Heavy Russian artillery blasts were answered in kind by the Germans on numerous sectors but the Red army appeared to be besting them at every turn.

(The Nazi-controlled Paris radio reported that Russian forces under cover of a smokescreen landed in the Novorossisk area from motor launches and were locked in fierce fighting with the Germans.)

U. S. Bombers Rock Catania

● **Cairo, INS** — United States heavy bombers yesterday severely blasted the Sicilian port of Catania in daylight, Middle East headquarters announced.

Nearly 50 Liberators participated in the raid and dropped more than 110 tons of explosives on the target.

Reconnaissance photographs showed extensive damage to a big power station and railway installations at Catania. One Liberator is missing.

The heavy American bombers were accompanied by Royal Air force fighters in their "highly successful" attack, the communique said.

The strong bombing force blew up an ammunition ship, scored direct hits on other shipping and set fire to an airplane hangar.

Moles and harbor installations were severely damaged. One mole where three ships were tied up was demolished.

"The whole dock area was left in flames," said the communique.

The bombers shot down a Junkers 88 and an Italian Macchi 200.

Hague-Backed Candidates Have Smashing Victory

● **Jersey City, N. J., INS**—Mayor Frank Hague of Jersey City today had won another smashing victory at the polls.

Hague-backed candidates in yesterday's local elections were swept into office in a move regarded as repudiation of efforts of Gov. Charles Edison to break Tague power.

In Hoboken and North Bergen, the Hague victories were by large majorities but a closely contested race in west New York resulted in the election of only three of five Hague-backed candidates.

George Offers Substitute for Ruml Tax Plan

● **Washington, INS**—Sen. Walter F. George (D) Ga., chairman of the Senate Finance committee today proposed a substitute for the Ruml plan pay-as-you-go tax measure as the Senate readied itself for debate on the issue.

George proposed cancellation of 75 per cent of either the 1942 or 1943 individual income tax liabilities with the 25 per cent balance being collected over a two-year period.

While George has had the proposal under consideration for some time, he did not decide to wage an active fight on the Ruml plan bill, which provides for a full year's cancellation, until today.

The decision followed a series of conferences among democratic leaders during which the administration decided to oppose the Ruml plan vigorously.

While his plan means partial doubling up of taxes in 1944 and 1945, George asserted that individual income tax payers could bear the burden.

A formal Finance committee report meanwhile, declared that it is important that income tax payers be placed on a current basis during the war.

An influential Senate leader predicted passage of the Ruml plan bill by nine votes. The measure then would go to conference with the House, where the Ruml plan has been rejected.

George predicted that passage of the modified Ruml plan bill —unless vetoed by the President —will bring an immediate request from the administration for new taxes. Mr. Roosevelt, he pointed out, has asked $16,000,000,000 in new taxes or savings.

Rabaul Raked By Allied Fire

● **United Nations Headquarters in Australia, INS**—A heavy aerial assault by Allied bombers on the Rabaul Japanese base in New Britain and other night raids on enemy bases in the Southwestern Pacific were disclosed today.

Intensified clashes between small advanced ground elements in the Green's Hill area near the enemy base at Mubo, New Guinea, also were reported.

Japanese planes caused some damage and casualties in a Dutch New Guinea raid and others attempting to attack Allied shipping off the northern coast of Australia were driven off.

Rabaul was assaulted by Allied heavy bombers under adverse weather conditions at dawn. Resultant fires were visible 60 miles as the planes bombed the Vunakanau airdrome. Many small fires appeared to indicate burning enemy aircraft.

● **Washington, INS** — The Navy announced today that Army and Navy bombers carried out new raids on Jap positions in the North and Central Solomons, bombing Kahili, Shortland Island, and Rekata Bay installations.

Fires were started at Kahili on the morning of May 11 by Army flying fortresses but results of their attack on Shortland Island were not observed, the Navy said.

Main Stem Flashes

—By "Barney" French—

● **Mary Everts** cooling her heels at the Vestal station while her arriving b. f., Pvt. Dayton Noteware, went into the arms of a flock of other receptionist women —his mother and sisters and others . . . But she got the last crack at him, and how.

Marion Card, free of scholastic duties at Syracuse U. for a spell, renewing acquaintances along the Main Stem with folks in the shops and enjoying herself to the fullest.

Jennie Randisi studying a map of California the while she hums that old refrain, "California, Here I Come" . . . And she means it! . . . Off to San Francisco to live soon . . . Which shows you how this weather drives folks away.

Albert Brewer of the Air Raid warden forces considering how well he did the other night in the black-out but wondering what can be done about those water holes on South street before the next one.

Sgt. "Chuck" Hibler meeting up with a member of Uncle Sam's sea forces while furloughing about town and ribbing the pal in blue with a query as to "when is that Navy going to get into this war?" . . . The old tune.

Betty Jane Thorpe tunefully attired for the day (in white crew cap and rain coat) and looking very chic withal . . . Full of bubbling enthusiasm for the contemplated trip to New York to visit the soldier b. f.

Reported Wounded

Staff Sgt. Victor Rose

Air Gunner Is Wounded

● **Vestal**—Staff Sgt. Victor L. Rose, 20, a gunner with a bomber squadron in England, today was reported "wounded in action in England May 1," according to a War department telegram sent to his parents, Mr. and Mrs. Clifton Rose, 233 Main St.

A graduate of Vestal Central High school where he was a star athlete, the youth left for Army service a year ago this month. Prior to his induction, he was employed in Endicott Johnson Corp.

The War department's telegram informed Mr. and Mrs. Rose that they would be notified of the youth's condition every 15 days.

Sergeant Rose has been in England since Jan. 19.

He has two brothers in service, Rexford, 22, first class seaman, USN, Great Lakes, Ill., and George, 18, trooper in the cavalry, stationed at Fort Riley, Kan. His oldest brother, Herman, 24, who was an aviation cadet in the Air Corps received an honorable medical discharge earlier this year.

U. S. Training Fighter Crews

● **Orlando, Fla., INS**—Specially selected crews using new type planes and equipment today are being trained in the latest night fighter plane tactics which eventually may wipe out surprise enemy bombing attacks under cover of darkness.

This development in the campaign to crush the Axis powers is being taught to pilots and plane crew members in the Army Air forces newest school of applied tactics, with headquarters at Orlando.

While both the British and Germans have been using night fighter planes for some time, the U. S. Army Air force in the past few months have improved on the strategy of knocking out bombers which fly at night.

Details of the methods and equipment used must remain secret, but the Army finally revealed that it has transformed the A-20, twin-engined attack bomber into a deadly night fighter.

House Leaders Fail to Avoid Trade Showdown

● **Washington, INS**—Efforts of House Democrats and Republican leaders to avoid a showdown fight on renewal of the reciprocal trade act collapsed today and Speaker Rayburn announced that administration forces would attempt to pass the legislation without amendment.

It was understood that Secretary of State Hull and other State department officials declined to agree to the proposal of legislative leaders that the act be extended only two years instead of three.

With final passage expected to come before night, indications were that the fight would center around the proposal to restrict renewal to two years.

Division Arrives

● **Cairo, INS**—The Sixth South African armored division has arrived in the Middle East, an official announcement said today.

Allied Moves to Take Burma, Hit Japs Predicted

By Kingsbury Smith, INS Staff Corresopndent

● **Washington, INS**—Possibility of a major Allied move to retake Burma late this summer and deal a staggering blow to Japan was seen today as President Roosevelt and British Prime Minister Winston Churchill held their fifth wartime conferences in Washington.

Belief that a powerful move against Japan is being planned by the President and Churchill was based on the Prime Minister's party of Field Marshal Sir Archibald P. Wavell, commander-in-chief of the British forces in India, and other officers of the British high command in India.

In view of the fact that the monsoon is now underway in Burma and may not end before the latter par of August or early September, it was believed that any major military operation to strike at Japan from India probably would not start before the end of the summer.

This belief was strengthened by the fact that the major campaigns in North Africa were planned approximately three months in advance by the President and Mr. Churchill.

There was no doubt that both the military and political aspect of the Indian situation would figure prominently in this latest historic meeting between the two leaders of the United Nations. Ambassador William Phillips, special Presidential envoy to India, returned a few days ago from that country and conferred yesterday with President Roosevelt.

The apparent attention being given to the Pacific situation aroused immediate speculation in diplomatic cricles in Washington as to whether a major invasion of the European continent might be postponed until next spring while the United States and Britain concentrated their attention in checking Japan in the Pacific.

British forces recently started a withdrawal from Burma, and there have been persistent reports that the Japanese were planning an invasion move against India. If Japan contemplates such a campaign, it is believed that it would not get under full swing until after the monsoon at the end of the summer.

If the Allied high command has received definite word of Japan's intention to invade India this autumn, diplomatic observers believe that it might well necessitate a concentration of United Nations forces in that country to check the Japanese move.

However, there still was a strong belief in usually well-informed diplomatic circles that the President and the British Prime Minister will not depart from the strategy of defeating Hitler first. These diplomatic sources were inclined to believe that the presence of the British Indian military and naval chiefs meant that the Allied high command intends to take measure to hold the Japanese off in the Pacific, especially in India, while the Allied invasion of the European continent is under way this year.

At the same time, some of the Pacific Allies, especially China and Australia, are known to have favored a shift in the grand strategy to concentrate on Japan following the ousting of the Axis forces from Africa.

Lt. Gen. Joseph C. Stilwell, commander of American forces in India and China, and Maj. Gen. Claire Chennault, commander of the American air forces in China, are still understood to be in Washington, and it is considered highly probable that they will participate in the military conferences on the Pacific.

White House Secretary Stephen T. Early said that the President and Churchill "had a long talk last night" after Churchill's arrival in Washington. He added that President Roosevelt and Churchill would be in almost continuous conference during the Prime Minister's visit to Washington. Early would not say how long Churchill would remain in the capital.

Nor would Early give any indication on what was transpiring at the conferences. The early general consensus in Washington, however, was that the President and Churchill were meeting to make vital strategic plans for an Allied invasion of the European continent this summer.

The big victory of Allied forces in Tunisia led to the "victory conference" in the fifth wartime meeting between Mr. Roosevelt and Churchill.

Churchill arrived in Washington late yesterday, accompanied by a staff of high ranking military and naval experts. He was greeted by President Roosevelt on his arrival and will be a White House guest for the duration of his visit.

Second Front In Axis-Held Europe Looms

● **London, INS**—Prime Minister Winston Churchill went to Washington to confer with President Roosevelt on plans for "a major military operation much greater than that in North Africa," well-informed quarters in London said today.

The general concensus of opinion is that the current Washington parley will be the final meeting of the Allied leaders prior to the opening of a second front in Europe.

These sources said the conferences will involve essentially the planning of strategy to defeat the Axis in broad details.

The President and Prime Minister, it was said, will extend the "war-winning" blueprint mapped last January at Casablanca.

No hint can be published, of course, of where the Allies next will strike the Axis, but, informed quarters said, it can positively be said that from the meeting will evolve a major military operation much greater than that which smashed the Axis from North Africa.

(The Algiers radio declared that "an event of international importance" will be announced at the conclusion of Churchill's Washington visit.)

Churchill and the President, it was said, will plan the exact extent and representation of the armies, air forces and navies of the Allied nations to participate in the operation. They will allocate the amount of shipping required to take all of the necessary supplies.

Decisions on the actual operations also will be taken with formulation of plans after the forthcoming campaign is concluded.

Suggestions from Washington that the meeting may be followed with a conference of Allied leaders with Premier Joseph Stalin of Russia were noted in London circles but the thought was expressed that this possibly still is impractical since Stalin has his hands full with plans for summer offensive and defensive operations in his war theater.

It was believed likely that President Roosevelt's special envoy to Russia, Joseph E. Davies, will outline the full scheme of the Allied plans to Stalin and fill him in on all details.

The British Prime Minister and President Roosevelt are expected to discuss in their current fifth conference since Hitler plunged the world into the bloodiest war in history the political and military problems which will arise from a continental invasion.

The decision to launch an invasion as early as possible was taken by the Allied leaders at the historic conference in Casablanca last January. Now the problems which it will entail must finally be decided upon.

May 12, 1943: Grim news about local soldiers made its way onto the front page. *Courtesy Jean Rose-Klein*

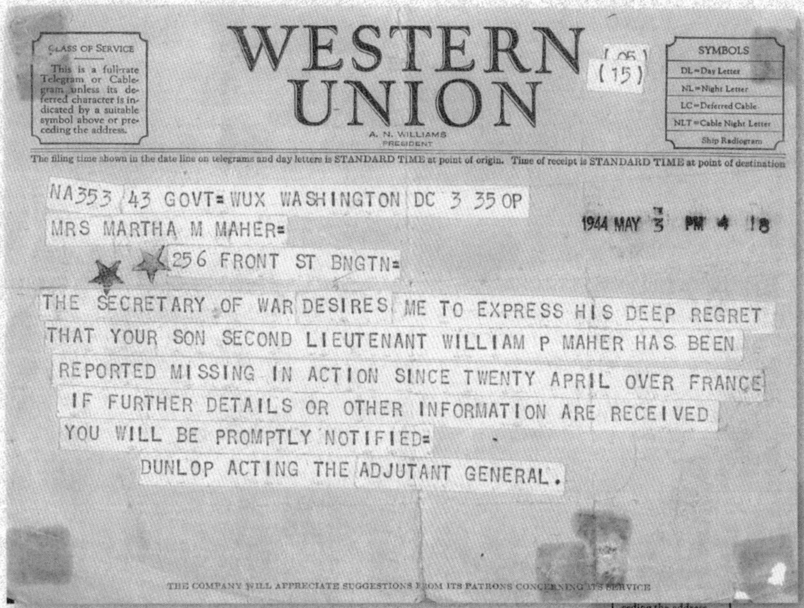

WESTERN UNION

A. N. WILLIAMS PRESIDENT

CLASS OF SERVICE
This is a full-rate Telegram or Cablegram unless its deferred character is indicated by a suitable symbol above or preceding the address.

(15)

SYMBOLS
DL=Day Letter
NL=Night Letter
LC=Deferred Cable
NLT=Cable Night Letter
Ship Radiogram

The filing time shown in the date line on telegrams and day letters is STANDARD TIME at point of origin. Time of receipt is STANDARD TIME at point of destination

NA353 43 GOVT=WUX WASHINGTON DC 3 35 OP
1944 MAY 3 PM 4 18
MRS MARTHA M MAHER=
256 FRONT ST BNGTN=

THE SECRETARY OF WAR DESIRES ME TO EXPRESS HIS DEEP REGRET THAT YOUR SON SECOND LIEUTENANT WILLIAM P MAHER HAS BEEN REPORTED MISSING IN ACTION SINCE TWENTY APRIL OVER FRANCE IF FURTHER DETAILS OR OTHER INFORMATION ARE RECEIVED YOU WILL BE PROMPTLY NOTIFIED=
DUNLOP ACTING THE ADJUTANT GENERAL.

THE COMPANY WILL APPRECIATE SUGGESTIONS FROM ITS PATRONS CONCERNING ITS SERVICE

Western Union telegram to Martha M. Maher informing her that her son, Second Lt. William P. Maher, had been reported missing in action. *Courtesy James P. Foley*

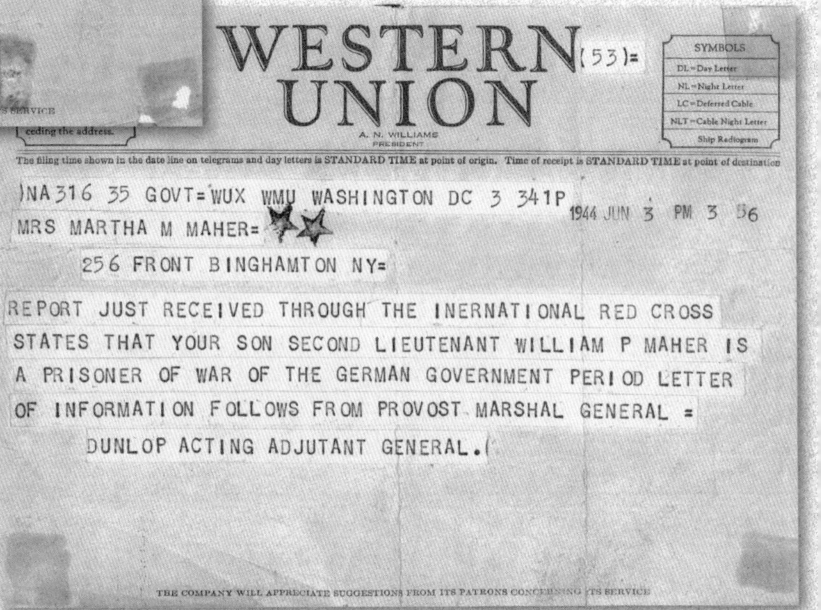

WESTERN UNION (53)=

A. N. WILLIAMS PRESIDENT

SYMBOLS
DL=Day Letter
NL=Night Letter
LC=Deferred Cable
NLT=Cable Night Letter
Ship Radiogram

The filing time shown in the date line on telegrams and day letters is STANDARD TIME at point of origin. Time of receipt is STANDARD TIME at point of destination

NA316 35 GOVT=WUX WMU WASHINGTON DC 3 341P
1944 JUN 3 PM 3 56
MRS MARTHA M MAHER=
256 FRONT BINGHAMTON NY=

REPORT JUST RECEIVED THROUGH THE INERNATIONAL RED CROSS STATES THAT YOUR SON SECOND LIEUTENANT WILLIAM P MAHER IS A PRISONER OF WAR OF THE GERMAN GOVERNMENT PERIOD LETTER OF INFORMATION FOLLOWS FROM PROVOST MARSHAL GENERAL =
DUNLOP ACTING ADJUTANT GENERAL.

THE COMPANY WILL APPRECIATE SUGGESTIONS FROM ITS PATRONS CONCERNING ITS SERVICE

A second telegram to Mrs. Maher, sent one month later, informing her that her son was a prisoner of war. *Courtesy James P. Foley*

From left, Joan Maher, Kathleen Maher (Foley), Mary Maher (bride), Sgt. Thomas Watson (groom) and Lt. William Maher. Thomas Watson and Mary Maher were maried Sept. 8, 1945, at St. Patrick's Church in Binghamton. Tom Watson served 20 years in the U.S. Army, including three years as a P.O.W. of the Japanese (1942-1945). He also was a survivor of the Bataan Death March. William Maher served with the U.S. Air Force based out of England. Lt. Maher's B-17 aircraft was shot down on his 20th mission over France. He, along with one other crew member, were the only survivors of the 10-man crew. Lt. Maher was a P.O.W. in Germany. *Courtesy James P. Foley*

First Pictures of Start of Invasion--by WIREPHOTO

—Page 3

BINGHAMTON PRESS

FOURTH INVASION **EXTRA**

Vol. 66, No. 48. SIXTEEN PAGES TUESDAY EVENING, JUNE 6, 1944. ★★ PRICE FOUR CENTS

WE CRACK WEST WALL, SECURE BIG BEACHHEADS

0 100
STATUTE MILES
ENGLAND
Liverpool
Hull
North Sea
HOLLAND
Norwich
WALES
Coventry
Amsterdam
Rotterdam
Cardiff
LONDON
Dover
Brussels
Dunkerque
Calais
Brighton
BELGIUM
Plymouth
Dieppe
Le Havre
Cherbourg
Caen
Marne
Brest
PARIS
Seine
FRANCE
Nantes
Loire
St. Nazaire
Tours
Dijon

WHERE ALLIES DROVE INTO FRANCE—Securing beachheads on a wide front, Allied forces were inside Caen (1), 10 miles inside the coast, early today, according to Berlin. Massed landings were made between Cherbourg (2) and Le Havre (3). The Seine Estuary at the latter point was scene of major assault and Nazi retreat, Berlin said. Dieppe (4) and Dunkerque (top arrow) were heavily blasted by air and sea. Chutists and glider troops landed far behind the coast over a stretch of more than 90 miles.

By the United Press

Supreme Headquarters, Allied Expeditionary Force, London, June 6—Allied invasion armies landed in Northwestern France today, drove at least 10 miles into the vaunted Nazi West Wall to the town of Caen, and after 12 hours of fighting held beachheads on a broad front along the coast of Normandy.

Prime Minister Winston Churchill told Commons late today that the invasion "is proceeding in a thoroughly satisfactory manner" and simultaneously a Supreme Headquarters spokesman said the American and Allied Armies had "gotten over the first five or six hurdles" in the greatest amphibious assault of all time. The German Transocean News Agency, however, broadcast a statement by a Nazi military spokesman which said that except for the Caen beachhead, all the invasion troops had been thrown back toward the sea.

Mr. Churchill, making his second appearance of the day in Commons to report on the invasion, said this evening in announcing satisfactory development of the invasion:

"The troops have penetrated in some cases several miles inland. Lodgements exist on a broad front."

He said Allied forces were fighting inside Caen, 10 miles inland and 30 miles southwest of Le Havre. Earlier Berlin broadcasts reported fighting on both sides of the town, as well as Allied landings all around a broad reach of the Normandy coast from the tip of the Cherbourg Peninsula to the Seine Estuary.

Gen. Dwight D. Eisenhower's Supreme Headquarters revealed that the Allied armies, carried and supported by 4,000 ships and 11,000 planes, encountered considerably less resistance than had been expected in the storming of Adolf Hitler's vaunted West Wall.

Nazi broadcasts reported Allied troops pouring ashore most of the day along a broad reach of the Normandy coast and to the east, and admitted that invasion landing barges had penetrated two estuaries behind the Atlantic Wall.

German opposition in all quarters was less than expected, it was learned at headquarters tonight, and an optimistic tone was evident.

Despite the Nazi propaganda claim of defensive successes everywhere except at the Caen beachhead, the DNB News Agency reported later that a strong air-borne force established itself on both sides of the Carentan-Valognes road southeast of Cherbourg. It was reinforced by air this morning and again around noon, DNB said.

The same source said German coastal fire turned back a 200-ship Allied armada in the area of St. Vaast-La Hougue, 15 miles southeast of Cherbourg.

The apparent key to the lightness of the Nazi opposition to invasion forces opening the battle was contained in a disclosure that thousands of Allied planes dropped more than 11,200 tons of bombs on German coastal fortifications in eight and a half hours last night and early today.

Simultaneously, the German DNB news agency re-

(Continued on Page Two)

Churchill Says Losses Less Than Expected, Progress Satisfactory

London, June 6 (AP)—Prime Minister Churchill announced today that Allied air-borne troops had captured several strategic bridges in France before they could be blown up and that "there is even fighting proceeding in the town of Caen."

"Air-borne troops are well established and the follows-up are proceeding with very much less loss than we expected," Mr. Churchill reported in a second statement of the day to the House of Commons.

Allied troops had penetrated in some cases several miles inland after effective landings on the coast on a broad front, he said.

The Prime Minister said he had visited the various centers where latest information was received and could state that "this operation is proceeding in a thoroughly satisfactory manner."

"Many dangers and difficulties which appeared at this time last night extremely formidable are behind us," the war leader reported.

"Passage of the sea has been made with far less loss than we apprehended.

"The resistance of batteries has been greatly weakened by bombing by the air force and the superior bombardment of our ships quickly reduced their power to dimensions which did not affect the problem."

Mr. Churchill, addressing the House of Commons after a visit to Gen. Dwight D. Eisenhower's headquarters in company with King George, described the landing of

(Continued on Page Five)

BULLETINS

London, June 6 (AP)—Transocean in a Berlin broadcast today said the Allies had established a 15-mile front from a mile to half a mile deep between Villers-sur-Mer and Trouville, seven miles south of Le Havre.

Stockholm, June 6 (INS) — Berlin's Wilhelmstrasse spokesman simplified the whole invasion drama in a characteristic manner today. The Chief Executive called on Gen. Dwight D. Eisenhower to "whip up" the fourth-term election by ordering the invasion on Europe, the spokesman said.

New York, June 6 (INS)—The Berlin radio reported this afternoon that new Allied landings have been made on the French coast in the area of Carentan, opposite the channel Island of Jersey, NBC monitors reported.

London, June 6 (INS) — Allied air activity reached new heights this evening when swarms of fighters and bombers roared overhead toward the continent, wrapping the London area in an unending drone of powerful motors.

London, June 6 (INS) — The Nazi-operated Paris radio, quoting "a last-minute flash from the battlefield," said tonight that "a vicious battle is raging north of Rouen between powerful Allied paratroop formations and German anti-invasion forces."

An Allied Air Base in England, June 6 (INS)—Many Allied assault troops are now beyond the initial danger zone of total exposure in France, reconnaissance fliers reported today.

New York, June 6 (AP)—The Berlin radio said that strong Allied air attacks have been launched on the Dieppe area.

New York, June 6 (INS)—A small group of German destroyers was "wiped out" by Allied warships in the preliminary phase of the Northern France invasion, a Blue network reporter announced.

London, June 6 (AP) — German forces launching a counter-attack knocked out 35 heavy Allied tanks at Asnelles in the Seine Bay area alone by noon, a DNB report from Berlin said today.

London, June 6 (U.P.) — The German Transocean news agency said today that about 80 medium-sized Allied warships were approaching the town of Ouistreham in the estuary of the Orne River.

London, June 6 (INS)—German fighter planes this afternoon began offering opposition to Allied invasion forces. Returning pilots reported numerous dogfights between Allied Typhoons and German Messerschmitts and Focke-Wulfs.

5th Army Plunges on 5 Miles Past Tiber

Allied Headquarters, Naples, June 6 (U.P.)—The Allied 5th Army drove the battered Germans in disorderly retreat across the Tiber River on a 17-mile front from Rome to the Tyrrhenian Sea today and sent powerful armored columns five miles beyond the river under orders to destroy the fleeing enemy.

Front dispatches said Nazi Field Marshal Albert Kesselring's broken 14th Army was offering only the feeblest sort of rearguard resistance as the Allied tanks and riflemen burst across the winding Tiber at a score of points north and west of Rome.

At many points the enemy retreat had turned into a disorganized rout under the raking fire of Allied planes and tanks, and 2,000 Nazis threw down their arms and surrendered to a fast-rolling British column that trapped them on the east bank of the river, near the seacoast.

Every bridge across the Tiber below Rome had been blown up by the fleeing Germans, but 11 of the 14 main spans inside the capital were intact and Allied troops were crossing in a steady stream.

Only in the northeastern outskirts of Rome did the Germans offer any determined resistance. A force of enemy tanks was reported battling desperately around the Littoria airport in an attempt to stem the swift Allied advance long enough for the main body of General Kesselring's troops to escape.

Official sources said the Vatican had been by-passed in all Allied operations in and around the city.

French troops on the 5th Army's

(Continued on Page Seven)

U. S. BOMBERS SINK TWO JAP SHIPS OFF DUTCH NEW GUINEA

Allied Headquarters, Southwest Pacific, June 6 (U.P.)—Allied bombers sank two Japanese vessels, including a destroyer, and probably another warship off northwestern Dutch New Guinea, in the drive to prevent the enemy from re-organizing its Geelvink Bay defenses, it was disclosed today.

Two other Japanese vessels, possibly merchantmen, were damaged and two troop-filled barges were destroyed.

Eisenhower Cheers Men

Allied Advance Post, England, June 6 (U.P.)—Gen. Dwight D. Eisenhower stood on a rooftop on invasion eve and watched a mighty airborne armada form in the dusky sky and wing toward France to begin the final phase of the war of liberation.

The Allied supreme commander radiated supreme confidence. It was contageous among those about him.

He had spent the greater part of the day among the troops, seaborne and airborne, going from group to group, chatting and laughing with the men.

At about 2:30 p. m. yesterday, General Eisenhower met a small group of British and American press and radio representatives and told us when the invasion of Europe would be launched—that the machinery already was in motion.

General Eisenhower talked to us for an hour and one-half. The conference took place in his command tent—a plain, bare-walled structure about 20 feet square.

Whistles Call Citizens To Prayer on D-Day

Albuquerque, N. M., June 6 (AP)—Sirens and whistles announced the invasion of Europe.

"I carried out my promise to the people of Albuquerque to notify them, and call them to prayer the minute the invasion began," said Mayor Clyde Tingley.

Ads Omitted to Provide More Invasion News

To permit widest coverage of invasion news and to make today's Binghamton Press available to more readers, all display and classified advertising is omitted.

THIS also assures extra copies for all who may wish them.

CURTAILMENT of newsprint, both by governmental restriction and manufacturers' allowance, makes elimination of advertising necessary to provide needed space for news and to provide the paper required for additional copies.

THE BINGHAMTON PRESS believes this service to its readers of primary importance. It wishes to express its regrets to Triple Cities merchants but knows they will appreciate the necessity for omitting their advertising from this issue.

Navy Surprises Nazis, Knocks Out Big Guns

By PIERRE J. HUSS
International News Staff Writer

Aboard a British Warship off the French Coast, June 6—Six hundred Allied naval guns in rhythmic succession opened fire on the French coast at 5:15 a. m. today.

Two thousand tons of naval shells were laid down along a stretch of the French coast west of Le Havre over a period of 10 minutes.

This ship opened up with the rest, hurling missiles of from 4- to 16-inch caliber in a terrific 10-minute barrage launched after an unmolested night crossing of the English Channel.

Apparently the Germans were taken by surprise. They began to reply from under a smoke screen laid down by aircraft to hide us.

Intermittently paratroops and airborne forces passed over and opened D-Day in a spectacular manner, covered by the tornadic bombardment.

From 7 a. m. the most sustained bombardment struck the Germans. It must have stunned them, silencing the majority of their batteries. The Luftwaffe was absent and apparently the Allied Air Force has complete mastery of the sky.

June 6, 1944: This is the fourth extra the Press put out to report on D-Day developments. *Courtesy David Silvanic*

THE WEATHER
Mostly cloudy and mild tonight and Thursday with some light rain Thursday.

BINGHAMTON PRESS

City Edition
Complete Financial News

Vol. 66, No. 179. TWENTY-FOUR PAGES WEDNESDAY EVENING, NOVEMBER 8, 1944. ★★★ PRICE FOUR CENTS

F. D. R. WINS 407 TO 124

Nation Approves His Conduct of the War; Democrats Have Clear Majority in House

Patton's Army Crosses Seille In New Drive For Saar Basin

U. S. 3d Army Outflanks Metz Bastion in Push Down Moselle Valley

FOUR VILLAGES TAKEN

Vossenack Reoccupied by Americans in Bitter Street Battle

MAP ON PAGE 8

By the United Press

Paris, Nov. 8—Lieut. Gen. George S. Patton's 3d Army opened a new offensive today on a broad front in the Moselle Valley which outflanked Metz, most powerful Nazi stronghold in northeastern France, and broke through the Seille River line at several points.

The first impact of the American drive between Nancy and Metz carried forward a mile or more and overran at least four villages.

Berlin, describing it as a "long awaited large scale offensive," said it was a strong bid to break through to the rich Saar coal basin of southwest Germany, some 40 miles to the northeast.

Vossenack Retaken

On the Aachen front the U. S. 1st Army drove the Germans back to the eastern outskirts of Vossenack, virtually completing the recapture of the village 28 miles southwest of Cologne after a bitter battle at close quarters in its streets.

United Press Correspondent Collie Small, with the 3d Army in the Moselle valley, reported that U. S. 12th Corps units under Maj. Gen. Manton Eddy charged the German positions at 6 a. m. after a heavy artillery bombardment.

Mounting the offensive under heavy skies that impeded air support, assault forces advanced over rain-sodden fields to score their first successes in breaking across the Seille, a Moselle tributary angling in a northwest-southeast direction above Nancy.

Nazis Use Shock Troops

Captured German guns and ammunition were turned against the Nazis in the preliminary shelling, softening the enemy positions for the attack. Berlin said the drive was preceded by a "strong" bombardment between Pont a Mousson and Chateau Salins.

German shock troops, apparently trying to throw Patton's attack off balance, "thrust deeply into enemy positions" south and southeast of Chateau Salins and in the forest of Parroy, Berlin said. They were credited with blowing up 23 U. S. pillboxes and taking an unspecified number of prisoners.

Third Town Lost

A German counterattack drove American 1st Army troops out of the hamlet of Kommerscheidt, some 13 miles southeast of Aachen, but the doughboys held firmly to high ground 500 yards to the northwest and edged closer to Schmidt, a mile to the southeast.

Kommerscheidt was the third town to be won and lost in the period of a few days at the top of the deepest Allied salient in Germany. The swaying street battle for Vossenack, a mile and a half northwest of Kommerscheidt, raged on into its third day on a rising scale of fury.

Both the Americans and the Germans threw reinforcements of tanks and infantry into the struggle for Vossenack, field reports said.

(Continued on Page Eight)

350 Allied Bombers Pound Nazi Oil Plant, Railyards

London, Nov. 8 (UP)—About 350 Flying Fortresses and Liberators attacked the Leuna synthetic oil plant at Merseburg and railyards at Theine today in a renewal of the winter bombing campaign against Germany.

More than 850 Mustang and Thunderbolt fighters escorted the Fortresses and Liberators.

The Election At a Glance

By the Associated Press

PRESIDENTIAL

Roosevelt leads in 34 states with 407 electoral votes (141 more than a majority); Dewey was in front in 14 with 124.

POPULAR VOTE

(101,263 of 130,810 voting units) Roosevelt, 20,647,097; Dewey, 18,193,492.

SENATE

Democrats elected 15 including Barkley, Wagner, Tydings, McMahon, Hayden, Thomas (Okla.), Thomas (Utah), and Lucas, outside the Solid South. Brien McMahon, one-time assistant attorney general, trounced John Danaher, the Republican incumbent in Connecticut. The Republicans had elected eight, including two in Oregon, and one each in Kansas, South Dakota, Vermont, Iowa, Wisconsin and Colorado.

HOUSE

Democrats elected 193 including 18 seats now held by Republicans. Republicans elected 109 including two seats now held by Democrats. Administration critics Clare Hoffman (Rep., Mich.) and Clare Boothe Luce (Rep., Conn.) were reelected, while Hamilton Fish, Republican House veteran of 12 terms, lost out.

GOVERNORS

Democrats elected 11 (Arizona, Arkansas, Florida, Idaho, Massachusetts, Missouri, North Carolina, Rhode Island, Tennessee, Texas and West Virginia) and led in five other states. Republicans elected eight (Connecticut, Iowa, Kansas, Maine—on Sept. 11—Nebraska, South Dakota, Wisconsin and Vermont) and were ahead in eight others.

Yanks Smash 30 Jap Ships, 440 Aircraft

U. S. Planes Hit Manila Bay Again, Sinking 5 More Vessels

MAP ON PAGE 8

Pearl Harbor, Nov. 8 (UP)—American carrier planes striking anew at the Manila area in preparation for the next phase of the liberation of the Philippines had raised their toll to 30 Japanese ships and 440 planes destroyed or damaged today.

At least five vessels were sunk, a heavy cruiser and a destroyer probably sunk and 23 other vessels damaged in attacks Saturday and Sunday on the enemy's waning sea and airpower by planes from Admiral William F. Halsey's 3d Fleet.

The battle of the Philippines already was shaping up as the most decisive campaign fought in the Pacific since the United States regained the initiative.

Tokyo, recognizing that her entire southern empire was threatened, announced that Gen. Tomoyuki Yamashita, who captured Bataan, Corregidor and Singapore, had returned to the command of Japanese forces in the Philippines area.

On Leyte, some 350 miles south of Manila, Gen. Douglas MacArthur's American invasion forces finally joined battle with elements of four Japanese divisions in what probably will prove the final and decisive struggle for the central Philippines island.

Units of the American 24th Division ran headon into elements of the 1st, 20th and 102d Japanese Divisions and remnants of the no-

(Continued on Page Eight)

House Goes Democratic In Big Gain

President's Party Picks up 20 New Seats in Chamber

NYE OUT, REED WINS

Roll-Call in Senate Is Likely to Stay Put; Gillette Trails

New York, Nov. 8 (UP)—The Democrats were assured of stronger control of the House of Representatives today with a gain of approximately 20 seats.

A United Press tabulation showed Democratic nominees had ousted 20 incumbent Republicans, elected their 219th man in returns completed at 3:30 p. m., and had filled at least four of the five vacancies now in the House. The Republicans won two seats now held by Democrats, leaving the Democrats a net gain of 22. There are 93 undecided contests.

The Republicans lost five seats in Pennsylvania, four in Connecticut, three in New York, two in Illinois and one each in Maryland, Kentucky, Minnesota, California, Missouri and Ohio.

The 342 candidates definitely elected included 202 Democrats, 138 Republicans, one Progressive and one American Labor Party member. The Democrats have 214 against 212 Republican seats in the present Congress, and need at least 218 for a bare majority.

The Democrats lost another seat, in California, when Gordon L. McDonough (Rep.) defeated Hal Styles (Dem.) for the seat which former Representative John M. Costello, (Dem.) lost to Styles in the primary election.

The Democrats shared in a notable victory but it will do them no good when the House is organized. Augustus W. Bennet, nominee of the Democratic, American Labor, Liberal and Good Government parties, defeated Republican Incumbent Hamilton Fish, Jr.,

(Continued on Page Nine)

LATEST FIGURES

HOUSE

Latest Associated Press returns on the 435 House of Representatives seats showed:

Democrats elected, 219. (Present Congress, 214; vacancies, 5.)

Republicans elected, 118 (Present Congress, 212.)

Progressives elected, 1. (Present Congress, 2.)

American Laborites elected, 1. (Present Congress, 1.)

Contests undecided, 110.

SENATE

Latest Associated Press returns on the 35 Senate contests showed:

Democrats elected, 15; holdovers, 36; total, 51.

Republicans elected, 8; holdovers, 24; total, 32.

Progressive holdover, 1.

Contests undecided, 12.

INJUNCTION ISSUED

Scranton, Pa., Nov. 8 (INS)—The Lock Haven Auto Co. was under a permanent injunction issued in federal court at Scranton restraining the Lock Haven firm from further violations of the Price Control Act.

THE CHAMP—Wearing his campaign navy cape and brown hat, President Franklin D. Roosevelt watches neighbors' torchlight parade in his honor last night when he was reelected to a fourth term in the White House. Behind the President are his daughter, Mrs. John Boettiger, and Mrs. Roosevelt. —Associated Press WIREPHOTO.

F.D.R.'s State Plurality Hits Total of 251,000; Wagner, Dye Winners

Albany, Nov. 8 (AP)—President Roosevelt had his home state's 47 electoral votes on ice today as returns from 9,086 of New York's 9,121 districts indicated a final plurality of about 250,000 over Governor Dewey.

In his hour of fresh triumph, the nation's first fourth-term Chief Executive shared vote-getting honors with his friend and fellow Democrat, U. S. Senator Robert F. Wagner.

Mr. Wagner galloped far ahead of Secretary of State Thomas J. Curran, Republican nominee for the veteran New Deal senator's seat.

In step with the Democratic victory swing, Marvin R. Dye of Rochester, a judge of the State Court of Claims, climbed to the highest rung in New York's judiciary ladder—the Court of Appeals bench—by defeating State Supreme Court Justice John Van Voorhis of Irondequoit.

Mr. Roosevelt, Mr. Wagner and Judge Dye received vital help from the American Labor Party and its offshot, the Liberal Party.

With only 35 districts unreported, all of them outside New York City, Mr. Roosevelt's plurality stood at 251,838 on the basis of unofficial returns.

The President rolled up 3,278,640 against 3,026,802 for Governor Dewey.

Unofficial returns from 3,322 of 5,421 districts outside New York City gave Mr. Roosevelt, 1,224,295; Mr. Dewey, 1,682,784, netting the Governor a 458,489 plurality.

New York City complete gave Mr. Roosevelt, 2,039,932; Mr. Dewey, 1,270,083 — a Roosevelt plurality of 769,849.

Returns from 9,011 districts gave Mr. Wagner 3,254,488, Mr. Curran 2,855,015 — a margin of 399,473 for the sponsor of the

(Continued on Page Nine)

SOVIET TROOPS LAND ON DANUBE ISLE TO OUTFLANK BUDAPEST

London, Nov. 8 (UP) — Radio Budapest said today that Soviet troops, outflanking the Hungarian capital from the south, had landed on a small island in the middle of the Danube River four miles away.

"Fighting is going on not far from Budapest," the broadcast said, adding that Soviet artillery and anti-aircraft guns already were firing from Dunaharaszti, suburban town on the east bank of the Danube also within four miles of the capital.

Berlin reported the Red Army had launched a strong assault against the 140-mile German defense line along the Tisza River northeast of Budapest and had seized two bridgeheads on the west bank, posing a new threat against the satellite capital.

The Soviet high command for the second straight day made no mention of the fighting around Budapest in its communiques. It was believed Marshal Rodion Y. Malinovsky was regrouping his 2d Ukrainian Army for the final assault on the city.

CHINA HAILS F. D. R. VICTORY

Chungking, Nov. 8 (AP)—President Roosevelt's reelection put Chungking in a happy mood today despite the worsening South China military situation. The news spread quickly throughout the capital and burdened its meager telephone system.

Democrats Get 3 of 26 G. O. P. Governorships

Tobin Wins Massachusetts; Missouri Republican Is Far Behind

Washington, Nov. 8 (AP)—Democrats captured three of the 26 Republican governorships in a notable election upset and today were threatening the G. O. P. hold on several others.

The turnover extended from Massachusetts in the East to Missouri in the Middle West and Idaho in the West. It generally followed the Roosevelt tide.

Maurice J. Tobin, 43-year-old Democratic Boston mayor, was conceded election as Massachusetts' chief executive succeeding Republican Gov. Leverett Saltonstall. Mr. Tobin was leading Republican Lieut. Gen. Horace T. Cahill by over 130,000 votes.

Idaho voters chose Democrat

(Continued on Page Eight)

F. D. R. Holds 70,000-Vote Margin in Returns From Pa.

Harrisburg, Nov. 8 (INS)—President Roosevelt took a commanding 70,000-vote lead today over Gov. Thomas E. Dewey in Pennsylvania and was holding ground with each tabulation of results in the 208 precincts yet to be counted.

Returns from 8,004 precincts, including New Deal strong points in Philadelphia and Pittsburgh, gave Mr. Roosevelt 1,733,071 compared with 1,662,461 for Mr. Dewey.

In Pittsburgh, he carried the city by more than 60,000 votes while Philadelphia fell to him by a final unofficial plurality of 132,028.

Democratic Representative Francis J. Myers, of Philadelphia, continued to hold a comfortable 72,534-vote lead over James J. Davis, of Pittsburgh, for the U. S. Senate.

Voters turned in 1,602,595 ballots for Mr. Myers in 7,856 precincts and 1,530,000 for the 71-year-old lawmaker who served Pennsylvania for 14 years after being secretary of labor for Presi-

(Continued on Page Nine)

Dewey Gets Only 14 States, Fails to Break F.D.R. Grip in East

By the Associated Press

See-saw swings in three key states today kept in doubt the size of President Roosevelt's fourth term victory.

The electoral vote totals stood at 407 to 124 at 3:30 p. m. after several shifts by New Jersey.

New Jersey shifted back to the Roosevelt column at midday, but in vote total approaching 2,000,000, the margin amounted to only 4,000. Outstanding ballots made the eventual decision uncertain.

The President was gaining in both Ohio and Michigan and there was a possibility that he might run his electoral vote up to 451 against 80 for Mr. Dewey. His third term electoral count was 449 to 82 for Wendell L. Willkie.

A mix-up at Detroit, blamed by officials on inexperienced election workers, resulted in "losing" 50,000 votes in about 100 precincts. A special canvass will have to be made, and the state's electoral votes appeared certain to remain in doubt until that is done tomorrow.

F. D. R. Leads in 34 States

At 2:30 p. m. the popular vote for President, from 102,660 of the country's 130,810 voting units, showed Mr. Roosevelt, 20,865,595, and Mr. Dewey, 18,343,397.

Mr. Roosevelt was leading in 34 states having a total of 407 electoral votes, as follows:

Alabama, Arizona, Arkansas, California, Connecticut, Delaware, Florida, Georgia, Idaho, Illinois, Kentucky, Louisiana, Maryland, Massachusetts, Minnesota, Mississippi, Missouri, Montana, Nevada, New Hampshire, New Jersey, New Mexico, New York, North Carolina, Oklahoma, Pennsylvania, Rhode Island, South Carolina, Tennessee, Texas, Utah, Virginia, Washington, West Virginia.

Mr. Dewey was leading in states with an aggregate electoral vote of 124 as follows:

Colorado, Indiana, Iowa, Kansas, Maine, Michigan, Nebraska, North Dakota, Ohio, Oregon, South Dakota, Vermont, Wisconsin, Wyoming.

Detroit for Roosevelt

At one stage Mr. Dewey had a lead of over 133,000 in the contest for Michigan's 19 electoral votes. But Wayne County (Detroit), cut into this steadily and by mid-morning it had dropped to about 50,000. The Republican candidate's Ohio lead was 25,000.

To the millions who voted with him in the Republicans' losing fight under the battle cry of "it's time for a change," went Governor Dewey's thanks and his expressed confidence that all will join in the hope that providence will guide Mr. Roosevelt and the nation to peace.

The victory vote with which the democracy's majority stamped approval on Mr. Roosevelt's conduct of the war thus far, sweeping as it was, still was less than the one he gained in his third term bid four years ago.

Along with the presidential victory, Democrats made sharp inroads in the Republican House membership which has been so close to a majority lately that the administration ran into trouble on bill after bill. Further, as most had expected, the Democrats clinched their majority in the Senate, which must pass on peace and other treaties.

Never before have foreign nations displayed so much interest in an American election—and indications at Washington were that a

(Continued on Page Nine)

Dewey Urges All to Accept Will of People

NEW YORK, Nov. 8 (AP)—Following is the text of Governor Dewey's statement conceding defeat:

"It's clear that Mr. Roosevelt has been reelected for a fourth term, and every good American will wholeheartedly accept the will of the people.

"I extend to President Roosevelt my hearty congratulations and my earnest hope that his next term will see speedy victory in the war, the establishment of lasting peace, and the restoration of tranquility among our people.

"I am deeply grateful for the confidence expressed by so many millions of my fellow citizens, and for their labors in the campaign.

"The Republican Party emerges from the election revitalized and a great force for the good of the country and for the preservation of free government in America.

"I am confident that all Americans will join me in the devout hope that in the difficult years ahead, Divine Providence will guide and protect the President of the United States."

President Roosevelt replied: "I thank you (Governor Dewey) for your statement."

Vice President-elect Truman—"It was a grand statement by Governor Dewey and it shows American sportsmanship in this political campaign."

Governor Bricker—"I join in the sentiment expressed by Governor Dewey.

BERLIN SAYS VOTING SHOWS 'U. S. WORRIED'

By the Associated Press

President Roosevelt's reelection caused no surprise, the Berlin radio said today.

"The large number of votes received by Dewey testify to the fact that Roosevelt's policy is worrying wide circles of the American people," said the broadcast, recorded by the Associated Press.

"A majority of the voters seem to have felt that the responsibility for a change in political and military leadership of the country in the present crucial stage of the war was too heavy a burden."

13 UNLUCKY FOR DEWEYS

New York, Nov. 8 (AP)—Gov. and Mrs. Thomas E. Dewey, in coming here to vote yesterday, rode from Albany in car No. 13 at the end of a 13-car train.

FIRST LADY UP LATE FOR VOTING RETURNS AND TORCH PARADE

Hyde Park, N. Y., Nov. 8 (AP)—Mrs. Roosevelt was up until an early hour today listening to election returns long after many of the guests who had crowded into the rambling family mansion had departed.

Earlier, wearing a light-colored tweed sports coat topping a long black dinner gown encrusted with silver beads and sequins about the low decolletage, she stood at the President's side, smiling radiantly and waving to Hyde Park neighbors from the portico of the house.

Ever the gracious hostess, she appeared more concerned with the comfort of many of the guests who had been standing in the crisp November night watching a torchlight parade. She urged guests into the high-ceilinged drawing room to warm themselves before a crackling fire.

ON ALL FRONTS

Wednesday, Nov. 8, 1944

THE WAR AGAINST JAPAN:

American carrier planes increase their toll to 30 Jap ships and 440 aircraft as new strikes are made in Manila area.

WESTERN FRONT:

General Patton's army launching a drive on a 25-mile front between Nancy and Metz have crossed the Seille River. In the Aachen area's see-saw battle, the Yanks lost a third town. The Americans had about completed recapture of Vossenack, center of bitter fighting for several days.

RUSSIAN OFFENSIVE:

Red troops have outflanked Budapest by landing on a Danube island and are also attacking the Nazi line northeast of city.

November 8, 1944: F.D.R. wins in a landslide. *Courtesy Jackie Deinhardt*

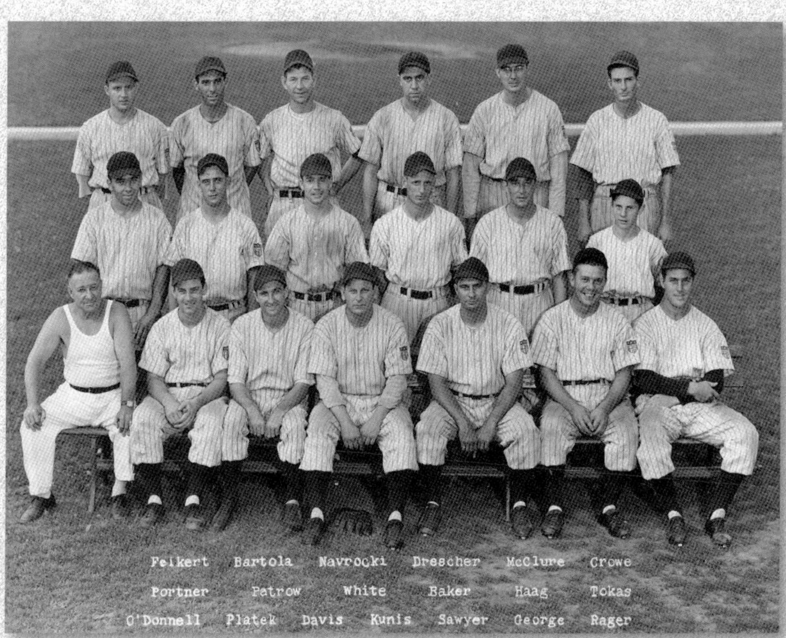
Feikert Bartola Navrocki Drescher McClure Crowe
Portner Patrow White Baker Haag Tokas
O'Donnell Platek Davis Kunis Sawyer George Rager

The Triplets baseball team, 1943. *Courtesy Ann Smith*

Benjamin's Dance Hall, Kirkwood Village, Kirkwood, 1944. A favorite for round and square dancers, it was run by Elta Benjamin (known as Benny). He is pictured in the center of the photo. The old barn was run by Benny from 1930 to 1944. This photo is the new hall built in 1944. *Courtesy Dorothy Diffendorf*

Nurses from what is believed to be the State Hospital or the nursing school in Binghamton pose for this photo in the early 1940s. Edith Schoonmaker Hibbard is pictured in the second row, second from the right. *Courtesy Virginia Hibbard*

EXTRA

BINGHAMTON PRESS

THURSDAY EVENING, APRIL 12, 1945. PRICE FOUR CENTS

ROOSEVELT DIES

Cerebral Hemorrhage at Warm Springs; Truman Quickly Sworn as New President; Cabinet Is Called Into Emergency Session

Warm Springs, Ga., April 12 (AP) --- President Franklin D. Roosevelt died unexpectedly today of a cerebral hemorrhage, at 3:45 p. m. (Central War Time) at his summer cottage here.

The shocking news of the fourth term President's death was announced to the press by Secretary William D. Hassett shortly before 5 p. m. (CWT)

"It is my sad duty," he told the reporters, "to announce the President died at 3:45 p. m., of a cerebral hemorrhage."

Hassett urged the reporters to rush to their telephones immediately as a simultaneous announcement was being made at the White House in Washington.

In quivering voice, in the presence of other members of the White House staff who came here with Mr. Roosevelt March 30, for what was to be a three weeks rest, Mr. Hassett said further details as to the cause of death would be given out later by Commander Howard Bruenn, naval doctor who was taking care of the nation's 31st President, in the absence of Vice Admiral Ross T. McIntyre, navy surgeon general.

There was no information immediately available here as to when Vice President Harry S. Truman, a formr Missouri Senator, would be sworn in as Mr. Roosevelt's successor.

In Washington, at the moment this was dictated Mr Truman and the cabinet were in an emergency meeting at the White House.

So insistent was Secretary Hassett that the news be made public immediately that details were left for future announcement.

The death of the President was announced a few short mniutes after it was rveald that high army officials had told senators the war soon would be over in Germany.

Cabinet members began assembling at 6 p. m., E.W.T., for an emergency session.

First to arrive were Secretary of Labor Perkins and Secretary of the Interior Ickes, veterans of every month Mr. Roosevelt served in the White House.

Mr. Roosevelt died in the bedroom in his little white bungalow atop Pine Mountain, where he had been ccming for 20 years to take the after-treatments for infantile paralysis with which he was stricken in 1921.

Long before his presidency, Mr. Roosevelt helped found the Warm Springs Foundation for polio victims. In recent months he had taken a deep interest

(Continued on Page Four)

BULLETIN

Washington, April 12 (AP)—Harry S. Truman of Missouri was sworn in as thirty-second president of the United States tonight at 7:09 P. M. (EWT).

HARRY S. TRUMAN
The New President

Born 1882 Died 1945

President Roosevelt

April 12, 1945: Roosevelt's death called for an extra edition. *Microfilm archives*

Weather Indications
Fair and Cooler

The Binghamton Sun

"FIRST IN THE HOMES OF SOUTHERN NEW YORK AND NORTHERN PENNSYLVANIA FOR MORE THAN A CENTURY"

Triple Cities **FINAL**

ONE HUNDRED AND TWENTY-THIRD YEAR NO. 166 — BINGHAMTON, N. Y., WEDNESDAY, MAY 2, 1945 — PRICE FOUR CENTS

HITLER DEAD, HAMBURG RADIO SAYS

Australia, Tokio Report Invasion of Borneo

Oil-Rich Territory Struck by Combined Aussie, U. S. Force

Report Unconfirmed by MacArthur in Notice of Advances on Vital Mindanao Port

Truth About Fate of Hitler Remains Unsolved Mystery

COMMONS TOLD BIG NEWS MAY BE THIS WEEK

Prime Minister Churchill Promises to Inform House If Break Comes

Der Fuehrer 'Fallen at His Post'; Admiral Doenitz Named Successor

New Leader Tells German People He Will Continue Struggle Against Bolshevism

(By Associated Press)

LONDON, May 1—The Nazi radio at Hamburg said tonight that Adolf Hitler had died this afternoon at his command post in Berlin and had been succeeded by Admiral Karl Doenitz.

The broadcast, recorded by the Associated Press listening post in London, said:

"From the Fuehrer's headquarters it is reported that our Fuehrer, Adolf Hitler, has fallen this afternoon in his command post at the Reichs Chancellery, fighting up to his last breath against Bolshevism."

Doenitz, commander of the German Navy, then was introduced by the announcer as "our new Fuehrer," and declared that Hitler had died "a hero's death."

ADOLF HITLER

YANKEES CAPTURE HITLER'S AUSTRIAN BIRTHPLACE TOWN

Braunau Taken by Third Army; Patton, Reds Are 40 Miles From Junction

RUSSIANS NEAR AREA WHERE HITLER WAS SAID TO HAVE DIED

Shock Troops Take 100 Rubbled Blocks of Nazi Capital; Victory Close

SEIZURE OF MINES THREATENED AGAIN

Walkouts of 72,000 Miners Cut Into Fuel Supply

Four Small Powers to Head Plan Drafting Commissions

No Snags Encountered as United Nations Conference Squares Away to Real Work

Admiral Karl Doenitz

Arnold's Forces Nearing Airfield on East Okinawa

Graziani Confirms Ligurian's Defeat After Death Rumor

'Object So Sublime' Sought in Punishment for Hirohito

President Requests No Celebrations on End of Nazi Battle

Rest for Wicked? Not on Jap Isles

May 2, 1945: Hitler's death foretold end of European conflict. *Courtesy Jackie Deinhardt*

Weather Indications
Showers, Not So Warm
Forecast and Summary on Page 2

The Binghamton Sun

"FIRST IN THE HOMES OF SOUTHERN NEW YORK AND NORTHERN PENNSYLVANIA FOR MORE THAN A CENTURY"

Triple Cities **FINAL**

ONE HUNDRED AND TWENTY-THIRD YEAR NO. 171 — BINGHAMTON, N. Y., TUESDAY, MAY 8, 1945 — PRICE FOUR CENTS

OFFICIAL ENDING OF WAR EXPECTED AT 9 A.M. TODAY

Nazis Plead for Reconciliation With Nations

No Recovery Possible Unless World's Hate Ends, Krosigk Says

Foreign Minister Lauds 'Heroic Fight' of Reich in Message—Calls Terms 'Harsh'

HIGH COURT RULES MINERS ENTITLED TO GET TRAVEL PAY

Legality of New Wage Bargain Thrown Into Doubt by Ruling of Justices

Americans Push Ahead on All Okinawa Lines Against Japs' Defenses

Japs Break Through Near Yank Air Base in West Hunan Province

'Old Glory' Displaces Swastika...

THE SPIRIT OF '76 MARCHES ON—The Allies have raised the flag of victory over the fallen Nazi Reich today in the same indomitable spirit which is evidenced in this photograph by Joe Rosenthal of Marines raising the Stars and Stripes over Mt. Suribachi on Iwo Jima and also in the insert above of Archibald M. Willard's famous painting of Civil War marchers, "The Spirit of '76." The same dauntless courage is now making strides toward achieving the victory in the Pacific.

Allies Rejoice Over Victory, Pledge Selves to Defeat Japs

HILARITY TEMPERED BY UNFINISHED WAR

New York City Crowds Roar Joy in Times Square

German General in Norway Orders Obedience to Terms

King George Relays Thanks of British to Eisenhower

Truman May Attend Manila Ceremonies

Announcement Due From Big 3 After Unexplained Delay

CZECH PARTISANS REPORT YANKS IN PRAGUE SUBURBS

Germans Fighting on as Nazi General Refuses to Comply With Surrender

President Truman, Churchill Wait Only for Stalin to Agree

LONDON, May 7 (AP).—Germany surrendered unconditionally to the Allies today, completing the victory in the European phase of the second world war—the most devastating in history.

Prime Minister Churchill will proclaim the historic conquest at 9 a. m. (Eastern War Time) tomorrow from 10 Downing st. and simultaneous announcements are expected from President Truman in Washington and Premier Marshal Stalin in Moscow.

Churchill then will report directly to Commons and ask for adjournment to Westminster Abbey for a service of thanksgiving.

The whereabouts of such war criminals as Himmler, Goering, even Hitler himself although he had been reported dead, were unknown or if they were known they had not been officially announced.

Signed at Eisenhower's Headquarters

Germany's formal capitulation came at 2:41 a. m. (French Time) in the red Reims schoolhouse, headquarters of General Eisenhower, supreme commander of the Allies of the West.

The crowning triumph came just five years, eight months and six days after Hitler invaded weak but proud Poland and struck the spark which set the world afire.

It marked the official end of war in Europe, but it did not silence all the guns, for battles raged on in Czecho-Slovakia.

Truman to Speak

Victory Won, Reds Urge Speed in Security Plans

May 8, 1945: The Sun prepares its readers for the end of the European war. *Courtesy David Silvanic*

END IN EUROPE

GERMANY QUITS

FIRST **EXTRA**

BINGHAMTON PRESS

Vol. 67, No. 23. TWENTY-EIGHT PAGES MONDAY EVENING, MAY 7, 1945. ★ PRICE FOUR CENTS

Unconditional Surrender to U. S., Britain, Soviet Is Signed by Nazi Army and Navy Commanders at Eisenhower Headquarters

By the Associated Press

Reims, France, May 7 -- Germany surrendered unconditionally to the Western Allies and Russia at 2:41 a. m. French time today. (This was 8:41 p. m., Eastern War Time Sunday.)

The surrender took place at a little red schoolhouse which is the headquarters of General Eisenhower. The surrender which brought the war in Europe to a formal end after five years, eight months and six days of bloodshed and destruction was signed for Germany by Col. Gen. Gustaf Jodl. General Jodl is the new chief of staff of the German Army.

It was signed for the Supreme Allied Command by Lt. Gen. Walter Bedell Smith, chief of staff for General Eisenhower. It was also signed by Gen. Ivan Susloparoff for Russia and by Gen. Francois Sevez for France.

Gen. Eisenhower was not present at the signing, but immediately afterward General Jodl and his fellow delegate, General Admiral Hans Georg Friedeburg, were received by the Supreme Commander.

They were asked sternly if they understood the surrender terms imposed upon Germany and if they would be carried out by Germany. They answered yes.

Germany, which began the war with a ruthless attack upon Poland followed by successive aggressions and brutality in internment camps, surrendered with an appeal to the victors for mercy toward the German people and armed forces.

After signing the full surrender, General Jodl said he wanted to speak and was given leave to do so.

"With this signature," he said in soft-spoken German, "the German people and armed forces are for better or worse delivered into the victors' hands."

"In this war which has lasted more than

(Continued on Page Ten)

Patton, Soviets In Last-Minute Mopup of Foe

Both Yanks and Reds Near Prague in Windup Push of War

Paris, May 7 (AP)—American and Russian armies beat through Czechoslovakia and Austria today in the final mopup of organized German resistance and embattled patriots in Prague said at 9 a. m. (E. W. T.) that U. S. 3d Army tanks were only 15 miles from that city.

[illegible]

(Continued on Page Ten)

LaGuardia Can Be Airline 'Czar'

New York, May 7 (AP) — Mayor F. H. LaGuardia, who announced yesterday he would not seek reelection, has been offered the presidency of the Air Transport Association, the New York Daily News says in a copyrighted story.

[illegible]

WEATHER

Increasing cloudiness and not quite so cool tonight. [illegible]

GENERAL EISENHOWER

HE TAKES NAZI SURRENDER—Full surrender of Germany was signed at 8:41 p. m. (E. W. T.) Sunday at General Eisenhower's headquarters, it was announced today.

—Associated Press Photo

Booming Post-War Production Seen

New York, May 7 (AP)—American [illegible]

Reich Announcement

London, May 7 (UP)—The text of a speech by German Foreign Minister Count Ludwig Schwerin von Krosigk as broadcast by the Flensburg radio and recorded by the BBC:

German men and women: The high command of the armed forces on orders of Grand Admiral Doenitz has today declared the unconditional surrender of all German fighting troops.

As leading minister of the Reich Government which the Admiral of the Fleet has appointed for dealing with war tasks, I turn at this tragic moment of our history to the German nation.

After a heroic fight of almost six years of incomparable hardness, Germany has succumbed to the overwhelming power of her enemies.

To continue the war would only mean senseless bloodshed and futile disintegration.

The government which has a feeling of responsibility for the future of its nation was compelled to act on the collapse of all physical and material forces, and

(Continued on Page Ten)

'Lord Haw Haw' May Be in Eire

London, May 7 (UP)—The Daily Mail suggested today that one of three men who landed near Dublin Saturday after a flight from Denmark might have been William Joyce, the "Lord Haw Haw" who broadcast for the Nazis throughout the war.

The Mail said one of the three was a passenger in mufti who spoke fluent English. It added that many persons were asking whether it was Joyce, but officials of Eire were silent.

It's Anti-Climax To U. S. G.I.'s

With the U. S. 1st Army in Germany, May 7 (AP)—The announcement of complete victory over the Germans comes as an anti-climax to American doughboys who have seen the German Army disintegrate.

They are now asking themselves "Where do we go from here?"

It is a strange ending to a strange war, an ending nobody could have quite visualized and without the dramatic conclusion most of us had pictured. Suddenly the war just melted away into nothingness and the guns were still.

May 7, 1945: The Press keeps extras flowing to keep citizens up to date on the end. *Courtesy Arlene Pewterbaugh*

THE WEATHER
Intermittent rain tonight and ending early tomorrow, then cloudy. Lowest temperature tonight near 55.

BINGHAMTON PRESS

City Edition
Complete Financial News

Vol. 67, No. 99. EIGHTEEN PAGES MONDAY EVENING, AUGUST 6, 1945. ★★★ PRICE FOUR CENTS

POWER OF UNIVERSE LOOSED AT JAPAN BY ATOMIC BOMB

Our Missile Has 20,000-Ton TNT Strength

TEXT OF ANNOUNCEMENT, PAGE 9

By the Associated Press

Washington—An atomic bomb, hailed as the most terrible destructive force in history and as the greatest achievement of organized science, has been loosed upon Japan.

"The atomic bomb," President Truman said, "is a harnessing of the basic power of the universe. The force from which the sun draws its power has been loosed against those who brought war to the Far East."

President Truman disclosed in a White House statement at 11 a. m., (E. W. T.), today that the first use of the bomb—containing more power than 20,000 tons of TNT and producing more than 2,000 times the blast of the most powerful bomb ever dropped before—was made 16 hours earlier on Hiroshima, Japanese army base.

The atomic bomb is the answer, President Truman said, to Japan's refusal to surrender. Secretary of War Stimson predicted the bomb will "prove a tremendous aid" in shortening the Japanese war.

Japs May Expect Rain of Ruin

Mr. Truman grimly warned that "even more powerful forms (of the bomb) are in development." He said:

"If the Japanese do not now accept our terms, they may expect a rain of ruin from the air the like of which has never been seen on this earth."

The War Department reported that "an impenetrable cloud of dust and smoke" cloaked Hiroshima after the first atomic bomb crashed down. It was impossible to make an immediate assessment of the damage.

President Truman said he would recommend that Congress consider establishing a commission to control production of atomic power within the United States, adding:

"I shall . . . make . . . recommendations to Congress as to how atomic power can become a powerful influence towards the maintenance of world peace."

Consider Peacetime Application

Both Mr. Truman and Secretary Stimson, while emphasizing the peacetime potentiality of the new force, made clear that much research must be undertaken to effect full peacetime application of its principles.

The product of $2,000,000,000 spent in research and production—"the great scientific gamble in history," Mr. Truman said—the atomic bomb has been one of the most closely guarded secrets of the war.

Franklin D. Roosevelt and Winston Churchill gave the signal to start work on harnessing the forces of the atom. Mr. Truman said the Germans worked feverishly, but failed to solve the problem.

Mr. Truman added:

"It is an atomic bomb. It is a harnessing of the basic power of the universe. The force from which the sun draws its power has been loosed against those who brought war to the Far East."

Hiroshima Is City of 318,000

The base that was hit is a major quartermaster depot and has large ordnance, machine tool and aircraft plants.

The raid on Hiroshima, located on Honshu Island on the shores of the Inland Sea, had not been disclosed previously although the 20th Air Force on Guam announced that 580 Superforts raided four Japanese cities at about the same time.

The city of 318,000 also contains a principal port.

The President disclosed that the Germans "worked feverishly" in search of a way to use atomic energy in their war effort but failed. Meanwhile American and British scientists studied the problem and developed two principal plants and some lesser factories for the production of atomic power.

The President disclosed that more than 65,000 persons are working in great secrecy in these plants, adding:

"We have spent $2,000,000,000 on the greatest scientific gamble in history—and won.

Ready to Destroy Warpower

"We are now prepared to obliterate more rapidly and completely every productive enterprise the Japanese have above ground in any city. We shall completely destroy Japan's power to make war."

The President noted that the Big 3 ultimatum issued July 26 at Potsdam was intended "to spare the Japanese people from utter destruction" and the Japanese leaders rejected it. The atomic bomb now is the answer to that rejection and the President said "they may expect a rain of ruin from the air, the like of which has never been seen on this earth."

Mr. Truman forecast that sea

(Continued on Page Two)

WHAT 3,000 TONS OF TNT DID

New York—(AP)—A faint idea of the power within the atomic bomb:

On June 6, 1917, a munitions ship blew up in a collision in Halifax, N. S., harbor; 1,500 persons were killed, 4,000 injured, 20,000 made homeless, two and one-half square miles of the city devastated.

That munitions ship carried 3,000 tons of TNT—about one-seventh of the equivalent of the new bomb.

Petain Savior Of Thousands, Prince Claims

Without Armistice, French Would Have Met Fate of Poles, Xavier Says

By the United Press

Paris — Prince Xavier of Bourbon-Parma testified today that Marshal Henri Philippe Petain's orders caused the release of thousands of Frenchmen from concentration camps in central France.

Prince Xavier, brother of Empress Zita of Austria and uncle of Archduke Otto, was the second defense witness at the treason trial of Petain, now in its third week. He returned recently from Dachau.

The prince said that if Petain had not signed the armistice with Germany in 1940, Frenchmen would have suffered the same fate as the Poles.

Xavier told the jury that the old marshal "wanted to wait until the Allies came, and then join in the attack against Germany."

Indo-China Defenseless

Gen. Charles Lacaille, the first witness today, testified that France had only 50 planes and no tanks in Indo-China for the defense of the country's colony in the Far East.

Lacaille testified that in the fall of 1943, a Trappist monk named Barmby, who worked for the French intelligence service, came to see him in Paris. He had a note from Gen. Henri Giraud to Petain, seeking Vichy support.

Petain replied that the proposals were "interesting," Lacaille said, but that he wanted to wait until the Allies landed in France before making any move.

Petain fell sound asleep while Lacaille droned on about the activity of the Armistice Commission at Wiesbaden.

Communists Attacked

Prince Xavier attacked French Communists, charging they "seem to claim a monopoly on the resistance movement. But the whole of France resisted."

As a member of the resistance, Xavier said, he went to Vichy to see Petain, who told him:

"I am doing what I can to save France in this deplorable situation. After peace comes, we will inevitably have to revert to the Republic."

He said Petain complained he could do nothing at Vichy because "all my letters are opened, my phone calls are tapped, and my public utterances controlled."

Character Is Praised

When court convened, defense chief Fernan Payen read a cable from Pierre Merillon, former member of the French embassy in Madrid, praising Petain as a man of sterling character.

Lacaille testified that he often heard Petain support the use of aviation and armor in strengthening France's armed forces. But there were only a handful of

(Continued on Page Two)

Hitler Dead? Radio Voice Says 'I'm Not'

Stockholm—(UP)—The newspaper Aftonbladet said yesterday that a man identifying himself as Adolf Hitler spoke over a clandestine radio station Saturday night.

The dispatch described the speaker's voice as "remarkably like Hitler's but with a notable difference." The radio station called itself Dietrich Eckardt and the newspaper suggested that it might be situated in Ireland.

Aftonbladet quoted the speaker as saying:

"Now the hour has come when I can speak to the German people again and answer the question, 'Does he live or not?' The world can be assured he lives."

—Associated Press Photo

HIRAM JOHNSON ▼

Hiram Johnson Is Dead at 79; Foe of Charter

Washington — (AP) — Hiram W. Johnson of California, militant opponent of the League of Nations and the San Francisco Charter for a United Nations Organization, died today at 79 years.

The veteran Republican Senator succumbed at Naval Hospital, where he had been confined for two and one-half weeks. His physician, Capt. Robert E. Duncan, U. S. N., said he died from a thrombosis of a cerebral artery.

The 79-year-old Californian died at 6:45 a. m., after having been in ill health for some time.

His political activities extended over a third of a century covering some of the most stirring events in the nation's history.

In Senate Since '16

A striking figure in the Senate since first elected to Congress in 1916, he played a leading part in defeating President Wilson's League of Nations Covenant and later in opposing United States adherence to the World Court.

His wife, whom he referred to as "the boss," was with him at the time of his death.

Senator McKellar (Dem., Tenn.), president of the Senate, today will appoint a committee to attend the funeral.

Senator Johnson, who served as governor of California from 1910 until his election to Congress six years later, described himself as a "progressive Republican" and was instrumental in writing into his state's constitution such provisions as the initiative, referendum and recall, the direct primary, woman suffrage and the wiping out of national party lines in municipal and county elections.

Backed, Fought F. D. R.

Although he always retained the Republican label in his Senate activities, he several times broke with that party, the most recent being his support of President Roosevelt in 1932.

During Mr. Roosevelt's second term, however, the veteran Californian opposed the President on several major issues and took the stump against him when he ran for a third term.

Peace Draft Is Licked, Its Backers Admit

Charge Army With Killing Own Program by 'Hogging' Policy

Washington — (AP) — Congressional backers of universal military training said privately today they have all but abandoned hope of winning their fight.

They plan to make an effort, when Congress reconvenes in October, to put through a program of compulsory training for all able-bodied youths, but they don't expect to get far.

The House Post-War Military Policy Committee, headed by Representative Woodrum (Dem., Va.), has recommended the program. It has the solid backing of the army, navy and veterans' groups, but is opposed by most churchmen, educators and organized labor.

Army Held Beating Itself

Members of the House Military Affairs Committee charged today that the army itself was defeating its request for compulsory military training after the war.

Members pointed to a mounting friction between Congress and the War Department over:

ONE—Heavy army spending.

TWO—Army insistence on keeping a force of 7,000,000 for the remainder of the war. Many congressmen believe that is far too much.

THREE—Charge that army stockpiling of food is partly responsible for the domestic shortage.

FOUR—The army's refusal to release the demanded number of railroaders, coal miners and shipyard workers to meet war and homefront needs.

Three House committee members—all proponents of peacetime training—said their hopes for such a program were fast fading. One said that the army's relationships with Congress "had sunk to their lowest level in history."

Civilian Control Predicted

"If we have a universal military training program after the war it will be in spite of the army and not because of it," he said.

Senator Edwin C. Johnson (Dem., Colo.), member of the Senate Military Affairs Committee, said the War Department's policies were causing a "growing mistrust" both among the public and in the service itself.

"The War Department's arbitrary attitude about releasing eligible men who are no longer needed and its apparent desire to hog everything in order to keep up its own establishment are causing a sharp decline in public sentiment for conscription," Mr. Johnson said.

T. R.'s Widow 84

Oyster Bay — (AP) — Mrs. Edith Kermit Roosevelt, widow of President Theodore Roosevelt, today quietly observed her eighty-fourth birthday with her family.

Power of Atomic Force Explained

By HOWARD W. BLAKESLEE
Associated Press Science Editor

NEW YORK — President Truman's statement that the atomic bomb is made of the force from which the sun draws its power explains the principle of this new explosive.

The sun's power is the sun's heat. For years scientists have known that this heat could not come from ordinary fires like any known on the earth's face. The sun just wasn't big enough to have lasted the billions of years during which there is plenty of evidence it has been burning at the present rate.

In ordinary fire, molecules of wood, coal or whatever else is blazing, separate. As they come apart, the energy which held them together, is released in the form of heat, light and other rays, like X-rays. Even a hot fire gives off a bit of X-rays.

The sun burns not by separation of molecules but by two more intensely hot methods. One is the atoms that form molecules separating from each other. This kind of separation releases incredibly greater amounts of heat and energy than molecule separations.

But an even greater source of sun power is the fact that the atoms themselves come apart to some extent. These atoms are made of electrons, protons and other electrical and non-electrical particles. Electrons and [illegible] separation releases even greater energies (including heat and all other sorts of rays) than the separation of atoms from each other.

Not all these inter-atomic forces are yet even known. Some are so powerful that they have only been guessed at. The popular phrase, smashing the atom, describes this sort of atomic disintegration where the atom itself flies apart.

For many years scientists have been able to disintegrate atoms in laboratories. There were no explosions, because billions of atoms would have to go off at one time, even to equal a firecracker. The reason is that atoms are so exceedingly tiny.

It has been clear to scientists for nearly a half century that if they could get enough atoms in a piece of solid matter, or even gas, the size of a pea, to break up all at once, the explosion would be terrible.

President Truman's announcement gives no clue to the method of producing the atomic bomb. The steps which were sensational just before the war, and which were given world-wide publicity then, are still strictly censored, even though the information is available in public records.

His statement does give one clue, which is in line with what scientists expected. This is that there are useful possibilities in the atomic power as well as destruction. What will explode, will also burn more slowly, to give heat for making steam or electricity.

The atomic bomb hunt started right after the war got under way when a German mathematician, a Jewish woman, Lize Meitner, calculated that something which had puzzled scientists for 10 years was really an explosion of atoms of one of the kinds of the metal uranium.

Within two weeks after she published this calculation the great physics laboratories in the United States, England and Germany had verified her prediction. She was banished from Germany shortly afterward, but Hitler put all available physicists at work on atomic bombs and atomic power at the Kaiser Wilhelm Institute, Berlin.

What the scientists found was that a rare form of uranium, known as 235, when bombarded with low electrical energy (in the form of neutrons) would react by splitting some of its atoms [illegible]

Up to that time no atom had ever been really smashed. A few electrons or other particles had been forced out by the smashing rays used, which might be X-rays or rays made of atomic particles.

When uranium atoms split in two, as the German woman predicted, a whole new world opened for atomic power. The energy released by an atom breaking in two was thousands of times greater than the energy when just a few pieces were chipped off.

This new situation started the United States and Britain on a hunt for atomic power and atomic bombs, and even before the United States entered the war, all this atomic work was placed under censorship. Since then not a single development has been published until today's bomb announcement.

5 Major Jap Targets Fired By B-29 Blast

Guam—(AP) — American fighter-bombers hit Tokyo and five surrounding prefectures today only a few hours after almost 600 Superfortresses set fire to five major targets along a 550-mile stretch of Japan in a pre-dawn assault.

A Tokyo broadcast said a few Superforts this morning dropped fire bombs and high explosives on Hiroshima, Honshu city of 350,000 northwest of Kure.

Radio Tokyo said 130 Iwo-based Mustangs swarmed over the Greater Tokyo area in two waves for an hour shortly before 9 a. m., bombing and strafing military and transport objectives. Urban areas of several cities also were said to have been attacked.

The first wave of 70 planes raided Saitama, Gumma and Tochigi prefectures, all north of Tokyo, the enemy broadcast said. The second wave of 60 Mustangs struck northern Tokyo itself and Chiba, Ibaraki and Tochigi prefectures, southeast, northeast and north of Tokyo.

Superfortress crews reported "good to excellent" results in their 3,850-ton pre-dawn raid on a synthetic gasoline plant at Ube and on the industrial centers of Maebashi and Nishinomiya-Mikage on Honshu, Saga on Kyushu and Imabari on Shikoku.

Radio Tokyo said some bombs also fell in the big Honshu war production center of Osaka, Japan's second largest city.

Maebashi was raided for about two hours and suffered a "considerable loss," Tokyo said.

Others in the force of no fewer than 580 B-29's mined enemy waters near Tsurga and Hagi on the southwest coast of Honshu and around Rashin, in northeast Korea, 21 miles from the Soviet border.

It marked the first time that the Superfortresses have attacked three of the four main Japanese home islands in a single assault.

A dispatch from the 3d Fleet revealed that it still was off the Japanese coast.

Stimson Says Bomb's Effect 'Staggers Mind'

Washington—(AP)—Secretary Stimson predicted today that the atomic bomb will "prove a tremendous aid" in shortening the war with Japan.

The war secretary made his statement as the army reported that an "impenetrable cloud of dust and smoke" cloaked Hiroshima after it was hit by the new weapon from the air.

An accurate assessment of the damage inflicted by the bomb is not yet available, however, the War Department said. As soon as details of its effectiveness are learned, the department added, they will be released.

Mr. Stimson said in his statement that the explosive power of the bomb is such as to "stagger the imagination." He added that scientists are confident of developing even more powerful atomic bombs.

Mr. Stimson said that security requirements do not permit disclosure of the exact methods of producing the bomb or the nature of its action. He did say, however, that uranium ore is essential to the production of the bomb.

Development of the bomb culminated three years of work by Allied scientists, industry, labor and military forces, Mr. Stimson said, adding that he was convinced Japan will not be in a position to use a similar weapon. While Germany worked "feverishly" to develop an atomic bomb, Mr. Stimson said, the Nazi defeat now has erased danger from that source.

Mr. Stimson promised that fur-

(Continued on Page Two)

U. S. Controls Patent on Bomb

Washington—(INS)—The War Department announced today that substantial patent control on the atomic bomb is held by the United States.

The announcement said that Great Britain and Canada had cooperated in this arrangement.

Uranium is the essential ore in production of the weapon, the War Department said, disclosing that steps have been taken to assure continued adequate supplies of the mineral.

End of World Fear Recalled By Doom Bomb

By the Associated Press

Comm. Herbert Agar, aide to U. S. Ambassador to Great Britain John G. Winant, said on June 29 that "if the war (European) had gone on for another six months, it is quite possible that this planet would have ceased to exist because it was probable that someone would have learned to break the atom without controlling it."

Commander Agar said "there was a danger that the Germans would learn how to split the atom first," and added: "I sincerely believe that in a very few years human beings will know how to destroy the human race."

Previously Lt. Col. John A. Keck of Greensburg, Pa., chief of the Enemy Equipment Intelligence Section of the U. S. Army Ordnance Division in the European theatre, had told of many highly advanced German secret weapons which had not yet reached the perfection stage when the war ended.

While revealing many German inventions Colonel Keck added that they were not all—that there were others which must remain secret because of the Pacific war.

Churchill Says:

London — (AP) — Germany possessed some atomic power secrets, Winston Churchill said tonight; but "by God's mercy British and American science outpaced all German efforts."

Woman Denies Kidnaping Boy

Buffalo—(UP)—Mrs. Venda Taylor Jones, 24, was committed to jail in default of $25,000 bail today after pleading innocent to a charge of kidnaping four-year-old Peter Watson.

82 DAYS OF HELL ON OKINAWA

The stench of dead Japs still pollutes the air of Okinawa as Lt. George Thompson of the Marines gives his grim account of the bloodiest slaughter of the Pacific. A series of six stories begins today in The Binghamton Press.

Turn to Page 7

WHAT EMMY GOERING SAW, DID

The wife of the Nazi fat man, Hermann Goering, Emmy was on the inside of the Nazi inner circle. Now, she is talking and The Press has three exclusive stories on what she has to say. The Curt Riess stories begin today.

Turn to Page 6

ERNIE PYLE IS IMMORTAL

Hal Boyle finds the vagabond soul of Ernie Pyle is anchored in Dana, Ind. The first of two stories by the writer of "War Correspondent's Notebook" appears today.

Turn to Page 18

August 6, 1945: The Press marvels at the destruction caused by the first atomic bomb. *Courtesy Jackie Deinhardt*

REDS DECLARE WAR ON JAPAN

THE WEATHER
Clear and cooler tonight, lowest temperature 50 to 55. Thursday sunny and pleasant with moderate temperatures.

BINGHAMTON PRESS

EXTRA

Vol. 67, No. 101. TWENTY-SIX PAGES WEDNESDAY EVENING, AUGUST 8, 1945. ★★★ PRICE FOUR CENTS

Japs Admit and U. S. Pictures Show:

HIROSHIMA IS NO MORE

Truman Smiles As He Announces Reds in Jap War

London—(AP)—The Moscow radio announced tonight that Russia was at war with Japan effective Aug. 9.

By the Associated Press

Washington—President Truman announced today that Russia had declared war on Japan.

Mr. Truman made the momentous announcement to a hurriedly summoned news conference.

He said he had only a simple statement to make but it was so important he could not delay it.

Then with a broad grin he declared:

Russia has just declared war on Japan.

That is all.

The disclosure that the Soviet Union at last had pitted its enormous might alongside Britain and the United States against the Pacific enemy had not been unexpected.

When it would come, however, had been a matter of conjecture for months.

Official Washington at once took this development, along with the unleasing of atomic bombing against the Pacific enemy, as a sure sign that Japan can not long continue to resist.

Leahy at His Side

The President sat behind his desk for a minute until the 30 or so correspondents all were gathered around him. Then he arose, flanked on the right by Admiral of the Fleet William Leahy, his personal chief of staff, and on the left by Secretary of State James F. Byrnes.

The President explained that he had no intention of holding a news conference but this matter was so important he felt that it couldn't wait.

Mr. Truman then made the simple one-sentence announcement of Russia's declaration of war. He added that was all he had to say.

The short announcement brought a gasp from reporters who had rushed to the White House in a stream of taxicabs and an exclamation of "my God" from some.

Potsdam Decision?

A number of naval aides and state department attaches were present when the announcement was made.

Whether the arrangements for Russian entry into the war on Japan were fashioned at Potsdam was not disclosed.

A communique signed by himself, Generalissimo Stalin and Prime Minister Attlee, released when the Potsdam meeting ended, made no specific mention of Japan. But it carried the significant statement that chiefs of staff had studied military matters "of mutual interest."

There had been multiple hints that the Soviets would align themselves with the Western Allies in crushing the Nipponese. Perhaps the most pointed was Russia's denunciation months ago of its non-aggression pact with Japan.

Petain's Spies Helped R.A.F., Air Chief Says

Paris—(AP)—Gen. Jean Bergeret, former Vichy air minister, testified today that French secret agents furnished the R. A. F. with details of German air force activities and were paid from a budget set up by Marshal Petain, now on trial for his life.

"Petain gave me the necessary funds in secret," said the defense witness on this 13th day of the marshal's trial on charges of intelligence with the enemy and plotting against the security of France.

Refused Air Bases

Bergeret said the Germans in 1941 demanded air bases in Syria in the Middle East and asked French fighters to defend Paris, but "Petain refused both demands and, because of him, they never were carried out.

He said French forces were reorganized in secret after the armistice to resume the fight against Germany, adding:

"Marshal Petain knew and approved all of this."

"When I left the air ministry in April, 1942, we had 54 aerial groups complete and ready for action," Bergeret said. "The air force was composed of 980 planes altogether. . . . But we never had any number of the air force on active service with the Germans."

He said Petain personally retired two French air generals who clamored for collaboration.

Return to Battle

The witness said that because of his work, financed and sanctioned by Petain, 27 French air groups totaling 19,000 men returned to the war against Germany in its final stages.

Bergeret said his main tasks were to maintain contact between the French air force and the Allies, to prepare for the resumption of fighting as soon as possible and to obtain German permission for France to possess sufficient planes. Pilots were trained and planes were maintained by secret methods, he swore.

Gen. Maurice Martin testified that both the United States and Great Britain informed France they would be unable to send her aid in the Orient and suggested that the Vichy regime accept Japanese demands on French Indo-China.

He testified that the French command in Indo-China had been determined to fight on in 1940.

The witness said Cordell Hull, then U. S. secretary of state, advised Vichy unofficially to accede to Japanese demands and close the supply route to Chungking. Mr. Hull was represented as saying the United States could send no arms.

Four Powers Sign Pact For War Trials

London—(UP)—An agreement on the trial of Nazi war criminals was signed here today by American, British, Russian and French representatives.

An official announcement of the formation of an inter-Allied tribunal was expected later today.

It was believed that the announcement will reveal acceptance by Great Britain, France and Russia of all the main points of the United States proposal for single trials of all major Nazi war criminals by a joint tribunal.

British Freighter Is on Fire at Sea

Halifax, N. S.—(INS)—The British freighter Argos Hill was reported today on fire at sea, about 200 miles off the Newfoundland coast.

Truman Signs World Charter

Washington—(AP)—Ratification of the United Nations Charter by this country was formally completed today with President Truman's signature on the Senate's instrument of approval.

Truman Takes Charge of Nip Atom Bombing

Terms Weapon 'Greatest Weapon for Peace, War Ever Devised'

Washington — (AP) — President Truman today took over from the White House personal direction of the atomic bomb campaign he believes foreshadows early victory over Japan. He returned to the United States from the Potsdam conference late yesterday.

The commander-in-chief voiced his victory hopes to newsmen accompanying him home from the Big 3 meeting in Berlin. He termed the devastating weapon—which wiped out 60 per cent of its first target, a Japanese city the size of Memphis—"the most powerful weapon for war and peace ever devised."

Quoting scientists' assertions that the discovery may be the greatest "of any age for the benefit of the people," Mr. Truman added that the atomic field "means a wonderful peacetime release of energy if its powers can be harnessed for commercial use."

Meanwhile, every device known to psychological warfare experts is being used to end the Pacific war without delay.

Radio broadcasts are pounding home to the Japanese people hour after hour the terrors of atomic destruction which confront them, and leaflets telling the same story have been prepared to be scattered over the islands.

The President himself will have opportunity in his radio report this week on the Potsdam conference to renew Allied demands for the Japanese to give up now, before they force the destruction of much of their country.

The immediate objective of the campaign appears to be to split the Japanese people from their warlord leaders and terrify them into revolution. Military and naval authorities are hoping for, but not planning on this.

Word of the frightful new destruction readied for the enemy came from Guam. There, U. S. Army Strategic Air Forces said today the single atomic bomb dropped on Hiroshima Monday wiped out 4.1 square miles of the city's total area of 6.9 square miles.

PRESIDENT TO SPEAK

Washington—(UP)— President Truman will report to the nation on the Big 3 Berlin conference tomorrow night at 10 o'clock (E. W. T.). The White House said the address would be broadcast on all radio networks. Presidential Secretary Charles G. Ross said Mr. Truman would make a 30-minute address, in which he would go into greater detail about the historic Potsdam parley than was related in last week's official communique on the meeting.

What Happened When Bomb Hit

Guam—(UP)—Here are the eyewitness stories of the men who dropped the first atomic bomb on Japan:

Col. Paul W. Tibbets, Jr., 30, of Miami, pilot of the Superfortress Enola Gay:

"We selected Hiroshima as the target when we made the landfall. There was no opposition, conditions were clear and we dropped the bomb visually at 9:15 a. m.

COL. TIBBETS

"Only Captain Parsons, Bombardier Maj. Thomas W. Ferebee of Mocksville, N. C., and myself knew what dropped. Others only knew it was a special mission.

"We knew immediately that we had to get the hell out of there and made a sharp turn in less than 30 seconds to get broadside to the target.

"Then—it was hard to believe what we saw.

"Below us, rising rapidly, was a tremendous black cloud. Nothing was visible where only minutes before the outline of the city with its streets and buildings and waterfront piers were clearly apparent.

"It happened so fast we couldn't see anything and could only feel the heat from the flash and the concussion from the blast.

"There were a couple of sharp slaps against the airplane. It felt like close bursts of flak. I yelled a warning to the crewmen, but we were all okay."

Capt. William Parsons, U. S. N., of Santa Fe, N. M., one of the designers of the bomb, who went along as "weaponeer repairer" to see that the bomb worked:

"The bomb resting in the bomb-bay looked like the final test one we exploded less than a month ago—July 16—in a remote corner of the Alamogordo, N. M., bombing range.

"I had a very personal interest in the mission. We knew when we started that success could only be measured in the first battle delivery on Japan.

"We knew it was worth a lot in terms of shortening the war. When the bomb fell away, we began to put as much distance between us and the ball of fire which we knew was coming, as quickly as possible.

"There was a terrific flash of light—even in the daytime. Visual shock was apparent from several miles.

"That was the first indication I had that the bomb worked. Each man said a 'My God!'

"What had been Hiroshima was going up in a mountain of smoke.

"First I could see a mushroom of boiling dust—apparently with some debris in it—up to 20,000 feet (four miles). The boiling continued three or four minutes as I watched.

"Then a white cloud plumed upwards from the center to some 40,000 feet (eight miles). An angry dust cloud spread all around the city.

"There were fires on the fringes of the city, apparently burning as buildings crumbled and the gas mains broke.

"I knew what the Japs were in for, but I felt no particular emotion about it.

"Last month in the New Mexico desert, when we set off a facsimile bomb suspended from a tower, it fused the sand for quite a radius because it generated heat like something in the stellar regions.

"The heat flash in New Mexico was felt for 20 minutes."

Dark Future Forecast for 'Age of Atom'

By WILLIAM H. STONEMAN
Special Cable
To The Binghamton Press and the Chicago Daily News

London — Only human decency can prevent atomic energy from obliterating civilization, and considering the amount of that human quality which has been displayed since the dawn of time, the future looks dark indeed.

This was the general conclusion of scientists, statesmen, editorial writers and just plain people today as they dwelt upon the greatest scientific development in history.

There was no joy in anyone's heart as he surveyed the prospects, only a vague glimmer of hope that this monstrosity might bring people to their senses.

Among the interesting comments brought to light today in British newspapers are the following:

H. H. Dale, president of the Royal Society, in a letter to the London Times emphasizes the fact that the methods used in developing the uranium bomb cannot be kept a secret indefinitely and that the only hope of mankind must lie in controlling the use of atomic energy by international agreement.

Allied Leaders Order Further Atomic Raids

Washington—(INS)—The Allied High Command today ordered fresh atomic bombing attacks on Japan.

The new devastating blows by the greatest weapon in history may come at any moment.

It is the consensus in Washington that the atomic bombings in themselves will serve as a new ultimatum to Japan to surrender unconditionally or be wiped off the face of the earth.

This development came as official reconnaissance photographs showed that the first atomic bombing attack on the important Japanese city of Hiroshima completely destroyed sixty per cent of the war center and wiped out five major industrial targets.

Reports from fliers who dropped the first atomic bomb on the flourishing center and its 318,000 population told of a city "dissolving" under the blow. Yet only a relatively few pounds of the mysterious and potent U-235 were contained in the missile.

Officials Deny Death Rays Peril for Years

Washington—(AP)—The War Department today denied published reports that areas devastated by the atomic bomb continue for years to react with death-dealing radioactivity.

15th Jap City On 'Death List' Is Burned Out

Guam (Thursday)—(UP)— Nearly 100 Superfortresses, hitting the Japanese home islands for the fourth time in 24 hours, sent incendiaries crashing into the "death list" city of Fukuyama shortly before midnight yesterday, it was announced today.

The new blow in a 'round-the-clock offensive by the 20th Air Force followed two late afternoon demolition strikes at the Nakajima Musashimo-Tama aircraft plant in Tokyo and the once mighty Tokyo arsenal, and a smashing daylight raid with more than 1,000 tons of explosives on the great steel center of Yawata.

62 Cities Blasted

Fukuyama was the 15th of 31 cities warned by the B-29 command to be blasted by incendiaries, and the 62d Japanese city to be burned out. Located 47 miles northeast of Kure on the inland sea, with a population of 57,000, it is a center for chemical production and aircraft works.

Earlier Gen. Carl A. Spaatz had announced from U. S. Strategic Air Force headquarters that some 50 Superforts had bombed the Nakajima plant which already had been 62 per cent destroyed. The B-29's met intense flak but no enemy aircraft.

Yawata 'Scratched off'

More than 225 Superfortresses set fire to Yawata, the Pittsburgh of Japan, with demolition bombs in the morning attack.

Preliminary reports on the Yawata attack indicated it was so successful that the great steel center could be scratched from the list of Japanese cities doomed to destruction by the Superfortress command.

It'll Be Decades Before One-Sixth Ounce Of Atomized Coal Heats House for Year

New York—(UP)—It will be a long time before atomic power comes into every-day use. Our leading industrialists agree on that almost unanimously.

"In time—a long time—it will be developed for peaceful pursuits," said Dr. M. Lelyn Branin, technical consultant of the Bituminous Coal Institute.

"It will undoubtedly be generations before the atom will make all the nation's steel, power the nation's locomotives, generate the electricity or furnish the billions of hours of industrial horsepower that coal does now, let alone heat the nation's homes."

Charles W. Kellogg, president of the Edison Electric Institute, said atomic power in its present stage of development was akin to lightning.

"We all know what lightning is, and can do, but we haven't learned yet how to control it," he said.

Most industrialists agreed with Dr. W. A. Gibbons, research director of U. S. Rubber Co. that "for the generation of large quantities of power and to overcome the geographical limitations in obtaining power, atomic energy seems to be the answer."

The weekly bulletin of the Anthracite Institute, whose members control $400,000,000 worth of mines, commented:

"It has been stated that coal could produce over 3,000,000 times as much energy if used atomically, instead of in combustion. Obviously this would revolutionize the generation of heat and power, since at this ration, one-sixth of an ounce of coal would equal the annual average fuel requirements of an average home, and 20 tons would replace current annual anthracite production.

"However, there are three unanswered questions which lead to the prediction that it will be many years before the breakers are torn down to make room for atomic factories.

"The first is, can atomic energy be controlled and directed? The second is that uranium and the other material now reportedly being used all have the heaviest, most complex atoms which are relatively unstable and comparatively easy to split. Carbon, on the other hand, has one of the lightest, least complex atoms, which would indicate much greater stability. The third all-important question is how much it would cost to process a piece of coal."

150,000 Are 'Seared To Death,' Corpses 'Too Many to Count'

PICTURES, Pages 3, 5 and 18. Other bomb stories, Page 2 and 23.

By the United Press

Guam — Tokyo conceded today that most of Hiroshima had been destroyed completely by a single American atomic bomb Monday and said blasted and blistered corpses "too numerous to count" littered the ruins.

"The impact of the bomb was so terrific that practically all living things, human and animal, were literally seared to death by the tremendous heat and pressure engendered by the blast," one Tokyo broadcast said.

American reconnaissance photographs confirmed that four and one-tenth square miles—60 per cent of the built-up area—of Hiroshima had vanished almost without trace in the world's greatest explosion.

Unofficial American sources estimated Japanese dead and wounded might exceed 150,000.

Five major war plants and scores of smaller factories, office buildings and dwellings were known to have been levelled. Only a few skeletons of concrete buildings remained in the obliterated area. Additional damage outside the totally destroyed section still was being assessed.

Unparalleled Holocaust, Say Japs

Radio Tokyo, breaking its silence of more than 60 hours after the raid, said the "indescribable destructive power" of the bomb had crushed big buildings and small dwellings alike in an unparalleled holocaust.

Inhabitants were killed by blast, fire and crumbling buildings, Tokyo said. Most bodies were so badly battered that it was impossible to distinguish between the men and the women.

As Tokyo painted a fearful picture of the catastrophe, some sources saw a possibility that Japan might reconsider her rejection of the Allied demand for her surrender before she is invaded.

"It shouldn't take the Japanese long to think this over," one ranking officer said. "We plan to present them with bursting atoms as often as possible."

Preparations were continuing through the Pacific for an invasion of Japan if necessary, however. Everywhere transports were on the move with supplies and troops.

Foe Cries 'Humanity Disregarded'

The Japanese, stunned by the destruction of Hiroshima, charged over the Tokyo radio that the United States was violating Article 22 of the Hague Convention and showing disregard for humanity by attacking a non-military city with the atomic bomb.

Hiroshima actually was an important quartermaster depot and garrison city for the Japanese Army.

The broadcast made no mention of the fact that Japan did not subscribe to the Hague Convention.

Radio Tokyo said both the dead and wounded had been burned beyond recognition and confessed that authorities still were unable to obtain a definite check on civilian casualties.

"Those outdoors burned to death, while those indoors were killed by the indescribable pressure and heat," Tokyo said. It called the city a "disastrous ruin."

"Medical relief agencies that were rushed from the neighboring districts were unable to distinguish, much less identify, the dead from the injured," the enemy broadcast said.

'Hands Full' in Hiroshima'

"With houses and buildings crushed, including the emergency medical facilities, the authorities are having their hands full in giving every available relief possible under the circumstances."

Radio Tokyo still referred to the atomic missile as merely a "new-type bomb." It said order gradually was being restored in the stricken city.

The Japanese cabinet was called into a special session at the official residence of Premier Kantaro Suzuki this morning to hear a report from its chief secretary, Hisatune Sekomizu, on the raid, Tokyo said.

Gen. Carl A. Spaatz, commander of the American Strategic Air Forces in the Pacific, said reconnaissance photographs revealed that fires touched off by the almost unbelievable heat of the bomb leaped block-wide streams and spread into the outskirts.

The city appeared desolated in the photographs. Bridges across seven channels of the Motoyasu River delta within the city were damaged.

Horizontal Blast Across City

Strangely, the photographs showed no crater. However, Tokyo had reported that the bomb was dropped by parachute and exploded in the air. It was likely that the entire force of the blast was directed horizontally across the city below.

Although the built-up area of Hiroshima came to six and nine-tenths square miles, the city as a whole totalled 12 square miles with a population of 318,000—an average of 26,500 persons per square mile.

Few, if any, of the more than 150,000 persons in the totally-devastated four square miles were believed to have escaped death or injury. The blast alone of the atomic bomb could kill persons within a four-mile range, and it

(Continued on Page Eight)

August 8, 1945: An extra notes that Russia takes up arms against Japan. *Courtesy Jackie Deinhardt*

FIRST

EXTRA

BINGHAMTON PRESS

Vol. 67, No. 103. FOUR PAGES FRIDAY EVENING, AUGUST 10, 1945. ★ PRICE FOUR CENTS

JAPAN AGREES TO ALLIED TERMS

Emperor Hirohito Asks the Governments Of U. S., Great Britain, China and Russia For Immediate Cessation of All Hostilities

San Francisco—(U.P.)—Tokyo radio said today that Emperor Hirohito told the United States, Great Britain and the Soviet Union he would accept terms of the Potsdam ultimatum "with the understanding that the said declaration does not compromise any demand which prejudices the prerogatives of His Majesty as a sovereign ruler."

Radio Tokyo in a broadcast recorded by the United Press began the historic declaration addressed to the Allies through Switzerland and Sweden but broke off without completing the text of the announcemen. An announcer asked listeners to "stand by."

The broadcast came soon after an announcement in which the enemy radio said the Japanese had lodged a protest with the United States against use of the atomic bomb.

Tokyo Radio announced the following communication:

"By the gracious command of His Majesty the Emperor who ever to enhance the cause of world peace desires earnestly to bring about an early termination of hostilities with a view to saving mankind from the calamities to be imposed upon them by further continuation of the war, the Japanese Government asked several weeks ago the Soviet Government, with which it had neutral relations then, to render good offices in restoring peace with the enemy powers.

"Unfortunately these efforts in the interest of peace having faced the Japanese Government in conformity with the August wish of His Majesty to restore the general peace and desiring to put an end to the untold suffering led by war as quickly as possible has decided upon the following—a Japanese Government are ready to accept the terms by the joint declaration which was issued at Potsdam by the heads of the governments of the United States, Great Britain and China and later subscribed by the Soviet Government with the understanding that the said declaration does not complies (sic) any demand which prejudices the prerogatives of this majesty as a sovereign ruler.

The Potsdam declaration was issued July 26 by President Truman, Prime Minister Churchill and President Chiang Kai-Shek. Soviet Russia associated herself with the declaration when she declared war on Japan two days ago.

The declaration, telling Japan she must surrender unconditionally or be utterly destroyed, was reinforced by President Truman last night in a radio broadcast to the people of the United States.

The Potsdam ultimatum contained these points:

ONE—Elimination "for all time" of the authority and influence of those who led Japan into her career of conquest.

TWO—Occupation of points in Japanese territory to be designated by the Allies until a "new order of peace and security" in the world is assured.

THREE—Limitation of Japanese sovereignty to the main Japanese islands of Honshu, Bokkaido, Kyushu, Shikoku and a few minor islands.

FOUR—Carrying out the terms of the Cairo declaration which would strip Japan of all her conquests.

FIVE—Complete disarmament of Japanese armed forces.

SIX—No enslavement of the Japanese nation.

SEVEN—Stern justice for war criminals.

EIGHT—Removal by the Japanese Government of all obstacles to a revival of democracy, freedom of speech, religion and thought.

NINE—Permission for Japan to retain such industries as will sustain her economy and permit reparation in kind.

TEN—Access for Japan to raw materials and world trade.

ELEVEN—A promise to withdraw occupying Allied forces when Japan has established a peacefully-inclined government "in accordance with the freely expressed will of the Japanese people."

London—(U.P.)—Usually reliable sources said today that the reported Tokyo demand for protecting the sovereignty of the emperor probably would be acceptable to Britain, insofar as that particular phase of the situation was concerned.

RISING SUN SETS — Emperor Hirohito sees his dreams of Pacific conquest shattered as the overwhelming military power of America, plus the atomic bomb, plus Russia's declaration of war, brought Japan to its knees today.

State Library Has Close Call In Albany Fire

Priceless Old Manuscripts Never Could Have Been Replaced

By TOM BENTON
Associated Press Staff Writer

Albany — Three million dollars worth of little known state property had a narrow escape from destruction this week, and the staff of the state library breathed a collective sigh of relief.

A spectacular fire which razed an abandoned school within 25 yards of the State Education Building, home of the library, brought the institution, with its almost preeless old manuscripts and other data, back into public notice.

The present library has been largely reconstituted since 1911, when another fire destroyed the west end of the state capitol which then housed the library.

Although intense heat from this week's blaze cracked 300 windows in the massive State Education Building, modern fire-proof construction did its part and the valuable collection of state history, family genealogy and education data, escaped undamaged.

Some of the manuscripts survived the 1911 fire, along with about 20,000 of 500,000 bound volumes. Acting state librarian Joseph Gavit and other members of the staff still sorrow at the destruction of the blaze 34 years ago.

Included in the loss then were the complete manuscripts of New York's colonial and state laws from 1664 to 1829, land records of 1607 to 1803 and one of the nation's most valuable collections of early American newspapers.

These never can be replaced.

The library has recovered amazingly, however, Mr. Gavit said, and many of the rare volumes which the staff despaired of acquiring again have been located.

Today's library contains about 1,000,000 volumes as well as a large number of manuscripts, Mr. Gavit said. Repercussions in the scholastic world from its loss would beggar description.

"It ranks in importance, although not in size, about sixth in the country," he said. "It is first, of course, among state libraries."

State's Birth Rate Increase To 15-Year Peak Laid to War

Binghamton Press Bureau,

Albany—The war has had a decided effect on New York State's birthrate, a Health Department report report revealed today.

Though the first six months of this year showed an increase of 4,000 births the report pointed out that births have dropped sharply since 1943.

Says the report, "An upward trend in the birthrate accompanied the outbreak of the war and the subsequent participation in it of this country, and in 1943, the annual number of births in this state for the first time passed the quarter million mark. The rate rose to 18.2, the highest in 15 years."

But the report adds that the transfer of hundreds of thousands of servicemen overseas was reflected in a sharp drop. "The may be reflected in due time in present partial demobilization another swing," it continues, "but the rate for 1943 is not likely to be equalled soon, not even after the imminent defeat of Japan."

Marriages recorded in Upstate New York have returned to the pre-war figures, after a rise in the beginning years in the war.

The death rate was the lowest during the first six months of 1945 than in any year except 1942. Infant mortality and maternal mortality have "never been lower."

Marine Mystery

Santa Monica, Cal.—(INS)—What caused thousands of lobsters to wash ashore near Santa Monica canyon is providing the Pacific coast with a first-class marine mystery. For several hours the crustaceans poured ashore, to the delight of scores of persons who brought gunnysacks, baskets and other containers to gather in the ration-free, cash-free delicacies.

Loses All Around

Worcester, Mass.—(U.P.) — Haled into court for disturbing the peace, Wilbert Larson explained to the judge that when he parked double he heard someone behind him blowing his horn. He got out to argue, he said, but discovered too late that the horn belonged to a police cruising car. He was fined $10.

Shorter in Winter

The Canadian Pacific railroad has about two and one-quarter miles less rails in its cross-country span in severe cold weather than in summer, due to contraction.

Communist List in Error

Washington — (AP) — The House Military Committee has acknowledged a second mistake in a recent listing of 16 army officers and non-coms as having alleged Communist or "fellow traveler" backgrounds.

It removed from its files yesterday the name of 1st Lt. Edward W. Finkelstein, New York, listed last month by Committee Counsel H. Ralph Burton as chairman of the Philadelphia District International Workers Order. Mr. Burton said the organization was a "subservient instrument of the Communist Party."

The committee now says Lieutenant Finkelstein was confused with "another person whose name is similar."

Soon after Mr. Burton's list appeared the committee announced that Capt. Henry Clovis Cullen, Napier Field, La., had been named through mistaken identity.

Cool Tourism

Los Angeles—(INS) — Southern California's all year club, which is busy with plans for a mammoth post-war tourist drive, has just learned that it has a new rival—Iceland.

Iceland officials asked the Office of War Information's outpost service bureau to send them all available data on how to plan and launch a tourist industry.

The OWI obligingly turned the request over to the all-year club, which complied.

Ancient Motor

Williamstown, Vt.—(U.P.) — The world's first electric motor was invented by Thomas Davenport of Williamstown, whose first step was to make a horseshoe magnet and wind it with the silk of his wife's wedding dress. That was the beginning of the electrically driven car.

Davenport, who devoted his life to science, died here a poor and unrecognized man.

Japs Did Best To Ferret Out Atom Secrets

Nipponese Scientists Spent Most of 1938 in U. S. Laboratory

Berkeley, Cal.—(AP)—A year before Pearl Harbor Japanese scientists attempted to obtain the latest American secrets on atomic power research, but were foiled by Nobel prize winner Dr. Ernest O. Lawrence, and his band of brilliant young physicists.

The story has been revealed by University of California scientists.

A group of Nipponese physicists spent most of 1938 and part of 1939 at the laboratory, with numerous other foreign physicists. At that time they were shown every courtesy, given blueprints of the cyclotron and aided in construction of a cyclotron of their own at the Imperial Pniversity, Tokyo.

Their stay was marred by only one incident. Dr. Donald Cooksey, asistant director of the radiation laboratory, caught a snooping Japanese. His actions caused him to be permanently barred from the laboratory.

However, when three eminent Japanese physicists, Doctors Iimori, Yasaki and Watanabe, made a hurried trip to the U. S. in 1940, they were barred from the laboratory by a new rule promulgated for their benefit.

During their two days at Berkeley, the American scientists filled the Japanese with a constant flow of accurate, but worthless information.

Dr. Lawrence disclosed yesterday that since December, 1943, 20 British scientists under Prof. H. S. Massey, University of London, have been working on atomic bomb research at Berkeley.

Since the start of the war the 4,900-ton cyclotron has been one of the country's most closely guarded secrets. The radiation laboratory at Berkeley has been a research center and not, as some had supposed, a link in the production chain of atomic bombs.

Wind Damage

The wind from a bomb reaches a velocity of 7,000 miles an hour at the start, and it's the wind, not the fragments of the bomb, that does the most damage.

August 10, 1945: As the war winds down, a small story notes the beginning of the baby boom. *Courtesy Arlene Pewterbaugh*

EXTRA **The Binghamton Sun** EXTRA

"FIRST IN THE HOMES OF SOUTHERN NEW YORK AND NORTHERN PENNSYLVANIA FOR MORE THAN A CENTURY"

ONE HUNDRED AND TWENTY-THIRD YEAR NO. 253 BINGHAMTON, N. Y., TUESDAY, AUG. 14, 1945 ★ PRICE FOUR CENTS

WAR'S OVER!

Key Men in Allied Drive to Victory...

Gen. Douglas MacArthur

Adm. Chester W. Nimitz

Jap Surrender Official; Truman Reports End of Four-Year Pacific Fight

'Japan has surrendered,' President Truman reported in a brief radio address at 7 P. M. tonight. The announcement was made simultaneously at Washington, London and Moscow, according to Allied agreement.

Surrender terms will be accepted by Gen. Douglas MacArthur when arrangements can be completed.

Mr. Truman read the formal message relayed from Emperor Hirohito through the Swiss Government in which the Japanese ruler pledged the surrender on the terms laid down by the big three conference at Potsdam.

Japan's official reply to Allied surrender terms was delivered to Secretary of State Byrnes late today.

Byrnes immediately left his office for the White House.

The secretary started out on his short but historic walk at 6:12 p. m. Eastern War Time.

The document was delivered to Byrnes by Max Grassli, charge d'affaires for Switzerland. Grassli was in Byrnes' office about five minutes.

When he came out reporters crowded around as he waited for the elevator and several said, "Was it the note you took in?"

With a big smile, Grassli nodded in confirmation.

About a minute later Byrnes left for the White House.

He reached there at 6:16 p. m., and walked rapidly through a side door stuffing a bundle of papers into the inside pocket of his coat.

Wild Frenzy of Joy Unleashed in Triple Cities by War's End

Swiss Radio Says Japs Give False Account of Reply

Enemy Conquests Hit Sources of Yank War Goods

600 Planes Smash Targets on Kyushu, Blast Shipping

Nippon Surrender Now Won't Mean Release of Men in Half Year

Tokio Radiocast of Coming Reply Awakens World

AP Newsfeatures

THIS MAP shows the chunk of the globe that had been carved out by the Japanese by the middle of 1942, when their stolen empire reached its greatest size. The dates on the flags show when organized resistance at those places ceased.

FIRST BRITISH DEFEAT

HARD LEARNED LESSON

(AP Newsfeatures)

YANKS TRAINED CHINESE

(AP Newsfeatures)

Thirteen generals were among a group of combat-seasoned Chinese, the first foreign officers ever to receive U. S. Army staff training in their homeland, who graduated from an infantry school in southwest China in July, 1944.

August 14, 1945: The headline signals it's time to start the wild celebrations. *Courtesy Arlene Pewterbaugh*

JAPAN QUITS

Children join in the World War II victory celebration in Binghamton, August 14, 1945. *Press & Sun-Bulletin archives*

HAPPY
DAYS
ARE
HERE AGAIN

"Happy Days are Here Again" was the sentiment during victory celebrations in Binghamton, August 1945.
Press & Sun-Bulletin archives

This jalopy stalled in the midst of the victory celebration in downtown Binghamton, August 1945. *Press & Sun-Bulletin archives*

Women use household items as noisemakers during victory celebrations in Binghamton, August 1945. *Press & Sun-Bulletin archives*

Smiles, flags and noisemakers were everywhere during the celebrations in Binghamton, August 1945. *Press & Sun-Bulletin archives*

Youngsters celebrate as a trumpet gets into the action in Binghamton, August 1945. *Press & Sun-Bulletin archives*

ROUFF
FURNITURE CO.
ESCAPE IN THE
DESERT & BLONDE
FROM BROOKLYN

Parade down Washington Avenue in Endicott to celebrate the end of World War II, August 1945. *Press & Sun-Bulletin archives*

Victory parade in Binghamton, August 1945. *Press & Sun-Bulletin archives*

Nippy Tonight

BINGHAMTON PRESS

Thursday Evening, Nov. 20, 1947 — THE TRIPLE CITIES' NEWSPAPER — Vol. 69—189 34 Pages 5 Cents

★ ★ ★
State Wage Floor

On Nov. 20, New York State quits asking payment of fixed minimum wages to some 800,000 employes in the state. The request becomes an order, with teeth, Dec. 1. You'll find the story on page 34.

Taking You to the Royal Wedding Today

SOLEMN MOMENT OF HISTORIC POMP—Archbishop of Canterbury (robed, wearing miter, bending forward) officiates at wedding of Princess Elizabeth and Philip, Duke of Edinburgh. Standing before the Archbishop, left to right, are King George VI, Elizabeth, Philip and the best man, the Marquess of Milford Haven. In the front row of witnesses are Queen Elizabeth (right), with Queen Mary at her right.

ROYAL MR. AND MRS.—Her royal highness Elizabeth, future queen of England, and her new husband, Philip, Duke of Edinburgh, leave Westminster Abbey minutes after their marriage in the sacrarium of the ancient edifice. After the wedding breakfast at Buckingham Palace, they hurried away to the Mountbatten estate of Broadlands in the south of England for their honeymoon.

Elizabeth Wed In Traditional Pomp, Splendor

By INEZ ROBB
International News Service Staff Writer

London—England's "fairy princess"—destined future queen of England—was married to her "Prince Charming" in a blaze of glory today and left London soon afterward with a regal sendoff for a honeymoon in Hampshire.

The scene of traditional magnificence and great splendor in Westminster Abbey was climaxed when Princess Elizabeth and her bridegroom, Philip Mountbatten, Duke of Edinburgh, left Buckingham Palace late in the afternoon for a rustic hideaway at Romsey.

A confetti and rose-leaves sendoff by the crowned heads of Europe marked the departure in an open coach drawn by four magnificent grays for Waterloo Station.

King George and Queen Elizabeth, along with royal guests at the marriage, pelted the newlyweds with confetti and rose leaves as they entered the coach in the inner quandrangle of Buckingham Palace.

The distinguished and magnificently dressed royal personages then dashed to the forecourt in full view of milling crowds to wave the bridal couple a farewell.

DAY OF EXCITEMENT

The couple's gaily bedecked train pulled out of the terminal at 4:20 p. m. (11:20 a. m. E. S. T.)

The honeymoon departure brought to an end a day filled with romance, glamour, jewels, excitement and a measure of grief as well. For more than 2,000 persons were injured in the bustle of London's celebrations—37 of whom were sent to hospitals.

A thin English sun on this gray November day did its best to struggle through the clouds as the royal bride and her bridegroom left the abbey.

Princess Elizabeth had been glamorous throughout—make no bones about it—and the groom, Philip Mountbatten, now Duke of Edinburgh and a royal highness of the British realm, was as handsome and sedate as could be.

An old woman among the spectators outside the abbey remembered the old adage and cried "Happy is the bride the sun shines on" when the pale orb showed itself through the murky sky.

CLUTCHES PHILIP'S HAND

No bride could have looked more radiant than the slim petite girl who left the abbey clinching tightly to the hand of her bridegroom—as she had clung to it from the moment in the solemn ceremony when the venerable Archbishop of Canterbury said:

"Whom God hath joined together let no man put asunder."

Frenzied cheers from thousands of her adoring countrymen and women lining the streets for a glimpse of the Princess sped her into the hushed abbey before Elizabeth promised to "love, cherish and obey" the man she has married.

The responses of both bride and groom were so low as to be inaudible to all but the few members of the royal family and their royal guests in neat rows of white chairs on each side of the abbey's sacrarium (which is the official spelling for what is commonly known as sanctuary).

MARY'S 'TYPICAL' HAT

There listening intent and tearless were her mother, Queen Elizabeth, and her wonderful old grandmother, Queen Mother Mary, who didn't disappoint the crowds by wearing any of these foolish new hats.

The dowager queen appeared in a typical "Queen Mary Hat" at her granddaughter's fabulous wedding.

This dreary gray land of hard austerity, this battle-scared and suffering world, dropped away for an hour in Westminster Abbey.

The King, in his serious intent to keep the marriage of his daughter on the nation's austere level, was defeated in the end by the ancient pomp of kings and the traditions of the abbey.

More than half the crowned heads of Europe witnessed the historic ceremony from box seats in the "sanctuary."

GUESTS ARE EARLY

There also were crown princes, princesses, regents and a slew of lesser and minor royalty to make a field day at any place in the abbey this afternoon.

The doors of the abbey on Parliament Square where the buildings are still pock-marked by the scars of the last war didn't open until 9:30 a. m. G. M. T. (4:30 a. m. E. S. T.), but long before that the guests had begun to gather.

Befurred ladies and men in silk skimmers were there as soon after breakfast as they could make it.

At 9:30 a. m. the abbey had an ancient, cold gray look.

Only the high altar, emblazoned under the weight of choice pieces of abbey gold plate (but not as much as eventually will be displayed when Elizabeth is crowned) was truly festive.

The only floral decorations in the vast abbey were two alabaster vases, one on each side of the altar.

Certainly the floral bill for decorations in the abbey won't strain His majesty's purse as they consisted only of two bouquets six feet high.

The white lilies, white and pink carnations and pale mauve chrysanthemums, beautifully arranged, won't nip the bride's father for more than a hundred dollars.

So far as delirious public approval of the affair goes, there just wasn't any let-up.

When Elizabeth and Philip got back to Buckingham Palace in the gloriously caparisoned glass coach after the abbey ceremony they found a tremendous crowd breaking through police and military cordons in the forecourt that just would not be held back.

RESPOND TO CHEERS

So out they came on the balcony overlooking the front palace yard and the long tree-lined Mall. And there they remained for a long four minutes in response to cries of "we want the princess" before they withdrew.

Mounted police reinforcements had to be called into action for the second time in the historic day to keep the crowds in some semblance of order.

But back to the proceedings in the abbey.

The great, glimmering golden altar of the ancient church needed

(Continued on Page Nine)

Dewey Hits Truman China Stand

Manchester, N. H.—(AP)—Gov. Thomas E. Dewey of New York today charged that President Truman was "seemingly abandoning the Chinese to Communist conquest," and asserted immediate aid should be sent to the Far East as even a two months' delay "may be too late."

Making his first comment on President Truman's special message to Congress, the Republican governor told a news conference he was "deeply disappointed in it" in that "no mention at all was made of China or the situation in the Far East."

"While European aid is urgent . . ." he said, "there is an even more urgent situation in China."

Dewey, who is making a two-day tour of New England, asserted "the dollar cost of giving necessary assistance to the Chinese people is a trifle compared with the cost of European aid."

"Yet," he declared, "the President either did not know of the situation or deliberately ignored it."

America's Answer To Russia's Abuse

Warren Austin, United Press delegate to the United Nations, has answered the accusations and vituperation of Soviet Delegate Vishinsky.

The same correspondents who interviewed Vishinsky Nov. 7 put the same questions to Mr. Austin, and his answers are detailed in Nat Barrows' story on page 6.

Also on the inside:

Faces Possible U. S. Indictment

Profits Stories False, Meyers Tells Probers

Washington—(UP)—Retired air force Maj. Gen. Bennett E. Meyers today denounced as "entirely false" charges that he reaped lush wartime profits through secret ownership of a subcontracting firm.

Justice Department spokesmen, however, said that they may seek criminal indictments against Meyers and also against his associates in the Aviation Electric Co. This is the firm that Meyers owned secretly.

The chubby former chief of the air force's materiel command testified before a Senate war investigating subcommittee.

Meyers vehemently denied testimony about his alleged ownership of Aviation Electric and "kickbacks" therefrom which had been given by B. H. LaMarre, who said he got $50 a week as the firm's president, and T. E. Readnower, its $25-a-week vice president.

"I will state without equivocation that LaMarre and Readnower's testimony is entirely false except for the repayments of loans from the corporation—loans that I made on notes from it—and except for personal repayments of loans made to Mr. and Mrs. LaMarre prior to Dec. 31, 1940," Meyers said.

Justice Department sources, in this connection, said they were making a sweeping inquiry into the activities of "everyone connected with him in the deal" to see if prosecution is warranted.

In Indianapolis last night Attorney General Tom C. Clark told reporters that the Justice Department would seek an indictment of Meyers on income tax evasion charges as soon as the subcommittee completes its hearings.

Justice Department spokesmen in Washington said they are working closely with the committee and are investigating the possibility of obtaining criminal indictments against Meyers on other charges as well.

Rents Head Control List

Washington — (AP) — The Senate Banking Committee decided today to go ahead immediately with a four-point anti-inflation program but delayed action on President Truman's request for standby price-wage and limited rationing control power.

Chairman Tobey (Rep., N. H.) said the committee will begin consideration next week of legislation to continue rent controls, restore installment buying curbs, tighten bank credit and possibly increase margins for buying on the commodity exchanges.

These four of the 10 points laid down by Mr. Truman in his program to combat high living costs already have been designated as the subject of hearings by the Senate-House Economic Committee.

Describing the price-wage and rationing recommendations of the President as "nebulous," Tobey told a news conference he expects to have more information about what the administration is seeking after a conference tomorrow with Treasury Secretary Snyder.

Today's Chuckle

At Dusseldorf, a local soccer team beat the team of the British Army. A German taunted a young Tommy.

"Do you realize it?" he exclaimed. "We've beaten you at your national game!"

The little cockney looked up with calm. "That may be," he answered. "But we've beaten you at yours!"

Win Pay Boost

Utica—(UP)—The Amalgamated Association of Street Railway Employes, A. F. L., won a 10-cent-an-hour pay increase for its members.

Blum Given Top Post In France

Paris—(UP)—Leon Blum, 75-year-old Socialist leader, today was named premier and agreed to attempt formation of a new middle-of-the-road government to guide France through a mounting political and economic crisis marked by violence and bloodshed.

Blum accepted the charge to form a new government from President Vincent Auriol. He will appear before the French National Assembly tomorrow afternoon.

The aging Socialist leader will succeed Paul Ramadier, who resigned the premiership last night amid a wave of new strikes and demonstrations. It was the fourth time that Blum had taken into his hands the fate of a crisis-torn France.

As premier, Blum was expected to steer—if possible—a middle course between the Communists and the rightist followers of Gen. Charles de Gaulle's Rally of the French People.

Blum agreed to take over the government at a time when nearly 750,000 persons were idle in strikes and political tension was rising throughout France.

Some 80,000 reservists were called back to the colors today without explanation. They recently had been demobilized from the conscription class of 1947.

Two More Are Killed In Italian Rioting

Rome—(UP)—Two persons were killed today in police gun battles with striking peasants in Puglia Province.

In Gravina, order was restored when police reinforcements broke up a mob besieging police headquarters. One man was killed and another wounded. Peasants armed with rifles, machine guns and spades abandoned their siege of headquarters to attack the headquarters of the Christian Democrat Party. Police defended the party office, and firing broke out before the crowd was dispersed.

The other death, bringing the toll in Italy's 18 days of disorders to 18, occurred in Serracapriola, 60 miles north of Gravina. Police used guns against another mob there.

Liz' Voice Tremulous, Philip's Deep in 'I Do's'

By JOAN SKIPSEY
SPECIAL CORRESPONDENT
Of The Binghamton Press and the Chicago Daily News

London—In tones almost of a little girl, Princess Elizabeth promised to love, honor and obey Philip Mountbatten, Duke of Edinburgh, at 11:41½ a. m. today.

In a deep, rich, confidence-inspiring voice never heard by the world before, Philip promised to cherish her "till death us do part."

Their words echoed in millions of hushed homes as the radio networks of the world relayed them from Czechoslovakia to British Columbia. But none will remember this day more vividly than the million Londoners who saw only a few minutes of pageantry and heard nothing but brass bands in the gray November morning.

ELATED BEAUTY

Some waited 18 hours bedded down with cushions and rugs in the dank night and drizzly dawn. A half minute's vision of the very dignified and serene princess on the right of her sailor-capped father on the way to the abbey, was their reward.

That half-minute revealed an elated beauty, radiant as her mother's diamond tiara crowning her white-veiled, luxuriant brown hair.

Most of the crowd seemed to feel this glimpse was worth every pang of hunger, and every twinge and cramp.

Cheers for victory never equaled today's. This is the best day austerity Britain ever had. In fact, for the millions who like a spot of glamor and romance, it was an occasion of undiluted joy.

THEY'LL REMEMBER . . .

They'll remember the policeman who, with coat flapping and the inevitably comic helmet, climbed nearly to the top of the huge Queen Victoria monument, opposite Buckingham Palace, to shoo away an enterprising photographer and then couldn't get down again.

"Speech, speech," cried the crowds with wicked delight.

They'll remember, most of all, that to their own slight surprise they somehow felt in on the intimate happiness of the most sensational family get-together in years, in which the uncles, cousins and aunts are all kings and queens.

Women Gasp At Gala Show

London—(AP) — The royal wedding was a women's show, from the bride in her glittering tiara of diamonds, to the old, old Cockney woman, who bedecked her bedraggled self with red, white and blue rosettes.

It was the women who cried out with close to tearful appreciation at the sight of the magnificent mounted guardsmen, whose sleek horses and red, white and gold uniforms first broke the monotony of the bleak day, the gray, tired crowds.

Women set up housekeeping along the route of the royal wedding. Hundreds heard Big Ben strike the hours 11 times. They camped all night on boxes, wrapped in blankets. They kept their children warm and shushed and fed them out of the British canvas carry-alls.

In This Case 11 Means 14

We have a 14-man football team on our hands.

The 1947 All-Southern Tier Conference team, announced today, contains 14 players. There were ties for three positions.

These 14 players, selected by conference coaches, will be our guests at The Press' football dinner next Monday evening at the Arlington Hotel. Lou Little will be guest speaker.

The story and pictures of the all-stars are on page 29.

To London You Go: Today's Pictures Today

It happened in London this morning, and you SEE IT.

Today's royal wedding pictures are in The Binghamton Press TODAY. Pages 1, 8, 9, 23 and 24.

Special writers cover the historic event in detail.

A great descriptive story starts on page 1. Another colorful story tells of the great crowds, page 8. Look at the picture with that story and see, even as they, Princess Elizabeth's coach and guards passing at Admiralty Arch on the way to Westminster Abbey.

There are other stories, page 8, that tell of the Duke of Edinburgh's last bachelor party, and a full description of the bridal gown, page 9.

November 20, 1947: The Press crowed about getting pictures from London on the same day. *Courtesy Carolyn Fitzgerald*

Mo' Sno'

Cloudy, colder with snow flurries tonight, low 28. Tuesday mostly cloudy, cold, high 40.

BINGHAMTON PRESS

Monday Evening, Nov. 29, 1948 — THE TRIPLE CITIES' NEWSPAPER — Vol. 70—195 32 Pages 5 Cents

★ ★ ★
Ungallant Knights

If young Mistress America is wont to complain of a lack of gallantry on the part of her man, she has only to consider the lot of the female in other lands. A story on page 22 gives the picture.

Geo. F. Johnson Dies at 91 Of Heart Attack at Home

Oct. 14, 1857 Nov. 28, 1948
GEORGE F. JOHNSON

Triple Cities Shocked At Passing of Its First Citizen and Benefactor

By LEWIS E. SWEET
Binghamton Press Endicott Bureau Chief

The Triple Cities was shocked today by the news of the death of its first citizen and benefactor.

Ninety-one-year-old George F. Johnson, beloved head of Endicott Johnson, died at 10:20 o'clock last night at his home in Park Place, Endicott.

The body of the man who did more than anyone else to bring prosperity to the Triple Cities will lie in state at his home tomorrow from 10 a. m. to 10 p. m. Friends are invited to call.

Mr. Johnson succumbed to a heart seizure. It was the last of many he had suffered in a valiant battle for life which began with a pneumonia attack in December, 1939.

The end came quietly and unexpectedly. With him were two of the nurses who had been in almost constant attendance over the last nine years.

His last visitors were George W. Johnson, his son and president of E-J; his nephew, Charles F. Johnson, Jr., E J vice-president, and his grandson, Frank A. Johnson, son of George W. Johnson.

The final decline in Mr. Johnson's health started shortly after his 91st birthday last Oct. 14. Mentally alert and physically more vigorous than on numerous birthdays during the last few years, Mr. Johnson greeted scores of callers on that day.

LAST APPEARANCE ON LABOR DAY

He had been well enough since then to attend several area football games, one of his numerous enthusiasms. He saw his last game four weeks ago.

Confined to his bed most of the time during the last month, Mr. Johnson had rallied somewhat last week. His death yesterday followed a notable improvement on Saturday.

Mr. Johnson had been more active during the summer months than during any summer in several years. His last public appearance was on Labor Day, when he was greeted with an ovation by 50,000 persons who jammed En-Joie Park for a record E J Labor Day celebration.

The world renowned industrialist and philanthropist was attended during his long illness by Dr. Edward M. Jones of Endicott.

MESSAGES POUR IN

Funeral services for Mr. Johnson were still pending this afternoon. Triple Cities leaders awaited word from the family as the signal to arrange a community expression of sympathy. The body was removed to the Allen Memorial Home, Endicott.

The Johnson family today asked mourners to omit flowers.

Messages of condolence were pouring into Mr. Johnson's Endicott home and Endicott Johnson offices today. Word of his death spread rapidly, and hundreds of workers drove and walked quietly by his home before factories opened this morning.

An unusual silence pervaded the usually noisy E J factories today. Thousands of workers—George F. knew thousands by their first names—recalled instances of "I knew him when." Workers, too, awaited a signal from the family to arrange their own expression of sympathy.

WIFE DIED IN 1947

The E-J founder is survived by two sons and two daughters. The sons are George W. Johnson and Walter L. Johnson of Vestal. The daughters are Mrs. Lloyd E. Sweet of Binghamton and Mrs. Zada Robertson of Boston.

An older brother, C. Fred Johnson of Johnson City, who is 93, also survives. Mrs. George F. Johnson died Oct. 1, 1947.

Mr. Johnson remained chairman of the board of directors of Endicott Johnson during the long years of his semi-retirement. He was last elected last March 15.

Mr. Johnson was forced to retire from his numerous activities when he was stricken by pneumonia in December, 1939.

His health had been a matter of concern for Triple Cities residents since early in 1940. Although his public appearances became less frequent, few days passed without inquiries by friends at his home or the tannery office in Oak Hill Avenue.

Nearly nine years of retirement never dulled Mr. Johnson's interest in the welfare of the Triple Cities in general and of his workers in particular.

George F. had lived to see a community of more than 50,000 persons develop in and around Johnson City and Endicott.

He had lived to see Endicott Johnson pay rolls reach their highest level in history.

Further, he had lived to see the Endicott Johnson organization increase from a band of a few hundred workers to an army of about 18,500 workers.

The Endicott Johnson personnel alone had grown almost as large as the total population of either Johnson City or Endicott.

Stricken by pneumonia on that Christmas Day in 1939, George F. astonished his medical attendants and his family when he staged a battle to live that won him a gradual return to health.

HIS DRIVING WILL

For days he lay at death's edge, victimized by recurrent heart attacks and pneumonia. It was months before he could leave his bed and again it was months before he could leave his room. Finally, he recovered sufficiently to return to his habit of making periodic inspections of the factory and the community.

His friends credited Mr. Johnson's remarkable recovery to the same impelling, driving will that had motivated his creation of E J, the industrial democracy, and its development to a peak previously unheard of in this country.

George F.'s victory over his pneumonia attack of 1939 came shortly after he had won what was probably his greatest victory, the

(Continued on Page Thirteen)

Defenses At Suchow Deserted

Army Pulled Out As Commy Peril Looms in South

By the Associated Press

Nanking—Nationalist troops have been ordered to abandon embattled Suchow, it was learned reliably today.

The outcome of the entire battle for this Chinese capital may depend upon the ability of the government's commanders to withdraw their 250,000 troops southward—to Red concentrations between Suchow and the broad Yangtze River.

Reliable Chinese sources reported that the order to withdraw the entire Suchow garrison to the south ...

[illegible]

Failure Confronts Madame Chiang

Washington—(AP)—Madame Chiang Kai-shek's arrival here this week is expected to touch off a fresh drive to get the United States to underwrite China's war against its Communist foes.

[illegible]

The generalissimo's wife has been invited to be the house guest of Secretary of State and Mrs. Marshall. She has indicated she will accept. Marshall's home is at nearby Leesburg, Va.

Although Mme. Chiang is to be given every courtesy, it is clear that American diplomats have little sympathy with her unofficial mission.

Rags-to-Riches Saga For Binghamtonians Written by Oil Strike

—Binghamton Press Photo

THAT GOLDEN GLOW — William Henry Pratt beams broodly at his wife, Thelma, in their modest home yesterday. Mrs. Pratt learned Saturday that she was an heir to oil-rich land in Illinois. That paper they're holding is a lease to the property.

Mrs. Pratt, Henry Street, Is Heir To Luxury-Promising Illinois Land

By WOODIE FITCHETTE
Binghamton Press Staff Writer

A Binghamton family that has known little but poverty and disappointment for the last five years has become the nation's Cinderella Family overnight and stands to spend the future in undreamed-of luxury.

The prospect of fantastic wealth came with an oil strike in Illinois.

The family is that of William Henry Pratt which lives in a little dreary-looking home at 142½ Henry Street. The family's income could conceivably become a staggering $2,000 a day.

Within the last few days, Mrs. Pratt—the former Thelma Little—was located through the relentless efforts of a private investigator, Joseph Chittenden of Endicott.

[illegible]

(Continued on Page Five)

Israel Asks United Nations Membership

Paris—(AP)—Israel applied formally today for membership in the United Nations.

[illegible]

Film Too Realistic

[illegible]

Demands Recount in 3 States

Truman Win 'Stolen,' Publisher Charges

Manchester, N. H.—(UP)—Publisher William Loeb of the politically independent Manchester Union charged in a front-page editorial today that President Truman's victory in the Nov. 2 election was "stolen."

[illegible]

Californian Denies Basis for Recount

[illegible]

Today's Chuckle

A mother was having a hard time persuading her 5-year-old daughter that a bath was healthful. Finally, she decided to appeal to the young lady's vanity.

"A daily bath will give you a beautiful figure," she coaxed. Then noticing the little girl's skeptical look, she questioned: "Don't you believe me?"

"Yes," the little lady promptly answered. "Only have you taken a good look at a duck lately?"

—Successful Farming

Soviet Told Veto May Wreck U.N.

Cadogan Proposes Pre-Vote Parleys To Prevent Misuse

Paris—(UP)—Sir Alexander Cadogan of Great Britain told the United Nations today that if Russia continued to abuse the veto power in the Security Council it might break up the U. N.

[illegible]

9 Killed In Floods, Rain, Snow

[illegible]

Butter Price Up By $3\frac{1}{2}$ Cents

[illegible]

Aid Heads for Europe Again

Dockers Back on Job, Speed Ship Loadings

New York—(UP)—Marshall Plan shipments to Europe were resumed for the first time in nearly three weeks today as 65,000 striking A. F. L. longshoremen returned to their jobs from Maine to Virginia.

[illegible]

Dealer Admits Friends Get Cars First

[illegible]

Kayo Kid Throws in Towel

Chores of Office Flatten Pug Elected as Mayor

[illegible]

... welterweight championship of West Virginia. He brought the same punch to politics.

Governor Herbert suspended Canaday from office Nov. 22 for a period of 30 days on eight charges of misconduct. The charges had to do with his handling of fines collected and with his try at buying a $265 water cooler for the Pomeroy office of the State Bureau of Unemployment Compensation.

Skyscraper 'Clock' Fools Visitors

Sightseers often set their watches after consulting a big bronze dial in the world's tallest building. It's all right, except that one hand shows the wind's velocity, the other its direction atop the skyscraper.

That's only one of the interesting things Frank Powell, manager of the Empire State Building observatories, tells about today on Page 23. His job is interesting—but a lot of work, too.

Also on the inside:

George F. Johnson's Life in Pictures, Stories: Pages 10, 11, 12, 13

November 29, 1948: The story detailed Johnson's fight for life since a pneumonia attack in 1939. *Microfilm archives*

JACK & JILL SHOP
KIDDIES CLOTHES
237 MAIN ST.
JOHNSON CITY
DIRECTOR OF FUNERAL
JOS. M.
KAMINSKY
CONTRACTOR & BUILDER
DIAL 6-4203

Russian Club dinner at St. Mary's FROC Church basement, 1946. The church, located on Baxter Street, was later called Dormition of the Virgin Mary Church. *Courtesy Marlene Yacos*

Lost child Ann Kocak, 7, daughter of Mr. And Mrs. Joseph Kocak, showing Patrolman C.M. Benedict her new toy automobile, Binghamton, 1947. *Courtesy Joseph F. Hidock, Jr.*

Friends from the Binghamton area, Pete Scott and Joe Battista, pose for the photo in 1948. Pete would later start the Pete Scott and the Montereys band. *Courtesy Pete Scott*

Marion King crossing Chenango Street in March 1947. Several of her family members worked at the Press. *Courtesy Mary-Ellen Bronson*

Birthday party for 10-year-old Mae Seetoo was given by Mrs. Percy (Clara) Cook in 1947. *Courtesy George Quon*

Friends pose for a photograph at the IBM Country Club in the 1940s. Starting at the bottom; Anna Sopchak Fedorchak, Martha Sopchak Hamilton, Stella Sopchak, Mary Matwey Yacos. *Courtesy Marlene Yacos*

Flood waters wreak havoc on the En Joie swimming pool and bath house during the flooding in 1948. *Courtesy Marlene Yacos*

ENDICOTT JOHNSON

Endicott Johnson Scout Factory baseball team at Johnson Field, 1948. *Courtesy Diane Stepneski*

Snowy

Snow flurries, windy, colder tonight, low 12. Thursday, snow flurries, continued cold, high 25.

BINGHAMTON TEMPERATURES

9 p. m.	12	3 a. m.	16	9 a. m.	34
10 p. m.	10	4 a. m.	21	10 a. m.	36
11 p. m.	11	5 a. m.	25	11 a. m.	40
Midnight	12	6 a. m.	26	Noon	42
1 a. m.	13	7 a. m.	27	1 p. m.	40
2 a. m.	14	8 a. m.	32	2 p. m.	39

BINGHAMTON PRESS

Wednesday Evening, Dec. 7, 1949 — THE TRIPLE CITIES' NEWSPAPER — Vol. 71—203 56 Pages 5 Cents

★★★

How to Whistle

The modern male shouldn't need a tin whistle to hail a taxi. If he doesn't know how to do his own whistling, a Page 22 story provides the know-how.

BRINK FINDS CORRUPTION, BRIBERY OF SOME POLICE BY CITY GAMBLERS

Downtown Fire Sears the Sky

—Press Photos by Swierkosz

ECLIPSE OF THE MOON BLOCK—Thousands watch as fire destroys interior of Moon block at Chenango and Lewis streets late yesterday, making some 60 persons homeless and causing damage estimated at more than $300,000. Burning cupola on corner of buildng is at right. At left, across Chenango Street, can be seen parts of Arlington and Carlton hotels. (Stories and more pictures on Pages 29, 35 and 45.)

F. D.'s Aides Are Cleared By Groves

Hopkins, Wallace Never Sought Atom Secrets, He Says

Washington—(P)—Lt. Gen. Leslie R. Groves testified today that neither Harry Hopkins nor Henry A. Wallace ever tried to get any atomic secrets or materials from him for the Russians.

Groves, who headed the wartime atomic bomb project, told House investigators that he had never, in fact, met Hopkins or had any correspondence with him.

As for Wallace, Groves said the former vice president never brought any direct pressure on him in connection with the atomic energy project and, as far as he knows, never put on any indirect pressure.

PROBE DIGGING DEEP

Groves was a witness before congressional investigators digging into a story of atomic materials going to Russia in lend-lease planes during the war and of a mysterious note signed "H. H." saying "had a hell of a time getting these away from Groves."

G. Harry Jordan, former air force major, told the House Un-American Activities Committee on Monday that he opened a Russian suit case at Great Falls, Mont., in the winter of 1943-44 and found "Oak Ridge" materials and the "H. H." note.

Groves told the committee:

1. The Russians got some atomic material during the war, but that he doesn't know how many shipments "because we don't know how many leaked through."

2. He found evidence of Russian spying within a month of the time he took charge of the atomic bomb project in 1942.

3. He knows the Lend-Lease Administration was under "pressure" to give the Russians "everything they sought" and that a "great deal of influence" was brought to bear. But he said he did not know who exerted the pressure.

Hopkins was at one time lend-lease administrator. A close friend of President Roosevelt, Hopkins went to Russia to consult with the Soviets on their needs to hold their front against the Germans.

Major Jordan's wartime job was to aid in lend-lease movement of planes to Russia. Great Falls was a main basing point on the air route to Russia via Alaska.

He has told of the Russians taking out suitcase after suitcase load

(Continued on Page Thirty)

Aluminum Strike Ends

Pittsburgh—(P)—The CIO United Steelworkers and the Aluminum Co. of America today signed a contract, which ended an eight-week strike of 17,000 workers in nine states.

The union announced the settlement which it said provides $100 a month pensions including social security, a company financed social insurance plan and a procedure for correcting wage rate inequities.

Cold War 'Half Won'

New York—(INS)—Marshall Plan Chief Paul G. Hoffman declared today that the United States has won "half" the cold war with Soviet Russia as a result of the European recovery program.

Rex Beach, Novelist, Is Suicide

Sebring, Fla.—(P)—Rex Beach, 72, nationally known novelist, was found dead of a pistol wound in the head at his home near here this morning.

His death was pronounced suicide by County Judge J. Howard Livingston and Sheriff Broward Coker.

Beach had been suffering from a throat cancer for three years. His body was found by a nurse who brought him breakfast, the sheriff said.

MR. BEACH

Mr. Beach married Edith Crater in 1907 and they moved to a house named "Topside" at Ardsley-on-Hudson, N. Y. Later they made their permanent residence at their ranch here.

He kept up a steady flow of novels, stories and articles. He was an enthusiastic fisherman and hunter and became interested in farming and cattle raising.

When Mrs. Beach died in 1947, the author said that one of his chief sources of inspiration had gone from him.

Major Coal Men Scoff At Contract

Washington—(P)—John L. Lewis' proud announcement that some mine owners have met his contract terms apparently left major coal operators unimpressed today.

They said the owners who signed with the mine leader produce comparatively little soft coal—less than 2,500,000 tons of the nation's annual total of 550,000,000. And they scoffed at suggestions that the new move might mean a major break in the long coal dispute.

Lewis made the announcement late yesterday. He said United Mine Workers members at the affected pits would return to work immediately on a five-day week.

The balance of the anthracite and bituminous coal industries went on a three-day week at Lewis' direction last Monday, as part of his over-all strategy to obtain new contracts. The old one expired last July.

From the signing operators, mostly in Kentucky, Lewis obtained these terms:

ONE—A 95-cent daily wage increase—first "fourth round" postwar pay hike won by a major labor leader this year. It would make the miner's basic daily pay $15.

TWO—A 15-cent increase in the operators' welfare fund royalty. That makes a total of 35 cents a ton, which goes for medical, hospital and death benefits and the $100 monthly pensions for 60-year-old UMW members.

The total boost in the production of coal, Lewis said, would be 23 cents a ton—less, he added, for the more efficient mines.

The United Mine Workers said after a two-hour conference with operators today that it still plans to keep the three-day work week in effect in the hard coal industry.

Floods in Costa Rica

San Jose, Costa Rica—(P)—Floods caused by torrential rains have caused great damage on the northeast section of Costa Rica.

Prosecutor Thinks Indictments Likely From His Evidence

By WOODIE FITCHETTE
Binghamton Press Staff Writer

District Attorney Robert O. Brink who is investigating gambling in Binghamton said today that he has uncovered evidence of corruption in law enforcement.

He said the evidence involves bribery and the "taking of unlawful fees by law enforcement officers."

Mr. Brink said that the investigation by a grand jury which has been meeting since Monday, "quite probably" will result in "felony indictments against divers persons not now in custody."

These statements were contained in an affidavit submitted by the district attorney to County Judge Daniel J. McAvoy at the arraignment of two habitual gamblers as material witnesses in the case.

The material witnesses are Joe Banovic, 8 Dickinson Street, and Louis A. (Lob) Fiato, 158-160 Henry Street.

Both men, who appeared with their attorney, John J. Cucci were attempting to raise $15,000 property bail.

Mr. Brink's affidavits, read at the arraignment by First Assistant District Attorney Samuel W. Bernstein, charged that both men had operated gambling establishments in Binghamton with police protection.

In the affidavits, Mr. Brink charges that both men paid for police protection, and that each had secret meetings with "certain police officers."

The district attorney announced on Nov. 29 that he had ordered a grand jury investigation of gambling in the city. The day before, sheriff's men raided four Binghamton horserooms and arrested six men on bookmaking charges. Thirty-eight other persons were picked up as players and have appeared before the grand jury.

CHARGES IN AFFIDAVIT ON BANOVIC

In the affidavit on Banovic, the district attorney charged:

". . . Joseph Banovic has admitted to investigators participating in (the) grand jury investigation that he has conducted a gambling establishment at 61 Clinton Street . . . for more than three years.

"That in the . . . gambling establishment a crap game has been conducted with a rake for the house, and professional gamblers furnishing what is commonly known as a bank or a book.

"The deponent (Mr. Brink) has evidence to present to this grand jury which establishes that . . . Banovic's gambling establishment has been protected by police officers.

"The deponent has been informed and verily believes that in consideration of such protection . . . Joseph Banovic and divers others have paid bribes, gratuities and unlawful fees to police officers.

"That further evidence has been brought to the deponent's attention, which is being brought to the grand jury's attention, establishing clandestine and secret meetings between . . . Joseph Banovic and certain police officers and their co-conspirators and certain others in order to effect the purposes hereinbefore set forth."

WOULD LEAVE STATE

Mr. Brink also said in his affidavit that he believes Banovic, if he were not held as a material witness, would leave "the jurisdiction of the state . . . before said grand jury can report and he can be apprehended in connection with indictments that may involve him."

The district attorney said, too, that "by reason of his friendship and close contact of . . . Banovic with other co-conspirators involved in the above mentioned charges, he may and undoubtedly will be subject to duress and undue influence by other defendants and conspirators . . ."

In the affidavit on Fiato, the district attorney charged that he believes "Fiato actively participated in said gambling racket."

The district attorney further charged:

"That evidence has already been presented to (the) grand jury against . . . Fiato on a charge of bookmaking. . . . That the deponent further is informed and believes that . . . Fiato during his operations of a bookmaking establishment in the city . . . received protection from police officers for

(Continued on Page Three)

3 Million Pilgrims

Vatican City—(U.P.)—An estimated 3,000,000 pilgrims will take part in more than 26 solemn ceremonies over most of which Pope Pius XII will preside during the 1950 Holy Year, the Vatican announced today.

U. S. Freighter Leaves Japan To Get Ward

Aboard Lakeland Victory, En Route to Tientsin, China—(U.P.)—The American freighter Lakeland Victory, with Army doctors and Christmas presents aboard, sailed for the Chinese Communist port of Tientsin today to pick up American Consul-General Angus Ward and his staff of the Mukden consulate.

The Lakeland Victory left Kobe, Japan, at 4 p. m. for a rendezvous with Ward and his staff this week-end at Taku Bar, a windswept roadstead 35 miles below Tientsin.

Taku Bar is the sea exit for Tientsin, which lies on the shallow Hai River. Ward and his staff—20 persons in all—are expected to arrive at Tientsin tomorrow or Friday aboard a special train from Mukden provided by the Chinese Communist government.

In the absence of contrary information, it was presumed the group left Mukden as scheduled yesterday for the 700-mile trip to Tientsin.

Australian Election Test of Labor Rule

Every eligible voter must vote in Australia Saturday. And the rule of the Labor Party is the big issue.

What it's all about and how it may change the world drift toward socialism are important to everyone in the U. S. as well as elsewhere.

The details are on Page 49.

Also on the inside:

Bitter News From Augostura

Colombia Quints Hoax, Just Jailbird's Dream

Bogota, Colombia—(P)—Two Bogota newspapers reported today the story of the birth of quintuplets in a remote Colombian village was a hoax.

Medellin dispatches had detailed at length the story of the birth of five sons to the wife of an illiterate mulatto farm laborer in the village of San Alejandro near the town of Augostura.

Today Medellin correspondents reported the couple have five children, all right—but their ages range from five to 13.

The correspondent of El Liberal said a prisoner in the Medellin jail, Luis Arroyave, invented the quintuplet story. He told authorities, the paper said, he wanted to get out to visit his "five nephews."

The story apparently was accepted and elaborated. The mayor of Augostura "confirmed" the tale. But El Tiempo, another Bogota paper, said the mayor thought he had been asked merely if the family had five children.

In this way, it was explained, a story got out that five boys were born Nov. 26 to 26-year-old Maria Arroyave.

Today's Chuckle

Little Joan: "Daddy, why do the ladies always bring their knitting when they come to the house?"

Daddy: "It gives them something to think about while they're talking."

Father Kills 3 Children

Alexandria, Va.—(INS)—An Alexandria father today shot and killed his three young children and then told police "I don't know why I did it."

Slain by a .20-gauge shotgun fired by John S. Conner, 40, were Stephanie Conner, 11; Michael, 8, and Cecelia, 4.

Conner's wife, an attractive woman of 35, fled unharmed as the man opened fire on the three children in the kitchen of the family home.

Mrs. Conner's screams alarmed neighbors, who summoned police. Conner surrendered quietly.

Union Puts Heat On College Bands

New York—(P)—The AFL American Federation of Musicians has turned on the pressure to keep student bands away from college basketball games in Madison Square Garden.

Koreans Offer To Free Yanks

Washington—(U.P.)—Secretary of State Acheson said today an American representative will be sent Sunday to the border of Communist-controlled North Korea to receive two captive Americans.

The North Korean radio broadcast an offer yesterday to release the two.

The two officials, Albert Willis of Brooklyn, N. Y., and Alfred T. Meschter of Kinderhook, N. Y., have been held since Sept. 22.

They were seized when the Korean crew of the American ship Kimball R. Smith mutinied and sailed the vessel to North Korea.

Quake in Italy

Gorizia, Italy—(P)—A strong earthquake was reported early today from the Carnia Mountains, north of here. The quake was said to have caused panic among the population in the mountains, Astra, the Italian news agency, reported.

New Military Spirit Feared

Angry German Women Battle War Toys Sale

Frankfurt, Germany—(P)—Angry German women halted—but only for the time being—a campaign against the sale of military toys here after dealers threatened to stone them.

The women, contending that the sale of such toys would reawaken the military spirit in German children, set up a loud speaker near the city market place yesterday under the auspices of the Frankfurt German Women's Association and broadcast their boycott appeals.

The dealers threatened to stone the balcony of the private home where the women had their loudspeaker, a representative of the women's group said. The homeowner, fearful for his property, asked the women to find another location, and they began looking for one right away.

A member of the women's association said toys like water pistols, rifles and tanks were on display. The tanks bore inscriptions on the undersides saying the toys were for sale to foreigners only.

December 7, 1949: Fire destroyed the Moon Block, a building at Chenango and Lewis streets. *Microfilm archives*

ELGINS
RUGS
ORIENTALS
DOMESTICS

Elgin's Rugs, located at 59 Main Street, Binghamton, circa 1950. *Courtesy Richard Gillespie*

Second-grade class, Sts. Cyril and Methodius School on Clinton Street, Binghamton, 1950. *Courtesy Pete Kofira, Jr.*

EXIT

Endicott Johnson Scout Factory workers gather for a group photo in the 1950s. *Courtesy Diane Stepneski*

1950 - 1959

Paving the way for growth

Pour-haps

Some cloudiness tonight and Friday.

BINGHAMTON PRESS

Thursday Evening, May 31, 1951 — THE TRIPLE CITIES' NEWSPAPER — Vol. 73—43 46 Pages 5 Cents

★ ★ ★ Love in June

Tomorrow begins the month when orange blossoms are worn and a pound of rice in the hand is worth two in the pudding. Page 2.

Russia Inclined to End Korea War As U. S. Strengthens, Says Sherman; Big 4 Conference Is Put Up to Stalin

Cardinal Dougherty, Catholic Church Dean In U.S., Is Dead at 85

Philadelphia — (AP) — Dennis Cardinal Dougherty, 85-year-old prince of the Roman Catholic Church died today at 10:15 a. m. at his residence.

THE CARDINAL

West Calls For July 23 Meeting

'Quit Bickering On Agenda' Note Handed Gromyko

Mac Eyed Armistice, Quiz Told

Admiral Asserts Pentagon Feared World Conflict

By Press Wire Services

Washington — Adm. Forrest P. Sherman said today Russia could call off the war in Korea at any time and may be inclined to do so as the United States becomes stronger.

Asks Guilty Verdict Be Set Aside

Bribery Case Defense Claims Judge Improperly Talked to Two Jurors

MRS. BERTHA WHITING — CARLTON PALMER

THE AIRPORT FROM THE AIR—Part of the estimated 30,000 persons who were present yesterday at the dedication of the Broome County Airport are shown in this aerial photo, snapped from the Gannett helicopter, flying low. Left, on the promenade of the administration building, is the speaker's platform. And, right, is the combined IBM and EJ Workers Band. (More pictures on Pages 3, 14 and 24.)

Senate OK Of Draft Bill At Hand

People Want Strong Air Force—Barkley

By KENNETH C. JOHNSON, Binghamton Press Staff Writer

Reds Fight Furiously, Slow Yanks

By GLENN CLEMENTS, Associated Press Staff Writer

Mobs of Shoppers Grab Everything

Barricades Thrown Up By Macy's in Price War

Iran Heats Oil Dispute To a Boil

Syrians Shoot Down Israeli Fighter-Plane

Shrine to Pick Potentate July 12

Today's Chuckle

Malik's Next Move In UN Is Big?

Enjoy Your VACATION

YOU'RE OUT of the sport roundup if you don't have the Triple Cities' only seven-day newspaper follow you on your vacation. But it's an easy matter to have The Binghamton Press and Sunday Press sport coverage right through the summer. Just give us your vacation address and The Press will be sent to you.

Telephone 2-3411

May 31, 1951: News of the Korean War leads this front page. *Microfilm archives*

The papers from this period are dominated by new construction. New highways, new airports, new schools, new bridges. Like much of the nation, Broome County was building a new future.

The aftermath of a tragic Labor Day 1951 fire demonstrated that eagerness to build. The blaze killed a firefighter and destroyed a state technical school housed in the armory. By Tuesday afternoon, local authorities were already drawing plans for a new facility.

The population in the three-county region around Binghamton grew by almost 16 percent in this decade, as IBM was entering its explosive growth phase and EJ was still a vibrant manufacturer.

The year 1957 was a big year for news. *Sputnik* was launched. Plans were announced for the $100 million "Roads of Tomorrow," which we now call Interstate 81 and Route 17.

Also that year, proof of a national commission that ran organized crime became public when state police raided a crime lord's home in Apalachin, a few miles west of Binghamton.

That same day, another story broke that spoke to the social condition of the nation. Willie Mays, perhaps the greatest ballplayer of all time, was finally allowed to buy a home in a white section of San Francisco.

Today's Weather
CLOUDY
Summary on Page 14

The Binghamton Sun

"FIRST IN THE HOMES OF SOUTHERN NEW YORK AND NORTHERN PENNSYLVANIA FOR MORE THAN A CENTURY"

TRIPLE CITIES
★ ★ ★ ★
FINAL

ONE HUNDRED AND TWENTY-NINTH YEAR NO. 268 | BINGHAMTON, N. Y., TUESDAY, SEPT. 4, 1951 | PRICE FIVE CENTS

1 DEAD, 7 HURT IN STATE TECH FIRE

Loss of Building, Equipment Near $1,000,000

DIES IN FIRE. Jerome Patrick Ryan, Binghamton fireman who would have been 37 this month but who lost his life as the result of the fire which early yesterday morning razed the old State Armory building on Washington Street. Ryan, who suffered concussion and second degree burns, died of asphyxiation when unable to grope his way out of the smoke and heat-filled basement of the structure.

—All Fire Photos by Chas. Treed, Sun Staff Photographer.

CITY LANDMARK GUTTED. A spectacular early morning fire yesterday razed one of Binghamton's revered landmarks and left practically homeless five-year-old State Tech that only last January was given a temporary one-year lease on life by action of the New York State Legislature. Both photos were taken just before the collapse of the roof, first and second floors of the building shortly after 4:30 am. In the top photo, the northeast tower, acting singularly like a smokestack, is silhouetted against the raging flames and black smoke probing grotesquely skyward. Photo at left shows three firemen vainly trying to overwhelm the all-consuming flames. The roof collapsed soon after the pictures were taken and led to the death of one fireman, Jrome Ryan of 22 Livingston St. (Additional photos on Pages 3, 5, 13, 16).

Old Armory Scene Of Spectacular Labor Day Blaze

Area Firemen Battle for Hours To Protect Surrounding Property —Cause Not Determined

By BOB DOLAN

A Binghamton fireman died, trapped in a cellar, and seven other firemen were injured early yesterday morning as flames gutted the New York State Institute of Applied Arts and Sciences, housed in the old State Armory building at 227 Washington St.

More than 100 firemen from Binghamton and surrounding communities used 16 fire trucks in an attempt to halt the three-alarm blaze. When it was brought under control after a four-hour battle, firemen said that it was "nearly a total loss." Unofficial estimates placed damage at more than $1,000,000.

The last fire equipment did not leave the scene until 10:33 o'clock last night, when the official recall signal was sounded on the alarm system.

Fireman Jerome P. Ryan, 36, of 22 Livingston St., a member of Engine Co. 5 at the South Washington Street station, lost his life after a floor collapsed just inside of the main entryway of the building at about 4:45 am., tumbling him into the basement. Ryan, who was with a group of firemen who were attempting to locate the center of the blaze, is believed to have crawled some 75 feet to the south end of the basement, where his body was found covered with debris in the partial shelter of a lavatory shortly after 8 am. Dr. S. Easton McManis, a Broome County coroner, said death was due to suffocation.

Seven Firefighters Hospitalized

Admitted to City Hospital was Fireman Martin O'Shea, 36, of 65 Broad Ave., who suffered a back injury when struck by falling debris as a wall collapsed. He was reported in fair condition.

Also admitted was Fireman Charles B. Jenks, 36, of 19 Mygatt St., who suffered a shoulder injury. He was also in fair condition.

The following firemen were discharged after treatment at City Hospital:

WILLIAM BUCKLEY, 37, of 86 Crestmont Rd., suffered burns of the left hand.

GEORGE SEDOR, 28, of 261 Murray St., puncture wound of the right foot when he stepped on a nail inside the building.

STANLEY MASTON, 37, of 36 LaGrange St., burns of the right hand and abrasions of the right thigh.

ARMAND MARIANO, 27, of 9 Allen St., injury to the right wrist.

JOHN CONOMIKES, 39, of 8 Bond St., injury to the right wrist.

Nearby Buildings Threatened

Fire Marshal Gerald E. O'Loughlin reported damage to two adjoining buildings: The Department of Labor building at 221 Washington St., where a number of windows were broken by the heat; and the Southern Tier Electric Supply Co., at 218 Water St., where the north wall of the building was damaged in the collapse of one wall of the burning building. Neither of the adjoining buildings suffered fire damage, he said.

After investigating the burned-out shell yesterday afternoon the fire marshal said that the fire had apparently started in the school auditorium on the northerly side of the building, and may have been burning for some hours before it was discovered. He said the alarm was phoned in by many persons almost simultaneously when heavy smoke was sighted.

The building had been closed by custodians at 4 pm. Sunday, he said.

The fire marshal said he would be unable to assign a cause for the blaze pending further investigation. The dangerous state of the Water Street wall of the building made it unsafe to proceed too far into the rubble yesterday afternoon.

All Companies Respond

The first alarm was telephoned in at 4:30 am. Firemen, led by Second Assistant Chief Gerald J. Ring, responded and probed the interior without locating the flames. Four minutes later, a second alarm was sounded as flames roared upward through ventilator shafts and stairways. Chief William D. Thomas and First Assistant Chief Frank J. Buckman were called to the scene.

The third alarm was sent in at 4:46 am., immediately after debris from the second floor crashed on the first, collapsing it and carrying Fireman Ryan to his death. Every Binghamton fire company was called to the scene, including the extra engine which usually stands by in Central Fire Station to answer other calls. Thirteen trucks, pumpers and aerial ladder trucks represented Binghamton's entire firefighting reserve on the scene.

Two Johnson City fire trucks were dispatched to the blaze by County Fire Controller Ernest S. Youngs at 4:37, and an Endicott truck followed.

Nearly all off-duty firemen and even some vacationing men answered the general call by the Binghamton Fire Bureau. Equipment from nearby communities was moved in under the county-wide mutual aid system to provide fire protection for sections of the city" left uncovered.

Shortly after the third alarm was sounded, the fire burst through the roof of the building in a number of places, sending embers showering over Binghamton for as much as a quarter of a mile. The blaze raced unchecked through the wooden interior, and appeared to be burning most strongly on the Water Street side of the building.

Close Call for Firemen

At about 5:30, a section of the wall facing on Water Street collapsed, tipping outward into the street and burying the base of one of the Fire Bureau's new 80-foot aluminum extension ladders in a mass of debris. Firemen on the spot dashed out of the way in time. About 45 minutes later, a remaining section of the wall collapsed, damaging the Southern Tier Electric building.

Firemen feared that the high, medieval-style tower on the north end of the Washington Street side of the building would follow the walls. Through narrow windows, interior timber structures trussing the brick exterior could be seen blazing, and blasts of terrific heat showered sparks and debris from the top of the tower. The comparatively few spectators who turned out in the early dawn to watch the blaze were kept at a distance by a cordon of police.

Throughout the blaze, the police and sheriff's ambulances stood by at the scene or took the injured

(Continued on Page 5)

Unofficial Loss Estimates

Building	$250,000
Machine Shop	$500,000
Electrical Laboratory	$120,000
Chemical Labratory	$ 75,000
Medical Labratory	$150,000
Furniture & Equipment	$ 50,000
Miscellaneous	$ 50,000
Total	$1,195,000

Ridgway and Joy Confer on Truce

Fighting Rages in Korea While Closed Conference Is Held

TOKYO, Tuesday, Sept. 4 (AP). — Gen. Matthew B. Ridgway conferred today with his chief negotiator for the suspended Kaesong truce talks.

The Supreme Allied Commander held a closed conference, beginning at 8:30 am. (5:30 PM., EST, Monday), with Vice Adm. C. Turner Joy while fighting raged in East Korea's jagged mountains.

The atmosphere over the Red-suspended truce talks was equally as tense. Lt. Gen. Nam Il, chief Red negotiator, tartly rejected Joy's latest denial of Red charges of Allied neutrality violations at Kaesong. The Reds broke off the talks Aug. 23. Nam, in a statement dated Sept. 3, ridiculed Joy's denial that an Allied plane dropped a flare in the neutral zone Aug. 29.

Joy arrived in Tokyo last night with two of his negotiators, Rear Adm. Arleigh Burke and Maj. Gen. L. C. Craigie.

Tension in Korea and Tokyo was the greatest since the Kaesong talks began July 10.

It obviously was just as great in the Red camp. Peiping radio today broadcast three statements by NAM in reply to Joy. None contained the slightest inkling that the Reds were thinking of taking up Ridgway's offer to resume the truce talks.

One statement angrily brushed aside Joy's denial of the flare dropping. The other sharply rejected Joy's denial that South Korean troops entered the Kaesong area Aug. 30 and killed Red military police.

The third statement on the alleged ground incident labelled Joy's denial "irresponsible and absurd."

In Korea, both sides stepped up the war.

Communist fighter planes swooped out of the clouds and bombed and strafed Allied ground troops in six attacks on the east-central front. It was the first Red attack by more than one plane and it whipped up fresh rumors of enemy plans for an all-out offensive.

On the ground, Allied troops on the east-central front stormed up two vital heights and routed the Reds from their last stronghold on the line north of the Punchbowl, where fierce battles were fought before the truce talks started.

There was a single note of optimism. Gen. James A. VanFleet, United Nations ground commander, said at Eighth Army Headquarters that he believed the Reds would settle for the present battle-line as the cease-fire zone if the truce talks are resumed.

When the talks broke off, the Communists were insisting that the 38th Parallel be made the cease-fire line. The battle line extends 25 to 30 miles into North Korea in the east.

Child Rescued After She Falls Into Well

NEWBERG, Ore., Sept. 3 (AP).—Rescuers reached 2½-year-old Marie Payne at 6:13 pm., this evening, about four hours after she had fallen 12 feet into a well.

The child was conscious as rescuers brought her up to daylight. She was taken to a hospital here.

The lower half of her body was covered with mud.

Rescue crews sank a shaft four feet long and three feet wide down 14 feet alongside the well. They carefully shoved a steel rod into the well hole at the point where they thought the girl was lodged.

She called to her father at the top of the hole that the rod had touched her. He relayed the information down to the rescue crew. Then they tunnelled across to the girl.

As soon as she was brought to the top of the rescue shaft, the little girl slipped into a "state of shock" Dr. C. A. Bump reported.

At the hospital, penicillin shots were begun to prevent pneumonia. The girl suffered only chill and shock. A half-hour after she arrived at the hospital, she drank half a bottle of milk which her mother had brought.

Weekend Deaths Hit New Record

(By Associated Press)

With a death rate of one about every 11 minutes, the nation's traffic toll for a Labor Day weekend reached a new record Monday night of 419 fatalities.

The old record of 410 deaths for a 78-hour Labor Day holiday was recorded in 1949.

The 1951 toll was well in excess of the 390 deaths the National Safety Council first had predicted for the period. Later, Ned H. Dearborn, council president, boosted the prediction to "more than 500" deaths before the millions of cars have cleared the holiday traffic by midnight Monday.

The period in which the deaths occurred was from 6 pm. (local time) Friday.

Score of Red Japs Are Seized by Police

TOKYO, Tuesday, Sept. 4 (AP).—Japanese police today arrested a score of suspected Communist leaders in raids across Japan.

They were charged with anti-occupation activities for publishing secretly articles opposing the Japanese peace treaty and rearmament of Japan.

British Detectives Get $33.60 Weekly

LONDON, Sept. 3 (AP).—Britain's secret service agents asked for a raise today, disclosing their salaries for the first time.

They applied to a government pay tribunal for an increase in their weekly salary of £12 ($33.60).

Chancellor of the Exchequer Hugh Gaitskell rejected their previous demand for £15/10 ($43.40).

NY Fairgrounds Are Overjammed

SYRACUSE, Sept. 3 (AP). — The gates to the state fairgrounds were closed today as an estimated 80,000 persons taxed facilities and a backlog of cars jammed highways for miles.

Fair officials gave an official estimate of over 80,000 but police said they believed there were more than 100,000.

The gates were reopened after being closed for a half an hour to unscramble the holiday traffic. Sound trucks and radios appealed to motorists to turn back and visit the fair some other time.

DANGEROUS RIDE

WEYBURN, Sask., Sept. 3 (AP).—Douglas Fee, power corporation foreman, narrowly escaped being crushed to death when he and 150 hydro poles rolled off a railway flat car. Fee, sitting on top of the piled poles when they rolled, suffered a broken foot.

Editor Asks U. S. Ban Tass Agency

WILMINGTON, DEL., Sept. 3 (AP).—Alexander F. Jones, president of the American Society of Newspaper Editors, proposed today that Congress ban representatives of Tass, the Russian news agency, from its press galleries.

He also urged that they be sent back to Russia.

Jones, executive editor of the Syracuse, NY, Herald Journal, wants Congress to take this action in retaliation for the jailing of Associated Press Correspondent William N. Oatis in Communist Czechoslovakia.

COURTESY CALL

SAN FRANCISCO, Sept. 3 (AP).—Japanese Premier Shigeru Yoshida paid a 25-minute courtesy call late today on K. G. Younger, head of the British delegation to the Japanese Peace Conference. No statements were issued and there was no hint of what they discussed.

Key Nations Agree On Treaty Rules

Acheson Seeks to Block Any Move By Russia to Stall Proceedings

SAN FRANCISCO, Sept. 3 (AP). — President Truman arrived here today and rode past the opera house where tomorrow night he will open the 51-nation peace conference for Japan.

Two hours after the President's plane touched the ground, 11 key nations reached an agreement on a set of rules for the conference procedure.

Secretary of State Dean Acheson, who had spent most of the day in last minute efforts to block any move the Russians might make toward stalling the proceedings, met Mr. Truman at the airport.

The 11 key nations who agreed along general lines to follow Acheson's suggestions for rules of order met in the U. S. delegation headquarters.

Kenneth Younger, British minister of state, presided at the informal meeting. Other nations represented were Australia, Canada, Ceylon, France, Indonesia, The Netherlands, New Zealand, Pakistan, the Philippines and the United States.

Younger said later "The meeting reached general agreement on procedure with the people who were there. But as you see it was not a fully representative group."

All 11 of the nations present are members of the Far Eastern Commission for Japan. A majority of them must sign and ratify the treaty. Russia, who also is a member of the commission, was not present and obviously was not invited.

It generally was believed the rules agreed upon called for limiting speeches to one hour, with five minutes allowed for a reply if any delegate is questioned.

The tough set of rules also would forbid amendments to the present draft of the treaty.

Acheson has been afraid the Russians might try to stall the meetings with lengthy oratory and ask for revisions.

ON WAY HOME

MADRID, Sept. 3 (AP). — U. S. Ambassador Stanton Griffis left by plane for New York tonight for medical examination.

U. S. Unions Win Praise Of Sec. Tobin

(By Associated Press)

American workers won the praise of Secretary of Labor Tobin on their Labor Day holiday yesterday for not succumbing to the lure of Communism.

They have never been moved by Communism's "idea of class conflict, and it's a safe bet they never will," Tobin said in a radio address.

Tobin headed a long list of Labor Day speakers across the nation on the traditional holiday as millions of Americans enjoyed the long weekend with trips to woods and beaches and ball parks, or just rested.

President Truman spent most of the day aboard a plane headed for the Japanese Peace Treaty Conference at San Francisco.

Tobin said most American workers still don't belong to unions but those who do have helped improve working conditions for all the employed.

"Collective bargaining has become the key to industrial peace in the United States," the Secretary added. "In general, labor and management get along in America. That's the thing to remember, even when the newspapers are full of strike news.

"The result of the democracy that unions bring to American industry has not been greater strife but greater stability."

September 4, 1951: The morning Sun announced the death of a fireman and the destruction of the old state technical school. *Courtesy Charlie Jenks*

Fair Deal

BINGHAMTON PRESS

Tuesday Evening, Sept. 4, 1951 — THE TRIPLE CITIES' NEWSPAPER — Vol. 73—123 30 Pages 5 Cents

★ ★ ★ GIs' Girls

Living has been fun for the sweethearts of GIs in Japan, but with the end of the occupation the girls will face a future of spinsterhood. For the story of these social outcasts, turn to page 20.

Drive Opens for New State Tech Here

Yanks Battling 83,000 German-Staffed Reds

Allied Blow Aims to Halt Any Drive

Europeans Giving Technical Advice To Enemy Troops

By the United Press

Tokyo—The UN revealed today that three U. S. divisions have been thrown into battle against 83,000 entrenched Communist troops to knock off balance a threatened Red offense in Korea by a Soviet "puppet" army including Germans and other East Europeans.

The U. S. Army's 7th and 2d Divisions and the 1st Marine Division are in the bloody fight against the Communists on the east-central and central front, Gen. James A. Van Fleet, United Nations ground forces commander, disclosed.

Van Fleet said that the Red forces in Korea now number 838,000 men backed by 1,000 planes, 500 tanks and heavy artillery and armored car units.

His announcement followed a statement by Gen. Matthew B. Ridgway's UN Supreme Headquarters here that a "large number" of Soviet Caucasian troops, including technical experts from East Germany and other European nations, are in North Korea and that a Red air and ground offensive is "strongly suggested."

Until now, only South Korean troops have been identified as being in action against the Reds.

Van Fleet said at 8th Army Headquarters that at the start of the present hot action in Korea Aug. 18, Red units included ...

Ridgway Note

Tokyo—(UP)—Gen. Matthew B. Ridgway is completing a note to the Communist high command which he hopes may break the deadlock in Korean truce negotiations, it was disclosed tonight.

There are strong indications that Ridgway may suggest that the ceasefire negotiations be switched to a new site.

High level officers of the UN command express confidence that the truce talks will be resumed despite the hysterically angry Communist complaints of repeated violations of the neutrality of Kaesong, where negotiations were held until the Reds broke them off Aug. 23.

30 Officers Have Army's Toughest Job

The Picture as Big Show Opens

How Will Soviet Try To Block Jap Treaty?

By PETER EDSON
NEA Service Writer

San Francisco—On the eve of this great medicine show to get a peace treaty signed with Japan, the $64 question is, "How will the Russians try to break it up?" First round diplomatic cocktail parties and pre-conference luncheon and dinner groups are kicking around these theories, since Andrei Gromyko isn't tipping the Russian hand: ...

Jap Pact

SAN FRANCISCO — Following is a summary of major features of the Japanese peace treaty:

Sovereignty

Japan would be restored to "friendly association" with the Allied powers as a fully sovereign equal, expected to apply for membership in the United Nations and to conform to the principles of the Charter.

Territory

Japan would be reduced to the four islands of Honshu, Hokaido, Kyushu and Shikoku, the so-called metropolitan area. In a return to her territorial status of 1854, Japan would be shorn of Korea, Formosa, the Pescadores, the Kuriles and South Sakhalin, as well as the former German-mandated Marianas, Marshall and Caroline Islands, which she received under the Versailles Treaty after World War I. Tokyo would also be required to agree to any United States proposal in the United Nations for establishing a United States-administered trusteeship for the Bonins, Ryukyus and related lesser islands.

Peace

Japan would accept the obligation to settle international disputes "by peaceful means" and to refrain from "the threat or use of force" against any other state in ways inconsistent with the purposes of the United Nations.

Security

While freed of Allied occupation troops within 90 days after the treaty became effective, Japan would be enabled to enter into security agreements providing for the stationing of "foreign armed forces" in Japanese territory. This provision anticipates such a pact with the United States soon after the treaty is signed. Recognizing Japan's right of individual as well as collective self-defense, the treaty places no restrictions ...

Reparations

Trade

Other Pacts

(Continued on Page Seven)

Respect Your Child's Fear

Turn to Page 19

STATE TECH'S SCORCHED REMAINS—Here are the ruins of the old armory building, which housed the State Institute of Applied Arts and Sciences in Binghamton. It was destroyed by fire yesterday. One fireman was killed and seven hurt in battling the blaze, which caused between $750,000 and $1,000,000 damage. (Fire stories on Pages 3 and 5. More pictures on Pages 3 and 16.)

Purchase Of Site Put To County

Institute Trustees To Check on Use Of North High Setup

By ROBERT L. McMANUS
Binghamton Press Staff Writer

A determined effort to have Binghamton Institute of Applied Arts and Sciences continued in new and permanent quarters started this afternoon, a day after the old Washington Street armory which housed the institute was destroyed in the city's costliest fire.

At a meeting of the institute's Board of Trustees this afternoon, a committee of three was authorized to ask the Broome County Board of Supervisors to purchase a site for a new institute.

DR. JARVIE

At the same time, institute officials were instructed to inspect North High School's machine shop and other facilities late today with a view to moving most of the institute's classes to the city school temporarily.

EQUIPMENT SOUGHT

In a third step aimed at getting the institute back into operation as rapidly as possible, it was voted to ask area industries to lend the technical school whatever machinery and equipment may be necessary for a temporary operation.

If the Board of Supervisors approves the suggestion, the Board of Trustees intends to ask Governor Dewey to accept the county-purchased land and some possible financial assistance from the City of Binghamton as the local contribution toward a new and permanent institute.

EDITORIAL, "Tragic State Tech Fire Should be Turned to Gain in Community's Planning for Eventual Auditorium," is on Page 6.

Mayor Donald W. Kramer, who attended the meeting along with State Senator Floyd E. Anderson and institute representatives, said that the city would cooperate in the drive "as fully as possible." He indicated a plan might be worked out under which some of the $250,000 insurance money the city will collect on the armory could be used for the institute development.

Cecil C. Tyrrell, director of the five-year-old technical school, said at best the opening of the institute's fall semester probably will be set back two weeks. Classes had been scheduled to resume next Monday.

QUARTERS OFFERED

Weekend Dead 707, New Mark

Party to End 'Em All Rocks Millionaires

By HAYNES THOMPSON
United Press Staff Writer

Venice, Italy—(UP)—An almost unknown Spanish millionaire gave a fabulous costume ball today that made Woolworth heiress Barbara Hutton say: "I wish I had his money." Don Carlos, "Good Time, Charley" De Beistegui y Iturbi ...

Jamaicans Spared Full Hurricane

Abbe Lane's Minks Stolen at Hotel

Self-Inflicted Gun Wound Kills Adamic

Flemington, N. J.—(UP)—Author Louis Adamic was found dead today in his burning farmhouse, and a coroner ruled his death was caused by a "supposedly self-inflicted" bullet wound.

German Prince Marries Blonde Princess

Royalty Weds in Medieval Pomp

Drunks Up in Air

Friendly Stranger Thief

Today's Chuckle

September 4, 1951: By the time the afternoon paper came out, the community was already planning to rebuild. *Courtesy Charlie Jenks*

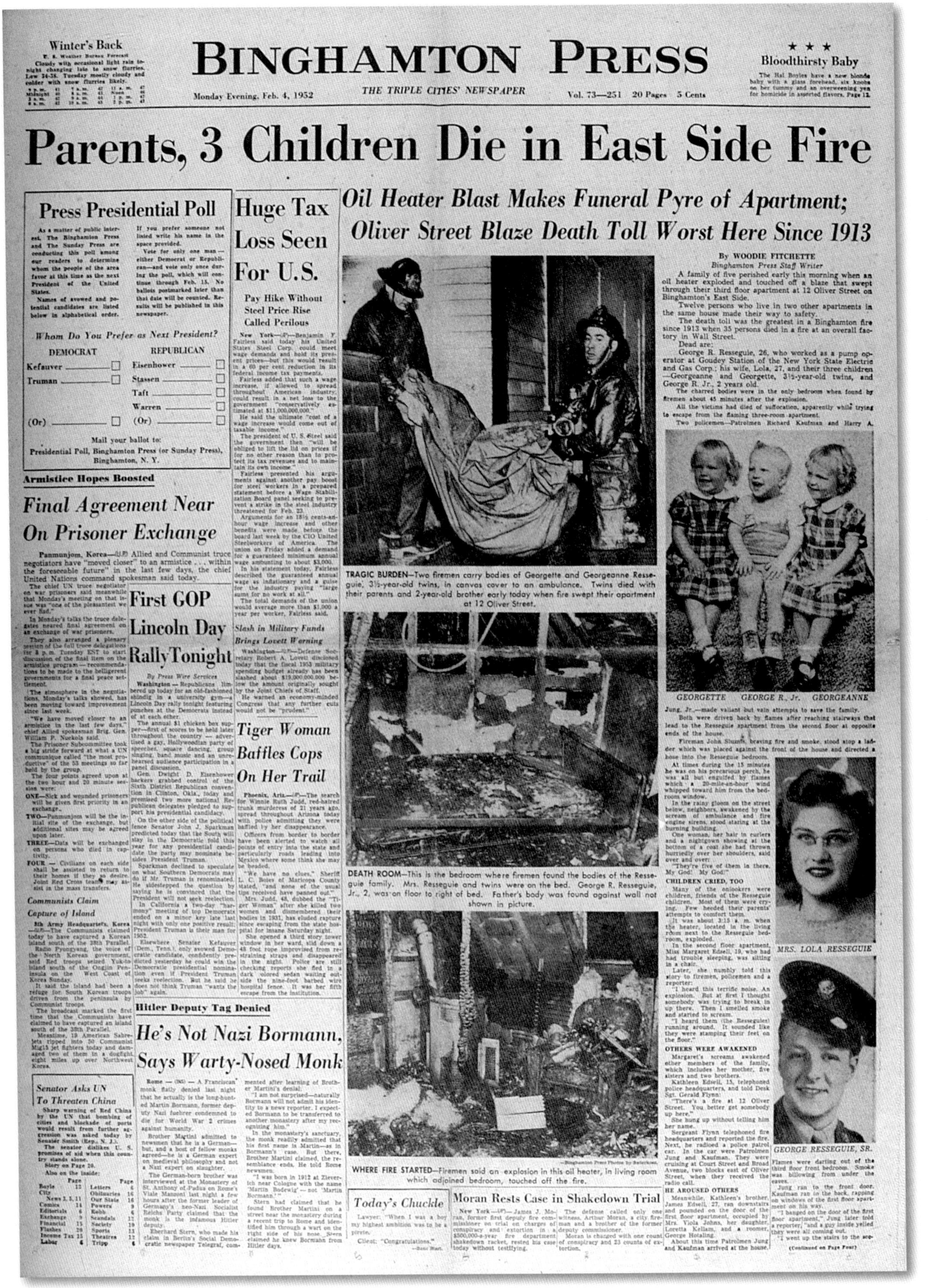

Winter's Back

U. S. Weather Bureau Forecast

Cloudy with occasional light rain tonight changing late to snow flurries. Low 34-38. Tuesday mostly cloudy and colder with snow flurries likely.

BINGHAMTON PRESS

Monday Evening, Feb. 4, 1952 — THE TRIPLE CITIES' NEWSPAPER — Vol. 73—251 — 20 Pages — 5 Cents

★ ★ ★

Bloodthirsty Baby

The Hal Boyles have a new blonde baby with a glass forehead, six knobs on her tummy and an overweening yen for homicide in assorted flavors. Page 12.

Parents, 3 Children Die in East Side Fire

Oil Heater Blast Makes Funeral Pyre of Apartment; Oliver Street Blaze Death Toll Worst Here Since 1913

By WOODIE FITCHETTE

Binghamton Press Staff Writer

A family of five perished early this morning when an oil heater exploded and touched off a blaze that swept through their third floor apartment at 12 Oliver Street on Binghamton's East Side.

Twelve persons who live in two other apartments in the same house made their way to safety.

The death toll was the greatest in a Binghamton fire since 1913 when 35 persons died in a fire at an overall factory in Wall Street.

Dead are:

George R. Resseguie, 26, who worked as a pump operator at Goudey Station of the New York State Electric and Gas Corp.; his wife, Lola, 27, and their three children—Georgeanne and Georgette, 3½-year-old twins, and George R. Jr., 2 years old.

The charred bodies were in the only bedroom when found by firemen about 45 minutes after the explosion.

All the victims had died of suffocation, apparently while trying to escape from the flaming three-room apartment.

Two policemen—Patrolmen Richard Kaufman and Harry A. Jung, Jr.—made valiant but vain attempts to save the family.

Both were driven back by flames after reaching stairways that lead to the Resseguie apartment from the second floor at opposite ends of the house.

Fireman John Sluzis, braving fire and smoke, stood atop a ladder which was placed against the front of the house and directed a hose into the Resseguie bedroom.

At times during the 15 minutes he was on his precarious perch, he was all but engulfed by flames which a 20-mile-an-hour wind whipped toward him from the bedroom window.

In the rainy gloom on the street below, neighbors, awakened by the scream of ambulance and fire engine sirens, stood staring at the burning building.

One woman, her hair in curlers and a nightgown showing at the bottom of a coat she had thrown hurriedly over her shoulders, said over and over:

"They're five of them in there. My God! My God!"

CHILDREN CRIED, TOO

Many of the onlookers were children, friends of the Resseguie children. Most of them were crying. Few heeded their parents' attempts to comfort them.

It was about 3:15 a. m. when the heater, located in the living room next to the Resseguie bedroom, exploded.

In the second floor apartment, Miss Margaret Edsell, 19, who had had trouble sleeping, was sitting in a chair.

Later, she numbly told this story to firemen, policemen and a reporter:

"I heard this terrific noise. An explosion. But at first I thought somebody was trying to break in up there. Then I smelled smoke and started to scream.

"I heard them (the Resseguies) running around. It sounded like they were stamping their feet on the floor."

OTHERS WERE AWAKENED

Margaret's screams awakened other members of the family, which includes her mother, five sisters and two brothers.

Kathleen Edsell, 15, telephoned police headquarters, and told Desk Sgt. Gerald Flynn:

"There's a fire at 12 Oliver Street. You better get somebody up here."

She hung up without telling him her name.

Sergeant Flynn telephoned fire headquarters and reported the fire. Next, he radioed a police patrol car. In the car were Patrolmen Jung and Kaufman. They were cruising at Court Street and Broad Avenue, two blocks east of Oliver Street, when they received the radio call.

HE AROUSED OTHERS

Meanwhile, Kathleen's brother, James Edsell, 27, ran downstairs and pounded on the door of the first floor apartment, occupied by Mrs. Viola Johns, her daughter, Loretta Kellam, and a roomer, George Hotaling.

About this time Patrolmen Jung and Kaufman arrived at the house. Flames were darting out of the third floor front bedroom. Smoke was billowing from under the eaves.

Jung ran to the front door. Kaufman ran to the back, rapping on windows of the first floor apartment on his way.

"I banged on the door of the first floor apartment," Jung later told a reporter, "and a guy inside yelled they were all coming out.

"I went up the stairs to the sec-

(Continued on Page Four)

TRAGIC BURDEN—Two firemen carry bodies of Georgette and Georgeanne Resseguie, 3½-year-old twins, in canvas cover to an ambulance. Twins died with their parents and 2-year-old brother early today when fire swept their apartment at 12 Oliver Street.

DEATH ROOM—This is the bedroom where firemen found the bodies of the Resseguie family. Mrs. Resseguie and twins were on the bed. George R. Resseguie, Jr., 2, was on floor to right of bed. Father's body was found against wall not shown in picture.

WHERE FIRE STARTED—Firemen said an explosion in this oil heater, in living room which adjoined bedroom, touched off the fire.

GEORGETTE — GEORGE R., Jr. — GEORGEANNE

MRS. LOLA RESSEGUIE

GEORGE RESSEGUIE, SR.

Press Presidential Poll

As a matter of public interest, The Binghamton Press and The Sunday Press are conducting this poll among our readers to determine whom the people of the area favor at this time as the next President of the United States.

Names of avowed and potential candidates are listed below in alphabetical order.

If you prefer someone not listed write his name in the space provided.

Vote for only one man—either Democrat or Republican—and vote only once during the poll, which will continue through Feb. 15. No ballots postmarked later than that date will be counted. Results will be published in this newspaper.

Whom Do You Prefer as Next President?

DEMOCRAT		REPUBLICAN	
Kefauver	☐	Eisenhower	☐
Truman	☐	Stassen	☐
		Taft	☐
		Warren	☐
(Or)	☐	(Or)	☐

Mail your ballot to:
Presidential Poll, Binghamton Press (or Sunday Press), Binghamton, N. Y.

Armistice Hopes Boosted

Final Agreement Near On Prisoner Exchange

Panmunjom, Korea—(U.P.) Allied and Communist truce negotiators have "moved closer" to an armistice . . . within the foreseeable future" in the last few days, the chief United Nations command spokesman said today.

The chief UN truce negotiator on war prisoners said meanwhile that Monday's meeting on that issue was "one of the pleasantest we ever had."

In Monday's talks the truce delegates neared final agreement on an exchange of war prisoners.

They also arranged a plenary session of the full truce delegations for 8 p. m. Tuesday EST to start discussion of the final item on the armistice program—recommendations to be made to the belligerent governments for a final peace settlement.

The atmosphere in the negotiations, Monday's talks showed, has been moving toward improvement since last week.

"We have moved closer to an armistice in the last few days," chief Allied spokesman Brig. Gen. William P. Nuckols said.

The Prisoner Subcommittee took a big stride forward at what a UN communique called "the most productive" of the 53 meetings so far held by the group.

The four points agreed upon at the two hour and 20 minute session were:

ONE—Sick and wounded prisoners will be given first priority in an exchange.

TWO—Panmunjom will be the initial site of the exchange, but additional sites may be agreed upon later.

THREE—Data will be exchanged on persons who died in captivity.

FOUR — Civilians on each side shall be assisted to return to their homes if they so desire. Joint Red Cross teams may assist in the mass transfers.

Communists Claim Capture of Island

8th Army Headquarters, Korea—(U.P.)—The Communists claimed today to have captured a Korean island south of the 38th Parallel.

Radio Pyongyang, the voice of the North Korean government, said Red troops seized Yuk-to Island south of the Ongjin Peninsula on the West Coast of Korea Sunday.

It said the island had been a refuge for South Korean troops driven from the peninsula by Communist troops.

The broadcast marked the first time that the Communists have claimed to have captured an island south of the 38th Parallel.

Meantime, 19 American Sabrejets ripped into 30 Communist Mig15 jet fighters today and damaged two of them in a dogfight eight miles up over Northwest Korea.

Senator Asks UN To Threaten China

Sharp warning of Red China by the UN that bombing of cities and blockade of ports would result from further aggression was asked today by Senator Smith (Rep., N. J.).

The senator dislikes U. S. promises of aid when this country stands alone.

Story on Page 20.

Also on the inside:

Huge Tax Loss Seen For U.S.

Pay Hike Without Steel Price Rise Called Perilous

New York—(AP)—Benjamin F. Fairless said today his United States Steel Corp. could meet wage demands and hold its present prices—but this would result in a 60 per cent reduction in its federal income tax payments.

Fairless added that such a wage increase, if allowed to spread throughout American industry, could result in a net loss to the government "conservatively estimated at $11,000,000,000."

He said the ultimate "cost of a wage increase would come out of taxable income."

The president of U. S. Steel said the government then "will be obliged to lift the lid on prices if for no other reason than to protect its tax revenues and to maintain its own income."

Fairless presented his arguments against another pay boost for steel workers in a prepared statement before a Wage Stabilization Board panel seeking to prevent a strike in the steel industry threatened for Feb. 23.

Arguments for an 18½ cents-an-hour wage increase and other benefits were made before the board last week by the CIO United Steelworkers of America. The union on Friday added a demand for a guaranteed minimum annual wage amounting to about $3,000.

In his statement today, Fairless described the guaranteed annual wage as inflationary and a guise for the industry paying "large sums for no work at all."

The total demands of the union would average more than $1,000 a year per worker, Fairless said.

Slash in Military Funds Brings Lovett Warning

Washington—(U.P.)—Defense Secretary Robert A. Lovett disclosed today that the fiscal 1953 military spending budget already has been slashed about $19,000,000,000 below the amount originally sought by the Joint Chiefs of Staff.

He warned an economy-minded Congress that any further cuts would not be "prudent."

First GOP Lincoln Day Rally Tonight

By Press Wire Services

Washington — Republicans limbered up today for an old-fashioned shindig in a university gym—a Lincoln Day rally tonight featuring punches at the Democrats instead of at each other.

The annual $1 chicken box supper—first of scores to be held later throughout the country — advertised a gay, Hollywoodian party of speeches, square dancing, group singing, band music and an unrehearsed audience participation in a panel discussion.

Gen. Dwight D. Eisenhower backers grabbed control of the Sixth District Republican convention in Clinton, Okla., today and promised two more national Republican delegates pledged to support his presidential candidacy.

On the other side of the political fence Senator John J. Sparkman predicted today that the South will stay in the Democratic fold this year for any presidential candidate the party may nominate besides President Truman.

Sparkman declined to speculate on what Southern Democrats may do if Mr. Truman is renominated. He sidestepped the question by saying he is convinced that the President will not seek reelection.

In California a two-day "harmony" meeting of top Democrats ended on a minor key late last night with only one positive result: President Truman is their man for 1952.

Elsewhere Senator Kefauver (Dem., Tenn.), only avowed Democratic candidate, confidently predicted yesterday he could win the Democratic presidential nomination even if President Truman seeks reelection. But he said he does not think Truman "wants the job" again.

Tiger Woman Baffles Cops On Her Trail

Phoenix, Ariz.—(AP)—The search for Winnie Ruth Judd, red-haired trunk murderess of 21 years ago, spread throughout Arizona today with police admitting they were baffled by her disappearance.

Officers from border to border have been alerted to watch all points of entry into the state and particularly roads leading into Mexico where some think she may be headed.

"We have no clues," Sheriff L. C. Boies of Maricopa County stated, "and none of the usual tips received have panned out."

Mrs. Judd, 48, dubbed the "Tiger Woman" after she killed two women and dismembered their bodies in 1931, has eluded capture since escaping from the state hospital for insane Saturday night.

She opened a third story tower window in her ward, slid down a 48 foot rope improvised from restraining straps and disappeared in the night. Police are still checking reports she fled in a dark colored sedan waiting outside the nine-foot barbed wire hospital fence. It was her fifth escape from the institution.

Hitler Deputy Tag Denied

He's Not Nazi Bormann, Says Warty-Nosed Monk

Rome — (INS) — A Franciscan monk flatly denied last night that he actually is the long-hunted Martin Bormann, former deputy Nazi fuehrer condemned to die for World War 2 crimes against humanity.

Brother Martini admitted to newsmen that he is a German—but, and a host of fellow monks agreed—he is a German expert on medieval philosophy and not a Nazi expert on slaughter.

The German-born brother was interviewed at the Monastery of St. Anthony of Padua on Rome's Viale Manzoni last night a few hours after the former leader of Germany's neo-Nazi Socialist Reichs Party claimed that the monk is the infamous Hitler deputy.

Eberhard Stern, who made his claim in Berlin's Social Democratic newspaper Telegraf, commented after learning of Brother Martini's denial:

"I am not surprised—naturally Bormann will not admit his identity to a news reporter. I expected Bormann to be transferred to another monastery after my recognizing him."

In the monastery's sanctuary, the monk readily admitted that his first name is Martin—as in Bormann's case. But there, Brother Martini claimed, the resemblance ends. He told Rome newsmen:

"I was born in 1912 at Zieverich near Cologne with the name 'Martin Bodewig' — not 'Martin Bormann.'"

Stern had claimed that he found Brother Martini on a street near the monastery during a recent trip to Rome and identified him through a wart on the right side of his nose. Stern claimed he knew Bormann from Hitler days.

Today's Chuckle

Lawyer: "When I was a boy my highest ambition was to be a pirate."

Client: "Congratulations."

Moran Rests Case in Shakedown Trial

New York—(AP)—James J. Moran, former first deputy fire commissioner on trial on charges of conspiracy and extortion in a $500,000-a-year fire department shakedown racket, rested his case today without testifying.

The defense called only one witness, Arthur Moran, a city fireman and a brother of the former deputy commissioner.

Moran is charged with one count of conspiracy and 23 counts of extortion.

February 4, 1952: A tragic fire is recorded; the Press wants to know how its readers would vote. *Courtesy Charlie Jenks*

Korea Must Accept What U. S. Wants, Says Rhee

No Reign Here
By U. S. Weather Bureau
Fair tonight and Wednesday. Low tonight 45-50. High tomorrow 73-78.

BINGHAMTON PRESS

Tuesday Evening, June 2, 1953 — THE TRIPLE CITIES' NEWSPAPER — Vol. 75—44 32 Pages 5 Cents

★ ★ ★
Vacation Boom
More people are getting longer vacations and more holidays this year, and resort owners are expecting their business to be the best in history. Sam Dawson gives collective bargaining credit for this is a story on Page 12.

Millions Cheer as Elizabeth Is Crowned

We Must OK Truce, Says Rhee

By the Associated Press

Seoul — President Syngman Rhee of South Korea today disclosed he had received a three-point message from U. S. President Dwight D. Eisenhower, and added: "We must accept anything that the U. S. President wants.

"Common sense and wisdom require that we cooperate with the U. S. at any cost," Rhee said, without saying what Mr. Eisenhower had told him.

The 78-year-old Republic of Korea leader's statement indicated that South Korean opposition to the secret UN command proposal for bringing an armistice in Korea is lessening.

Rhee also said he is looking for someone to take the place of Maj. Gen. Choi Duk Shin as the South Korean delegate on the UN armistice negotiation team.

TRUCE STAND HAZY

Rhee declined to elaborate on his apparently conciliatory statement. He spoke to correspondents at a parade of the British Commonwealth Division honoring the coronation of Elizabeth II.

Nor did he make it precisely clear whether he is ready now to accept the Allied truce proposal, to which he and his government had expressed vigorous opposition.

South Korea's prime minister yesterday had threatened a break with the Allies and go-it-alone policy for South Korea but deferred action until after Thursday's critical truce session.

The Communists are expected to reply to the Allied proposal at Thursday's meeting.

The 78-year-old Rhee's statement came on the heels of a report from Washington that he had proposed to Mr. Eisenhower a mutual defense pact plus substantial U. S. financial and military aid as South Korea's price for accepting Allied truce terms.

NO REPLY YET

The ROK president said he had not yet replied to the message from Mr. Eisenhower but that he would do so "very soon."

The violent opposition of the Rhee government since the proposal was submitted last month precipitated a crisis so serious that it threatened to wreck chances for a truce in the nearly 3-year-old Korean war.

The armistice negotiations at Panmunjom have been in recess since May 25 and the Communist reaction to the Allied plan will not be known until Thursday when they are resumed.

Big 3 Conference Delayed by British

Paris—(UP)—A foreign ministry spokesman said today that the conference of President Dwight D. Eisenhower, Prime Minister Sir Winston Churchill and the premier of France in Bermuda, scheduled for mid-June would be postponed several days at the request of the British Government.

Commies Slam UN Lines

Seoul—(AP) — More than 4,000 North Korean and Chinese Reds slammed against 11 Allied main line positions and a handful of outposts today as big-scale Communist attacks exploded in Eastern and Central Korea.

American and South Korean infantrymen smashed 10 of the main line attacks, nine on the bloody Easter Front and one on the Central Front.

Fighting for trench line positions just in front of Luke the Gook's Castle on the Eastern Front, still raged.

There South Korean troops of the 12th Division were counterattacking for a second time against Reds who hammered their way to Allied lines.

An 8th Army briefing officer said the bitter fighting on the Eastern Front was the heaviest in that section in more than a year.

Today's Chuckle

Mrs. Newly-Rich went up to compliment the author after his talk about his new book. "I feel we have such mutual interests," she cooed. "You have written a book and I have read one."

Long Live the Queen

—AP WIREPHOTOS via Radio from London.

London's Multitudes Go Wild as Queen's Coach Appears in Trafalgar Square Today

First Coronation Of Woman Since 1837 in England

By INEZ ROBB
International News Service Staff Writer

Westminster Abbey, London—Britain crowned her new and endearing sovereign Elizabeth II today with an ancient and beautiful ritual viewed by her son and heir, little Prince Charles.

It was Britain's first coronation of a woman since Victoria, 116 years ago.

The 4-year-old Charles in white satin short pants and scrubbed face looked on in wonder at the solemn ceremony he too must undergo some day.

Amid all the pomp and glory of the Abbey ceremony there was a touching moment when the queen clung lovingly to the hand of her husband, Philip, Duke of Edinburgh, as he humbly knelt in homage to Elizabeth, his sovereign.

It was the one personal gesture she permitted herself.

Thrice at dramatic moments the sun won out in a battle with rain which drenched and chilled London.

The sun burst through angry black clouds when Elizabeth drove from Buckingham Palace to Westminster Abbey, the old traditional shrine.

It broke leaden skies again when the 27-year-old queen, resplendent and regal, was being anointed as head of a commonwealth of a quarter of the world's peoples.

And again the sun bathed the ancient Abbey and surrounding Parliament Square in a warm glow shortly after the tired queen and her tall husband drove away at 3:15 p. m. (10:15 a. m., EDT) on the triumphant processional return along streets jammed with 3,000,000 persons.

TIRED QUEEN SMILES

Cheering multitudes acclaimed the newly-crowned sovereign as she drove in the ancient royal state coach through the heart of gaily-garlanded but rain-drenched London in the company of her dashing consort.

The tired but beautiful queen smiled cheerfully as the carriage rolled along the two-mile-long route.

Ten thousand troops from all parts of the Commonwealth led the way along a route lined with 14,000 troops from every branch of Britain's armed services.

The rain began again as the return procession passed through Hyde Park toward Marble Arch. The royal couple was partly obscured behind slightly steamed, closed windows of the state coach but the queen was seen smiling, although no longer waving.

Philip sat rigidly alongside her. In her hands she held the sparkling sceptre and golden orb, consecrated by prayer and sacrament to a lifelong service to God and her people.

SLIGHT BUT REGAL

Scotland Yard reported a total of 3,062 casualties an hour before the queen began her ride back to the palace. Most of them were crowd crush-fainting cases. One hundred and fourteen were hospitalized.

Radio carried the story and the queen's clearly audible words to millions. Millions more in Europe saw the coronation on television.

Her majesty was a slight figure in her gorgeous robes and jewels. She was regal as she went through the long ceremony.

Dr. Geoffrey Fisher, the officiating Archbishop of Canterbury, matched her in perfection. And the Duke of Norfolk, the Roman Catholic earl marshal who arranged the whole crowning and consecration of a queen in the Anglican church rites could congratulate himself on masterminding a show without a bobble.

It was a supremely serious and dedicated-looking young queen on whose dark curls the archbishop placed the golden Crown of St. Edward at the climax of the ceremony.

CHARLES EXEMPLARY

It was another milestone, too, in the most fascinating love story of the century—that of 50,000,000 Britons for one slight girl and mother, Elizabeth II.

By his exemplary behavior young Prince Charles deserved a big lollipop on his return home after 60 minutes in the Abbey under the watchful eyes of grandmother Queen Elizabeth, the queen mother.

The young prince stood erect in the royal box, his hands clasped before him and his chubby face grave, as the crowning ceremony ended and a triumphant "God Save the Queen!" roared from the throats of assembled noblemen and women from every corner of his mother's realm.

As the queen was being anointed the Abbey was bathed in a brilliant warm light. Guns boomed, bells rang merrily.

Elizabeth, radiant, but at times looking fatigued near the end of the ceremony, was crowned and then faced her husband from the throne.

Philip handed his coronet to a page. Grave-faced, he approached the dais carefully, climbed the steps, his eyes riveted on his wife. The queen lowered her eyes.

The handsome, blond prince carefully pledged allegiance in a strong voice. He put his hands between those of the queen's and promised to be her "liege man of life and limb."

Elizabeth kept her eyes averted until Philip's oath was completed. Then she glanced for a split second at her husband.

Philip leaned forward and kissed her on the cheek, slightly dislodging the five-pound crown. Elizabeth immediately set the gleaming, jeweled St. Edward's Crown in place.

This part of the ritual obviously puzzled little Charles. He turned to Queen Mother Elizabeth and asked questions, breaking them off when the silver trumpets blared.

QUEEN TIRES VISIBLY

The chaste peck on the queen's fair cheek by Philip was a sweet moment for both. It also symbolized the life of heavy responsibility ahead for both.

The queen was extremely composed throughout the long, difficult ritual which lasted two hours and a half, but she tired visibly. Her head kept slightly tilting forward under the weight of the big crown. Sometimes her hands fluttered, and the heavy bejeweled sword of state wobbled in her grip.

There was a small incident when a baron paid homage to his queen. One of the supporting nobles leaned forward on his knees a little too far and fell onto his face. He quickly recovered his position.

The long ritual consisted of prayers by the queen at her faldstool (prayer stool) and her thrilling recognition by the Archbishop of Canterbury when he proclaimed "Sirs, I here present unto you Queen Elizabeth, your undoubted queen."

Then there was the queen's oath to govern her peoples "according to their respective laws" and to maintain the Protestant Reformed religion; the anointing while the choir sang Handel's "Zadok the Priest," and the presentation of the emblems of majesty—spurs, sword, robe royal of cloth of gold, orb, ring, scepter, rod and other regalia.

The Archbishop of Canterbury

(Continued from Page Seven)

Balcony Scene

London—(INS)—Queen Elizabeth II, brushing away a possible tear, appeared on the balcony of Buckingham Palace this afternoon to hear "God Save the Queen" roar out from 30,000 of her subjects.

The queen came out on the balcony holding 4-year-old Prince Charles by the hand. She was followed by 2-year-old Princess Anne and by husband, Prince Philip.

—AP WIREPHOTO via Radio from London.

Somber Queen, Crowned, Sits on Throne

Elizabeth Trembles As She Enters Abbey

By ROBERT JONES
Associated Press Staff Writer

Westminster Abbey — (AP) — The fragile features of Queen Elizabeth II were set and unsmiling as she moved slowly into Westminster Abbey for her crowning today. She seemed to tremble slightly as she glided through the great gold and white doors.

She had a fleeting smile for the massed ladies of her household as they swept into a deep curtsy, but she gulped nervously at the Abbey doors.

Her handsome husband, the Duke of Edinburgh, was entirely at ease. Walking swiftly and looking about him with a smile at the curtsys and bows which greeted him, the duke moved straight up to the treasurer of his household and great friend, Lt. Gen. Sir Frederick Browning, and chatted briskly and quietly with him before taking his place in the procession.

The procession already had started to move down the Abbey before the queen—a slight, lonely figure with a circlet tiara of diamonds glistening in her hair—moved out to take her place.

She was composed but looked straight ahead, her hands clasped lightly together in front.

Four-Year-Old Charles Proves He's Prince Royal

By ALVIN STEINKOPF
Associated Press Staff Writer

Westminster Abbey, London—At that golden moment for which he, too, is destined, the little boy was indeed a prince royal today.

The Duke of Cornwall, Prince Charles of Britain, heir to the throne, did his mother proud. He was a good boy.

It was only sometime later—after the Crown of St. Edward had been placed on the head of Queen Elizabeth II and even after his father, the Duke of Edinburgh, had advanced to the altar for Communion—it was only then that the blond darling of England acted like a 4-year-old.

Prince Charles sucked his thumb.

His granny, Queen Mother Elizabeth, who had the task of minding the youngster, whispered quick words to him and his royal dignity returned. Charles was again a dutiful son and heir.

They saved a seat for the boy. He had been promised he could sit with all those grown-ups if he would behave. A great craning and creaking of 7,500 necks at the time of the queen's anointment signaled the arrival of her son.

Dressed in a white shirt and knickers, his hair meticulously parted, Prince Charles sat in the royal gallery with the Queen Mother.

Two chubby hands grasped the gallery ledge and he peered over the railing at the wonderful things going on. In a few minutes, the Queen Mother gave him something to stand on and Charles had a better view of the fascinating heralds and all those other things that dazzled even his elders.

He now was a solemn lad and a somewhat puzzled one. He turned around many times to find out what was happening.

His aunt, Princess Margaret, answered the questions that spring from childhood. And the questions became more and more abundant.

But at the moment of crowning there was not a better boy in all of Christendom.

Later, the sole child in an assembly of so many older people became noticeably the liveliest person in the royal gallery. He became seriously engaged with the problem of a handkerchief that he found projecting from his left sleeve. He examined his hands with great diligence and care. He gazed most thoughtfully at the thumb which had found his mouth.

More News Of Coronation

How Wally and Duke in Paris, Moscow and other world capitals react, Page 2.

Queen's message, Page 2.

Eight full columns of pictures, Page 10. More pictures on Pages 7, 8, 11.

The actual coronation ritual, Page 11.

Sketch of queen in her priceless coronation gown, Page 19.

Story, map and pictures of the Mt. Everest conquest, Page 23.

Upstate Red Probe Starts July 13, Covering Defense Plants, Unions

Binghamton Press Bureau

Washington—The House Un-American Activities Committee called today for a broad investigation of alleged Communistic activities throughout a wide area of upstate New York.

Chairman Harold A. Velde (Rep., Ill.) said it would be aimed at uncovering the extent of Communist influence in vital defense plants and toward exposing individual Communists in public educational institutions.

Hearings are scheduled to start July 13 at Albany before a subcommittee of the Un-American Activities group headed by Representative Bernard W. (Pat) Kearney, Gloversville Republican, and retired National Guard major general.

Kearney will direct the subcommittee including one other Republican and a Democrat. The other members are expected to be named later today.

Representative Velde said the hearings would last for "three or four days" and that they would be "concentrated in the capital area."

However, it was learned that the inquiry also may cover a wide range of activities in upstate New York, including left-wing labor unions and the American Labor Party, as well as alleged Communists in the state government and public schools.

It could affect atomic energy installations of General Electric Corp. in the Syracuse, Schenectady and Troy areas and other

(Continued on Page Thirteen)

British Climbers Conquer Mt. Everest

After one futile attempt two climbers in the latest British expedition have finally reached the top of the world's highest peak—Mt. Everest. Story, pictures and map, Page 23.

Also on the inside:

June 2, 1953: Queen Elizabeth's coronation almost crowds out news of the Korean War. *Courtesy Donna Lupardo*

Cool Comfort
By U. S. Weather Bureau

Partly cloudy, cooler tonight, low 60-65. Tuesday, fair, less humid, little change in temperatures high 80-85.

8 p. m.	82	7 a. m.	71	11 a. m.	78
Midnight	78	8 a. m.	69	Noon	80
3 a. m.	73	9 a. m.	71	1 p. m.	82
6 a. m.	71	10 a. m.	73	2 p. m.	84

BINGHAMTON PRESS

Monday Evening, July 27, 1953 — THE TRIPLE CITIES' NEWSPAPER — Vol. 75—90 22 Pages 5 Cents

★ ★ ★
Summer Manhunt
This is sad news for the working girl in search of an eligible bachelor. They can't be snagged. Page 12.

ALL SHOOTING ENDS IN KOREA

★ ★ ★ ★ ★ ★ ★ ★ ★

3,313 GIs Among POWs to Be Freed by Reds

Diplomats Take Over In Korea

Indochina, Rhee, Red China in UN Are Top Problems

By JOHN M. HIGHTOWER
Associated Press Staff Writer

Washington — Diplomats took over the battle for Korea today, and with the lifting of the pressures of open war a new set of problems and dangers arose to plague Allied and Communist governments alike.

Foremost among these on the Allied side is the threat of an eventual angry struggle between the United States and Britain over admission of Red China to the United Nations.

As for the Communists, there is speculation already about the impact of the armistice on relations among Russia, Red China and North Korea—a situation about which Western governments know little but hope for much.

It is too early to tell yet whether the uneasy truce that settled over Korea's shell-churned battlefront means the beginning of a new and more peaceful era in the worldwide conflict between the Communist and free nations. But officials here have no doubt that it poses many problems which were beyond action while the fighting raged.

FIRST ARENA

The first arena of the diplomatic struggle over these problems is due to be the United Nations General Assembly, at a special session in New York next month. The Assembly's primary task will be to set the stage for a political conference on Korean—and perhaps wider Far Eastern—issues. That conference, under the truce terms, must convene by late October.

In these sessions the major objective of the United States, and presumably of other friendly nations, will be to seek the Korean unification which both sides failed to win in the war.

The Western allies conceive of this as unification under a non-Communist government. That means they want the Reds to give up North Korea, and it raises the critical question. If the Reds are willing to consider this at all, what price will they ask?

Authorities here do not know the answer, but they have an idea that what the Reds may ask is a seat for Red China in the United Nations, displacing Nationalist China; an end to trade embargoes against Red China, and satisfaction of Red China's claims on Formosa.

NO CHOICE

This prospect effectively kills off any optimism in official quarters about the chances of early unification of Korea. For while the British have seemed to favor a UN seat for Red China once the Korean fighting ended, there is such overwhelming opposition to it in the U. S. Congress that the Eisenhower administration appears to have no choice but to fight any deal along that line.

The issue of Formosa is an even more bitter one for the United States, which recognizes the Chinese Nationalist government established there and also considers that Formosa in hostile hands would be a threat to the American defense system in the Western Pacific.

The United States, Britain and France agreed early this month that they would maintain their policies of barring Red China from the UN and embargoing strategic materials to that coun-

(Continued on Page Four)

Allies Hold 96,300 Commie Prisoners

Munsan—(AP)—The secret record of the Panmunjom truce negotiations released today showed that the Communists have told the Allies they will return 12,736 prisoners of war—including 3,313 Americans.

The Communists gave this breakdown of the captives they will release: 3,313 Americans, 8,186 Koreans, 922 British, 12 French, 228 Turks, 15 Australians, 40 Filipinos, 14 Canadians, 22 Colombians, 6 South Africans, 1 Greek, 1 Belgian and 3 Japanese.

This makes a total of 4,577 prisoners of non-Korean nationality to be returned.

The Allies informed the Communists that about 5,000 Chinese prisoners and 69,000 North Korean captives will be returned to the Reds in the big exchange of prisoners.

SECRET SESSION

The information was exchanged in a secret staff officers session held at Panmunjom July 22. Marine Col. James C. Murray spoke for the Allies and North Korean Col. Lee Pyong Il for the Reds.

The UN said that about 7,800 North Koreans and 14,500 Chinese captives, the rest of their total of 93,800 prisoners, will be turned over to the neutral nations repatriation commission. These prisoners have renounced communism and do not want to return to their homelands.

Both sides have agreed to send prisoners of war who refuse repatriation to camps in the demilitarized zone between the opposing armies. They will be guarded by Indian troops.

South Korea has threatened to open fire on Indian troops if they land in South Korea. President Syngman Rhee and his government regard India as pro-Communist.

There have been reports that the Indian troops would be flown directly to the neutral zone.

The Communists said yesterday they would return 300 prisoners a day, including sick and wounded. They did not give the number of disabled men they still hold.

APPROXIMATE FIGURES

The UN command informed the Reds they will turn back the Communists captured at the rate of 2,400 able-bodied prisoners daily, plus 360 sick and wounded each day until all the disabled are released. The Allies said they hold about 3,000 sick and wounded in UN camps.

The Allied staff officers, however, told the Reds the figures "are approximate but may be used for planning purposes."

The truce document requires that all prisoners desiring to return home be exchanged within 60 days after the signing.

The Allied officer at the session yesterday, Col. L. C. Friedersdorff, told the Communists the UN feels the proposed Communist rate of exchange of 300 prisoners daily "is unduly small in view of the numbers which we will deliver to you each day."

The Red staff officer, Chinese Col. Wuang Chien, replied that the Reds are "willing to complete repatriation of prisoners of war at the earliest date" and promised to "continue to study the situation of our transportation."

Not Returning

Washington—(INS)—When will the boys come home from Korea? Not very soon. In some cases, it may be many months.

That's the consensus of defense and military leaders who nonetheless mapped plans today to trim an estimated 100,000 off the roster of man-power requirements immediately.

Both Defense Secretary Charles E. Wilson and Gen. Mark W. Clark, supreme Allied commander in the Far East, agreed that there will be no early or large-scale withdrawal of American forces from Korea.

UN Meets On Korea In 3 Weeks

United Nations—(AP)—The UN General Assembly will meet three weeks from today to tackle the next big hurdle in the Korean problem—the setting up of a special political conference.

The conference provided for in the armistice agreement must meet within 90 days. Its chief job will be to try to transform the armistice into a permanent peace. Just what subjects will come up remain to be decided.

The 60-nation General Assembly will determine which nations will have a seat at the conference and will fix the time and place it will meet. Some delegates want the Assembly to work out the conference agenda too, but others have indicated they want to leave that to the conference itself.

The call for the Assembly meeting on Aug. 17 went out quickly to members last night, but Assembly President Lester B. Pearson of Canada and other leaders thought it best to allow ample time for private consultations before the formal meetings begin.

Pearson expressed the hope that some plans might be agreed upon informally before the session opens. If this is done, Pearson said, the meeting might be concluded in a week or a little more.

Ike Requests 200 Million For Korea Aid

Washington — (AP) — President Eisenhower today formally requested Congress to provide an initial $200,000,000 for Korean relief. He said security interests of the United States "clearly indicate the need to act promptly."

Acting less than 24 hours after signing of the armistice at Panmunjom the President said:

"The extent of devastation suffered by the people and the economy of Korea is staggering."

In a special message to Congress, Mr. Eisenhower spoke of a confidential survey of Korean economic conditions made more than three months ago by Henry J. Tasca, the President's special representative on Korean economic affairs.

"The completed survey has been reviewed by the National Security Council," Mr. Eisenhower said. He added:

"On the basis of its analysis and recommendation, I am convinced that the security interests of the United States clearly indicate the need to act promptly not only to meet immediate relief needs but also to begin the long-range work of restoring the economy to health and strength."

Flood Control Fund

Washington — (AP) — President Eisenhower signed a bill appropriating $440,093,600 to the Army Engineers for use in the fiscal year which began July 1. Most of the money is for flood control, navigation and power projects.

Reds Flood India With Anti-U. S. Lies

Booklets and magazines from Red China are jamming India's bazaars and bookstalls. They present a 100% false picture.

And two Red newspapers do even worse.

The details are on Page 11.
Also on the inside:

Lied at Red Trial, N. Y. Cop Fired

New York — (AP) — Lt. Arthur Miller was dismissed from the Police Department today on his conviction at a departmental trial of lying when he denied membership in the Communist Party.

Police Commissioner George P. Monaghan said the dismissal was on the basis of Miller's conviction last week, and also because he was absent five days without official leave.

The commissioner said that, in view of the evidence at the trial, Miller "would have been dismissed even though he had not been unofficially absent."

'Best Road Out of Terrible Mess'

San Francisco—(AP) — Vacationing at Bohemian Grove, north of here, former President Herbert Hoover had this to say today of the armistice in Korea:

"This is the best road out of a terrible mess. It offers hope of rebuilding American economic life. But above all, mothers, fathers, wives, brothers and sisters will prayerfully rejoice in the cessation of killing."

U. S. Takes Armistice News Calmly

Prayer Replaces Celebration, Doubt Tempers Joy

By the Associated Press

It looked like any other Sunday night on most main streets of the nation.

The surface was calm, but underneath—in the hearts of the American people — there was a stirring.

Doubts tempered joy. Prayers replaced demonstrations. Relief mingled with sorrow. Tears watered cheers.

A truce had been signed in Korea. That was last night's news.

Other wars had been marked at their end by riotous celebrations of Americans released from the tensions of sacrifice.

But there was no such release this time.

In Washington, a father spoke: "I'm glad this war is over, and I hope my son is going to come home soon."

In New York, a teenaged sergeant chorused:

"I am glad it is over and that nobody else has to see it."

In Portland, Me., a brother of a Marine, commented:

"The truce has taken so long we're inclined to be skeptical about it."

MIXED FEELINGS

These were the words of a nation.

They came from its President, Dwight D. Eisenhower, whose son is a major in Korea; from 18-year-old Sgt. Daniel Van Luve of San Francisco; and from Anthony Mezoian, brother of Marine Pfc. George Mezoian.

But they expressed the mixed feelings of millions.

It was not a night of jubilation. The big cities had little or no public reaction to the news.

Many places had taken extra police precautions, but outwardly it was an ordinary Sunday night.

Typical was this Associated Press report from Boston, which reflected a bit more activity than in most other large cities:

"Residents took truce news calmly. City sounded air and fire sirens, some church bells. Boat whistles joined in. Most people seemed bewildered at sudden noise but car horns gradually stirred some pedestrians to an occasional cheer. No gathering at corners or other demonstrations like end of World War 2."

DINERS IGNORE IT

Diners in a Washington, D. C. cafe ignored a television announcement of the truce signing.

Some 300 people entered the huge Episcopal Cathedral of St. John the Divine in New York to hear trumpet fanfares and a doxology.

At Scranton, Pa., special prayers were offered for a lasting peace by 75,000 persons from 23 states and three foreign countries attending an annual novena at St. Ann's Catholic Monastery.

Several state and municipal officials asked for moments of prayer today.

Practically to a man, members of Congress who commented on the signing of the armistice said, in effect: wonderful, but what of the future?

"We have only opened a new chapter in a long book—the fight

(Continued on Page Twelve)

Returns to Moscow

Berlin—(AP)—U. S. Ambassador Charles E. Bohlen took off from Templehof Airbase for Moscow today after a vacation in the West.

Press Photo by Swierkosz

SOLEMN MOMENT—Sgt. Wayne Clark and his wife of 20 Jefferson Avenue, Endicott, pause on the Courthouse Square here at the moment of today's cease-fire in Korea. Sergeant Clark, on leave, is a provost marshal investigator at Fort Dix, N. J.

They'd Hate to Die With Truce So Near

By JOHN RANDOLPH
Associated Press Staff Writer

Central Front, Korea—I had promised Item Company I would bring them a bottle of whisky the minute that agreement was reached on the armistice.

They didn't see me coming until the last 20 yards on the steep and muddy hill northeast of Kumhwa.

Under my arm, like a football, I was carrying the fifth of 100 proof bond wrapped safely in a dirty GI khaki towel.

Sergeant Ippolito spotted me floundering and gasping up the final slope. He looked a long moment—then he started to yell, his voice breaking with excitement.

"He's got it! He's got the bottle! It's an armistice, by God—they've got an armistice!"

Helmeted heads craned out of bunkers and foxholes and dirty bearded faces turned my way and Ippolito ran down the slopes to meet me.

A horrible suspicion of doubt crossed his face and he stopped short.

"You wouldn't kid us, would you? It's true, ain't it?"

DEEPER SHADOW

"I wouldn't kid you," I said. "It's true. It's official. The UN command this afternoon announced an armistice had been agreed upon. They sign it tomorrow at 10 a. m. The cease-fire is 12 hours later—10 p. m. tomorrow."

Another and deeper shadow crossed Ippolito's face.

"Tonight . . . You mean we gotta sweat out tonight . . . Jesus Christ I hope we make it." Then he shoved that awful fear out of his mind, brightened again and shouted:

"The lieutenant! Lieutenant! They got an armistice — He brought the bottle just like he said."

29 ETERNITIES

The others were crowding around now, maybe a dozen of them, and I was escorted to the muddy hole covered with logs that was the company command post.

Lt. Don C. Patton, the company executive, leaned out from under the sandbagged logs. Patton is a bronzed young man with a big brown mustache and a

(Continued on Page Four)

East Germans Rush for Ike's Relief Food

Berlin — (AP) — An estimated 100,000 hungry East Germans poured across the border into West Berlin today to get "forbidden" food offered under President Eisenhower's relief program.

Residents of all parts of the Soviet Zone crossed the open East-West city border and entered West Berlin by foot, railway and subway on the first day of the two-week program.

They lined up by the thousands before 11 West Berlin borough halls to get five-pound food packages.

Only One Left, Now

Cleric Loses Third Son In Service of U. S.

Marietta, Okla. — (AP) — The Rev. Cled Wallace, Church of Christ minister, has lost a third son within 10 years in the service of his country.

He said yesterday he had been notified Ens. Henry Wallace, 25, a jet pilot on the carrier U. S. S. Lake Champlain was shot down over North Korea three days ago.

"Now we have only one son left," the minister said. He is Cled, Jr., who lives in Houston.

The first son to die was 1st Lt. John W. Wallace, a B24 pilot shot down on a mission in Italy during World War 2.

Then Capt. D. W. Wallace, another Air Force officer, was discharged in 1944 with a serious illness contracted during the war. A few months later he died following a heart attack.

"He was a war casualty, too, as surely as though he had been shot down," Mr. Wallace said.

"My boys never were afraid of anything," the father added philosophically, "and we try to have that same courage."

Ike Grateful, But Wants Total Peace

Washington — (AP) — President Eisenhower hailed the Korean truce signing last night with a prayer of thanksgiving but solemnly declared "we have won an armistice on a single battleground—not peace in the world."

"We may not relax our guard nor cease our quest," he said in a nationwide television and radio address an hour after the truce had been sealed at Panmunjom, ending the 31-month war.

A few moments before he went on the air from the White House, the President—a happy smile on his face—made a remark which undoubtedly was being echoed by hundreds of thousands of other parents all over America.

SON IN KOREA

"I'm glad this war is over," Mr. Eisenhower said quietly, "and I hope my son is coming home soon."

His son, Army Maj. John Eisenhower, has been on active duty in Korea since last July. The only break in his service for a brief return to the United States came when he traveled to Washington to attend his father's inauguration.

In his TV-radio address over all networks, the President started by saying:

SPEAKS GRAVELY

"Tonight we greet, with prayers of thanksgiving, the official news that an armistice was signed almost an hour ago in Korea."

Peace in Korea has been the President's main objective. He pledged during the campaign he would work unceasingly for it. He traveled to the battlefront shortly after he was elected in November.

(Continued on Page Four)

Today's Chuckle

Most of the men who have to pay big income taxes are rather hardened to such things. They started early by taxing their brains.

Fighting Halted By Truce

Big Commie Guns Belch Out Death 'Til Last Minute

MAP OF TRUCE zone, Page 4. Highlights of the Korean war and more truce stories, Page 17.

By the Associated Press

Seoul — Shooting stopped along the Korean battlefront at 11 o'clock tonight (9 a. m. Monday EDT), bringing to an abrupt halt 37 months of death and destruction. The shooting stopped 12 hours after the formal signing of the armistice agreement at Panmunjom.

While ground fighting was all but nil the final hours, mounting Communist artillery fire took its toll of Allied soldiers up to the last minute.

At 11 p. m., a hush fell over the front.

The last man to die may never be named. Nor, perhaps will the last hero.

The front, usually aflame at this hour of night, just grew dark.

Men heaved sighs of relief, but with great caution.

As the clock ticked off the seconds, they grew more brave.

AP correspondent John Randolph said the ceasefire came on the central front amid silence after a smashing artillery duel between Allied and Red guns that began in midafternoon and built up a deafening crescendo shortly before 11 p. m.

YANKS YELL

Randolph said all firing stopped at 10:43 p. m.

A few seconds after 11 p. m. wild yells broke out from American GIs.

All day and into the night the Reds sent artillery and mortar barrages screaming into Allied lines east of Kumhwa on the central front.

The barrages mounted in fury as the hours went by. Sometimes shells ripped front and rear line positions at the rate of four a minute.

Allied artillery boomed back trying to silence the guns.

Even as the shooting ended, litter jeeps and ambulances wound down dusty hill trails from outpost ridges, bringing moaning, broken men to rear hospitals.

ALLIES REPLY

Only five minutes before the guns fell silent, American and South Korean artillerymen tried to muffle the Red guns once and for all with a time-on-target barrage.

Using massive supercharges of powder, nearly 12 battalions of Allied artillery opened simultaneously.

The valleys roared and shook as the shells burst deep behind the Red lines.

The Communist shelling stopped—at about the same moment the Allied barrage lifted.

If the Reds had not insisted on shooting it out, there would have been little or no firing on the closing day.

The 8th Army had warned division commanders only to fire defensively. The order was meant to save lives.

GENERALS SIGN

Generals of the UN command and the Red armies signed in 10 minutes an armistice document that took two years and 17 days to write.

Hardly had they completed the signing when these ominous, clashing warnings were sounded:

The Chinese Red Peiping radio boasted that the Communists had won "a glorious victory" and cautioned Red soldiers to remain "highly vigilant and guard against any disruptive actions from the other side."

UN commander Gen. Mark Clark told his troops flatly there will be no "immediate or even early withdrawal" from Korea and declared that the UN is staying on—"a reminder to the enemy.

(Continued on Page Four)

More Taft Treatment

New York — (INS) — New York Hospital announced today that Senator Taft (Rep. Ohio) would remain there for further treatment rather than return to Washington this Wednesday as scheduled. A hospital bulletin said merely that, "further treatment now appears warranted."

July 27, 1953: A local soldier and wife are grateful the war is over. *Microfilm archives*

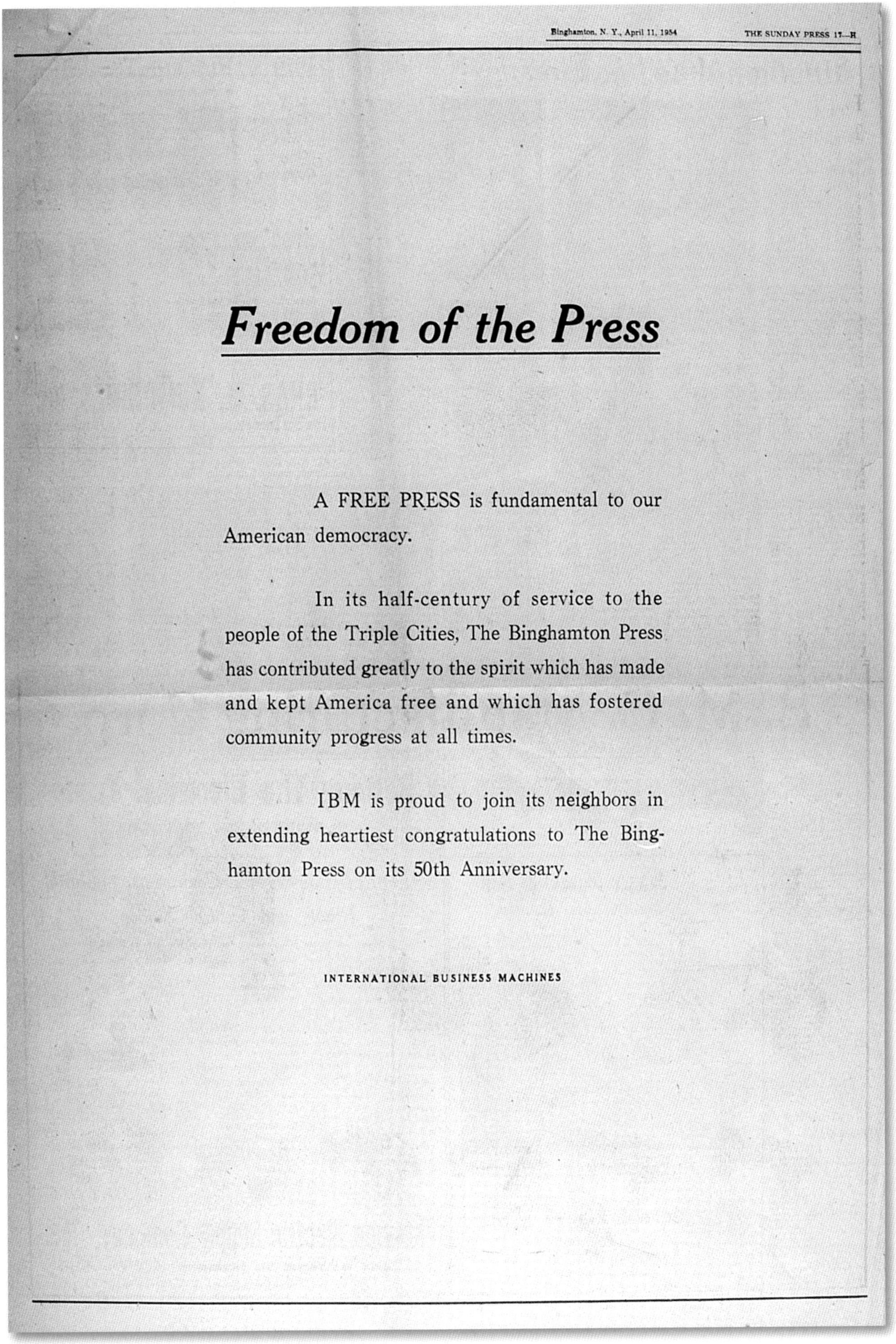

Binghamton, N. Y., April 11, 1954 THE SUNDAY PRESS 17—H

Freedom of the Press

A FREE PRESS is fundamental to our American democracy.

In its half-century of service to the people of the Triple Cities, The Binghamton Press has contributed greatly to the spirit which has made and kept America free and which has fostered community progress at all times.

IBM is proud to join its neighbors in extending heartiest congratulations to The Binghamton Press on its 50th Anniversary.

INTERNATIONAL BUSINESS MACHINES

April 11, 1954: IBM took out a full-page ad to salute the Press in a 50th anniversary edition. *Courtesy Charlie Jenks*

Day of Wreckoning

By U. S. Weather Bureau

Partly cloudy and cool tonight. Low 35-40. Sunday partly cloudy and cool with chance of a few light showers. High 55-60.

5 p.m.	15	7 a.m.	46	11 a.m.	55
Midnight	37	8 a.m.	52	Noon	57
3 a.m.	33	9 a.m.	51	1 p.m.	60
4 a.m.	47	10 a.m.	55	2 p.m.	62

BINGHAMTON PRESS

Saturday Evening, Oct. 16, 1954 — THE TRIPLE CITIES' NEWSPAPER — Vol. 76—159 18 Pages 5 Cents

★ ★ ★

Are You a Success?

Symbols of success change as frequently as women's fashions, but the real thing never changes, although few people know what it is. Story on Page 10.

94-Mile Winds Wallop Area, Kill Two

★ ★ ★ ★ ★ ★ ★ ★ ★ ★ ★ ★

75 Dead in 8 States, Canada; Thousands Homeless

—Press Photo by Bolss.

A CRUSHING BLOW—Fury of Hurricane Hazel, first hurricane ever to strike the Southern Tier, felled this tree which crushed garage and 1953 Oldsmobile at home of Leo Exley, 244 Harrison Street, Johnson City. Wind gusts were as high as 94 miles an hour, averaged 72. (Other storm pictures on Pages 2, 3, and 9.)

Howler Still Rages In North

By Press Wire Services

Hazel, the killer hurricane, stabbed through Canada's industrial heartland today, blazing a new trail of destruction and causing one of the worst disasters in the history of Ontario Province.

Hazel, the eighth and worst tropical storm of the season, has taken at least 75 lives in the United States and Canada, and was still raging northward towards the Hudson Bay area. In its wake along the eastern seaboard of the United States were at least 67 dead. Eight were known dead in Canada and many others were feared drowned or trapped by rampaging rivers.

Spawned near the tropical Windward Islands, it accounted for up to 100 deaths in the Republic of Haiti before smashing into the U. S. mainland yesterday, leaving a grim 2,000-mile path of destruction extending to the northern wastes of Canada.

FEAR 26 MORE DEAD

Police in Weston, Ontario, estimated that the death toll there might be 26. Ten persons in two automobiles were reported drowned when the vehicles were swept into the swollen Humber River. Five firemen dumped into the river from their overturned truck were believed to have drowned.

Hundreds of persons in Toronto and in the area of the Humber and Don rivers were missing. Flash floods swept through the city, swirling away houses and leaving thousands homeless.

Flood damage to homes, factories and stores in the city of more than 1,100,000 persons was expected to run into millions of dollars.

Seven inches of rain fell in Toronto in 24 hours. The towns of Woodbridge and Holland were isolated. Telephone service and roads were cut off. The Canadian National and Canadian Pacific Railways halted all trains to Western Canada. Two trains were derailed and others were marooned by washouts.

WORST LOSS OF YEAR

The destruction left in the wake of hurricane Hazel was expected to exceed the damage caused earlier this year by hurricane Carol which took more than 90 lives and hurricane Edna which killed 14 persons. The damage was expected to run into hundreds of million dollars.

Thousands were left homeless along the east coast of the United States in Hazel's 750-mile path. Entire cities were left without

(Continued on Page Nine)

First Hurricane in History Of Tier Roars for 3 Hours

QUEBEC
Quebec
St. Lawrence R.
CANADA
Montreal
ME
VT.
N.Y.
N.H.
Toronto
Lake Ontario
Syracuse
Albany
MASS.
Buffalo
Binghamton
CONN.
R.I.
PENN.
Pittsburgh
Williamsport
Philadelphia
NEW YORK
N.J.
MD.
W. VA.
Atlantic City
WASHINGTON
HAZEL
Atlantic Ocean
Richmond
Roanoke
VIRGINIA
AP
0 100
STATUTE MILES

HAZEL'S DESTRUCTIVE PATH—Arrow on map shows how hurricane Hazel ravaged eight-state area, District of Columbia and Canada.

By AL SCHWARTZ

Binghamton Press Writer

Life was returning to normal today in the Southern Tier after the area was rocked last night by the first hurricane in its recorded history.

A nightmarish three-hour period starting about 7:30 p. m. saw power knocked out through most of the Southern Tier as winds reached a screaming pitch of 94 miles an hour.

Motorists were warned off the streets as scores of falling trees blocked roads and brought down live wires.

Hurricane Hazel, which charged into the area at better than 50 miles an hour, also was responsible for two deaths in the Norwich area.

TWO DIE IN CAR

Mr. and Mrs. Frank E. Henderson of North Norwich were killed when a 1,500-pound chimney capstone fell from a five-story building and crushed their car as they were stopped in traffic.

Most Tier roads were reopened today and a spokesman for the New York State Electric & Gas Corp. said that power generally would be restored by tomorrow morning, although in scattered cases delays in resumption of service would be longer.

Telephone service was not badly hit, according to New York Telephone Co. officials.

They estimated that service to some 900 telephones was knocked out by the storm in the Broome-Tioga area and several hundred telephones also were knocked out in other Tier areas.

They said most service would be restored by nightfall.

ESCAPED DISASTER

The weatherman at Broome County Airport said today that much of the Tier "escaped disaster" when a forecast of heavy rains did not materialize.

He said the rains would have loosened trees and building foundations and resulted in far more damage than occurred.

He said Hazel was the first hurricane in the recorded history to strike the Tier.

Winds twice reached a frenzied record-breaking 94 miles an hour, at 8:54 p. m. and at 9:46 p. m. Shortly before 9 p. m., they reached a record-breaking average of 72 miles an hour.

The center of the storm passed through the Tier before 10 p. m.

After that time winds began tapering off. By midnight wind velocities approached normal.

CONTROL TOWER CLEARED

The control tower at the Broome airport was evacuated for more than an hour at the height of the storm, because of the fear of breaks in the huge glass windows.

The winds tore a small two-place training plane owned by the Tri-Cities Aviation School loose from its moorings and flipped it over. The plane's wing tips were left behind.

Falling wires resulted in more than 30 calls for rural volunteer fire departments in Broome County alone.

A fire in the Town of Conklin, the cause of which had not been ascertained this morning, swept through a farm implement storage building and caused an estimated $6,000 in damage.

High winds also tore down a new house nearing construction in Crocker Hill Road, Town of Chenango, and blew it into the road.

BARN BLOWN IN ROAD

A barn was blown into the road in the old Vestal Road near Route 26 and blocked traffic for most of the night.

A portion of the roof of the Pine Inn off Route 26 in the Town of Maine was peeled back by Hazel and some of the roof fell into the tavern which was experiencing brisk Friday night trade.

The Electric & Gas Corp.

(Continued on Page Nine)

Pittsburgh Area Is Hit By Floods; Eight Dead

Pittsburgh—(AP)—Torrential rains and high winds—partially due to hurricane Hazel's backlash—flooded hundreds of small Pennsylvania streams, driving thousands from their homes and causing damage already estimated in the millions of dollars.

At least eight persons are dead.

One of the worst hit sections was the Turtle Creek Valley on the fringes of Pittsburgh where raging creek waters swept through five towns last night, rising 4 to 6 feet in less than four hours.

The big industrial city of Pittsburgh braced itself for high water from the Ohio, Allegheny and Monongahela Rivers. The crest was expected late in the afternoon.

The Weather Bureau said the Ohio River will probably crest about five feet above the 25 foot flood stage in Pittsburgh. That would cause damage only in a small section.

Most of the affected communities are located along the Monongahela and Allegheny rivers above Pittsburgh. The Weather Bureau said about 6 inches of rain fell over the Western Pennsylvania watershed yesterday.

The Pennsylvania Railroad said east-west passenger service was delayed as much as three hours during the night. The delay was caused by washouts along the tracks. Most of the service has been restored.

A Pennsylvania diesel nosed into highwater at Red Bank, 63 miles north of Pittsburgh, injuring four crewmen who were repairing tracks.

The railroad said the diesel was not submerged. The men were treated for shock but reported in good condition.

Butler, a community of 24,000 about 35 miles north of Pittsburgh, was one of the hardest hit communities. The eastern section of the town was submerged under five to eight feet of water. No injuries were reported.

Butler firemen and a unit of the National Guard worked through the night removing

(Continued on Page Nine)

Salk Vaccine Report Due In Spring

Washington—(AP)—The National Foundation for Infantile Paralysis said today there will be only one "authoritative" report on whether the Salk vaccine is effective against paralytic polio—and it won't be ready until next spring.

Foundation officials said reports on children involved in last summer's nationwide test of the Salk polio vaccine are being made available only to a University of Michigan research group making an "independent" evaluation of the trials.

Radio Boss Seeks All $8,000,000

Los Angeles—(AP)—Suit to have an $8,000,000 fortune declared wholly his has been filed by Jacob (Jay) Paley, cofounder of the Columbia Broadcasting System.

The suit was filed yesterday against the Bank of America as executor of the estate left by Paley's wife, Mrs. Lillian Paley, 62, who died last Jan. 2. Paley told the court the bank is claiming a half interest in personal property standing in his name on the groud that oe-half of property acquired outside California but brought into the state by a married couple becomes subject to testamentary disposition by either husband or wife.

Reds Hurl Big Staff Of Diplomats at Tito

Communist nations are changing their tactics in their efforts to woo Tito's Yugoslavia away from the West. Vastly increased diplomatic staffs are a key sign of the new program. Page 10.

Also on the inside:

John Roosevelt Makes GOP Plea

Tampa, Fla.—(AP)—John Roosevelt finished two days of campaigning for Florida Republicans with renewed pleas for voters to elect a GOP Congress to carry out President Eisenhower's program.

The son of the late Franklin D. Roosevelt told his audience here yesterday not to believe charges that President Eisenhower is interested only in the welfare of big business.

Ike Links Farmer Prosperity to GOP

STEVENSON questions propriety of campaigning by Secretary of Defense Charles Wilson. Page 5. Democrats threaten to oust Republicans from Wyoming Senate and House. Page 14.

Indianapolis—(AP)—President Eisenhower bid for the nation's farm vote last night, saying election of a Republican Congress will help assure American farmers "a foundation of enduring prosperity."

Speaking to a wildly cheering, capacity crowd of 15,000 in Butler University Field House, the President jabbed at the Truman administration for what he termed the farmers' "serious loss in buying power" in 1951-52.

And—in a separate speech at a smaller rally of GOP colleagues—he sounded a challenge to Republicans to spur "our horses . . . and to get going" in the party's drive to maintain control of Congress in the Nov. 2 elections.

Mr. Eisenhower stopped over in the Indiana capital in the midst of the farm belt on his way back to hurricane-lashed Washington from Denver, where he ended an eight-week work and play vacation yesterday.

CAMPAIGN STEPUP

His private plane, the Columbine, landed at Washington National Airport at 12:13 a. m. today, several hours after the hurricane had swept north.

The Chief Executive's major address last night—broadcast nationwide by radio and telecast in 15 farm states—marked another stepup in his personal campaign to swing voters into the Republican column this fall.

During the first 21 months of his administration, he said, "we have gone far toward building for our agriculture a foundation of enduring prosperity, in an America at last at peace."

He said there never had been more constructive farm legislation than that passed by the GOP-controlled 83d Congress, and he blamed "the old farm law" for a "steady decline in farmers' buying power."

WILD OVATION

The Chief Executive got a wild two-minute standing ovation when he was introduced by an official of the national Institute of Animal Agriculture, an organization described by the White House as non-partisan.

Most of the President's address dealt with the farm situation, but he also said:

"My heart truly goes out to every one of our citizens who has no job, or who, in other ways, suffers these hardships.

(Continued on Page Nine)

Roosevelt Promises Farm Aid

HARRIMAN AFFIDAVIT tells what happened at Yalta conference. Page 6.

Oneida—(AP)—Representative Franklin D. Roosevelt, Jr., says "there's going to be a big change in the farm picture" if the Democrats are returned to power in New York State on Nov. 2.

The Democratic-Liberal nominee for attorney general spoke to about 300 persons at a Democratic dinner here last night, directing his remarks principally to upstate dairy interests.

"We are going to do more than slap you on the back and tell you about your 'prosperity,'" he said. "We are going to do more than drink a glass of milk for the movie cameras."

Roosevelt today entered the fourth day of a seven-day campaign swing Upstate. His schedule called for speeches in Oswego today and Ithaca tonight.

Renewing his charge that the GOP state administration had "neglected" the farmer, Roosevelt predicted that "this monopoly of Republicans in upstate New York is going to be broken." He declared:

"I hope upstate New York starts to apply the two-party system and gets real representation rather than the silent treatment they have been getting."

Hurricane Grounds Harriman in North

Ogdensburg—(AP)—Averell Harriman, blocked by Hurricane Hazel from flying to New York on schedule last night, flies back today after rapping Republican leaders on unemployment, farming and electric power issues.

The Democratic-Liberal nominee for governor, encouraged by his receptions in normally Republican upstate New York, planned to make three more upstate trips next week.

He had expected to take off for New York last night from Massena by chartered plane but airline officials postponed the flight after getting reports of high winds.

Harriman, after the campaign tour to Buffalo, the Southern Tier and central and upper New York, said unemployment had become a serious problem and accused the Republicans of a "do nothing" attitude about it.

Bitter Attack by Governor

F.D.R. Film Gangsters Democrats, Says Dewey

New York—(AP)—Gov. Thomas E. Dewey last night said that all the "gangsters and hoodlums" mentioned in Franklin D. Roosevelt, Jr.'s, campaign film about harness racing scandals "were important figures in the Democrat machine."

Dewey, the retiring Republican governor, bitterly assailed Roosevelt, Democratic candidate for attorney general, for what he called "distortion and misrepresentation" in the television film.

Dewey said that Tommy Lewis, the Bronx labor leader whose murder touched off a sweeping state investigation of harness racing this year, was a dinner companion of Roosevelt and Carmine G. De Sapio, the Tammany Hall leader, at a Democratic fund raising dinner two years ago.

The campaign movie, he added, disqualifies Roosevelt "for any public office till he learns to get his facts and ethics straightened out."

It was Dewey's first major campaign speech, and he called for the election of U. S. Senator Irving M. Ives, whom Dewey is backing to succeed him as governor.

"I don't want to see the gangsters of Tammany Hall take over

(Continued on Page Nine)

Ives Charges Foe Twists The Truth

Niagara Falls—(AP)—Senator Irving M. Ives, describing Averell Harriman as off on "flights of fancy" in the election campaign, challenged his opponent today to "come down to earth" and discuss issues.

Ives, the Republican candidate for governor, said in a speech prepared for delivery here that Harriman had been campaigning "entirely on distortion and deceit."

Noting that Harriman had never run for office before, Ives contended the Democratic nominee had introduced "a brand-new and original scheme of campaigning." In speech after speech, the senator went in, "he takes off on his flights of fancy."

HITS ROADS VIEW

Ives said Harriman "has simply not been able to find anything wrong to talk about." The senator claimed he had been giving "forthright views on the issues," and added he was waiting for Harriman "to come down to earth and give you his."

Specifically, Ives argued that Harriman had complained "in cities served by our great new Thuway" that nothing had been done about state roads.

And he quoted Harriman as saying the GOP administration had done nothing to bring defense orders into the state. During the first six months of 1954, Ives declared, 18.6 per cent of all Defense Department contracts went to New York State firms.

SILENCE ON REDS HIT

Last night Ives asked why "the Democrat platform this year omits any mention of communism." He attacked Harriman by calling him a multi-millionaire "Johnny-come-lately" ignorant of labor problems.

The senator described Harriman as "my multimillionaire opponent" and said "until this election nobody had ever heard of

(Continued on Page Nine)

Kansas City Site Of Horse Show

Kansas City—(AP)—Kansas City's pride in being a cow town busted out all over today with the opening of the annual American Royal Livestock and Horse Show.

An auburn-haired University of Missouri sophomore, 20-year-old Marlene Hickman of Clinton, Mo., was named at a coronation ball attended by 10,000 last night to reign as queen of the week-long event.

UN Asked to Stop It

Soviet Charges U.S. Aggression on China

United Nations—(AP)—Russia accused the United States last night of aggression against Red China and called on the UN General Assembly to put a stop to it. The United States promptly branded the charge a lie.

In a letter to Dr. Eelco N. Van Kleffens, Assembly president, Russia's Andrei Vishinsky held the United States responsible for coastal attacks on the Chinese mainland and ship seizures near Formosa, seat of the Chinese Nationalist regime. He asked the Assembly to condemn the alleged American aggression.

A quick replying statement issued by chief U. S. Delegate Henry Cabot Lodge, Jr., declared: "To say that the United States has engaged in any aggressive action in the area of Formosa or anywhere else is a plain lie."

Vishinsky sent his letter one day after the UN circulated a complaint from Red Chinese Premier Chou En-lai charging the United States with aggression and asking the Assembly to call a halt to American aid to Chinese Nationalists.

The United States refused to accept delivery of the Chinese complaint, which was circulated to UN members over American objections. Diplomatic sources said since the United States does not recognize the Peiping regime it does not need accept communications from it.

The UN Security Council considered similar aggression charges preferred by Red China in 1950, but turned down a Peiping request that it condemn the United States.

Mob Burns USIS Office

London—(UP)—Mobs smashed into the United States Information Service (USIS) office in Amman, Jordan, and set it afire, an Arab radio broadcast said today.

The broadcast said police opened fire and there were "some injuries."

The riots broke out as Jordan's voters elected 40 members of the House of Representatives. It was the third election since the annexation of Arab Palestine in 1949.

Today's Chuckle

Definition of Rhode Island: Texas after taxes.

October 16, 1954: Hazel was the first hurricane to be recorded as striking the Tier. *Microfilm archives*

Ex-slide-ing Report
Weather Bureau Forecast
Clearing and colder tonight. Low near zero. Tuesday fair and continued cold. High 15-20.

BINGHAMTON PRESS

Monday Evening, Dec. 6, 1954 — THE TRIPLE CITIES' NEWSPAPER — Vol. 76—201 30 Pages 5 Cents

★ ★ ★
Take Own 'Medicine'

The doctors of today not only prescribe relaxing, they also practice it. And relaxing can mean a nap or many other things. How they do it is told on Page 10.

WORST DOWNTOWN BLAZE IN THREE YEARS

$800,000 Fire Ruins Ackerman Building

Chi-Reds Hold Many More GIs, Freed Canadian Reveals

PICTURE ON PAGE 16

Hong Kong — (AP) — Squadron Leader Andrew R. (Andy) MacKenzie, a Canadian flier shot down in the Korean war and just freed from imprisonment in Red China, says the Chinese are still holding some American war prisoners in his prison camp.

The 34-year-old air ace reported upon reaching Hong Kong yesterday that the Americans he knows about—all Air Force fliers—had been allowed to write home and it was known in the United States that they were prisoners.

He added that they do not include any of the 13 Americans recently sentenced by Peiping on spy charges.

Canadian and U. S. officials did not permit disclosure here of the number or names of the captured men. The location of the camp also was withheld.

(In Washington, an Air Force casualty officer said three Americans were known to have been in the camp with MacKenzie. They were Capt. Harold E. Fischer of Swea City, Iowa; Lt. Lyle W. Cameron of Lincoln, Nebr., and Lt. Roland W. Parks of Omaha, Nebr.)

MacKenzie reached freedom two years to the day after he was shot down near the Yalu River in North Korea while flying as an exchange officer with the U. S. Air Force.

Canadian diplomats had asked about him when they met the Chinese Communist delegation to the Geneva conference last Ju... on Korea and Indochina. ...Reds promised at that time to release him. They finally notified the Canadian Foreign Ministry informally on Nov. 23 that he would be at the border of this British colony yesterday.

Appearing thin but otherwise healthy, he arrived in the custody of three Red Chinese guards. He wore a blue, padded Chinese uniform.

Allies Held Near OK On Flier Resolution

United Nations — (UP) — The United States and its 15 Korean war allies were reported close to agreement today on details of a resolution calling for the release of 11 U. S. fliers and other allied personnel in Red China's hands.

Informed quarters said the United States and Britain had resolved some points of differ-

(Continued on Page Sixteen)

Eden Accuses Chinese Reds

London —(UP)— Foreign Secretary Anthony Eden today accused the Red Chinese of "direct violation" of the Korean armistice in jailing the 11 American airmen it has charged with "espionage."

Eden said he was speaking on behalf of "the government and all civilized nations."

Eden's view was given before the House of Commons in reply to Socialist John Baird who asked why instructions were given to British United Nations representatives to "condemn the Chinese people's government because they have punished United States spies."

Eden snapped back that he refused to accept the reference to "United States spies."

I Named Suspects: Dr. Steve

By Press Wire Services

Cleveland—Dr. Stephen Sheppard testified today he mentioned "possibly four or five" suspects after his brother was arrested on a charge of murdering his wife.

"I did not accuse anyone," however, the witness said.

Dr Steve engaged in a heated verbal duel with Assistant Prosecutor Thomas Parrino as the lawyer entered this phase of his cross examination.

Dr. Steve was the first defense witness in the trial of his brother, Dr. Samuel Sheppard, who is accused of nacking to death his wife, Marilyn, on July 4.

Parrino asked, "When was the first time you named any suspects?"

"The first time I was asked to

(Continued on Page Sixteen)

Navy Says Monty Puts Carrier in Wrong Sea

Washington—(AP)—Assistant Navy Secretary James Smith said today of Field Marshal Montgomery's commentary on aircraft carriers that there is "a fairly substantial difference on the problems as seen by an Englishman with European responsibilities compared with the problems visualized from this building."

Smith expressed his views at a Pentagon news conference which he opened up by saying that "It might be of some interest to run over some of the principles that were presented by Field Marshal Montgomery last week" at the California Institute of Technology.

In an address there, Montgomery said among other things that "We see the day of the aircraft carrier approaching its end."

Smith, when asked why Montgomery believed carriers are going out of the picture, said "I think you are always influenced by what you have been exposed to for a number of years."

The Navy official said Montgomery was speaking of the defense requirements for Europe and the Mediterranean area, which Smith called a "short range war." But, Smith said, when war in the Pacific is considered, the ranges required for air strikes are long and there are no readily available land bases for air operations.

Santa to Deliver Toys Worth Billion

Santa's pack is expected to set an all time toy record this year. And the manufacturers are happy as they rush their new wares to the display counters.

Details aplenty are on Page 25.
Also on the inside:

ALL HANDS BATTLE ACKERMAN BUILDING FIRE AT COMMERCIAL AVENUE, LEFT, AND HENRY STREET, FOREGROUND
—Press Photo by Swierkosz
(More pictures of the blaze appear on Pages Three and Twelve.)

Firemen Hampered By Cold

Firefighter Suffers Broken Ankle In Fall Off Ladder

By LARRY HALE
Binghamton Press Writer

Binghamton firemen this afternoon continued to pour water into the burning ruins of the fire-ravaged 60-year-old Ackerman Building at State and Henry streets.

Damage in the three-alarm fire, which broke out early today, was estimated unofficially at more than $800,000 and involved 15 business firms which had quarters in the building.

Nine hours after the fire was discovered, firemen still were using up to 10 streams of water in efforts to extinguish the flames.

ALL FIREMEN CALLED

All 168 available city firemen, including those on the two off-duty shifts, and all fire equipment were assigned to the fire which was discovered at 3:42 o'clock by two city policemen.

The coldest weather of the season — 9 degrees — hampered fire fighters. Water from fire hoses formed icicles on hose nozzles and fire trucks, on firemen's helmets and gear, and turned the State-Henry street intersection into a lake of ice.

Blow torches were used to melt ice from equipment.

One fireman, John R. McMahon, suffered a fractured right ankle when he fell from a 10-foot ladder onto the sidewalk in Henry Street.

SPREAD IN SHAFT

Fire Chief Frank J. Buckman said cause of the fire has not been determined. But, he added, the fire apparently started in the cellar of the building near the main heating plant and spread to the upper floors and roof through an elevator shaft.

Fire Marshal Gerald E. O'Loughlin said that the owner of the building, E. L. Kittredge of Glenwood Road, was in the cellar as late as 1 a. m. repairing a coal stoker in the heating unit.

The fire was discovered by Police Sgt. Andrew Barvinchak and Patrolman Frank McCarthy. The patrolman, whose beat covers the State and Henry streets area, said he had smelled smoke since about 3:15 o'clock but had been unable to locate the source.

ALARM SOUNDED

Shortly after 3:30 o'clock, Sergeant Barvinchak stopped to talk to the patrolman and was told about the smoke odor. Upon investigation, they discovered smoke pouring out of the building's roof on the Commercial Avenue side. They immediately turned in an alarm from a box at the intersection.

Fire officials turned in a second alarm at 3:46 o'clock and 12 minutes later sent in a third alarm.

Simultaneously, Ernest S. Youngs of Port Crane, county fire coordinator, was notified and he sent five volunteer fire companies and equipment into Binghamton from neighboring areas to man city fire stations on a stand-by basis.

WORST SINCE 1951

The fire was the most disastrous since Labor Day of 1951 when the old State Armory in Washington Street was destroyed at a loss of $1,000,000 and the death of one city fireman.

The 32 receiving and sending circuits of the Western Union Telegraph Co., situated on the building's second floor, were destroyed at a loss estimated by Charles Eggleston, office manager, at $50,000.

The New York Telephone Co. began installing temporary circuits between Binghamton and Syracuse in the Chenango Street

(Continued on Page Three)

Oil Stove Explodes

5 Children Trapped In Beds, Die in Fire

Franklin, Mass. — (AP) — Five helpless children, trapped in their bedroom by flames, died a few minutes before midnight in a roaring farm house fire.

The five, ranging in age from 2 to 7, were the son and daughters of Mr. and Mrs. Reginald de Baggis.

De Baggis, 30 a polisher at the Attleboro plane of Swank Jewelry Co., rescued his English war wife, Maureen, 29, and their youngest child, 6-month-old Diane.

The five who perished were Shirley, 7, Donald, 6, Margaret, 4, Joanne, 3, and Regina, 2. Dr. Walter Crowley, medical examiner, said they apparently suffocated although some of the bodies were charred.

De Baggis said a kitchen oil stove exploded as the family was preparing for bed about 11:45.

The five older children were asleep directly above the kitchen. Their parents and the baby were downstairs in a room adjoining the kitchen.

Nearly an hour went by before firemen wearing gas masks were able to enter the smoking bedroom. They found the five pitiful bodies—the three older children in a double bed, the two smaller ones in a large crib.

4 Elderly Women Perish in Fire

Germantown, Md. —(AP)— Four elderly women died in a fire that broke out early today at a rest home in this town 25 miles northwest of Washington.

Volunteer fire fighters managed to evacuate most of the patients despite subfreezing weather and intermittent snowfall. Fifteen other persons were reported injured.

The Montgomery County coroner's office listed these persons as dead in the fire at the Marylander Rest Home:

Sally Turpin, 96; Matilda Kohler, 84, and Mrs. Yates Duke, 73, all of Washington, and Mrs. Dora Ward, 86, of Rockville, Md.

HIS EYES SAW HORROR—Five of his children killed before his eyes in their blazing home, Reginald De Baggis is restrained by his wife and neighbors as he struggles to make a last desperate rescue attempt. Priest is Father Rudolph Masciarelli.
—Associated Press WIREPHOTO.

Pontiff Continues To Rally

Vatican City—(AP)—The Vatican gave new evidence today that Pope Pius XII is continuing to improve, announcing that the ailing Pontiff will close the Marian Year celebration on Wednesday with a blessing broadcast from his sickbed.

The 78-year-old head of the Roman Catholic Church, still critically ill with gastritis, spoke a similar blessing into a microphone yesterday. It was relayed by loudspeaker from his bedside to a throng of 50,000 in St. Peter's Basilica and by the Vatican radio and other networks to much of the world.

The Vatican press spokesman announced today that "the Pope's slow and gradual improvement continues." A Vatican source said earlier that the Pope had spent his third fairly restful night since he rallied from the severe collapse last Thursday which brought grave fears for his life.

Until his illness, the Pope had been scheduled to officiate at the ceremonies Wednesday which will end the special year of celebrations proclaimed by the Pontiff in honor of the Virgin Mary. Instead, Clemente Cardinal Micara, the Pope's vicar general for the City of Rome, will celebrate the Pontifical Mass in the city's oldest shrine to the Virgin, the Basilica of St. Mary Major.

As in yesterday's broadcast, a microphone will be brought to the Pontiff's bed and his blessing "urbi et orbi"—to the city and the world—will be relayed to the church loudspeakers and broadcast by the Vatican radio. Radio networks of other nations again are expected to pick up the Vatican broadcast.

Prior to his broadcast yesterday, the Pope was able to swallow a little broth. It was the first food he had taken by mouth in a week.

At one point in his short broadcast, the voice of Catholicism's stricken leader faded slightly, but mostly he spoke firmly and in cadence.

Some Resistance Shown in Poland

Vienna, Austria— (AP) —Amid some resistance from the nation's farmers, Poland elected 230,000 unopposed Communist candidates yesterday to local town and country councils.

The Warsaw radio said today that from 97.2 to 87.7 per cent of the eligible voters cast their ballots.

Socialists Oust Coalition

Extremists Get Nowhere In West Berlin Elections

Berlin—(UP)—West Berlin Socialists captured 64 of the 127 seats in the city's parliament today, crushing Communists and Nazi-tainted rightists who had hoped to get a foothold in the city government.

The anti-rearmament Socialists retained their position as the city's strongest party and ousted a rightwing coalition from power.

But West Berlin's Christian Democrats, in winning 44 seats, made sweeping gains in Sunday's elections to assure themselves of representation in a new Socialist-Democrat coalition.

Dr. Otto Suhr, incoming speaker of parliament who has been nominated by his party for mayor of West Berlin, said the Socialists will not attempt to use its one-seat majority in parliament to rule alone.

A record total of 1,554,766 voters turned out for the election and gave the Socialists 44 per cent. Christian Democrats received 30 per cent, at the expense of the moderate rightist Free Democrats, their chief coalition partners in Chancellor Konrad Adenauer's federal government.

The Communists, attempting to return to West Berlin's political life for the first time since 1946, failed to win anything near the required 5 per cent vote.

The extreme rightist German Party, which includes many former Nazis and which campaigned with rallies marked by jackbooted guards and anti-Jewish slogans, also did not receive the 5 per cent minimum.

McCarthy Fails To Show Up

Washington—(AP)—The Senate investigations subcommittee began closed hearings on alleged Communist infiltration in defense plants with Senator Carl Mundt (Rep., S. D.) presiding and Chairman Joseph McCarthy (Rep., Wis.) absent.

Mundt showed up about 2:15 p. m., 15 minutes after the scheduled starting time and told newsmen Mrs. McCarthy had called him and asked him to preside. She said McCarthy's sore elbow still was bothering him.

He has been under treatment for the bruised and infected elbow, injured when a handshaker pushed it against a glass table top, and canceled a scheduled speech in Cincinnati Saturday night because of it.

Honduras Rule Grabbed By Dictator

Tegucigalpa, Honduras— (AP) — Vice-President Julio Lozano took over as dictator of this Central American republic today.

The short, 60-year-old businessman assumed power constitutionally after a boycott by two parties prevented congress from picking a president from the two top contenders in last October's general elections.

Broadcasting from the Blue Room of the presidential manor at midnight, Lozano decreed himself chief of state and named the newly elected national congress as an advisory council. He said it will draft a new constitution.

He prohibited all gatherings, demonstrations, publications and broadcasts which might "tend to disrupt the peace."

Armed troops and police marched through the capital last night and were posted at all strategic sites. Trucks and jeeps patroled city streets. A truck with machineguns stood guard at the cordoned-off Congress Building.

President Juan Manuel Galvez, who was not a candidate for reelection in October, is in Miami, Fla. He left on Nov. 16 for medical treatment, leaving Lozano in charge as acting president, and has not announced whether he would return.

Fire at Chief's Home

Boston — (UP) — District Fire Chief Harry W. Murphy followed the fire engine in answer to an alarm last night. The $1,000-fire was in Murphy's home.

Today's Chuckle

Three little ink drops were crying, because their mother was in the pen and they didn't know how long the sentence was going to be.

Vote on Yoshida Expected in Diet

Tokyo— (AP) —Prime Minister Shigeru Yoshida, fighting back in the face of a no-confidence motion filed against him in the Diet, said tonight he will take his case to the people if the move succeeds.

The vote is expected tomorrow (late tonight, EST).

Yoshida, speaking through the secretary-general of his Liberal Party, Hayato Ikeda, threatened anew to dissolve the Diet (parliament) if his opponents win.

December 6, 1954: The fire was at Commercial Avenue and Henry Street. Larry Hale, who later became the editor of the paper, wrote the story. *Courtesy Charlie Jenks*

Flood waters continue to rise at En Joie Park in 1956. Notice the bandstand is completely surrounded by floodwaters. *Courtesy Marlene Yacos*

Charlie Jenks, local fireman for 27 years, shows off the deer he shot in 1954. *Courtesy Charlie Jenks*

MRS.
AMERICA
MRS.
NEW Y
STAT

Phyllis Bell, local resident, won the titles of Mrs. Binghamton, Mrs. Southern Tier and Mrs. New York State in the 1950s. In this 1956 photo, she has been crowned Mrs. Southern Tier. *Courtesy Bonnie Lyon*

Green's
RESTAURANT
Tavern
Bar
1504
TRANSCUCENT
MODERNITE
LEVINSON'S
WORKERS OUTFITTERS

Budweiser's Clydesdales have their picture taken July 1, 1956, in front of Green's Tavern. Edward J. Green (Barge) and Ann Green Burnell operated the bar from 1950 to 1956 and lived above the bar until it was sold. *Courtesy Ann Green Burnell*

Vestal Lawsuit

Contractors for Vestal's Sewer District 4 charge "anticipatory breach of contract," sue the town for $100,707. Story Page 5.

THE DAILY BULLETIN

Serving Endicott, Endwell, Vestal and Western Broome — Eastern Tioga Counties

The Weather

Fair and cool tonight; low 50 to 55. Tomorrow, considerable cloudiness with possible showers and moderate temperatures; high 73 to 78.

Vol. 97, No. 25 | 46 Pages—3 Sections | Endicott, N. Y., Wednesday, August 22, 1956 | Telephone 5-3355 | 5 Cents

Ike Takes Charge at Convention

Art Exhibition, Elaine Malbin Delight Golden Year Crowds

An art show in IBM Field House proved to be a smash hit last night. Area residents jammed the exhibit 3,500 strong to see the million dollar IBM collection of works of American artists from 1720 to 1920.

During and after the outdoor Golden Year concert staged in a temporary theater on the grounds of IBM Country Club, people were filing through the foyer and adjacent corridors of the field house viewing the unique collection of oil paintings.

A Young Patron of the Arts

Ronald Janicki gazes in awe at one of the paintings displayed in the IBM Field House. Many oldtimers found paintings, which they recognized from their old textbooks, but Ronald has still to explore the works of famous 1720 to 1920 painters in his history classes. The one million dollar exhibit attracted many unexpected visitors.

Many of the guests took notes. Oldtimers recognized some of the pictures from having seen them in their history books in school many years ago. Paintings by Rembrandt, Peale, Samuel F. B. Morse, and many other artists brought back familiar scenes of the American heritage.

The show will continue for three more days. It will be open daily from 1 to 10 p. m. through Friday.

More than 3,00 guests also attended the outdoor concert. Elaine Malbin won round after round of applause. Miss Malbin, the $1,350 substitute for Rise Stevens, reminded many observers of Lily Pons—both in voice and gesture.

She captivated her audience with her voice, petite beauty and personality. She presented songs from "Kismet," in which she sang on Broadway and selections from "My Darling Aida," another of her Broadway successes.

She sang selections from the title role of "Madam Butterfly," which she will interpret this fall when the new NBC Opera Co. makes its first American road tour, and presented various modern songs from Victor Herbert.

Exposition Slated

An exposition telling the story of Endicott's first 50 years in separate displays will open the second day in the 50th anniversary observance tonight. The grand opening of the exposition will be conducted at 7 o'clock in the Recreation Center. Following the opening the 500 pioneer residents of the village, guests of the Golden Year celebration, will be honored at a reception in the center.

Heading the list of hostesses for the reception will be Mrs. Charles F. Johnson Jr. Mrs. Claire Carey arranged the reception and Dr. Joseph Van Riper of the Harpur College Faculty is chairman of the exposition.

Twelve area industries will exhibit the contrasting picture of the advanced industrial nature of the community today in elaborate displays which will occupy one-half of the recreation center.

Some 180 costumed dancers and singers of 18 different national groups — represented in the population of Endicott—will perform on a newly-constructed 75 foot stage in front of the En-Joie Park Stadium tonight at 8:30 p. m. Approximately 7,000 guests can be accommodated in the vast stadium and the area about the stage can accommodate an overflow crowd of several thousand.

Play Will Open

The hilarious Broadway comedy, "The Tender Trap," will open tonight, too. The opening performance will be held at 8 o'clock in the auditorium of the Union-Endicott High School where 1,200 seats will be available to the public free of charge. "The Tender Trap," to be presented by the Susquehanna Players, will be repeated again Friday at 8:30 p. m.

Climaxing the second day in the week long Golden Year celebration will be a fire works display in En-Joie Park tonight at 10. Dorr W. Warner, general chairman of the Golden Year observance, assured the public that an expert crew will be on hand to stage the 45 minute aerial show.

Tomorrow area merchants will open an Old Fashioned Days sale at 9:30 a. m. The Historical Industrial Exposition will continue through tomorrow from 2 p. m. to 7 p. m.

Mardi Gras Dances

At 9 p. m. tomorrow the Mardi Grass Masquerade will start with three open air dances. Three local ten piece bands will provide music for the dances to be conduced at Main Street and Washington Ave.; Liberty Ave. and Main St.; and the North end of the McKinley Ave. viaduct. More than $2,000 in prizes will be awarded to wearers of the funniest and best costumes.

The grand drawing for the $3,200 Pontiac Catalina Hardtop will be held at 11 p. m. Holder of the winning ticket must be present at one of the three Mardi Gras dances to qualify. Free tickets for the community wide raffle are being distributed at all Golden Year activities.

Lovely Guest and Endicott's Lovely Queen

Miss Elaine Malbin accepts flowers with a winning smile, from Miss Patricia Gallagher, right, Queen of Endicott's Golden Year celebration. Miss Malbin captivated her audience last night with her voice, beauty and sensational personality at the open air concert at the IBM Country Club.

Schedule of Events

(All Events Free)

Tonight

7:00 p. m.	Reception for pioneer residents and grand opening of the Historical-Industrial Exposition at EJ Recreation Center.
8:00 p. m.	First performance, "The Tender Trap," by the Susquehanna Players at Union-Endicott High School.
8:30 p. m.	First performance, Heritage Group choral and dance routines representing 16 nationalities at En-Joie Stadium.
10:00 p. m.	A 45-minute aerial fireworks display.

Tomorrow

9:30 a. m.	Opening of old-fashioned days sale by Endicott merchants.
1:00 p. m.	Art exhibit at IBM Field House.
2:00 p. m.	Historical-Industrial exposition.
9:00 p. m.	Mardi Gras Masquerade begins with open air dances at Main and Washington, Main and Liberty and McKinley Avenue viaduct, with $2,000 in prizes for best and funniest costumes.
11:00 p. m.	Grand drawing for the Golden Year gift, a $3,200 Pontiac Catalina hardtop at the Mardi Gras. Holder of the winning ticket must be present to to qualify.

Big Three Meets Again to Plan Suez Appeal to Egypt

LONDON (AP)—The Western Big Three met today to decide how to confront Egypt with their Suez Canal plan, backed by 17 of the 22 nations at the London Conference.

There was no indication President Nasser of Egypt would accept their proposal despite its solid backing. It calls for international control of the waterway he seized last month.

Secretary of State Dulles first met for 40 minutes with V. K. Krishna Menon of India, whose rival plan leaving Egypt in control of the canal won support from only four nations assembled here. One nation is undecided.

Then Dulles conferred with Foreign Secretary Selwyn Lloyd of Britain and Foreign Minister Christian Pineau of France.

French sources said the Big Three were determined to arrange for presenting their proposal to Nasser without delay. It was possible two separate groups would be chosen to present Egypt with the rival Indian and U. S. plans.

It appeared as delegates went back into session that the best the Big Three could hope for would be Egypt's acceptance of India's plan for an international group to give advice only to the Egyptian canal management.

The conference was nearly over. The only business before today's session was appointment of a committee to inform Nasser of decisions reached. Presumably, the committee would also suggest the opening of negotiations.

In brief, this was the outcome of the week-long conference:

Seventeen nations endorsed the proposal presented by Secretary of State Dulles for an international board, associated with the U.N., to run the 103-mile canal. The 17 were the United States, Great Britain, France, Australia, New Zealand, Pakistan, Iran, Ethiopia, Turkey, Denmark, Norway, Sweden, Japan, Italy, West Germany, the Netherlands and Portugal.

GE Testing 1st Giant Generator

SCHENECTADY (AP)—The General Electric Co. today was testing the first of 16 giant hydro-electric generators that are to be installed at the New York Power Authority's Barnhart Island project in the St. Lawrence River.

Chairman Robert Moses and other Authority representatives inspected the unit yesterday.

IBM Reaches Accord With Sperry-Rand

NEW YORK (AP)—International Business Machines Corp. and Sperry Rand Corp. have settled their differences over office equipment patents and licenses, at a cost of 10 million dollars to IBM.

In an out-of-court settlement yesterday, Sperry Rand dropped its 30-million-dollar antitrust suit against IBM and IBM, in turn, withdrew a counterclaim charging Sperry Rand with patent infringement. Since Sperry Rand asked triple damages under the Sherman Anti-Trust Act in its suit, the potential cost to IBM was 90 million dollars.

At the same time, the two firms agreed to exchange licenses to make electronic data processing machines and punched card accounting machines under patents existing on Oct. 1, 1956. Since IBM is expected to make more machines under Sperry Rand's patents than vice versa, IBM will pay Sperry Rand a fixed royalty of $1,230,000 for eight years as a credit against production royalties.

Police Probe Fourth Threat

ALBANY (AP)—Police in this capital city today had a record of four groundless bomb threats within 22 hours.

About 200 persons were evacuated from the Palace Theatre late yesterday afternoon when a man telephoned that a bomb was hidden there.

Earlier, the same threat was made about an S. S. Kresge Store in the downtown shopping district.

On Tuesday, anonymous calls sent police to the 34-story Alfred E. Smith State Office Building and to a 17-story bank building.

Nixon's Selection as Running Mate Looks Certain for Approval

By JACK BELL

SAN FRANCISCO (AP)—President Eisenhower took command of the Republicans' centennial convention today amid indications he will cement its choice of Vice President Nixon as his running mate.

The only question seemed to be whether he would do so by remaining silent, or by restating his oft-voiced views that the convention should be "open" and that he would be delighted to run again with Nixon.

A convention showdown on Harold E. Stassen's campaign to ditch Nixon remained a possibility.

The mood of the delegates was such that only an outright expression of preference for someone else would induce them to sidetrack Nixon. And there was absolutely nothing to indicate Eisenhower would do that.

Ike Certain Choice

Eisenhower himself is certain to be renominated unanimously at the convention session late today. Immediately after that, the delegates will choose the vice presidential nominee.

Eisenhower had no known plans to visit the convention hall until his acceptance address tomorrow night.

But his influence was all-encompassing. Following his arrival from Washington last evening, he arranged to receive at a downtown hotel a long line of party leaders and hopeful GOP candidates for office. First in line was GOP National Chairman Leonard W. Hall.

Most party leaders thought Eisenhower would not go beyond what he has said publicly—that Nixon is "perfectly acceptable" to him as a running mate. Eisenhower never has foreclosed other candidates, however.

No Announcement

Atty. Gen. Herbert Brownell Jr. indicated he expects no Eisenhower announcement on a running mate prior to the convention's actions. Brownell said he didn't look for any "excitement" as a result of the President's day-early visit to San Francisco.

Gov. Christian A. Herter of Massachusetts, who has been Stassen's chief candidate to replace Nixon although Herter will put Nixon's name in nomination, said he doesn't think Eisenhower will have any list of men acceptable to him as running mates.

Eisenhower, all smiles, got a rousing reception on his arrival here. His appearance gave the Republicans something to cheer about and they turned out by the thousands as he drove to a downtown hotel from the airport.

Nixon headed the list of greeters at the airport. He got a warm handclasp and a few words from the President. Stassen, in the receiving line, also got a presidential smile and a word or two.

Eisenhower told the airport crowd he had been reading the papers in Washington and he suddenly decided that "this was too interesting a place to stay away from till Wednesday"—when he originally had planned to come. So, he said, he persuaded his family to come out with him a day earlier.

With Eisenhower on the scene, the delegates perked up and got ready for today's big nominating show.

Without a dissenting voice delegates whipped through yesterday a platform promising spending cuts, a balanced budget and tax reductions aimed primarily at the lower and middle income groups.

Chances Dim For Stassen Floor Appeal

SAN FRANCISCO (AP)—Determined objections apparently stood in the way today of Harold E. Stassen's request to address the Republican national convention before it nominates a vice presidential candidate.

"He will not get the chance to talk," Sen. William Jenner of Indiana said. "If no one else objects I will."

Jenner announced dispatch of a telegram to Rep. Joseph W. Martin Jr. of Massachusetts, the chairman of the convention, protesting against letting Stassen speak to the delegates. Stassen is not a delegate.

Technically, objection by Jenner or any other delegate would block Stassen since the rules require unanimous consent to permit any non-delegate to speak.

Martin said in a separate interview he had heard there would be "plenty" of objections to Stassen's request to be heard by the convention even though Vice President Nixon, whose renomination Stassen opposes, urged that he be allowed to speak.

Martin added that he understood some "big delegations are going to object" to Stassen's request.

Stassen, on leave as President Eisenhower's disarmament adviser, has been waging an apparently futile fight to drop Nixon from the GOP ticket and to replace him with Gov. Christian A. Herter of Massachusetts.

He advised Martin yesterday he would "deeply appreciate" an opportunity to speak to the convention today after it nominates its presidential candidate but before it selects its vice presidential nominee.

Crockenberg Rites to Be Held Friday

Funeral services will be held Friday morning for Robert C. Crockenberg, former Endicott restaurateur who died suddenly last night following a heart attack.

Mr. Crockenberg, who was 44 years old, was stricken shortly before 9:30 p. m. while in the locker room at the Binghamton Country Club. He was taken to Wilson Memorial Hospital in the Broome County Sheriff's ambulance, but was pronounced dead on arrival.

A former proprietor of the old Drake's Restaurant in Washington Avenue (now the Belvui) Mr. Crockenberg was owner of DeLano's Restaurant at 22 Chenango St., Binghamton; of Mary's Restaurant, 11 Castle Creek Road, Binghamton RD, and a co-proprietor of the Horse Shoe Grill at 217 Washington St.

He also in past years operated the Community Coffee Shop and Crockey's Restaurant in Binghamton.

Sheriff's men said Mr. Crockenberg had been playing golf at the Country club just prior to his attack. They said investigation disclosed he had suffered a previous heart attack last winter in Florida.

Besides his wife, Mrs. Helen L. Crockenberg of 9 Castle Creek Road, he is survived by four sisters, Mrs. Paul Carl of Binghamton, Mrs. William Bittle and Mrs. Walter Cleary of Philadelphia, Pa. and Mrs. Edward Sullivan of Scranton, Pa.; and three brothers, Ferdinand P. Crockenberg of Sidney, and Leo J. and Walter N. Crockenberg, both of Binghamton.

Funeral services will be held Friday morning at the McDevitt Brothers Funeral Home, 88 Front St., Binghamton, and at St. Christopher's Church, of which he was a member.

Friends may call at the funeral home today from 7 to 9 p. m., and tomorrow from 2 to 5 and from 7 to 9 p. m.

Stevenson Calls GOP Tax Cut Plans 'Election Talk'

LIBERTYVILLE, Ill. (AP)—Adlai Stevenson today labeled a Republican promise of tax cuts as just "so much election talk."

The Democratic Presidential nominee, completing plans for a flying tour of the country next week to lay the groundwork for a strenuous campaign, said the tax cut promise was a contradiction" of President Eisenhower's own position that he is "against tax cuts" and favors applying any surplus revenue toward "retirement of the public debt."

"I am perplexe that the Republican national convention should make this promise, when President Eisenhower has said repeatedly he is a gainst a tax cut," Stevenson said.

In a separate statement, Stevenson, meeting reporters in the recreation room of his farm home near here, expressed sarcasm at the Republican platform committee chairman, Prescott Bush's emphasis on a balanced budget.

"The Republican convention applauded loudest when Sen. Bush said 'We have balanced the budget.'

"This was certainly an accurate reflection of what interests the Republican leaders most—not the education of our children, not a fair break for farmers, not the growing menace of Communism in the world, not America's wandering influence—but 'a balanced budget'."

Drowns After Dive

BUFFALO (AP)—Forty-nine year old Francis Elliott of Buffalo drowned yesterday in the Niagara River. Authorities said he failed to come to the surface after apparently striking his head on something following a dive.

Main Stems

Mr. and Mrs. George (Endicott Florist) Camp pleased with their new boy, born last week in Ideal Hospital. The baby was confined to Ideal Hospital for a while and is now at home with the couple.

John (Bulletin Carrier) Griffith, son of **Mr. and Mrs. F. Irving Griffith**, returning hale and hearty from Lark Lamoka after a week's recreation. He's back on the job in the Overton tract of Nanticoke Avenue area.

Jack Bergen of Sullivan Bros. Furniture Store recuperating at Lourdes Hospital after an op. He'd gladly read cards and such from friends.

Airman 2/c Nicholas Napolitano Jr. home from Westover Air Force Base, weekending with parents at 3111 Argonne Ave., Endicott, and visiting Miss Patti Underwood of Washington Avenue.

Lary and Gary Crandall of Vestal, twin sons of **Mr. and Mrs. Franklin Crandall**, visiting their grandmother, **Mrs. Marjorie Crandall** in Endicott.

C of C Raps Sales Tax

Triple Cities Chamber of Commerce members today were planning action to be taken if a 2 per cent sales tax for either the county or city of Binghamton should become a reality.

In 1952, when the proposed was last brought before the Broome County Board of Supervisors and was rejected, all three chambers banded together to fight the levying of the tax.

The chambers were of the opinion that the tax would hurt business. Many were bitter about the collecting of the tax which would compel a new set of books and make merchants "tax collectors for the city or county government."

Prior to the negative vote of 22 to 7 by the supervisors, the Binghamton, Johnson City and Endicott chambers banded together in a general committee to battle against imposition of the tax.

Chairman was Ray Hancock of Johnson City and there was a vice chairman from both Endicott and Binghamton.

When queried today about the Endicott chamber's opposition to a county-wide 2 per cent sales tax, Stephen W. Ryder, president said that it would be discussed at the next meeting in September.

"Because of the Gollden Year celebration we haven't had a directors' meeting but we plain a session next month. However, the chamber has been opposed to a sales tax in the past and it is assumed that we will continue tto oppose such a tax," Mr. Ryder said.

William Sliker, executive secretary of the Johnson City chamber, said that he is of the opinion that the members will probably take the same stand that was taken in 1952.

"We haven't made any attempt to contact Endicott on the matter," Mr. Sliker said, "because they are all busy with the anniversary celebration. But I expect within a week or two we will discuss taking action on the proposed tax."

Edgar Severson, president of the Binghamton chamber, said that he would rather wait until he had talked with his directors before commenting on the issue.

He said that in 1952 he was a member of the unit and was opposed to the sales tax.

The sales tax was revived last eek by Binghamton Mayor Donald W. Kramer. He said he was going to urge the supervisors to make it countywide but if the proposal was rejected, he would ask the City Council to approve a citywide tax.

The mayor has authorized the corporation counsel to prepare the legislation for presentation to City Council.

When it was voted in 1952, councilmen rejected a proposed 1 per cent tax by a vote of 7 to 6. The mayor said that the tax would have more support this year and estimated that as many as 10 members of Council might vote in favor of a 2 per cent city tax.

Old Fashioned Days Sale Tomorrow, Friday—See Section Today

August 22, 1956: The Daily Bulletin was in its 97th year serving Endicott. It would soon merge with the Binghamton Sun. *Courtesy Dolly Escovar*

DEDICATION CEREMONIES WILL START TRAFFIC ROLLING ON THREE TRIPLE CITIES HIGHWAY PROJECTS

Tomorrow's the Big Day! New Bridge to Open

THE SUNDAY PRESS
BINGHAMTON PRESS SUNDAY EDITION
Section C Nov. 18, 1956

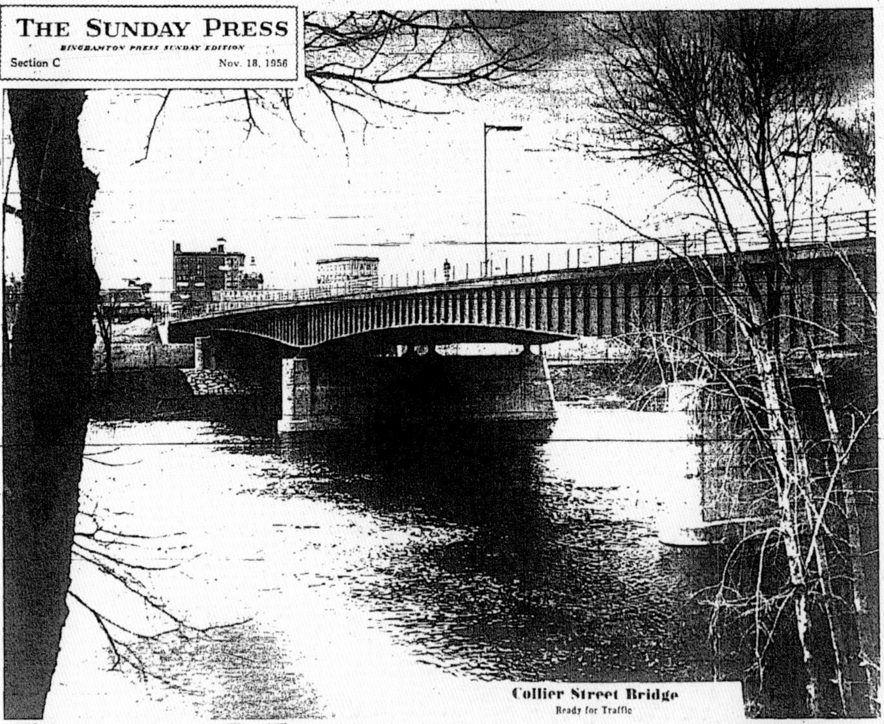

Collier Street Bridge
Ready for Traffic

Only 1 More Arterial Link Remains to Be Constructed

By LARRY HALE
Sunday Press Writer

Traffic will begin flowing across Binghamton's new Collier Street Bridge tomorrow, an event forging the key link in Binghamton's urban arterial highway system.

The $6,400,000 structure will replace the antiquated Washington Street Bridge as the principal span across the Susquehanna River in the center of Binghamton.

It will be the largest, as well as the newest, of nine bridges across the Susquehanna and Chenango rivers in the city.

The six-lane bridge was conceived in 1947 by the State Department of Public Works. The construction contract was awarded on Dec. 31, 1954, the final day of the Dewey administration. Building of the span began three months later.

The bridge will be opened with formal ceremonies beginning at 10:30 a.m. tomorrow.

Tomorrow also will mark the opening of two smaller, but highly important, highway projects in the Binghamton area.

These are the new traffic interchange at Pickle Hill and the Bevier Street overpass of Brandywine Highway. Total cost of both projects is $791,947. The Pickle Hill project, particularly, has resulted in a traffic bottleneck throughout construction. It involves elevating Chenango Street over the Brandywine Highway, Route 7.

John W. Johnson, state superintendent of public works, will speak at ceremonies dedicating the Collier Street Bridge. He is expected to inspect the two other projects, although no special ceremonies are scheduled there.

Planning and construction of the Collier Street Bridge was marked by sporadic wrangling and controversy involving, at various times, a group of Fifth Ward merchants and city and state officials.

A major project carried out in connection with the building of the bridge was the displacement of about 300 families, as well as business firms and other institutions to make way for the new span. Among these was the Eldredge Park School for physically handicapped children.

Three of the key personnel who played an important part in the planning and construction of the span have left the scene.

Bertram D. Tallamy, who was state superintendent of public works when the project was conceived, later became head of the State Thruway Authority and now has been appointed to direct a federal highway construction program.

Frank W. (Jack) Donovan, who supervised much of the project as Binghamton District engineer for the State Department of Public Works, retired last Dec. 31.

Frank J. Weber, who was the state's on-the-site representative during most of the construction, died Sept. 25 after serving as assistant district engineer for [illegible]

The Collier Street Bridge first was proposed in 1947 by the State Department of Public Works as part of a multimillion dollar arterial highway program to relieve critical traffic conditions in Binghamton.

One proposal [illegible] construction of an arterial highway from the [illegible] at State Hospital [illegible] of Vestal.

Completion of the new bridge leaves only one link to be built in the arterial system. This is a "river bank" route along the north shore of the Susquehanna between the new bridge and the Brandywine Highway at Court Street.

The river-route link has been estimated to cost between $1,000,000 and $5,000,000. Although no starting date has been scheduled, an appropriation of $65,000 has been included in the tentative 1957 city budget as a down payment on the city's share of land acquisition costs. Total cost to be paid by the city is estimated at $1,300,000.

The proposed bridge drew objections from the start from the Fifth Ward Businessmen's Association, which sought to have Washington Street Bridge reconstructed into a [illegible] [illegible] as the [illegible] Susquehanna River [illegible]

Mayor Donald W. Kramer [illegible]

State officials held firm against the merchants' protests, as well as those made by some councilmen, and insisted that the new bridge be built upstream from the Washington Street structure. State officials argued that the new span was designed to relieve traffic congestion at Memorial Circle.

In November, 1954, City Council approved the bridge [illegible] a vote of 10 to 2, with First Ward Republican Daniel J. Keane Jr. and Fifth Ward Republican [illegible] Frank [illegible]

(Continued on Page 3C)

★ ★ ★ Here's Program For Tomorrow's Span Ceremonies

Traffic will roll over the $6,400,000 Collier Street Bridge shortly after 10 o'clock tomorrow morning after brief ceremonies in which state and city officials will participate.

John W. Johnson, superintendent of the State Department of Public Works, and Mayor Donald W. Kramer will be main speakers.

The ceremonies will be climaxed with the cutting of a ribbon at the center of the bridge by Kathleen McMahon, a member of the Binghamton Girls Club.

George F. Knowlton Jr., chairman of the Highway Committee of the Chamber of Commerce, will be master of ceremonies.

Invocation will be offered by the Rev. Thomas F. Whalen of St. John the Evangelist Roman Catholic Church, and the benediction will be pronounced by the Rev. Cordal N. Leaty, rector of Christ Episcopal Church.

Music will be provided by Central and North high school bands.

Matter of Fact

You'd Almost Say Holiday Was Near

By TOM CAWLEY

IN THESE parts, you know it's Thanksgiving week because [illegible] the [illegible] and streamers hanging from their [illegible] are [illegible] [illegible] the Christmas [illegible] downtown. . . . The mail is full of toy catalogs. . . . Another small girl says without any [illegible] [illegible] or disillusionment, "I know that YOU'RE Santa Claus, not anybody who comes down any dumb chimney," and seems faintly amused at the [illegible] been playing these last [illegible] years.

MR. CAWLEY

★ ★ ★

The first fall of snow—you can tell in your bones it isn't going to "stick"—brings out every sled on the block, and there's a symphony of raspy scraping of rusted runners on wet sidewalks. . . . The out-of-town papers get a Thanksgiving Day play because there are no local papers, pausing for a breath on a nice day. . . . There are subtle female hints in the daughter department about Christmas gifts.

★ ★ ★

THE banquet managers of the hotels try to keep their bookkeeping straight as reservations for holiday parties pile in. . . . A guy says, "Good grief, you mean to tell me it's Thanksgiving ALREADY!" . . . The pictures of those long-legged basketball players in short pants move with more frequency through the sports pages. . . . The Most Valuable Player awards are made in the big leagues, which is a prelude to pitcher-reporting time only a few snow flurries away.

★ ★ ★

The night sounds include the sip-sip-sip of tires on a wet pavement. . . . The night sounds include an automatic furnace turning on as it reacts to the thermostatic control. . . . The department store windows feature expensive-looking frocks designed strictly for partying. . . . The window girl dummies look fresh and appealing, but did you ever see anything more desolate than a man dummy wearing a dinner jacket?

★ ★ ★

THE [illegible] are beginning to appear. . . . The bright-looking kids in our [illegible] are home from college for the weekend. . . . The market windows show up full of plucked turkeys and was there anything ever so depressing in appearance than an unplucked turkey, hanging head down?

★ ★ ★

The Salvation Army band at Court and State huddled together in a chill drizzle, but blowing and pounding gloriously for a glorious cause with no complaints for the weather. . . . The cars splash muddy water from a sink in Washington Street asphalt, and a cop murmurs, "Those guys have no respect for a pair of nylons," as he assists the dripping lady to the curb.

★ ★ ★

YOU know it's Thanksgiving week when the children walk home from school are loaded with paper turkeys, paper pumpkins, paper [illegible] stalks lovingly made [illegible] to be presented with great pomp to parents. . . . You know what week it is because [illegible] of a [illegible] after 4 weeks of [illegible] feeling [illegible]

Workmen Put Finishing Touches on Chenango Street Bridge
Pickle Hill Project Is Final Link in Brandywine Arterial Highway

Bridge Opening to Cue Unveiling of 761 Signs

"Operation Striptease" will get under way tomorrow morning when scores of state and city employes unveil the 761 new signs that will govern the revised traffic pattern in Binghamton for the Collier Street Bridge and its approaches.

[illegible]

> Traffic flow map, showing direction in which traffic will move to and from Collier Street Bridge, appears on Page 3C.

He said that the signs will be uncovered as closely as possible to the time the bridge is opened to traffic to avoid confusion.

While attention is centered on the opening of the new Susquehanna River span the work crews [illegible] [illegible] the burlap covers [illegible] new signs.

Harried motorists who are able to negotiate the new traffic maze without difficulty may have trouble in finding a parking place.

In conjunction with the new traffic pattern, restrictions on parking will remove 104 curb meters from the Seventh and Eighth Wards in addition to [illegible] removed for [illegible] the bridge approaches.

Scores of non-metered parking places also will be removed on both sides of the river.

Mr. Burns said that the parking meters involved either will be removed or "bagged" [illegible] morning. Other [illegible] parking in [illegible] areas also will be in place.

Signs governing the new traffic pattern will read "Stop," "One Way," "Do Not [illegible]

(Continued on Page 3C)

Car Hits Tree, 2 Youths Hurt

Two youths were injured last night when a car struck a tree at South Washington Street and Woodland Avenue.

They are Michael DeFrancesco, 16, of 125 Gaylord Street, and William Luckenbill, 18, of 21½ Baxter Street. **Both suffered knee injuries and both were discharged from City Hospital after receiving emergency treatment.**

Young DeFrancesco had been driving west and had attempted a turn into South Washington Street when the car struck the tree. Although Young DeFrancesco holds a junior operator's license, Young Luckenbill is a licensed driver.

Vestal's Hexagonal Schools Stir Wide Interest

Sunday Press [illegible] Photo by Gerson

New Willow Point School Nears Completion

Vestal school children soon will be going to classes in two new elementary buildings incorporating the most revolutionary architectural design and construction in this area and possibly in the state.

So unconventional are these buildings, both in design and, more importantly, in economy of construction, that Vestal has become a focal point of interest for other school districts hard-pressed for classroom space and for funds with which to construct traditional schools.

In addition, officials of the State Education Department, including Commissioner James E. Allen, have expressed "great interest" in the outcome of the building program and have indicated they will visit the two schools for an on-the-spot inspection of the facilities soon after the buildings are put in use.

Basically, the schools are hexagonal clusters of pie-slice-shaped classrooms joined together by connecting corridors.

The one-story buildings are of monolithic concrete and structural steel construction with extensive plate glass windows providing a maximum of natural light.

The Ross Corners school will have 10 classrooms, a combination auditorium-cafe-

(Continued on Page 2C)

November 18, 1956: Three bridges opened on one day. The biggest, the Collier Street Bridge, is now called the State Street Bridge.

Microfilm archives

Swell-egant

WEATHER BUREAU FORECAST
Generally fair tonight and Sunday with some daytime cloudiness. Low tonight 35-40. High Sunday 60-65.

BINGHAMTON PRESS

Saturday Evening, October 5, 1957 — THE TRIPLE CITIES' NEWSPAPER — Vol. 79—150 16 Pages 5 Cents

Read It in The Press
Hear It Over WINR

Red Moon Circles World in 96 Minutes

Other Poles Join Student Riot Near Red Headquarters

Warsaw —(AP)— Angry students and other Poles battled police, security troops and militia in Warsaw's streets last night in the second violent antigovernment demonstration in two days.

Big Soviet Victory Over U. S.

By JOSEPH L. MYLER
United Press Writer

Washington—American scientists, caught flatfooted by Russia's epic launching of the first man-made moon, indicated today the United States may speed up its own earth satellite program.

Area Hams Hear Beeps Of Satellite

560 Miles Out in Space; Russians Win Space Race

By the Associated Press

A Soviet-launched artificial moon roared around the earth today circling the globe every 96 minutes 560 miles out in space.

Scientists proclaimed the pioneer satellite the first dramatic step toward exploring the universe. They also credited the Soviet with winning the world race into space.

Radio signals from the tiny moon were reported picked up in the United States, Britain, Canada and the Soviet Union.

Although there were reports that the satellite had been spotted by Americans, scientists at the Smithsonian Astrophysical Observatory at Cambridge, Mass., said they are certain its not visible to observers.

Dr. Fred L. Whipple, director of the observatory, said computations have determined that the moon, streaking around the world at 18,000 miles an hour, is invisible because of the relation of its course to the position of the sun.

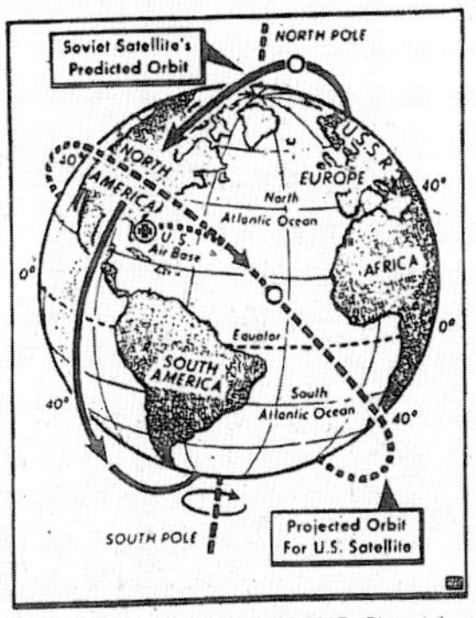

Soviet Satellite's Predicted Orbit
NORTH POLE
NORTH AMERICA
EUROPE
Atlantic Ocean
AFRICA
Equator
SOUTH AMERICA
South Atlantic Ocean
SOUTH POLE
Projected Orbit For U.S. Satellite

HOW SATELLITE ORBITS WOULD DIFFER—Diagram shows how the north-to-south orbit of the Russian-launched earth satellite differs from the west-to-east orbit planned for the satellites to be launched by the U. S. Russia last night announced the launching of the first man-made moon.

Facts, Figures

'Moon' Sidelights

Teamsters, Hoffa In Double Trouble

By Press Wire Services

Miami Beach — The 1,400,000-member Teamsters Union which often uses its power to aid other striking unions, had one foot out of the door of the AFL-CIO today, and the other in the hot water of a Senate investigation.

Little Rock Youth Gets Rifle Butt

Reds Convict Yugo Writer

Grid Special On WINR

To keep football-interested Triple Citians abreast of Saturday grid activities on the local front, Jim Adelson, WINR sportscaster will be giving forth on two special shows starting today.

At 6:10 and 11:10 p. m. you'll get the full story—

MR. ADELSON

with the bright details and sidelights as only Jim can tell them—on WINR, 680 on your radio dial.

A-Blast Postponed

Crossing Crash Fatal

Mrs. Stengel, Cow Save Day

Yankees High-Hat Wisconsin Welcome

What's Next, Little Rock?

Week for Handicapped

Essay Contest Shows Inflation Worries

Christmases Have Merry

It's Simple Satellite, Only Radio in It, Says Russian

Let's Chuckle

October 5, 1957: *Sputnik* and the Press' relationship with WINR were big news items on a football Saturday. The paper owned the radio station and later a television station with the same call letters. *Microfilm archives*

Cool, Man

WEATHER BUREAU FORECAST

Cloudy, cool today, a few light showers likely, brisk northwesterly winds, high 45-50. Clearing, cooler tonight, low 28-33. Monday fair, continued cool, high 45-50. Weather map on Page 2 C.

AIRPORT TEMPERATURE

3 p. m. 42	7 p. m. 39	11 p. m. 38
4 p. m. 40	8 p. m. 38	Midnight 37
5 p. m. 40	9 p. m. 38	1 a. m. 37
6 p. m. 39	10 p. m. 38	2 a. m. 37

THE SUNDAY PRESS

BINGHAMTON PRESS SUNDAY EDITION

Vol. 9—7 6 Sections 15 Cents Sunday, October 20, 1957

★★★★★ Latest News, Sports

The Tier's Only LOCAL Sunday Paper

$100,000,000 'ROADS OF TOMORROW' SLATED FOR BROOME

PENN-CAN SLICES BINGHAMTON; ROUTE 17 CUTS CITY, JC, VESTAL

★ ★ ★

'Service' Our Aim: Federick

The concept of "service to the community" underlies the state's proposal to aim the Penn-Can Highway and new Route 17 Expressway directly through urban areas of the Triple Cities, Joseph C. Federick said last night.

MR. FEDERICK

Mr. Federick, Binghamton District engineer of the State Department of Public Works, noted that such highways are intended to carry traffic safely and rapidly over long distances.

But, he said, "what is of much greater importance, the purpose of the highways is to serve the metropolitan community."

"It cannot be too strongly emphasized that these new highways must serve the community. If they do not, their fundamental purpose has not been fulfilled."

HIT URBAN AREAS

Of the 41,000 miles making up the nation's interstate highway system (of which Penn-Can would be a part), 6,000 miles are to be built within urban areas, Mr. Federick said.

The proposed location of Penn-Can through Binghamton and vicinity "adds this locality to those progressive communities that will derive maximum service and benefit from these new facilities," the engineer said.

He said the expressway plans have been integrated with "the basic community pattern" as prepared by the Broome County Planning Board.

FACTORS CONSIDERED

Thus, he said, such factors as "land use, population densities, planning neighborhoods, recreation and educational facilities, public buildings, and the thoroughfare plan" were considered.

In addition, he said, the restrictions of topography had to be considered.

Earlier this year, the state had proposed that a Penn-Can link between Five Mile Point and Hinman's Corners be built in such a way that it would pass through Hillcrest—a plan strongly opposed by Hillcrest residents.

Under the plan disclosed last night, Penn-Can and the Route 17 Expressway would share a joint right-of-way from Five Mile Point to Binghamton's Stow Flats and then split up, with

(Continued on Page 7 A)

JUDSON ST.
BRANDYWINE
BEVIER ST.
DeFOREST ST. BRIDGE
MOFFATT AVE.
CHENANGO ST.
N. SIDE POOL
PENN-CAN
STOW FLATS
FRONT ST.
CHENANGO RIVER
NEW RT. 17
CUTLER ICE CO.
VALLEY ST. PLAYGROUND
FRANKLIN ST.
VALLEY ST.

—Photo by Swierkosz. Art Work by Bryan.

State Proposes Penn-Can, Route 17 Expressway Merger at North Side Pool

Hillcrest 'Bypassed'; Johnson Field, Pool In 13th Ward to Go

By LARRY HALE
Sunday Press Writer

A dazzling plan for two high-speed superhighways through the heart of the Triple Cities was unveiled last night by the State Department of Public Works.

The breath-taking project—bringing the Penn-Can Highway directly through Binghamton (not through Hillcrest as originally proposed) and plunging a new Route 17 Expressway through Binghamton, Johnson City and Vestal—would cost more than $50,000,000.

Together with new connecting links, some of them already approved, it would add up to $100,000,000 worth of road-building in Broome County—by far the biggest public works program ever contemplated in the area.

The state agency has approved the plan. It now rests with the U.S. Bureau of Public Roads for a decision.

Johnson Field, home of the Triplet baseball team, would be struck out by the new Route 17. Both the infield and the outfield would be converted to humming traffic lanes.

595 PROPERTIES IN THE PATHS

The ball park is one of 595 properties in the paths of the proposed superhighways.

Among other casualties would be Binghamton's spanking new $163,000 North Side Veterans Memorial Swimming Pool at Stow Flats, which was dedicated in ceremonies last May 30.

State officials said Johnson Field and the municipal North Side pool easily could be rebuilt near their present locations with federal and state reimbursement.

Under the state-proposed plan, Penn-Can and the new Route 17 Expressway would share a six-lane right-of-way from Five Mile Point over State Hospital Hill and through sections of Binghamton's 12th and 13th Wards to Stow Flats.

From that point, almost exactly at the swimming pool, Penn-Can would veer north across the Chenango River—on twin bridges—and parallel Upper Front Street, running along the river flats.

The Route 17 Expressway, narrowing to four lanes, would cross the Chenango River southwest of Stow Flats and pass through Binghamton's First Ward, Johnson City's North Side, Oakdale, Endwell, over the Susquehanna River, and through Twin Orchards, Vestal Gardens and Vestal.

The speed limit would be 50 miles an hour on both expressways. For a continuous flow of traffic, there would be no stop lights.

Each traffic lane would be at least 12 feet wide. All-weather shoulders, 12 feet wide, would be on both sides of each superhighway. Both highways would be graded for an additional lane on each side for possible future use.

Malls would divide opposing traffic streams to prevent head-on collisions. The malls would vary in width from more than 100 feet to a minimum of 20 feet in Johnson City.

COULD CAUSE BATTLE ROYAL

The new "roads of tomorrow" obviously would have a profound effect on the traffic patterns and the commerce of the community. They are laid out as the fulfillment of the dreams of motorists and truckers.

The plan also could whip up a controversy that might make this year's battle against an earlier proposed Hillcrest routing of the Penn-Can Highway seem like a tempest in a teapot.

For instance, 566 houses accomodating 650 families would be torn down or removed for the expressway routes.

Also knocked out would be Binghamton's Calvary Baptist Church, recently rebuilt after a fire; state police barracks at Five Mile Point, a portion of Phelps Park in the city's 13th Ward; the Vestal American Legion clubhouse, both of the drive-in theatres in this area and 22 other commercial establishments.

On the other hand, state officials said the 20.6 miles of the two expressways would be on land classified as vacant, farm or scattered residential along 71.5 per cent of the right-of-way in the area.

The $2,500,000-a-mile expressway program was recom-

(Continued on Page 3 A)

To Regain Prestige

U. S. Must Send Men Into Space, Say Savants

Washington —(AP)— Some American scientists believe the only way the United States can regain prestige in the wake of Russia's earth satellite launching is to be first in sending a man into space.

"Some of us believe we should do this any way we could," said one of these scientists, adding that the launching of an American space satellite would not have the desired effect.

The specialists holding this view say they feel the United States could launch a manned space vehicle if the program received popular and financial support. A "really strong" scientific effort in this field, they say, could yield results within 12 to 18 months.

This group of scientists professes to be deeply concerned over what they believe to be American indifference to Soviet Russia's technological strides.

These persons long have been interested in the study of outer space. Other scientific groups have considered space flight to be largely in the realm of science fiction.

A number of American space scientists earlier this month attended the tenth annual assembly of the International Astronautic Federation in Barcelona.

There, they heard Russian delegates say, when asked about further Sputnik plans, "Watch Nov. 7—we'll do something then that's never been seen before." That is the fortieth anniversary of the Bolshevik revolution.

Some of the American scientists suspect the Reds will try something spectacular, such as a shot at the moon. There have been a number of published reports to this effect.

"The Russians have greater capability than we have to do this, and if they want to they can do it," said one American. "It looks like we are going to take another scientific blow."

The space science group believes the U. S. has failed to recognize the speed at which technology is advancing. And it says that U. S. industry is just beginning to realize the rapid rate of change.

"It's quite unlikely we will ever fight the war we are preparing for, and it's likely we will lose the war we are fighting now unless we wake up to the situation," one of the scientists said.

"We are not in shape to fight this war. It is a war of minds, and the troops are the scientists and the press."

Democrats Blast GOP Arms Cut

Washington — (AP) — The Democratic Advisory Council yesterday accused the Eisenhower administration of having undertaken "unilateral disarmament at the expense of our national security . . . in the face of Russia's rapid progress in science and technology."

If continued, the council said, the present policy "will, by 1960, take the United States far toward political isolation, continue to weaken our military position relative to the Russians, and leave those nations of the still free world which are capable of industrial development looking to Moscow for capital and technical assistance."

The council's views were contained in a statement issued after the first session of a two-day meeting here. The statement was approved by all 17 council members present, including Adlai Stevenson, two-time Democratic presidential nominee. Paul M. Butler, national committee chairman, said former President Harry S. Truman, one of the seven council members unable to attend, had endorsed the statement.

The council's statement basically followed the recommendations of a foreign policy advisory committee headed by former Secretary of State Dean Acheson.

Israeli Jet Fires on Airliner

Cairo—(AP)—The American pilot of the Air Jordan passenger plane reported last night an Israeli jet fighter fired on the plane five times over Jordan territory in a vain effort to force him to land in Israel.

The Air Jordan craft was not hit. It landed safely at Cairo with its 14 passengers and 4 crew members unharmed.

Capt. Jesse Stallworth of Pine Bluff, Ark., said in an interview the incident occurred about 50 miles north-northeast of Aqaba, Jordan, in midafternoon as he was flying the DC3 on flight 201 from the Jordanian sector of Jerusalem to Cairo.

He said the Israeli jet crossed his path, made two passes around the plane and indicated it should head from the Arab nation toward Israeli territory.

"When I tried to continue on my regular course, the Israeli plane opened fire at us five times," Stallworth said. "Each time he fired approximately 25 rounds of ammunition. The shots came so close we flew through puffs of smoke, but apparently we weren't hit. Frankly I don't see how he missed us."

Let's Chuckle

Some people are so prejudiced they won't even listen to both sides of a phonograph record.

Light Plane Crash Fatal To Iowa Man

Johnstown, Pa. —(AP)— Two hunters and a squad of volunteer firemen yesterday found one man dead and another seriously injured in the wreckage of their light plane on a nearby mountain knoll.

State police identified the victims as Marvin L. McMains, the dead man, of Des Moines, Iowa; and Earl Howard, 41, the pilot, of Ames; Iowa.

Howard was rushed to Memorial Hospital in Johnstown where he was listed in serious condition with head injuries.

The single-engine Beechcraft Bonanza crashed in a rugged, wooded area on Laurel Hill Mountain near Keefer's Corners about seven miles south of Johnstown.

It was not immediately learned when the plane crashed, but residents of the Keefer's Corners section reported hearing a low-flying plane Friday night. Volunteer firemen searched at the time but found no trace of a plane. Early yesterday the wreckage was spotted from the air.

Cleaner Air Week

Albany — (AP) — Branding air pollution a hazard to the health, welfare and efficiency of New Yorkers, Gov. Averell Harriman yesterday designated this week as Cleaner Air Week in the state.

Sunday Press Index

October 20, 1957: News of how highways would slice the Triple Cities dominated the front page. *Courtesy Rudy Bystrak*

GOOD MORNING!

A man can't expect a train of thought to help him unless he works up enough steam to operate it.

The Binghamton Sun

"FIRST IN THE HOMES OF SOUTHERN NEW YORK AND NORTHERN PENNSYLVANIA FOR MORE THAN A CENTURY"

TODAY'S WEATHER

LOCAL FORECAST — Cloudy, windy and mild with occasional rain. High 55-60. (Official Map and Summary on P. 12)

ONE HUNDRED AND THIRTY-SIXTH YEAR No. 23 — BINGHAMTON, N. Y., FRIDAY, NOVEMBER 15, 1957 — ★ ★ ★ FINAL — PRICE FIVE CENTS

65 HOODLUMS ROUNDED UP IN APALACHIN

Mays Gets Home In San Francisco

AP Wirephoto

HAPPY ENDING — Willie Mays (shown above with his wife), Giants' center-fielder, finally got his home in an all-white San Francisco neighborhood. It was sold to him by Walter A. Gnesdiloff (bottom right), who turned down Mays' offer earlier because of what he called heavy pressure exerted on him by persons in the neighborhood.

SAN FRANCISCO, Nov. 14 (AP)— Negro baseball star Willie Mays bought a $37,500 home in a San Francisco all-white area today, ending a controversy that flared as some neighbors objected on racial grounds.

The property owner, who had announced earlier he would sell to the San Francisco Giants' world famed center fielder, accepted a check to close the deal with Mays.

"The opposition from neighbors is practically all over. Some people just don't understand."

Gnesdiloff said earlier that he had turned down Mays originally because heavy pressure was put on him in the neighborhood.

When he heard Howden's report, Willie commented with relief that he hoped to complete the deal at once. He said he plans to return to New York with his wife in a few days to dispose of the home they own there.

"It's a nice place, with a good view and we want to live here," Mays said of the San Francisco home he is buying. It is a new place on a high hillside.

Mays and his wife had been badly upset by the incident, which she said was their second such turndown in San Francisco since the Giants moved to the West Coast.

ROUGH LANDING

MASSENA, N.Y., Nov. 14 (AP)—Both engines of an Eastern Airlines plane were torn off today in a rough landing at Massena Airport. No one was injured, Eastern reported.

Senate Probe Witnesses Invoke Fifth

WASHINGTON, Nov. 14 (UP) — C. Don Modica, bespectacled former philosophy tutor who said he "couldn't get a job as dishwasher" now, took the Fifth Amendment today when called before a Senate investigation of New York racketeering.

Modica, who refused to say whether he had tutored the children of the late Albert Anastasia and other gangsters, followed another Fifth Amendment witness — Nunzio Squillante, alleged "enforcer" of a trash collection racket.

Headed Picket Crew

Squillante was pictured by a Long Island department store operator as the apparent leader of a union picket crew which persuaded him to sign a garbage hauling contract with the non-union General Sanitation Co. headed by Squillante, in 1954.

In a high-pitched voice that contrasted strangely with his rugged features, Squillante refused to testify about this or even to say whether he had ever heard of the Fifth Amendment which he was invoking.

Modica likewise refused to answer questions of the Senate Rackets Investigating Committee on the ground they might tend to incriminate him.

Committee counsel Robert F. Kennedy covered considerable ground in questioning the reluctant witness whom he frequently called "the professor."

Kennedy said Modica had told staff interviewers that he was "very close" to the Anastasia family, and had been one of the last to see him after Anastasia was shot and killed in a New York hotel barber shop last month.

"Mrs. Anastasia is the godmother of his (Modica's) daughter," Kennedy said.

Link to Anastasia

White Student Strikes Negro In Little Rock

LITTLE ROCK, Ark., Nov. 14 (AP)—Officials at racially integrated Little Rock Central High today said that a white boy had been suspended for striking a Negro boy. The incident occurred Tuesday.

Village Ordered To Supply Water

CHICAGO, Nov. 14 (AP)—A judge today told the village of Maywood to supply water to a Negro family until the court settles the question of whether the water was turned off because they are Negroes.

The superior court suit brought by Mr. and Mrs. Jessie Carmichael contends officials of the suburban community denied them water because of their race.

But the village counsel, Louis Ancel, said violations of ordinances governing new dwellings—not any race question—are involved.

The Carmichaels, through their attorneys, sought an injunction forbidding the village from continuing to deny them water.

Judge Norman C. Barry said he wants village officials to supply the water, pending another hearing on the injunction Monday.

AP Wirephoto

MODICA ON STAND. Don (The Professor) Modica appears before the Senate rackets committee. He refused to answer questions about his alleged activities with gangsters in the garbage hauling business in New York.

Small Arms Being Sent To Tunisia

WASHINGTON, Nov. 14 (AP)—The United States and Britain brushed aside strong French protests today and ordered a token shipment of small arms sent to Tunisia.

First Shipments To Arrive Today

TURKEY ACCUSED

Reserve Bank Lowers Discount Rate

WASHINGTON, Nov. 14 (AP)—The Federal Reserve Board, now said to be convinced that inflation is subsiding, today took a firm step to ease the tight money market.

HARRIMAN 66

United Nations Votes New Arms Meeting

UNITED NATIONS, N.Y., Nov. 14 (AP) — The United Nations called today for new talks to break the disarmament deadlock despite the Soviet Union's announcement it will refuse to take part in them.

By a vote of 56-9 the 82-nation General Assembly approved a Western resolution asking for new negotiations in the five-nation UN Disarmament Subcommittee with priority given Western proposals.

Only the Soviet bloc opposed the resolution. Fifteen nations abstained and two were absent.

Assembly Meets Today

Outside Move On

Bakery Union Chief Won't Resign Office

Searchers Recover 15 Bodies From Sea

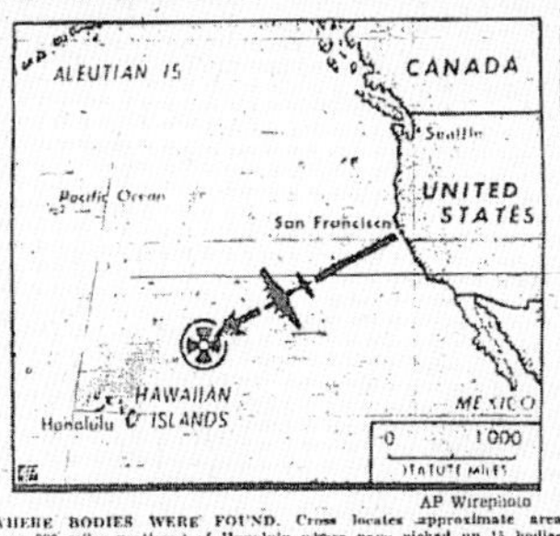

ALEUTIAN IS
CANADA
Seattle
Pacific Ocean
UNITED STATES
San Francisco
HAWAIIAN ISLANDS
Honolulu
MEXICO
0
1000
STATUTE MILES

AP Wirephoto

WHERE BODIES WERE FOUND. Cross locates approximate area some 900 miles northeast of Honolulu where navy picked up 15 bodies in water where a Pan American Airways plane disappeared last week.

HONOLULU, Nov. 14 (AP) — Fifteen bodies, all shoeless and most with lifejackets from the lost airliner Romance of the Skies, were sighted today from an 11 by 3 mile debris-scattered area of the Pacific 955 miles northeast of here, the aircraft carrier Philippine Sea reported.

May Have Tried to Land

Ike Searches for Money To Meet Space Needs

Truman Predicts Tax Cut

★ ★ ★

Soviets Solve Re-entry Puzzle

New Rights Board Meeting in Dec.

Eastern Coast Racketeers in Confab Here

By DAVE ROSSIE

A conclave of 65 hoodlums from various parts of the United States, Cuba and Puerto Rico, including several described by police as "the hierarchy of crime on the Eastern Seaboard" was broken up yesterday by state police in a day-light raid on a palatial Apalachin residence.

Biggest "catch" in the police net was Vito Genovese, 59, of Atlantic Highlands, NJ, questioned recently in regard to the gangland slaying of Albert Anastasia in a New York City barbershop.

All were released shortly before 1:30 this morning.

"We haven't a thing on them," said Sgt. Croswell, "but we made it clear we wanted them out of this area."

Parking Lot Filled

Plenty of Money

Five Area Hoods

(Continued on Page 13)

Won't Force Resignation

Brother's Sacrifice Melts Air Secretary

WASHINGTON, Nov. 14 (AP)—Air Force Secretary James Douglas tonight tossed the rulebook out the window and voided the forced resignation of a lieutenant who wants to give one of his kidneys to save his twin brother's life.

The officer is Lieut. Samuel Merriman of the Oklahoma Air National Guard who is stationed at Hondo Air Force Base, Texas.

November 14, 1957: Willie Mays, perhaps the greatest ballplayer of all time, finally was allowed to buy a house in an all-white neighborhood in San Francisco. And the gangland convention proved there was a national mob. *Microfilm archives*

GOOD MORNING!
Uprooting a bad habit is never effective unless you stick a good one in the hole.

The Binghamton Sun

"FIRST IN THE HOMES OF SOUTHERN NEW YORK AND NORTHERN PENNSYLVANIA FOR MORE THAN A CENTURY"

TODAY'S WEATHER
LOCAL FORECAST—Increasing cloudiness followed by some rain by night. High 48-53.
(Official Map and Summary on Page 2)

ONE HUNDRED AND THIRTY-SIXTH YEAR No. 24 — BINGHAMTON, N. Y., SATURDAY, NOVEMBER 16, 1957 — ★ ★ ★ — FINAL — PRICE FIVE CENTS

NEWSMAN BOOTED BY BARBARA'S SON

Senators Say Mafia Trying to Rule Nation

Burglars Ignore Cups and Caps; Annoy Pruzzlers

No wonder we didn't have a winner this week! The judges admit Pruzzle No. 8 of the new series was one of the toughest we have ever had. Out of more than 4,000 entries, many of them submitting more than one solution, nobody came close to gathering in the $200 jackpot. So it's upped to $225 for No. 9 with the hope this one will be a cinch and that one of you good people will come through and get something extra to be thankful for a week from Thursday. A great many thought a burglar would be less likely to steal a "cap" than a "cup" without thinking that the word "ordinarily" leaves a loophole. Of course a burglar would steal a gold cup, or trophy, but he wouldn't bother with a cap — or would he? "Fears" and "tears" stumped a lot of Pruzzlers. Tears arise from a mental disturbance but fears are the mental disturbance. There were some others, "past" for "pact," that old one about "poem" and "poet," and the "bitter-fitter" thing. A boxer could be bitter after losing a fight but it stands to reason he wouldn't be fitter. It all seems simple enough when you think it over. So try it again, and good luck.

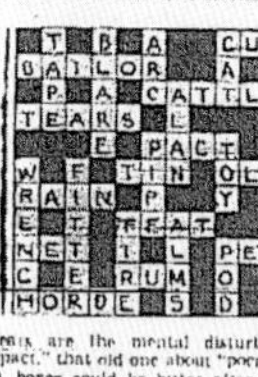

McElroy to Name Space Manager

WASHINGTON, Nov. 15 (AP)—Secretary of Defense McElroy, acknowledging Russia has seized the lead in satellites and missiles, announced plans today to put a new general manager in charge of such futuristic projects as anti-missile missiles and space vehicles.

One major purpose of the move is to avoid pulling and hauling among the armed services — a rivalry which some critics say has hampered progress on missiles and satellites.

Killian Sworn In

In another effort to catch up with the Soviets, Dr. James R. Killian Jr., president of the Massachusetts Institute of Technology, was sworn in this morning as President Eisenhower's scientific-military co-ordinator.

McElroy told his first full dress news conference at the Pentagon that it "seems rather obvious to me that we are behind the Russians" in missile and satellite development.

He then said that within a month the Defense Department hopes to appoint a single manager for what he called "upstream" type projects such as the anti-missile missile and military application of space vehicles.

Under this new manager, McElroy said, the Defense Department would have direct operating responsibility for research, development and engineering of future space vehicles or weapons up to the point where they can be turned over to a single military service for actual use.

The defense chief said he hoped such an arrangement would avoid wasteful competition among the military services in the early stages of weapon development.

A new title and expanded authority was announced for William M. Holaday, the secretary's guided missile aide. McElroy said Holaday would become director of guided missiles. It appeared that Holaday would continue to have supervision over missile programs that are operational or in an advanced stage of development.

McElroy said the best man available would be obtained for the new job of space chief and that he might be drawn from either civilian or military ranks.

The Pentagon developments overshadowed to some extent Dr. K[illegible] entrance into the [illegible] as Eisenhower's $2[illegible],000 a year assistant for science and technology.

Mysterious Objects Are Dismissed

WASHINGTON, Nov. 15 (AP) — The air force said today it has looked into five recent reports of mysterious lights and strange objects from the sky—and there isn't a flying saucer in the lot.

The air force report gave the most severe description — hoax — to the most vivid of the stories that began circulating after Soviet satellites turned the attention of Americans skyward. This was a Kearney, Neb., man's account of being shown around the interior of a spaceship by its German-speaking crew.

But the air force technical investigators also dismissed as exaggerations or misunderstood natural phenomena stories of a huge glowing object touching ground near Levelland, Texas, and causing automobiles to stall; somewhat similar reports from near Alamogordo, NM; bright lights seen from a coast guard cutter in the Gulf of Mexico and by planes patrolling near White Sands, NM.

KC Star Enjoined In Monopoly Suit

KANSAS CITY, Nov. 15 (AP)—The Kansas City Star was enjoined from engaging in business practices which the government charged were monopolistic and ordered to dispose of its radio and television broadcasting facilities under terms of a consent decree filed in Federal District Court today.

Signing of the decree in the chambers of Federal Dist. Judge Richard M. Duncan ended three years of anti-trust litigation against the Star in which the newspaper was charged with attempting to monopolize and monopolizing dissemination of news and advertising in the Kansas City area.

ORDERED DEPORTED

BUFFALO, NY, Nov. 15 (AP)—Giuseppe La Marca, 32, who is wanted in Italy for a list of crimes dating from the end of World War II, has been ordered deported from the U. S., the Immigration Service announced today.

PLEAS FOR SCHOOL

OYSTER BAY, NY, Nov. 15 (AP)—The President of the State University tonight renewed his plea for a four-year, science-engineering college on Long Island.

May Be Tied To Teamsters; Inquiry Near

WASHINGTON, Nov. 15 (AP) — Members of the Senate committee investigating criminal activities in New York City's garbage collection industry today disclosed that they intend to find out whether the Mafia, or Black Hand criminal society is involved with the giant Teamsters Union "generally," and is trying to take over the country.

"We know there is a lot of corruption and racketeering in the Teamsters," Sen. Irving Ives of Norwich, vice-chairman of the Senate Investigating Committee said, "and I think we ought to find out how much the Mafia is responsible."

Have Some Information

Chief committee counsel Robert F. Kennedy immediately revealed that "we have some information on that," and added that he expects to develop it later.

He said he had seen the list of those present at the Apalachin meeting of gangland's hierarchy "and some of them we are interested in." He indicated some of those attending would be quizzed by staff investigators.

"We've got to determine if the government is bigger than hoodlums and crooks," chairman McClellan (D-Ark) declared, "or if they are running this country. We've got to, we have to, or the hoodlums are going to take over . . ."

In actual testimony before the committee today, Vincent (Jimmy) Squillante, who has been pictured as the big man in the New York rackets despite his diminutive 122 pounds, refused to answer whether he was a member of the Mafia, or a dealer in narcotics.

The 5 foot 1½ inch Squillante, alleged overlord of a 50 million dollar a year trash collecting industry, pleaded the fifth amendment in answer to a series of questions, including one as to whether he actually was the godson of the slain Albert Anastasia, as he has boasted on occasion.

Questioned on Fund

He was called before the rackets investigating committee after a staff investigator told of a garbage collectors' fund established last year for the defense of Squillante "in any shape or form."

The investigator, James P. Kelly, testified the $57,855 fund was set up at a June 7, 1956 meeting of the Greater New York Cartmen's Assn., a trade organization for garbage and refuse collectors in New York City. The association has been pictured in previous testimony as under Squillante's domination.

Minutes of the meeting read by Kelly quoted Squillante as telling association members that the fund should be used for five purposes:

"1. Defense of the association and its members.

"2. Defense of Vincent J. Squillante in any shape or form.

"3. Defense of any cartman . . .

"4. Publicity advertising . . . research.

"5. Any charitable action for the benefit of mankind."

Laika Wasn't Coming Back

MOSCOW, Nov. 15 (AP) - A Soviet scientist said today the dog Laika was allowed to die aboard Sputnik II because the Russians have not yet solved the problem of re-entry into the earth's atmosphere.

Alexei Pokrovsky told a news conference attended by six other leading Soviet scientists there never was a plan to bring the dog back to earth, as even some Russians scientists had suggested.

He said the dog died painlessly of oxygen deficiency when equipment that regenerated oxygen in the whizzing earth satellite had completed its work.

Povrovsky, director of the laboratory where dogs are trained for space flight, said several more satellites with animals aboard must be launched before the first human space flight is attempted.

"We must first solve the problem of returning animals safely to earth before we can risk human life," he said.

Army Raises Draft Call for January

WASHINGTON, Nov. 15 (AP)—The Army today raised its draft call for January to 10,000 men and forecast even higher induction quotas through next June.

The January figure is 3,000 more than the quota announced for December.

Asst. Secretary of the Army Hugh Milton told reporters that increased drafts are necessary for the first six months of 1958 even though the Army is now dropping 100,000 men in line with manpower cut-backs ordered some months ago by former Defense Secretary Wilson.

48 Killed In British Crack-up

NEWPORT, Isle of Wight, Saturday, Nov. 16 (AP)—A four-engine British Solent flying boat crashed in flames on a wooded hillside near Newport last night and 43 of the 58 persons aboard were believed killed.

Only 15 are known to have survived.

Firemen pulled a number of survivors from the wreckage. Some were in serious condition.

The big plane, belonging to the British Aquila Airline, crashed with 50 passengers and crew of 8 shortly after taking off from Southampton on a trip to Lisbon, Portugal.

Trees were set ablaze and a police officer who rushed to the scene said the only recognizable part of the plane was the tail, "sticking up above the flames."

It was the second accident involving an Aquila plane this year. Last March one of the line's Solents hit a rock while taking off from Majorca. On that occasion all the 60 aboard climbed on the wing of the plane and were rescued by launches.

2 More Bodies Found in Ocean

HONOLULU, Nov. 15 (AP)—The sea yielded up two more broken bodies today and there was more evidence that all 44 persons aboard probably died swiftly and violently when Pan American's Stratocruiser "Romance of the Skies" met her fate with terrific force a week ago.

That made 39 bodies recovered, 17 of them yesterday.

The navy carrier Philippine Sea radioed from the search scene that the plane struck the sea so hard it disintegrated and the victims died within the hour if not immediately.

The report added this grim note: "Some sharks were seen in the area."

OFFER EXCHANGE

WASHINGTON, Nov. 15 (AP)—The United States has called on Russia to stop banning travel by U. S. citizens to nearly one third of Soviet territory, offering a similar relaxation on Russians' traveling here in return.

TEST COMPLETED

WASHINGTON, Nov. 15 (AP)—The Defense Department said a test vehicle was launched today at the missile test base at Cape Canaveral, Fla.

PHOTOG KICKING PRINCIPALS. Charles Carson (with camera in top picture), a news photographer for the New York Journal American, shows his damaged [illegible] graphic to Endicott Acting Police Justice Michael S. L. Buran as he swears out a warrant for the arrest of Joseph Barbara, Jr., 21, of Apalachin, whom he accused of kicking the camera and his hand. Standing in top picture are (left) Edward Newman, a reporter for the Journal American, and Lee Sands (between Carson and Buran), an Endicott detective. In photo below, Barbara (center) is arraigned before Justice Buran in Police Court, where the defendant pleaded not guilty. At the left of Barbara is his attorney, Edwin Lachman. At right are Broome County District Attorney Louis M. Greenblott and Assistant District Attorney Stephen Smyk.

Ask Federal Permission

States Want to Tax to Build Schools

WASHINGTON, Nov. 15 (AP)—State governors today formally offered to launch state-aided school construction programs in place of President Eisenhower's federal aid plan, in return for the right to collect local telephone and some other taxes.

An administration spokesman said the idea will get serious consideration. Some other officials suggested privately it might influence Eisenhower not to repeat his school construction recommendation when Congress meets in January.

The Eisenhower plan sent to congress last session called for a four-year program costing 352 million dollars a year. There was no final action on the plan. The tax on local telephone service now collected by the federal government brings in about 370 million dollars in annual revenue.

The governor's proposal was announced by Gov. Lane Dwinell of New Hampshire after a two-day session of the joint federal-state action committee drafting proposals to restore some federal functions to the states and cities.

The eight-member governors committee, dis[illegible] of the conference of state governors, released a statement affirming the conference's position that states and localities should bear the responsibility for public school construction costs.

Labor Organization Suspends Bakers

WASHINGTON, Nov. 15 (AP)—The AFL-CIO suspended the Bakery Workers Union from AFL-CIO membership today on grounds of corruption.

President James G. Cross pleaded in vain for the union kept on [illegible] against the ouster.

He told a news conference the action was illegal, that the AFL-CIO has no business ordering a member union to throw out duly elected officers.

Cross was one of the AFL-CIO leaders specifically [illegible] accused of [illegible] having [illegible] deals with employers.

And Cross said—perhaps significantly—that the Bakers Union has a mutual assistance pact with the Teamsters Union, whose members transport the products of 90 per cent of the bakeries that the union has organized.

The Teamsters [illegible] are under AFL-CIO suspension on charges of corruption.

Kasper Must Serve Another 6 Months

KNOXVILLE, Tenn., Nov. 15 (AP)—John Kasper was sentenced to another six months in prison today by a federal judge who, in a sharp but patient reprimand, blamed Clinton's school integration troubles squarely on the Northern segregationist.

The sentence was imposed by U. S. Dist. Judge Robert L. Taylor, who was lenient with the six residents of the nearby Clinton area who were convicted with Kasper in July of criminal contempt of court.

Youngster Kicks Photographer; Charges Pressed

By ED FRANK

The 21-year-old son of Joseph Barbara, Sr., host to 58 mobsters Thursday in Apalachin, was accused yesterday of kicking a New York City newspaper photographer who was attempting to get pictures of the Canada Dry Bottling Co. plant in Endicott.

Charles Carson, a photographer for the Journal-American, swore out a warrant for the arrest of Joseph Barbara, Jr., also of Apalachin, after he said he was kicked in his hand and his camera damaged by the husky youngster.

Barbara, Carson said, chased him around a number of parked cars in the Badger Avenue parking lot of the plant and then down Badger Avenue.

"I told him to stop," Carson said, "or I'd jam my camera down his throat." After that, he said, Barbara called off the chase.

The photographer was with three reporters who visited the bottling plant operated by the senior Barbara shortly before 5 pm.

He was looking around for a likely picture, Carson said, when Barbara came storming out of the plant and asked him what he was doing. Before he could reply, Carson said, "he kicked me in the hand carrying the camera."

Barbara Asks for Film

Carson, a 54-year-old veteran newspaper photographer, said he ran around the cars with Barbara right behind him. As he dashed down Badger Avenue, Barbara asked for the film.

"I took the film holder out of my camera," Carson said, "and tossed it to the ground. Then he wanted the one in my pocket. I told him it hadn't been used, but he wanted it anyway, so I threw that one out."

"Conservatively, I'd say he kicked at me 12 times during the chase, landing three times."

The photographer insisted that had Barbara asked him not to take any pictures of the plant, he would have gone along with him. "It was dark, anyway, and besides it wasn't much of a shot. I don't think my paper would have even used it."

OTHER PICTURE, STORY ON P. 3

Carson said he was willing to forget the matter, but a telephone call to his newspaper in New York City by Edward Newman, a Journal American reporter working with Carson, found instructions to press charges.

With him at the time were Newman, Carl Pelleck of the New York Post, and Jerry Nerney, a reporter for the Endicott Daily Bulletin.

Picks Up Holders

Miss Nerney said Barbara seemed to "come out of nowhere." She picked up one of the film holders tossed by Carson in his flight. "Barbara asked me to give it to him," Miss Nerney said, "and I told him he'd have to come and get it. He didn't, though."

After police were called by the Bulletin reporter, Carson and others went to headquarters where a warrant was issued by Acting Police Justice Stephen S. L. Buran.

Barbara was called at the bottling plant, police said, and he came to headquarters of his own accord accompanied by his attorney, Edwin Lachman, a village trustee.

Arraigned before Justice Buran on a third degree assault charge, he pleaded innocent. At the request of District Attorney Louis M. Greenblott, Justice Buran stayed the proceedings for presentation to a grand jury "for further investigation."

Although third degree assault is a misdemeanor and is not often carried to the grand jury, Mr. Greenblott said his office has the authority to make such a switch and thought it best under the circumstances.

Bail was fixed at $1,000 cash by Justice Buran. Unable to immediately raise the money, Barbara was freed in the custody of his attorney until this morning, when bail is expected to be posted.

Has Bruised Knuckle

Carson got off with a bruised knuckle on his right hand, and damage to his speed graphic was said to be minor. He was examined by a physician before arraignment, but said he did not require hospital treatment.

He told The Sun he has been a newspaper photographer for 25 years, 10 of them with the Journal American. Only once before he said, was he ever kicked.

"I've been chased before," he said, "and I had a counterfeiter kick at me in Federal Court. He was handcuffed to another prisoner, though, and wasn't able to do much damage."

As a result of the State Police raid Thursday in Apalachin which netted 58 hoodlums, the top boys in the East Coast rackets, the Journal American assigned Carson and Newman to the area to do a "color story" on Apalachin.

They were in the hamlet that overnight gained fame, most of the afternoon, talking with residents and getting statements. All in all, it was a bad day for Carson, for he got few pictures there, also.

"The people would talk, all right," he said, "but they didn't want to be photographed."

Barbara, a husky former Union-Endicott High School football player who weighs well over 200 pounds, was subdued in court. After the incident at the plant, he talked quietly to reporters and appeared to be rather hospitable.

A worker at the bottling works said he had been under a strain all day, with reporters from this area and out-of-town papers asking questions incessantly.

Baby's Slayer Says

'I Always Wanted to Kill'

RENO, Nev., Nov. 15 (AP)—A petulant-lipped 15-year-old reform school fugitive freely admitted today he smothered a 22-month-old baby girl in Los Angeles because of a long-standing impulse to kill someone.

"I always wanted to kill somebody—first it was my father," said blue-eyed John Lawrence (Larry) Miller. He was captured here today after a 950-mile flight over three states in three stolen cars.

"At first I was going to cut her up—but I got the willies."

The body of little Laura Wetzel, her clothing removed, was found by police Monday in a Los Angeles suburb shortly after young Miller, waving a rifle and knife, frightened her parents away from making their own grim discovery. The child was not molested sexually.

Larry, a fugitive from a Whittier, Calif., reform school, signed a confession witnessed by Reno Police Capt. Daryl Read, then talked matter-of-factly about the crime to newsmen.

"The little girl just happened to be the only one around," he said.

". . . I suffocated her with one hand over her mouth . . .

"I always wanted to kill somebody. I was always meeting somebody, some man, I didn't like and wanted to kill."

Then, reflecting back on the grisly incident, he added solemnly: "I haven't wanted to kill anybody since."

Earlier, however, after his capture at a Reno filling station, young Larry had said he would have fought it out with a stolen pistol—if he only knew how to use it. The pistol was found under the seat of his stolen car.

Larry, who was in reform school for auto theft and burglaries, said "I lost my love for my parents a long time ago," beginning with his placement in a military school.

Mrs. Charles Wetzel, of Rolling Hills Estates, Calif., mother of the slain child, wiped away tears on being told of the capture and said:

"I hope he's locked up forever and ever so he won't ever hurt anybody else."

"I didn't feel bad about killing her," Larry's signed confession concluded, "but afterward I knew I messed up my life."

South Greets Ike With Friendship

AUGUSTA, Ga., Nov. 15 (AP)—President Eisenhower was greeted just about exactly as usual—in an outwardly friendly manner—on his arrival in the Deep South today for the first time since he ordered troops into Little Rock, Ark.

This is the President's 16th visit to Augusta for a golfing holiday since his 1952 election, and his coming this time was completely without incident.

Abel Given 30 Years In Hope He May Talk

NEW YORK, Nov. 15 (AP)—Russian Col. Rudolf I. Abel, abandoned to his fate by his Soviet masters, today was sentenced to 30 years in prison as a spy. He could have gotten the death penalty.

Defense Atty. James Donovan, seeking mercy for the wispy little masterspy, held out the remote hope that Abel some day may have a change of heart and tell what he knows about the Red spy apparatus he so faithfully served. Abel declined to testify in his own behalf at his recent trial.

May Be Used in Exchange

Dr. Donovan added, the time may come when Abel can be used in an exchange to save the life of an American spy who might fall into Russian hands.

Abel also was fined $3,000 by Federal District Judge Mortimer W. Byers. He said the sentence best served "the interest of the United States in the present and foreseeable future."

From the moment of Abel's arrest last June 21, the Soviet government moved a hand to lend him aid. Traditionally, a spy expects no mercy when he is captured. But in prior espionage cases, the Russians have made determined efforts to aid nationals seized in this country.

Abel, 55, frowned but displayed no emotion at the sentence. He wore the same stoic, composed air that he maintained throughout a three-week trial. It ended Oct. 25 in his conviction in Brooklyn federal court.

November 16, 1957: More coverage of the Barbara mafia story. *Microfilm archives*

Joseph Barbara Sr., host to the 1957 underworld convention at Apalachin, is wheeled into the post office building in Syracuse for arraignment in Federal Court on tax evasion charges. At right is his attorney, Harry S. Travis. Pushing the wheel chair is Harry Flesher. *Press & Sun-Bulletin archives*

Joseph M. Barbara Jr., son of the late Apalachin meeting host, grins after receiving a suspended sentence and a one-year probation on a criminal contempt charge in New York City. Barbara Jr. refused to answer questions about the 1957 gangland meeting. *Press & Sun-Bulletin archives*

Joseph Barbara Sr. hosted a gangland convention at his house in Apalachin on Nov. 14, 1957. State police caught the crimelords attending a steak cookout. *Press & Sun-Bulletin archives*

Joseph Barbara's house in Apalachin. State police caught the crimelords attending a cookout here in 1957. *Press & Sun-Bulletin archives*

Pete Scott and the Montereys, a rock 'n' roll band from Binghamton, 1960. *Courtesy Pete Scott*

Mr. And Mrs. Richard M. Nixon visit Broome County in 1960. *Press & Sun-Bulletin archives*

Union-Endicott football field is under water during the 1960 flooding. *Courtesy Marlene Yacos*

Raymond F. Martin, patrolman, Binghamton Police Civil Defense Drill. The schools closed, business closed and no traffic was allowed. *Courtesy David R. Martin*

1960 - 1969

A decade of big news

Say It Isn't Sno

THE EVENING PRESS

THE HOMETOWN NEWSPAPER OF THE SOUTHERN TIER

Binghamton, N. Y., Thursday, Jan. 19, 1961 — Volume 82 — 238 — 30 Pages — 5 Cents

Read It In the Evening Press, Hear It Over WINR, See It on TV 40, 78, 81

EJ Management Wins Its Battle--- List to Sell Stock to Pension Fund

JFK Sees Ike, Takes Notebook

Last Briefing Involves World Trouble Spots

KENNEDY LISTENS—President-Elect John F. Kennedy listens to President Eisenhower as they pose at the White House today at the end of a conference on world problems.

MRS. JOHN F. KENNEDY — Back in Capital for Big Day

Rocky Bids to End Rail Tieup

Need Court Approval For $2,520,000 Deal

By JAMES HEAVEY

Movers, Fitters Make Jackie's Home Hectic

By HELEN THOMAS

'Everybody' in Capital For Inaugural Glitter

Slushy Time Is In Prospect For Inaugural

6 Yanks Held As Castro Foes

The Gown: Slim Skirt, Blousy Top

Johnson's Reception His Biggest

Halaby Named To Head FAA

Queen Names Archbishop

Abbas Wants Army to Go

Conklin Appointed

Are Teenagers Really 'Spoiled'?

Green Marks The Lobbyist

Jackson Seeks Divorce

Marriage 'Experts' Fail in Own Home

Traveling Music

4 Children Die In Rural Fire

Let's Chuckle

January 19, 1961: As JFK prepared to take office, word that EJ would remain in local hands dominated the news. The paper started calling itself The Evening Press in September 1960 to reflect circulation growth that had expanded well past Binghamton. *Courtesy Dolly Escovar*

The events in the 1960s threatened to overwhelm us all, as the news ranged from the horror of assassinations to the excitement of men on the moon.

In the three-county area around Binghamton, the population continued to swell. A 7 percent increase by the end of the decade put the population at 314,696. Tioga County grew at the fastest rate.

The Binghamton Press, recognizing it served a much larger area than the city, changed its name to The Evening Press in 1960. By 1965 the paper outgrew its Chenango Street home and moved to the Vestal Parkway.

For the people who worked at the paper, the name change and the move were big events. But measured against the news of the decade, they were small items indeed:

John and Robert Kennedy and Martin Luther King Jr. were killed. Opposition to the Vietnam War stopped Lyndon Johnson from seeking a second term. The Civil Rights Act outlawed many practices that had suppressed millions of black Americans for the decades following the abolition of slavery.

In one of the biggest tragedies in Binghamton's history, six babies died at Binghamton General Hospital when a nurse mistakenly put salt in infant formula instead of sugar. The story made worldwide headlines.

Endicott Johnson closed factories and tanneries. Its business waned and by the end of the decade, the company passed into the hands of the McDonough Corp. EJ's new leader, Harold McGowan, promised a return to boom times. It was a promise he could not fulfill.

As EJ was deteriorating, IBM was booming. And in 1961, in a move that would eventually have profound effects on the region's economy, the SUNY-Binghamton campus opened in Vestal.

Inaugur-ice-ion

WEATHER BUREAU FORECAST
Variable cloudiness, windy, cold with snow flurries tonight and Saturday. Low tonight zero to 5 below. High Saturday 5-10.

BINGHAMTON TEMPERATURES
[illegible]

THE EVENING PRESS

THE HOMETOWN NEWSPAPER OF THE SOUTHERN TIER

Binghamton, N. Y., Friday, Jan. 20, 1961 — Volume 82 — 239 — 30 Pages — 5 Cents

★ ★
Read It
In the Evening Press,
Hear It Over WINR,
See It on TV 40, 78, 81

Kennedy Calls for New Peace Quest At Snow-Blanketed Inauguration

—Associated Press WIREPHOTO.

NEW PRESIDENT IS SWORN IN — Chief Justice Earl Warren administers oath of office as President of United States to John F. Kennedy in Washington today. Lyndon B. Johnson, the new Vice-President, is at right. Holding Bible at center is James R. Browning, clerk of Supreme Court.

Takes Oath With Plea To World

TEXT of Kennedy address, Page 6.

By UP-International

Washington — John Fitzgerald Kennedy began his presidency in a time of awesome troubles today by summoning the world's peoples, Communist and non-Communist, to "a grand and global alliance" against "tyranny, poverty, disease and war."

At 12:51 p. m., Kennedy, at 43, the youngest man ever elected president and the first Catholic, solemnly took the oath of office as the nation's 35th chief executive. To the 172-year-old oath he added, as George Washington had done, the words, "So help me God."

Then, head bared to a freezing wind in a city glittering under a 7-inch blanket of snow, he addressed himself not only to his countrymen but to "my fellow citizens of the world."

'PAY ANY PRICE'

Solemnly to the Communist nations he said, "Let us begin anew" the quest for peace. To all nations, whether they "wish us well or ill," he made this promise:

We shall pay any price, bear any burden, meet any hardship, support any friend or oppose any foe in order to assure the survival and success of liberty."

Standing on a red carpet in the imposing stand erected for his inauguration on the east steps of the Capitol, in the presence of his wife and parents and two former presidents, he called for a new beginning toward a world of peace and justice.

The new President had begun the most solemn day of his life by attending a special Mass "in honor of the Holy Spirit" at 9 a.m. Then he had ridden to the capitol from the White House with his predecessor, Dwight D. Eisenhower who, at 70, was the oldest man ever to serve in the White House.

SELDOM SMILES

During the long ceremonies preceding the oath-taking, he conversed seriously with Mr. Eisenhower. He smiled seldom.

The ceremony was slow in getting started, and he took the historic oath 40 minutes later than the scheduled time. Before and after the invocation, Kennedy made the sign of the cross.

Two of the three living former presidents, Mr. Eisenhower

(Continued on Page 9)

—Associated Press WIREPHOTO.

THE KENNEDYS—John F. Kennedy and his wife, Jacqueline, appear at last night's inaugural gala in Washington.

Lectern Smokes At Start

Washington — (UPI) — Smoke wisped out of the speaker's lectern today at John F. Kennedy's inauguration.

The smoke blew into the faces of Mr. Kennedy, outgoing President Eisenhower and others in the forefront of the inauguration platform.

There was a noticeable smell of burning wire, much like an electrical short circuit. It appeared to get slightly worse as Richard Cardinal Cushing of Boston delivered the invocation.

EXPERTS CALLED

A technician and a fireman tinkered with the electrical connections in order to find the trouble. Senator John J. Sparkman, inaugural chairman, also showed concern during the invocation and signaled for a technician.

Secret service agents moved in immediately.

There was brief delay as the cause was sought but Sparkman finally went ahead and introduced Marian Anderson to sing "The Star-Spangled Banner" despite the continued smoking from inside the lectern box.

There was a gush of blue smoke for a second but firemen apparently located the trouble.

Some observers thought they detected a small fire break out at the bottom of the lectern.

GUARDS CRAWL

A fire extinguisher was summoned quickly and guards crawled around on the red-carpeted floor trying to find the source of the smoke.

Mr. Kennedy, Mr. Eisenhower, Vice-President Lyndon B. Johnson, and outgoing Vice-President Richard M. Nixon all appeared to show some concern at first but then later grinned, then chuckled together when the trouble was apparently rectified and the smoke stopped.

During the incident, Mr. Eisenhower fished into an outside pocket for a handkerchief, which he transferred to his overcoat pocket.

Heroes of Big Snow Open D. C. Streets

Washington—(UPI)—A miracle of toil today won Washington's all-night battle against a eight-inch snow storm which had threatened to bog down the presidential inaugural ceremonies for John F. Kennedy.

An unsung army of workers had cleared all traces of snow from the historic parade route down Pennsylvania Avenue by dawn. The work crews then switched to the swearing-in site at the Capitol Plaza for back-breaking dig - out operations there.

Inaugural Day dawned sunny and bright after a nightmarish night of toil by work crews of laborers and army troops to clear the snow deposited by the severe storm.

The storm had passed by early morning.

By 6 a. m., the Pennsylvania Avenue parade route from the Capitol to the White House had been cleared with chemicals, snow equipment and sheer hard work. A force of 3,000 laborers and troops, 500 dump trucks, 200 snowplows, dozens of wreckers and army graders and tons of salt and sand were thrown into the all-night struggle.

An estimated 10,000 cars were stalled and abandoned in Washington. Forty-two vehicles were hauled away from one block of the Pennsylvania Avenue parade route. Five hundred cars were

(Continued on Page 9)

★ ★ ★

N. Y. City, Pa. Areas Crippled by Blizzards

By the Associated Press

A staggering blizzard pounded metropolitan New York today, numbing the lifelines of a city already crippled by transportation tieups.

Stabbing winds and mounting snowdrifts turned usually bustling midtown sections into scenes of arctic desolation. Scant traffic crawled on nearly empty streets.

Schools were closed, and businesses and industry hit by lack of manpower. An average 12-inch snowfall plastered the city, and the wind heaped it into man-high drifts in places, burying parked cars.

Suburban communities were paralyzed by the storm. Poughkeepsie's Mayor Victor Waryas proclaimed a state of emergency, with all firemen and police ordered to their stations. Mail service, industry and schools were shut down.

At New Rochelle, the gale-swept snowdrifts closed roads, virtually imprisoning the city. Plows fought to open main arteries, but the drifts piled up immediately behind them.

Airports shut down, the runways blocked with snow. Huge planes stood caught in the mounds, looking like toys a child had abandoned in a drifted yard.

What little traffic moved did so at a snail's pace.

A 26-mile-an-hour wind was blowing, with gusts ranging much higher. Two subway lines were closed.

Middletown reported a 29-inch snowfall. Schools in the outlying areas, as well as the city, suspended operations, as did many banks, factories and other industries.

The Newburgh-Beacon News suspended publication of all four of its editions today because of the snowstorm. It was the first shutdown in the daily's 76-year history.

Reports of closed schools and industries came from Sullivan, Ulster, Rockland, Orange, the Albany area and other suburban counties in New York.

Stewart Air Force Base, near Newburgh, closed down.

In New York City, in addition to the closing of public schools, the board of higher education suspended classes in municipal col-

(Continued on Page 9)

102 Escape Death In Jetliner Crash

PICTURE ON PAGE 11

New York — (UPI)—"Let's get the hell out of here."

And with that cry, 102 did. They were the lucky ones.

They scrambled in panic through broken windows, escape hatches and holes torn in the fuselage of the giant DC8 jet Mexican airliner that crashed and burned last night at Idlewild Airport.

Diplomats and businessmen, wives and children, the rich and the not rich climbed over seats and cocktail tables and squirmed, jumped or squeezed out of the burning plane.

Then they ran for their lives.

FLAMES CAST GLOW

It was a near-miracle that more than 100 got out within minutes after the huge jet gunned down the runway in a swirling snowstorm, lifted off the ground, faltered and smacked into a marshy area next to the airport.

Flames engulfed the four-engine giant with a whoosh as the kerosene-type fuel caught fire, casting a glow through the snowstorm on the figures staggering through the marsh grass for safety.

Firemen who sped to the blaze first said no one could have survived the blasting flames. They could not get within 60 feet of the plane because of the intense heat.

Then the survivors began to trickle into airport waiting rooms, restaurants near the airport and onto a nearby highway, where passing motorists helped them to shelter.

MANY INJURED

Twenty were reported alive, then 30. The figure grew to 53, then to 63 and up to 92. Then it jumped over the 100 mark in accounting for the 98 passengers and crew of eight.

It was hours after the crash that the police department tally showed that of the 106 aboard, four died and 102 were found alive.

Many of those who escaped were injured and seven hospitalized. One was critically hurt, three were in poor condition and one was reported in fair condition. Injuries to two were not determined.

The four victims were identified as the plane's captain, Ricardo Gonzales, First Officer Antonio Ruiz Bravo, Second Officer Javier Backa Alvarez, and Gloria Sanchez, a stewardess.

The Aeronaves de Mexico plane took off for Mexico City in a driving snowstorm at 8:15 p.m. There was a 600-foot ceiling, visibility was 5/16th of a mile. Winds were 27 miles an hour and snow was blowing in the 20-degree temperature.

"I don't think the plane got more than 30 feet off the ground," Joyce Groper, 28, of Chestnut Hill, Mass., said. "It came back down and it burst into flame the instant it touched.

LOST HER SHOES

"We all went forward and jumped down to the ground through the hole in the side of the plane there. One woman broke her ankle jumping.

"We all were deathly afraid of an explosion and we ran as best we could over the rough ground and the snow.

"I lost my shoes but I didn't notice it at the time."

Her husband, Irving, said as they got away from the plane it became a huge mass of flames. They were taken to St. Joseph's Hospital by a passing motorist who found them on Rockaway Boulevard.

What's on 'Tap' For Traveling Ave?

U. S. security agents are going to be especially careful about arrangements for Averell Harriman on his overseas missions for the new administration.

They remember the wiretapped eagle the Russians installed in Harriman's Moscow office.

Also on the inside:

2,000 Books To Go to Africa

Buffalo—(AP)—A Nigerian student at the University of Buffalo will return home in June with more than 2,000 books he has acquired while attending college.

He is Samson Obi, and he plans to start a public library in his home town Oba, Nigeria, where he says there is a great need for books. His fellow students conducted a drive and gathered most of the books for him.

Men, Missiles, Girls, Bands in Big Parade

Washington—(AP)—Men and missiles, bands and beauties converged on Pennsylvania Avenue today for the big parade that transforms staid old Washington into a rollicking youth of a town every four years.

Horn tooters and horseback riders, soldiers and sailors assembled by the thousands for the march down the avenue, from the Capitol to the White House, to celebrate the Inauguration of President John F. Kennedy.

And many thousands who just plain love a parade gathered to watch the procession move along the trail of presidents.

A tremendous over night work effort cleared the parade route of all vestiges of the eight-inch snow storm which had hit the city yesterday and last night.

As in every inaugural parade, this one put its star attraction up front. Only the usual introductory array of police and marshals, backed by the army band and a battle group of infantrymen, preceded the presidential limousine.

Open sedans and limousines

(Continued on Page 5)

Ike Pension $25,000 Plus Expenses

Washington—(UPI) — President Eisenhower leaves office today with a $25,000 annual pension, a $50,000 yearly expense account and free mailing privileges.

But he will have to pay taxes on his pension.

Congress may give him back his five-star general rank. A move is under way to restore the rank, without the usual $20,000 pension, in view of the allowances he gets as ex-president.

Pastor Says He's Church Firebug

Palo Alto—(AP)—A Baptist minister stunned his parishioners yesterday by admitting, officers said, that he had burned down two of his churches. He said he didn't know why.

Officers booked on arson charges the Rev. Leonard Ross Rhoads, 44, whose First Southern Baptist Church in Palo Alto was leveled by a roaring blaze Dec. 13. Deputy District Attorney Harry Parker said the minister also admitted burning down his church at Fontana Nov. 16, 1956.

Ex-Yugoslav Official Freed

Belgrade, Yugoslavia — (UPI) — Former Vice-President Milovan Djilas was released on parole today from the prison where he had served nearly five years for criticizing Communist policies in connection with the Hungaran revolt.

An eyewitness said the 47-year-old patriot appeared to be in good health.

No Veil for Lyndon

"The chief embarrassment in discussing this office," said the scholarly Woodrow Wilson of the vice-presidency, "is that in explaining how little there is to be said about it one has evidently said all there is to say."

When he was nominated for the post, Teddy Roosevelt glumly wrote an old army friend: "I have been forced to take the veil."

No outsider knows what words passed between John Kennedy and Lydon Johnson that night in Los Angeles when the Texan agreed to join Kennedy on the Democratic ticket, but it's a safe bet both spoke of it in far different terms.

How will Johnson handle the Vice-Presidency?

That question is examined by AP newsfeatures writer Arthur Edson as he takes a look at the historical evolution of the job in

The Sunday Press

B52 Explodes Over Utah, 5 Are Killed

Monticello, Utah—(UPI)—A B52 intercontinental jet bomber exploded six miles above the southern Utah badlands last night, apparently killing five crewmen.

Two officers survived a long parachute drop of 36,000 feet, an ordeal they described as "colder than hell." Then they hiked to a highway and hitched a ride into town. Neither was badly injured.

There was no nuclear bomb on the plane, the Air Force said.

The State Highway Patrol said four bodies had been recovered from the wreckage, but a fifth crew members remained unaccounted for.

Fragments of the $8,000,000 eight-jet bomber scattered over several acres of rocky ground 12 miles north of here. Fires burned for several hours at three separate spots.

The two survivors told a doctor who treated for abrasions that a severe vibration, much like turbulent weather, shook the plane as it winged north from Biggs Air Force Base, El Paso, Tex., on a round-trip training mission. One wing apparently caught fire and then exploded.

Architects Face Charge on Trip

New York — (AP) — Two board of education architects have been accused of a $2,340 "freeloading" trip to Miami Beach in 1959 at a school building contractor's expense.

Scheduled to be arraigned in Ridgewood, Queens, Felony Court are Louis Schneiderman of Brooklyn and Benjamin Kurtz of Hicksville. They are charged with illegal acceptance of gratuities.

Retail Trade Is Up 2-6%

New York — (AP) — Retail trade in the week ended Wednesday increased moderately over the previous week and the corresponding week a year ago, Dun & Bradstreet, Inc., reported today.

Dollar volume was 2 to 6 per cent higher than a year ago.

Favorable weather and extensive reduced-price sales were credited for the increase.

Year-to-year gains were registered in apparel, floor coverings, furniture and linens. They offset declines in major appliances, draperies and housewares.

Lumumbists Warned by UN

Leopoldville — (UPI) — The United Nations has sent a strong note to pro-Lumumba authorities in Stanleyville warning them not to mistreat 12 Belgians arrested there in retaliation for the transfer of ousted Premier Patrice Lumumba to a prison in Katanga Province.

A UN spokesman said the note was issued by UN chief representative Rajeshwar Dayal of India. He said the prisoners included three women.

Let's Chuckle

Americans: People who spend money they don't have to buy things they don't need to impress people they don't like.

January 20, 1961: Kennedy's inauguration. *Courtesy Dolly Escovar*

Count Down

WEATHER BUREAU FORECAST

Partly cloudy and colder with a few snow flurries tonight. Low tonight 8-13. Wednesday partly cloudy with a chance of a few snow flurries. High Wednesday 20-25.

BINGHAMTON TEMPERATURES

9 p. m.	28	7 a. m.	22	11 a. m.	23
Midnight	26	8 a. m.	22	Noon	24
3 a. m.	27	9 a. m.	22	1 p. m.	26
6 a. m.	24	10 a. m.	22	2 p. m.	27

THE EVENING PRESS

THE HOMETOWN NEWSPAPER OF THE SOUTHERN TIER

Binghamton, N. Y., Tuesday, Feb. 20, 1962 — Volume 83 — 265 — 32 Pages — 5 Cents

★ ★ ★
For timely . . . accurate news reporting, tune
WINR-Radio
680 on your dial

GLENN COMPLETES ALL THREE ORBITS, RECOVERED OK AND FEELING FINE

★ ★ ★ ★ ★ ★

Voice in Space

—Associated Press WIREPHOTO.

BLASTING SPACEWARD—Atlas rocket blasts from the launch pad at Cape Canaveral missile test center carrying the Mercury capsule with astronaut John Glenn for his trip around the earth.

Cape Canaveral, Fla.—(AP)—Space agency officials released the following unofficial transcript of conversations with John H. Glenn, Jr.:

Some purely technical conversations have been eliminated.

GLENN: Five-four-three-two-one-zero, liftoff. The clock is operating. We are under way. Roger. Read you loud and clear. Roger.

MERCURY CONTROL: We are pragaming . . . OK.

GLENN: It is a little bumpy along about here. Roger.

MERCURY CONTROL: Flight path is good.

GLENN: Checks OK. Minus 7, on your mark.

MERCURY CONTROL: Roger. Reading you clear, John.

GLENN: Coming into high gear a little bit. A little contrail went by the window or something.. Roger. 102 . . . 101 . . . oxygen 78 . . . 101 . . . amps 24, still OK. We are . . . out some now, getting out of the vibration area.

MERCURY CONTROL: Flight path very good.

GLENN: Pitch four three. Coming out real fine. Flight very smooth now.

MERCURY CONTROL: Roger. Flight path is good.

GLENN: Cabin pressure is holding at six one. OK. Have had some oscillations, but they seem to be damped.

GLENN: The clock two minutes. G's are building to six.

MERCURY CONTROL: Roger. Reading you loud and clear. Flight path looks good. Pitch 25. Standby for station.

GLENN: B E C O. B E C O (booster engines cut off). I see the tower go. I saw the smoke go by the window.

MERCURY CONTROL: Roger. We confirm staging TM (telemetry).

GLENN: Roger. Still have about 1½ G's. . . . The tower went right then. I have the tower in sight way out.

MERCURY CONTROL: Roger, we confirm on 5. . . . Tower is green.

GLENN: 1½ G's.

MERCURY CONTROL: Flight path looks good.

GLENN: Retro jettisoned. Emergency retro jettison slips off.

MERCURY CONTROL: Flight path looks good.

GLENN: The steering is good.

MERCURY CONTROL: Roger. Understand everything looks good.

GLENN: G's starting to build again. . . . Roger Bermuda, stand by. This Friendship 7.

MERCURY CONTROL: Roger. Reading you loud and clear. Flight path looks good.

MERCURY CONTROL: Roger. Reading you loud and clear. Cape is go. We are standing by for you.

GLENN: Roger. Cape is go and I am go.

GLENN: All systems go. Cabin pressure holding steady. All systems are go.

MERCURY CONTROL: Roger. 20 seconds. . . . Flight path looks

(Continued on Page 13)

—Associated Press WIREPHOTO.

CLIMBS INTO CAPSULE—Astronaut John Glenn climbs into Mercury space capsule from platform on the 11th floor of gantry which surrounds Atlas rocket at the launch pad at Cape Canaveral.

Cape Canaveral, Fla.—(AP)—Astronaut John H. Glenn, Jr., was plucked safely from the Atlantic Ocean at 3:01 p. m. today by a destroyer, the Noa, after he flew three times around the world in his space ship. He was on the deck of the ship at 3:04.

Cape Canaveral—(UPI)—John H. Glenn, Jr., broke the space trail for the free world today with a magnificent leap into orbit that carried him three times around the earth to a splash down in the Atlantic about 6 miles from a recovery ship.

The 40-year-old marine rose into space atop a flame-spewing Atlas rocket at 9:47 a. m.

At 2:28 p. m., EST, 4 hours and 41 minutes later, he had completed the three orbits of his mission.

Ten minutes later, his spacecraft's 63-foot main parachute opened at 21,000 feet and dropped the craft and its pilot into the sea.

Recovery forces sighted them at 2:40 p. m. while they were still in the air.

Glenn splashed down at 2:43 p. m.

The destroyer Noa, flanking the aircraft carrier Randolph in the main recovery area, estimated it was 6 miles from the capsule.

Glenn's total time in the sky from launch to splash-down was computed at 4 hours and 56 minutes. This was just six minutes more than space officials had estimated before the flight.

The destroyer NOA spotted Glenn's capsule floating at the end of the brilliant red and white parachute.

The capsule then landed in the ocean at 2:43 p. m. about six miles from the destroyer NOA which first spotted it floating down.

The space craft began its descent off the west coast of America when braking rockets fired at 2:20 p. m. The ton-and-a-half cabin arched into dense layers of the atmosphere at an altitude of about 55 miles above the East Coast.

In the space of five minutes its speed was cut from about 17,500 to 270 miles an hour, and air friction heated its blunt re-entry heat shield to nearly 3,000 degrees.

Glenn's own comment on his glowing spacecraft was, "Boy, that was a real fireball."

In diving back into the atmosphere the astronaut again underwent gravity forces about 7½ times normal.

By the Associated Press

Cape Canaveral, Fla.—Astronaut John H. Glenn, Jr., reported that despite minor difficulties with his capsule control system, he was in good condition to complete his full three-orbit mission around the world.

While officials were considering the possibility of terminating the flight after two orbits, the astronaut told the Kauai tracking station in Hawaii that he was in good shape and was having no trouble controlling his craft.

Asked how he felt about a third orbit, Glenn replied:

"Affirmative. I am 'go' for the third orbit."

The Hawaii station confirmed Glenn's judgment, advised the Mercury control center at Cape Canaveral, and Glenn was given the green light to continue.

Glenn said the roll of his capsule "seems to be about 20 degrees off." He completed the second orbit at 12:54 p. m.

The whole world watched and listened as the marine lieutenant colonel whirled on around the globe. "I feel fine," he said.

He did encounter some minor trouble with his space control system, but officials of the National Aeronautics and Space Administration said it was not serious.

Glenn's rocket blasted off from Cape Canaveral at 9:47 a. m. and he completed his first orbit in 88.29 minutes.

There are three ways the spacecraft can be controlled. One is the regular automatic system, one is all manual, and the third is the fly-by-wire system which is a combination of the two.

HIS TROUBLE was in the automatic system and he switched to the fly-by-wire method.

Scientists planned to return Glenn's Friendship 7 spacecraft to earth after three sweeps around the earth at 17,530 miles an hour. The three-orbit mission was to last four hours, 50 minutes.

This would bring Glenn, who is 40, down for a landing near Grand Turk Island in the Bahamas about 2:37 p. m.

Glancing down at the earth at altitudes ranging from 100 to 160 miles, Glenn had a breath-taking panoramic view stretching 1,800 miles from horizon to horizon. He described the view as "tremendous" and "a beautiful sight."

On the initial orbit, Glenn ate a space meal of beef and vegetables from a squeeze bottle, controlled the altitude of his capsule several times and made frequent instrument readings to ground stations.

When he passed over Australia, he sighted the lights of the city of Perth. Nearly all lights had been turned on by residents of the city as a good-will gesture to the space pioneer.

"Thank everybody for turning them on," Glenn told fellow

(Continued on Page 13)

Glenn's Big Day

Cape Canaveral, Fla. — (AP) — With a confident wave, astronaut John H. Glenn, Jr. set out again today to conquer the biggest objective any marine has ever tackled—the first American "beachhead" in orbit around the earth.

Glenn's green eyes, visible through the opening in his round, white space helmet, seemed to say "I'm going to make it this time" as he walked from his special training quarters at 5:01 a. m.

Just 25 days ago, Marine Lt. Col. Glenn started on this same journey, only to be thrwarted by a heavy cloud cover just 20 minutes from launch time.

Then had come more delays because of weather and technical bugs. But now the waiting was over.

The strong-jawed veteran of two wars had said calmly back on Jan. 27 that there would be another day—and that day had come.

Glenn didn't say anything as he passed, but Lt. Col. John A. Powers, a space agency spokesman, told reporters "John feels great."

The astronaut, showing no outward sign of any strain, smiled and waved three times with his extended right arm as he hustled to the van.

About 100 reporters, security officers, cameramen and others watched quietly as Glenn climbed four steps into the van. Just before entering, he paused and laid a friendly hand on the shoulder of Charles Buckley, a security officer from New Bedford, Mass.

As soon as Glenn, his doctor and several technicians disappeared into the van, there was a meshing of gears and the truck began a slow, four-mile drive to the launch pad at 5:03 a. m.

Glenn and his standby pilot, 36-year-old Navy Lt. Cmdr. Scott Carpenter, turned in early last night in the blue-walled room they shared on the second deck of the hangar.

At 2:20 a. m., Glenn was awakened by Dr. William K. Douglas, the Air Force flight surgeon who has said "I'm as close to this man as I am to my brother."

Then began the ritual that always precedes a space flight.

After a shower and shave, Glenn sat down to a steak breakfast with a group of men who have become his friends over the nearly three years he has been preparing for this day. The meal began at 2:45 a. m.

These breakfasts have been lighthearted affairs, with the astronaut holding the place of

(Continued on Page 13)

★ ★ ★

'Tremendous Note of Joy' Sweeps Glenn Household

Arlington, Va.—(AP)—"A tremendous note of joy."

That was a friend's description of the atmosphere in the home of Astronaut John H. Glenn, Jr., today as fast-flowing reports showed full success in the early stages of the launching of the husband and father into space flight.

As for the tense early moments of the lift-off, the Rev. Frank A. Erwin, pastor of the Little Falls United Presbyterian Church which the Glenns attend, told reporters:

"It was quiet; everybody had his own thoughts."

But in the last second before flame at the base of the great rocket signaled the actual start, another friend reported, the spaceman's wife voiced her assurance as to how he met the great moment.

"I know John's just really smiling now," Mrs. Thomas H. Miller quoted her.

Mrs. Glenn and the two teenage children, David, 16, and Lyn, 14, with several friends and neighbors watched all the proceedings on three television sets in the living room.

Erwin came out to report to newsmen what was going on inside.

He said as the launch proceeded nobody said anything—"It was no time to say anything."

Asked if there were any prayers, Erwin said, "There were some prayers I am sure. No verbal ones."

Meanwhile, in New Concord, Ohio, Glenn's parents watched and prayed in the quiet atmosphere of their home as their son rose into space atop a fiery rocket.

Dr. Glenn McConagha, acting president of Muskingum College and family spokesman, quoted Mrs. John Glenn, Sr., as saying, "I was very thrilled to hear John's voice on a recording."

Carlino Cleared

Story on Page 11

Close U. S. Family Life Surprises Women

Movies Mislead Jap Study Team

Houston, Tex.— (AP) —Nine Japanese housewives are beginning to think they have seen too many American movies.

"We discovered to our great surprise that mothers and children are very close and that great emphasis is put on the importance of family life," said Mrs. Tomeno Kudo, leader of a study team from the province of Hokkaido.

The women are on a tour of the United States to study a great American problem—the family budget.

"We have visited a number of American homes, three in San Francisco and two in Los Angeles," Mrs. Kudo said through an interpreter yesterday.

"Maybe we had seen too many highlife movies but we thought American mothers were not so close to their families as they are."

The women started their Houston visit by delving into the mysteries of the charge account.

They visited a bank, a downtown department store, a supermarket, a discount house and Houston's largest shopping center.

"We have found that American women are very frank and natural in their homes and they are perfectly at ease with us talking about their budgets and their problems," Mrs. Kudo said.

She said Japanese and American women have a common problem — keeping up with the Joneses.

"In Japan we call it monkey-like mimicry," she said. "It is causing some housewives to suffer."

Mrs. Kudo, who is president of the Muroran-Ski Kanan Women's Association, seemed particularly interested in knowing if steps are taken to make sure American women can afford the things they buy on credit.

"Japanese women are not so well protected because we have no bodies like your Better Business Bureau," she said.

Fighting Fire With Fire

South Viet Nam forces are using new tactics against Communist guerrillas. They're using guerrilla tactics.

The thinking behind this change in the methods of jungle figting is explored on Page 20.

Also on the inside:

Let's Chuckle

Wife, joyfully to husband: "We won't have to pay all those household bills, dear. This letter just came for you. It says 'Final Notice.'"

Bulletin

Hamburg, Pa.—(AP) — Harry Hamilton, about 35, of Syracuse, was killed today when a tractor-trailer in which he was riding collided with a truck on the Harrisburg, Pa.-New York highway.

Hamilton, who state police said may have moved to Binghamton a few weeks ago, died at Reading Hospital of injuries suffered in the accident, about 12 miles north of Reading in eastern Pennsylvania.

JFK Asks Billion Federal Pay Boost

Washington—(AP)—President Kennedy has urged Congress to provide a $1,000,000,000 pay raise over three years for the government's white collar workers. The aim, he said, is to put federal pay on a par with that outside so that competent people can afford to work for Uncle Sam.

The President said in a special message today he was proposing "federal pay reform, not simply a federal pay raise."

For the whole field of white collar workers, the increase would amount to 10 per cent of the present $10,000,000,000 annual payroll. But for individuals, the raises would range from 3.7 per cent to about 33 per cent for the three-year period. The first increase would come Jan. 1.

Kennedy said he is proposing a wholly new, "common sense" approach to the problem of putting

(Continued on Page 13)

February 20, 1962: The Evening Press reported on the nation's joy as we closed in on the Soviets in the space race. *Courtesy Glenn Heath*

Weather Bureau report

Monday, cloudy with rain, possibly beginning as [illegible] or snow. High 38-43. Monday night, rain ending followed by partial clearing. Low 38-40. Tuesday, partly cloudy with seasonal temperatures. High 40-45.

Summary and weather map on Page 18.

The Sun-Bulletin

Monday, March 12, 1962

Binghamton, N.Y. 7 Cents

Tragedy at General Hospital

SIX BABIES ARE DEAD; FORMULA IS PROBED

Sun-Bulletin photo by [illegible]

Police Lt. John Gillen and Patrolman Eugene McGoff inspect the cans which held hospital's sugar and salt. Note tiny label on sugar can at left. Police will examine the contents of the cans.

Rusk warns Gromyko on harassment

GENEVA (UPI) — Secretary of State Dean Rusk last night told Soviet Foreign Minister Andrei Gromyko in their first round of talks here that "we did not like" recent Berlin incidents provoked by the Communists.

Rusk gave a four-hour dinner for Gromyko and British Foreign Secretary Lord Home and their top aides. It was the opening of Big Three talks here.

Rusk told newsmen after the meeting broke up just before midnight that "we talked about Berlin, particularly the recent Soviet harassments in and near Berlin.

"We told them we did not like them," he said.

Gromyko's version of the talks was: "We dealt in general terms with Berlin but we did not treat it in any detail. ... This was just the beginning."

Rusk refused to draw any conclusions from the opening meeting. He said the Allies must wait a day or two "to determine Soviet intentions."

Lord Home, asked if any progress had been made, said "You have to get used to a lot of meetings of this kind. This was preliminary. There will be a lot more."

* * *

[illegible]

Sun-Bulletin photo by Renee Myrae

Mrs. Lillie Colvin

... Practical nurse suspended

Nurse employed for two months

[illegible]

4 more infants on critical list

By ESTELLE NEMOY
Sun-Bulletin Reporter

Six babies have died at Binghamton General Hospital during the last three days. Four more were in critical condition last night.

Hospital officials were investigating the possibility that the deaths were due to a substitution of salt for sugar in the feeding formulas.

Six other infants who are believed to have been fed some of the formula containing salt are under special care at the hospital. Teams of doctors are watching their conditions closely.

A nurse who made herself a cup of instant coffee in the formula room yesterday morning discovered table salt in the sugar container there, hospital officials said. This touched off the realization that the deaths of the infants might be connected.

The dead babies ranged in age from three days to eight months. They are:

THE VICTIMS

- **Kathryn Fleming, eight-month-old daughter of Mr. and Mrs. Gerald W. Fleming, 789 Chenango St., Port Dickinson.**
- **Glenn Stewart Jones, five-week-old son of Mrs. Althea Jones, 6 Court St.**
- **Lisa Marie Bealo, week-old daughter of Mr. and Mrs. Frank Bealo, 21 Meadow St. Mr. Bealo is a photographer for The Sun-Bulletin.**
- **Randy Alan Mower, three-day-old son of Mr. and Mrs. John F. Mower, Box 134, Corbettsville.**
- **Debra Ann Walker, four-day-old daughter of Mr. and Mrs. Robert P. Walker, 47 Murray St.**
- **Barry John McPeek, week-old son of Mr. and Mrs. George W. McPeek, 54 Gerard Ave.**

The tragedy was described to newsmen at a hastily called press conference at 6 o'clock last night. Doctors, nurses and the general public were stunned.

Carl N. Wathne, acting hospital administrator, said the sugar container in the formula room had been filled last Tuesday. He identified the licensed practical nurse who refilled it as Mrs. Lillie Colvin of 147 Susquehanna St. She was suspended from duty yesterday, pending further investigation.

Mrs. Colvin was questioned last night by Broome County District Attorney Stephen Smyk. Mr. Smyk said no charges had been placed against her. He said the investigation would continue. Mr. Wathne said the can in the formula room was refilled from a container in the hospital's main kitchen. The large salt and sugar cans were next to each other in the kitchen, but each was labeled, he said.

Carl N. Wathne

The two large cans were taken to the Binghamton Police Station last night and locked in a cell. Mr. Smyk said their contents would be analyzed today.

Mrs. Colvin said she was sure she filled the formula room container from the sugar can.

Salt dose peril to heart

According to pediatricians, an overdose of salt will upset the chemical balance in the body and cause a strain that could cause heart failure in a very young child.

Autopsies were ordered on the six babies who died.

The State Social Welfare Department, which has general supervision of hospitals, announced that its Syracuse director, C. Walter Driscoll, would begin an investigation here today.

The State Health Department said Dr. Cleveland A. Sergeant, Binghamton health officer, had been asked to investigate on its behalf. A department official said in Albany that a doctor from the State Health Department would be sent here today, if necessary, to lend assistance.

Official statement

A statement on the tragedy was issued yesterday by William S. Chittenden, treasurer of the hospital board of managers, and Mr. Wathne. It said:

"This morning, March 11, Mrs. May Pier, licensed practical nurse working in the formula room, fixed herself a cup of instant coffee in the formula room. She used some of the contents of the sugar can which is used for the preparation of the formula on pediatrics and maternity floors.

"She tasted the coffee and discovered that [illegible]. She then tested some of the contents of the can and was of the opinion that it was salt. She immediately called Mrs. [illegible] Galewaler, who is the supervisor in maternity, and told her of her discovery.

"Mrs. Galewaler called Mrs. (Margaret) Maxey, who is the nursing supervisor in charge today. Mrs. Maxey immediately called Dr. (Jason K.) Meyer, medical director of the hospital, at approximately 9:45 a.m.

"Dr. Moyer called me at my home right away calling my attention to the fact that we had a problem on maternity and pediatrics floors since perhaps salt had been used in place of sugar in the preparation of the formula.

"I then came to the hospital immediately, just before 10 a.m. I went immediately to pediatrics and maternity and met Dr. Moyer in the corridor on his way to pediatrics. I came back to the office and talked with Mrs. Maxey, the nursing supervisor in charge today at the hospital.

"I then called Mr. (John H.) Nermile, counsel for the board of managers of the hospital. Upon his arrival we initiated an investigation to determine how the salt had come to be placed in the sugar container used in the formula room.

"Our investigation indicates that the sugar can used in the formula room had been refilled on Tuesday, March 6, from the

See BABIES, Page 3.

Convulsions first warning

Parents of two dead infants were informed by doctors

The parents of two of the babies who died at General Hospital over the weekend said their doctors told them their babies went into convulsions, the first indication that anything was wrong with them.

Mrs. George W. McPeek of 54 Gerard Ave. said her doctor informed her last Thursday night shortly after 7 o'clock that her 7-day-old son, Barry John, was having convulsions. She said that the doctor told her the baby apparently was lacking in calcium and also that the baby was thought to be hemorrhaging.

The baby died 4:30 Friday morning. Mrs. McPeek was still in the hospital. She said that Dr. John H. Ford called her husband George at 1:45 p.m. yesterday to inform him of the possible formula mix-up.

[illegible] Mower [illegible] he was told that his baby, Randy, [illegible] old, had gone into convulsions [illegible] day.

The baby, who had been born Wednesday morning, had undergone a blood transplant the same afternoon, Mr. Mower said. He said the transplant was needed because of an Rh negative factor involved. The baby died Saturday night.

He said his wife was more fully informed of the situation than he was, but "she was so broken up she couldn't talk to me."

The McPeeks have one other child, [illegible]. The Mowers have three sons, [illegible], William, 7, and Mark, 2.

Doctors said yesterday that at least two of the six babies who died over the weekend were probably not connected with the formula [illegible].

Love, luggage laugh at Reds—

BEBRA, Germany (P)—The star[illegible] line story of a young West German man who carried his East German fiancee to freedom in a traveling bag was told by West German police at this Iron Curtain border town yesterday.

The West German man, 20, obtained a pass to visit the industrial fair at Leipzig. He arranged a meeting with his fiancee.

In Leipzig they bought a traveling bag large enough to hold the petite 19-year-old girl.

They boarded a westbound train and when it came to Eisenach about 10 miles from the border, the girl slipped into the bag. [illegible] the East German border checkpoint of Wartha where the train [illegible] the girl [illegible]

[illegible] with a second bag.

Then he returned to his compartment and waited [illegible]

'How my baby died'

By FRANK BEALO
Sun-Bulletin Photographer
As told to John Tang[illegible]

We brought the baby home Wednesday afternoon along with a quart bottle of formula. The formula was still warm and we had all the bottles ready.

The baby had been fed at 10 o'clock in the morning and we arrived home with her about 1 o'clock. We were late leaving the hospital because of a delay in checking out.

My wife and my sister, Mrs. [illegible], 20 Meadow St., were giving the baby her 2 p.m. feeding, but the baby wouldn't take the bottle. She appeared to choke and gag. The formula wouldn't come up or go down. She made a funny noise like gurgling. She couldn't take the milk down.

My wife and my sister kept trying for a while and managed to get about one ounce of formula down. The baby was supposed to get four ounces at a feeding.

Then we decided to give the

See MY BABY DIED, Page 3.

THE WORLD THIS MORNING

GENEVA — Secretary of State Dean Rusk met for four hours with Soviet Foreign Minister Andrei Gromyko and British Foreign Secretary Lord Home in the opening of Big Three talks. Rusk said he warned Gromyko "we did not like" Soviet harassments in Berlin. He also was quoted as having said continued incidents could disrupt the talks.

ALGIERS — As French-Algerian peace talks continued in Evian, France, violence continued in Algeria. French troops and European civilians fought a gun battle in the streets of Algiers working class district of Bab-el-Oued. The district is the stronghold of the rightist Secret Army, which opposes Algerian independence. French troops were alerted for a major attack by the Secret Army. On Page 2.

LUANG PRABANG — Laos King Savang Vatthana criticized the United States for cutting off aid to Laos and trying to force his rightwing government to join a coalition with neutralist and pro-Communist factions. He called on [illegible] to support royal Premier Prince Boun Oum. On Page 2.

ROME — Mrs. Jacqueline Kennedy left for New Delhi, India after a weekend stopover in Rome that included a 30-minute private audience with Pope John XXIII. The First Lady and the pontiff conversed in French with no interpreters. A crowd of 20,000 pilgrims in St. Peter's Square cheered and almost mobbed her as she left. On Page 2.

20 Pages
140th Year No. 120

[illegible]

Second-class postage paid at Binghamton, N.Y.

Have The Sun-Bulletin delivered to your home daily
Dial RAymond 4-4311

Today is Monday, March 12 [illegible]

On this day in history:

[illegible]

March 12, 1962: The Sun-Bulletin had early reports about a tragedy that made news around the nation. *Microfilm archives*

Mild and Woolly

WEATHER BUREAU FORECAST

Cloudy with occasional rain followed by partial clearing and scattered snow flurries later tonight and Tuesday. Low tonight 28-33. High Tuesday 33-38.

THE EVENING PRESS

THE HOMETOWN NEWSPAPER OF THE SOUTHERN TIER

Binghamton, N. Y., Monday, March 12, 1962 — Volume 83 — 282 — 26 Pages — 5 Cents

Net Paid Circulation 77,496 For February, 1962

Hospital Battles to Halt Babies' Deaths at Six

Salt Error Is Cited, Infants Are Watched

By JERRY HANDTE and JOE PIERSON

A round-the-clock battle to halt the infant death toll at six was being fought in General Hospital today after discovery that a blunder may have changed life-giving nursery formula into deadly salt solution.

Teams of doctors, nurses and technicians routed the blood supply of four infants outside their bodies in an effort to cleanse it of potentially lethal high sodium content.

Six other infants are being watched carefully.

A cup of instant coffee brewed by a practical nurse yesterday morning tasted terrible.

"Sugar" in the coffee, from a can in the formula room for the Maternity and Pediatrics floors, turned out to be salt.

Hospital officials said it appeared that the can was mistakenly filled with salt instead of sugar in the hospital's main kitchen last Tuesday, after infant formulas for that day already had been prepared.

Three babies died in the hospital early Friday morning.

There were three more deaths Saturday.

IT APPEARED that the formula containing common table salt instead of ordinary granulated sugar had been fed to some infants Wednesday, Thursday, Friday, Saturday and yesterday, until Mrs. May Pier of 214 Reynolds Road, Oakdale, tried to drink the telltale cup of coffee.

Carl N. Wathne, assistant administrator of the hospital, suspended Mrs. Lillie Colvin of 147 Susquehanna Street from her job as a practical nurse in the Infants Department, which includes both Maternity and Pediatrics.

Mr. Wathne, in a statement read at a special press conference last night, said Mrs. Colvin was the one who refilled the formula-room sugar can in the main kitchen last Tuesday.

The assistant administrator said Mrs. Colvin told him she filled the can, but that she was sure she filled it correctly from a large sugar can in the kitchen.

Sugar and salt are kept in the kitchen in large labeled cans which stand side by side, Mr. Wathne said.

DR. JOHN KILEY of Albany Medical College, an expert on dialysis (chemical treatment of the blood and other body fluids outside the body to counteract chemical or metabolic ailments), hurried to Binghamton last night to direct efforts to save the lives of three critically ill infants. He was asked to come by Dr. Jason K. Moyer, hospital medical director.

Dr. John H. Ford, chief of the Pediatrics Section, told reporters that the dead babies apparently "were loaded with common table salt."

"The whole place is shook up," he said, when asked how

(Continued on Page 3)

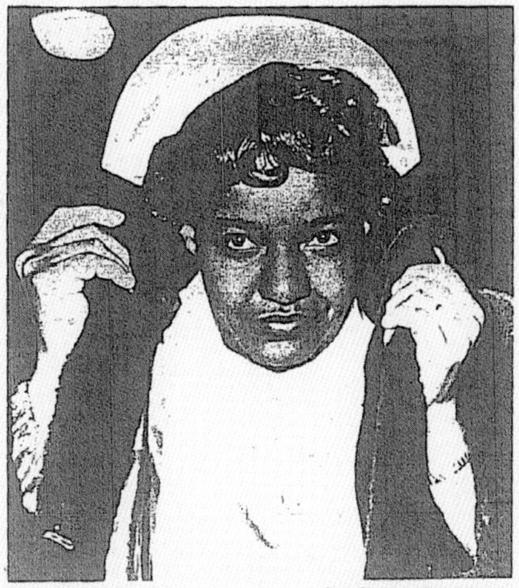

—Press Photos by Gene Swierkosz

FOCUS OF INVESTIGATION—Mrs. Lilllie Mae Colvin, suspended practical nurse, leaves General Hospital last night after questioning about a mixup in which salt was substituted for sugar in making infant formulas, possible cause of six deaths at the hospital in two days.

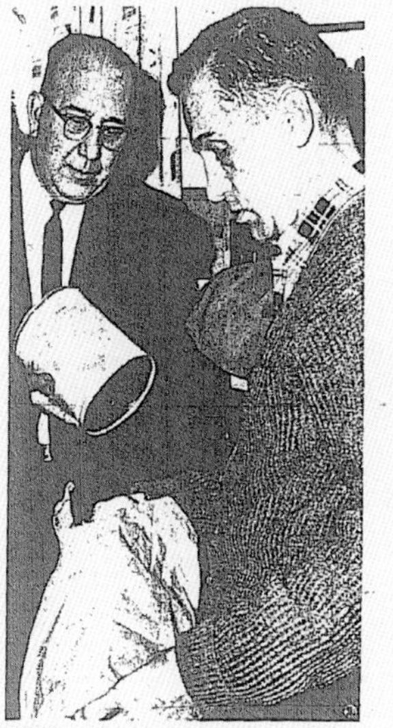

POSSIBLE DISASTER SOURCE—Detective Lt. John V. Gillen, left, holds the used can in which sugar normally is stored in the General Hospital formula preparation room. District Attorney Stephen Smyk holds a bag in which the can was taken to police headquarters for shipment to state laboratories for analysis.

Rusk Eager For A-Pact

By the Associated Press

Geneva—U. S. Secretary of State Dean Rusk and Soviet Foreign Minister Andrei Gromyko met today to sound each other out on conflicting East-West positions on Berlin, nuclear testing and disarmament.

British Foreign Minister Lord Home bowed out temporarily and let Rusk press the Western views on the issue. The American Secretary and Gromyko got together over the luncheon table in the Soviet delegation's villa.

A British spokesman said Home's temporary withdrawal from the foreign minister's sessions was a logical development since the Americans and the British are speaking in Geneva with one voice.

Rusk, Gromyko and Lord Home—here for the opening of the 17-nation disarmament conference Wednesday — conferred last night at dinner but reports were that little progress was made.

The West called on Russia to stop harassing Allied air traffic to Berlin lest increasing tensions there endanger the disarmament negotiations.

GROMYKO denied knowledge ...

Harassing By Reds Continues

By UP-International

Berlin—Western officials today reported new Soviet harassment of Western aircraft in the air lanes over East Germany to West Berlin.

The officials gave no details of the harassment because of a news blackout ordered on the Soviet tactics, but the Russians were believed to be scheduling flights in the corridors at the times and altitudes Allied planes were scheduled to fly.

Western officials expressed fear the new Soviet harassment tactics could lead to incidents in the three 20-mile-wide air corridors which link West Berlin, located 110 miles inside Communist territory, with the West.

They said the Russians kept their tactics within legal limits by announcing their flight plans at the Air Safety Center as they are supposed to. But the Soviets were said to be coinciding their flight plans deliberately with those of Western aircraft.

Informed sources said also that West Berlin's Tempelhof Airfield has had sporadic trouble reaching aircraft in the air corridors on some frequencies of ...

★ ★ ★

Reds Have Goat Tag Ready

By UP-International

Moscow — The Soviet press and radio has started laying the blame on the West in advance in the event the Geneva Conference fails to show progress on Berlin, disarmament and a nuclear test ban.

Pravda, the Communist Party newspaper, said today the U. S. decision to resume nuclear tests ...

(Continued on Page 11)

Homefolks Welcome Powers

French Strike Against OAS

Paris—UPI—Strikes were called in France and Algeria today to protest continued terrorism spurred by the approaching cease fire in the Algerian war.

More Snow In Midwest

Seek 'Protection'

Fire From Right Helps, Says ADA

Escaped Lion Slain by Cops

Asks Stamp

FIRST LADY PAYS HOMAGE TO GANDHI

India Cheers Jackie

New Delhi, India — (AP) — Indians welcomed Mrs. John F. Kennedy warmly today and watched with interest as she placed a wreath of white roses at the shrine of Mohandas K. Gandhi.

BEFORE LEAVING the memorial, the wife of the U. S. president was shown a marigold tree planted by Eisenhower on

(Continued on Page 11)

—Associated Press WIREPHOTO

MRS. J. F. KENNEDY, POPE JOHN XXIII ... At Vatican where Pope granted audience

The Dazed Leaned On Her

Lexington, Ky.—(AP)—Gertrude Landmesser has looked on misery and death for 20 years.

(Continued on Page 11)

Parades Criticized

Bad Day for the Irish And for Catholics?

New York — (AP) — A Roman Catholic priest — himself of Irish descent — suggests St. Patrick's Day parades can have "bad effects" for Catholics.

The Rev. Edward T. Cooke, writing in the current issue of Information magazine, a national Catholic monthly published here by the Paulist Fathers, says St. Patrick's Day celebrations are harmful to the church, to Catholic schools and to the Irish.

Father Cooke, curate in Our Lady Queen of Peace Church in Maywood, N. J., noted that he had marched in New York's St. Patrick's Day parade four

(Continued on Page 11)

Let's Chuckle

Sign in a gift shop: "For the man who has everything —a calendar to remind him when the payments are due."

Most Stores Are Open Tonight for Your Shopping Convenience

March 12, 1962: The afternoon paper reported on how the tragedy was being contained. The nurse was suspended and later reinstated.

Microfilm archives

District Attorney Stephen Smyk plays the part of Mrs. Lillie Mae Colvin, on witness stand in rear, as she describes to him how she filled a small sugar can from a 20-gallon sugar bin in General Hospital's kitchen, April 1962. Also in rear is Broome County Coroner Vincent M. Maddi. *Press & Sun-Bulletin archives*

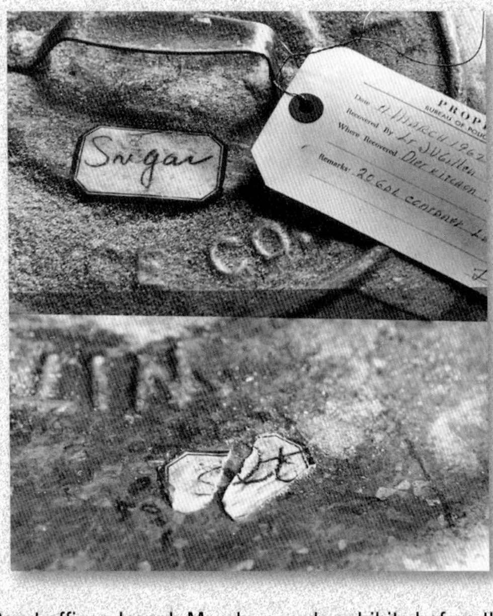
Sugar

Close-ups of a sugar can label, top, and salt can label on containers from General Hospital's kitchen in 1962. Confusion of the cans, which resulted in a container from the baby formula room being filled with salt instead of sugar, led to the deaths of six infants. *Press & Sun-Bulletin archives*

IN GOD WE TRUST

County Court officer Joseph Murphy guards exhibits before the start of coroner's inquest in Binghamton, April 1962. The exhibits include two large cans, used to store sugar and salt in the hospital kitchen, and smaller shiny cans and spoons used to measure the formula that led to the death of six infants. *Press & Sun-Bulletin archives*

Hot to Beat

WEATHER BUREAU FORECAST
Generally fair, warm and humid tonight. Chance of showers. Low 65-70. Tuesday mostly cloudy, scattered showers or thundershowers. High 83-88.

THE EVENING PRESS

THE HOMETOWN NEWSPAPER OF THE SOUTHERN TIER

Binghamton, N. Y., Monday, August 6, 1962 — Volume 84 — 99 — 40 Pages — 5 Cents

★ ★ ★ Read It In The Evening Press, Hear It Over WINR, See It on TV 40, 78, 81

Broome Population Boost of 30%, Big Employment Spurt Are Predicted

By JACK MORTON

Broome County's economy will become "much improved, stable and diversified by 1980," according to a firm of economists.

The economists predict the county's population will rise 30 per cent during the period to 256,000 and that the number of jobs available will climb about 28 per cent to a total of 112,400.

The report states that there will be a change in the type of jobs available. For example, the economists predict that Endicott Johnson Corp., which now employes some 12,000 persons, will need only 10,000 by 1970 and 7,000 by 1980.

This is a general conclusion and one of the major highlights of a report given to the Broome County Board of Supervisors by Hammer & Co. Associates of Washington, D. C. and Atlanta, Ga.

The report contains the results of a study the Hammer firm made into the county's economic future over the next two decades. The firm was hired for the job by the County Planning Board with state and federal grants totaling about $14,000.

The Planning Board will use the information in drawing up a master plan for future development of the entire county.

Generally, the economists see a bright future for the county, if several programs are carried out by community leaders.

Several defects and one "glaring weakness" in the county as it now exists are described, along with assets that can bring prosperity if properly used.

(Details of the economists' report are on pages 4, 5, 9, 10 and 17.)

Highlights of the report:

1—The work force of Endicott Johnson will undergo a 42 per cent decline from the present level. This will result from modernization, some automation and possibly decentralization.

2—The county has too many separate units of government, resulting in uncoordinated planning and inadequate control over development. "Urban sprawl" is threatening the area because of this and for other reasons.

3—There are defects in the housing picture in the county and new houses cost too much. Efficient, economic building practices used successfully elsewhere should be adopted.

4—The amount of land developed in the immediate Triple Cities area will increase by 50 per cent by 1980.

5—Median family income in the county by 1980 will reach $8,500. Extremely low-income families will almost disappear and the number of families making more than $9,000 will grow to 41 per cent of the total.

6—International Business Machines Corp. already has the most "economic impact" of any industry, and IBM and other growth firms will become even more dominant in the future.

7—The county must expand its higher education facilities or lose some of its industries to other communities.

8—The street system in the Triple Cities is the area's "most glaring weakness" and contributes to blight.

9—Retail trade at present is the second highest employer in the county and promises to become even more important.

10—The county has many assets that can be used to compete with other metropolitan areas successfully, including strategic location, trans-

(Continued on Page 4)

Details on Pages 4, 5, 9, 10 and 17

Soblen May Go to Israel

By the Associated Press

London—The conviction grew today that runaway Russian spy Dr. Robert Soblen will be returned to Israel this week to continue his fight to escape a life sentence in a U. S. prison.

Speedy Abortion Sought

By the Associated Press

Stockholm—Mrs. Sherri Finkbine sees a Swedish doctor today, seeking speedy abortion of the baby she fears has been deformed by the drug thalidomide.

PILLS END MARILYN'S LIFE

Misfit's Last Exit

Recalls Jean Harlow . . . 11

By the Associated Press

Hollywood — Marilyn Monroe's body lay unclaimed today in the county morgue—in a tragic climax to a lifetime of personal torment.

FOUND DEAD — Actress Marilyn Monroe, 36, found dead in her home in Brentwood, a Los Angeles suburb, as she left Columbia-Presbyterian Medical Center in New York in March of 1961 after a 23-day checkup.

JIM DOUGHERTY . . . Her first husband

BEDSIDE TABLE—A policeman points to an assortment of medicine bottles on the nightstand beside the bed of Marilyn Monroe's home where she was found dead.

Russians Not Told Of Blast

Festival Upset . . . 2

By UP-International

Moscow—The Soviet Union resumed nuclear testing yesterday with a tremendous high-altitude explosion near the Arctic island of Novaya Zemlya but the Russian people were not told about it through their newspapers and radios.

SITE OF SHOT

(Continued on Page 4)

Wheeler Arraigned

New York—(AP)—Maynard C. Wheeler, president of Commercial Solvents Corp., was arraigned today on a fugitive warrant issued in Texas in connection with Billie Sol Estes' alleged illegal operations in chemical fertilizer.

How Is JFK Holding Up?

President Kennedy is rounding out his second year in office. How is he holding up, and what sort of record is he making?

Relman Morin assesses the President on the basis of the first half of his term in five articles, the first of which appears on Page 15.

Also on the inside:

Power Lawyer Urged for Senate

New York—(AP)—James B. Donovan, the attorney who arranged the prisoner exchange of U2 pilot Francis Gary Powers for Soviet spy Rudolph Abel, was proposed today as a Democratic candidate for the U. S. Senate.

Maybe She Called Him A Big Ape Once Too Often

Cincinnati—(AP)—Penny and Big Boy were lovers. But he done her wrong and now it's all over.

Dr. Kelsey To Testify On Drug

Washington—(AP)— The Senate Judiciary Committee called Dr. Frances Kelsey for testimony today on President Kennedy's proposed amendments to drug control legislation.

Final Tragedy Inevitable?

EDITOR'S NOTE: AP Hollywood columnist Bob Thomas knew Marilyn Monroe from the beginnings of her Hollywood career.

By BOB THOMAS

(Continued on Page 8)

World Mourns Lost Sex Goddess

Hollywood—(AP)—From London, from Paris and around the world came reverberations of the shock caused by the death of Marilyn Monroe.

The news even penetrated the Iron Curtain. In Moscow, Tass reported

(Continued on Page 8)

Rail Unions Fight Rules

Chicago—(AP)—Five on-train rail brotherhoods pleaded with a federal judge today to issue an injunction before they are forced to create a national crisis by calling a strike.

Negro Voter Hike Appeal

Albany, Ga.—(AP)—Negro leaders vowed last night to step up a voter registration drive designed to erase segregation barriers in this south Georgia city.

(Continued on Page 8)

Let's Chuckle

Rich food and late hours are what make a lot of people thick and tired.

August 6, 1962: The story predicted 256,000 people would live in Broome by 1980, and the gradual decline of Endicott Johnson and growth for IBM. *Microfilm archives*

Girls from the East Jr. High School graduating class, Binghamton, 1962. *Courtesy Virginia Hibbard*

Boys from the East Jr. High School graduating class, Binghamton, 1962. *Courtesy Virginia Hibbard*

Fred Stein, former publisher of The Press, breaks ground for the new building in Vestal, 1963. Standing with Fred are Kimball Davis, Ed Scala, Irwin Cronk, Fred Cockenie, Henry Baldwin, Glen Bartle, Sam Pearis, Herb Rand, John Burns and Stu Dunham. *Courtesy Rudy Bystrak*

WEATHER: Considerable cloudiness and mild with occasional rain or showers today. High 70-75. Partly cloudy and mild tonight. Low, 53-58. Fair and warm tomorrow. High, 75-80. (Map, Page 13).

The Sun-Bulletin

Tuesday, June 4, 1963
Binghamton, N.Y. 7 Cents

WORLD MOURNS DEAD POPE

John XXIII ends 4-day fight for life; statesmen, churchmen lead tributes

Plane with 101 vanishes in Alaska; wreckage seen

JUNEAU, Alaska (AP)—A military chartered airliner with 101 aboard vanished off the coast of Alaska yesterday and the Coast Guard said last night a Canadian plane had reported sighting what appeared to be wreckage.

The only detailed information concerning the sighting came from an amateur radio operator at Sitka, Frank Getman, who told radio station KSEW, Sitka, he heard over an aircraft frequency that the plane sighted no survivors. He said the information he heard was that the wreckage included partially inflated liferafts.

The purported wreckage was said to be near Graham Island, approximately 100 miles west of the Canadian mainland on the north end of Queen Charlotte Island.

The plane was carrying men, women and children.

The Northwest Airlines DC7, a piston-engined aircraft, last radioed 30 to 40 miles at sea off Prince of Wales Island, requesting a change of altitude from 14,000 to 18,000 feet. Air traffic men trying to reply minutes later got no answer.

The last confirmed message from the plane was at 2:06 p.m., about 2½ hours after it left McChord Air Force Base, Wash., with 96 military passengers, including dependents, and a crew of six.

Army officials at Anchorage said some of the military men aboard the DC7 were soldiers destined for posts in Alaska under regular rotation.

An air search began immediately. Four search planes left Elmendorf and another took off from Eielson AFB, Fairbanks, Alaska. The Military Air Transport Service, in charge of the charter, diverted a C124 en route from McChord to Alaska.

The Coast Guard sent two planes and the Strategic Air Command diverted two KC135 jet tanker-transports to the search.

Unpledged electors face probe

WASHINGTON (UPI)—A senatorial inquiry into an unpledged elector movement aimed at denying President Kennedy Southern support in 1964 was ordered yesterday by Sen. Estes Kefauver, D-Tenn.

Kefauver said in a statement the Senate's constitutional amendments subcommittee he heads will seek public testimony today on the effect and legal aspects of efforts in five states to free presidential electors from even the moral obligation of voting for the candidate heading either party's national ticket.

The subcommittee will vote June 12 on a series of proposed constitutional amendments to change the electoral system.

Kefauver named Alabama, Mississippi and Georgia as states in which he said new election laws permit the choice of unpledged electors. He added that at least one house of the state legislatures in Florida and Louisianna has passed similar bills.

"This could result in the removal of these states, representing a total of 53 electoral votes, from the electoral equilibrium which has heretofore existed, with the possibility that the presidential election could be thrown into an entirely different arena, the House of Representatives," he said.

Unless one candidate collects 268 electoral votes in 1964, the decision on the winner would be passed to the House, where each state delegation would have a single vote in chossing the President.

Kennedy won in 1960 with 303 electorial votes, including 27 from Alabama, Georgia and Louisiana. This was 34 more than the 262 total he needed then. Florida gave its 10 votes to former Vice President Richard M. Nixon. Mississippi, Alabama and Oklahoma—where a Nixon elector exercised his legal right not to vote for the Republican nominee—contributed a total of 15 to Sen. Harry F. Byrd, D-Va.

Many lands, faiths join in grieving

NEW YORK (AP)—Leaders of all faiths, heads of government and world statesmen joined yesterday in a solemn tribute to Pope John XXIII — the Pope of good will whose appeal was "Catholic," or universal, in the full sense of the term.

The five American members of the Roman Catholic church's college of cardinals said sadly that the world would miss the 81-year-old pontiff, who died in Vatican City yesterday.

President Kennedy said the concern of the Pope for human spirit "transcended all boundaries of belief or geography."

Comment came from far and wide, from Jew and Gentile, from every corner of the political arena. All voiced sorrow and regret at the Pontiff's passing.

Religious leaders were unanimous in their opinion that Pope John's great contribution was unity and understanding among the various faiths. Political leaders praised his attempts to achieve peace.

* * *

Soviet Premier Khrushchev sent a telegram of "profound condolences" to the Vatican. Tass said Khrushchev's message added: "We retain good memories of John XXIII, whose fruitful activities for the maintenance and strengthening of peace have earned him wide recognition and won him the respect of peace-loving peoples."

President Kennedy, the first Roman Catholic President, said the Pope's "wisdom, compassion, and timely strength have bequeathed humanity a new legacy of purpose and courage for the future."

He said the Pope brought compassion and understanding to the most decisive problems of a tumultuous age.

"He was the chosen leader of world Catholicism but his concern for the human spirit transcended all boundaries of belief or geography," the President added.

U Thant, secretary general of the United Nations, praised Pope John's recent encyclical on peace, "Pacem in Terris." He said it "spoke for all men and to all men in restating his belief in the dignity of the individual, in fundamental human rights, in justce and in an effective international order.

"His was truly an ecumenical message for far-sighted significance," Thant said.

* * *

Dr. Eugene Carson Blake, highest ranking officer of the Presbyterian Church of the U.S.A., called the Pope's death "a loss, not only to the Roman Catholic Church, but to a fragmented and anxious world seeking meaning and unity in the midst of chaos. More than any of his predecessors since the Reformation, John sought to replace suspicion with trust, contention with cooperation."

Bishop Fred Pierce Corson, president of the World Methodist Council, which represents nearly 50 million Methodists, said, "All Christendom mourns the death of a great and good man."

He called him "the most widely known and best loved leader of the 20th century."

"His life and noble works will long endure as an inspiration for man's immortal quest for peace and justice," said Rabbi Julius Mark, president of the Synagogue Council of America.

SUN-BULLETIN—UPI

Pope John XXIII
. . . in a photograph released May 22

Eventful 4½-year reign ends

VATICAN CITY (AP)—Pope John XXIII, who touched the heart of a divided world with his untiring work for unity and peace, died last night as the sun set over 100,000 grieving faithful gathered beneath his window.

The 81-year-old supreme pontiff of the world's half-billion Roman Catholics, in the words of Vatican Radio, "passed away religiously and serenely" on the fourth day of his agonized struggle with death.

His closest relatives and associates were at his side in the papal apartment overlooking St. Peter's Square, where only nine minutes before an extraordinary outdoor Mass for him had ended.

"My time will come at night," the Pope had once said. "By day I have church business."

True to his prediction, Pope John—by official Vatican reckoning the 281st spiritual ruler of the world's Catholics—died at 7:49 p.m. (2:49 p.m., EST).

The mourning begun in St. Peter's swept around the world, across barriers of nature and man. World leaders displayed rare unanimity in their praise of Pope John, and church leaders of many sects joined in prayers for him.

* * *

Death came to the humble Italian tenant farmer's son four years, seven months and six days after he began his reign as spiritual leader of the world's Catholics. For his simplicity, his love and his yearning for all men to live as brothers, he became known as the "Pope of unity and peace."

In the last throes of death, he expressed his hopes for peace, Christian unity and social justice many times.

He worked untiringly for these ends even in the last months of his mortal illness.

* * *

Death was caused by a stomach tumor complicated by peritonitis. The Pope was stricken a year ago with the tumor, which caused hemorrhaging, but he continued working at his heavy tasks almost to the end. Two weeks ago the pontiff suffered a grave relapse.

The final crisis began Friday morning, when peritonitis—inflamation of the lining of the abdominal cavity—set in. He was close to death then.

But the strong heart of this son of an Italian peasant continued to pump life through his veins. The Vatican doctors were astonished at his vitality. He rallied a number of times sufficiently to bless those about him and to console them. He was, he told prelates and relatives at his bedside, ready to go "sweetly toward the end."

Often in excruciating pain, the pontiff fought off death for almost four more days. He first rejected the use of morphine to ease his pain, offering up his suffering as a sacrifice for the aims which had been closest to him — world peace and Christiain unity. Later he was given pain-killers.

In the final hours, the Vatican said, the pain was "atrocious." The dying pontiff clutched a crucifix to his breast. Only unconsciousness brought him relief. In the moments of consciousness the Pope appeared to concentrate on prayer.

* * *

Of the many milestone acts of his reign, the pontiff seemed to set the greatest store by the Ecumenical Council he summoned last autumn to deal with the distant goal of Christian unity.

Pope John's death now automatically terminates this major undertaking. When a sucessor is chosen by a solemn conclave of the College of Cardinals, one of the first major decisions to be faced will be whether to continue the council, which had been in recess since Dec. 8 and was scheduled to resume Sept. 8, or whether to leave it in suspension.

More on Pope John inside: The world was his parish—an obituary . . . A new type of religious leader—an assessment by Methodist Bishop Corson . . . Everybody liked him — a report by George Cornell . . . TC pair attended last appearance . . . All on Page 5.

De Gaulle plans tough Bonn line

By NORA BELOFF
London Observer Service

LONDON — When General de Gaulle visits Chancellor Adenauer at the beginning of next month, he is expected to confront the West German leader with a difficult choice.

He will tell him that either he must repudiate Vice Chancellor Ludwig Erhard's pro-British policy or the general will have no more use for the Common Market.

Charles de Gaulle

In principle the Rome Treaty is indissoluble; in practice a rigidly uncooperative attitude by any of the major powers can paralyze the projected economic union.

Things went badly for the French at the Brussels conference of foreign ministers last week when all their partners ganged up against them and in favor of regular meetings of the six and Britain.

But the French are still confident when it comes to the crunch the chancellor will once again succumb to General de Gaulle.

* * *

Another meeting of the six foreign ministers will be held on June 17. Between now and then the commission and the smaller delegations will try to work out a face-saving formula, but both Vice Chancellor Erhard and French Foreign Minister Maurice Couve de Murville are convinced the matter cannot be settled until their leaders meet in July.

The collision seems to have been the consequence of an unexpected toughening on the German side.

French sources said last week that there will be no modification of the French attitude. Although they agree with their partners that in the long run Britain should come in, they say the subject cannot be reopened "for several years."

* * *

The French protest, with some justice, that the quarrel has been wrongly presented in London and Washington as a division between the outward and the inward-looking—or the protectionist and the liberal—members of the community.

On agriculture, now the principal point of conflict, the French are more liberal than the Germans. And before reaching new agreement on raising the levy on poultry, which has caused such a furor in Washington, the French got four of their partners to agree to a more accommodating formula. The veto this time was by the Germans.

Officials in Bonn assert bravely that the federal government was not too dihearlened by the new French veto at Brussels on closer links between the Common Market and Britain. They are still moderately optimistic about the prospects of a British tie-up with the market.

Mrs. Rocky makes her first public bow

ALBANY (AP)—Mrs. Nelson A. Rockefeller smiled, shook hands and exchanged pleasantries with a substantial segment of Albany's leading citizens last night as she made her first, formal public appearance since her marriage to the governor of New York State.

Gov. and Mrs. Rockefeller the former Margaretta (Happy) Filter Murphy, were among 400 guests at a dinner of the Albany Civic Planning Committee, which works for the improvement of the capital.

Mrs. Rockefeller was the center of attention and the initial reaction was one of curiosity—to get a look at the new First Lady of New York State.

Happy Rockefeller

TC leaders voice regret

Officials, clergy comment on Pope's passing

These were the reactions of Triple Cities civic and religious leaders to the death of Pope John XXIII yesterday:

Binghamton Mayor John J. Burns:

"He was one of the greatest Popes of all time. His tremendous impact on the world in the cause of peace and brotherly love and social justice will live long after him."

Endicott Mayor E. Raymond Lee:

"I think Pope John XXIII has set an example for the world in the restoration of tolerance between different religious beliefs. His aims to establish peace have been an inspiration not only to the free world, but even included the Communist bloc.

"His passing has been a sad affair for the Catholic Church, because his leadership will long be remembered by the entire Christian world."

Johnson City Mayor James W. McCabe:

"I feel that the world has lost a tremendous leader for peace, and a tremendous leader for understanding among the religious denominations. As has happened in the past, it will happen this time that a leader will be picked who will continue his efforts toward peace and understanding."

The Rev. Dan Thomas, pastor, First Presbyterian Church:

"All the world mourns the passing of one of the greatest Popes of all time. He has, by the depth of his humility and the breadth of his sincerity, communicated not only with Roman Catholics, but all Christian men, everywhere."

The Rev. Robert Davern, director, Broome County Catholic Charities:

"I can think of no human who has accomplished more for God and men in four years of history. His love for all men seemed to embrace the entire planet. The flame of his loving spirit will spread out and touch even more as he leaves this world. He was certainly a man sent by God to show us his goodness and lead a troubled world back to its maker."

The Rev. George Flint, president, Broome County Council of Churches an dpastor of the Tabernacle Methodist Church:

"The Pope's death is a distinct loss to be mourned by Protestants as well as Catholics. It is my prediction that he will go down as one of the greatest influences in religious history."

Rabbi Jacob Hurwitz, Temple Israel:

"The entire world mourns the

See TC LEADERS, Page 5.

How a Pope is chosen

VATICAN CITY—A successor to Pope John XXIII will be chosen by the College of Cardinals between June 18 and June 21.

The cardinals, princes of the Roman Catholic Church, will decide on a new Pope by "inspiration," "compromise" or secret ballot. It took two years and nine months to elect Gregory X in 1271, but only a few hours to name Julius II in 1503. The last seven Popes have been selected within four days. They must begin deliberations between 15 and 18 days after the death of the Pope.

After nine days of funeral rites for the dead Pope, the cardinals gather a staff of doctors, barbers, waiters and personal assistants to tend to all their needs while they are locked in an area of some 200 rooms in the Vatican. This area is then sealed up, windows whitewashed, telephones disconnected. The cardinals do not emerge from their conclave until they can announce, "We have a Pope."

There are two ballots in the morning and two in the afternoon. To choose a Pope requires a majority of two thirds of the cardinals present. Today there are 82 living cardinals—more than ever voted for a Pope in the history of the church.

Although theoretically any male Catholic is eligible to be named Pope, the supreme pontiff has been chosen from the college itself for centuries. While Italians outnumber any other nationality in the college, the 29 living Italians represent the smallest ratio in history.

THE WORLD THIS MORNING

VATICAN CITY: Pope John XXIII, probably the best loved Pope of modern times, died after four days of agonized struggle with a stomach tumor and peritonitis. He was 81 years old, had ruled for less than five years, but had captured the world's imagination and heart with his efforts and appeals for peace, Christian unity and social justice.

NEW YORK: Churchmen and statesmen led lamentation for Pope John XXIII, with spokesmen for all faiths joining in tribute and world leaders including Soviet Premier Khrushchev and President Kennedy leading official condolences.

JUNEAU: A military-chartered airliner carrying 101 people was reported missing over Alaska. Search planes at once began hunting it.

PARIS: President De Gaulle is expected to offer Konrad Adenauer an ultimatum soon—stop the pro-British tendencies rising in West German government circles, or face a French torpedoing of the European Common Market and Bonn-Paris ties.

WASHINGTON: Sen. Estes Kefauver D-Tenn., announced he plans an investigation of an unpledged elector movement aimed at denying President Kennedy support in the South in 1964. Electors are not bound in law to vote for their party's nominee.

BIRMINGHAM: A federal judge postponed a decision on whether to issue an injunction, as government request, to forbid Alabama's Gov. George Wallace to attend—and try to block—enrollment of Negroes at the University of Alabama next Monday.

ON PAGE 2.

18 Pages

141st Year No. 179

Second-class postage paid at Binghamton, N.Y.

Today is Tuesday, June 4th, the 155th day of 1963 with 210 to follow.

The moon is approaching full phase.

The morning stars are Venus, Jupiter and Saturn.

The evening star is Mars.

Sun rises today at 5:29 a.m. and sets at 8:36 p.m.

On this day in history:

In 1800, the finishing touches were put on the White House.

IN 1896, Henry Ford wheeled his first car from a brick shed in Detroit and drove it around the darkened city streets on a trial run.

In 1942, the Battle of Midway began and the Japanese fleet suffered its first decisive defeat of World War II by the United States.

In 1944, U.S. and British soldiers occupied Rome, the first Axis capital to fall to the Allies.

June 4, 1963: The Sun-Bulletin marked the death of Pope John XXIII, whose Second Vatican Council ushered in momentous changes in the Roman Catholic Church. *Courtesy David Silvanic*

Chatter Proposal

WEATHER BUREAU FORECAST
Cloudy, windy, cold with snow flurries tonight and Sunday. Low tonight 27-32. High Sunday 38-43.

BINGHAMTON TEMPERATURES

THE EVENING PRESS

THE HOMETOWN NEWSPAPER OF THE SOUTHERN TIER

Binghamton, N. Y., Saturday, November 2, 1963 — Volume 85 — 173 — 36 Pages — 7 Cents

★ ★ ★
Read It In The Evening Press,
Hear It Over WINR,
See It on TV 40, 75, 78, 81

—PRESS PHOTO BY LEO FAHEY

COUNTY'S 34TH FATALITY—Sheriff's Sgt. G. William Norton stands beside wreckage of tractor-trailer in which John Stegich, Jr., 22, of Mohawk, died early today in Route 79 near Harpursville. (Story on Page 5.)

Suicides of Nhu, Diem Claimed by Viet Rebels

Were Shot, Others Say; Streets Gay

Saigon, South Viet Nam—(UPI)— President Ngo Dinh Diem and his brother Ngo Dinh Nhu were assassinated by rebel soldiers early today while they were being taken to military headquarters in Saigon in an armored personnel carrier, reliable military sources said.

Earlier, the Saigon radio said the brothers committed suicide after being captured.

By Press Wire Services

Military rebels in Viet Nam announced today the death of President Ngo Dinh Diem and his brother Nhu, and proclaimed a new government led by Buddhists.

Some accounts filtering from South Viet Nam's capital—where thousands danced joyously in the streets — said the Ngo brothers committed suicide, others that they were shot to death.

Suicide was the story broadcast by the rebel-held radio Saigon.

MR. NHU

This terse account, as pieced together by diplomatic sources in Bangkok and in Washington, was that the 62-year-old chief executive and his brother, 52, killed themselves upon being recaptured after once escaping.

A BANGKOK diplomat said the two were reported to have swallowed poison on the way to jail in an armored car from a church in Saigon's Chinese quarter where they had taken refuge.

There was no independent confirmation. Some diplomats wondered whether the two would have so breached their Roman Catholic faith as to take that way out, for the church condemns suicide.

The American Broadcasting Co. announced it had received word from its Saigon correspondent that a nervous officer shot the brothers after taking them into custody at the church.

Some news dispatches filtered from Saigon after a long blackout about the 18-hour revolu-

(Continued on Page 2)

Associated Press WIREPHOTO

MONUMENTAL JEERING—Vietnamese crowd jeers as pedal-cab driver carts head of demolished statue through streets of Saigon following overthrow of the Diem regime. Monument was demolished by the crowd because of resemblance to Mrs. Ngo Dinh Nhu, South Viet Nam's former first lady.

Secluded Mrs. Nhu Has Statement Ready

Los Angeles — (AP) — Mrs. Ngo Dinh Nhu, secluded behind her double-locked hotel door, prepared a statement late last night on reports her husband, South Viet Nam's strong man, Ngo Dinh Nhu, and President Ngo Dinh Diem had committed suicide after their surrender in a military coup.

But she withheld the statement while keeping track of news reports. Her travel plans depend upon them.

She intended to attend Mass at the nearby Roman Catholic Church of the Good Shepherd during the morning.

EARLIER, she snapped "Never" to a newsman's question as to whether she would seek asylum in the United States were the coup successful.

"I cannot stay in a country whose government stabbed me in the back," she said.

She blamed the coup on American intervention.

(Immigration Service officials said Mrs. Nhu could be granted a visa extension if she is unable to return home.)

Messages of condolence on the overthrow of her brother-in-law's government poured into the hotel switchboard all day.

MRS. NHU received the first report of the possible suicides at about 9:45 p.m. (12:45 a.m. E.S.T.), approximately three hours after they reportedly occurred in Viet Nam.

Her original travel plans were to leave Los Angeles early next week for Tokyo, Hong Kong and Saigon, the final leg of her five-week round-the-world tour.

When word of the suicides reached her, an aide said, "this changes the picture entirely."

The aide speculated that Mrs. Nhu may have had an inkling a revolt was brewing when she decided last Monday to return to Los Angeles from San Francisco instead of continuing on to Tokyo as planned.

UPI TELEPHOTO

PROVISIONAL PRESIDENT—Nguyen Ngoc Tho, a civilian and former vice-president has been named provisional president of Viet Nam following yesterday's overthrow of the Diem regime.

Won't Drop Run

Albany — (AP) — The Public Service Commission says the New York Central Railroad has dropped a plan to discontinue operation of its pacemaker between Buffalo and Albany.

Desert Fighting Explodes

UP International

Figuig, Morocco—Bitter fighting exploded again today on the Algerian-Moroccan border and each side charged the other with breaking the midnight cease fire agreed on in Mali Thursday.

The Moroccans accused the Algerians of launching a new offensive at 6 a.m. against this border oasis town, 37 miles northeast of the Algerian desert base at Colomb Bechar.

The Algerians charged the Moroccans unleashed attacks at almost exactly the same hour against the village of Beni Ounif, about a mile from here but on the Algerian side of the border.

The charges and counter charges were made after both Algeria and Morocco had announced that the cease fire was being observed.

Algerian President Ahmed Ben Bella said late last night he had ordered his forces to respect the cease fire.

THE MOROCCAN army commander in the Figuig area said he had given similar orders to his forces.

Hours after the fighting should have stopped, however, both sides reported it had resumed.

Mortar shells were falling in downtown Figuig at 7 a.m. and Moroccan sources said an estimated 3,000 Algerian troops about a mile outside of town were attacking with tanks, mortars and recoilless rifles.

AN ALGERIAN spokesman at Colomb-Bechar charged that the Moroccans were attacking in force at Beni Ounif.

The Algerian spokesman said Moroccan artillery continued to bombard Beni Ounif for half an hour after the cease fire was to have gone into effect, and that the attack was resumed at 6:15 a.m.

He said the Algerian army had launched a counterattack and that "violent fighting" was going on.

Two Moroccan battalions—upwards of 1,200 men, supported by 300 civilian volunteers—were resisting the Algerians.

Both sides were using heavy mortars, recoilless rifles and tanks, as well as small arms.

MOROCCAN SOURCES said two Moroccan soldiers were killed and one was wounded in an attack yesterday in which they estimated the Algerians lost at least 100 men dead or wounded.

Figuig's Moroccan mayor said there were "many" Moroccan civilian casualties in yesterday's attack.

Moroccan King Hassan II told newsmen in Rabat yesterday the Algerians had encircled the town, forcing its garrison to withdraw half a mile to the west.

Correspondents who arrived here last night found the Moroccans firmly in control of the town, although the thunder of artillery and mortar fire could be heard from what seemed to be every side.

Gas Leak May Get Blast Blame

Indianapolis, Ind. —(UPI)— Investigators today worked on the theory that leaking gas ignited by a concession stand stove caused the Halloween evening explosion that killed 64 persons at an ice show here.

A total of 340 persons were injured in the disaster, one of the worst in the history of this city. Officials said there was a possibility the death toll would rise. At least 16 of the injured remained in critical condition.

State Fire Marshal Ira Anderson, who headed a four-man blue-ribbon investigating team, said food-heating equipment at refreshment counters in the coliseum may have ignited butane gas leaking through a broken valve.

As cranes pulled apart the debris inside the big coliseum at the Indiana State Fairgrounds, investigators found a half-dozen butane gas tanks. Two of them were ruptured. At least four were impounded.

There were "wild rumors" galore, Anderson said. Some said no permits had been issued for the butane gas. Anderson said investigators were checking out reports a concession worker "discovered hissing gas, saw the fog and yelled 'clear out.'"

Space Pair Will Wed Tomorrow

Moscow — (UPI) — Cosmonette Valentina Tereshkova and her sweetheart in space, Andrian Nikolayev, will be married in Moscow tomorrow, it was announced officially today.

The Foreign Ministry, confirming a story that had been an open secret here for days, said the nuptials will be followed by a party in the official House of Receptions in Lenin Hills.

Western reporters were invited to the celebration but the wedding, in one of Moscow's two "palaces of marriage," was declared off limits to them. However, the ceremony was expected to be televised throughout the Soviet Union.

An earlier announcement had said the 26-year-old chestnut-haired former textile worker and Nikolayev, 33, would be wed. But the exact date and place had been unspecified.

2 of Snow, More Ahead

Jamestown — (AP) — A two-inch blanket of snow greeted early risers in Jamestown and vicinity today.

The wet heavy snow, first of the season, arrived during the night. The weatherman predicted an additional three to seven inches of snow in some sections near Lake Erie by nightfall.

They Buzzed The Traffic Right Away

Weed, Cal. — (UPI) — Several hundred thousand bees gave this Northern California community more than a taste of honey yesterday when 150 hives were dumped in the highway.

The bees escaped at the intersection of U. S. Highways 99 and 97 when a flatbed truck carrying their hives collided with a logging truck, the highway patrol reported.

The bees took control of the intersection, forced local inhabitants to retreat indoors and stopped all traffic.

"There must have been millions of them," a patrol spokesman said.

"They stung a lot of people."

Faith in Action, A Graphic Message

One of the less publicized features of this newspaper is the graphic portrayal of religious faith in action.

This week's illustration by Woodi Ishmael is the first of a group telling the story of how a missionary's befriending of a native boy bore fruit in later years. Page 6.

Also on the inside:

Judy's a Doll, 17, and Teen Queen

By Press Wire Services

Dallas, Tex.—A living doll—Judy by name — is the new Miss Teenage America, but a bubbly sprite from Santa Rosa, Cal., Karen Valentine, has the first television contract.

It was a multi-ring circus last night, with a national TV audience estimated at 40,000,000 in on the fun. Emcee Bud Collyer called it "the liveliest spot in the nation."

Judy Doll, 17-year-old blue-eyed brunette representing Akron, Ohio, was crowned "teen queen for 1964."

"I'm just glad to represent you all, and hope I can be a wonderful queen," Judy told the other 49 contestants. "You've made me so happy, but I know you all deserve this, too."

Pixie-like Karen Valentine, 16, captured the audience — as she has done everyone this week.

"I've just never seen anyone as cute as that gal," one man said, after seeing her uninhibited, shoulder-wiggling and eye-rolling version of "Blame it on the Bossa Nova." "Wonder if I could adopt her?"

Showman Ed Sullivan telephoned from New York after seeing Karen's act and invited her to his program.

First runner up to the new teen queen was Jeanine Zavrel, an energetic 16-year-old representing Washington, D.C. A blue-eyed dark brunette, Jeanine sang a folk ballad of "Two Brothers."

Second runner-up was Eileen Melody Speerin, 15, rosy-cheeked charmer from New York City. She danced her strenuous acrobatic ballet in spite of a painful cut and bruised foot which she injured Thursday during rehearsals.

Judy's prizes include a four-year scholarship to a college of her choice, a new car, a trip around the United States, 50 shares of stock in a soft drink company, and cosmetics and clothes.

An above-average student in her senior year, Judy hopes to major in interior decorating and design in college.

ROSES AND CROWN FOR A TEEN QUEEN —UPI TELEPHOTO

★ ★ ★

U. S. Denies Role in Coup, Says Tho Well Qualified

Washington — (UPI) — President Kennedy, who had urged a change in policies and personnel in South Viet Nam, today had a new regime to work with in that Communist-plagued southeast Asian land.

Administration officials said the man who became president in the provisional Saigon government — former Vice-President Nguyen Ngoc Tho—was well qualified to head a caretaker government and cut out the repressive measures of the Diem government against the country's Buddhist majority.

Tho, a 55-year-old career civil servant, had served as vice-president under Diem since 1956. He is a former Vietnamese ambassador to Japan and secretary of state for economy.

EARLY in the day yesterday the State Department asserted categorically that the United States played no part in the uprising nor did it have advance information that a revolt was imminent.

They acknowledged, however, that the Kennedy administration's hints for reforms could have encouraged the rebellion. Once the revolt got going, all U. S. aid to Viet Nam was ordered held up.

The provisional government to be established under the protection of the military junta is expected to win early recognition from the United States after a few days of observation.

BUT THERE was little doubt

(Continued on Page 2)

Spy's Farewell: 'Nonsense'

New York— (AP) —Three accused Soviet spies expelled by the United States flew home to Russia last night after one ridiculed the espionage charges as nonsense.

The one-word description was offered by Yuri A. Romashin, 28, third secretary of the Russian delegation to the United Nations, as he and two other delegation employes departed from Idlewild Airport.

Let's Chuckle

Diplomacy might improve if we could find a key to fit a deadlock.

November 2, 1963: Early reports already questioned the reported suicides of Vietnamese leaders. *Microfilm archives*

Dull-a-Mite

WEATHER BUREAU FORECAST

Rather cloudy, mild, chance of occasional showers tonight. Low 45-50. Saturday cloudy, warm, chance of scattered showers. High 55-60.

2 a. m.	48	7 a. m.	45	11 a. m.	50
4 a. m.	48	8 a. m.	44	Noon	54
5 a. m.	48	9 a. m.	44	1 p. m.	56
6 a. m.	47	10 a. m.	46	2 p. m.	58

THE EVENING PRESS

THE HOMETOWN NEWSPAPER OF THE SOUTHERN TIER

Binghamton, N. Y., Friday, November 22, 1963 Volume 85 — 190 42 Pages 7 Cents

★ ★ ★

Read It In The Evening Press, Hear It Over WINR, See It on TV 40, 75, 78, 81

President Is Assassinated; Texas Governor Wounded

President John F. Kennedy slumped down in back seat of car after being shot today in Dallas. Mrs. Kennedy leans over President as unidentified man stands on bumper.

—Associated Press WIREPHOTOS.

President John F. Kennedy, left, and Gov. John Connally of Texas, right, shortly before they were shot, the President fatally, in Dallas, Tex., today. In center is Mrs. Kennedy.

Suspect Is Held

By UP-International

Dallas—President Kennedy was assassinated today in a burst of gunfire in downtown Dallas. Texas Gov. John Connally was shot down with him.

The President, the nation's 37th chief executive, cradled in his wife's arms had been rushed in his blood-spattered limousine to Parkland Hospital and taken to an emergency room. An urgent call went out for neurosurgeons and blood.

Vice-President Lyndon Johnson was in the same motorcade and was immediately surrounded by Secret Service men until he could take the oath of office as president.

The President, 46 years old, was shot once in the head. Connally was hit in the chest.

Young Man Quizzed

Police found a foreign-make rifle. Sheriff's officers were questioning a young man picked up at the scene.

The President was conscious as he arrived at the hospital. A Father Huber from Holy Trinity Roman Catholic Church was called and administered the Last Rites of the church.

A Secret Service agent and a Dallas policeman were shot and killed today some distance from the area where President Kennedy was assassinated.

No other information was immediately available.

Johnson, who now becomes President was in a car behind the Kennedys and Connallys.

He was to be sworn into office as soon as possible.

He rushed to the hospital and was whisked away by Secret Servicemen. His whereabouts were being kept secret.

Mrs. Kennedy was still at the hospital. She was not shot.

The White House spokesman refused to comment on her condition.

Shot in Right Temple

President Kennedy was shot in the right temple.

"It was a simple matter of a bullet right through the head," said Dr. George Burkley, White House medical officer.

The shooting occurred as Mr. Kennedy and his wife, riding with Governor Connally and Mrs. Connally, were riding in the White House "bubbletop" limousine through a crowd of 250,000 people in downtown Dallas.

As it neared the triple underpass leading toward the Trade Mart where Mr. Kennedy was to address a lunch, three bursts of gunfire sounded.

Motorcycle police raced up the grassy knoll of a park nearby where a man and a woman were huddled.

Mr. Kennedy died 30 minutes after the shot was fired.

Johnson left the hospital moments after he was informed of the President's death.

Traveling behind a police escort, with his wife, Lady Bird, Johnson headed under heavy guard for seclusion somewhere in midtown Dallas.

Presumably Johnson and his staff will go right to work on plans for taking a formal oath of office to succeed the slain President.

The President was the fourth U. S. president to be slain in office.

Connally Condition

Governor Connally was reported in serious condition and in great pain.

"Take care of Nellie," his wife, he gasped to an aide.

The identity of the assassin or assassins was not immediately known.

Sheriff's officers took a young man into custody at the scene and questioned him behind closed doors.

A Dallas television reporter said he saw a rifle being withdrawn from a window on the fifth or sixth floor of an office building shortly after the gunfire.

Mr. Kennedy was shot at 1:25 p. m. He died at approximately 2 p. m.

Throughout the Texas trip, when Mr. Kennedy and Johnson had been in the same motorcade, as an obvious security measure they have ridden in separate cars. The Johnson car has always been some distance from the Kennedy car, sometimes by as much as 60 yards.

Mrs. Connally was also in the famous

(Continued on Page 4)

★ ★ ★

Area Shocked

The news that President Kennedy had been shot brought expressions of shock and disbelief among downtown shoppers this afternoon.

"You're kidding—you can't mean it," one woman said.

Everybody expressed shock, some expressed anger.

"I can't imagine anybody resorting to this in this day and age," said one man.

The news passed through the crowds on Court Street with lightning speed.

The foreman of a crew of city employes, after he and his men had mulled over the news for a minute, said: "Come on, let's have a coffee break. I can't work."

A Catholic priest who heard the news while eating lunch crossed himself and started to pray.

In one restaurant the television set suddenly blared forth with the ominous announcement, stopping all activity.

"You wouldn't think it would happen in Lyndon Johnson's state, where he should be liked," a woman said.

But a few feet away, another woman said:

"Texas is full of crazy people who'd do something like this."

★ ★ ★

Mother, Father Told Grim News

Hyannis Port, Mass. — (UPI) — President Kennedy's mother and father were advised today that he was shot.

A workman at the Kennedy family compound heard the news on the radio and rushed into the house to tell Mr. and Mrs. Kennedy.

Mrs. Kennedy is 72. Her husband Joseph, who suffered a stroke in December, 1960, is 75.

The elder Kennedy was napping when informed of the shooting. His niece, Ann Gargin, 32, who was about to leave for Detroit, canceled her trip.

Attorney General Robert F. Kennedy, the President's younger brother and closest adviser, was having lunch at home when word of his brother's shooting reached him.

Kennedy's personal secretary said the Attorney General was remaining at the Kennedy Hickory Hill Estate in McLean, Va.

Senator Edward M. Kennedy, (Dem.-Mass.) the President's other brother, was presiding over the Senate today when word came that the President had been shot. An aide told him and he rushed from the Senate chamber.

Fire Loss $100,000

Colonie—(UPI)—A huge barn on South Shaker Farms was leveled by a fire last night which caused almost $100,000 damage. About 20 cows were in the barn when it collapsed, but another 30 cows were led to safety.

Off-Track Betting Favored Upstate

Nineteen upstate New York communities approve off-track betting, according to an informal poll of the man-on-the-street.

The Associated Press tally showed that the margin was smaller than in New York City.

For further facts gleaned from the poll, turn to page 12.

Also on the inside:

Reds Refuel Convoy Spat

By the Associated Press

Moscow—The Soviet Union accused the United States today of trying to make the rules for Soviet policing of Western convoy traffic on the Berlin Autobahn. The Russians warned they would not permit this.

A Russian note to the U. S. Government rejected an American protest over the stalling of a U. S. Army convoy for 42 hours Nov. 4-5 because the Americans refused to dismount from their vehicles and be counted.

The Soviet reply renewed the threat of more interference with Allied troop convoys on the 110-mile life line highway between West Berlin and West Germany. The Allies insist they have the right to move on the Autobahn as they like. The Kremlin note said:

"THE CLAIMS of the American authorities to establish at their dicretion the range of duties and manner of action of Soviet representatives at the checkpoint in checking American servicemen are in general absolutely untenable.

Since Oct. 10 the Russians have held up three American

(Continued on Page 4)

★ ★ ★

Market Closes

New York—(AP) — The New York Stock Exchange closed at 2:10 p. m. for the day.

The action was taken by the board of governors.

The stock market reacted with a violent downturn late this afternoon to news that President Kennedy had been shot. Trading was very heavy.

Volume for the day was estimated at about 5,500,000 shares.

Washington—(AP)—The Senate recessed "pending developments" today as word reached the capitol that President Kennedy had been shot in Dallas, Tex. The House was not in session.

Sen. Mike Mansfield (Dem., Mont.), the Democratic leader, made the motion at 1:56 p. m.

November 22, 1963: The Evening Press put news of the assassination of President Kennedy in the same day's paper. *Courtesy David Silvanic*

CLOUDY AND WINDY Details on Page 35

The Sun-Bulletin

★ FINAL 7¢ ★

Binghamton, New York — Saturday, November 23, 1963 — 40 Pages, Two Sections — 142nd Year, No. 30

KENNEDY DEAD

★ ★ ★

Pro-Castro man held on charge of murder

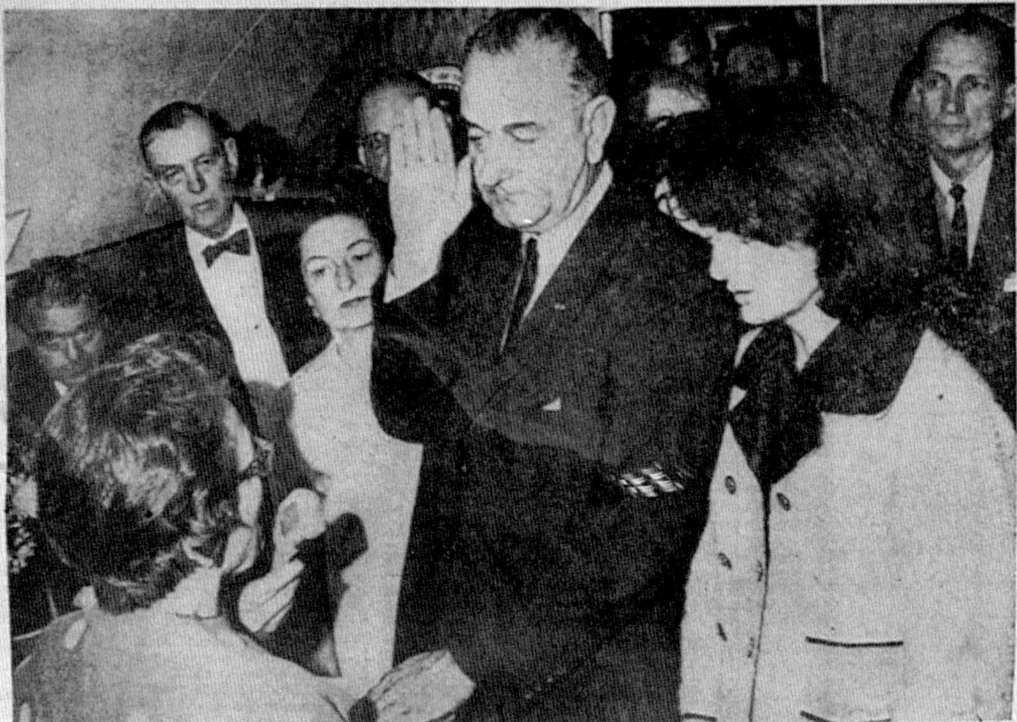

A new President takes the oath

Lyndon B. Johnson, with his wife Ladybird on one side and the grief-stricken widow of his predecessor on the other, is sworn in as the new President of the United States. The oath was administered by Federal District Judge Sarah T. Hughes of Dallas, aboard the Presidential plane, just before the group flew back to Washington in the late afternoon. (UPI Telephoto by Capt. Cecil Stoughton, official White House photographer).

November 23, 1963: The photo of Johnson's swearing-in became one of the lasting images from that terrible day. *Courtesy Carolyn Fitzgerald*

—Copyright, the Dallas Morning News via AP WIREPHOTO.

GUNMAN MOVES IN TO SHOOT OSWALD — Jack Ruby, Dallas nightclub owner, steps out with a gun in hand a moment before Lee Harvey Oswald, charged with the assassination of President Kennedy, was shot in the stomach at the Dallas city jail yesterday.

—Copyright, 1963, the Dallas Times Herald and Photographer Bob Jackson via AP WIREPHOTO.

BULLET SLAMS INTO BODY—Oswald begins to collapse as a bullet smashes into his abdomen. Oswald died several hours later only a few feet from the hospital room where the President died Friday. He never regained consciousness.

Books on JFK's Slaying Closed--in Dallas

The Weather

WEATHER BUREAU FORECAST

Fair, cold tonight. Low 20-25. Tuesday, increasing cloudiness, milder. High 38-48.

BINGHAMTON TEMPERATURES

THE EVENING PRESS ★

THE HOMETOWN NEWSPAPER OF THE SOUTHERN TIER

Binghamton, N. Y., Monday, November 25, 1963 — Volume 85 — 192 — 44 Pages — 7 Cents

JFK 'Rest in Peace' Mass Held

Johnson Orders Full Probe

By Press Wire Services

Dallas—Police in Dallas closed the books today on Lee Harvey Oswald and the world will never know what was in his mind. He was shot to death as President Kennedy's assassin by a self-appointed executioner before a nation-wide television audience.

While the martyred President was being buried in Arlington National Cemetery, mourned by the world, the Communist-Castro sympathizer accused of slaying him lay on a cold marble slab in a morgue.

He died with his lips sealed. He took to the grave with him the reason Mr. Kennedy was killed if, as police are convinced without doubt, he was the assassin.

(While Dallas police were quick to call the case closed, federal officials felt otherwise.

(President Johnson ordered a full probe of Oswald's slaying, and the FBI proposed further investigation into the presidential assassination with the hope of eventually giving the American people the whole story.)

The 24-year-old pro-Castro Marxist was being transferred in handcuffs from City Jail to a maximum security cell at the County Jail House when Jack Ruby, a one-time Chicago street brawler and owner of a Dallas strip-tease night club, leaped from a crowd of newsmen and policemen with a curse, jammed a snub-nosed .38 caliber pistol into Oswald's side and fired one shot.

"YOU SON of a bitch," he shouted. Oswald jerked back. So did the police bodyguards

(Continued on Page 4)

Grandmother Is Not Told

Boston — (UPI) — President Kennedy's 98-year-old grandmother has not been told, and probably never will be, of the President's assassination.

Mrs. John F. Fitzgerald celebrated her 98th birthday Oct. 31 and was cheered by messages of congratulation and a bouquet of flowers from the President and Mrs. Kennedy.

"Her mind si keen, very keen and we are afraid she'd understand this awful thing all too well," Miss Katherine Fitzmaurce of Worcester, the woman's constant nurse, said.

A Shamed Dallas Probes Conscience

Degraded twice in 48 hours!

That's the burden a shamed Dallas is bearing today as it examines its conscience trying to answer a difficult question: How could it happen?

Story on page 13.

Also on the inside:

★ ★ ★

Texas DA: 'No Doubt'

Dallas, Tex.—(AP)—"This Is it—I've sent men to the electric chair on less evidence than we have against Lee Harvey Oswald."

WADE

torney Henry Wade made the claim as he revealed the evidence which convinced Dallas police they had an airtight case against the accused assassin of President John F. Kennedy.

"There is no doubt in my mind that Oswald was the killer," Wade said.

Nine hours before Wade spoke to newsmen last night, Oswald, 24, was fatally shot by Jack Ruby, owner of a Dallas lounge. The shooting occurred in the police head . rters basement in front of hundreds of police, secret service, FBI men and newsmen, as Oswald was being escored to an armored car for transportation to new jail quarters.

WADE SAID TWO facts stood high in the mass of evidence linking the slim, brown-haired Oswald to the slaying.

First, a palm print on the underside of the rifle which fired the bullets that killed Mr. Kennedy was identified as Oswald's.

Secondly, Wade said, Oswald had definitely been placed inside the building at the time the shots were fired from there at Mr. Kennedy.

"The gun was here, his prints were on the gun, the gun was the gun that killed Kennedy, his palm prints were on the box which the killer sat, and witnesses put him on the sixth floor at the time of the shooting."

Asked if he believed Oswald was slain to keep him from talking, Wade said police were looking into that angle but so far no connection has been established between Oswald and Ruby.

"There is no concrete evidence to go on that there is anyone else connected with the assassination," Wade said, but added that some aspects of the case may still be investigated.

The district attorney said that because Ruby's slaying of Oswald was an assassination "I am certain that I can get the death penalty for Ruby. Ruby walked up to a man who was handcuffed and defenseless and cold - bloodedly assassinated him."

Wade added several specific details to evidence previously brought out.

HE SAID Oswald bought the Italian-make assassination rifle last March from a Chicago mail order firm, at a cost of slightly more than $12. The FBI, he said, confirmed the serial number of the mail order rifle matched that of the rifle that fired the shots at Mr. Kennedy.

Wade said they found a photograph showing Oswald holding the rifle at what he called an "at attention" stance. In one hand, Oswald held the rifle and in the other copies of the Daily Worker and a Fascist publication, the militant.

There was no evidence that showed Oswald was a member of the Communist Party, Wade said. "However, there was lots of material dealing with communism, such as the Daily Worker, and there was even more material dealling with the Fair Play for Cuba organization."

Police said earlier Oswald

(Continued on Page 4)

Johnson Wrote Caroline, John

Washington — (AP) — The first two letters Lyndon B. Johnson signed as President were to the two children whose father is buried today.

The letters to Caroline Kennedy, 6 years old Wednesday and John F. Kennedy, Jr., 3 years old today, told them at the beginning they perhaps are too young to understand it all now.

Mr. Johnson wrote them last Friday just after his return from Texas and only hours after he had been sworn in to succeed their slain father in the highest office of the nation.

—Associated Press WIREPHOTO.

PRESIDENT'S CASKET AT CAPITOL—Horse-drawn casket of President Kennedy halts before U. S. Capitol as symbolic riderless horse stands alongside.

GOP Delays Meeting

Minneapolis—(AP)—The Republican National Committee has postponed its scheduled meeting in Minneapolis Dec. 10-14, at which it was to have worked on plans for next year's GOP convention. Republican officials said the meeting will be held in January, with precise dates to be announced later.

Casinos Closed

Las Vegas, Nev. — (UPI) — This city's gambling casinos were closed today for only the third time in history in honor of slain President Kennedy. The only other times the city's gambling ceased was for about four hours in 1945 upon the death of President Roosevelt and for 12 hours on Good Friday in 1940.

Oswald Aid Denied

Washington — (UPI) — Senator John G. Tower (Rep., Tex.) said yesterday he did not help Lee Harvey Oswald, accused assassin of President Kennedy, return to the United States from Russia: "The facts of the matter are just exactly opposite," Tower said in a statement.

Cushing Conducts Rites; 1,200 Attend

By UP-International

Washington—The soul of John Fitzgerald Kennedy was commended unto God today at a simple Roman Catholic funeral Mass attended by world leaders.

Last rites for the assassinated President were conducted at St. Matthew's Cathedral by Richard Cardinal Cushing of Boston, the lifelong friend and pastor who performed Mr. Kennedy's marriage ceremony and baptized his children.

Mr. Kennedy's flag-draped coffin was borne to the cathedral from the White House, six blocks away, by the same horse-drawn caisson that brought the body from the Capitol, where an estimated 240,000 to 250,000 persons had passed by the bier.

JACQUELINE KENNEDY, who was at her husband's side when a sniper's bullet cut him down Friday, followed on foot behind the caisson. Walking behind her to the mournful cadence of muffled drums were President Johnson, former Presidents Eisenhower and Truman, foreign heads of state and other dignitaries.

After the services, the cortege was to proceed to Arlington National Cemetery, where the commander of PT-109 will rest forever among fellow comrades-in-arms of World War 2 and other heroic dead.

The "rest in peace" Mass for America's first Roman Catholic President was offered in the presence of 1,200 persons who had come from near and far to make a final gesture of love or respect.

"LIFE IS NOT taken away . . . life is but changed," intoned white-hair Cardinal Cushing, as he offered the ancient Catholic prayer for the departed:

"Be merciful, we beseech Thee, O Lord, to the soul of Thy servant, John Fitzgerald Kennedy, whom You have just called out of this world. . . . He put his hope and trust in You: do not then let him undergo the pains of hell, but bring him to happiness without end."

By the side of the grief-numbed young widow was Attorney General Robert F. Kennedy, the late President's brother and closest to him of all in the closely knit Kennedy family.

AMONG THE mourners were such diverse world leaders as Prince Philip of Britain; Anastas I. Mikoyan, Soviet first deputy premier; President Charles de Gaulle of France; Chancellor Ludwig Erhard of West Germany; King Baudouin of Belgium; President Eamon de Valera of Ireland; and Sir Alec Douglas-Home, new prime minister of Britain.

Across America, millions of Mr. Kennedy's countrymen said their own prayers for the repose of his soul. President Johnson declared a national day of mourning and "earnestly recommended" that every American attend his place of worship "to pay homage to the memory of a great and good man."

ST. MATTHEW'S Cathedral, which was Mr. Kennedy's parish church, is a drab red-brick building with a 200-foot-high dome. Standing since 1898, and begrimed by the soot of the downtown area it occupies, it is far from impressive in its external appearance.

But its interior is a glittering example of Romanesque-Byzantine architecture, with pillars of magnificent red-and-white Carrara marble and richly colored mosaics of Venetian glass. Its showpiece is a magnificent high altar of white marble, carved in India and decored with colored insets in the same manner as the famed Taj Mahal.

Mr. Kennedy's coffin rested in front of this altar and just

(Continued on Page 4)

NATO Pays Its Tribute

Paris — (UPI) — The North Atlantic Treaty Organization's Permanent Council paid solemn tribute to the memory of President Kennedy today and pledged its support to President Johnson.

The council met for 15 minutes while the flags of all 15 members of the alliance flew at half-staff outside the NATO headquarters building.

NATO Secretary General Dirk U. Stikker said, "To our friends in the United States we only say: their grief is ours. They and we have lost a leader of outstanding ability, transparent sincerity and utter dedication."

November 25, 1963: Powerful images of Jack Ruby shooting Lee Harvey Oswald dominated the front page. *Courtesy Kate Sands and Harry Dodd*

CLOUDY WITH SHOWERS

Details on Page 31

The Sun-Bulletin

★ FINAL 7¢ ★

Binghamton, New York | Tuesday, November 26, 1963 | 142nd Year, No. 32 | 44 Pages

Now he too belongs to the ages

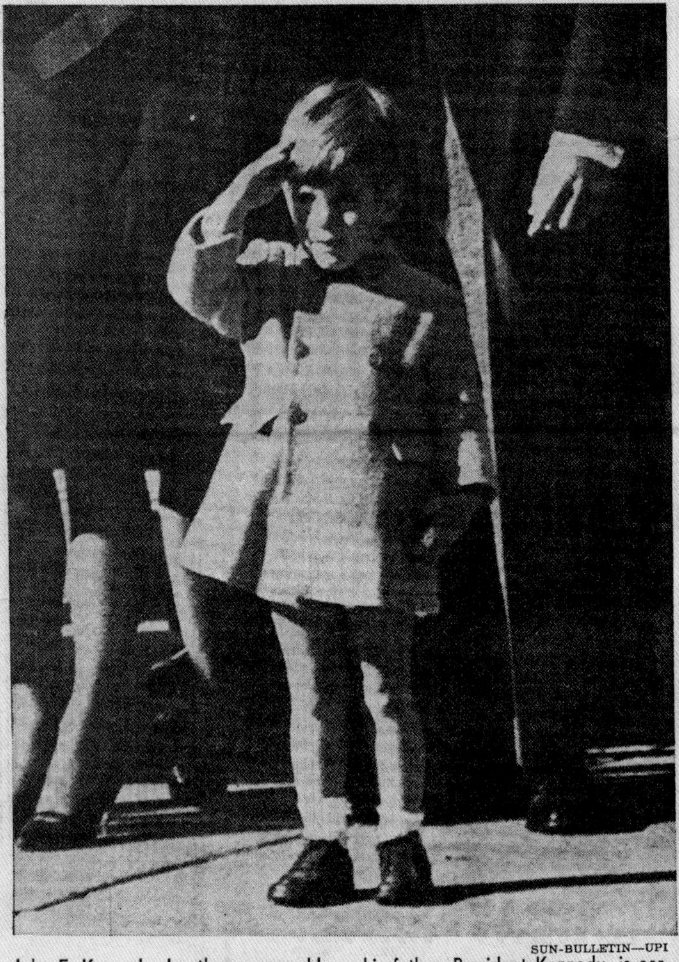

SUN-BULLETIN—UPI

John F. Kennedy Jr., three years old yesterday, salutes as the casket of his father, President Kennedy, is carried from cathedral.

Taps, salutes bid Kennedy farewell

By MERRIMAN SMITH

ARLINGTON NATIONAL CEMETERY (UPI) — America buried John Fitzgerald Kennedy on Arlington's green slopes Monday, consigning his body to the land he loved and his soul to the God he worshiped.

After the last rites of a funeral Mass that broke the composure of his grieving widow, the martyred President was borne across the Potomac River to the national shrine of honored dead.

There, before the stricken family and before foreign presidents and princes, he found his final rest. An eternal light will burn at the tomb looking out on the Lincoln Memorial.

An estimated 800,000 hushed mourners lined the streets to pay their respects as the slain President was brought from the Capitol to the White House, from there to St. Matthew's Cathedral, and at last to the still green cemetery.

★ ★ ★

Joining the family and all America in its grief were kings, presidents, ministers and princes from nearly every country of the world, Communist as well as free, from Charles de Gaulle of France to Anastas Mikoyan of Russia.

At the grave site, the farewell of "taps" mourning across the Virginia countryside and the crash of rifle volleys in final salute climaxed a day of sounds. The sounds, above all, convinced those who had refused to believe the young President was dead.

There had been the dirges ... the muffled drums ... the sad skirling of bagpipes ... creaking caisson wheels on hushed streets ... the cadenced march of military men ... the sobs of mourners.

★ ★ ★

At one brief point, it became too much for the veiled Jacqueline Kennedy.

It was only at the cathedral that her grief overwhelmed her in public. Upon leaving the low pontifical Mass, she suddenly bent forward as though in pain, sobbing into her handkerchief.

Others wept openly or within.

Under sunny, cloudless skies, but with a chill in the air, the young dead President than was taken across the river and under the trees of Arlington.

There, in sonorous tones, Richard Cardinal Cushing of Boston, who had married "Jack" Kennedy and his beautiful bride 10 years ago, commended his soul to God.

"Let his soul and all the souls of the faithful departed rest in peace," the archbishop prayed.

Through the funeral hours, bells of churches of every faith were tolled.

★ ★ ★

And always throughout the capital, along all routes of procession, were the silent, sympathetic people.

They were there hours before Mrs. Kennedy and other members of the official party emerged from the White House to join her husband's body at the Capitol where it had lain in state throughout the night.

An estimated 140,000 people had passed by the bier before the casket had to be taken away.

They lined the route as the horse-drawn caisson carrying the flag draped casket moved slowly back to the White House.

It was there that Mrs. Kennedy, leaving her limousine, began the pilgrimage on foot to the cathedral. By her side were the President's brothers, Atty. Gen. Robert F. Kennedy and Sen. Edward Kennedy.

She walked head high behind the casket, never faltering, in the chill wind.

Following her were the 1,200 invited for the Mass. Among those on foot were such men as De Gaulle, President Johnson, Prince Philip of rBitain, King Baudouin of Belgium, 82-year-old President Eamon de Valera of Ireland and Mikoyan.

Former Presidents Eisenhower and Truman joined the mourners at the cathedral as did Caroline and John Jr. There were about 1,200 mourners in all.

From the church the casket was taken to Arlington on the caisson which had borne it through the city streets these last two sorrowing days.

So long was the procession of limousines in the funeral cortege that the grave side services were underway before the last was able to arrive.

There, in the shadow of the onetime mansion of Robert E. Lee, came the 21-gun salute, the three volleys of musketry by the firing party, and the sad sound of "taps."

A little boy salutes

By ROBERT M. ANDREWS

WASHINGTON (UPI)—A little boy at his grieving mother's side saluted the passing casket.

And in that moment, he suddenly became the brave soldier his father would have wanted him to be on this day, of all days.

For Monday, John F. Kennedy Jr. turned three.

His world was strangely different, in little ways a child notices but does not understand.

Where was his daddy? The tall man with the laughing blue eyes who had a big desk and saw lots of important people and stooped to spank him good-naturedly and took him on helicopter rides and called him "John-John."

This was supposed to be the day of The Party. The cake with three candles to blow out, the friends singing boisterous "Happy Birthdays," the gifts.

★ ★ ★

He did get a letter, as did his sister Caroline, from Lyndon Johnson, the man they call President now. No one outside the White House knew what the letters said.

But home, the White House,

See JOHN JR., Page 25

November 26, 1963: John F. Kennedy Jr. salutes his father. *Courtesy David Silvanic*

Aspirin overdose kills city girl, 7

STORY ON PAGE 5.

CLOUDY AND COLDER Details Page 38

The Sun-Bulletin

★ FINAL 7¢ ★

Binghamton, New York, 13902 Thursday, February 13, 1964 40 Pages—Two Sections 142nd Year, No. 97

Soviets demand 'release' of U.S.-'kidnaped' defector

GENEVA (UPI) — The Soviet Union angrily implied Wednesday that agents of the United States engineered the defection of Russian security officer Yuri Nossenko. The Soviets hinted he had been kidnaped and demanded his immediate return.

The Soviets also charged that Switzerland aided "provocative foreign agents" in arranging Nossenko's defection.

The Swiss government promptly rejected the Soviet charge, which cast a pall over the future of Soviet-American relations and the 17-nation disarmament conference.

The U. S. State Department reported Monday that the 36-year-old Nossenko, believed to be carrying top-secret information on Soviet nuclear weapons and defenses, asked for asylum in the United States a week ago. He disappeared from the Soviet delegation to the disarmament conference on Feb. 4.

Wednesday's charge by chief Soviet disarmament negotiator Semyon K. Tsarapkin was the first official Soviet comment on Nossenko.

"If it be true that Nossenko is really in the hands of the United States authorities, this can only mean that Swiss authorities not only do not provide delegates to international conferences with sufficient protection, elementary security and guarantees, but also allow the provocative activities on their soil of foreign agents, he said.

Swiss Foreign Minister Frederick T. Wahlen was said to have "blown his top" when informed of the Soviet charge.

Wahlen called Soviet Ambassador Alexander I. Lochtchakov to his office and delivered a note which called the allegations untrue and incorrect.

Nossenko's whereabouts are not known publicly. Spokesmen for the American mission to the conference denied knowing anything about Nossenko or his disappearance. It was presumed here that he flew to the United States last week, but the State Department has said nothing more than that Nossenko asked for asylum.

SUN-BULLETIN—UPI

BEFORE

These are the Beatles — Ringo Starr, George Harrison, John Lennon and Paul McCartney — the famous mop-topped British rock'n'rollers.

SUN-BULLETIN—UPI

AFTER

And these are—the same quartet, after being "cropped" by UPI staff artist Nat Curry, wielding an airbrush on the photos. Neat, huh?

Beatles at Carnegie Hall

NEW YORK (UPI) — They turned high-brown Carnegie Hall over to England's no-brow Beatles Wednesday night.

The old hall has had its share of enthusiastic audiences since it was opened on May 5, 1891. Its 5,200 occupants Wednesday night (2,600 for each of two eBatle concerts) maintained the tradition.

The British rock 'n rollers were on stage for 45 minutes, having been preceded by a group of self-styled "folk 'n' rollers" called the Briarwoods — four gentlemen and a lady.

The usual screaming, whistling and stomping accompanied the appearance of the Beatles. Signs hung from parts of Carnegie's five balconies. "Beatles we love you," read one. "Betles 4-ever," said another.

Among those attending the second concert was Mrs. Happy Rockefeller, wife of the New York governor. She was with a daughter by a previous marriage, Wendy.

"She's just as excited as any child," Mrs. Rockefeller said.

Seats had to be placed on the stage to accommodate the overflow crowds attending possibly the first rock 'n' roll show ever held at the hall. Aside from the shouting, the audiences were orderly.

The Beatles arrived by taxicab, took one look at the 1,500 youngsters gathered in 56th Street, and fled into the hall.

Among the onlookers were some anti-Beatles, members of a student organization called "SWAT" — Students War Against Trash.

Nixon hits rights chiefs' 'extremism'

CINCINNATI (UPI) — Former Vice President Richard M. Nixon called upon "responsible" civil rights leaders Wednesday night to take over from the extremists."

Nixon said Congress soon will pass a "significant bi-partisan" civil rights bill, but he warned "much of the good of that law will be destroyed if the irresponsible tactics of some of the extreme civil rights leaders continue."

The 1960 Republican presidential candidate, who was accused by some of being evasive on the civil rights issue during the 1960 campaign, dealt at length with the issue in his speech at a Republican Lincoln Day dinner.

In his prepared text Nixon also unleashed an attack on President Johnson's handling of foreign affairs. It was his second major pronouncement on foreign policy this week.

Nixon said "America has had the worst series of foreign policy failures under President Johnson that we have experienced in any period since World War II."

The New York attorney addressed 1,100 rank-and-file Republican workers at a $5-a-plate dinner in a community he carried easily in 1960 against the late President John F. Kennedy.

Looking back to that contest, Nixon predicted in a news conference that this year's election would be decided on issues and not personalities.

He called for televised debates between the two candidates, saying he felt the 1960 debates with Kennedy "rendered a great service" to the public by stimulating political interest even though they may have cost Nixon the election.

Nixon, who said he is not seeking the Republican presidential nomination but would run if drafted, told the Republican gathering "The great issue of the 1964 campaign is foreign policy."

February 13, 1964: The newspapers were ready for a little fun. A UPI artist used an airbrush to give The Beatles haircuts. *Microfilm archives*

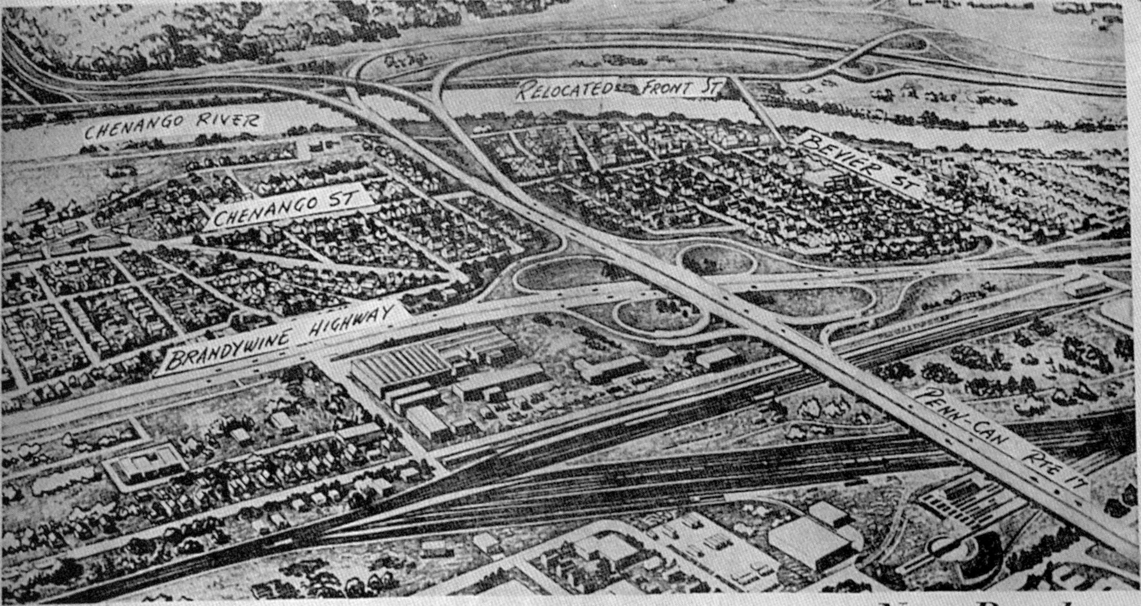

RELOCATED FRONT ST
CHENANGO RIVER
BEVIER ST
CHENANGO ST
BRANDYWINE HIGHWAY
PENN-CAN RTE 17

TOMORROW (▲)

WHERE 81 AND 17 PART COMPANY—Sketch above shows new highway pattern that will result with completion of Chenango River crossing of Penn-Can Highway and Route 17. Photo below shows progress to date. The highways come through North Side from Five-Mile Point on joint roadbed, then split, with Penn-Can heading north to Canada, Route 17 west to Lake Erie.

TODAY (▼)

EXISTING FRONT ST
CHENANGO RIVER
CHENANGO ST
BRANDYWINE HIGHWAY
PENN-CAN RTE 17
BROAD AVE

—PRESS AIR PHOTO BY BOB GARVIN.

Builders' Prospects Stunning For 1964

By JOHN E. GIBBONS

Executive Secretary, Associated Building Contractors of the Triple Cities, Inc.

The year 1965 promises to witness the largest building construction volume ever undertaken in Broome County and immediate adjacent areas.

Industrial construction, office and commercial buildings, public and school construction are contemplated to be bid or negotiated by contractors at an average rate of over $4,000,000 per month during 1965.

MR. GIBBONS

This is coupled with building construction in excess of $14,000,000 which already is under contract and remains to be completed in 1965 or later.

THE COMBINATION of building construction and heavy and highway construction will insure the greatest single volume year in the history of this area.

This anticipated volume for building construction only includes a relatively minor amount of demolition work in connection with Binghamton's Urban Renewal Project 1.

The bulk of construction related to urban renewal is anticipated in 1966 although it is expected that businesses in the process of relocation will have a more immediate effect on construction requirements.

THE BUILDING construction industry considers itself reasonably well - geared to meet this influx of new work in 1965.

The availability of skilled labor plays a key role in this optimism.

Historically, the building season has been limited to 7 or 8 months of the year.

In the last two decades techniques have been developed to protect work and workmen and extend the construction season in many cases to a 12-month operation.

NATURALLY, certain phases of construction cannot be undertaken in the severest of weather but improved job schedules allow much more work to be completed via winter protection methods.

Therefore, the same skilled work force can complete a greater volume of construction by lengthening the season.

Also, greater emphasis is being placed on apprenticeship training to meet long term needs by the Associated

(Continued on Page 27)

New Road Boom Really Is Rolling

By JACK MORTON

Highway construction in the Triple Cities area this year will reach an unprecedented $50,000,000 pace.

New Penn-Can Highway contracts to be awarded over the next three months will continue the construction boom that began with the start on $32,000,000 worth of roads in 1963 and 1964.

The Triple Cities for some months has been getting the benefits of the big payrolls and high levels of employment brought on by new highway construction.

The new projects, which are expected to total about $16,000,000, are likely to continue these conditions through at least two more construction seasons.

• •

THE CHANCES are the highway building boom will last longer. Gov. Nelson A. Rockefeller has indicated he will push for speedy completion of Route 17 Expressway between Binghamton and Lake Erie.

When contractors start on the projects, probably soon after the weather breaks in the spring, the Penn-Can will be under construction all the way from Binghamton State Hospital Hill to Whitney Point. This is a distance of almost 19 miles.

Penn-Can projects already account for almost $27,000,000 of the construction under way. These include a project from the Hospital Hill to the Chenango River at Stow Flats and another northward from Stow Flats to Hinman's Corners.

The new projects will extend from Hinman's Corners for the 12 miles to Whitney Point.

Meanwhile, the Pennsylvania Department expects to complete construction this summer on 23 miles of the Penn-Can between Scranton and Ashley, Pa. Pennsylvania officials hope to have the highway open at summer's end from the New York State line to Ashley, which is a couple of miles south of Wilkes-Barre.

• •

OTHER TRIPLE Cities projects that will still be under construction this summer include the North Shore Drive. This $5,000,000 arterial extends from Collier Street Bridge along the Susquehanna River to Court Street and then northward with a viaduct to Frederick Street.

A project that was not begun until last summer was construction of a new bridge over the Susquehanna River between the Towns of Kirkwood and Conklin, about three miles north from the Pennsylvania State line.

This bridge will provide a connection between Route 7 (Conklin Road) and the hamlet of Conklin, on the Conklin side of the river, with the hamlet of Kirkwood, Route 11 and the Penn-Can Highway on the Kirkwood side of the river.

Another project on which construction will start this summer is a new section of Route 26 between Whitney Point and the Cortland County Line. The project, for which a contract was awarded last October, will cost about $680,000.

• •

EAST OF Broome County, construction on two major

(Continued on Page 27)

THE EVENING PRESS
Business Review and Forecast
Fri., Jan. 29, 1965 25
Section 1

Optimism Tempered With a Dash of Caution

By J. A. LIVINGSTON

Special Press Writer

What's to keep prosperity rolling? That is the question, as we move along in 1965. This has been a 20-year boom.

It began right after World War 2 and has persisted with only four minor interruptions—1949-50, 1953-54, 1957-58, and 1960-61. The setbacks were so mild we introduced a new term: Recession instead of depression.

MR. LIVINGSTON

The latest advance has been a gallop. It started in February, 1961—the month after President Kennedy's inauguration—and has hardly stopped for breath since.

It is now the second longest peacetime upcycle on record, exceeded only by the unprosperous recovery from the Great Depression.

• •

BUT THIS RAISES a critical question: Is it petering out?

The majority of economists who responded to my year-end questionnaire think so. Their predicted pattern for the year is: First half up, second half up also, but not so fast. This leads to the inference: Recession in '66.

Here are seven reasons for apprehension:

ONE—The automobile industry has had three superlative years in a row. Adding on a fourth would be like filling an inside straight in poker. It can be done, but the experts advise: "Don't bet your all on it!"

TWO—Housing continues to dip. The continued rise in foreclosures and the persistent vacancy rate of more than 7 per cent hardly foreshadow any immediate reversal.

THREE—The United States has not yet solved its balance-of-payments difficulties and, even more emphatically, neither has Great Britain. A sterling crisis could upset international money markets and perhaps put pressure on the dollar.

FOUR—As a corollary, the Federal Reserve System is inhibited. Modern economic thought—a la Keynes—dictates that central banks should make money and credit cheap and plentiful when business is not expanding rapidly enough to take up slack in employment.

But if interest rates were to fall in the U. S., foreign banks, business firms and investors would pull out funds—"hot money"—from this country. This would put pressure on America's gold supply and perhaps cause a "dollar crisis."

FIVE—Closing of military bases, if not carefully planned and spaced, can cause pockets of unemployment and a fear psychology. Indeed, retrenchment in defense spending—highly desirable, in itself—is a source of uncertainty.

SIX—Labor unrest is possible. The rivalry between David J. McDonald, president, and I. W. Abel, secretary-treasurer, for the presidency of the United Steelworkers increases the chance of a strike. Whoever is elected will want to prove he deserved it—by winning a signal wage boost.

SEVEN—Moreover, in anticipation of trouble in steel, many manufacturers and retailers are building up inventories. Not only are they ordering steel but also products made of steel. This could lead to an up-down inventory cycle.

So much for the question: What's to cause a slowdown? Now to: What's to keep prosperity rolling?

Recoveries are often propelled along by unexpected strengths generated by recovery, itself. This is possible in 1965.

Corporate profits have made the Great Leap Upward: From $22,000,000,000 after taxes in 1961, to $25,000,000,000 in 1962, to $27,000,000,000 in 1963, and in 1964 to well above $30,000,000,000. This is a major breakthrough.

• •

THE RETURN ON invested capital has been increasing. This courses through the economy in unexpected ways and places. It induces corporate boards of directors and entre-

(Continued on Page 27)

January 29, 1965: This page was in a special business section and showed how new highways would reshape the landscape. *Courtesy Jackie Deinhardt*

THE PRESS
EVENING
SUNDAY

—PRESS PHOTO BY LEO FAHEY.

THE EVENING PRESS' $5,000,000 PLANT IN EAST VESTAL, ALMOST SEVEN MONTHS OLD, WEATHERS FIRST WINTER.

the EVENING PRESS

Business Review & Forecast

Friday, January 28, 1966

SECTION C

Press Building Is Tourist Attraction

—PRESS PHOTO BY PAUL KONECNY.

HEART OF THE PLANT—Pressmen check editions coming off new, two-story press. At $1,800,000, it is the most expensive item in the new plant.

$5,000,000 Plant Draws Thousands

By JOE PIERSON

A newspaper plant is a fascinating complex of departments and activities devoted to the unusual task of producing a new product every time it publishes.

When The Evening Press opened its $5,000,000 plant in the Vestal Parkway about seven months ago, therefore, it was perpared for a crush of requests for guided tours.

Such tours, of course, were conducted at the newspaper's former cramped and inadequate quarters at 19 Chenango Street.

But the attraction of touring a vibrant new building housing one of the most modern newspaper plants in the country is much greater.

"IT'S REALLY SOMETHING the way people want to see this," said Jacque DuMond, Press promotion director who conducts most of the tours.

He said about 4,000 persons have toured the new Press facilities. They have included school children and members of service clubs, technical and engineering societies, scout organizations, church groups and others.

Last summer, a newspaper publisher and an architect from Tehran, visited the new Press plant in search of building ideas.

The visiting architect, Hooshang Poroushani, said he was especially impressed with the lighting, heating and air-conditioning systems.

The Press tour starts in the carpeted, wood-paneled lobby that contains striking light fixtures hanging from the ceiling.

GUESTS USUALLY ARE impressed first with the lighting and colors. Lighting in all rooms except the press room and paper storage room is by luminous ceilings. The colors of the walls, floors, desks, chairs and even the telephones were selected for compatibility.

The roominess of the various departments also impresses visitors, especially those familiar with the cramped confines of the former Press plant.

A highlight of the tour is an inspection of the new 12-unit Goss Mark I Headliner press—the heart of the plant and, at $1,800,000, its most expensive component.

Spectators are able to watch the workings of the two-story-high press from a second floor, glassed-in deck.

The old press, which was in the basement of

(Continued on Page 5C)

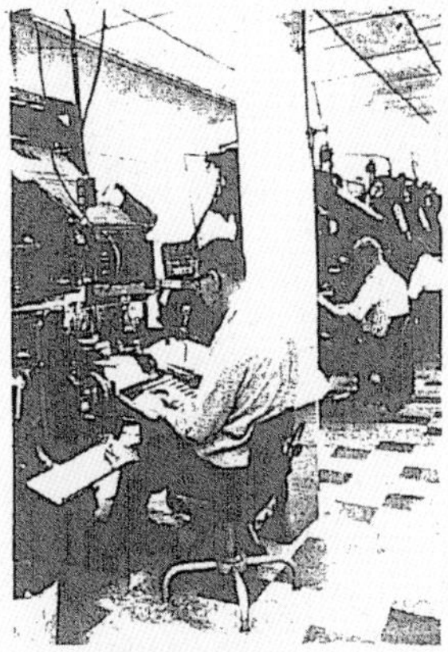

PRESS PHOTO BY GENE SWIERKOSZ

COMPOSING ROOM—Linotype operators work at their machines in composing room of the new plant.

UPI
UNIFAX

—PRESS PHOTO BY GENE SWIERKOSZ

NEWS FROM THE WORLD—A copy girl checks news coming in on one of eight machines in the wire room. With all machines operating, a day's average production consists of about 1,200 feet of news that must be checked. In the foreground are wire-photo machines, which send about 100 to 150 photographs a day.

—PRESS PHOTO BY JOHN ROLAS

FORMER HOME—The Press Building (and annex) in Chenango Street was home for the Press until last July, when the operation was moved to the Vestal Parkway plant.

—PRESS PHOTO BY GENE SWIERKOSZ

THIS IS PART OF SPACIOUS EDITORIAL DEPARTMENT, PROVIDING CONSIDERABLY MORE ELBOW ROOM THAN FORMER QUARTERS.

January 28, 1966: The paper included a special report on itself in its annual business review. *Microfilm archives*

'Snowblower' Goes Wild--No Letup for Tier

Story Below

Get the Drift
WEATHER BUREAU FORECAST
Partly cloudy, windy and cold with a few snow flurries tonight. Low 10-15. Tuesday, generally fair but windy and cold. High 15-20.

THE EVENING PRESS

THE HOMETOWN NEWSPAPER OF THE SOUTHERN TIER

Binghamton, N. Y., Monday, January 31, 1966 — Volume 87 – 247 — 24 Pages — 10 Cents

Juror Stricken

The nine-month Krebiozen trial may end in a mistrial as one of the jurors suffers asthma attack. Page 12A.

U.S. Resumes Bombing of N. Viet Nam

THROUGH THE SNOW—Young man in hooded coat plods between snowbanks at Courthouse Square in Binghamton, one of few persons moving downtown early today after 15-inch snow hit Southern Tier, the second snowy weekend in a row.

Offensives On Ground Stepped Up

Cong War Lull . . . 4A

By the Associated Press

Saigon, Viet Nam — The United States unleashed its bombers against North Viet Nam today after holding off air attacks for 37 days while vainly trying to bring the Communists to the peace table.

The first waves of U. S. Navy and Air Force planes hit bridges, ferries, barges, warehouse areas and storage facilities well south of the Hanoi-Haiphong industrial area. Later flights pummeled highway No. 1, a main artery along the coast, wrecking a truck convoy and destroying a bridge, a U. S. spokesman reported.

The later attacks were centered around Vinh, on North Viet Nam's central coast.

ON THE GROUND, U. S. and South Vietnamese forces stepped up their offenses against the Viet Cong, but the Communists inflicted heavy losses on a militia unit and Red guns hammered Allied positions.

A U. S. spokesman said navy pilots claimed destruction of a bridge about 10 miles southeast of Dong Hoi and damage to the approach to the Quang Khe ferry landing about 20 miles northwest of Dong Hoi.

Bad weather prevented estimates of the damage in other raids. Spokesmen declined to say how many sorties were flown or what types of bombs were dropped.

One navy plane was shot down as the raiders encountered heavy ground fire. But a U. S. Air Force helicopter rescued the pilot unharmed under machine-gun fire. He was Lt. Comdr. Sylvester Chumley of Lemoore, Cal.

Chumley's A4 Skyhawk jet went down about a mile off Dong Hoi. The Communists peppered the water around him for 35 minutes as he waited to be rescued.

"I'm glad to see you guys. Now, can you turn off that machine-gun fire?" Chumley told his rescuers. The rescue plane was piloted by Lt. Col. Robert E. Freshwater of Canton, Ohio.

RADIO HANOI claimed the North Vietnamese shot down Five American planes and damaged 10.

Resumption of the bombing had been expected for several days because of repeated state-

(Continued on Page 9A)

Marine Killed

(Marine Pfc. John G. Monks of Binghamton was killed in action Thursday near Chu Lai in South Viet Nam, a Marine Corps spokesman confirmed today. Story on Page 1B

LBJ Makes New Peace Bid to UN

RED CHINA
N. VIET NAM
HANOI
Haiphong
LAOS
GULF OF TONKIN
VINH
HAINAN
VIENTIANE
DONG HOI
U.S. SEVENTH FLEET
THAILAND

UPI TELEPHOTO Map.

RAIDS RESUMED—Map locates targets hit as the United States ended its 37-day pause in air raids against North Viet Nam today with strikes against military and communications targets near Vinh and Dong Hoi. Heavy antiaircraft fire was encountered by U. S. Navy and Air Force planes operating from land bases and the Seventh Fleet carriers Ranger and Kitty Hawk.

By the Associated Press

Washington — President Johnson made a new Vietnamese peace bid to the United Nations today a few hours after American bombers resumed air strikes against North Viet Nam.

The renewal of bombing "does not mean the end of our pursuit of peace," Mr. Johnson told the nation and the world in a special broadcast.

The President announced that he had directed Ambassador Arthur Goldberg to seek an immediate meeting of the UN Security Council in order to make a full report on the Vietnamese situation and to present a resolution for new action toward peace.

The resolution, the President said, "can open the way to the conference table."

"THIS REPORT and this resolution," Mr. Johnson declared, "will be responsive to the spirit of the renewed appeal of Pope Paul; that appeal has our full sympathy."

Mr. Johnson said he had ordered renewal of the bombing to save the lives of American, South Vietnamese and Allied soldiers fighting communist guerrilla forces in South Viet Nam. Those forces are supplied and reinformced by infiltration from the North.

He said he had carefully considered the counsel of his advisers. He declared:

"These advisers tell me that if continued immunity is given to all that supports North Vietnamese aggression, the cost in lives — Vietnamese, American and Allied — will only be greatly increased.

"In the light of the words and actions of the government in Hanoi, it is our clear duty to do what we can to limit these costs."

THE PRESIDENT asserted that bombing of North Viet Nam was renewed after it was determined that there was no readiness for peace on the part of Hanoi.

Nor has there been any support or understanding from Peking for U.S. efforts to open the road to peace, Mr. Johnson asserted.

He said that the United States does not regret its 37-day pause in the bombing of North Viet Nam—a pause that ended today. And, he declared:

"The end of the pause does not mean the end of our own pursuit of peace. That pursuit will be as determined and un-

(Continued on Page 9A)

Take War to UN, Morse Urges U. S.

Washington — (AP) — Senator Wayne Morse has urged the United States to bring the Viet Nam struggle before the United Nations Security Council, a move strongly opposed by Senator John C. Stennis.

"We haven't any unilateral right to determine what a Viet Nam settlement should be," the Oregon Democrat said yesterday, 12 hours before it was announced that American planes had begun bombing North Viet Nam targets again, ending a 37-day lull.

"I want a United Nations' resolution calling for arbitration," Morse, a member of the Senate Foreign Relations Committee and outspoken critic of the administration's Viet Nam policies, said. "I want a United Nations' takeover for peacemaking purposes."

IN OPPOSING Morse's views, Stennis, a Mississippi Democrat who heads the Senate preparedness subcommittee, said that to refer peacemaking to the UN Security Council members "would be giving them a problem they could not solve.

"We'd better go on and do it under our command," argued Stennis. "I don't want to turn it over to anyone."

The discussion of possible UN arbitration apparently stemmed from a suggestion Pope Paul VI made Saturday. Asked about arbitration, the Pope said:

"Who knows whether finally an arbitration by the United Nations, entrusted to neutral nations, might tomorrow — we could hope for such a thing even today—be able to resolve the terrible question."

THE WHITE HOUSE, then in the midst of decision-making on the resumption of bombing in North Viet Nam, promised to study the Pontiff's suggestions.

Morse and Stennis aired their disagreements on an unusual 90-minute television-radio program Congress and The War.

Also appearing were Senators Karl E. Mundt (Rep., S. D.) and Joseph S. Clark (Dem., Pa.) and Representative Hale Boggs (Dem., La.).

No Letup in Wild Winds Across Blizzard-Socked Tier

By TOM CAWLEY

A violent blizzard all but paralyzed the Southern Tier and northern Pennsylvania today.

It was the worst 24 hours of weather, barring flash-flood days of the past, the region has experienced in modern history.

Forty-to-50-m.p.h. winds toyed viciously with a 15-inch snowfall and forced most normal daily activity to a dead-center standstill. The Weather Bureau sees no letup in the gale winds tonight or tomorrow.

After a review of his records, Chief Meteorologist Gean DiLauro, Jr., said, "It is the worst blizzard-like condition in a half-century."

THE WEATHER BUREAU clocked peak gusts of 50 m.p.h. The wind settled back from gusts to steady blowing of 40 m.p.h. It scooped up the 13.3 inches that fell in the city and the 15.1 inches that fell on the hillsides and rearranged the snow in drifts across roads, streets and homes.

There was one snow-related highway death on Route 17 near Waverly.

Gales from the north played with a historic snowstorm that had moved north and east during the weekend. The combination neutralized transportation, education, all planned social activity and put off such events as midwinter graduation ceremonies, funerals and military physical examinations.

Key to the paralysis was the blow to transportation. Highways were hopelessly clogged with drifting snow. Airport opera-

(Continued on Page 3A)

Top Space Year Just 'Preface'

Washington — (AP) — President Johnson said today that American space achievements last year were a brilliant preface to the coming years of stations in space and voyages to the planets.

In a special message to Congress, Mr. Johnson said 1965 with its walk in space and the rendezvous of two manned U. S. spacecraft was the most successful year in the nation's aeronautics-space history.

"As our space program continues," the President told Congress, "the impact of its developments on everyday life becomes daily more evident. It continues to stimulate our education, improve our material well-being, and broaden the horizons of knowledge. It is also a powerful force for peace.

"The year 1965—the year of Gemini, Ranger and Mariner—is a brilliant preface to the coming years of Apollo, stations in space, and voyages to the planets."

The military space section of the report included this development on space surveillance: Research is under way on the best means of determining the physical characterisitics of "uncooperating objects in earth orbit" through observation by ground-based radar.

Storm, Cold Keep Clutch On Seaboard

By Press Wire Services

A wild winter storm thrashed the Eastern Seaboard for the second-straight day today. The South lay frozen under the deepest snows of the century, gale winds lashed coastal communities and heavy snow fell through the night in New England.

The number of storm-connected deaths since Thursday climbed to at least 75 in 16 states.

A state of emergency existed in Delaware and a state of near emergency in Virginia, where icy winds stirred the snow into 15-foot drifts. Prince George County in Maryland was under an emergency weather alert and New York City declared a snow emergency for the second time in eight days.

TEMPERATURES fell below freezing through central Florida. Chattanooga, Tenn., recorded 5 degrees below zero; it was zero at Rome, Ga., and Huntsville, Ala., and 2 below at Mus-

(Continued on Page 9A)

State Is Numbed, Choked by Drifts

Albany — (AP) — Blustery winds and brittle cold swept across New York State today in the wake of a Dixie-born snowstorm that stranded motorists and closed highways, schools and businesses with near-blizzard conditions.

Up to 18 inches of snow were reported in Rochester last night and accumulations of about a foot were widespread. Gusts of up to 60 miles an hour piled the snow to depths of several feet in some areas, however shutting down roads and airports.

The mayor of Oswego on Lake Ontario proclaimed a state of emergency as the storm spread 8-foot drifts through city streets.

The city had received 82 inches of snow since Thursday and up to 7 more inches were forecast.

In many localities, the high winds made it difficult to determine exactly how much snow fell during the day.

Schools and industries in

(Continued on Page 9A)

High 9 Plans Hoffa Case Review

Washington — (AP) — The Supreme Court agreed today to a limited review of James R. Hoffa's conviction in 1964 on jury tampering charges.

In a brief order, the court said it would hear the Teamster Union president's appeal on one question alone.

That is: "Whether evidence obtained by the government by means of deceptively placing a secret informer in the quarters and councils of a defendant during one criminal trial so violates the defendant's Fourth, Fifth and Sixth Amendment rights that suppression of such evidence is required in a subsequent trial of the same defendant on a different charge."

Heart Disease Battle Turning

Houston, Tex. — (AP) — A founder of the American Heart Association says science is turning the corner in its battle against cardiovascular diseases.

Dr. Paul Dudley White of Boston, a cardiologist, softened his optimism yesterday, however, by warning that coronary heart disease is on the increase.

Japan Still Seeks Peace

By Press Wire Services

Tokyo—The Japanese government said today it will continue its efforts for peace in Viet Nam despite resumption of bombing of North Viet Nam.

In Moscow, the Soviet news agency Tass reported without comment today on the resumption of American bombing raids over North Viet Nam.

Communist China charged the United States "recklessly resumed" bombing North Viet Nam "after the utter failure of its 'peace hoax'" in a dispatch by the official New China news agency.

No Place for Indians At Albany Powwow

The New York State Legislature, according to David H. Beetle, Press Albany Bureau news analyst, is designed for the chiefs not the Indians.

His three-part series on the Legislature begins today on Page 6A.

Also on the inside:

Publisher Dies

Huntsville, Ontario—(AP)—Paul Herman Rice, 65, publisher of the weekly Huntsville Forester since 1958, died yesterday at his home.

UPI TELEPHOTO

MEDIC, MEDIC!—A marine shouts for a medic to aid his comrade, injured at Thach Tru during "Operation Double Eagle." The amphibious operation, largest of the Viet Nam war, sent thousands of Marines ashore against light Viet Cong opposition.

Let's Chuckle

During a coffee break: "I have to watch my weight or I won't fit into my car pool."

January 31, 1966: War and weather news recorded a miserable January day. *Microfilm archives*

HOTEL
ARLINGTON
HOTEL
CARLTON
HOTEL

Carlton Hotel on Chenango Street was torn down by urban renewal wreckers in 1966. The Arlington was razed in 1969. *Press & Sun-Bulletin archives*

Miss Universe Sylvia Hitchcock during the Johnson City Jubilee parade in 1967. *Courtesy Marlene Yacos*

Centennial Parade in Binghamton, 1967. *Courtesy Marlene Yacos*

Centennial Parade in Binghamton, 1967. *Courtesy Marlene Yacos*

Among the citizens marching in Binghamton's Centennial Day in 1967 are from left: John Sullivan, Mary Ellen McGory, Mr. and Mrs. Frank A. Nytch, Frank A. West, Michael Anderjack and Duke Alexander holding his toy Manchester terrier. *Press & Sun-Bulletin archives*

Dixie music at the Court House in Binghamton during Binghamton's centennial festivities in July 1967. *Press & Sun-Bulletin archives*

Windy and cold today with a possibility of an inch of snow. High, 30-35. Partly cloudy tonight with a few snow flurries. Low, 20-25. Sunday fair, not as cold. High, 32-37. Details, Page 37.

The Sun-Bulletin

FINAL

50c per week
Home-delivered

Binghamton, New York 13902 40 Pages (In 3 Sections) SATURDAY, JANUARY 28, 1967 145th Year, No. 82 10 Cents

3 ASTRONAUTS BURN TO DEATH ON APOLLO PAD

SEE PAGES 2 and 3

Virgil (Gus) Grissom, Edward White and Roger Chaffee in front of Apollo launch stand

January 28, 1967: A grim setback for the U.S. space effort.

18—H THE SUNDAY PRESS Binghamton, N. Y., July 2, 1967

Fine Weather For Celebrating

Perfect, sunny centennial skies are our hope for Binghamton and vicinity throughout the entire series of centennial events. Warm, sunny days perfect for parading. Cool, starlit nights ideal for partying. Lots of enthusiastic people to enjoy all the proceedings.

THE PRESS

Binghamton, New York "Centennial Edition" July 2, 1967

Centennial Chuckle

Millions of people have participated in a 100th anniversary. A few have participated in two, but to this day we know of none who have made three. We all seem to be "out of town" when that third one rolls around.

Our Congratulations to City of Binghamton, One of Nation's Fastest Growing Markets

THE PRESS
EVENING
SUNDAY

Press Moved to Present Building in July of 1965

In July, 1965, The Evening Press moved bag, baggage, typewriters, and typesetters to a more centrally located home in the middle of its expanding circulation area. It built a modern $5,000,000 plant in Vestal Parkway East leaving the founder's building at 19 Chenango Street.

The new building, which includes approximately 85,000 square feet of working space, is considered one of the most modern newspaper plants in the country. From the carpeted, wood-paneled lobby and throughout the entire building the colors of the walls, floors, desks, chairs and even the telephones have been selected for compatability. The building is completely heat and air-conditioned.

Guests usually are impressed first with the lighting and colors. Lighting in all rooms, except the pressroom and paper storage room, is by luminous ceilings. The roominess of various departments impresses visitors, especially those familiar with the confines of the former Press Building.

The heart of the plant is a new 12-unit Goss Mark 1 Headliner press which can print full-color newspapers of up to 144 pages at a rate of 60,000 an hour. One feature of the new press that is duplicated in only a few other newspaper plants in the country, is an electronic system for controlling the ink mist that generally fills the air in newspaper pressrooms. This mist, a troublesome by-product of most publishing plants, is suppressed with an electronic charge.

The old press, which was in the basement of the Press Building, was a common sight for Chenango Street pedestrians who peered through the windows to watch the whirring mechanism. In the new building visitors are able to watch the workings of the two-story high press from a second floor, glassed-in observation deck.

Another complicated machine automatically casts, trims, washes and delivers to the pressroom the heavy lead castings used to print the paper.

New equipment installed in the new plant in addition to the press includes mailing room equipment providing high-speed routing of newspapers from pressroom to delivery trucks.

In contrast to the former plant the new Press building provides employes with a spacious, well-appointed and air-conditioned home.

The exterior of the building preserves the campus atmosphere provided by Harpur College on the other side of the Vestal Parkway.

The 300-foot-long front of the building is made of Avondale stone and brick. The other sides of the structure also are of brick. The building is set back 100 feet from the Parkway. Landscaping of the 5½ acre site included the planting of 56 large trees and numerous shrubs.

Parking is provided for customers and guests in the front of the building and employes in the rear. Access is provided from both the Parkway in the front and the Old Vestal Road in the rear.

A newspaper plant is a fascinating complex of departments and activities devoted to the unusual task of producing a new product every time it publishes. When The Evening Press moved into its new Vestal Parkway plant, it was prepared for a rush of requests by visitors of all ages. Over 14,000 persons have toured the new Press facilities. They have included school children and members of service clubs, technical and engineering societies, scout organizations, church groups and others. Newspaper people from all over the world have visited The Press looking for new ideas that can be incorporated into their operations.

"We're pleased with the way the new plant has helped increase the efficiency of our operations, and we are confident it will help us give better service to our readers and advertisers for many years to come," said Fred W. Stein, editor and publisher of The Press.

The Press also owns and operates radio station WINR, which it acquired in January 1957 and WINR-TV, Channel 40, which went on the air in November 1957.

The radio and tv studios are at 70 Henry Street, with transmitting facilities on Windy Hill, east of Binghamton.

MR. STEIN

First Press Hit Streets April 11, 1904, With Latest in Journalistic Techniques

The first issue came off the press in the Kilmer Building at Chenango and Lewis Streets. At the same time excavators were preparing the land for construction of the Press Building, which still is the tallest office building in town.

The striking thing about the first issues of the Press is that, even today, 50 years later, they give off a flavor of freshness and urgency.

This, despite the journalistic pro's peculiarities of the period, is due to the adoption of the latest in news techniques which were introduced here for the first time. The Press was one of the first small-city newspapers to raise the photographer and his function to the working level of the editor and the writer.

The first issue was printed in two colors. It featured cartoons and photographs turned out by the most expansive Engraving Department between New York and Buffalo.

The gigantic mechanical task of getting a newspaper underway from scratch was handled by the most capable crew that could be gathered, and the atmosphere of the new venture affected the entire staff.

They just had to win!

KILMER BUILDING, CHENANGO AND LEWIS STREETS

Circulation Records Set

Following the first edition, Press circulation started to grow, and it has never stopped. While some of our circulation records covering the early days are not complete, available figures show a very exciting increase year after year. Beginning with the first edition, circulation figures are:

1904	21,500
1910	24,100 est.
1915	26,711 est.
1920	29,100 est.
1925	34,593
1930	37,007
1935	38,095
1940	42,451
1945	50,507
1950	57,196
1955	61,761
1960	71,508
1965	78,273
1967 (May)	80,178

It All Started in 1904

MR. KILMER

Willis Sharpe Kilmer was a bouncy 36 when he started his paper. He was also extremely wealthy. With his father, Jonas M. Kilmer, he had built a patent medicine business (Swamproot) into a multi-million dollar trade.

Kilmer set a new pattern. First of all, The Binghamton Press declared itself politically independent and recognized the vital journalistic fact that there is nothing as objective as a photograph. Willis Kilmer introduced pictorial journalism on a lavish scale in a town where reproduced photographs on a daily basis were rare indeed.

Contemporaries of the younger Kilmer have described him as a firm, impatient person who wanted the least time lag between a decision and the execution of a plan.

Within 24 hours after Mr. Kilmer had decided to start a newspaper, he was buying the best equipment and employing the best available personnel.

It took just 90 days from the decision until The Press reached the street, with 44 pages, on April 11, 1904.

We Changed Our Name 7 Years Ago

To fit more accurately the role the paper was playing as a fully regional publication and having outgrown the restriction of being The Binghamton Press alone, a name change was made to The Evening Press on September 23, 1960.

Press circulation had fanned throughout the Southern Tier. Portions of northern Pennsylvania and Binghamton were fast becoming the center of a 3-county metropolitan market. The decision to alter the name from the Binghamton Press to The Evening Press conformed to this new metropolitan concept.

Under Mr. Stein, The Press on September 11, 1949, began to publish the first successful Sunday paper ever to be issued in Binghamton.

The Evening Press and The Sunday Press are now the hometown newspapers for over 80,000 families in Broome, Tioga, Susquehanna, Chenango, Delaware and Otsego Counties.

We Joined Gannett In 1943

In the summer of 1943, The Press became a member of the Gannett Group of newspapers, which purchased this newspaper from the Kilmer Estate.

There were no strangers in the transaction. Frank E. Gannett, head of the Group had lived in this section of New York State. Among his first newspapers were the Ithaca Journal and the Elmira Star-Gazette of the Southern Tier.

Frank E. Tripp, Chairman of the Board of the Gannett Newspapers and a widely read columnist, had been one of the first members hired for the original staff of The Press in 1904.

As a member of the Gannett Group, The Press began to expand its staff and facilities. The vast demands involved in telling the full story of World War 2 required physical expansion.

The first 10 years under Gannett ownership saw the largest single increase in circulation of any 10-year period in the paper's history.

FRANK E. GANNETT

First Press Building Was Occupied in 1905

The citizens of 1903 watched with wonder and expressions of marvel as floor was piled upon floor of the Press Building at 19 Chenango Street.

They had seen the wreckers tear down the graceful old white home of Cyrus Strong where it stood in the midst of a green lawn, and then they watched the diggers mine deeply into the earth to make room for a cavernous press room.

Then the first floors began to take form until they added up to 12 and the city had its first (of only two in the whole century) "skyscraper."

Stone cutters from the quarry yards of Nick Carlucci & Sons did their work on the spot, shaping and chiseling under the watchful eye of T. I. Lacey & Sons. They tailor-made each piece of limestone (quarried over the state line in Pennsylvania) where it was to be erected.

The piece de resistance was the lobby—pure marble and a sight to behold as the first lamps were lit to bound their rays off the glossy surfaces. The 12-story building housed the newest newspaper in town in 1905, filled itself with lawyers, merchants and chiefs from top to bottom and was the home of The Press until 1965, when the newspaper moved to the Vestal Parkway.

Its builder and original owner was Willis Sharpe Kilmer. In the 1940s, his estate sold it to Cornell University and since the late 1940s it has been owned by a series of real estate investors.

With the Security Mutual Building around the corner at Exchange and Court, it was the highest downtown ever climbed.

PRESS BUILDING, 19 CHENANGO STREET
HOME OF THE PRESS FOR 60 YEARS

Stein Made Editor in 1941

When Fred W. Stein rose to the top editorial post in 1941, he became the first full editor The Press ever had.

He took over additional responsibilities in January 1959 when he was made editor and general manager, and in 1961 Mr. Stein became the first man to hold the positions of both editor and publisher.

In the corporate structure of the Gannett Group of Newspapers he became a member of the group Board of Directors, and Vice-President of the Binghamton Press Company, Inc., the paper's corporate name, as well as its secretary.

Under Mr. Stein, The Press has experienced continued expansion and growth. He was closely involved in the planning and construction of the new Press Building in Vestal Parkway East which the newspaper now occupies.

Pearl? We Called Shot

With the rise of Adolf Hitler and Benito Mussolini and the warfare between the Western Allies and the Nazis and the Fascists, The Press supported aid to Britain and lendlease as practical measures of national defense. Watching, with the rest of the observers of the world, the moves of Japan, The Press on December 6, 1941, headed its lead editorial: "Will It Be Sunday?" The Japs attacked the United States at Pearl Harbor on Sunday, December 7.

July 2, 1967: On an inside page, the Press told its story as part of a celebration of the city's centennial. *Courtesy David Silvanic*

'Deny Violence Its Victory,' LBJ Appeals

Story Below

Salute Gen. Clearing

WEATHER BUREAU FORECAST

Fair, much cooler tonight. Low in mid 20s. Tomorrow, mostly sunny. High in upper 40s to 50. Precipitation probability near zero.

6 p.m.	[illegible]	6 a.m.	[illegible]	11 a.m.	[illegible]
7 p.m.	[illegible]	8 a.m.	[illegible]	Noon	[illegible]
Midnight	[illegible]	9 a.m.	[illegible]	1 p.m.	[illegible]
3 a.m.	[illegible]	10 a.m.	[illegible]	2 p.m.	[illegible]

THE EVENING PRESS

Binghamton, N. Y., Friday, April 5, 1968 Volume 89–302 3 Sections 44 Pages 10 Cents

★ ★

Let's Chuckle

Tolerance is the ability to listen enthusiastically to someone telling your favorite story.

Hunt Is Pressed for King's Assassin

★ ★ ★ ★ ★ ★

Angry Negroes Riot, Are Told to Get Guns

By UP-International

Bands of Negroes, enraged over the murder of Dr. Martin Luther King, Jr., burned, looted and clashed with police in more than a dozen American cities last night. Three persons were killed and dozens were injured.

Meanwhile, black power advocate Stokely Carmichael called today for Negroes to arm themselves with guns and take to the streets in retaliation.

National guard troops were summoned in Nashville and Memphis, Tenn., and Raleigh and Greensboro, N.C. The outbursts were especially violent in New York's Harlem ghetto, Washington, Tallahassee, Fla., and Nashville.

A white youth was suffocated in a firebombing in Tallahassee; an elderly man died in a fire in Harlem and a white man died today of injuries suffered in the Washington violence.

SCATTERED VIOLENCE also was reported in Charlotte, Winston-Salem, New Bern and Wilmington, N. C.; Hartford, Conn.; Detroit; Boston, Itta Bena and Jackson, Miss.; Tampa and Miami, Fla.; and Birmingham and Tuscaloosa, Ala.

In some areas, there was firebombing and looting. In others, young Negroes clashed with police, using rocks, guns, and, when ammunition

(Continued on Page 8A)

FLAMES OF ANGER IN HARLEM — Firemen battle blaze in Harlem furniture store, looted and set afire by enraged Negroes after slaying of Dr. Martin Luther King, Jr., in Memphis last night.

Johnson Leads Nation In Mourning

By Press Wire Services

Memphis, Tenn. — Authorities pressed a manhunt today for the killer of Dr. Martin Luther King, Jr., whose assassination touched off Negro violence in a number of American cities and brought a national outpouring of grief and sorrow.

King, 39, leading advocate of nonviolence and Nobel Prize winner, died in a Memphis hospital last night less than an hour after he was shot in the neck by a white gunman while standing on the balcony of his motel.

President Johnson led the nation in mourning and tribute. In a nationwide television and radio appearance he called upon "every citizen to reject the blind violence that has struck down Dr. Martin Luther King."

But violence flared in Memphis and the convulsive reaction also reared in Nashville, Newark, Washington, Boston, New York's Harlem and Bedford-Stuyvesant and more than a half dozen smaller towns and cities.

THE ASSASSINATION caused Mr. Johnson to delay this morning, for the second time, his departure for Hawaii.

Mr. Johnson originally had planned to leave for Hawaii last night and postponed it to early today, then postponed it again for a meeting with civil rights leaders.

At the same time, Attorney General Ramsey Clark and three other federal officials

(Continued on Page 8A)

DR. MARTIN LUTHER KING, JR.
. . . In Last Public Appearance Wednesday Night

'Like a Firecracker'

Special Press Correspondence

Memphis—"He didn't say a word; he didn't move," said the Rev. Andrew Young, executive vice-president of the Southern Christian Leadership Conference.

"It sounded like a firecracker."

The shot, he said, had hit Dr. Martin Luther King, Jr., in the neck and lower right part of his face.

Dr. King bled profusely from the huge wound as he lay face-up on the concrete walkway before he was taken away by a fire department ambulance. His eyes appeared at first half-closed and then open but staring.

JAMES BEVEL, one of Dr. King's closest aides, said after the ambulance departed: "I think he's gone."

"I heard the ping and looked around and he was lying on his back," said Chauncey Eskridge, one of Dr. King's legal advisers.

"When I looked up, the police and sheriff's deputies were running all around. The bullet exploded in his face," said the Rev. Jesse L. Jackson, who was with Dr. King on the balcony of the hotel.

"He had just bent over. If he had been standing up, he wouldn't have been hit in the face. When I turned around, I saw police coming from everywhere. They said, 'Where did it come from,' and I said, 'Behind you.' The police were coming from where the shot came."

He said, "It was similar to the Kennedy incident. The police were all around, but there was no military protection against ambush, and he was ambushed."

On South Main, where the building in which the sniper

(Continued on Page 10A)

REV. ANDREW YOUNG
. . . Shows Where Shot Hit

★ ★ ★

Bulletin

Washington —(UPI)— President Johnson today proclaimed Sunday a national day of mourning for Dr. Martin Luther King. He urged the nation to pray for an end to racial hatred. "In our churches, in our homes, in our private hearts, let us resolve before God to stand against the divisiveness in our country and all its consequences," the President said.

The President said he plans to address a joint session of Congress, hopefully by Monday night, to deal with problems stemming from the assassination.

★ ★ ★

'The Will of God'

MRS. MARTIN LUTHER KING, JR.
. . . Leaves Atlanta for Memphis

Atlanta, Ga. — (AP) — "I do think it's the will of God," said Mrs. Martin Luther King, Jr., a few hours after the death of her husband. "We always knew this could happen."

Mrs. King flew to Memphis early today in a plane chartered by Senator Robert F. Kennedy to claim the body of her slain husband.

A spokesman for Kennedy said he chartered the plane at Mrs. King's request after the senator telephoned to ask if there was anything he could do.

MRS. KING was in seclusion of her home last night, receiving only a few close friends in her bedroom. Friends and relatives greeted the streams of mourners, who passed 15 policemen guarding the house.

The slender, attractive wife of the civil rights leader was composed but seemed dazed. She wept occasionally and accepted a few phone calls, one from President Johnson.

Mrs. King, who is recuperating from major surgery, re-

(Continued on Page 8A)

Exchanges Honor King

New York —(AP)— The New York and American stock exchanges paid tribute today to the memory of Dr. Martin Luther King, Jr., the civil rights leader who was assassinated in Memphis last night.

Trading was halted on the floors of both exchanges at 11 a.m. and one minute of silence was observed.

At the opening of the session, the New York Stock Exchange ticker tape carried this message:

"The New York Stock Exchange shares the shock and the deep sorrow of the nation and the entire world at the tragic death of the Rev. Dr. Martin Luther King."

ON THE AIR

WINR RADIO 68

Tonight

5:45—Area news and sports
6:30—Perspective on the news
10:05 — Album Time, Hello Young Lovers, Nancy Wilson

WINR TV 40

6—News Central 40
6:30—Huntley - Brinkley News (color)
7:30—Tarzan, "Trina," Ron Ely (color)
8:30—Star Trek, William Shatner, Leonard Nimoy, and DeForest Kelley (color)
9:30—The Hollywood Squares (color)
10—American Profile: Home Country U.S.A. (color)
11—News Central 40
11:30—The Tonight Show (color)

★ ★ ★

Johnson Confers, Appeals

By Press Wire Services

Washington — President Johnson called on the nation today—all men and all races — to "stand their ground to deny violence its victory" in the wake of the slaying of Dr. Martin Luther King, Jr.

The President's statement was issued after a hastily summoned meeting at the White House of civil rights leaders, government officials and members of Congress.

He voiced again his sorrow at the death of the Negro apostle of nonviolence, assassinated by a rifleman last night in Memphis, Tenn.

MR. JOHNSON meanwhile kept in abeyance his plans to fly to Honolulu later in the day for Vietnam policy talks.

The President's statement said:

"The dream of Martin Luther King has not died with him.

"Men who are white—men who are black—must and will join together now as never in the past to let all the forces of division know that America shall not be ruled by the bullet but by the ballot of free and just men."

Mr. Johnson said that when he heard last night "the terrible news of Dr. King's death my heart went out to his people — especially to the young Americans who, I know, must wonder if they are to be denied a fullness of life because of the color of their skin."

HE SAID HE had called to the White House the leaders of the Negro community for consultation, and went on to say:

"No words of ours — no words of mine—can fill the void of the eloquent voice that has been stilled."

Roy Wilkins, executive director of the NAACP; Whitney Young, executive director of the Urban League; Housing Secretary Robert Weaver and Supreme Court Justice Thurgood Marshall were among the Negro leaders who assembled at the White House.

The extraordinary meeting came after a night of violence in more than a dozen of the nation's cities.

EVEN AS THE leaders were arriving at the White House, Black Power militant Stokely Carmichael was telling a news conference several blocks away that Negroes "will have to get guns" and take to the streets to avenge King's death.

Mr. Johnson, again postponing plans to go to Honolulu for Vietnam strategy talks, was on the telephone early this morning setting the high-level meeting in hopes of averting further violence.

Top administration leaders joining Mr. Johnson at the meeting included Vice-President Hubert H. Humphrey, Defense Secretary Clark Clifford and Undersecretary of State Nicholas Deb. Katzenbach.

OTHERS ATTENDING the session in the Cabinet Room

(Continued on Page 10A)

Appeal to Nation

Must Find Love, Not Hate: Jackie

New York—(UPI)—Mrs. John F. Kennedy issued an emotional appeal to the nation today to let the assassination of Dr. Martin Luther King "make room in people's hearts for love, not hate."

Mrs. Kennedy, herself widowed by an assassin's bullet, issued the following statement from her apartment here:

"I weep for Mrs. King and for her children for this senseless, senseless act of hate which took away a man who preached love and hope.

"When will our country learn that to live by the sword is to perish by the sword?

"I pray that with the price he paid — his life — he will make room in people's hearts for love, not hate.

"Some people would never kill—but even to speak of an-

(Continued on Page 10A)

Graves Unchanging

Portland, Ore. —(AP)— Even though his company, Burial Vault, Co., has become a subsidiary of Pacific Northwest, Co., there will be no changes in personnel or policy, Kenneth Graves, the president, said yesterday.

More Stories on Death Of Dr. King Inside

Other stories on the tragic assassination of Dr. Martin Luther King, Jr., including his speeches, personality, dreams for the future and world reaction to his death, appear on the following pages: 4A, 5A, 6A, 8A, 10A, 11A, 14A, 15A and 15B.

Also on the inside:

April 5, 1968: The violent reaction to Martin Luther King Jr.'s death dominated the news. *Courtesy Dolly Escovar*

High 'n Dry
WEATHER BUREAU FORECAST
Fair and mild tonight. Low in the 50s. Mostly sunny and warm tomorrow. High in the 80s. Rain chance near zero.

BINGHAMTON TEMPERATURES

6 p.m.	70	4 a.m.	50	8 a.m.	50
9 p.m.	66	5 a.m.	50	9 a.m.	52
Midnight	56	6 a.m.	50	10 a.m.	56
3 a.m.	52	7 a.m.	50	11 a.m.	60

THE EVENING PRESS

Binghamton, N. Y., Wednesday, June 5, 1968 Volume 90--47 4 Sections 72 Pages 10 Cents

★

Let's Chuckle

Definition of a tough town: It's one where nobody asks you what time it is. They just take your watch.

KENNEDY IS IN INTENSIVE CARE AFTER 3 HOURS UNDER SURGERY

★ ★ ★

LBJ Leads U.S. Prayer For Senator

By Press Wire Services

Washington—President Johnson today led a horrified nation in praying for the recovery of Senator Robert F. Kennedy, who was critically wounded in an assassination attempt in Los Angeles. Lawmakers voiced fear "the world's gone mad."

Mr. Johnson, who succeeded to the office of president when John F. Kennedy was slain before his eyes in Dallas four years ago, said "there are no words equal to the horror" of this newest tragedy.

"All America prays for his recovery," Mr. Johnson said. "We also pray that divisiveness and violence be driven from the hearts of men everywhere."

Our thoughts and our prayers are with Senator Kennedy, his family and the other victims," the president added.

THE PRESIDENT, who spent much of the night watching television accounts of the tragic shooting and its aftermath, also ordered the Secret Service to immediately assign a detail to guard the other presidential candidates and their families.

George Christian, White House press secretary, said Mr. Johnson talked with Senator Edward M. Kennedy, who had rushed to his brother's bedside in Los Angeles. The President also was in touch with Theodore Sorensen, one of Kennedy's advisers.

Reaction from public figures came swiftly in the wake of today's shooting of Senator Robert F. Kennedy with ex-

(Continued on Page 15A)

★ ★ ★

'God Help Us'-- World Reaction

By the Associated Press

Waves of shock, dismay and sorrow went round the world today at news of the shooting of Senator Robert F. Kennedy.

"God help us," said a GI in Vietnam. "What the hell is going on back there?"

"I feel just like the last time," said another, referring to the assassination of President John F. Kennedy.

Members of the Kennedy family in Europe were on the telephone to the United States. An aide to Sargent Shriver, the new U.S. ambassador to France and the senator's brother-in-law, said Shriver was trying to reach members of the family in Los Angeles.

IN LONDON, Princess Lee Radziwill said she had spoken to her sister, President Kennedy's widow, but "she tells me the news is pretty confused so far."

News of the shooting caused "acute sorrow" at the Vatican, the chief press official there said. He said Pope Paul VI was being kept informed constantly of the condition of the senator, who is a Roman Catholic.

"It's a nightmare—it's terrible," said a Russian woman on a Moscow street.

"It is a great pity that you live in such a country where

(Continued on Page 15A)

ON THE AIR

WINR RADIO 68

5:45—Area news and sports
6:30—Perspective on the news
10:05—Album Time

WINR TV 40

6—News Central 40
6:30—Huntley-Brinkley News (Color)
7:30 — The Virginian, "The Good-Hearted Badman" (Color)
9—The Music Hall (Color)
10—Run for Your Life, "Three Passengers for Lusitania" (Color)
11—News Central 40
11:30 — The Tonight Show (Color)

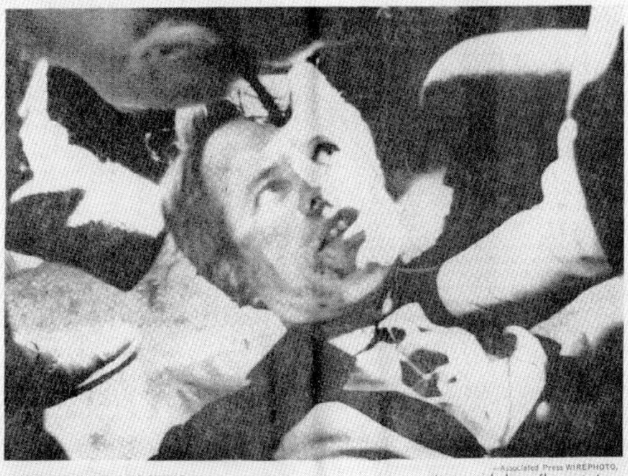

—Associated Press WIREPHOTO.

MOMENTS AFTER SHOOTING—Senator Robert F. Kennedy lies gravely wounded on floor at Ambassador Hotel in Los Angeles, moments after he was shot during celebration of his victory in yesterday's California primary election. (Copyright, 1968, Los Angeles Times.)

Horror in Kitchen: 'I Saw Arm Come Out . . . Holding Gun'

By RICHARD DREW
Copyright, Pasadena Independent Star-News

Los Angeles — (AP) — Senator Robert F. Kennedy had just finished making his victory speech and was taking a short cut through the kitchen to a press room when I saw an arm come out of the crowd. It was holding a gun.

As soon as I saw the gun —it was pointing right at me for a second—I ducked and tried to get out of the way.

Just then I heard two shots. Then there was a half-second pause and then three more.

As I looked up, Senator Kennedy started to fall back and then was lowered to the floor by his aides. There were about 50 of us in the kitchen when the shots were fired, mostly Kennedy men and the press.

For a few seconds everyone stood back, not getting too close. It was about then that I saw another man lying on the floor.

At almost that instant people began to close in around the victims and someone started screaming, "Get a doctor. Please get a doctor." That was all I could hear over the yelling and crying.

Rafer Johnson (former decathlon star, now a Kennedy aide) and Roosevelt Grier, the pro football tackle, grabbed a man in a blue jump suit and they and about a half-dozen guards began grappling with him, trying to disarm him.

Kennedy was still lying on the floor and there was blood all over him. Finally some doctors came into the kitchen —along with a huge group of supporters—and began trying to treat him while they waited for an ambulance.

Someone in the crowd gave him a rosary and he clutched it in his hand.

The crowd in the kitchen kept growing and Kennedy's aides began screaming and pushing to get people away from the senator.

A police ambulance arrived and Kennedy was lifted onto a stretcher and they started carrying him out. Another shooting victim lay on a kitchen table.

A momentary calm came over most of the people in the room. It was then that I found I had blood on my coat. Apparently I was standing so close to him that it spattered on me.

Cushing Offers Prayers

Boston — (UPI) — Richard Cardinal Cushing, Roman Catholic archbisohp of Boston, celebrated a special morning mass for Senator Robert F. Kennedy and said he was dedicating the entire day today to prayer for his recovery.

Cardinal Cushing, a lifelong friend of the Kennedy family, said he was "tremendously shocked" at the attempt on Kennedy's life.

"It is some kind of indication of the extent of crime in the country when an attempted murder like this can take place under such circumstances," Cardinal Cushing said.

The prelate, who presided at the funeral of the senator's assassinated brother, the late President John F. Kennedy, said, "it is really impossible for me to express in words the sympathy I have for the entire family.

"I pray that it will never happen again!"

Radio Hanoi Gives View

Singapore — (AP) — Radio Hanoi reported the shooting of Robert F. Kennedy to North Vietnamese today and commented:

"This is to show the dirty face and tactics of U.S. politicians who will not hestiate to spill blood in order to even the score."

The remainder of the newscast, monitored here, gave an account of the shooting in Los Angeles and the arrest of an unidentified man.

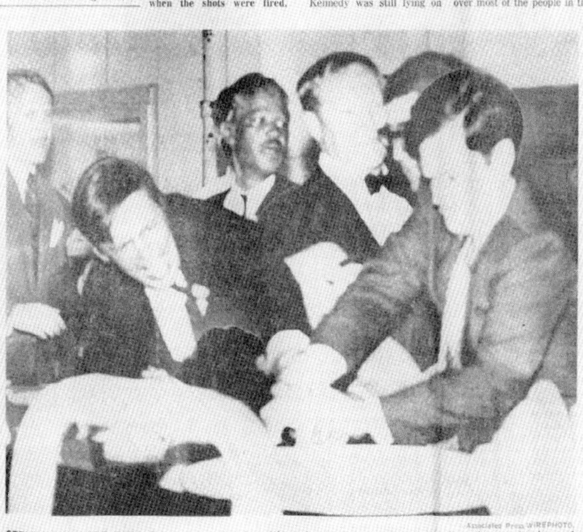

—Associated Press WIREPHOTO.

STRUGGLING FOR GUN—Two men struggle with a third trying to wrest gun from him in kitchen of hotel where Senator Kennedy was shot. Suspected assailant's head is just to left of cluster of hands.

Shot Making Victory Talk

By BOB THOMAS
Associated Press Writer

Los Angeles—Senator Robert F. Kennedy underwent more than three hours of surgery today after an unidentified young gunman fired a bullet into his brain. He then was transferred to an intensive care unit.

Deputy Los Angeles mayor Joe Quinn emerged from Good Samaritan Hospital to give the brief word, saying there would be a hospital briefing with details later. He added that Kennedy's personal physician is flying here from Leahy Clinic in Boston. Kennedy was shot shortly after midnight (PDT) just after proclaiming victory in California's Democratic presidential primary election.

Quinn said it would be two or three days before it could be determined if Kennedy's brain was severely damaged. Surgery lasted about 3 hours and 40 minutes.

Six neurosurgeons struggled in a lengthy and delicate operation to remove a .22 caliber pistol slug from the brain of the critically wounded, unconscious senator from New York.

After an hour and a half of surgery, life signs

(Continued on Page 15A)

—Associated Press WIREPHOTO.

SUSPECT — Los Angeles police released this photo of man they are holding as suspect in shooting of Senator Kennedy. He was described as being about 25 years old, 5 feet 5 in height, weighing about 120 pounds and of swarthy complexion.

More stories and pictures on Pages 16A and 17A.

Retirement Finances Important to All Ages

Consider the facts . . . that this year alone inflation could wipe out $2,000,000,000 in buying power of America's elderly citizens . . . that today's pace of price rises easily could cut in half the value of the retirement nest-eggs of many young Americans.

Consider the facts and you'll no doubt agree with business columnist Sylvia Porter that it's time for Americans of all ages to plan their retirement finances now.

Don't miss this important "clip and save" series of six columns, starting today on Page 9C.

Also on the inside:

June 5, 1968: A dramatic photo of a dying Bobby Kennedy showed the horror of his assassination. *Courtesy Kate Sands and Harry Dodd*

Wet Vote Gains

U. S. WEATHER BUREAU FORECAST

Cloudy, occasional rain tonight and tomorrow. Low around 40. Low tomorrow 45. Rain chance 70 per cent tonight and tomorrow.

THE EVENING PRESS

★ ★

Let's Chuckle

Advice to men over 40: Keep an open mind and a closed refrigerator.

Binghamton, N. Y., Wednesday, November 6, 1968 Volume 90–177 4 Sections 68 Pages 10 Cents

Illinois Hands Nixon Presidency After Ohio, California Cliffhangers

★ ★ ★ ★ ★ ★

Democrats Keep Rule of Congress

WASHINGTON (AP) — Democrats have retained control of a Congress that may be called on to elect the next president and vice president.

But the cross currents of an extraordinary election left in utter doubt the crucial questions whether the House would get the presidential decision and if it does whether a Democratic majority would elect the party's nominee, Hubert A. Humphrey.

Democrats were assured a numerical majority in both branches of Congress, keeping a grip on the key Senate and House offices and committee chairmanships that play major roles in shaping and handling legislation.

Their margins were reduced, however, in both chambers. They had controlled the old House, 246 to 186, with three vacancies, and the Senate, 63 to 37.

Returns tabulated so far gave Democrats 234 of the 435 seats in the new House and Republicans 183, with 18 races still undecided.

In the 100-member Senate, where 34 seats were to be filled, Democrats were assured of control with 54, including holdover members, and Republicans 39. In the undecided races, Democrats led for five seats and Republicans for two.

If no presidential ticket wins a majority of the electoral vote, the House elects a president and the Senate a vice president.

But the election in the House would be by states, with 26 votes needed for victory. The makeup, and in addition the disposition, of each state delegation are what would count.

Early estimates were that Humphrey might be able to count on 13 states with predominantly Democratic delegations, and Republican Richard M. Nixon on 15 dominated by members of his party.

Three state delegations were tied and the status of the others was clouded by various factors. Some states were carried by third party candidate George C. Wallace and in others newly elected members had pledged themselves in various ways to vote for the candidate favored by popular vote, regardless of party.

In any case, switches among the electors, most of whom are legally free agents, could settle the election by Dec. 16, when they meet in their respective states.

Wallace, who won at least 39 electoral votes, repeatedly has said the election would never be allowed to go to the House, although he has denied making any deals with the other candidates.

The 91st Congress, it was evident, will look much like its predecessor, although the GOP gains and the return of Southern Democrats who frequently vote with Republicans would give it a somewhat more conservative cast.

Most party leaders and committee chairmen were returned.

GOP Regains All State Reins

Albany — (AP) — Smashing through Hubert Humphrey's presidential tide in New York, Republicans found themselves almost certain masters of the State Legislature today.

The GOP strengthened its hold in the Senate, capturing 33 of the 57 seats, according to unofficial figures compiled by The Associated Press.

And Republicans stunned the state political flock by toppling many strong Democrats from the Assembly and apparently seizing control in the 150-member house.

An unofficial count of noses gave the Republicans 77 seats and Democrats 73. It appeared that the Republicans fully realized their objective—to increase their current 70-member bloc beyond 76. To rule in the Assembly, a party must command 76 votes.

Tuesday's legislative vote ran sharply counter to the pattern laid down in Hubert Humphrey's 550,000-plus victory over Republican Richard M. Nixon in the presidential race in this state.

The result also made losers out of the political experts who had declared right up to election night that the GOP would need a strong Nixon showing to help win back the Assembly.

Thus, barring a reversal resulting from some recounts, the Republican party stood today to have the enormous state power it enjoyed for three decades until 1964 and the Johnson landslide.

In the startling turn of events in the Assembly, some strong figures, including Democratic Ways and Means Chairman Harvey Lifset of Al-

(Continued on Page 10A)

★ ★ ★

Burns Shocked By Losses

By HOWARD CLARK

Albany, N. Y.—(AP)—Several well-known Democratic legislators fell in Tuesday's election, and no one professed more surprise than State Democratic Chairman John Burns.

"I'm shocked. Surprised. I don't know what to say," he commented from his head-

JOHN J. BURNS

quarters in a New York City hotel. "We just thought some of them were safe."

"Some of them (the Democratic officeholders) are in tough Republican districts, and they always are in jeopardy," he said. "But we just didn't expect Albany County."

Voters in Albany County, a Democrat stronghold for decades, rejected Assemblyman Harvey Lifset, third-ranking Democrat in the Assembly and chairman of the powerful Ways and Means Committee; Assemblyman Frank P. Cox, an eight-year legislator, and State Sen. Julian B. Erway, a 14-year veteran.

Losing in normally Republican districts were Assemblyman Victor Waryas of Poughkeepsie and Assemblyman Louis E. Wolfe of Plattsburgh. "They were just buried," Burns said.

Burns did find a bright spot, however. "I'm glad the top of the ticket ran well," he said in reference to the state victory of Democratic presidential candidate Hubert H. Humphrey.

"I just don't know what happened everywhere else."

Reject Police Unity

Buffalo — (AP) — Despite approval by voters in Erie County's three cities, the electorate in 16 villages and 25 towns decided yesterday they did not want a consolidated police force.

ON THE AIR

WINR RADIO 68

5:55—Area News
6:05—Winner Radio
7:05—Vestal Plaza Show
11:35—National Radio Pulpit

WINR TV 40

6—News Central 40
6:30—Huntley-Brinkley News (color)
7—Richard Diamond, "One Dead Cat"
7:30 — The Virginian, with James Drury in the title role (color)
9—The Bob Hope Special (color)
10 — The Defenders, "Loud and Clear"
11—News Central 40
11:30—The Tonight Show, with Bill Cosby, Carol Burnett (color)
12:55—WINR - TV Nightwatch News

Wyszynski In Rome

Rome — (AP) — Stefan Cardinal Wyszynski arrived in Rome today by train on his first trip out of Poland since the Communist government picked up his passport three years ago.

Foreign travel was prohibited to the Roman Catholic primate of Poland after his bishops addressed a letter of forgiveness and reconciliation to German bishops during the Vatican Council.

PRESIDENT-ELECT RICHARD M. NIXON

Washington — (AP) — Republican Richard M. Nixon was elected 37th president of the United States today, bursting by Democrat Hubert H. Humphrey with narrow windup victories in California, Illinois and Ohio.

★ ★ ★

Minneapolis, Minn. — (UPI) — Hubert H. Humphrey today conceded the presidential election to Richard M. Nixon.

By JACK BELL and BARRY SCHWEID

Associated Press Writers

Washington—Republican Richard M. Nixon smashed to victory early today in California and Ohio and pushed within a whisker of election as the 37th president of the United States.

The two states pumped a massive 66 electoral votes into Nixon's growing lead over Democrat Hubert H. Humphrey in a sizzling, photo-finish race.

If Nixon scrambles to a win in Illinois—and he was in the lead—he would have the big prize that eluded him in a razor-thin loss to John F. Kennedy in 1960.

In popular votes Nixon and Humphrey were in a virtual tie.

But in the more important electoral votes, Nixon had surged at 8:40 a.m. EST to a lead of 261 to 172. The number necessary for victory is 270.

Humphrey's only chance—and it was diminishing rapidly—was to deny Nixon an Electoral College victory and have the House decide the presidency.

To accomplish this, Humphrey had to keep Nixon's total beneath 270. Nixon, meanwhile, could end it all by taking Illinois or by beating out Humphrey in any one of three other undecided states: Maryland, Missouri or Washington.

Even if Humphrey won all four he still would be short of an electoral majority.

Humphrey's total stood frozen for hours. American Independent George C. Wallace, who said on the eve of balloting that the race really was between him and Nixon, was a distant third with 45, all in the Deep South.

Nixon knocked off Humphrey in Ohio by the thinnest of margins. With 98 per cent of the vote counted Nixon had 1,766,384 to 1,658,933 for the Democratic vice president—an edge of 107,451.

In California, with 95 per cent of the precincts reporting Nixon had 3,183,897 and Humphrey 3,054,577.

Nixon's press chief, Herbert G. Klein, had claimed Nixon would carry the state by 300,000 votes.

Humphrey went to bed early in the morning without mak-

(Continued on Page 10A)

★ ★ ★

Nixon Followed The Script

By JACK W. GERMOND

Gannett News Service

Washington—Despite its Hairbreadth Harry quality, Richard M. Nixon's apparent victory in the presidential election followed the Republican scenario with remarkable accuracy.

He won handily in the Border and "New South" states, the far West and Midwest and held his losses in the Northeast and the major industrial states to a tolerable level.

Although it took more than 12 hours to determine it, the results in most states followed the line the political oddsmakers had established.

The suspense came because the late surge for Democratic Nominee Hubert H. Humphrey, the same surge that gave him runaway margins in much of New England, made genuine contests out of states that Nixon had been figured to win all along and ultimately did win — notably California, Illinois, Ohio and New Jersey.

THE PRINCIPAL surpise in the Nixon electoral package, and a mild one at that, was the eight votes from South Carolina that had been expected to go to George C. Wallace of the American Independent Party but—presto, courtesy of Strom Thur-

(Continued on Page 10A)

Bombing Halt Tied by Nixon Aides to Closeness of Vote

NEW YORK (AP) — Richard M. Nixon, described as maintaining "cheerful confidence," was acknowledged by aides early today as finding the presidential race closer than expected—perhaps because of the Vietnam bombing halt.

Herbert K. Klein, director of communications for the Republican presidential candidate, said the contest with Democrat Hubert H. Humphrey was tighter than anticipated and asserted, "the bombing halt, I think, played a role."

Nixon, spending the long election night in a 35th floor suite at the Waldorf-Astoria Hotel, was said by Klein to be standing behind his public pledge to support the popular vote winner should the election be thrown into the House of Representatives.

But Klein said the possibility that Nixon would wind up

(Continued on Page 10A)

★ ★ ★

Electoral Vote

By the Associated Press

Humphrey has carried 11 states and the District of Columbia with 172 electoral votes: Connecticut, Rhode Island, West Virginia, Massachusetts, Maine, Minnesota, Pennsylvania, Texas, New York, Michigan, Hawaii, and the District of Columbia.

He is leading in three states with 31 electoral votes: Maryland Missouri and Washington.

Nixon has carried 29 states with 261 electoral votes: Kentucky, Vermont, Indiana, Oklahoma, Florida, Nevada, Idaho, Colorado, Ohio, Kansas, Tennessee, Wyoming, Virginia, Delaware, Arizona, Utah, New Mexico, New Jersey, South Dakota, Oregon, North Carolina, South Carolina, California, New Hampshire, Nebraska, Wisconsin, North Dakota, Montana and Iowa. He is leading in two states with 29 electoral votes: Alaska and Illinois.

Wallace has carried five states with 45 electoral votes: Alabama, Arkansas, Mississippi, Georgia and Louisiana.

State by state table on Page 10A.

GREETINGS FOR FOLLOWERS — Vice - President Hubert Humphrey greets Democratic Party workers and friends in his hotel headquarters yesterday.

Vice-President Goes to Bed Without Knowing Outcome

MINNEAPOLIS, Minn. (AP) — Hubert H. Humphrey went to bed this morning not knowing whether he was to be the 37th president of the United States or just another former vice president.

"I feel sufficiently at ease so that I want to get a good night's rest," the beaming Humphrey told several hundred shouting supporters at his hotel election headquarters.

Humphrey supporters had been waiting in the hotel ballroom more than six hours when the vice president showed up.

It's fair to say," Humphrey went on, "that we have done much better than most observers thought we would and about as good as I thought we would. There are critical states yet to be heard from—Ohio, Illinois, California and Washington.

"This is a donnybrook. Anything can happen."

Humphrey said several already seen fit to retire in confidence"—and that when his wife, Muriel, asked him whether he wanted her to get up and appear with him, he replied, "Well, dear, let's wait until we can announce a victory statement completely."

Humphrey said he had always been "a rather optimistic man—and tonight I feel that way.

"I feel that by the time the turn of day comes tomorrow, you and I are going to be a lot happier."

Humphrey, thanking his supporters, said the American people "have been mighty good to us. They have given us a great vote of confidence."

Thus, Humphrey followed in the footsteps of Democratic candidates of history like John F. Kennedy and Woodrow Wil-

(Continued on Page 10A)

Update Election System Now--for 1972

This is the year the nation found out how it really elected its presidents, says Carl T. Rowan, and decided it didn't like it.

Mr. Rowan details some of the problems and suggests changes in the electoral system be made now, in time for the 1972 election. He tells all on Page 6A.

Also on the inside:

November 6, 1968: Despite the closeness of the presidential vote, perhaps the most surprising news was that the Republicans controlled the New York Assembly. *Courtesy Dolly Escovar*

Souper Day

Variable cloudiness, windy and cold with a chance of a few snow flurries today. High in the mid 20s. Precipitation chance 20 per cent today, 10 per cent tonight.

U.S. WEATHER BUREAU FORECAST
AIRPORTTEMPERATURES

3 p.m.	20	7 p.m.	18	11 p.m.	15
4 p.m.	20	8 p.m.	17	Midnight	14
5 p.m.	19	9 p.m.	16	1 a.m.	13
6 p.m.	18	10 p.m.	15	2 a.m.	12

THE SUNDAY PRESS ®

The Hometown Newspaper of the Southern Tier

Volume 20 — 18 Binghamton, N. Y., January 12, 1969 8 Sections 30 Cents

Let's Chuckle

If you want to make somebody believe something, whisper it.

McDONOUGH TAKES CONTROL OF EJ

White, Johnson Quit; McGowan New Chief

BERNARD P. McDONOUGH

By PHIL HAND and DAVE BEAL

Bernard P. McDonough last night finally succeeded in taking over control of the Endicott-Johnson Corp.

In the largest administrative shakeup in the shoe company's history, EJ's top executives, including Frank A. Johnson and Eli G. White, resigned and were replaced by Mr. McDonough and his supporters.

Eight of EJ's 14-member board of directors resigned and were replaced by six new directors. Five of the new directors are officers or directors of McDonough companies.

MR. WHITE was replaced as president and chief executive officer by Harold P. McGowan, formerly a group vice-president and director of EJ.

Mr. Johnson, whose family founded and operated the firm for most of its corporate life, was replaced as chairman of the board by Mr. McDonough.

The massive executive changes came after a board of directors meeting in Endicott yesterday which was not concluded until after 8 o'clock.

Mr. McGowan, after the meeting, said there is no plan to close, move or make substantial changes in the company at this time.

"WE DON'T PLAN to make any changes at this time, openings or closings," he said. "We have one plan and that is to be successful making shoes."

O. Russell Kennedy, group vice-president of EJ, also resigned last night along with these directors:

Joseph M. Beil, Jr., chairman of the board of New York State Electric & Gas Corp.; Wayne W. Cawley, retired president of Cadre Industries; Philip L. Carret, chairman of the Pioneer Fund which ownes 25,000 shares of EJ stock; John C. Clark, director of Clark-Cleveland Inc.; Robert V. Horton, limited partner with Goldman, Sachs & Co.

Named to the board of directors during the meeting were: Mr. McDonough; Donald E.

(Continued on Page 7 A)

HAROLD P. McGOWAN ELI G. WHITE FRANK A. JOHNSON

We'll Boom--McGowan

By STEVE HAMBALEK

"We're going to build Endicott Johnson into a fantastic success," Harold P. McGowan said last night at his first press conference as the new president and chief executive officer of the shoemaking firm.

The press conference took place in the office of Frank A. Johnson in the company headquarters in Endicott's East Main Street, about two hours after Mr. Johnson left the building, no longer the chairman of the board.

The top job at EJ came to Mr. McGowan 22 years after he joined the company as the office manager of its Keystone Shoe Co. in Archbald, Pa., where he was born, the seventh of 10 children of a coal miner.

While scores of veteran EJ executives vanished for a variety of reasons under three other company presidents in the last 10 years — Mr. Johnson, P. J. Casella and Eli G. White, who resigned last night — Mr. McGowan climbed and climbed.

IN 1957, WHEN Frank Johnson was named president of the company, Mr. McGowan, 48, was promoted to administrative assistant in the EJ accounting department. In 1959 he was named assistant treasurer and then controller.

In 1963 he was made administrative assistant to Mr. White. Three years later he was elected group vice-president for NADCO, EJ's national distribution company, which included the Specialty Sales Division and the All-Weather and Leisure Footwear sales.

And in March of 1968, Mr. McGowan was elected to the EJ board of directors.

As of last night Mr. McGowan was the president and chief executive officer of two, competing shoe companies.

It was only nine days ago that he announced that he was leaving EJ to head the Weinbrenner Shoe Corp. in Milwaukee.

LAST NIGHT Mr. McGowan said that he would resign from the Milwaukee post immediately.

Asked if he had any hobbies, Mr. McGowan said, "My hobby is work. No other hobbies."

Mr. McGowan summed up his personal philosophy as follows:

"I never had any goals. It never was my goal to be president. I always figured that somebody was trying to get my job and I always made sure that I did that job better than anyone else. No close plays at second.

"I came through the depression. I get up in the morning and I get wheeling," he said.

Mr. McGowan will be 49 on May 25. He stands 6 feet two

(Continued on Page 7 A)

Swedish Tie OK'd By Hanoi

By UP-International

Tokyo — North Vietnam announced early today it has accepted neutral Sweden's offer to establish diplomatic relations with the Hanoi government.

The Communist Vietnam News Agency broadcast a message to Stockholm by Hanoi Minister for Foreign Affairs Nguyen Duy Trinh "warmly" welcoming the Swedish decision announced Friday to establish diplomatic relations with North Vietnam.

LENNART PETRI

Lennart Petri, Swedish ambassador in Peking, is mentioned as the man most likely to represent the Swedes in Hanoi.

"Our people and our government are firmly convinced that the establishment of these diplomatic relations will help strengthen further the solidarity, friendship and cooperation between Vietnam and Sweden and will make a positive contribution to the safeguarding of world peace," Trinh said in a cable sent to Swedish Foreign Ministry.

Sweden is the first non-Communist nation in Europe to establish diplomatic relations with North Vietnam. Its move has been denounced both by the United States and South Vietnam. The Saigon government said Friday the Swedish action would "aid the Communists."

The announcement came as no surprise to Paris diplomatic circles.

The North Vietnamese delegation to the Vietnam talks had issued a statement Friday night "warmly welcoming" recognition announced by neutral Sweden.

The delegation statement said that its nation's "firm foreign policy" had been the establishment of relations with all other countries irrespective of their internal social structure.

Aid Cuts Last Resort, Finch Says

NEW YORK (AP)—Robert H. Finch, President-elect Nixon's designated secretary of health education and welfare, said Saturday he would withhold federal funds an "ultimate weapon" to advance desegregation in the public schools.

Finch said, however, that there are other means of approaching the problem of desegregated schools and that he intends to examine each case separately. He made the statements in answer to questions at a news conference in Nixon's Pierre Hotel headquarters.

The withholding of federal education money as a means of achieving desegregation "has always been there as an ultimate weapon," Finch said.

Asked if he would use this measure, he repeated "as an ultimate weapon."

"You do not come in with a meat ax and get genuine compliance," he said.

Button Up!

By UP-International

A major storm and a series of small ones spread more snow over much of the north half of the nation yesterday. In the third full week of unrelenting winter severity, cold penetrated southward to the Gulf of Mexico.

A snow blanket ranging in depth from a few inches to Marquette, Michigan's 54 inches covered most Northern states.

Snow fell yesterday in the Pacific Northwest, which was being battered by still another ocean gale, the Rockies, the Plains, the upper Mississippi Valley, the lower Great Lakes, and the Appalachians from West Virginia to New England.

Travelers warnings were posted in parts of California, Oregon, New York and Pennsylvania.

Frigid polar air continued pushing into the northern Plains and upper Midwest with temperatures as low as 30 below zero forecast for parts of Minnesota.

Pacification Record Claimed

Saigon — AP — The number of South Vietnamese living under direct control of the Viet Cong hit a record low of 12.3 per rent at the end of 1968, the U. S. Command said Saturday.

As of Dec. 31, slightly fewer than 2 million of the country's 17 million people were recorded as living in areas that were neither secured nor contested by government forces.

The monthly report on progress in pacification — the so-called "other war" in which the Saigon government seeks to wrest control of the countryside from the enemy forces — said 76.3 per cent of the people lived in areas that were relatively secure and 11.4 per cent in contested areas.

All of these figures represented high-water marks of progress under the complicated and oft-criticized Hamlet Evaluation System used by American advisers to the government's pacification program.

In rural areas alone, the report said, 65 per cent of the people life in relatively secure areas, an increase of 4.3 per cent over November. Under the formula, rural areas include everything outside self governing cities which by themselves have some 3.3 million people.

Thus the "rural" figure includes many people who live in cities that while not autonomous, are actually urban areas broken up into villages and hamlets.

Top U.S. officials admitted

(Continued on Page 8 A)

—Associated Press WIREPHOTO

VILLAGERS HELP—Peasant women help haul the poncho-covered body of a South Vietnamese Ranger killed during an assault on enemy positions in My Hoa village southwest of Da Nang. When heavy fighting broke out, the women joined the rangers and helped care for the wounded.

Oil Strike to End?

Los Angeles — The Oil, Chemical and Atomic Workers Union said yesterday it has reached tentative agreement with the Union Oil Co. that could settle a nationwide oil strike.

Tennessee Williams Now Catholic

KEY WEST, Fla. (AP)—Playwright Tennessee Williams, whose widelyread plays are salted with four-letter words and graphic sexual detail, has converted to Catholicism—saying "I wanted my goodness back."

The 57-year-old author, whose full name is Thomas Lanier Williams, took his vows Friday at St. Mary's Star of the Sea Church.

"I had never met the man before last Sunday," said the Rev. Joseph LeRoy, who baptized Williams.

Father LeRoy said Williams was ill with the flu when Dakin Williams, the author's brother, approached him last Sunday and told him Tennessee was interested in joining the church.

"I saw him, told him what was involved in a profession of faith to the church, and he replied that he had been a Catholic in spirit all his life. He felt convinced that God was calling him to be a Catholic," said the priest.

Williams, who won a Pulitzer Prize for "A Streetcar Named Desire" and "Cat on a Hot Tin Roof," had been an Episcopalian.

Humphrey Recommends Fred Harris

Washington — AP — Vice-President Hubert H. Humphrey recommended Senator Fred Harris of Oklahoma yesterday to become the national chairman of the Democratic Party.

The Vice-President's choice is all but certain to be accepted. As the last Democratic candidate for president, he is titular head of the party.

In a telegram to members of the Democratic National Committee, Humphrey said, "I hope he will have your support."

Lawrence F. O'Brien's resignation as chairman was announced Jan. 7 in a letter to Humphrey.

Israel, Jordan Hit In New Attacks

Tel Aviv —AP— Israel turned to air power twice yesterday in fighting along the Jordan River cease-fire line.

Jet fighters first hammered Arab commando positions in Jordan, a spokesman said, in reprisal for a rocket attack by the guerrillas soon after dawn on an Israeli army vehicle near Kubbutz Gesher, six miles south of the Sea of Galilee.

Military sources said the jets later streaked across the river to support Israeli forces in a two-hour mortar and artillery battle near the King Abdullah Bridge, three miles north of the Dead Sea.

Trouble also arose on Israel's western flank, in the teeming Gaza Strip. An explosive charge blew up beneath an Israeli automobile in occupied Gaza City while another blast shook a soft drink bottling plant on the main street. The army said there were no casualties and damage was slight.

A dispatch from Amman said four fighters — Super Mysteres of French make and American-made Skyhawks — attacked farms in the Manshiyeh and Northern Shuna areas with napalm, bombs and machine guns.

A spokesman in Amman, Jordan's capital, said the raiders inflicted damage, but no one was killed.

Radio Amman said that, in the subsequent battle near the King Abdullah Bridge, Jordanian gunners hit three Israeli tanks. It said Jordan suffered no casualties.

The army reported one Israeli soldier was wounded.

Progress Reported

New York — (UPI) — A spokesman for the New York Shipping Association, struck 22 days ago by the International Longshoremen's Association, said yesterday "considerable progress" was made in new bargaining sessions, but he warned "there are still many problems to be worked out."

Sunday Press Index

January 12, 1969: Frank Johnson was the last of the Johnson family to play a role in the shoe company his family founded. *Microfilm archives*

Sunny today. Chance of showers. High near 80. Clear tonight. Low near 55. Cloudy tomorrow. High near 80. Rain chances, 40% tonight, 20% tomorrow. Details, page 31.

The Sun-Bulletin

FINAL

Tonight's deadline for junior drivers: 9:04 p.m.

Binghamton, New York 13902 | 36 Pages | MOONDAY, JULY 21, 1969 | 147th Year No. 226 | 10c per copy

MAN ON MOON!

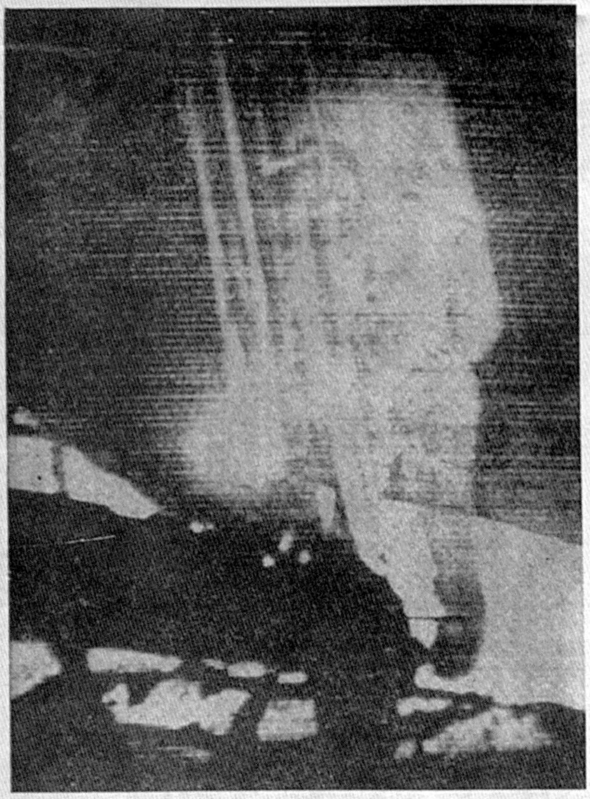

Ed Aldrin steps from LM ladder to moon's surface to join Neil Armstrong. Picture televised from moon.

SUN-BULLETIN—UPI

SPACE CENTER, HOUSTON (UPI) — Man reached the moon yesterday at 4:17:45 p.m. EDT. Then, for the first time, he set his foot on the soil of an alien world.

The first step, by 38-year-old civilian Neil A. Armstrong, hit the lunar dust at 10:56:20 p.m. EDT, about 6½ hours after Armstrong and Edwin E. "Buzz" Aldrin Jr. landed their spaceship Eagle on the lunar surface.

"That's one small step for man, one giant leap for mankind," were Armstrong's first words as his foot touched the lunar soil which he likened to powdered charcoal.

A worldwide television audience watched man's first footfall in a world other than his own.

The step was a dramatic moment in a day jammed with such moments — the landing itself, and Armstrong's superb calm when he overrode the automatic pilot of the lunar lander which was taking the spaceship toward a boulder field, and manually steered himself and Aldrin, an Air Force colonel, free of almost certain disaster.

The first view that millions of earth viewers saw of the moonwalk was Armstrong's foot pawing the air as he descended the nine rungs on the aluminum ladder leading to the lunar surface.

It was a world of harsh sunlight and black shadows, but the picture was amazingly clear.

Nixon speaks to astronauts

"There's going to be no difficulty in moving around," he said, first testing man's equilibrium on the lunar surface, where gravity is one-sixth that of earth.

While Armstrong handled the camera, Aldrin, 39, then crawled from the space ship and joined Armstrong on the lunar surface at 11:16 p.m. EDT. The world got even a better picture of the second man to step onto the moon.

TURN TO BACK PAGE

6 killed, 4 hurt in Afton crash—P. 3

July 21, 1969: Notice the date of the paper: "Moonday, July 21, 1969." *Courtesy Carolyn Fitzgerald*

DIRECTORY

Student Timothy Smith leads other students in song before the start of an anti-Vietnam teach-in held February 1968 in the lobby of the administration building at the State University in Binghamton. *Press & Sun-Bulletin archives*

General W. M. Mantz honors Guy Zonio, a veteran Endicott Johnson employee, for the company's production of 1million boots for use by troops in Vietnam, February 1969. The general, commander of the Defense Personnel Support Center in Philadelphia, accepted the boots at a ceremony at the Boys and Youth Plant in Johnson City. *Press & Sun-Bulletin archives*

Three Lane Construction Corp. laborers take a break and enjoy a rare view of Binghamton in 1969. Left to right: Edward L. Zaharris, Joseph A. Santangelo and Thomas A. Quaranta Jr. *Press & Sun-Bulletin archives*

A crowd looks on in Johnson City as state and local officials open the 4.5-mile link of the Route 17 Expressway between Binghamton and the Endwell area. *Press & Sun-Bulletin archives*

ENDICOTT, N.Y.
PAST

Broome County Executive Edwin L. Crawford, on rostrum at right, speaks to a group largely made up of military veterans and auxiliary members during ground-breaking ceremonies for a $6.6 million Veterans Memorial Arena in downtown Binghamton, 1971. In the background are the city hall and the taller state office building behind it, under construction in the Governmental Plaza west of the Arena site. *Press & Sun-Bulletin archives*

Construction of Veterans Memorial Arena in downtown Binghamton, circa 1971. *Press & Sun-Bulletin archives*

1970 - 1979

Everything changes in the '70s

Flurry Chance

Partly cloudy tonight and tomorrow with chance of flurries, low near 5, high in mid to upper teens. Precipitation chance 50 per cent tonight and tomorrow. Details on Page 7B.

THE EVENING PRESS

A Gannett Newspaper ★ ★

Binghamton, N.Y., Tuesday, January 9, 1973 Volume 95—230 3 Sections 44 Pages 15 Cents

Let's Chuckle

TV viewers are still waiting for an announcer who will surprise them with information about a soap that won't do a darn thing but get the dirt off.

$25 Million Downtown UR Plan OK'd

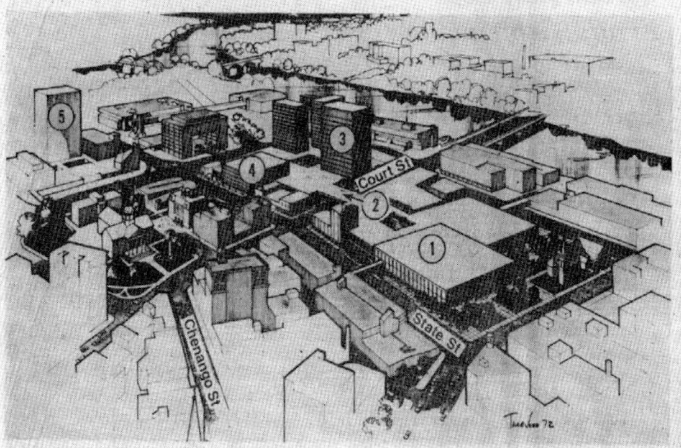

Court St
State St
Chenango St

BINGHAMTON'S FUTURE? — The above drawing shows the $25 million construction project planned by the MonDev development firm for downtown Binghamton. The project includes (1) a department store; (2) a pedestrian walkway over Court Street; (3) an office tower with two high rise apartments behind it; and (4) an office or hotel building. At upper left in picture, (5) is the new governmental complex south of Hawley Street.

By DAVE MACK

Officials of MonDev—Binghamton, Inc., the Binghamton Urban Renewal Agency and the Binghamton Parking Authority today signed agreements for construction of a $25 million, 7-acre multi-use project in downtown Bingnamton.

According to Keith Bryant, vice president of planning and development for MonDev, the project will be built over a two to three-year period, beginning in the fall of this year.

Agreements for land disposition and cooperation between MonDev and the Parking Authority were signed in Binghamton by I. Roche Ranson, president of MonDev Corp., Ltd., of Montreal, Canada, and Binghamton Mayor Alfred J. Libous, chairman of the Urban Renewal Agency.

MonDev—Binghamton, Inc., a wholly-owned subsidiary of MonDev—USA, was designated owner-developer-manager of the project.

MonDev—USA is a subsidiary of MonDev, Ltd.

The project was designed by the Chicago architectural firm of The Office Of Mies van der Rohe.

According to MonDev, it will cover four city blocks and will include a major department store, quality retail stores, office towers, luxury apartments and interior parking space.

Interior space layout was developed by J.F.N. Interior Design Consultants of New York City.

★ ★ ★

The seven-acre Binghamton project, covering four city blocks, will include a major department store, quality retail stores, office towers, luxury apartments and interior parking space. – MonDev.

★ ★ ★

The total retail space will be about 300,000 square feet.

The plan calls for a department store with a floor area of about 150,000 square feet. It is to be built at the northeast corner of the area.

The area is bounded by Henry Street on the north, Water Street on the west, Hawley Street on the south and State Street on the east.

Washington Street, which runs parallel to Water and State streets, will cease to exist between Hawley and Henry streets.

This closed-off street will become a closed pedestrian mall.

The mall will include a bridge over Court Street for pedestrians at the second floor level of Court Street buildings.

Underground parking will be provided beneath the portion of the development south of Court Street.

Of the existing buildings inside the project area south of Court Street, only the Bache Building, the Woolworth Building, the J. C. Penney Building and Hamlin's Building will remain standing.

North of Court Street plans call for demolition of all buildings between State and Washington Streets fronting on Court Street, except for the Banker's Trust Building.

Buildings facing Court Street between Water and Washington streets will remain standing. The five buildings on the west side of Washington Street immediately north of Court Street will also remain.

Second floor-level ramps are planned between the city's two new parking buildings on Water Street and on State Street, and the retail area north of Court Street. MonDev officials said they have not yet completed negotiations with a tenant for the department store.

Negotiations are under way, they said, with possible tenants for the department store

(Continued on Page 3A)

Sniper Escapes; Cops May Have 'Goofed'

NEW ORLEANS (AP) — Police Supt. Clarence Giarrusso says a sniper involved in the slayings of six persons slipped through a 200-man cordon from his hotel rooftop perch Monday either through "police negligence" or because he was super smart.

Giarrusso said Monday night he was convinced more than one sniper was responsible for killing the six and injuring 17 others in a two-day battle. But when pressed by newsmen, Giarrusso admitted there could have been just one sniper — the man killed by police gunfire Sunday night.

A floor-to-floor search of the 18-story DownTown Howard Johnson's hotel was made by 100 officers Monday night. They found no one and all but about a dozen officers left the scene.

Police kept the hotel closed today, but the central business district, which was cordoned off by police Monday, is to be opened to normal activity today, Mayor Moon Landrieu said.

As the floor-by-floor search of the hotel began, Giarrusso said, "If they don't turn up anyone...then he got away."

How could he have filtered to freedom through the scores of officers surrounding the hotel?

"There's a gamut of possibilities ranging from police negligence to a superbrain sniper," Giarrusso replied.

The theory of two or more snipers was based on "some" evidence, Giarrusso said, stressing that after a sniper was killed on the rooftop Sunday night, there were reports of gunfire coming from the roof and three officers were slightly wounded.

However, the superintendent admitted the possibility that the three were wounded by gunfire from fellow officers stationed in surrounding buildings.

He said he had other evidence, but would not elaborate.

A sharpshooter in an armor-plated Marine helicopter killed the sniper whose body lay on the rooftop all night and most of the day Monday.

The body was removed Monday evening and fingerprinted. Giarrusso said there was a tentative identification, but "I'm not going to announce anything tentative. When we are positive, I'll tell you."

He said he believes the shooting spree was part of a national conspiracy of black militants.

When asked what evidence he had to back up his statement, Giarrusso declined to comment.

Landrieu said the police operation has now moved from the hectic action at the hotel to the painstaking in-

(Continued on Page 11A)

Tanker Crew Lost

SINGAPORE (AP) — Ten crewmen from the Cypriot oil tanker Anson are believed lost in the sinking of their ship after a collision with the Liberian tanker Atlantic Faith.

S. Viet Role Shift Possible

By PETER LISAGOR

The Press—Chicago Daily News

WASHINGTON — The Nixon administration is again "threatening" to turn the Vietnam war over to the South Vietnamese, whether a cease-fire agreement is reached with Hanoi or not.

The word "threatening" is used advisedly. For in the past, administration officials have argued that North Vietnam would better serve its interests by a negotiated settlement with the United States, rather than risk dealing with an adequately trained and supplied Saigon force.

The argument apparently had small appeal for Hanoi. But now, some administration sources here believe, the North Vietnamese may be in a more compliant mood, partly because the South Vietnamese may be ready to assume major responsibility for the military and political outcome of the war.

In any case, these sources hold, President Nixon and his advisers may finally feel compelled to declare that the Vietnamization process is complete.

Outgoing Defense Secretary Melvin R. Laird indicated to the House Armed Services Committee Monday that the President may be headed along that course.

Within a few weeks, when

(Continued on Page 11A)

B52s Get Jet Guardians

SAIGON (AP) — President Nixon has authorized U. S. fighter escorts to attack North Vietnamese MIGs or surface-to-air missile sites above the 20th parallel if they threaten American B52s below the northern limit Nixon has placed on the bombing of North Vietnam, reliable sources reported today.

The U. S. Command announced today that an Air Force F4 Phantom shot down a MIG21 along the 20th parallel Sunday when it threatened a flight of B52s.

The Command said that the MIG was downed "northwest of Thanh Hoa," which is only 10 miles below the 20th parallel, and spokesman refused to say just how far northwest of the city. This was interpreted as a tacit acknowledgment that the dogfight extended above the parallel.

U.S. sources outside the Command indicated today that Hanoi Radio was not lying when it reported last week that U.S. fighters escorting reconnaissance planes attacked antiaircraft defenses in Hoa Binh Province south of Hanoi. The U.S. Command denied at the time that American planes had bombed preselected targets above the 20th parallel, but it refused to comment on reconnaissance operations and what action fighter escorts might have taken.

The MIG21 downed Sunday was credited to Capt. Paul D. Howman, 28, of Wooster, Ohio, and 1st Lt. Lawrence W. Kullman, 25, of Hartly, Del. The pilots reported they fired two missiles at the enemy jet after detecting it on their radar, and one of the missiles blew it up.

It was the fifth MIG reported downed by U.S. crews since Dec. 18. The U.S. Command said a total of 183 North Vietnamese jets have been downed during the war.

Thirty-nine B52s dropped about 1,100 tons of bombs in the North Vietnamese panhandle during the 24 hours ending at 8 a.m. today, U.S. sources said. The Command said the targets included supply caches and supply routes 25 to 45 miles south of Than Hoa and 10 to 30 miles northwest of Dong Hoi, another port 45 miles above the demilitarized zone.

During the same period, the Command said, U.S. fighter-bombers made 128 strikes in the panhandle, destroying supply trucks and setting fuel depots afire.

In South Vietnam, nearly 50 B52s dropped more than 1,200 tons of explosives on troop concentrations in a staging area that North Vietnamese forces used for attacks in the triborder region of the central highlands, where the frontiers of South Vietnam, Laos and Cambodia meet.

It was the second day of heavy raids in the region between Highway 14 and the border, 10 to 20 miles northwest of Kontum. This indicated a new North Vietnamese buildup, perhaps in preparation for an attack on Kontum.

Premier Pham Van Dong of North Vietnam ordered new austerity measures and heightened military alerts for his coun-

(Continued on Page 11A)

★ ★ ★

2nd Paris Session Ends in Coolness

PARIS (AP) — Henry A. Kissinger conferred with Le Duc Tho for six hours today in the second session of their Vietnam peace talks as Hanoi declared in a broadcast that "there has not been any sign showing that the negotiations will reach any results."

President Nixon's national security adviser was the host of the meeting in an American-owned villa overlooking a golf course in suburban St. Nom la Breteche. As at Monday's meeting on Communist ground, there was no public handshaking between the two sides, reflecting the apparent chilly atmosphere of the talks following the massive American bombing raids on North Vietnam.

But Tho and his advisers emerged smiling from the villa at the end of the meeting, in marked contrast with their grim expressions when the meeting began. Kissinger also directed a wan smile toward waiting newsmen and photographers when he left the villa a few minutes later.

Both sides maintained their mutually agreed news blackout over the subjects under discussion.

The unfriendly atmosphere which surrounded Monday's meeting continued today. None of the North Vietnamese were outside to greet Kissinger on his arrival Monday, so none of the Americans were visible when Tho and his staff arrived today.

Nhan Dan, the official newspaper of the North Vietnamese Communist party, said today that Hanoi's representatives had returned to the negotiations "with the seriousness and good will to bring about a correct solution to the Vietnam problem."

But Nhan Dan made clear that Hanoi was still demanding that the U.S. sign the draft peace agreement Kissinger and Tho worked out in October.

Meanwhile, technical experts of the two sides also were meeting for the seventh day today.

Food Price Jump Highest Since '47

WASHINGTON (AP) — Wholesale farm prices posted the biggest monthly increase in 26 years last month with a climb of 6.8 per cent, the government reported today.

The report, by the Labor Department's Bureau of Labor Statistics, blamed weather damage to crops as the main reason for the big increase.

The sharp climb in food prices boosted the government's over-all wholesale price index 1.8 per cent in December, the largest in 22 years. The increase was slightly less, 1.6 per cent, on a seasonally adjusted basis.

Prices of a broad range of industrial raw materials rose three-tenths of 1 per cent while wholesale consumer finished goods ready for market at retail had climbed 1.2 per cent, the report said.

The big increase in prices of farm products, largely uncontrolled by federal price regulations, included boosts of 21.1 per cent for grains, 16.9 per cent for eggs, 13.6 per cent for hay and oil seeds, 9.4 per cent for livestock, 7.8 per cent for plant and animal fibers, eight-tenths of 1 per cent for poultry and one-tenth of 1 per cent for milk.

The only declines was 5.1

(Continued on Page 11A)

—Associated Press WIREPHOTO.

THE SUN THAT NEVER SETS—This photograph, taken at Japan's Showa Base in Antarctica, shows the up-and-down position of the never-setting sun at the South Pole. Aimed at the horizon to the south of the base, the camera's shutter was opened at 20-minute intervals, left to right, to record the location of the sun. It now is midsummer in the Antarctic.

Blast Destroys Jewish Agency

PARIS (AP) — An explosion destroyed the offices of the Jewish Agency in Paris today and wrecked 11 cars parked in the street outside.

The agency arranges for the emigration of jews to Israel. The incident came a few days before the expected arrival in Paris of Israeli Premier Golda Meir to attend a meeting of the Socialist International.

Inside THE PRESS

If he had it to do all over again, Sen. George McGovern would conduct a "cooler" presidential campaign: he'd travel less, use television more and be less open with the press. Page 10A.

January 9, 1973: The city and Canadian developer Mondev began a long, eventually fruitless dance over downtown redevelopment.

Courtesy Rudy Bystrak

The region's leaders put resources into urban renewal in an attempt to keep the good times flowing in the valley of the Susquehanna. It was an uphill fight as good roads and better automobiles allowed the population to spread out.

Broome's population dipped by the end of the decade as Chenango and Tioga grew.

Binghamton again made national headlines with a tragedy. Three firefighters drowned in the Susquehanna River. Press photographer Paul F. Konecny took one of the most powerful news photos ever taken when he saw a firefighter's hand rise out of the water.

The tragedy overshadowed news of the opening of the Oakdale Mall. The shopping center, within sight of Route 17, soon ended Binghamton's long reign as the retail hub of the Southern Tier.

World and national news dominated the decade. The Vietnam War ended. Richard Nixon became the only president to resign. Elvis died. Three Mile Island became the nation's worst nuclear accident.

Refund Pot Rocky's Hiding Place From Tax Cutters

Charles Holcomb, Gannett News Service's Bureau Chief in Albany, reveals that Gov. Rockefeller's proposed $150 million income tax refund is this year's big gimmick, a way of hiding funds for use in the next election year and keeping it out of the hands of the tax-cutters in the legislature.

By CHARLES R. HOLCOMB
Gannett News Service

ALBANY — Gov. Nelson Rockefeller's proposed income tax refund reserve skims $150 million off current income tax proceeds to be saved for use in the election year 1974-75 budget.

It also maneuvers local governments out of $27 million in state revenue-sharing aid they would otherwise get.

And at the same time, it keeps a potentially fat cash surplus out of the hands of the would-be tax cutters in the legislature.

Rockefeller startled legislators and reporters alike by including in his 1973-74 budget request — unveiled last week — $150 million reserve fund to pay off extra heavy income tax refunds he expects in the first quarter of the 1973-74 fiscal year, which starts April 1.

He said that after the federal government had revised its withholding tax tables, New York did, too, early in 1972, to prevent "underwithholding." But the taxpayers didn't take advantage of an "option" to claim more exemptions and so the result, he said, was substantial "overwithholding."

This "unprecedented situation," he said in his budget message, resulted in "substantial and artificial "inflation of 1972-73 receipts."

Therefore, he said, it was necessary to set up a $150 million reserve fund to pay off this flood of refunds early in the 1973-74 fiscal year.

The reserve fund is an ingenious financial device — his budget experts decline to accept the label "gimmick" — that may enable the governor to avoid having an embarrassment of riches as the 1972-73 fiscal year draws to a close.

Here is how it works.

Cash surpluses on hand March 31 must be paid into the Tax Stabilization Reserve Fund, and can't be spent unless revenues fall below estimates.

This is the "rainy day" fund that was tapped for $66 million to finance a $23 million deficit in March 1971 and for another $43 million to pay for part of a $483 million deficit last March 31.

The governor tries to end the fiscal year with as close to a zero surplus as possible. He is required to have the budget balanced, but excess funds go untouchably into the rainy day Fund and therefore become useless.

Suddenly he is faced with a big surplus in the current fiscal year.

Federal aid was a gamble that more than paid off; federal revenue sharing was still a dream a year ago when he budgeted $400 million in federal aid, but New York wound up getting $442 million.

The economy bounced back from recession faster and more strongly than expected, increasing tax revenues. And as a result, all the emergency increases he rammed through at the late 1971 special session — in income, liquor, gasoline and cigarette taxes — also yielded a bumper crop.

(Continued From Page 1A)

Rain Likely

Rain likely tonight, low in mid-30s. Cloudy, windy and mild tomorrow with chance of showers, high around 45. Precipitation chance 60 per cent tonight, 50 per cent tomorrow. Details on Page 10B.

THE EVENING PRESS

A Gannett Newspaper

Binghamton, N.Y., Monday, January 22, 1973 Volume 95—229 2 Sections 28 Pages 15 Cents

Let's Chuckle

It is easier to believe a lie that one has heard a thousand times than a fact no one has heard before.

—Associated Press WIREPHOTO

HAIRY EXPERIENCE—Boni Peterson, a junior at Hillcrest High School in Dallas, Tex., found her physics class anything but dull when she received 200,000 volts from an electrostatic generator that caused her hair to stand on end. The charge was harmless and painless.

Jet Down; Toll May Be 202

By the Associated Press

LAGOS, Nigeria—A Jordanian jetliner bringing home 202 Moslem pilgrims from Mecca crashed while landing today at Kano in northern Nigeria.

"It is feared most of those aboard have died," a spokesman for Nigerian Airways said.

The world's worst air disaster took the lives of 176 persons in the crash of a Soviet Aeroflot jet near Moscow last Oct. 14.

Mecca, the holiest place of Moslems, is in Saudi Arabia.

The Royal Jordanian Airlines Boeing 707 left Saudi Arabia from Jidda, near Mecca, on the 2,100-mile flight to Kano.

Officials in Lagos, 730 miles south of Kano, said communications with Kano were down and for this reason R. A. B. Dikko, Nigeria's commissioner of transport, was flying to the scene of the crash at Kano's airport.

These officials said it was not likely that a full report on the crash will be available before Tuesday.

Saigon, D.C. Predict Cease-Fire This Week

WASHINGTON (AP) — As captured enemy documents signaled a midweek initialing of a cease-fire accord, Henry A. Kissinger heads back to Paris today to join allied and Communist officials in the last steps toward ending the Vietnam war.

Before the presidential assistant left Andrews Air Force Base, he was to get last-minute instructions from President Nixon at a breakfast-hour White House meeting.

Officially, the White House continued to portray the purpose of Kissinger's return to the French capital as "completing the text of an agreement" to end the fight.

But a flurry of developments Sunday bolstered the belief that an agreement soon will be signed, calling for a cease-fire, the return of prisoners of war, and machinery to reshape the South Vietnamese government. The major developments:

—Senior South Vietnamese officials said captured documents from the Communist high command stated that an agreement will be initialed at 8 a.m. EST Wednesday, that it will be formally signed on Saturday and that a cease-fire will go into effect on Sunday, Jan. 28.

—While shying away from specific dates, Washington sources indicated that Nixon has set a goal of wrapping up the Vietnam agreement this week and that, barring unexpected snags, the President is confident of hitting that target.

—South Vietnamese Foreign Minister Tran Van Lam told an interviewer as he departed for Paris that Vice President Spiro T. Agnew will be in Saigon on Jan. 28, presumably to demonstrate that Washington and Saigon were entering the post-war era shoulder-to-shoulder.

—Agnew himself said he couldn't answer when asked whether he will be heading for Saigon, saying the President would have to make "that announcement."

—Congressional sources reported that Nixon plans a meeting with Capitol Hill leaders within the next few days, providing him a forum to brief them on details of a peace accord.

—The Viet Cong foreign minister, Mrs. Nguyen Thi Binh, arrived in Paris and said the Communists are ready to "do everything possible to achieve a quick settlement." But, she said, "everything depends on the United States." Mrs. Binh said the proposed agreement offers the United States "an honorable way out of its dirty war."

Amid these developments, the White House maintained its lid on official discussion of Vietnam negotiations. When asked about reports that a pact would be initialed within days, a spokesman said he would have no comment on "speculative stories."

Kissinger declared in October that "peace is at hand." But a sudden impasse in the presidential assistant's negotiations with Hanoi Politburo member Le Duc Tho deflated that optimism.

Since then, Nixon, Kissinger and other White House officials have carefully avoided optimistic statements.

Not once in Saturday's inaugural address did Nixon use the word "Vietnam." But three times he said America's involvement in that long conflict is ending and that the nation stands "on the threshhold of a new era of peace."

Kissinger and Tho interrupted their talks on Jan. 13, when the U.S. negotiator returned to Washington for consultation with Nixon. The next day, Nixon dispatched Gen. Alexander M. Haig Jr., his chief liaison officer with South Vietnamese President Nguyen Van Thieu, to Saigon and four other Asian capitals to outline terms of a tentative agreement.

Prospects for Busy Week

- *Captured papers claim initialing of peace agreement Wednesday; signing Saturday and cease-fire on Sunday.*
- *Vice-President Agnew expected to be in Saigon Sunday.*
- *President Nixon expected to confer with congressional leaders.*
- *Viet Cong express eagerness for early settlement.*

★ ★ ★

S. Viet Troops Ambushed

SAIGON (AP) South Vietnamese forces have suffered a major defeat in the past few days, with two army battalions overrun and cut to pieces and relief forces repeatedly ambushed northwest of Saigon.

Fields reports said at least 80 soldiers, some of them wounded, had drifted back to government lines in the past two days. Some had been given safe conduct passes by the Communists after agreeing to throw away their weapons.

It was not known how many more were trying to escape nor was there any accurate count of the dead and wounded from the two battalions of the 5th Division which apparently fell into an enemy trap six days ago. The government has admitted so far to 56 of its troops killed and 132 wounded since Friday.

South Vietnamese commanders, after a series of emergency conferences, rejected a Viet Cong offer of a

(Continued on Page 7A)

Terrorism Renewal Predicted . . . 8B

Patience Ends Siege

By BETTY FLYNN
The Press-Chicago Daily News

NEW YORK — The sign atop the Riopiedras movie theater on Broadway in Brooklyn promised "el Super Show" for the weekend.

Hundreds of them watched as the four gunmen who commandeered John and Al's Sports Shop across the street shortly after 5 p.m. Friday meekly surrendered to police after a bloody, two-day battle in which a police officer was killed.

"They were convinced the only way to paradise was death," said William Johnson, a black special assistant to Police Commissioner Patrick Murphy. "We had to spend many hours pecking away at that philosophy to convince them that they should live."

It was patient, disciplined police work that avoided the bloodbath that so many expected yesterday, particularly after the escape by nine remaining hostages from the two-story building under siege for nearly two days in this Puerto Rican slum ghetto.

Shortly after the battle Johnson described how the police persuaded the gunmen to give up.

The gunmen, apparently members of a Muslim sect bent on dramatizing oppression of the black minority in this country, burst into the small store shortly after 5 p.m. Friday. They took 12 persons hostage, nine men and three women. A co-owner of the store, Sam Rosenblum, 56, was shoved out onto the street when police were alerted by a store-to-precinct buzzer—common to the area.

It was early Friday evening

(Continued on Page 7A)

—Associated Press WIREPHOTO

FREE AGAIN—Jerry Riccio, co-owner of a Brooklyn sporting goods store, dances for joy on rooftop after he led eight other hostages to freedom. They had been held in the store for nearly two days by four gunmen.

Teacher Strikes Span Three Cities

By the Associated Press

A strike by public school teachers in St. Louis—the first in the city's history—was called for today as similar walkouts continued in Philadelphia and Chicago.

Members of St. Louis Teachers Union Local 420 and the St. Louis Teachers Association, with both groups representing 2,800 members, authorized the strike in separate votes Sunday.

The St. Louis teachers have been demanding raises in bargaining sessions which have been under way since November. Their demands include a raise in the starting salary from $7,200 to $8,200. They also want a paid hospitalization program and a collective bargaining agreement.

Elsewhere, court proceedings were to begin today against 24 officials of the Philadelphia Federation of Teachers, the group leading a walkout which has started into its third week.

The union officials were named in criminal contempt proceedings for refusing to obey a court order to end the walkout.

The teachers are demanding a $9,300 starting salary and the school board is offering $8,900.

Negotiators for teachers in Chicago, who have been on strike since Jan. 10, say three major issues remain unsettled in that walkout and that the school board can not "buy us off with a salary increase alone."

Texas Abortion Law Upset

WASHINGTON (AP) — The Supreme Court today struck down the Texas abortion law and said a decision to possibly end a pregnancy within the early stages "must be left to the medical judgment of the pregnant woman's attending physician."

The 7 to 2 ruling was delivered by Julice Harry A. Blackmun over the opposition of Justices Byron R. White and William Rehnquist.

The court's judgment was based on "the right of privacy." Blackmun said whether it be founded in the concept of personal liberty or in restraint on government "is broad enough to encompass a woman's decision whether or not to terminate a pregnancy."

However, Blackmun went on, the right "is not unqualified" and the state can step in to protect health and prenatal life and to impose medical standards.

Blackmun's opinion rejected the theory pressed by abortion foes that a fetus is a "person" within constitutional terms and must be protected by the state.

Blackmun added: "We need not resolve the difficult question of when life begins. When those trained in the respective disciplines of Medicine, philosophy and theology are unable to arrive at any consensus, the judiciary, at this point in the development of man's knowledge, is not in a position to speculate as to the answers."

Inside THE PRESS

The Pentagon is eager to invade your bedroom. At least it wants to install a warning radio in every home to alert residents to tornadoes, nuclear attacks and floods. It would be voluntary for now. See Page 4A.

The second of Adam Smith's "Super Money" series also appears today on Page 4A.

January 22, 1973: News of the imminent end of American military involvement in Vietnam captured headlines. *Microfilm archives*

weather
Cloudy.
High in 30s.
Details, Page 2A

The Sun-Bulletin

Binghamton, N.Y. 13902 — A Member of the Gannett Group — 151st year, No. 78

wednesday
Jan. 24, 1973
12 cents a copy

Peace

WASHINGTON (UPI) — President Nixon last night announced agreement on a Vietnam cease-fire to begin at 7 p.m. Saturday, and the return of all U.S. troops and prisoners of war from Vietnam within 60 days.

Mr. Nixon announced the end of America's tormenting, 12-year involvement in the war in a nationwide radio and television address from the White House after special negotiator Henry A. Kissinger concluded the agreement with North Vietnamese representatives in Paris earlier in the day.

Dr. Kissinger will make public details of the accord, achieved after four full years of formal and secret negotiations, today. Secretary of State William P. Rogers will sign the agreement Saturday in Paris, along with foreign ministers of North and South Vietnam and the Viet Cong.

The President told the nation that the agreement would "end the war and bring peace with honor in Vietnam and in Southeast Asia."

He said that the accord had the "full support" of South Vietnam President Nguyen Van Thieu and his government, and that it met all the conditions for a peace settlement that Mr. Nixon laid down last May 8, including provision for South Vietnam to determine its own future.

Simultaneous announcements of the cease-fire were made by Thieu in Saigon and by the North Vietnamese foreign ministry in Hanoi.

THE SUN-BULLETIN—UPI

President Nixon: 'Peace with honor'

what's inside

1. The longest war—its effect. Page 2A.
2. War ends for U.S. Saturday. Page 3A.
3. Jack Germond's analysis. Page 4A.
4. The toll in Broome County. Page 5A.
5. Hope for missing in action. Page 6A.
6. Reaction—relief for all. Page 6A.

January 24, 1973: President Nixon called the end of hostilities "Peace with honor." *Courtesy Carolyn Fitzgerald*

The Kopernik Observatory is one of the major scientific and cultural institutions in Greater Binghamton. It was a lifelong dream of Dr. Edward Kozlowski, who helped find the resources to build the observatory in Vestal.
Courtesy Jay Sarton

KOPERNIK
OBSERVATORY
1973

Dr. Edward Kozlowski, Astronaut James Lovell, contractor Edward L. Nezelek, architect James Kilcy and Richard H. Miller, a teacher and eventually Town of Union supervisor and state assemblyman, dedicate the observatory.
Courtesy Valentina Kozlowski

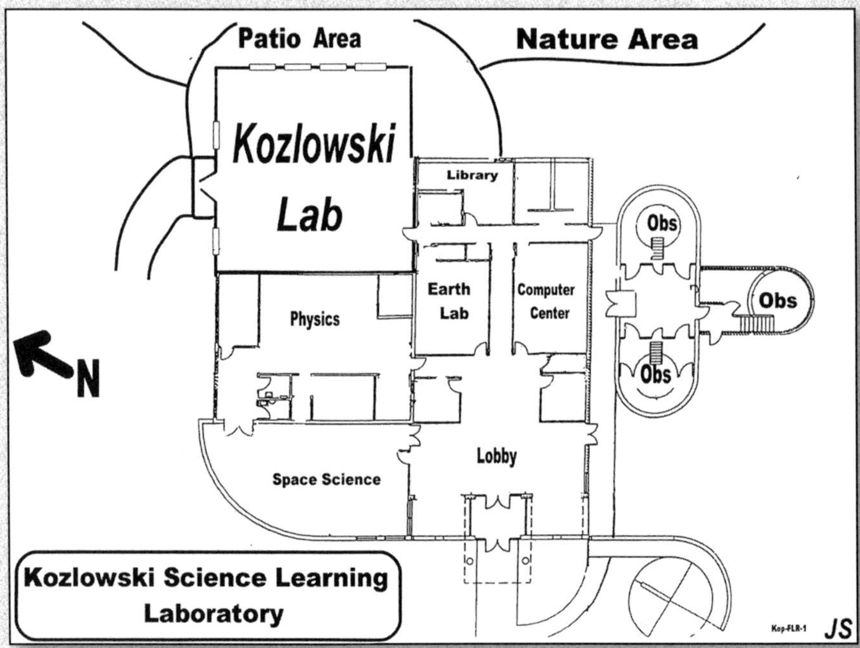
Patio Area
Nature Area
Kozlowski Lab
Library
Obs
Obs
Obs
Earth Lab
Computer Center
Physics
N
Lobby
Space Science
Kozlowski Science Learning Laboratory
JS

The observatory uses its instruments to educate students and the general public, who flock to the site from around the world.
Courtesy Jay Sarton

cloudy
High in 50s
Details, Page 2

The Sun-Bulletin

Binghamton, N.Y. 13902 — A Member of the Gannett Group — 151st year, No. 161

tuesday
May 1, 1973
12 cents a copy

Nixon on Watergate: 'I take responsibility'

WASHINGTON (UPI) — President Nixon told the nation last night that he must accept the responsibility for the attempt to bug the Democratic National Headquarters at the Watergate complex.

In a nationally televised address after he fired White House counsel John W. Dean III and accepted the resignations of two top aides and of Attorney General Richard G. Kleindienst, Mr. Nixon declared that those who perpetrated the crime — and those who sought to cover it up — must be punished.

But as for the responsibility for permitting the situation to come about, that, he declared is his alone and said, "I accept it."

He said it would be easy to blame the subordinates to whom he had assigned the responsibility for running his re-election campaign. But that would be the "cowardly" thing to do, the President said.

"I will not place the blame on subordinates," he said, on people whose zeal exceeded their judgment and "those who did wrong in the name of a cause they deeply believed to be right."

"The responsibility belongs here, in this office," the President said. "I accept it.

"I want the American people, I want you to know beyond a shadow of a doubt that during my term of office, justice will be preserved, fairly, fully and impartially."

The President said the case raised two questions — how could it have happened, and who was to blame?

Mr. Nixon acknowledged that he had always run his own campaigns. But in 1972, he said, "crucial decisions" on foreign and domestic matters were the overriding interest.

He said that he decided that during the campaign "the presidency should come first" and delegated campaign responsibilities to aides.

Tracing the history of the Watergate affair, the President said he first learned of it on June 17 — the day of the break-in. He was in Florida, resting from his summit meeting in Moscow.

"I was appalled," Mr. Nixon said, "at this senseless, illegal act."

He said he was "shocked" that employes of the Committee to Re-elect the President had been "among those guilty" of the break-in and attempted bugging.

He said he immediately ordered an investigation. That probe was conducted by Mr. Dean, although the President did not say so specifically in his broadcast.

Mr. Nixon said he "repeatedly" asked if any member of his administration was involved and was "repeatedly" assured none was.

"I believed the reports I was getting. I discounted the stories in the press that tended to implicate members of my administration," he said.

"Until March of this year I remained convinced that the denials were true," he said, and that the charges of involvement and of a cover-up by high officials were false.

When it appeared that the denials were false, Mr. Nixon said, he conducted his own investigation, which culminated yesterday in the resignations of Mr. Kleindienst, White House chief of staff H.R. Haldeman and adviser John Ehrlichman and the firing of Mr. Dean.

To replace Mr. Kleindienst as attorney general, Mr. Nixon appointed Defense Secretary Elliot L. Richardson.

Mr. Nixon said last night that he had invested full authority for the continuing official investigation in Mr. Richardson, who he said would be "fair and fearless."

He said there would be "no whitewash at the White House."

Although he insisted that the officials whose resignations he has accepted had been convicted of no crime, he left little doubt that they were under serious scrutiny.

He said, however, that Mr. Kleindienst had "no involvement in this affair whatsoever."

But he said the resignations were accepted out of a desire to have "rigorous legal and ethical standards" at the White House, and he said he was confident these standards would be "observed and enforced."

Accepting the resignations, the President said, was "one of the most difficult decisions I have had in the White House."

"I wanted to be fair. But I knew that in the final analysis that faith in this office, and faith in the personal integrity of this office, should take precedence."

He said the resignations were "necessary to restore confidence" in the White House.

Mr. Nixon said the Watergate affair already had "claimed far too much of my time and attention." Whatever its outcome, he said, "I must now turn my full attention, and I will do so once again, to the larger duties of my office."

Mr. Nixon's statement announcing that he had fired Mr. Dean and accepted the resignations of the three others was read to reporters by press secretary Ronald L. Ziegler early yesterday at the White House, while Mr. Nixon remained in seclusion at his Camp David retreat in the Maryland mountains, apparently preparing last night's address.

The President returned to Washington at 7:55 p.m.

In the morning statement, Mr. Nixon expressed "regret and deep appreciation" in accepting Mr. Kleindienst's resignation.

The President said Mr. Kleindienst felt he could not continue to head the Justice Department "now that it appears its investigation of the Watergate and related cases may implicate individuals with whom he has a close personal and professional association."

Among those believed to be targets of the grand jury investigation are Mr. Dean, Mr. Ehrlichman, Mr. Haldeman and Mr. Kleindienst's former boss — former attorney general John N. Mitchell, who was the President's campaign manager at the time of the burglary.

Mr. Haldeman and Mr. Ehrlichman remained in their White House offices, and there was no indication when their resignations would take effect. White House officials said they would remain for a "transition period."

Some seven hours after yesterday morning's announcement, the United States Information Agency announced the resignation of Gordon Strachan as its general counsel. He had joined the USIA last December after leaving the White House, where he had been Mr. Haldeman's liaison with the Nixon campaign committee.

Mr. Strachan testified before the Watergate grand jury last week, reportedly about money kept in a White House safe under Mr. Haldeman's jurisdiction.

what's inside

THE SUN-BULLETIN — UPI

President tells newsmen last night: 'I hope I'm worthy of your trust.'

May 1, 1973: President Nixon took responsibility for Watergate, but in a way that said he should have paid more attention to his subordinates.

Courtesy Dolly Escovar

mild
High in 60s
Details, Page 2.

The Sun-Bulletin

friday
April 5, 1974
15 cents a copy

Binghamton, N.Y. 13902 A Member of the Gannett Group 152nd year, No. 149

$221 million boost urged in state's aid for schools

By PETER J. WALSH
Gannett News Service

ALBANY — A $221 million boost in school aid and a major simplification of the aid formulas were recommended to the Legislature by a special task force yesterday.

More than half the increase — an estimated $120 million — would be funneled into the Big Five cities of Yonkers, Buffalo, Rochester, Syracuse and New York City by granting them so-called BOCES aid for the first time.

BOCES aid, through Boards of Cooperative Educational Services, are now denied the five big cities.

Although detailed figures for local school districts will not be published until Sunday, the task force recommendations ran into immediate criticism from Long Island and Westchester legislators whose school enrollments are declining.

They said they believed the formula treats their districts unfairly and said they would like an aid boost of up to $260 million.

(Broome County superintendents of schools have voiced similar fears.)

The new formula, if adopted, will do the following:

• Boost the ceiling — the amount of spending per pupil the state will share with the local district — from the present $860 to $1,200.

• Replace the complicated method of distributing state aid with a system giving districts the difference between $15 for every $1,000 true property value for each child and $1,200. For example, a district with $10,000 true property value for each student would get $1,200 minus 10 times $15 — or $150 — totaling $950 in aid for each student.

• Pay school districts twice as much for the education of handicapped students as for "normal" pupils, thereby providing a financial incentive to the districts to educate the handicapped in local schools.

• Pay districts 25 per cent more for the education of socially or culturally disadvantaged students.

• Provide aid for summer school and evening students, a recommendation of the Board of Regents that could be the first step toward year-round schools.

• Provide a minimum increase of eight per cent per pupil over this year's spending levels to every district, regardless of wealth. Since it would be calculated on the number of students, some wealthy districts with declining enrollments could acutally lose money.

• Limit the maximum aid increase to a district to 16 per cent of this year's levels, except where a district's enrollment increased.

The local impact

In Binghamton the true value per child is $37,038. Under the new formula the district would get $644.43 per student in 1974-75. The district is now getting $585 per student in state aid. However, adjustments in the weighting of handicapped or disadvantaged students could whittle away this seeming bonus.

Maine-Endwell, by contrast, has a true value per child of $26,226. This would mean $816.61 per student aid next year compared to $957 now. The guarantee of an increase of 8 per cent per student in state aid will not help Maine-Endwell if enrollment falls too far.

Nixon may float a loan to pay taxes

By JULES WITCOVER
Washington Post Service

WASHINGTON — President Nixon's payment of about $465,000 in back taxes and interest probably will wipe out his cash holdings and require him to borrow money or sell some of his property.

According to documents released by the White House last Dec. 8 covering President and Mrs. Nixon's personal finances, they had cash holdings of $432,874 as of May 31, 1973, including $250,000 in certificates of deposit.

According to an audit through last May 31 by Coopers & Lybrand, a New York accounting firm, the cash holdings constituted nearly half the net worth of the First Family — $988,522. Investments in land, buildings and furnishings made up most of the rest, the audit said.

The Nixons' home at San Clemente is the largest item in their holdings. Mr. Nixon bought the 28.9-acre estate for $1.5 million in 1969, with a $625,000 loan from his old friend, Robert H. Ablanalp, to pay the down payment and the first principal and interest payment on the mortgage.

A year later, the President sold 23 acres of the estate to Mr. Ablanalp and his other close friend, C. G. (Bebe) Rebozo, for $1,249,000, leaving Mr. Nixon with 5.9 acres and the 14-room house. Thus the net purchase price was $251,000. Mr. Nixon has reported he spent $68,000 of his own money on improvements.

In December 1968, shortly after his election as president, Mr. Nixon bought two homes in Key Biscayne, Fla., adjacent to one owned by Rebozo, for $252,800.

On Jan. 1, 1969, the audit by Coopers & Lybrand said, the Nixons' assets totaled $307,141. Thus, in the 4½ White House years covered by the audit, their net worth more than tripled.

Also as of last May, Mr. Nixon's total cash income in his White House years was $2.9 million, against which he had expenses of $2.5 million. Of this, $800,000 was in salary, at $200,000 a year, and $200,000 in expenses, at $50,000 a year.

Most of the rest of his income, according to the audit, came from the sale of real estate, including sale of stock in Fisher's Island in Biscayne Bay just south of Miami Beach, another Rebozo enterprise, sale of his New York apartment and of two Florida lots.

THE SUN-BULLETIN—UPI

Aaron hits No. 714

Hank Aaron of the Atlanta Braves ties Babe Ruth's home run record with his 714th career home run yesterday at Cincinnati. He may hit the record breaker tomorrow against the Reds. See stories about Aaron and baseball's historic moment on Pages 43 and 13.

April 5, 1974: Hank Aaron's record-tying home run made the front page. *Courtesy David Silvanic*

showers
High in 70s
Details, Page 12.

The Sun-Bulletin

friday
August 9, 1974
15 cents a copy

Binghamton, N.Y. 13902 A Member of the Gannett Group 152nd year, No. 257

Nixon resigns

Ford to be sworn in at noon

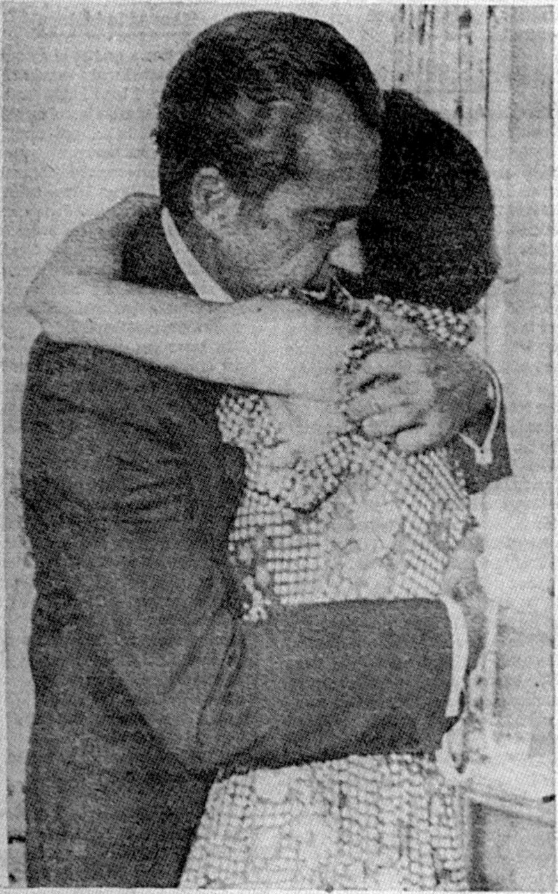

President Nixon and his daughter Julie hug at the White House shortly before he announced he would resign the Presidency.

THE SUN-BULLETIN—UPI

Gerald R. Ford greets well-wishers at his Alexandria, Va., home.

'I have never been a quitter. To leave office before my term is completed is abhorrent to every instinct in my body. But as President I must put the interest of America first.'

Richard M. Nixon
August 8, 1974

August 9, 1974: The Watergate drama draws near to a close. *Courtesy Dolly Escovar*

Susquehanna

Keep On truckin'

Magazine

parade

SUNDAY

the press & sun-bulletin

a gannett newspaper binghamton, n.y. june 29, 1975 volume 26-43 8 sections 50 cents metro

Good morning

Cloudy

Details on 2A.

Sweet revenge
The Yankees have their revenge on the Boston Red Sox and New York is back in first place in the American League East. 1B.

Tennis upset
There'll be no Jimmy Connors-Ken Rosewall showdown as set up by the seedings at Wimbledon. No. 2 Rosewall bowed out yesterday, an upset victim of fellow-Australian Tony Roche. 1B.

Refugees arrive
Binghamton's first Vietnamese refugees — two young dentists from Saigon — arrived at their new home on Oak Street yesterday. The couple, married earlier this year, are the first of what may be several dozen Vietnamese families coming to Broome County. 3A.

Pele at White House
President Ford gets a kick out of a soccer lesson with superstar Pele. 5A.

McHugh frustrated
Rep. Matthew F. McHugh is among Washington's frustrated freshman Democrats. Mike Doll explains on 1D.

Trapped in school
Those who compare high school with prison are not far off the mark, David Rossie argues on 3D.

Touch of pharaohs
At SUNY Binghamton they're making bronzes the way the Egyptians did. 17C.

Workers, unite!
Workers of the world were once told to unite. Now it's businessmen of the Southern Tier who are organizing. There's a new group nearly every week. 16B.

Let's chuckle
One of the best ways to surprise your husband on your anniversary is to mention it.

What's inside

Panel: Change foreign policy roles

WASHINGTON (UPI) — A government commission told President Ford yesterday that after Henry A. Kissinger steps down no future secretaries of state should be permitted to serve simultaneously as presidential assistant for national security affairs.

Kissinger was specifically exempted from this recommendation in a 278-page report by a presidential-congressional commission, which cited his "extraordinary abilities."

The recommendations, including ways to improve the government's foreign policy machinery, ease frictions with Congress and draw executive departments more directly into the decision-making process, drew severe criticism from Senate Democratic leader Mike Mansfield.

"Even a cursory reading of the commission's report is likely to impress the reader with its timidity and its paucity of substance," Mansfield, a commission member, said in a statement included in the body of the report.

"On the whole ... I fear that the ratio of effort to result has not been up to expectations. A surfeit of words masks an absence of clarity. Thin gruel is being served in a very thick bowl."

But chairman Robert D. Murphy dismissed Mansfield's criticism at a news conference by noting the senator had attended none of the commission meetings since the beginning of the year.

The commission, which included Vice President Nelson A. Rockefeller, was created by Congress in 1973 and spent what sources estimated was $2 million. The report was given to Ford to implement.

It cited two reasons why one man should no longer hold the dual posts

"The first is simply that the responsibilities of that assistant are heavy and important enough to require the undivided attention of even the ablest public servant," it said.

"The second is that an assistant to the president must be a facilitator of decision, a conduit for the president, a force for balance and evenhandedness in the presentation and consideration of issues."

White House aides reportedly are trying to strip Kissinger of his dual jobs. But Kissinger, who retained his original White House post when he became secretary of state in early 1973, has made it clear he wants to keep both titles.

The report at a glance

WASHINGTON (AP) — Here at a glance are the main recommendations of the Murphy Commission on organization of the government for the conduct of foreign policy.

- Future secretaries of state should not double as the president's national security adviser.
- Appointment of a senior assistant to the president for economic policy who would participate in both National Security Council deliberations and domestic policy making.
- Establishment of an International Economic Policy Advisory Board composed of private citizens.
- Creation of an independent study group on international economic issues under the auspices of the Council of Economic Advisers.

STAFF PHOTO BY DON BLACK

Convoy collision

New Jerseyite Peter Dorsa is in stable condition at Binghamton General Hospital after being hit yesterday by a truck. Dorsa was standing on a Route 81 North shoulder in front of his National Guard truck when it was struck from the rear by another guard truck.

Serling loses fight for life

Serling's career a succession of triumphs, 3A.

Rod Serling died yesterday afternoon at Strong Memorial Hospital in Rochester following complications during open heart surgery Thursday.

The 50-year-old television writer and creator of "The Twilight Zone" was pronounced dead at 2:15 p.m.

His wife, Carolyn, his daughters, Mrs. Steven Croyle of Ithaca and Ann, and his brother, Robert J. Serling of Potomac, Md., were with him.

A team of surgeons tried unsuccessfully yesterday morning to take Mr. Serling off a heart-lung machine that he had been on since Thursday evening following more than 10 hours of open heart surgery.

He had entered the operating room at 8:45 a.m. Thursday for two coronary by-pass operations in which two veins from the thigh were grafted onto the coronary arteries to allow alternative routes for blood flowing to the heart.

After sewing up the wound and taking Mr. Serling off the life-supporting machine, he suffered a heart attack. Surgeons reopened the wound and applied direct heart massage, putting him back on the machine and performing a third by-pass procedure.

Mr. Serling came out of the operating room about 7 p.m. Thursday in guarded condition, supported by drugs and the machine.
pital and particularly for the dedication and skill of his physicians."

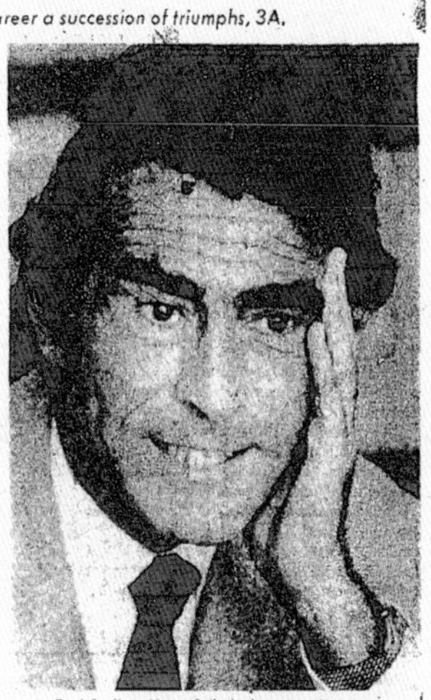

Rod Serling: Heart failed after complications.

The family, who will have a private funeral service, prefers contributions be made in Mr. Serling's memory to the American Heart Association. Arrangements were incomplete last night.

Mr. Serling was transferred from Tompkins County Hospital in Ithaca to Strong June 13 after suffering a mild heart attack in early May. He was a visiting professor of writing at Ithaca College.

Salesman held for Nazi crimes

BUENOS AIRES (AP) — Authorities are holding a man believed to be Walter Kutschmann, a former Nazi Gestapo officer accused of executing 38 Polish Jews in 1941, government sources said yesterday.

Information supplied to Argentine police by the Jewish Documentation Center in Vienna said Kutschmann and his men also were responsible for the deaths of between 1,500 and 2,000 other Jews in 1942.

The man held, who is 61, has been living in Argentina since 1947 under the name of Pedro Ricardo Olmo and is now sales manager for Osram, an Argentine manufacturer of lamps and appliances.

He was arrested after police received a report from Simon Wiesenthal, a Nazi hunter who runs the Jewish Documentation Center, the sources said.

Wiesenthal said in Vienna after the arrest that he was gratified by the prompt action of Argentine police and hoped West Germany would now request the man's extradition.

"He cannot be tried in Argentina for crimes he committed as a member of the Nazi SS against Polish Jews," Wiesenthal said, "but he can be tried in West Germany."

He said West Germany had issued a warrant for Kutschmann's arrest several years ago and he said the warrant was still valid.

The Osram factory in Argentina is a subsidiary of West Germany's Osram firm and a company official in Munich said Olmo had been suspended as sales manager until the allegations against him can be checked out. The official said Osram executives in Buenos Aires contacted Olmo by telephone yesterday and he acknowledged that he had changed his name from Kutschmann when he came to Argentina, but denied that he had been a Gestapo officer in Poland.

The official also said Olmo denied at that time that he was in police custody but attempts to reach him later by telephone failed.

A spokesman at the West German Embassy in Buenos Aires said the embassy had no file on Olmo and he knew of no immediate plans for an extradition request.

One of several highly placed sources in Buenos Aires said Wiesenthal's information "has been passed to very high levels, and there is no information we can give. But we can confirm that Olmo has been detained."

Federal police said they had no information on the case, and there was no public record of charges.

Dr. Walter Kutschmann
...or Pedro Ricardo Olmo?

June 29, 1975: Rod Serling was raised in Binghamton and references to time here frequently showed up in his work. *Microfilm archives*

Cloudy

Fair tonight, low near 50. Cloudy and breezy Tuesday, high in the mid to upper 60s. Chance of rain 10 per cent tonight, 20 per cent Tuesday. Details Page 11B.

THE EVENING PRESS

A Gannett Newspaper

METRO 25

Binghamton, N.Y., Monday, Sept. 29, 1975 Volume 99—123 2 Sections 32 Pages 25 Cents

Let's Chuckle

Some of us couldn't do with a three-day workweek. It takes us that long to get started.

City Fire Chief, Captain Drown Searching for Missing Fireman

★ ★ ★

An Editorial

THE TRAGIC STRING of events that claimed the lives of Binghamton Fire Chief John F. Cox, Captain Donald W. McGeever and Fireman John C. Russell are almost too shocking to comprehend.

Words alone can be of little comfort to the many loved ones and friends of the dead firemen. The community, however, realizes that the men died heroically, upholding the honor of their uniforms.

Russell, 26, of Deposit, is presumed dead after a valiant effort to rescue two men whose raft flipped going over the Rockbottom Dam in the raging Susquehanna River.

Chief Cox, 57, of 23 Mozart Street, and Capt. Donald W. McGeever, 53, of 25 Schubert Street, were in a boat with a third fireman this morning, searching for Russell's body. They were drowned when that boat was overturned and their companion, Lt. Robert Dale, was in serious condition at General Hospital.

The story of the efforts of dozens of police and firemen who strained to save the men in the river, shouted over police radios by frantic men, was heartbreaking. The power of the swollen river was simply too much for them.

The drama brings home to the community, once again and in a cruel manner, the dedication of the uniformed forces to their jobs.

The community cannot blink the fact the deaths of the three firemen were unnecessary. Would that two young men had not decided to test the power of the Susquehanna in flood.

It was their rescue that set the grisly train of events in motion. A swift and swollen Susquehanna cannot be toyed with by strong men in a boat, much less adventurers on a raft.

—PRESS PHOTO BY PAUL F. KONECNY

DESPERATE REACH — A hand of one of three firemen who plunged into the Susquehanna River below the Rockbottom Dam ... an attempt to grab an overturned boat. Later rescue attempts were too late for Fire Chief John F. Cox and Capt. Donald W. McGeever.

Rescue Boat Flips at Dam; One Saved

By SUSAN SCHWARTZ

Two Binghamton fire bureau officials — the fire chief and a captain — drowned today in the flood-swollen Susquehanna River at Rockbottom Dam as they tried to recover the body of another fireman who drowned there yesterday.

Fire Chief John F. Cox, 57, of 23 Mozart St., Binghamton, and Capt. Donald W. McGeever, 52, of 25 Schubert St., Binghamton, were pronounced dead at Binghamton General Hospital shortly before 11 a.m. today after they were pulled from the river by firemen and police.

10 Storm Deaths . . . 10A

Fire Lt. Robert Dale, 31, of 34 Elm St., Binghamton, was thrown into the river along with Cox and McGeever when their rescue boat capsized near the dam. He was rescued, and was reported in serious condition in the hospital's Special Care Unit today.

The rush of water over the Rockbottom Dam creates a backflow condition at the dam's base counter to the flow of the river. The backflow sucks anything floating toward the dam and traps it there.

The force of the backflow than normal because of the near-flood condition of the river as a result of tropical storm Eloise.

It was this same condition at the base of the dam that last night presumably cost Fireman John C. Russell his life while he participated in the rescue of two young men who had ridden over the dam on a raft.

JOHN F. COX

Cox, McGeever and Dale drove their boat into the maelstrom at the foot of the dam today in an effort to search for Russell when the 18-foot aluminum craft was seized by the tow, sucked into the spillover and capsized about 9:30 a.m.

After attempts to rescue them with a 100-foot fire truck ladder failed, a sheriff's department rescue boat was dispatched from shore carrying Sgt. Beverly Tripp and Special Deputy Donald Stark of the Broome County Sheriff's Dept.

DONALD W. McGEEVER

Firemen manning a second fire bureau rescue boat and cooperating with Cox, McGeever and Dale in the rescue attempt, put in toward the dam to try to rescue their comrades. They tossed ring buoys with lines attached, but the men struggling in the water could not reach them.

About a half hour later the second fire bureau boat was joined by a rescue craft oper-

(Continued on Page 3A)

2 Lose Challenge to River That Always Wins

By TOM CAWLEY

The last time I saw John Cox was at 2 o'clock this morning. He was standing on the south bank of the Susquehanna River talking into one of those little portable radio transmitters. He wanted to find the body of a 31-year-old fireman who had drowned in the angry stream trying to rescue two persons who had decided to go rafting on an exciting day.

This afternoon not only Cox, who was chief of the Binghamton Fire Bureau, is dead, but one of his most trusted aides, Capt. Donald W. McGeever, is dead, too. They were in a boat trying to find John Russell's body. John Russell was a Fire Bureau private-in-the-ranks everybody liked.

Somewhere around 9:30 this morning, Cox and McGeever made their move in an outboard-powered boat toward the Rockbottom Dam, where Russell had died. Russell's life jacket, a brilliant orange flag, still was bobbing in the wild currents of a flood-swollen river.

The Cox and McGeever boat overturned. They died in the Susquehanna River. A third man in the boat, Fire Lt. Robert Dale, survived. He was in serious condition in Binghamton General Hospital today.

At 10:50 a.m., their friend, Ass't Police Chief Philip J. Vanderbeck, looking at the river (now placid, flowing politely) said to a reporter:

"Both Chief John Cox and Capt. Don McGeever are deceased."

Vanderbeck is the type of policeman who uses language like that. He wouldn't think of saying, "John and Don are dead." He said, formally, dressed in a gray suit, white shirt and wearing a blue tie, and accompanied by Police Lt. Joseph Lynch, "Both Chief John Cox and Capt. Don McGeever are deceased."

What he was saying is that the Susquehanna River, which started taking lives uncountable centuries ago, still is taking lives. It all started at 6:30 last night when Anthony Tokos, an employe of Crowley's Foods saw two young men launch a rubber raft from the north shore of the river.

He was looking out a window of the Crowley plant.

"The minute I saw," Tokos said, "I knew there was trouble. By the time I had dialed the operator and somebody answered, I don't know who, whether it was the police or the firemen, they were over the dam."

> *"Both Chief John Cox and Capt. Don McGeever are deceased."--Asst. Police Chief Philip J. Vanderbeck.*

By that time, the sun on a late September afternoon was setting, and the clouds were moving in the west, drizzling rain. The firemen arrived and put out their own boat. In the rescue boat were Russell, the father of three children, and two other firemen.

They were on the edge of making a successful rescue when their boat capsized. Two of the firemen made it to shore. So did the two men who were being rescued. Russell died.

At 3 o'clock this morning, somebody said to Fire Capt. Walter O'Neill, who was standing on the riverbank and looking at Russell's life jacket dancing a macabre dance in the dam's undertow, "Why don't you go home and get some sleep?"

He said, "I think I'll hang around for a while. He is a brother and we've got to find him."

Chief Cox and Capt. McGeever were standing there, too, wondering how soon daylight could come and they could get out in a boat and find young Russell.

As soon as the daylight came, and as soon as the police could keep the morbid spectators away, Cox and McGeever, following a tradition that was established the day the first volunteer Fire Department was organized in the tiny village of Binghamton, shoved out in their own boat. It was a losing challenge to a river that always wins.

Cox leaves a wife and three children. McGeever leaves a wife and six children.

★ ★ ★

Body Reported Found

Broome County sheriff's deputies this afternoon reported finding a body in the Chenango River about one mile downstream from the site of a plane crash yesterday afternoon in which a 4-year-old girl was reported missing.

Deputies said the body, found snagged in brush along the riverbank, was identified as that of 4-year-old Amy Mitchell, of 30 Stuyvesant St., Binghamton, who was riding with her parents in their light plane when it crashed near Chenango Bridge. (Early story, Page 3A).

Tucson OKs Pay Raise

TUCSON, Ariz. (AP) — Nearly 800 police officers and fire fighters have ended a six-day strike, reporting back to work with a pay raise. But Mayor Lewis Murphy called the settlement "Tucson's darkest hour" and said it was achieved by the use of scare tactics.

After a four-hour debate behind closed doors Sunday night, the city council approved on a 4-3 vote the contract ratified by the Police-Firemen's Association.

Under the new contract, an immediate raise of 7.5 per cent was granted police officers ranked sergeant or higher, fire fighters ranked captain or higher and civilian municipal workers in administrative posts.

Other employes received a 5 per cent increase.

Inside THE PRESS

The death penalty and Justice Douglas are major questions as Supreme Court returns. Page 11A.

There are some rule changes for credit cards in the works. Page 13A.

NOT FAR ENOUGH — A ladder of a Binghamton firetruck was extended in an attempt to retrieve the firemen from the waters. The futile attempt was followed by the entry of a Broome County Sheriff's Department boat, that soon overturned.

September 29, 1975: The Press records one of the great tragedies to befall the Binghamton Fire Bureau. *Press & Sun-Bulletin archives*

Colder

Mostly cloudy tonight with a chance of frost. Low tonight in the low to mid 30s. Mostly sunny Friday, high near 50. Chance of rain 20 per cent tonight, 10 per cent Friday. Details Page 15B.

THE EVENING PRESS

A Gannett Newspaper

METRO

Binghamton, N.Y., Thursday, Oct. 2, 1975 Volume 99—126 2 Sections 42 Pages 20 Cents

Let's Chuckle

One woman to another: "George's idea of Women's Lib is for me to get a job."

— PRESS PHOTO BY JOHN ROLAS

FOR THE FIREMEN — Members of a grieving community filled St. Thomas Aquinas Church in Binghamton today at services for Fire Chief John F. Cox, Capt. Donald W. McGeever and Fireman John C. Russell. Mrs. Cox is in front pew, second from left, and Mrs. McGeever is in the front pew at center next to the fireman.

1,000 Bow at Rites for 3 Firemen

— PRESS PHOTO BY PAUL F. KONECNY

CARRYING A COMRADE — White-gloved pallbearers from the Binghamton Fire Bureau carry Donald McGeever's casket into church.

By LOU GANIM

The City of Binghamton — its residents, firemen, policemen, political officials and friends — said farewell today to three men who died in the line of duty.

The funeral was held today for three of the city's firemen, whose lives were taken early this week by the raging, flood-swollen waters of the Susquehanna River.

The names of the three men — one the chief, one an officer and the third a new member of the force — became fa-

Cawley Column . . . 1B

miliar to almost all residents of Broome County this week.

The tragedy brought more than 1,000 persons to pay their respects at today's services held at St. Thomas Aquinas Church on the city's West Side.

Among that number were more than 200 firemen from across the state and neighboring states.

Besides representatives of all the fire companies in Broome County, there were firemen from Utica, Rochester, Cortland, Norwich, Canandaigua, Auburn, New York City, Hornell, Montrose, Pa., and Boston, Mass.

Those men came to Binghamton today to share in the common grief of a community.

They came to pray for Binghamton Fire Chief John F. Cox, Capt. Donald W. McGeever and Fireman John C. Russell.

Only the bodies of Cox and McGeever, who drowned Monday in the waters near Rockbottom Dam, were at today's service. The body of Russell, who was lost in the river Sunday night and for whom Cox and McGeever were searching, has not been found.

As the service began, Acting Fire Chief Thomas Joseph, Mayor Alfred J. Libous, Assemblymen James R. Tallon Jr. and members of City Council were among those who formed an honor guard inside the Roman Catholic church's entranceway as the families of the three fallen firemen were escorted toward the altar.

Following Mrs. Cox, Mrs. McGeever and Mrs. Russell was a procession of relatives and close friends. Then came the line of visiting firemen and policemen who had come to honor their dead comrades.

Speaking from the altar, the acting fire chief read from the Book of Wisdom.

Joseph said, ". . . and after a time he became perfect, and his soul was pleasing to God. Therefore He sped him from the midst of wickedness. The people saw, yet they did not take this into account and they did not understand."

The funeral Mass was sung by the Rev. John J. Mulranen, pastor of St. Thomas Aquinas Church.

Father Mulranen, who delivered the eulogy, said, "The tragedy is but an indication of the courage of these three men. The message of their deaths will be lost if we fail this morning to accept the challenge of their total lives to sacrifice in our homes."

(Continued on Page 3A)

Inside THE PRESS

Oakdale Mall Found Nice . . . and Big

By STEVE LOHR

The huge crowd that showed up for last night's opening of the Oakdale Mall seemed to agree — they were impressed by the new 610,000-square-foot enclosed shopping center and they'd rather shop at the mall than anywhere else in the area.

These were the opinions of nearly all of the 20 people questioned last night, selected randomly from the thousands whose cars almost filled the mall's parking areas. They came more to look than spend, but most said they'd buy if something caught their eye.

"It's nice. We didn't come here for the premiere so this is the first time and it's much bigger than I thought," said William R. Mihalko, 30, of 19 Pamela Drive, Johnson City, who came with his wife and three children. (On Aug. 17, Interstate Properties Inc., the developers, held an open house, which about 30,000 browsers attended.)

"I absolutely prefer this to the downtowns. It's so much more convenient. You park in one spot and do it all. That's my idea of shopping," said Mihalko.

Tracey Williams, too, said she'd rather go to the big, new mall than the area downtowns. Though she had been to a shoe store, card shop and department store ("and they were nice"), the 11-year-old, who lives at 15 Bel Air Drive, Binghamton, was more impressed by the trees. In fact, Miss Williams, her sister and parents were standing near one of the mall's 13 indoor fig trees, which don't bear fruit.

The mall's developers and shop owners are banking on reviews like those received last night to spur a projected $70 million in total sales during the first year and justify the $250,000 weekly payroll for the 1,800 to 2,300 retail workers expected to be employed there. Eighteen stores opened last night.

A few of those asked said they would attract distant shoppers as well as local buyers. "Yes, I definitely think it should bring in outsiders. We've been going to Corning and look how far that is," said Eleanore S. Salisbury, 3 Home Ave., Binghamton.

Her husband, James D. Salisbury, said that might

(Continued on Page 18A)

October 2, 1975: News of the Oakdale Mall's opening, which would have profound effects on Binghamton retailers, properly took second place to the firefighters' funerals. *Press & Sun-Bulletin archives*

200 YEARS OF FREEDOM
1776 ~ 1976

SUNDAY
the press & sun-bulletin
BICENTENNIAL EDITION

a gannett newspaper binghamton, n.y. july 4, 1976 volume 28-44 14 sections 50 cents metro

Israeli blitz frees 104

TEL AVIV (UPI) — Israeli commandos staged a lighting airborne raid on the Entebbe, Uganda, airfield last night and freed 104 hostages held by pro-Palestinian hijackers, the Israeli army said.

Israeli sources in Paris said the Israeli jets landed safely in Nairobi, Kenya, after the raid and that surgical units rushed to the airport, indicating possible wounded.

Employes at the airport in Nairobi told reporters they had seen a few soldiers being treated but they did not appear to be badly wounded.

An Air France spokesman in Nairobi said the commando unit "apparently has eliminated" the hijackers. Air France officials in Paris said the planes took off from Nairobi soon after landing and headed back to Tel Aviv, where they were expected to arrive about 1 a.m. today.

"Israeli forces extricated and freed the hostages and Air France crew from the airport at Entebbe," an Israeli army statement said.

Asked whether all 61 Israelis and 43 French nationals held hostage had been freed, an army spokesman said: "We're being very precise about the announcement and we have nothing further to say at this time."

He said more information will be released later in the morning. There was no official word on the fate of the hijackers, or whether any of the commandos or hostages has been wounded in the rescue.

In Nairobi, France's ambassador to Kenya, Olivier Beleau, said the Israelis carried out the operation on their own and France had not been asked to participate.

"We did not know anything about it, the Israelis did everything themselves. We still are not sure how many of the hostages have been freed and we have no word whether the crew are free," he said.

See ISRAELI, Page 10A

Stunned
Village mourns loss of 6 girls in crash

By WES ALBERS
Staff Writer

DERUYTER — DeRuyter, population 650, will go through the motions today — church services, family reunions, homemade ice cream, country drives.

But it will be a celebration without heart.

July 4, 1976, was defused for this town by the deaths Friday night of six girls — all related — in a spectacular one-car accident near here.

The Eric Fostveit, Clair Dorward Sr., and Clair Dorward Jr. families gathered yesterday to plan Tuesday's joint funerals at 2 p.m. from the Wells R. Smith Funeral Home in DeRuyter.

The townspeople stopped to shake heads, trade rumors and reflect.

"Good morning" was replaced by "Isn't it terrible about the accident?"

"We heard the ambulance," said postal clerk Jean Hills. "Of course, we didn't know what it was at the time. It goes by lots of times and you don't think anything about it. Then my son came home and said, 'Mom, there's been a bad accident. I think it was the Dorwards.'"

The Fourth of July was meant for towns like DeRuyter, 30 miles north of Binghamton.

Clinging to Route 13 on the Cortland County line, the town is real Americana, complete with tree-lined main street, white frame houses trimmed with flags, a corner gas station and a country-type store.

"We're a small, very close-knit community," said Mayor John O'Mara. "Everybody's children grow up playing together. We all belong to the same clubs ... it's kind of a shock. You read about disasters in other communities, but you never think it can happen here."

About 7:30 p.m. Friday, a late-model, dark-blue car driven by John W. Bates, 19, of Brague, Okla., missed a curve on East Lake Road, then hit a utility pole, two trees and a stump. Seven of the car's nine passengers were ejected.

The young people had been swimming at DeRuyter Reservoir.

"I was one of the first out there," said O'Mara. "Everywhere you looked there were just bodies ... unbelievable. As people in town heard of it, they just kind of came out of their houses, met in the street and walked up and down. The atmosphere was incredible."

Killed were Clair Dorward Jr.'s daughters Judi, 18; Terri, 15; Denise, 11; and Sherri, 14. Also killed were Linda Dorward, 15, Clair Dorward Sr.'s daughter, and Lori Fostveit, 12, the Dorward girls' cousin.

Judi Dorward graduated from DeRuyter Central School last weekend, according to store clerk Emily Lawrence.

Three persons were in Syracuse hospitals: James Dorward, 6, in fair condition at Crouse-Irving Memorial Hospital and Richard Dorward, 4, in fair condition at St. Joseph's Hospital Health Center, both sons of Clair Dorward Jr.; and Bates, 19, in serious condition at Crouse-Irving.

State police said they are investigating possible charges against Bates.

All of Clair Dorward Jr.'s children were involved in the crash.

"They didn't have much, but they had children," O'Mara said.

"It really puts the damper on the holiday," Mrs. Lawrence said. "With all the tragedy, maybe it will do some good. Maybe we'll learn something. My daughter just got her driver's license. This has really scared her."

"You're kind of stunned at first," said O'Mara. "Then it starts to soak in. You start asking 'why?'. Maybe we'll never know exactly why."

Mrs. Lawrence summed it up for her townspeople as she fielded customer's questions about flower arrangements and memorials: "Well, I guess DeRuyter won't ever forget its Bicentennial weekend."

STAFF PHOTOS BY DON BLACK

Boy Scouts show the colors on Court Street.

What a day for a parade.

By BARRY HOLTZCLAW

One of the largest crowds ever to watch a Binghamton parade — estimates ranged from 25,000 to more than 35,000 — rubbed shoulders along a 20-block route yesterday to start the Bicentennial weekend in Broome County with a big display of community spirit.

It took three-and-one-half hours for the parade's 150 units, including 58 floats and 16 bands, to complete the route.

The celebration was amiable and relaxed, enhanced by sunny skies and a cool breeze.

Police said the large crowd was friendly and well-behaved. Some onlookers waved flags and wore red, white and blue, but most of the vast crowd avoided overt patriotic symbols and such traditions as standing or saluting passing flags.

Only a handful of firecrackers were heard during the long morning. There were no signs of protestors.

Flags waved from downtown lightpoles, but the unadorned buildings of the city's shopping district contrasted sharply with the Centennial celebration of a century ago, when red-white-and-blue bunting was draped from every building.

The only visible bunting — made of plastic — surrounded the viewing stand for dignitaries in front of the First-City National Bank of Binghamton.

The parade route, along Main and Court streets from Helen Street on Binghamton's West Side to State Street downtown, was packed with people of all ages.

People leaned out of apartment windows and thousands more watched the proceedings on live television.

Mickey Mouse balloons waved alongside Bicentennial flags and bagels competed with popcorn and cotton candy as morning snack favorites.

Residents along Grand Boulevard were roused about 8 a.m. by the sounds of horns and drums as the first groups began assembling for the parade, which began on time at 9 a.m.

Several thousand people had gathered along Court Street by the time the first contingent of police arrived there at 8 a.m. to begin closing off traffic.

About 275 National Guardsmen assisted Binghamton police with traffic control.

The neighborly, small-town atmosphere along the two-and-one-half-mile parade route rang with applause for floats and groups that heralded the county's cultural diversity.

Combining the twin themes of the parade — patriotism and community spirit — the marchers ended their trek at the Broome County Veterans Memorial Arena, where a three-day folk festival highlighting the county's ethnic heritage began yesterday afternoon.

The state's American Legion Com-

See COUNTY SALUTES, Page 6A

Lester R. Mosher, a member of state Bicentennial commission, rides on the Sons of American Revolution float in yesterday's parade.

Members of the Bainbridge-Guilford band supply spirited music at Spirit of '76 parade in downtown Binghamton.

Good morning

Showers

Details on 2A.

Henry Bloomer
Uncle Sam

Wimbledon champ

Wimbledon had its youngest champion in 45 years - Bjorn Borg, the winner over Ilie Nastase in the windup of the world's premier tennis tournament yesterday. 1B.

Uncle Sam

Henry Bloomer is Johnson City's Santa Claus, Blinky the Clown at carnivals and this area's personal Uncle Sam. Johanna Petroccia took a closer look at this colorful institution and found the man who hides beneath such outrageous trappings. 1C.

Ford's 51st veto

President Ford has vetoed a mineral royalties bill that was given prominence by a report that a Wyoming senator offered to deliver delegates if Ford approved the measure. 2A.

Bicentennial bonus

Today's SUNDAY contains three special Bicentennial sections in addition to the regular magazines and news and feature sections.

Let's chuckle

The trouble with good advice is that it usually interferes with our plans.

What's inside

July 4, 1976: The nation's bicentennial was marked with a special edition. There were three special sections inside. *Courtesy Dolly Escovar*

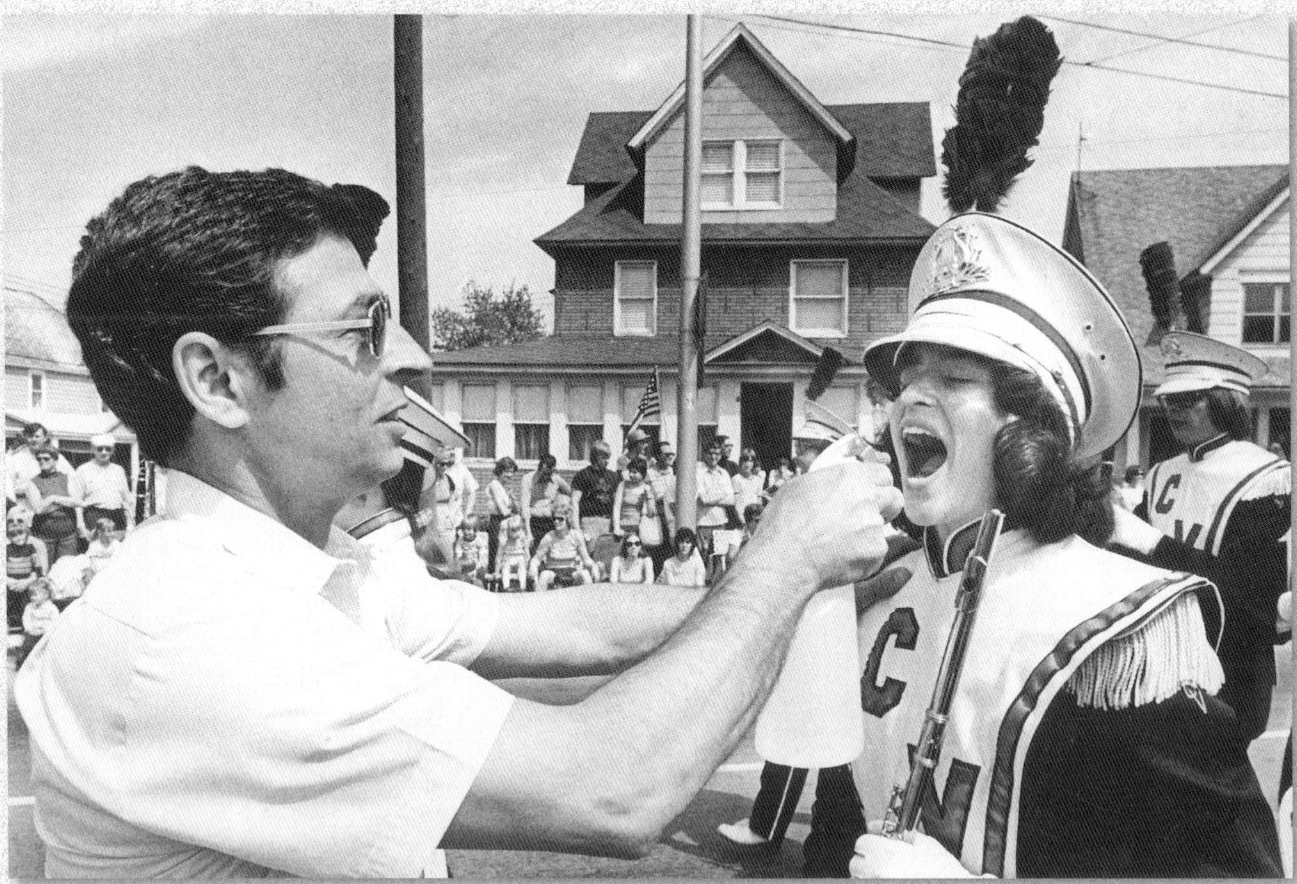

Joseph Fiesi gives Jennifer Ryan a squirt of water before the Chenango Valley High School band's performance in May 1976. *Courtesy Broome County Historical Society*

Laura Kroetsch, a sixth-grader who served as narrator of a play about Alexander Hamilton, and Anthony Kritausky, a fifth-grader, help Binghamton School Superintendent Richard P. McLean cut a birthday cake honoring the U.S. Bicentennial and the 221st birthday of Hamilton, January 1976. *Courtesy Broome County Historical Society*

Elvis Presley during the first of a two-day stint at the Broome County Veterans Memorial Arena, May 1977. His performance lasted 60 minutes and the crowd responded enthusiastically. He died a few months later. *Press & Sun-Bulletin Archives*

Ford backs Carter's canal plan

Will work for treaty, Page 2

Wednesday, August 17, 1977

The Sun-Bulletin

Sunny, 70's, Details, Page 2 | Binghamton, N.Y. 13902 | A Gannett newspaper | 20c

Elvis dead; fans mourn

FILE PHOTO

Elvis Presley: His act made millions swoon.

MEMPHIS, Tenn. (UPI) — Elvis Presley, the gyrating king of rock 'n' roll who changed the face of music forever when he growled "You Ain't Nothin' But A Hound Dog" two decades ago, died yesterday of an erratic heartbeat.

The fabulously wealthy, 42-year-old singer — "Elvis the Pelvis" when he burst upon the world in the mid-1950s and "The King" now — died face down on the floor of a bathroom at Graceland, his 18-room mansion.

He had visited a dentist Monday night and played racquet ball with members of his entourage until 6 a.m. His doctor said he may have died at 9 a.m., but his body was not discovered by road manager Jerry Esposito until 2:30 p.m.

Dr. Jerry Francisco, Shelby County medical examiner, said an autopsy indicated Presley died of "cardiac arrythmia," which he described as a "severely irregular heartbeat."

He said Presley had high blood pressure and "some coronary artery disease. These two diseases may be responsible for the cardiac arrythmia."

"The precise cause of death may never be discovered," said Francisco, the man who performed the autopsy on Dr. Martin Luther King Jr.

Sources close to Presley said he had been a heavy cocaine user for a year and there reportedly is an investigation into his drug use.

But Francisco and Dr. George Nichopolous, Presley's personal physician, reported no trace of drugs other than the medicine Presley took for hypertension and a colon problem.

Efforts to revive Presley at Baptist Hospital were abandoned at 3:30 p.m. Rumors swept from coast to coast and mourning began when his death was confirmed.

Radio stations throughout the world began playing hours of his songs. Politicians and entertainers eulogized him. Record stores, which for the past 22 years have sold more than 400 million of his albums, were jammed.

Cars moved bumper-to-bumper down Elvis Presley Boulevard in front of Graceland. A growing crowd pressed against the heavy wrought-iron gates, decorated with musical notes.

Sheriff's deputies lined the inside of the 10-foot-high brick wall ringing the 13-acre estate to prevent any rush on the grounds by grief-stricken mourners.

"What did he die of?" asked a teen-ager lined up to buy a stack of albums in Atlanta.

"He died of rock 'n' roll, man," answered the older man ahead of him.

The Memphis telephone system nearly collapsed along with the King. Officials appealed to the grief-stricken public to make no unneccessary calls.

Teen-agers in the 1950s went into frenzies, but parents, seeing his long, shiny hair and sideburns, his sneer and his hooded eyes and most of all his grinding hips, went into shock.

So much did those hips offend parents that when he appeared for the second time on the Ed Sullivan Show, television audiences were not permitted a full-length view of him.

He had finished a tour little more than a week ago, and was to begin another today. He was to have been in Syracuse Saturday. He appeared in Binghamton in May.

Some called him the most important figure in popular music in the century.

More stories, photos Pages 10-12

Dixie judge to head FBI

Frank Johnson
...heads for DC

WASHINGTON (UPI) — U.S. District Judge Frank M. Johnson Jr. of Montgomery, Ala., a Republican who issued a series of tough antidiscrimination decisions in the late 1950s, has been selected as the new director of the Federal Bureau of Investigation, government sources said yesterday. He will replace Clarence Kelley.

Administration officials confirmed President Carter has decided to appoint Johnson to the FBI post. The official announcement will be made at 2:30 p.m. today at the White House.

Johnson worked for the election of Republican Dwight Eisenhower as President in 1952 and became a federal judge in 1955 as an Eisenhower appointee. In 1956 he headed a three-judge panel that ruled, 2 to 1, that Montgomery city buses had to be integrated. It was a big victory for Martin Luther King but was unpopular with the white population.

He subsequently participated in a number of unpopular but landmark rulings dealing with desegregation, voting and mental health while gaining a reputation for making tough decisions.

Sources said Johnson, a reluctant candidate, had been Atty. Gen. Griffin Bell's final choice to replace Kelley.

Bell was known to have sought Johnson's services as either FBI director or his chief deputy for some time.

Johnson, 58, became a close friend while Bell was on U.S. 5th Circuit Court of Appeals. For many weeks after Bell took office he turned down the position of Bell's deputy, the second highest job in the Justice Department. Bell finally chose former Pittsburgh Mayor Peter Flaherty.

As late as last week, Bell hinted in news conferences and interviews he was still seeking Johnson for the FBI job but indicated he felt Johnson still was not interested.

Johnson, a native of Haleyville, Ala., rose from private to captain in the Army infantry in World War II, and was wounded in action. He obtained his law degree from the University of Alabama and was admitted to the bar in 1943, the same year he entered the Army. Who's Who lists him as Republican.

Bell bypassed five candidates chosen by a nine-member selection committee Carter formed at Bell's insistance after Bell decided that choosing an FBI director was too big a job for him alone.

The five were William Lucas, Wayne County sheriff in Detroit; John van de Kamp, Los Angeles County District Attorney; Neil Welch, head of the Philadelphia FBI office; John Irwin Jr., a Massachusetts state judge, and Harlington Wood Jr., a Chicago District Court judge, who later withdrew.

August 17, 1977: The Sun-Bulletin startled its readers with news that Elvis had died. *Courtesy Dolly Escovar*

The Evening Press

★★★ Wednesday, August 17, 1977, Binghamton, N.Y. 20 Cents

The King of Rock is dead

Sales show Elvis' songs will never die

By JERRY HANDTE

The death of Elvis Presley cost the Broome County Arena its greatest box office draw ever, manager Charles Theokas said today.

"If John Denver played our building 20 years from now — and I'm not knocking John, he's a great talent — he couldn't sell out the house twice like Elvis did in May," said Theokas.

Record stores this morning were swamped with fans — mostly in the 30-35 age group — buying up all the Presley albums, tapes and 45 rpm singles their pocketbooks could stand.

The one exception was Audio Service Stereoland in Binghamton, where Presley records move well with the 30-and-older group.

At five other stores, employees said Presley fans were calling up and coming in to the shops "in droves."

The first $60 in sales today at Recordland in the Oakdale Mall was all Elvis music.

Hi-Fi Record and Tape Center in Johnson City had six calls in the first half-hour this morning.

"I'm lucky I've got a saleman coming in this morning. I'm almost out," a manager said.

Last night at Discount Records in Vestal five albums, two tapes and four 45 rpm singles were sold.

The Sound Spot in Binghamton Plaza began to sell Presley at 7 last night, and was cleaned out by mid-morning today.

The first three telephone calls to Woody's Record Shop in Endicott today were to reserve Elvis records.

The reaction was quieter and maybe more personal today at 218 Bevier Street on Binghamton's East Side, home of 19-year-old Mike Igo.

Igo never met the legendary singer of 1950s music except to quickly hand Presley a portrait in oil the fan had done of the star, in exchange for a souvenir scarf.

See FANS, 28A

Concorde ban is ruled out

NEW YORK (AP) — The Port Authority of New York and New Jersey was ordered today by a federal judge to allow the supersonic Concorde jet to land at Kennedy Airport under noise rules now in effect for all other jets.

U.S. District Judge Milton J. Pollack enjoined the Port Authority, which operates New York area airports, from continuing its ban against the British and French supersonic jet.

Pollack said the Port Authority's 17-month delay in ruling on whether the Concorde could land here was "excessive and unjustified" and that the ban was "discriminatory, arbitrary and unreasonable."

Because the Port Authority has refused to make a decision on the Concorde, Pollack ruled that the plane "thereby has been deprived of an opportunity to show that it is environmentally acceptable at this international airport."

Pollack's ruling came in a 40-page decision that followed a hearing July 12, which had been ordered by the U.S. Court of Appeals.

Pollack said his decision will not take effect for 10 days, to allow time for appeal. An appeal is expected quickly, once again throwing the case to the appeals court.

The Concorde has been flying between Europe and Washington's Dulles International Airport since May of 1976.

Elvis shown performing in Memphis in 1974

By LES SEAGO

MEMPHIS (AP) — Elvis Presley - the one-time truck driver who as a rock 'n' roll singer was idolized by fans and denounced by preachers as the devil's tool - is dead of a heart ailment at age 42.

Doctors denied Presley's death was drug-connected.

Dr. George Nichopoulos, longtime physician to the swivel-hipped, throaty baritone who was known as the "King of Rock 'n' Roll," said an autopsy revealed a constriction in one of the main arteries to the heart, which restricted blood flow and brought on a heart attack.

"What caused it? Any one of a number of things," he said following Presley's death yesterday.

Nichopoulos said his patient, who carried about 175 pounds on a six-foot frame as a young man but recently had been reported grossly overweight, had been taking a number of appetite depressants, but did not have a drug problem.

Presley's uncle, Vester Presley, chief of security at Elvis' Graceland mansion, said early today that the singer's father, Vernon Presley, decided to open the casket for public viewing from 3 p.m until 5 p.m.

Jim Stewart, night supervisor at Memphis Funeral Home, said the body would be taken to Graceland. The funeral home said it understood from the family that the public would be permitted to pay its last respects.

Presley's uncle said Elvis' former wife, Priscilla, whom he divorced in 1973, arrived at the mansion at about 3 a.m. today.

"She is taking it hard. She is in a total state of shock."

Dr. Jerry Francisco, the Shelby County medical examiner, discounted rumors that Presley, who had been a virtual recluse at his white-columned Graceland mansion for 20 years, had suffered from a drug problem.

"There was no indication of drug abuse at all," Francisco said. "I was aware of the rumors and that is why I mention it."

He said the only evidence he found of drugs in the autopsy involved those Presley was taking for mild hypertension and a colon problem.

Francisco said there would have been visible needle tracks if illegal drugs were involved.

Delbert "Sonny" West, who was a Presley bodyguard for 16 years, said in Chicago just hours before Presley died that the singer was heavily addicted to drugs and haunted by fears that drove him into seclusion.

West was interviewed by Chicago Sun-Times columnist Bob Greene about a the recently released book, "Elvis: What Happened?" that West and two other former bodyguards have written about Presley.

"He was on pills all day long, and he would give himself shots in the arm or the leg with those little plastic syringes," West said in the interview. "He would have us give him shots in the rear end. We prayed for this man many times. His drug habit is so severe that I'm convinced he is in danger of losing his life."

Presley, whose recording of "Heartbreak Hotel" helped to put him on top of the entertainment world 21 years ago, was discovered unconscious at Graceland in suburban Memphis yesterday afternoon.

See MD, 5A

Presley is shown in 1957, mid 1960s, 1971 and this year.

1st intimate interview

Aide: Elvis lived on drugs

By BOB GREENE
Chicago Sun-Times

"Sometimes I couldn't believe it. Elvis would be sitting there, his eyes closed, his head hanging down, his mouth open — and he couldn't even manage to get his eyes open. He was on pills all day long, and he would give himself shots in the arm or the leg with those little plastic syringes. He would have us give him shots in the rear end. We prayed for this man many times. His drug habit is so severe that I'm convinced he is in danger of losing his life."

The speaker is Delbert "Sonny" West, for 16 years a confidant and bodyguard to singer Elvis Presley. Yesterday — only hours before Presley's death, in the first newspaper interview on the subject ever given by a member of Presley's entourage — West outlined a startling list of particulars about the Presley lifestyle, a list that bore out repeated rumors of Presley's deteriorating physical and mental well-being. As the interview was being typed, news of Presley's death was reported by the wire services.

Among the areas touched on in the interview, West said:

- Presley's drug habit was so severe that he had to take pills to get up in the morning, to go to the bathroom, to stop going to the bathroom, to perform, and to go to sleep.
- Presley believed that he was a "supernatural power" put on earth as a kind of modern-day Jesus, and felt that he had psychic healing powers.
- Presley enjoyed taking friends to funeral homes and mortuaries to examine embalmed bodies.
- Presley lived in mortal fear of assassination and had instructed his bodyguards to "rip the eyeballs out" of any Presley assassin before the assassin could be brought to trial.
- Presley had a fascination with firearms and once bought 32 handguns in one month. He owned a Thompson submachine gun and an M16 rifle, and often

See CONFIDANT, 5A

U.S. reduces Union, Vestal aid

By DAVE MACK

Broome County's most affluent communities — the towns of Union and Vestal — will lose 15 and 17 per cent, respectively, of their federal general revenue sharing allocations for fiscal 1978.

The county will gain 7 per cent over last year, budget officials say, while the rest of the county appears to stand to lose a little or break even at best.

Figures have not yet been received for the City of Binghamton, Director of Finance Ellsworth Dearborn said today.

In Union, however, Comptroller Steven Osser said word was received last week from the federal Office of Revenue Sharing the town would drop to $409,677 for 1978 from the $482,820 it received in 1977.

In the current fiscal year, revenue sharing money was used to pay for the town's share of the cost of the Binghamton-Johnson City joint sewage treatment plant and to pay salaries in the highway department. Where the money will come from next year has not yet been determined, Osser said.

The town has an overall budget for 1977 of about $6,727,000.

In Vestal, revenue sharing will drop from about $204,000 to about $169,000, a loss of about 17 per cent, according to Allan Lyons, Vestal's comptroller. Vestal's current budget is about $3.5 million.

See AID, 3A

City merchants still have faith

By MARYLU CARNEVALE

Despite Sears Roebuck & Co.'s plans to move its Binghamton store to the Oakdale Mall next year — and the possibility that J.C. Penney Co. may follow suit — some downtown merchants have faith that Binghamton is on the road to recovery.

For some, that may be a blind faith.

Statistics recently released by the state Department of Commerce show gross sales in department stores in the Binghamton area grew about 3 per cent in 1976 to $71.3 million from the $69.2 million in 1975.

The year before, the growth rate was only about 4 per cent for the five-county area.

The figures were not adjusted for inflation, indicating sales in department stores may have dropped slightly while the number of stores — and certainly the amount of retail space — has grown dramatically with the opening of the Oakdale Mall nearly two years ago.

Jack Zelter, who along with his son Donald, runs Roger's Apparel, said there seems to be a large amount of excess retail space in the Triple Cities area.

"There is too much retailing space and not enough people — shoppers," he said. "Too many stores are running into the mall and they aren't going to make enough money to stay open."

See CITY MERCHANTS, 3A

Inside

Gradual clearing and breezy tonight, cooler with a low near 50. Mostly sunny early tomorrow followed by some afternoon cloudiness, windy and a little cooler, high near 70. Chance of rain near 20 per cent tonight and tomorrow. (Details on Page 2A.)

ENJOY

George Atkinson sued Pittsburgh Coach Chuck Noll for slander when Noll referred to him as a "criminal element," but the defensive back enjoys the notoriety. Page 1C.

George Atkinson

BAND AID

Is competition a vital part of music education? That's the controversy surrounding the prize-winning band at Vestal High School. Page 1B.

One of Trophies

VETO HIT

Gov. Hugh L. Carey, under fire for his veto of the death penalty, spurs new criticism by vetoing a bill for special penalties for crimes against elderly. Page 15A.

Hugh Carey

A Gannett Newspaper
VOLUME 101-90

August 17, 1977: The Press recounts how Elvis played to two sold-out shows at the Arena in May of that year. Arena Manager says singer John Denver is good, but he's no Elvis. *Courtesy David Silvanic*

FINAL

The Evening Press

Friday, September 29, 1978, Binghamton, N.Y. 20 Cents

Pope dies after 34-day reign

Heart attack kills man of love, humor

Pope John Paul I

VATICAN CITY (AP) — Pope John Paul I, the humble "little man" elected pontiff of the Roman Catholic Church 34 days ago, died of a heart attack during the night, the Vatican announced today. The 65-year-old pope's reign was one of the briefest in history but his warmth and good humor had nonetheless endeared him to millions.

An official Vatican announcement said John Paul, who had a history of health problems, died at about 11 p.m. yesterday (5 p.m. EDT) while reading the 15th century book of meditations "The Imitation of Christ."

In death he still had his usual smile, said a senior cardinal.

The body was discovered this morning at about 5:30 (11:30 p.m. EDT yesterday) by his private secretary, the Rev. John Magee of Ireland, who went to the bedroom after noticing the pontiff was not in his private chapel at the usual time, the announcement said. The bed light was still on.

A doctor was immediately summoned, and he attributed death to "acute myocardial infarction." Monsignor Canisio Van Lierde, the pope's vicar for Vatican City, blessed the body.

"Providence took him away from us so suddenly," said Carlo Confalonieri, the 85-year-old dean of the College of Cardinals. "We are all with our eyes turned upward wondering about the inscrutable designs of God."

By noon, the body of the church's 263rd pontiff lay in state beneath a fresco of angels in the Vatican's Clementine Hall, just a few rooms away from the bedroom where he died. A stream of people, from cardinals and political leaders to foreign tourists and housewives, filed past.

See POPE, 6A

Local reaction, Page 6A

Possible successors, Page 6A

Editorial, Page 10A

Death stupefies leaders

By The Associated Press

Roman Catholics and non-Catholics in the United States and throughout the world expressed shock and sadness as they were stunned by the death today of Pope John Paul I, who they called a warm, loving man.

"We were stupefied, shocked," said the Rev. Giuseppe Bosa, apostolic administrator of the Venice diocese, where John Paul had served before becoming pope.

In Washington, President Carter said the late pontiff "captured the imagination of his church and of the world."

"He held out the promise of combining his predecessors' finest qualities, reaffirming what is enduring and strong in the Catholic tradition, while expanding the frontiers of the church to cope with the needs of the modern world," Carter said in a statement.

"We are all made poorer by his death," the president said.

New York Gov. Hugh Carey, who early last month attended the funeral of Pope Paul VI in Rome as part of the official U.S. delegation, said in Albany that John Paul had "brought a promise of new greatness to the papacy with his rare combination of grace and humility as well as innovation and tradition."

"I pray not only for the repose of his soul, but for the hope we find another with his great gifts," Carey said in a statement.

Cardinal Terence Cooke of New York, attending a meeting in San Francisco, characterized the pope as a "humble, loving and pastoral leader."

See CHURCH, 6A

John Paul I as the 263rd pope. AP

A Swiss Guard stands at attention near the pope

'Always caused concern'

Pope had history of illness

VATICAN CITY (AP) — Pope John Paul I, whose death was attributed to a heart attack, had often been in frail health, but he was not known to have a history of heart ailments.

"His health has always caused concern," his 32-year-old niece Pia Lucciania told The Associated Press in a telephone interview Aug. 29, three days after his election as pope. "He has to be careful about what he eats and about cold and heat. He is delicate, but, I advise you, he is not a traveling hospital."

When he was born Oct. 17, 1912, Albino Luciani was so tiny that his mother Bortola summoned a priest to baptize him that same day and in the same room where he was born.

"Albino was born such a frail thing that everybody thought he could hardly survive," his niece said.

She said her uncle twice entered a sanatorium for treatment of a "general lung condition" and underwent surgery four times — to remove his tonsils, to set a broken nose after a fall and twice for gallstones. The family once feared he might be suffering tuberculosis but doctors ruled that out, she said.

John Paul also suffered from rheumatism. Shortly before being elected pope Aug. 26, he spent several weeks at a seaside convent in Venice sunbathing to alleviate the pain.

6 had shorter reigns

At least six of the 263 popes of the Roman Catholic Church had shorter reigns than Pope John Paul I, who died in the 34th day of his papacy.

Pope Stephen II died three days after his election in 752. Both Marcellus II, in 1555, and Urban VII, in 1590, had 13-day papacies. Boniface VI was pope for 15 days in 896, Leo XI served 17 days in 1605 and Theodore II 20 days in 897.

The longest papacy was that of Pius IX, who reigned for 32 years beginning in 1846.

Dogma unchanged

Pope John Paul I made no major pronouncements on Christian dogma or ethics, but had urged efforts to save troubled marriages.

In an address to a group of American bishops eight days ago, the pope said he intended to follow the course of his immediate predecessor, Paul VI. "His teaching is ours," the pontiff said.

Asking for priority to help save marriages, the pope told the American bishops, "In particular, the indissolubility of Christian marriage is important."

The pope had yet to take a stand on the controversial issues dividing the Roman Catholic Church, including birth control, abortion and priestly celibacy.

Rail strikers ignore Carter

WASHINGTON (AP) — Striking rail clerks, ordered to work by President Carter, stepped up picketing instead today, slowing or halting rail traffic nationwide after a federal judge refused to enforce Carter's command.

"The strike is continuing," union president Fred Kroll said early today, just 8½ hours after Carter predicted his order for a 60-day cooling-off period "will take the railroad workers back to the job."

Kroll said he would not ask his members to obey the president until winning guarantees the strikers would not be punished by railroad employers.

"If I get the protection through the court, I will get them back as quickly as possible," said Kroll.

The union chief suggested that as a matter of "true fairness and evenhandedness, Congress might consider seizing the railroads for the United States government for the duration of the dispute, as well as ordering workers back to their jobs."

More than 300,000 rail workers were off the job, declining to cross picket lines of the Brotherhood of Railway and Airline Clerks.

The industry said the expanded picketing would disrupt every major rail carrier in the country, inconveniencing and sometimes stranding commuters, tying up shipments of food, cars, coal and other vital freight and forcing scattered layoffs because of parts shipment cutoffs. At least 42 states were affected.

The Delaware and Hudson Railway, which along with Conrail serves the Southern Tier, has not been affected by the strike so far. However, a company spokesman said he anticipated a decrease in traffic within the next few days.

See RAIL, 12A

Carling killed by drugs

ATHENS, Pa. — Bradford County Coroner Gordon Farr said he has ruled the cause of Roxanne L. Carling's death as homicide, caused by drugs that caused drowsiness and eventually asphyxiation.

Farr ruled on the cause of death after medical and police officials examined laboratory reports this morning issued earlier this week by the Allegheny County Medical Association in Pittsburgh.

The reports, requested almost a month ago, were turned over to state police at Towanda, Pa., on Tuesday.

Examining doctor Arthur B. King, of the Robert Packer Memorial Hospital in Athens, was out of town and unavailable to examine the reports until today, Farr said.

Carling, 17, of Van Etten, and Craig J. Morse, 23, of Athens, Pa., were found dead in Round Top Park near Athens on Sept. 3, 10 days after Morse is believed to have abducted Carling from her car on Route 34, south of Van Etten. Carling was on her way to work in Sayre when she was abducted.

See CORONER, 4A

Inside

Clear tonight, overnight low in the mid-30s. Sunny tomorrow with increasing cloudiness late in the afternoon, breezy and milder, daytime high in the upper 50s. (Details on Page 2A.)

SEEKS CHANGE

Native South African Paul Tracey wants to use his music to counteract the stereotype made-in-Hollywood image of Africa held by most Americans. Page 1B.

Paul Tracey

RAPS PRESS

Philadelphia Mayor Frank Rizzo, often at odds with the city's newspapers, has criticized black reporters for not representing his side. Page 4B.

Frank Rizzo

VISITS CITY

Bill Foster, whose Duke basketball team was still in its "infancy" when it reached the NCAA finals this year, is in Binghamton — and playing them one at a time. Page 1C.

Bill Foster

A Gannett Newspaper
VOLUME 102-119

September 29, 1978: The death of Pope John Paul I surprised readers and set the stage for selection of John Paul II. *Courtesy Carolyn Fitzgerald*

The old Press building, downtown Binghamton, circa 1980.
Courtesy Broome County Historical Society

The race is on in the Yegatta Regatta. Rafters began their journey near what is now the Polar Cap Ice Rink in Chenango Bridge and floated toward the confluence with the Susquehanna River, June 1980. *Press & Sun-Bulletin archives*

Rafters struggle to get their floats over a shallow spot in the Chenango River during the Yegatta Regatta, an annual party on the river that benefited the American Cancer Society, May 1980. *Press & Sun-Bulletin archives*

FREE THE HOSTAGES
FOWLER & WILLIAMS, INC.

Fowler and Williams Trucking Co. makes a statement with the side of one of its trailers during the Iran Hostage Crisis, 1980. *Courtesy Broome County Historical Society*

1980 - 1989

President Reagan dominates the news

Monday, May 19, 1980

The Sun-Bulletin

Final

Cloudy, 60s; Details, Page 8B — Binghamton, N.Y. 13902 — A Gannett newspaper — 25c NEWSSTAND

Up, up and away! Volcano blows top

UPI PHOTO

Billowing clouds of steam and ash hurl skyward yesterday from Mt St Helens. Explosion could be heard 150 miles away.

Seven die in major Mt. St. Helens eruption: Page 2A

Miami torn; 19 killed, 100s injured

Page 3A

Local dumps may poison your water

Page 8-9A

Indiantown Gap receives 1st Cubans

Page 6A

May 19, 1980: The Sun-Bulletin had switched to a front page of pictures and headlines. The format helped drive circulation growth. *Microfilm archives*

Ronald Reagan was the big story in the 1980s.

— American hostages in Iran were freed as he was taking office.

— He survived an assassin's bullet.

— His calm words soothed a nation grieving from the explosion of the space shuttle.

And, he visited Endicott.

Reagan became the first president to visit Broome County in 48 years when he appeared at Ty Cobb stadium in 1984. He came to Endicott on a campaign swing, telling local Republicans that the region had much to teach the nation.

Reagan won in a landslide. In Broome, Reagan beat Walter Mondale by about 55,000 votes to 37,000 votes.

One of the leading politicians who greeted Reagan in Endicott was Warren M. Anderson of Binghamton. Anderson, the longest serving majority leader of the New York Senate, was the most powerful Republican in the state.

During his tenure, SUNY-Binghamton grew to one of the top institutions in the country, complete with a world-class concert hall named after Anderson's father. Interstate 88 connects Binghamton with Albany because of his efforts, and the state named the highway after him.

He helped pick his successor, then-city councilman Thomas W. Libous.

In 1985, after years of circulation losses for the afternoon paper, The Evening Press and the Sun-Bulletin combined.

Tuesday, Dec. 9, 1980

The Sun-Bulletin

Final

Complete and final stock listings, 24A-25A

Colder, 30s; Details, Page 6B — Binghamton, N.Y. 13902 — A Gannett newspaper — 25c NEWSSTAND

EX-BEATLE JOHN LENNON SHOT TO DEATH

Singer gunned down in NYC; police have suspect in custody...2A

LENNON

Tough rules push up M-E student dropout rate

Page 3A

County panel urges aide for health dep't. chief

Page 4A

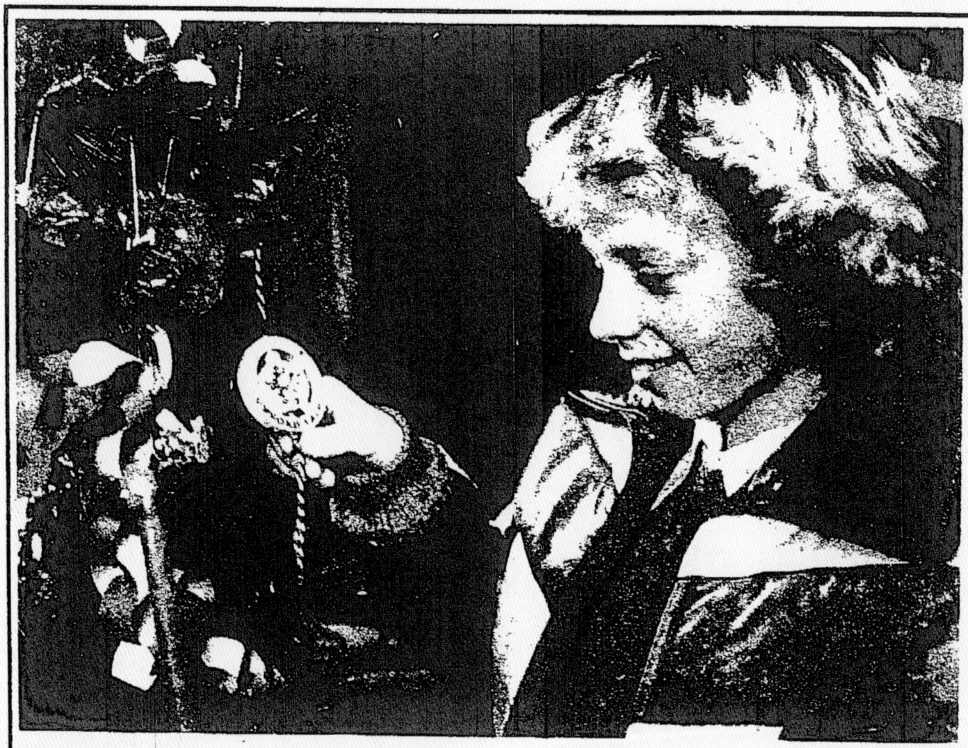

JOHN J. GUGLIELMI PHOTO

Looking a lot like Christmas...

Mary Brozovic, 11, of 142 Greenridge St., Johnson City, takes a close look at some of the handmade ornaments on one of the Christmas trees at the Roberson Center's 1980 Christmas Forest. This particular tree was designed with Czechoslovakian ornaments. For more photos, see Page 5A

December 9, 1980: The last of the major assassinations that began in the '60s. *Microfilm archives*

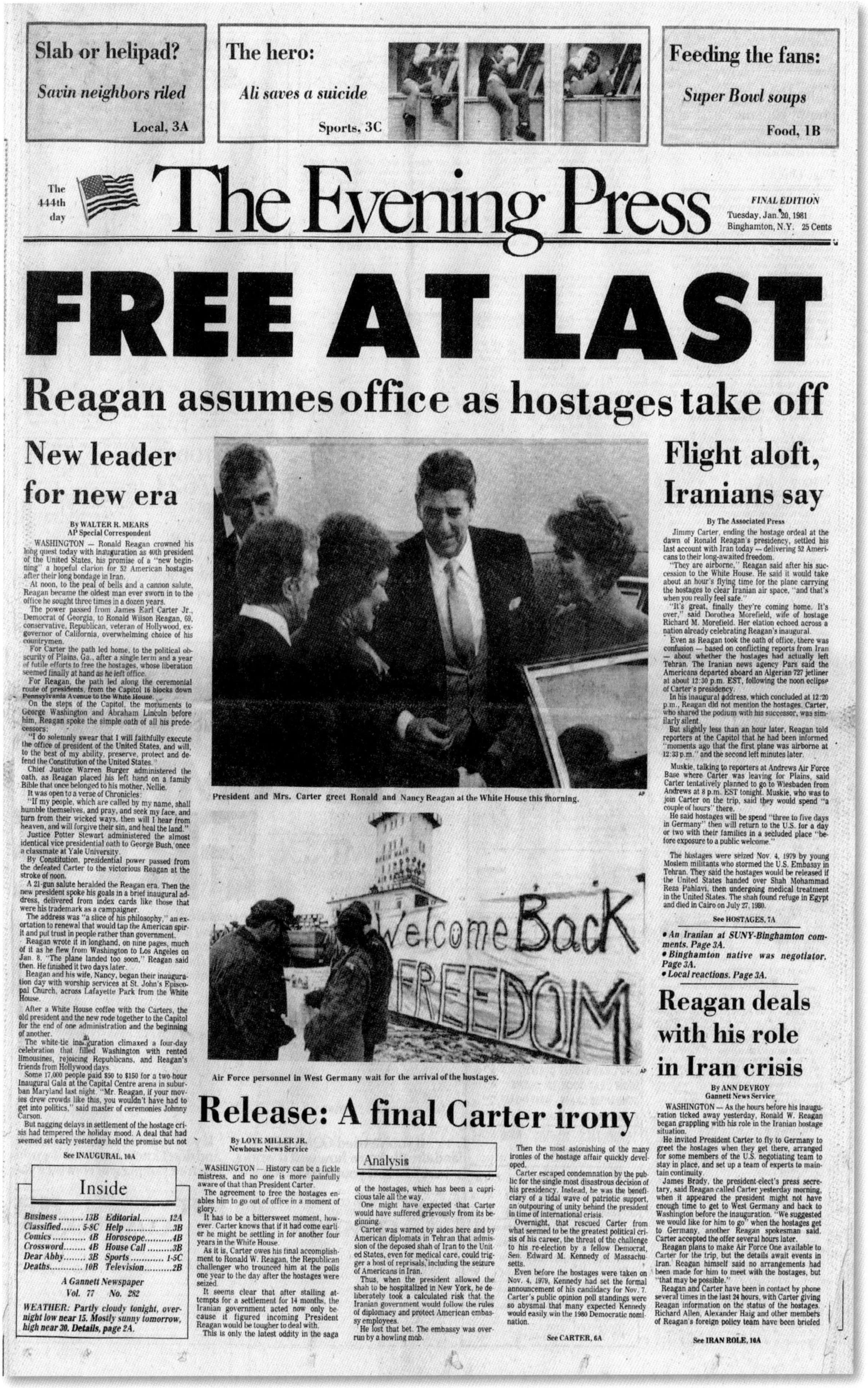

Slab or helipad?
Savin neighbors riled
Local, 3A

The hero:
Ali saves a suicide
Sports, 3C

Feeding the fans:
Super Bowl soups
Food, 1B

The 444th day

The Evening Press

FINAL EDITION
Tuesday, Jan. 20, 1981
Binghamton, N.Y. 25 Cents

FREE AT LAST

Reagan assumes office as hostages take off

New leader for new era

By WALTER R. MEARS
AP Special Correspondent

WASHINGTON — Ronald Reagan crowned his long quest today with inauguration as 40th president of the United States, his promise of a "new beginning" a hopeful clarion for 52 American hostages after their long bondage in Iran.

At noon, to the peal of bells and a cannon salute, Reagan became the oldest man ever sworn in to the office he sought three times in a dozen years.

The power passed from James Earl Carter Jr., Democrat of Georgia, to Ronald Wilson Reagan, 69, conservative, Republican, veteran of Hollywood, ex-governor of California, overwhelming choice of his countrymen.

For Carter the path led home, to the political obscurity of Plains, Ga., after a single term and a year of futile efforts to free the hostages, whose liberation seemed finally at hand as he left office.

For Reagan, the path led along the ceremonial route of presidents, from the Capitol 16 blocks down Pennsylvania Avenue to the White House.

On the steps of the Capitol, the monuments to George Washington and Abraham Lincoln before him, Reagan spoke the simple oath of all his predecessors:

"I do solemnly swear that I will faithfully execute the office of president of the United States, and will, to the best of my ability, preserve, protect and defend the Constitution of the United States."

Chief Justice Warren Burger administered the oath, as Reagan placed his left hand on a family Bible that once belonged to his mother, Nellie.

It was open to a verse of Chronicles:

"If my people, which are called by my name, shall humble themselves, and pray, and seek my face, and turn from their wicked ways, then will I hear from heaven, and will forgive their sin, and heal the land."

Justice Potter Stewart administered the almost identical vice presidential oath to George Bush, once a classmate at Yale University.

By Constitution, presidential power passed from the defeated Carter to the victorious Reagan at the stroke of noon.

A 21-gun salute heralded the Reagan era. Then the new president spoke his goals in a brief inaugural address, delivered from index cards like those that were his trademark as a campaigner.

The address was "a slice of his philosophy," an exortation to renewal that would tap the American spirit and put trust in people rather than government.

Reagan wrote it in longhand, on nine pages, much of it as he flew from Washington to Los Angeles on Jan. 8. "The plane landed too soon," Reagan said then. He finished it two days later.

Reagan and his wife, Nancy, began their inauguration day with worship services at St. John's Episcopal Church, across Lafayette Park from the White House.

After a White House coffee with the Carters, the old president and the new rode together to the Capitol for the end of one administration and the beginning of another.

The white-tie inauguration climaxed a four-day celebration that filled Washington with rented limousines, rejoicing Republicans, and Reagan's friends from Hollywood days.

Some 17,000 people paid $50 to $150 for a two-hour Inaugural Gala at the Capital Centre arena in suburban Maryland last night. "Mr. Reagan, if your movies drew crowds like this, you wouldn't have had to get into politics," said master of ceremonies Johnny Carson.

But nagging delays in settlement of the hostage crisis had tempered the holiday mood. A deal that had seemed set early yesterday held the promise but not

See INAUGURAL, 10A

President and Mrs. Carter greet Ronald and Nancy Reagan at the White House this morning. AP

Welcome Back
FREEDOM

Air Force personnel in West Germany wait for the arrival of the hostages. AP

Flight aloft, Iranians say

By The Associated Press

Jimmy Carter, ending the hostage ordeal at the dawn of Ronald Reagan's presidency, settled his last account with Iran today — delivering 52 Americans to their long-awaited freedom.

"They are airborne," Reagan said after his succession to the White House. He said it would take about an hour's flying time for the plane carrying the hostages to clear Iranian air space, "and that's when you really feel safe."

"It's great, finally they're coming home. It's over," said Dorothea Morefield, wife of hostage Richard M. Morefield. Her elation echoed across a nation already celebrating Reagan's inaugural.

Even as Reagan took the oath of office, there was confusion — based on conflicting reports from Iran — about whether the hostages had actually left Tehran. The Iranian news agency Pars said the Americans departed aboard an Algerian 727 jetliner at about 12:30 p.m. EST, following the noon eclipse of Carter's presidency.

In his inaugural address, which concluded at 12:20 p.m., Reagan did not mention the hostages. Carter, who shared the podium with his successor, was similarly silent.

But slightly less than an hour later, Reagan told reporters at the Capitol that he had been informed "moments ago that the first plane was airborne at 12:33 p.m." and the second left minutes later.

Muskie, talking to reporters at Andrews Air Force Base where Carter was leaving for Plains, said Carter tentatively planned to go to Wiesbaden from Andrews at 8 p.m. EST tonight. Muskie, who was to join Carter on the trip, said they would spend "a couple of hours" there.

He said hostages will be spend "three to five days in Germany" then will return to the U.S. for a day or two with their families in a secluded place "before exposure to a public welcome."

The hostages were seized Nov. 4, 1979 by young Moslem militants who stormed the U.S. Embassy in Tehran. They said the hostages would be released if the United States handed over Shah Mohammad Reza Pahlavi, then undergoing medical treatment in the United States. The shah found refuge in Egypt and died in Cairo on July 27, 1980.

See HOSTAGES, 7A

- *An Iranian at SUNY-Binghamton comments. Page 3A.*
- *Binghamton native was negotiator. Page 3A.*
- *Local reactions. Page 3A.*

Release: A final Carter irony

By LOYE MILLER JR.
Newhouse News Service

Analysis

WASHINGTON — History can be a fickle mistress, and no one is more painfully aware of that than President Carter.

The agreement to free the hostages enables him to go out of office in a moment of glory.

It has to be a bittersweet moment, however. Carter knows that if it had come earlier he might be settling in for another four years in the White House.

As it is, Carter owes his final accomplishment to Ronald W. Reagan, the Republican challenger who trounced him at the polls one year to the day after the hostages were seized.

It seems clear that after stalling attempts for a settlement for 14 months, the Iranian government acted now only because it figured incoming President Reagan would be tougher to deal with.

This is only the latest oddity in the saga of the hostages, which has been a capricious tale all the way.

One might have expected that Carter would have suffered grievously from its beginning.

Carter was warned by aides here and by American diplomats in Tehran that admission of the deposed shah of Iran to the United States, even for medical care, could trigger a host of reprisals, including the seizure of Americans in Iran.

Thus, when the president allowed the shah to be hospitalized in New York, he deliberately took a calculated risk that the Iranian government would follow the rules of diplomacy and protect American embassy employees.

He lost that bet. The embassy was overrun by a howling mob.

Then the most astonishing of the many ironies of the hostage affair quickly developed.

Carter escaped condemnation by the public for the single most disastrous decision of his presidency. Instead, he was the beneficiary of a tidal wave of patriotic support, an outpouring of unity behind the president in time of international crisis.

Overnight, that rescued Carter from what seemed to be the greatest political crisis of his career, the threat of the challenge to his re-election by a fellow Democrat, Sen. Edward M. Kennedy of Massachusetts.

Even before the hostages were taken on Nov. 4, 1979, Kennedy had set the formal announcement of his candidacy for Nov. 7. Carter's public opinion poll standings were so abysmal that many expected Kennedy would easily win the 1980 Democratic nomination.

See CARTER, 6A

Reagan deals with his role in Iran crisis

By ANN DEVROY
Gannett News Service

WASHINGTON — As the hours before his inauguration ticked away yesterday, Ronald W. Reagan began grappling with his role in the Iranian hostage situation.

He invited President Carter to fly to Germany to greet the hostages when they get there, arranged for some members of the U.S. negotiating team to stay in place, and set up a team of experts to maintain continuity.

James Brady, the president-elect's press secretary, said Reagan called Carter yesterday morning, when it appeared the president might not have enough time to get to West Germany and back to Washington before the inauguration. "We suggested we would like for him to go" when the hostages get to Germany, another Reagan spokesman said. Carter accepted the offer several hours later.

Reagan plans to make Air Force One available to Carter for the trip, but the details await events in Iran. Reagan himself said no arrangements had been made for him to meet with the hostages, but "that may be possible."

Reagan and Carter have been in contact by phone several times in the last 24 hours, with Carter giving Reagan information on the status of the hostages. Richard Allen, Alexander Haig and other members of Reagan's foreign policy team have been briefed

See IRAN ROLE, 10A

Inside

A Gannett Newspaper
Vol. 77 No. 282

***WEATHER:** Partly cloudy tonight, overnight low near 15. Mostly sunny tomorrow, high near 30. Details, page 2A.*

January 20, 1981: Iranians let 52 American hostages go the day Ronald Reagan became president. *Courtesy David Silvanic*

A Press Special

Inauguration

A new beginning: Section D

The Evening Press

FINAL EDITION
Wednesday, Jan. 21, 1981
Binghamton, N.Y. 25 Cents

'We are going to express the thanks of a grateful nation to the brave hostages...'
—Former President Carter

Jimmy Carter

The ex-hostages

'Between us we're going to straighten things out and we're going to take the high road.'
—President Reagan

Ronald Reagan

What a day it was

Three ex-hostages leave medical plane at Frankfurt Airbase early this morning.

Renewal and freedom seize U.S. feelings

WASHINGTON (AP) — In one extraordinary hour, two emotions sweep America: a sense of renewal and an appreciation of freedom. It is a clean end to an ugly piece of business — and a new beginning.

Ronald W. Reagan, 69, the oldest man ever to take the presidency, the first divorced man and first professional actor in that office, succeeds a drawn and gray Jimmy Carter.

It falls to Reagan to announce the news America wanted.

The hostages are free. The hostages are airborne. The hostages are on their way to Athens, Algiers, Frankfurt — and home.

For America, this sunlit Tuesday is a day of change and liberation.

Carter goes home, a two-day stubble of whiskers on his chin. He dances cheek-to-cheek with his Rosalynn to the rhythm of a country band on the streets of Plains, Ga.

Reagan takes the 35-word oath of office, swearing to preserve, protect and defend the Constitution, and offers "this breed called Americans" a speech of hope.

His inaugural address is vintage Reagan: "We have every right to dream heroic dreams," he says. "It is not my intention to do away with government. It is rather to make it work — work with us, not over us; to stand by our side, not ride on our back."

The celebration of freedom originates with the liberty flight, on the 444th day of their captivity in Iran, of the hostages.

Seized by a band of Moslem fanatics on Nov. 4, 1979, they had been prisoners in a war of wills that became Carter's obsession.

But, perhaps by the Iranians' deliberate calculation, the hostages' release is delayed until Carter surrenders the presidency to Reagan.

So Reagan, dressed in a flashy cutaway, gets the chance to lift a glass of California wine at an inaugural luncheon in the Capitol and announce: "Some 30 minutes ago, the planes bearing our prisoners left Iranian airspace and they're now free of Iran."

He offers this toast: "To all of us together, doing what we all know we can do to make this country what it should be, what it can be, what it always has been."

Across America, church bells peal.

About 400,000 people line Pennsylvania Avenue for the inaugural parade. Many of them hold transistor radios to their ears to keep up with the hostage drama.

Reagan's gleaming limousine proceeds down the avenue. Four years ago, Jimmy and Rosalynn Carter, holding hands, walked.

Now the Carters ride to Andrews Air Force Base

See FREE, 12A

END OF CAPTIVITY
A Press special report on the ex-hostages' freedom appears on Pages 12A and 13A, and a story on Page 3A.

President Ron~ld Reagan and Nancy wave after inauguration in Washington yesterday.

Ex-hostages enjoy taste of freedom

WIESBADEN, West Germany (AP) — The 52 former hostages, enjoying their first taste of freedom in 14½ months, settled into a U.S. military hospital today and made their first telephone calls to the United States.

"First of all there was a very heavy run on the telephones," State Department spokesman Jack Cannon said.

The Americans, 50 men and two women, checked into the hospital at dawn, after their dramatic release from Iranian captivity and a freedom flight to West Germany via Algeria.

Just after noon, some of the hostages appeared on the balconies of the hospital, bantering with hospital personnel. Orderlies tossed up a copy of the military newspaper *Stars and Stripes* to a group of four young men who autographed the newspaper and threw it back down.

Two other men, wearing pajamas and bathrobes, hopped over the railings separating each room's balcony and joined the other four. They waved when they noticed photographers about 200 yards away.

See FREED, 13A

Reagan released as well

End to crisis relieves foreign policy burden

By WALTER R. MEARS
AP Special Correspondent

WASHINGTON — President Reagan has been liberated, too.

He never said what he would have done had Iran held the American hostages into his administration. Now action won't be necessary.

Instead, Reagan took office freed of the agonizing marathon crisis that had defied Jimmy Carter for more than a year.

The 52 captives' release cleared Reagan's foreign policy agenda of a burden that could have become as troublesome for him as it was for his predecessor.

It was a subject Reagan had addressed repeatedly during the campaign that led him to the White House.

Analysis

Sometimes he spoke cautiously, sometimes in tough terms. One theme was consistent: Reagan blamed Carter foreign policy failures for the hostage seizure in the first place.

"I believe that this administration's foreign policy helped create the entire situation that made their kidnap possible," he said two weeks before the election. "And I think the fact that they're still there is a

See REAGAN FREE, 12A

Inside

A Gannett Newspaper
Vol. 77 No. 283

WEATHER: Partly cloudy, not as cold tonight, overnight low in the teens. Increasing cloudiness with a chance of flurries tomorrow, milder with a daytime high in the 30s. Chance of precipitation 10 percent tonight, 30 percent tomorrow. Details, Page 2A.

Fadden murder trial to get outside jury

By RUSSELL LEE KAHN

MONTROSE, Pa. — Jurors in the Susquehanna County trial of Robert S. Fadden, charged with murdering three members of his girlfriend's family Aug. 19, will be chosen from another county, a judge has ruled.

Susquehanna County Judge Donald M. O'Malley granted a change of venue in the trial because he said jurors chosen from Susquehanna County would be prejudiced by publicity given the case.

In his decision O'Malley said extensive publicity given to the related murder trial of Fadden's girlfriend, Roxanne Severcool, "would make the selection of an impartial jury difficult from Susquehanna County."

A jury will be selected in a neighboring county — probably Tioga County, Pa., — and brought to Susquehanna County for the trial, the decision said.

Fadden, 25, formerly of Montrose, has pleaded innocent to three counts of murder, one count of attempted murder, one count of assault and two counts each of burglary and theft in the three slayings.

Roxanne Severcool, 18, was found guilty at the end of a trial last week on three counts of first-degree murder. She will be sentenced to life in prison.

She was accused of helping plan the shooting deaths of her parents, Mary and Lester Severcool, and her brother, Theodore. Another brother, James Severcool, was shot but survived.

Fadden, who is accused of doing the actual shooting inside the family's Springville, Pa. home while Severcool waited in another room, will go to trial in February or March, his attorney said.

In an accompanying letter on the change of venue, O'Malley indicated to Henry X. O'Brien, the chief justice of the Supreme Court of Pennsylvania, that the Fadden jury probably will come from Tioga County, Pa.

O'Malley said in the letter that he has spoken with Robert Kent, Tioga County judge, about empaneling a jury from his area.

In a related matter, the state Supreme Court has denied Fadden's petition for review of the Susquehanna County Court decision rejecting his request for a new lawyer. Fadden is represented by Charles J. Aliano.

Fadden also has filed a motion regarding his arrest on the charges. He claims he was forced to make incriminating statements by state police and FBI investigators.

A seven-man, five-woman jury in Roxanne Severcool's trial remained deadlocked over the sentence to be imposed after nine hours of deliberations last week.

A unanimous verdict was required to impose the death sentence, and, under Pennsylvania law, a deadlocked jury meant an automatic sentence of life imprisonment.

Severcool's attorney, Robert Dean, said he will appeal the conviction.

January 21, 1981: The Press adds more details to the inauguration of Reagan and drops the flag that marked each day of the hostages' captivity. *Courtesy Dolly Escovar*

Eggleston:

No support for Crabb

Local, 5A

Hoosiers do it:

2nd crown for Knight

Sports, 1C

Seafood treats:

Luxury for Lent

Food, 1B

The Evening Press

FINAL EDITION

Tuesday, Mar. 31, 1981
Binghamton, N.Y. 25 Cents

This sequence of photographs shows President Reagan waving to bystanders outside the Washington Hilton Hotel as he is shot and shoved by Secret Service agents into his limousine. AP

Reagan is OK

Secret Service probes failure

By MERYL GORDON
Gannett News Service

WASHINGTON — The Secret Service will conduct a "complete in-house investigation" into why its agents were unable to prevent President Reagan from being shot outside the Washington Hilton hotel yesterday, said spokesman Jack Warner.

"When there is an attempt on the president or any other person we're responsible for, we have to shoulder that burden," he said.

"We closely monitor the public arena as we travel with the president," Warner said. "But the fact that we live and work in a democracy has to be taken into consideration. We are living in a free society."

No special precautions beyond normal Secret Service protection were taken for the president's speech yesterday, he said. "This was not considered an unusual day."

Warner said the Secret Service keeps detailed files on people considered dangerous to the president and that the shooting suspect, John W. Hinckley Jr., "is not in our files."

He said Hinckley apparently acted alone, but wouldn't rule out the possibility of accomplices until the investigation is complete. "It appears that he was by himself," Warner said.

"We receive threats frequently," he said. "We have about 400 people in our files that we consider to be serious threats. We have information on 25,000 people that we are interested in because of a potential to become a threat."

He said that Reagan's "threat level is not any higher than any other of the former presidents."

According to news reports, Hinckley was arrested in Nashville, Tenn., on Oct. 9 during a visit to that city by President Carter, but Secret Service agents said last night they weren't aware of it.

Warner wouldn't say how many agents were

See SECRET SERVICE, 3A

Citizens express horror, outrage

By LORRAINE VENTURA

"If someone's intent on taking a shot at somebody, he's going to do it. This is just another illustration of that," Patrick D. Monserrate, Broome County district attorney, said this morning at Dunkin Donuts, 225 Main St., Binghamton.

Monserrate and others in Binghamton and surrounding areas today reflected on yesterday's assassination attempt on Ronald Reagan, some expressing horror and outrage that once again an American president had been shot.

"I was very upset. I like him (Reagan) very much," Penny A. Strong, 20, of Pierce Creek Road, Binghamton, said. "I want to know his motive for the shootings, whether it had to do with all of (Reagan's) cuts, which I agree with because I'm not governmentally funded."

Janice Downie, RD1, Oneonta, part-time staff nurse at Hartwick College, said: "We turned the TV on to watch *General Hospital*. The news caught my eye. I just feel so badly that this type of thing continues to happen in our society and nobody seems to be able to control it. Things seem to deteriorate. I would

See CITIZENS, 5A

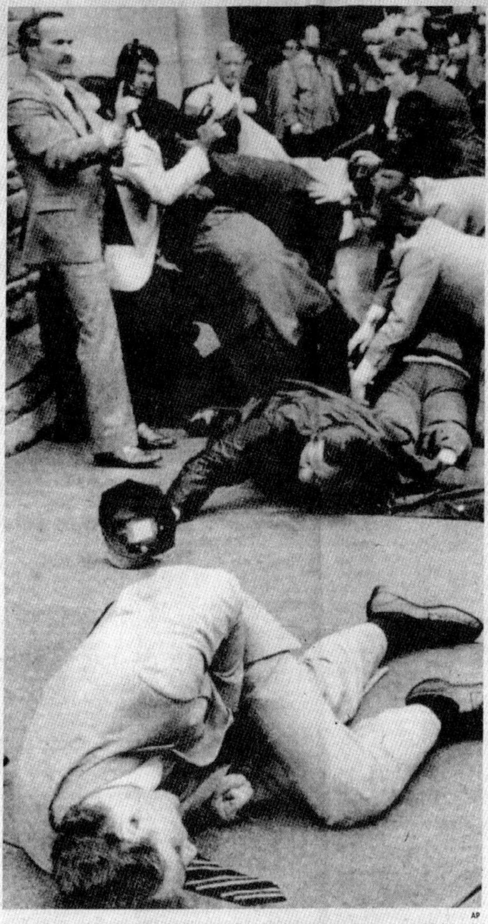

AP

Secret Service agent Timothy J. McCarthy lies wounded in foreground. Lying behind him is Washington, D.C., Patrolman Thomas K. Delahanty. In the background on the sidewalk is James Brady, presidential press secretary.

President in command

By JAMES GERSTENZANG
The Associated Press

WASHINGTON — President Reagan, in "exceptionally good condition" and "excellent spirits," resumed the duties of the presidency today from a hospital bed after an assailant's bullet was removed from his chest.

Less than 24 hours after he was shot outside a Washington hotel, the 70-year-old president was joking with nurses at George Washington University Hospital and impressing his doctors with his physical stamina.

At 7:15 a.m. EST, top White House aides visited Reagan's room and found him sitting up in bed, brushing his teeth after breakfast. Deputy White House press secretary Larry Speakes said Reagan used his breakfast tray to sign a dairy price support bill the aides had given him.

"He could probably put in a full day, if he gets a nap this afternoon," said Dr. Dennis O'Leary, a hospital spokesman. ". . . I would not be surprised to see him up walking around in a couple of days."

O'Leary said Reagan "is doing extremely well," could be discharged from the hospital in a week or two, "then a couple of months until he's back riding horses."

O'Leary said White House press sec-

See PRESIDENT, 3A

Inside

- *Press Secretary James S. Brady is making 'extraordinary progress.' Page 2A*
- *Nancy Reagan returned to President Reagan's bedside this morning after a night of little sleep. Page 3A.*
- *Vice President George Bush has been carefully coached to fill in for the president if needed. Page 2A*
- *Reaction poured in from home and abroad, and Hollywood postponed its Oscar awards. Page 2A.*
- *President Reagan should make sure his security precautions are sufficient enough in this violent world. Editorial, Page 12A.*
- *The president's wound is a common injury that never posed him serious problems. Page 2A*

Hinckley's vague past hints of troubled man

DAVID SHAPIRO
Gannett News Service

WASHINGTON — On March 23, John W. Hinckley Jr. quietly left a Lakewood, Colo., hotel that had been his home for 16 days, not bothering to tell the owner he was checking out for good.

He paused only to wave to Ginger Aucour, a chambermaid he had become friendly with during his stay because of their common interest in country and western music.

"I guess he was waving goodbye," Aucort would recall later. "He was just your basic loner, but he was very friendly."

Seven days later, Hinckley, 25, was arrested outside the Washington Hilton Hotel, accused of shooting President Reagan, presidential press secretary James Brady, a Secret Service agent and a Washington policeman.

The Justice Department formally charged last night that Hinckley attempted to assassinate the president and assaulted a Secret Service officer.

See HINCKLEY'S, 3A

AP

John Warnock Hinckley Jr.
...1981 Colorado Highway Dept. photo

March 31, 1981: President Reagan is shot. *Courtesy Rudy Bystrak*

Did wife know about poison?
Local, 3A

Gymnast soars to gold medal
Sports, 1C

Ball strike at decisive point
Sports, 1C

FINAL EDITION

The Evening Press

Wed., July 29, 1981
Binghamton, N.Y. 25 Cents

Prince, Di marry like a 'fairy tale'

LONDON (AP) — Prince Charles and Lady Diana Spencer were wed this morning in the music-filled color and splendor of a 1,000-year-old monarchy, embarking on life as man and wife on waves of love from a devoted people.

"O let the nations rejoice and be glad!" erupted the massed choirs when the Archbishop of Canterbury pronounced the couple wed under the soaring dome of St. Paul's Cathedral.

After the age-old, 80-minute ceremony, the royal couple rode back to Buckingham Palace in an open carriage, wending through a crowd of almost 1 million people who roared their good wishes and waved a sea of Union Jack flags. Church bells rang across the realm.

"This is the stuff of which fairy tales are made," observed the archbishop.

The union of the 32-year-old Prince of Wales and Lady Diana, the 20-year-old kindergarten teacher with the captivating smile, was the first time in three centuries that the heir to the British throne has married an English-born woman.

Besides the masses of spectators here, at least 500 million others were believed to have watched the ceremony on television around the world.

"I've never seen anything like it," one veteran bobby said of the crowds. "We've got the whole of Britain . . . here." Authorities had feared possible terrorist attacks or other violence during the great event, but no major incidents were reported.

At St. Paul's altar, the nervous heir to the British throne pronounced, "I, Charles Philip Arthur George, take thee, Diana Frances, to be my wedded wife, to have and to hold from this day forward . . ."

Diana, standing in a cloud of white, cast a sidelong glance and smile at her bridegroom.

Then, speaking scarcely above a whisper, she repeated the vow. She slipped up once, repeating Charles' full name in the wrong order, promising to marry "Philip Charles Arthur George." Charles also erred at one point, dropping the word "worldy" when he promised to share his "worldly goods."

The Prince of Wales then placed the band of Welsh gold on the bride's hand, and the archbishop, the Rt. Rev. Robert Runcie, declared them wed.

The throngs in the sunshine outside, listening to the ceremony on loudspeakers, broke a hushed silence with loud cheers.

See WEDDING, Living 1B

Inside

- *Rioting rages in Liverpool for third straight night. Back Page.*
- *Lady Di's jitters amid the glitter. Rossie, 3A.*
- *The wedding cost an estimated $2 million. Living, 1B.*
- *What did Lady Di's dress look like? Living, 1B.*
- *Britain was a land of celebration, mostly. Living, 1B.*
- *The history of Great Britain's royal weddings. Living, 1B.*

Prince Charles kisses the hand of his bride, Diana, at Buckingham Palace, and poses with her for an official portrait.

Auto industry turns around, earns profits

DETROIT (AP) — This is shaping up as a disastrous sales year for American automakers, worse even than 1980.

But despite unrelentingly high interest rates that have kept many potential buyers at home and continuing pressure from foreign competitors, the U.S. makers have recorded a dramatic financial turnaround.

For the second quarter, they recorded an industrywide profit of $566.3 million, a huge jump from their $1.5 billion loss in the second quarter of 1980.

General Motors Corp. completed the latest round of quarterly earnings statements Monday, reporting a $514.6 million profit for the second quarter, which ended June 30. Last week, Ford Motor Co. reported a surprising $60 million profit.

Chrysler Corp. earned $11.6 million, a paper-thin profit by industry standards but enough to push the company into the black for the first quarter since earning $43.1 million in the fourth quarter of 1978.

American Motors Corp., with a $19.9 million loss, was the only U.S. maker in the red, but the performance was an improvement on the $84.9 million deficit recorded a year earlier.

For the first six months of this year, the automakers have cut combined losses to $34.3 million — down from a whopping $1.96 billion in the first half of last year.

See AUTO, 15B

O'Neill virtually concedes tax battle

WASHINGTON (AP) — House Speaker Thomas P. O'Neill Jr., saying Democratic congressmen have been "engulfed by telephone calls" urging support for President Reagan's tax cut, today all but conceded the long-awaited showdown.

In his gloomiest assessment yet of Democratic chances, O'Neill declined to repeat his earlier prediction that Democrats would defeat Reagan's tax plan and substitute a proposal of their own.

"All I can say is we are experiencing a blitz . . . a telephone blitz like this nation has never seen," O'Neill said. "It's had a devastating effect."

But deputy White House press secretary Larry Speakes said today that an administration count of the likely vote in the House showed the outcome "too close to call."

He said White House aides worked "into the wee hours this morning" on the issue and continued calls to members until 10 p.m. yesterday.

"It is right down to the wire," Speakes said. "We feel we have gotten a number of people in the last 24 hours. We feel the momentum going our way."

The spokesman said Reagan would make telephone calls "to reach maybe two dozen fence-sitters" during the day, although only one member of Congress was scheduled to visit the president.

A victory in the Democratic-controlled House would give the president a double-barrelled triumph. The Senate was poised today to approve his three-year, 25-percent tax cut.

O'Neill said Reagan's forces seemed to be making inroads among moderate and liberal House Democrats as well as the conservatives who have supported him in earlier floor victories on budget cuts.

"The Congress of the United States always responds to the will of the people and because (members) have been engulfed by telephone calls, they may think (the president's tax plan) is the will of the people," O'Neill said.

O'Neill said he and other Democratic leaders would work hard right up to the time of the vote later today to try to keep Democrats from defecting from their own two-year, 15-percent tax cut.

Reagan's appeal for Americans to contact their congressmen and senators jammed Capitol switchboards yesterday with tens of thousands of calls and generated a five-fold increase in telegram traffic.

O'Neill accused the White House of making "all kinds of deals" to win Democratic votes and of mobilizing large corporations to get their employees to call wavering congressmen.

See O'NEILL, Back Page

McClain: 'Kids got death sentence'

By KEITH GEORGE

"No punishment on Earth could ever bring my kids back," Cheryl McClain said today as a jury prepared to consider murder charges against her former husband.

McClain, 33, now of Conklin, indicated the depth of her feelings against Chester M. Chandler Jr. when she said she did not even want to discuss what she thinks his punishment should be.

Last week McClain told the jury how she listened, bound, gagged and bleeding from stab wounds, as Chandler talked to her children Mark, 10, and Bonnie, 5, while he stabbed them to death last Oct. 8.

"My children got the maximum punishment, and for nothing," she said. "They didn't do anything wrong, and they are dead."

McClain agreed to talk with a reporter in the courtroom after being assured her remarks would not be published until the case went to the jury.

"I wouldn't want to do anything to interfere with the trial after all this time," she said today, a few minutes before a court clerk announced opening of the 12th day of the murder trial.

After hearing explanations of the law from Broome County Court Judge Robert W. Coutant, jurors were taken to lunch under guard of court officers sworn to keep them from outside influences. They were expected to be sequestered until reaching a verdict.

"None of this, whether he's guilty of manslaughter or murder, is going to bring my kids back," said McClain. She was divorced from Chandler about a year before he broke into her home on on Gorman Road, Kirkwood, attacked her and killed the children.

Dressed in a white sweater and dark slacks, she sat on a wooden bench in the courtroom, near the jury box, with a sister, other family members and friends.

McClain said she believes state lawmakers should restore the charge of first-degree murder and the death penalty for killing of people other than police.

See McCLAIN, 3A

Cheryl McClain
...fights for harsher laws

Fugitive Bani-Sadr flees Iran for France, asylum

PARIS (AP) — Abolhassan Bani-Sadr, Iran's fugitive ex-president, escaped to France today in an Iranian military plane.

The French government granted the 47-year-old Bani-Sadr political asylum. Tehran Radio later reported that the Iranian government officially demanded his extradition in a request presented to the French Embassy in Tehran.

Disguised by having shaved off his mustache, Bani-Sadr landed in an Iranian Air Force 707 jet at the Evreux military air base 60 miles west of Paris at 4:30 a.m. After being given political asylum, he was driven to his daughter's apartment in a Paris suburb.

Pars, the official Iranian news agency, claimed that the plane was hijacked, but details of the escape were not clear.

Bani-Sadr told reporters outside his daughter's apartment house his flight was organized by the Mujahedeen Khalq, the Islamic Marxist guerrilla group that has become the

See BANI-SADR, Back Page

Inside

A Gannett Newspaper
Vol. 78 No. 107

WEATHER: Partly cloudy tonight. Partly sunny tomorrow, high in the mid-70s. Details, Page 2A.

SS cuts adequate, actuaries say, but administration wants more

WASHINGTON (AP) — Benefit cuts already voted by Congress are enough to keep Social Security solvent through the end of the decade unless the economy falters, the system's actuaries say.

Nevertheless, the Reagan administration wants further reductions.

Only if the economy deteriorates would the combined trust funds run short of cash to pay benefits during the next five years, the actuaries say.

Social Security's trustees warned Congress in their annual report July 6 that even under a moderate economic projection the trust funds could become insolvent by 1985. The trustees said that only under optimistic assumptions could the trust funds get by, and then only by a thin margin.

But those projections ignored the impact of Social Security cuts voted by both houses of Congress, including plans to wipe out payments to college students and the $122 minimum monthly benefit.

The actuaries found that those cuts, which would save at least $22 billion by 1986, would keep the trust fund in the black until 1989 under moderate economic projections, Deputy Social Security Commissioner Robert J. Myers said yesterday.

See SOCIAL, Back Page

July 29, 1981: A story inside the paper pegged the wedding's cost at $2 million. *Courtesy Rudy Bystrak*

LIFESTYLE
Short hairdos in style for this summer—1B

LOCAL
$100 donation lets dog come home again—5A

SPORTS
Whalers fire Cunniff as hockey coach—48A

Sun-Bulletin

Friday
May 25, 1984
2 Sections
Binghamton, N.Y.
13902
A Gannett newspaper
35¢ newsstand

FINAL

SUNNY

House OKs aid for El Salvador

Cutoff of funds to CIA-backed guerrillas in Nicaragua also approved — 2A

Maiden ride KEITH HITCHENS PHOTO

Binghamton Mayor Juanita M. Crabb and Ryan Whalen, 3, of 30 McNamara St., Binghamton, yesterday take a ride on the newly-refurbished carrousel at Recreation Park. **Story, page 3A.**

Unemployment rate in Tier falls to 32-month low—37A

Fowler's appraisal increased after sale to Binghamton

Page 3A

Greene suspends 2 teachers accused of serving drinks

Page 3A

Judge settles suit in Stouffer's fire

Page 2A

The inside story:

Check paid for church's pump — 4A
Prison escapees sought in Tier — 4A
Municipal investment curb eyed—5A
Congress raises debt ceiling — 12A
Boycotters plan own Games — 13A
Hall leads Corning Classic — 48A

David Kennedy
. . . autopsy released

RFK's son's death ruled accidental

Page 2A

May 25, 1984: This was the final tabloid version of The Sun-Bulletin. The broadsheet version and The Evening Press merged in October 1985.

The Sun-Bulletin

Binghamton, New York 13902/Founded in 1822

FINAL

THURSDAY
September 13, 1984
Three sections
35 cents newsstand

SUNNY
High: 75
Low: 60
Details on Page 2A

SPORTS

Rozelle snubs USFL teams/1B

Mets' Gooden whiffs 16/1B

USA icers fall to Sweden/1B

SCORES

AMERICAN LEAGUE
Toronto 2, New York 1
Baltimore 3, Detroit 1
Chicago 4, Oakland 2
Boston 5, Milwaukee 4
Kansas City 3, Minnesota 2
Cleveland 7, California 1
Texas 8, Seattle 1

NATIONAL LEAGUE
Chicago 11, Montreal 5
New York 2, Pittsburgh 0
Philadelphia 3, St. Louis 1, 1st
Philadelphia 6, St. Louis 5, 2nd
Cincinnati 7, San Francisco 4
Atlanta 4, Houston 1
Los Angeles 8, San Diego 1

The fury of Diana Waves pound the shore near Wrightsville Beach, N.C., as Hurricane Diana, stalled just off the coast, causes giant tides that damaged the pier railing in background. The first storm fatality was reported yesterday. **Story on Page 11A.**

AP PHOTO

Ferraro, Pa. bishop feud on religion/4A

BUSINESS

UAW says GM stalling/16B

STATE

Bottle bill has birthday/8A

Reagan cites Tier's lesson to the nation

By BARRY KATZ
Staff Writer

President Reagan, speaking before an estimated 25,000 people at an overflow political rally in Endicott yesterday, vowed to block Democratic presidential candidate Walter Mondale's plan for tax increases and offered, instead, the promise of tax simplification.

Reagan also offered a mild endorsement for House candidate Constance E. Cook of Ithaca, who expects her campaign to be boosted by the Reagan visit, and much stronger praise for state Senate Majority Leader Warren M. Anderson, R-Binghamton, who is running for re-election.

The president also pledged to commit the necessary campaign resources to carry New York in the November election — a signal to state Republicans who had worried since last month that national campaign strategists had written off New York.

"We're in New York to win," Reagan said.

The visit is expected to help the Broome County Republican organization by attracting new campaign workers and increasing Republican voter registration.

Reagan's speech, meanwhile, brought scathing criticism from Gov. Mario M. Cuomo, who spoke last night at a Democratic fund-raising dinner in Johnson City.

Cuomo blasted Reagan for boasting about 6 million new jobs created in the last 20 months but failing to mention the number of jobs lost; for talking about the U.S. military victory in Grenada but failing to mention the military debacle in Lebanon; and for bragging about the Reagan administration's crackdown on crime but failing to mention Reagan-initiated budget cuts in drug education programs.

Reagan arrived in Broome County shortly after 3 p.m., then toured IBM-Endicott for a look at facilities for manufacturing the company's most advanced computers. The president arrived about 4:30 p.m. at Ty Cobb Stadium, behind Union-Endicott High School.

Endicott police estimated the tightly packed crowd at nearly 25,000; U.S. Secret Service officials reported the crowd at about 40,000. Hundreds more were left standing outside the gates.

By 1 p.m. lines of people four, five and six abreast, all waiting to enter the stadium, snaked the entire length of the high school and beyond.

Full coverage on Pages 3A-5A.

When room ran out inside, the crowd was asked to press closer.

Endicott Police Department estimates of 200 police personnel — some in helicopters, some on horseback, others perched on nearby rooftops — patrolled the stadium area and IBM vicinity.

Reagan, who spoke for nearly 20 minutes, keyed his speech on the economic transition of Broome County's "Valley of Opportunity" from a shoe industry economy to one dominated by high-technology industries.

Reagan renewed his attack on the tax side of Mondale's plan to reduce the federal deficit by raising taxes and cutting spending.

"We're not going to enact their tax plan, not on your life," Reagan said. "Our pledge is for tax simplification to make the system more fair, and easier to understand, so we can bring yours and everybody's income tax rates further down, not up."

At the conclusion of Reagan's speech, volunteers released thousands of red, white and blue helium-filled balloons that rose above the Susquehanna River and floated into the southwest sky.

After being hugged by the Union-Endicott "tiger" mascot and thanking students for a gift football jersey, Reagan remarked that the school's fight song, played during the rally, was the same one played by his high school in Dixon, Ill., many years ago.

JOHN BOHN PHOTO

Republican Sen. Warren M. Anderson of Binghamton reaches to shake hands as President Reagan approaches the podium for his speech at Ty Cobb Stadium yesterday.

Cuomo says Young made outrageous requests

By PHIL FAIRBANKS
Binghamton Bureau

Gov. Mario M. Cuomo presented his case on the federal deficit yesterday and, in the same breath, chastized Broome County Executive Carl S. Young for making unrealistic demands on the state.

"It's an outrage," the governor said.

He was referring to Young's claim that the governor's veto of legislation to restore a Home Relief bonus would cost Broome County nearly $1 million over the next two years, and could result in a budget deficit and an increase in county property taxes.

Cuomo told Democrats at the Fountains Pavilion in Johnson City that the state has increased aid to counties from $800 million a year to more than $1.2 billion. The increase includes a state takeover of local Medicaid costs.

"We made them rich and now they have this endless need," Cuomo said. "I'm disappointed with Carl. I really thought he was better than that. I thought he could count, I thought he could remember."

The governor used Young's statement to demonstrate the need to evaluate requests at budget time. He compared the state to the federal government and characterized the national recovery as a "credit card" recovery — borrowing now and paying back later.

"If I went home now to Queens and with my credit card put a new roof on the house, got Matilda a new fur coat, put new asphalt on the driveway and a new Buick on the asphalt and then called Matilda in and said, 'Now, don't you feel better than you did last year.' The problem comes when you have to pay the bill."

On other issues, Cuomo:

- Said he could not foresee any circumstance which could prevent the opening of the contaminated Binghamton State Office Building, which has been closed since a 1981 transformer fire contaminated the 18-story building with dioxin and other toxic chemicals.
- Opposed state assistance for a proposed stadium in downtown Binghamton. He said the stadium is not a serious enough need to warrant state money.
- Supported the concept of a cut in state taxes but would not commit himself to a reduction.
- Criticized the Republican-controlled state Senate for its support of a bail-out of the Long Island Lighting Co., owner of the Shoreham nuclear plant. "The Republicans believe we should have socialism for free enterprise," he said.

Real story shows chucklin' is good for America

By RICK MARSI
Staff Writer

Maybe you were busy making a living yesterday. Maybe crowds make you nervous. Or maybe you just got busy cleaning out bird houses and forgot the prez was in town.

For whatever reason, if you missed Broome County's biggest body count since Al Boscov rose tall in the saddle and declared Court Street resurrected, all is not lost. This reporter was on the spot, at Union-Endicott's Ty Cobb Stadium, digging out facts you need to know.

All afternoon — to the unamplified strains of Warriors, Blue Devils, Black Knights, Golden Sabers and other tuba-toting teens — I battled big-shot national reporters for the real story on the president's day in Bingaman . . . Bingington . . . Bingerville . . . Whatever.

SUNSPOT

When I say the *real* story, I mean it.

The good stuff — the inside dope secret service personnel tried to stifle — goes beyond the man, beyond the myth. It's the guts of America. Here it is:

- With a zest for life that would have made Ed McMahon's heart swell, Bill Flynn, master of ceremonies for the presidential rally, said, "Hoooooooo" (as in garden hoe) 32 times.

Every time a high school band stopped playing, Bill stepped to the mike and said, "Hoooooooo".

"Why does he do that?" a youngster in the bleachers asked his mother (the kid was way too young for the Carson show). "To get people excited," his mother said.

This reporter heard alot of people saying that Bill Flynn is good for America.

- Ronald Reagan and state Senate Majority Leader Warren M. Anderson are good buddies. Andy introduced the prez and said the prez was great. The prez turned right around and said Andy was great.

Then, while Endicott Mayor Marion Corino waxed proud about the valley of opportunity, Andy whispered something important in the president's ear. Darned if the president didn't whisper back. He chuckled, too. Andy chuckled back.

And then, for a sweet, short second — like good ol' boys swappin' lies and swattin' flies — they just sat there, Andy and the prez, grinnin' and chucklin'.

Chucklin' is good for America, this reporter heard many people say.

- Secret service people wear black loafers. This is amazing because the rest of the world wears loafers that are sort of reddish brown.

Lack of space prohibits a more detailed description of secret service attire. To view a decent facsimile, visit a funeral or other sad occasion.

- The prez has charisma that just won't quit. "I showered three times before I came, I was so excited," said one middle-aged woman, as the president's motorcade pulled into view.

People all around said showers are good for America.

KEITH HITCHENS PHOTO

Lisa Tomik, mascot of Union-Endicott High School's football cheerleaders, leads cheers for President Reagan yesterday.

Reagan saw IBM but not IBMers

By JEFF PLATSKY
Business Editor

Like a good student, President Ronald Reagan obediently trailed his guide through parts of IBM-Endicott yesterday. But when it all ended the president acknowledged that much of the lesson, understandably, was lost.

"I wish I could say I understood everything I've seen," Reagan said, as he departed building 47 of the huge IBM complex in Endicott.

With that comment he was off, without mingling with or addressing the 80 employees who had gathered to see him. After a wave of the hand, he was whisked off to a rally at Union-Endicott High School's Ty Cobb Stadium, about one-quarter mile from the Endicott IBM plant.

His 30-minute visit to buildings 46 and 47 was over. He had seen the type of high technology that has spurred much of Broome County's development over the century.

The president's trip through IBM was an extremely abbreviated version of the new employee tour, but Patrick A. Toole, IBM Systems Technology division president, managed to pack nearly a century's worth of company history into a compact presentation. It was complete with displays that were hauled from the company's Heritage exhibit across the street.

Toole told President Reagan of the Endicott plant's rich history. Generally, Reagan's face remained expressionless throughout the tour.

For the event, IBM converted a cafeteria into an exhibit hall. All but essential personnel were cleared from the two buildings that the president visited.

Reagan arrived at the plant with U.S. Sen. Alfonse D'Amato and Endicott Mayor Marion L. Corino at 3:43 p.m., only slightly behind schedule.

Before the president's arrival, many employees milled about the hallways, waiting for the president to arrive. Workers who had hoped to catch a glimpse of Reagan were disappointed. The areas that he visited were shielded from onlookers by curtains. Yards of the dark blue material was used throughout the building.

Security, which is always tight at IBM, was extra tough for the president's visit. Overtime was seemingly of no concern yesterday.

Near the end of the 30-minute tour, Reagan was asked to test a computer that recently had been completed. "You sure you want me to do this?" Reagan quipped. "If it doesn't work, we're both in trouble," Toole said.

With a touch of a button, paper from the high-speed printer came flying from the top of the machine with the message, "Mr. President, Thanks for coming."

INSIDE

September 13, 1984: Front pages about President Reagan's visit were popular keepsakes among our readers. *Courtesy Dolly Escovar*

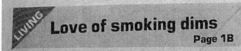

LIVING Love of smoking dims Page 1B

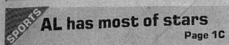

SPORTS AL has most of stars Page 1C

The Reagan visit

A memento from us

The Evening Press joins thousands of Broome County residents in commemorating President Reagan's unforgettable visit yesterday to Endicott — the first such trip here by an in-office U.S. chief executive in nearly 50 years — by publishing an 8-page keepsake section today.

It is section D of today's newspaper and it represents the collective effort of a staff of editors, reporters and photographers who were "on location" from the minute Reagan arrived at Edwin A. Link Field at 3:10 p.m. until Air Force One left about 2½ hours later to carry the president back to Washington.

Four Sections **FINAL EDITION**

THURSDAY

Sept. 13, 1984

The Evening Press

Binghamton, N.Y. 35¢ Newsstand

World

THOUSANDS FLEE from villages around Mt. Mayon in the Philippines as the volcano roars with a series of explosions. Page 2A.

EL SALVADOR'S PRESIDENT says he is imposing new regulations to halt abuses by security forces. Page 6A.

VIETNAM WILL RELEASE prisoners held since the end of the Vietnam war, but only if the U.S. takes all of them. Page 14A.

Nation

SEN. JESSE HELMS is blocking efforts to break a stalemate over ratifying a treaty to outlaw genocide. Page 3A.

A HOUSE MEMBER says the EPA is flouting federal law by delaying a list of toxic waste sites posing imminent threats to health. Page 3A.

WALTER F. MONDALE is back in the Deep South trying to shake Ronald Reagan's hold on voters. Page 4A.

SENIOR CITIZENS are taking to the streets in about 90 cities to demonstrate their concern for the health of Medicare. Page 5A.

State

THE STATE IS NOT letting political contributions influence the way it rents office space, a spokesman says. Page 7A.

NEW YORK'S bottle deposit law celebrates its first anniversary with evidence of cleaner streets but headaches for some people. Page 13A.

FOR THE SECOND TIME time this year, a judge orders former state Sen. Vander L. Beatty of Brooklyn to go to prison. Page 13A.

A NEW REPORT exaggerates instances of corruption in New York City's school system, Chancellor Nathan Quinones says. Page 13A.

Local

BROOME COUNTY EXECUTIVE Carl S. Young returns some criticism, charging Gov. Mario M. Cuomo with manipulating figures on state assistance to Broome and other counties. Page 11A.

FOR MAYOR JAMES B. MCNULTY, yesterday's campaign stop in Scranton, Pa., by Democratic vice presidential nominee Geraldine Ferraro was a call to a mission of sorts on the subject of abortion. Page 11A.

MORRIS GITLITZ, a prominent Binghamton lawyer and community leader for more than 40 years, dies at his Binghamton home. Page 11A.

Business

CONSUMERS RUSH to the banks for new car loans as the nation's installment credit surged by $7.1 billion in July. Page 15A

INTEREST RATES will rise by 2.4 percent by next spring because of the rising national deficit, a major economic forecasting consulting company said. Page 15A.

Sports

THE AMERICAN LEAGUE is on the verge of dominating as the NL did in the 1960s and '70s, a commentary. Page 1C.

METS PITCHER Dwight Gooden nails down the major-league rookie strikeout record, with his 16 last night against the Cardinals giving him 251 for the season. Page 1C.

BROOME COUNTY'S high school football teams take to the road in their openers tomorrow night. Page 1C.

Weather

CLOUDY TONIGHT and tomorrow with a 40 percent chance of showers, low around 60, high 70 to 75. Page 2A.

Tomorrow

COLUMNIST ROBERT SAMUELSON says higher-priced U.S. steel, caused by import restrictions, is making a lot of people angry. Commentary Page.

· A Gannett Newspaper ·
Vol. 81 No. 139

Inside

If you have a story idea, question or comment regarding national, state or world news, call News Editor Rodney Lee at 798-1184 between 7 a.m. and 2 p.m. For comments and questions regarding editorials, call acting Editorial Page Editor Thomas N. Tobin at 798-1110 between 9 a.m. and 5 p.m.

Reagan's foray to Endicott raises Republicans' morale

Cuomo: President is beatable

By PHIL FAIRBANKS
Binghamton Bureau

Gov. Mario M. Cuomo likes to compare the presidential campaign to a trial: The case against the Republicans is winnable but the Democrats must try it correctly to beat Ronald Reagan in November.

Gov. Cuomo

"If it's picture to picture, he'll beat us by 20 points," Cuomo said during a visit to Broome County yesterday. He arrived just minutes after Reagan ended a campaign tour of Endicott.

To beat the Republicans, Cuomo thinks the Democrats should avoid the Reagan image and concentrate instead on the Reagan record, emphasizing the federal deficit and the death of American soldiers in Lebanon.

"The polls don't mean a whole lot at this stage," he said during a press conference at the Fountains Pavilion in Johnson City. "They mean that Walter Mondale and Geraldine Ferraro haven't gotten the American public to think about the deficit, haven't gotten them to think about Lebanon, gotten them to think about the next four years."

The Democrats, Cuomo said, must get Reagan to tell the whole story of his first term in office. They must get the president to talk about the 1982 recession, high interest rates and unemployment.

He described Reagan as a "perfectly packaged candidate" with a unique ability to dodge issues and still appear credible.

Mondale, he said, is the right individual to make the case against Reagan and that the seven weeks remaining before the election is sufficient time to get the message to the American public.

"We don't focus early," he said. "The American people are not keen about American campaigns and subtle issues. They don't like spending time figuring out Lebanon or deficits. And they usually don't do it until the very end."

See CUOMO, 10A

• Gov. Cuomo will be in the media spotlight during his speech today at Notre Dame University in Indiana. Page 7A.
• Broome County Executive Carl S. Young hits back at Cuomo on state aid. Page 11A.

A campaigning President Reagan basks in the warmth of the reception he got yesterday at Endicott's Ty Cobb Stadium.

By BARRY KATZ

In one brief sweep through Endicott yesterday, President Ronald Reagan breathed new life into a less-than-visible come-from-behind congressional campaign, boosted morale among state Republicans concerned about their national status and injected the county Republican organization with more enthusiasm than it's seen in years.

The effects of Reagan's visit — a tour of IBM-Endicott and a speech at a jam-packed political rally at Union-Endicott High School — are likely to be long-term.

Local Republicans already have identified a corps of new volunteers, and indications are that more people are willing to register Republican, party officials said.

For his part, Reagan — the first president to visit Broome County in 48 years — managed to get in a few jabs at his own opponent, Democrat Walter F. Mondale. Reagan promised to block Mondale's plan to increase taxes as part of Mondale's strategy to reduce the federal deficit. All without mentioning Mondale by name.

Yet for all the hoopla, Reagan was sometimes halting in his delivery.

In general, the crowd responded in kind, appearing unusually subdued given the nature of the event — the first visit to Broome County by an in-office president since 1936. While applause interrupted his speech about 35 times, the clapping was not sustained. His welcome applause lasted about two minutes.

Reagan's endorsement of congressional candidate Constance E. Cook was not nearly as hearty as the praise he lavished on state Senate Majority Leader Warren M. Anderson, R-Binghamton. Cook disagrees with Reagan

See REAGAN, 10A

• Mondale concedes he trails in the Deep South but predicts "we're going to start gaining." Page 4A.
• Vice President Bush says blacks' concerns about President Reagan should be eased by steps taken by the administration. Page 4A.
• Reagan's presidency hasn't been for everyone, despite what he may say; Gov. Cuomo's vision of what defines our "valley of opportunity" is more sensible and more believable than Reagan's. Editorials, Page 8A.
• The president's daughter Maureen is coming to Broome County. Page 10A.
• Polls show Reagan in command. Page 10A.

Pope urges ecumenism, brotherhood in the world

MONCTON, New Brunswick (AP) — Pope John Paul II, in a corner of Canada still pained by the memories of religious bitterness, pleaded today for brotherhood and an ecumenical spirit in the world.

"May the Holy Spirit guide us . . . towards full unity!" he declared in a passionate call for progress toward Christian ecumenism.

The pontiff, on the fifth day of a 12-day Canadian tour, paid tribute to the tragedy-tested faith of New Brunswick's French Acadian people, likening it to the endurance of his Polish countrymen through centuries of suffering.

He was speaking to Roman Catholic clergy gathered in Moncton's granite cathedral, Our Lady of the Assumption.

Around him, a series of stained-glass windows depicted the sad history of the Acadian people, French settlers who were deported from eastern Canada by the English during the 18th century French-English wars.

They were exiled to the American South and other distant colonies. Eventually many returned, but families had been separated, homesteads seized and the Roman Catholic Church suppressed by Anglicans of English descent.

In the past century, the French Catholic culture has revived in New Brunswick, half of whose 700,000 people are Catholic. Church officials say 60 percent of the province's Catholics practice their religion regularly — a relatively high level.

Pope John Paul II meets Catholic educators yesterday in St. John's, Newfoundland.

The pontiff flew to this rain-drenched city of 55,000 people after a one-day stop in Newfoundland. On his way to the cathedral, he rode past soaked but enthusiastic crowds.

His schedule here also included an outdoor Mass, before a flight tonight to Halifax, Nova Scotia.

In Newfoundland, the pope said parents have a "legitimate claim" to tax dollars to help pay the cost of religious schools.

In a major statement on religion and schools last night, the pope said society should "support with public funding those types of schools that correspond to the deepest aspirations of its citizens."

Diana rips Carolinas

WILMINGTON, N.C. (AP) — Hurricane Diana blasted into the Carolinas today with 110-mph winds and tides 10 feet above normal, ripping down a water tower, catching people who had left shelters off guard and sending whitecapped waves down flooded streets.

The state suffered "some very great damage," with the worst in Brunswick and New Hanover counties, said Gov. Jim Hunt, although details were sketchy because of the difficulty in reaching affected areas. He said he was asking President Reagan to declare the state a major disaster area.

The town of Southport had "been hurt and hurt bad," said Police Chief Bill Corey.

An estimated 75 percent of Carolina Power & Light Co.'s customers around Wilmington, or as many as 30,000 houses, were without power, the utility said. Flooding and debris blocked some access roads to coastal communities wthat were in the direct path of the storm.

No injuries were reported today, but one man died of a heart attack while trying to secure his house and a social services worker died in a traffic accident on his way to work as the storm rushed ashore.

The National Weather Service called Diana "the worst hurricane since Hazel" in the Cape Fear area. Hazel struck Oct. 5-18, 1954.

The highest sustained winds began easing after the storm moved over land, dropping to an estimated 75 mph at 11 a.m. today, down from Monday's 130 mph. Below 74 mph it would be downgraded to a tropical storm. It was moving west-northwest, producing gale-force winds as far south as North Myrtle Beach, S.C., where a state of emergency was declared.

At 11 a.m. today, radar showed the eye of the storm was 20 miles in diameter, not as well defined and barely moving, centered near latitude 34.1 north and longitude 78.3 west, about 30 miles southwest of Wilmington.

The first Atlantic hurricane of the season ended a day of indecisive spinning offshore when it suddenly charged the coast last night. The eye of the storm touched land at 1:15 a.m. today at Fort Fisher, south of Wilmington and across the Cape Fear River from Southport, the National Weather Service reported.

Many residents who had evacuated Tuesday returned yesterday, when the hurricane stalled off the coast, to survey damage to their homes and they were caught along with sightseers by the storm's lurch to land.

Ferraro probe to finish by election

WASHINGTON (AP) — The House ethics committee will complete its investigation of Rep. Geraldine A. Ferraro before the Nov. 6 presidential election, said a source knowledgeable about the probe.

The source said the inquiry into Ferraro's financial disclosure statements could be shelved if she amends the statements and provides the committee with data she has refused to give it over a six-year period.

The source noted that in its other disclosure case this year, the panel gave Rep. George Hansen, R-Idaho, the chance to amend his statements before it completed the process that led to Hansen's formal reprimand by the House on July 31.

The source made the comments yesterday after the ethics committee voted 12-0 to investigate allegations made against the Democratic vice-presidential candidate by the Washington Legal Foundation.

That conservative public interest law group charges that Ferraro violated the Ethics in Government Act by not revealing her husband's assets and liabilities on the required disclosure forms she has filed annually since coming to Congress in 1979.

The CBS Evening News, meanwhile, reported that the Justice Department has opened a preliminary investigation to determine if federal law was violated by Ferraro's request for an exemption from including details of her husband's finances in her House financial disclosure report.

The foundation also alleges that Ferraro failed to disclose information about herself, including more than $60,000 in capital gains and interest in 1978 and $2,962 in 1981 income from a real estate firm she owns with her husband, John Zaccaro.

• Ferraro's Scranton, Pa., campaign stop is a call to action for that city's mayor. Page 11A.

September 13, 1984: President Reagan's visit to Endicott dominated the front page of the Press. *Courtesy Dolly Escovar*

Anitec Fire on Clinton Street. The photo was taken from Route 17.
Courtesy Sharon Nieminski

INTERNATIONAL BUSINESS MACHINES

IBM lab building on North Street, 1983. *Courtesy Marlene Yacos*

4-34-1
WEST ENDICOTT
FIRE DEPARTMENT
DIST. 1

Fire department truck in a 75th anniversary parade in Endicott, 1981.
Courtesy Marlene Yacos

Binghamton's State Office Building was the scene of one of the world's first recognized indoor pollution disasters. In the pre-dawn hours of February 5, 1981, a fire in an electrical switch gear caused a small explosion that punctured a nearby electrical transformer. The transformer leaked oil containing polychlorinated biphenyls into the fire. The heat created a toxic soot that contained dioxins and dibenzofurans, two deadly chemicals, which was sucked throughout the building by the ventilation system. The building was closed for more than a decade and the cleanup cost more than it did to construct the building. Here, John Greenbaum, a substitute teacher with the Binghamton School District, poses outside the building five years after the incident, February 1986. *Press & Sun-Bulletin archives*

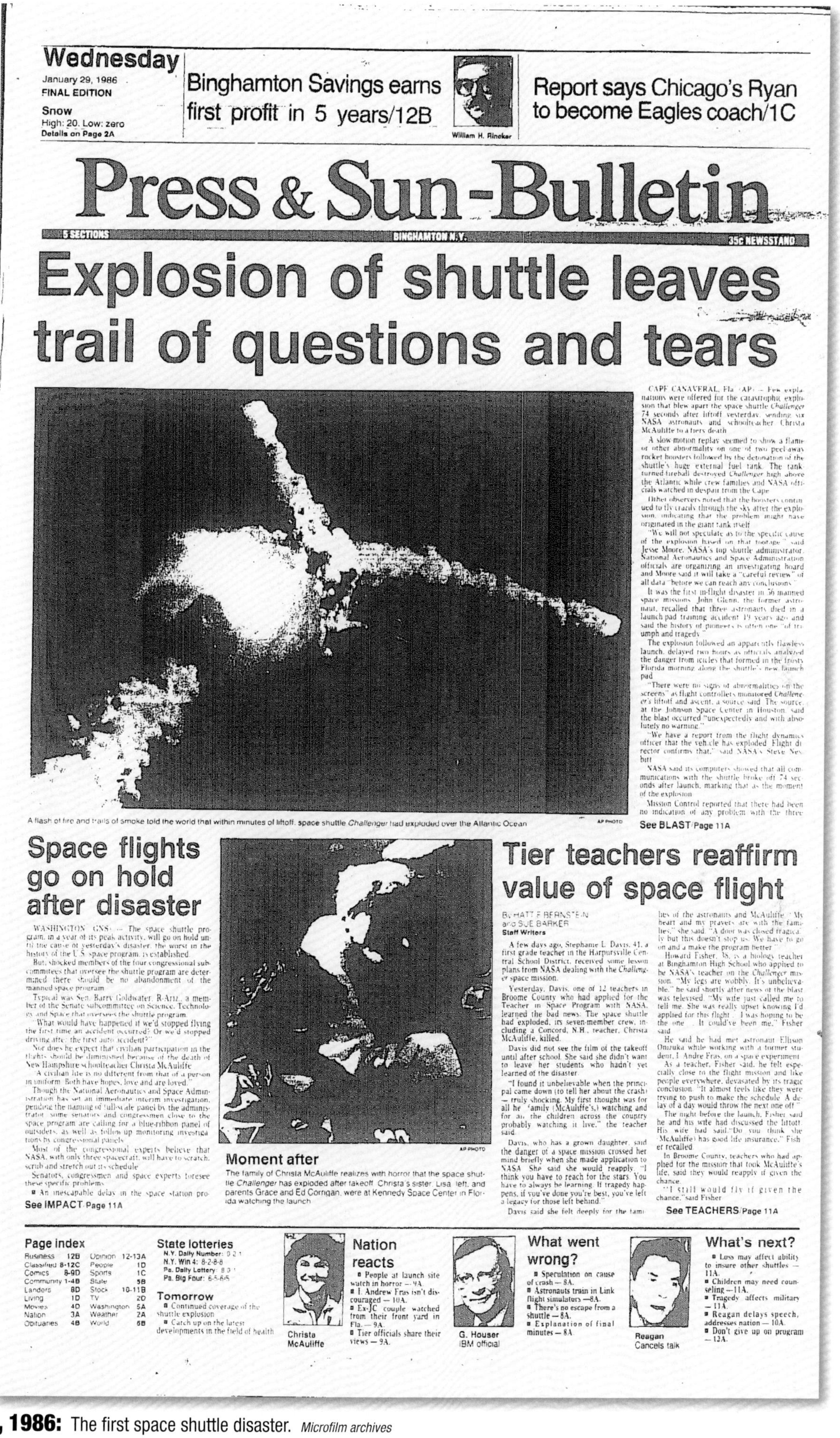

Wednesday

January 29, 1986
FINAL EDITION

Snow
High: 20. Low: zero
Details on Page 2A

Binghamton Savings earns first profit in 5 years/12B

William H. Rincker

Report says Chicago's Ryan to become Eagles coach/1C

Press & Sun-Bulletin

5 SECTIONS — BINGHAMTON N.Y. — 35c NEWSSTAND

Explosion of shuttle leaves trail of questions and tears

A flash of fire and trails of smoke told the world that within minutes of liftoff, space shuttle *Challenger* had exploded over the Atlantic Ocean — AP PHOTO

CAPE CANAVERAL, Fla. (AP) — Few explanations were offered for the catastrophic explosion that blew apart the space shuttle *Challenger* 74 seconds after liftoff yesterday, sending six NASA astronauts and schoolteacher Christa McAuliffe to a fiery death.

A slow-motion replay seemed to show a flame or other abnormality on one of two peel-away rocket boosters followed by the detonation of the shuttle's huge external fuel tank. The tank-turned-fireball destroyed *Challenger* high above the Atlantic while crew families and NASA officials watched in despair from the Cape.

Other observers noted that the boosters continued to fly crazily through the sky after the explosion, indicating that the problem might have originated in the giant tank itself.

"We will not speculate as to the specific cause of the explosion based on that footage," said Jesse Moore, NASA's top shuttle administrator. National Aeronautics and Space Administration officials are organizing an investigating board and Moore said it will take a "careful review" of all data "before we can reach any conclusions."

It was the first in-flight disaster in 56 manned space missions. John Glenn, the former astronaut, recalled that three astronauts died in a launch pad training accident 19 years ago and said the history of pioneers is often one "of triumph and tragedy."

The explosion followed an apparently flawless launch, delayed two hours as officials analyzed the danger from icicles that formed in the frosty Florida morning along the shuttle's new launch pad.

"There were no signs of abnormalities on the screens" as flight controllers monitored *Challenger's* liftoff and ascent, a source said. The source, at the Johnson Space Center in Houston, said the blast occurred "unexpectedly and with absolutely no warning."

"We have a report from the flight dynamics officer that the vehicle has exploded. Flight director confirms that," said NASA's Steve Nesbitt.

NASA said its computers showed that all communications with the shuttle broke off 74 seconds after launch, marking that as the moment of the explosion.

Mission Control reported that there had been no indication of any problem with the three

See BLAST/Page 11A

Space flights go on hold after disaster

WASHINGTON (GNS) — The space shuttle program, in a year of its peak activity, will go on hold until the cause of yesterday's disaster, the worst in the history of the U.S. space program, is established.

But, shocked members of the four congressional subcommitees that oversee the shuttle program are determined there should be no abandonment of the manned space program.

Typical was Sen. Barry Goldwater, R-Ariz., a member of the Senate subcommittee on Science, Technology and Space that oversees the shuttle program.

"What would have happened if we'd stopped flying the first time an accident occurred? Or we'd stopped driving after the first auto accident?"

Nor does he expect that civilian participation in the flights should be diminished because of the death of New Hampshire schoolteacher Christa McAuliffe.

"A civilian life is no different from that of a person in uniform. Both have hopes, love and are loved."

Though the National Aeronautics and Space Administration has set an immediate interim investigation, pending the naming of full-scale panel by the administrator, some senators and congressmen close to the space program are calling for a blue-ribbon panel of outsiders, as well as follow up monitoring investigations by congressional panels.

Most of the congressional experts believe that NASA, with only three spacecraft, will have to scratch, scrub and stretch out its schedule.

Senators, congressmen and space experts foresee these specific problems:

■ An inescapable delay in the space station pro-

See IMPACT/Page 11A

AP PHOTO

Moment after

The family of Christa McAuliffe realizes with horror that the space shuttle *Challenger* has exploded after takeoff. Christa's sister, Lisa, left, and parents Grace and Ed Corrigan, were at Kennedy Space Center in Florida watching the launch.

Tier teachers reaffirm value of space flight

By HATTIE BERNSTEIN and SUE BARKER
Staff Writers

A few days ago, Stephanie L. Davis, 41, a first grade teacher in the Harpursville Central School District, received some lesson plans from NASA dealing with the *Challenger* space mission.

Yesterday, Davis, one of 12 teachers in Broome County who had applied for the Teacher in Space Program with NASA, learned the bad news: The space shuttle had exploded, its seven-member crew, including a Concord, N.H., teacher, Christa McAuliffe, killed.

Davis did not see the film of the takeoff until after school. She said she didn't want to leave her students who hadn't yet learned of the disaster.

"I found it unbelievable when the principal came down (to tell her about the crash) — truly shocking. My first thought was for all he family (McAuliffe's,) watching and for all the children across the country probably watching it live," the teacher said.

Davis, who has a grown daughter, said the danger of a space mission crossed her mind briefly when she made application to NASA. She said she would reapply. "I think you have to reach for the stars. You have to always be learning. If tragedy happens, if you've done you're best, you've left a legacy for those left behind."

Davis said she felt deeply for the families of the astronauts and McAuliffe. "My heart and my prayers are with the families," she said. "A door was closed tragically but this doesn't stop us. We have to go on and a make the program better."

Howard Fisher, 38, is a biology teacher at Binghamton High School who applied to be NASA's teacher on the *Challenger* mission. "My legs are wobbly. It's unbelievable," he said shortly after news of the blast was televised. "My wife just called me to tell me. She was really upset knowing I'd applied for this flight ... I was hoping to be the one ... It could've been me," Fisher said.

He said he had met astronaut Ellison Onizuka while working with a former student, I. Andre Fras, on a space experiment.

As a teacher, Fisher said, he felt especially close to the flight mission and like people everywhere, devasated by its tragic conclusion. "It almost feels like they were trying to push to make the schedule. A delay of a day would throw the next one off."

The night before the launch, Fisher said he and his wife had discussed the liftoff. His wife had said:"Do you think she (McAuliffe) has good life insurance," Fisher recalled.

In Broome County, teachers who had applied for the mission that took McAuliffe's life, said they would reapply if given the chance.

"I still would fly if given the chance,"said Fisher.

See TEACHERS/Page 11A

State lotteries

N.Y. Daily Number: 9 2 1
N.Y. Win 4: 8-2-8-8
Pa. Daily Lottery: 8 3 1
Pa. Big Four: 6-5-6-5

Tomorrow

■ Continued coverage of the shuttle explosion
■ Catch up on the latest developments in the field of health

Christa McAuliffe

Nation reacts

■ People at launch site watch in horror — 9A.
■ I. Andrew Fras isn't discouraged — 10A.
■ Ex-JC couple watched from their front yard in Fla. — 9A.
■ Tier officials share their views — 9A.

G. Houser
IBM official

What went wrong?

■ Speculation on cause of crash — 8A.
■ Astronauts train in Link flight simulaturs —8A.
■ There's no escape from a shuttle — 8A.
■ Explanation of final minutes — 8A.

Reagan
Cancels talk

What's next?

■ Loss may affect ability to insure other shuttles — 11A.
■ Children may need counseling — 11A.
■ Tragedy affects military — 11A.
■ Reagan delays speech, addresses nation — 10A.
■ Don't give up on program — 12A.

January 29, 1986: The first space shuttle disaster. *Microfilm archives*

Tuesday
October 20, 1987
FINAL EDITION

Cloudy
High: 54. Low: 43
Details on Page 2A

Football Tuesday
Taylor runs 'em down/4C
- Second look at the NFL/4C
- College football notebook/5C

Giants' Lawrence Taylor

Yanks bump Piniella, hire you-know who/1C

Chuck Berry shares some of his secrets/1D

Press & Sun-Bulletin

4 SECTIONS | BINGHAMTON, N.Y. | 35¢ NEWSSTAND

508: Fear melts down market; impact is felt worldwide; IBM plunges $33 a share

Tier investors bury brokers; many sit tight

By JEFF PLATSKY
Business Editor

It was hard to tell where the action was on Endicott's Washington Avenue yesterday — off-track betting or the brokerage house across the street.

Individual investors were checking stock prices as always, but yesterday there seemed to be more of an urgency to their pecking on the quote machine. Curses were common as declines of 10 percent and more popped on the screen.

"This is the first time we've had a bigger crowd than OTB," said John E. Cheevers, the president of Cheevers, Hand & Angeline, 101 Washington Ave., Endicott.

Anxiety levels rose as the Dow Jones Industrial Average plunged. Frenzied investors were calling brokers as reports of the record-breaking dive spread.

"We've been on the phone all

See LOCAL/Page 5A

INVESTMENT BROKERS
IBM 103 1/4
DOW 508.57

CHUCK HAUPT PHOTO

John E. Cheevers, president of Cheevers, Hand and Angeline Inc., 101 Washington Ave., Endicott, displays the record-breaking dive in the Dow in the brokerage house's window. The market "is changing so fast it's hard to keep up," he said.

Dow drops a stunning 508 points

By BILL SING
Los Angeles Times

Fear and panic of historic proportions overwhelmed the stock market yesterday, forcing the Dow Jones industrial average to a stunning decline of 508.32 points, by far its biggest one-day plunge in history.

The Dow Jones average lost nearly a quarter of its value, nearly doubling the percentage drop on Oct. 28, 1929, a crash that preceded the Great Depression. With yesterday's plunge, the Dow has lost half the ground it has gained since the bull market got under way on Aug. 12, 1982, when the Dow stood at a mere 776.92.

Meanwhile, the frantic selling that swept through stock markets around the world yesterday continued with ferocity this morning as

See DOW/Page 8A

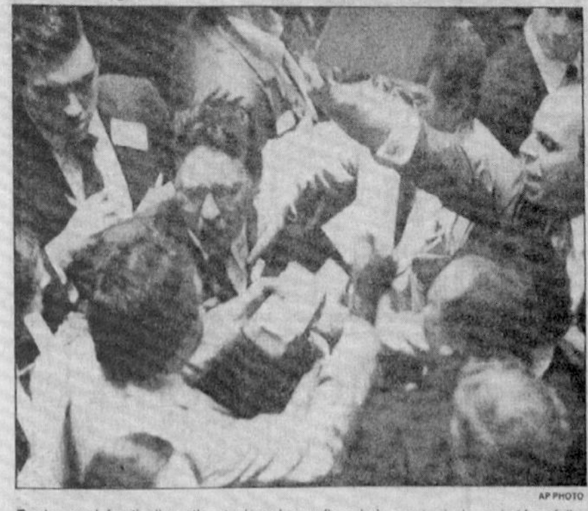
AP PHOTO

Traders work frantically on the stock exchange floor during yesterday's market free-fall.

What caused it, what it means to you, and what happens next?

Gannett News Service

QUESTION: What happened yesterday?

ANSWER: In simple terms, the stock market crashed. The most popular measure, the Dow Jones average of the stock value of 30 top industrial companies, plunged by 508 points, by far the biggest ever numerically and second-largest percentage-wise. The Dow finished the day at 1,738.74, the lowest it's been since early 1986. Other important indicators of market value also tumbled.

Q: What caused it?

A: A combination of factors. On the economic front there are fears of higher interest rates and higher inflation, worry about the value of the dollar, concern about the budget deficit and the trade deficit.

See ANSWERS/Page 8A

Full report inside

- Economy shudders as market hits bottom — Page 4A.
- Foreign markets follow the fall — Page 4A.
- There are still safe ways to invest — Page 4A.
- How to 'talk stock market' — Page 4A.
- N.Y. loses money fast — Page 5A.
- Tier foundations fear fewer donations — Page 5A.
- It's bad, but it's not 1929 — Page 5A.
- Gulf called spark that blasted stocks — Page 8B.

Local stocks sink

Stock	High	Low	Close	Change
Allied	35⅞	27½	28	-11⅛
Amer. Hm. Prod.	76¾	65½	65½	-11½
AT&T	32	20	23¼	-6¾
Nynex	68½	60	60¾	-11½
Brockway	52	47½	47½	-5⅝
Becton Dcknsn	51⅛	48¼	48¼	-7⅝
Chase Manhatn	35½	28	28	-8¾
Chemical NY	35⅝	25¾	25¾	-9⅞
Columbia Gas	44¾	37	37	-8¼
Contel	29⅜	26½	26¾	-5⅞
Dover	60	57	58⅜	-5¾
GAF	48	35	35	-17½
Gannett	41	31½	32¾	-10¼
GE	50	38¾	41½	-9¼
Hercules Inc.	49½	40	45¾	-9⅜
E.F. Hutton	28¾	23	23¾	-6⅝
IBM	130½	102	103½	-33
IrvingBank	61¾	48	48½	-16⅞
KMart	33	25	25	-9
MarineMidland	81½	78	78	-4
Merrill Lynch	32⅛	24	25	-8⅞
Morton-Thiokol	42¾	35½	35½	-11¾
NYSEG	24½	22½	22¾	-⅜
Pepsi Co	32½	27½	27½	-5¾
Piedmont	63⅜	60	60	-4
Proc. & Gamble	82¾	60	61	-23¼
Rymer	13½	12½	12½	-1¼
Sears	39⅜	30¾	30¾	-10¾
Singer	42¾	34¼	34¼	-10⅜
Union	7⅛	5¼	5¼	-2¼
USAir	38½	33⅛	33⅛	-6⅜

U.S. warns aggressors with attack on Iranian oil platform

Casualty risk considered in target choice

By JAMES GERSTENZANG
Los Angeles Times

WASHINGTON — President Reagan, calling the Navy attack on an Iranian offshore oil platform "aprudent yet restrained response"to the missile strike on a U.S.-flagged tanker last week, warned theTehran regime yesteday that theUnited States will not tolerate "unprovoked attacks" in the Persian Gulf.

"The United States has no desire for a military confrontation with Iran, but the government of Iran should be under no illusion abou-tour determination and ability to protect our ships and our interests," Reagan said, describing the intense barrage from four U.S. destroyers as "a lawful exercise of the right of self-defense."

Administration officials said the president had ruled out nearly adozen options presented to him, choosing one that would minimizethe risk to military personnel and Iranian civilians while sending a forceful signal of protest to Tehran.

"Our purpose was to demonstrate capability," a senior administration official said of the mission, which

See POLICY/Page 7A

Analysts say U.S. commits to stay in gulf

By RICHARD WHITMIRE
Gannett News Service

WASHINGTON — The latest swap of attacks with Iran makes it nearly impossible for the U.S. Navy to step out of the Persian Gulf conflict in the near future.

"There's no way the U.S. can leave this area without giving Iran an unacceptable victory," said Anthony Cordesman, a Middle East arms analyst, "unless Iran can be brought to a cease-fire (with Iraq)."

Privately, Navy Secretary James Webb has pushed for a flexible Persian Gulf strategy: assembling ships for a quick show of power and then leaving. For Webb, the current situ-

ANALYSIS

ation is approaching a worst-case scenario: Iran enjoys the tactical advantage of choosing when and where to attack, and the United States is locked into maintaining its escort service and responding to attacks.

The Iranians, for example, could continue to fire Silkworm missiles

See STRATEGY/Page 7A

State lotteries

N.Y. Daily Number: 0-8-5
N.Y. Win 4: 6-1-7-9
N.Y. Cash 40: 1-14-23-25-32-35
N.Y. Win-10: 4-8-10-15-16-18-20-24
30-31-33-35-42-44-54-55-56-58-78-80
Pa. Daily Lottery: 0-2-0
Pa. Lotto: 23-10-11-06-02-25 **Alt** 24

Page index

Donald Woomer and Linda Despot are all smiles.

Man, girlfriend to share $46 million with wife

By BRAD BUMSTED
Gannett News Service

HARRISBURG, Pa. — Flashing a thumbs-up sign, Donald R. Woomer Sr., a self-employed plasterer, and his live-in companion Linda K. Despot, a bookkeeper, collected a $1.4 million check yesterday — the first annual installment of their $46 million jackpot, the largest lottery prize ever in the United States.

"It's unreal," said Despot, holding 46 roses — one each for the $46 million won in last Wednesday's "Super 7" drawing. "Super," said Woomer.

Though he lives with Despot, Woomer is

SUNSPOT/The lighter side of the news

still married. When asked whether his wife will share the winnings, he said, "I imagine so." His wife could not be reached for comment yesterday.

Woomer kissed the check handed to him by a state lottery official.

Woomer, 55, and Despot, 37, said they chose their lucky number using a combination of family birthdays and random numbers. Woomer purchased the winning ticket Oct. 13, Despot's birthday, at a Sheetz Store, a convenience store in Hollidaysburg. It was one of 25 tickets he purchased.

They plan to spend the money together and will "do some traveling and help our families," Woomer said. Asked how long they'll remain together, Despot said: "25 years for sure." The remainder of the money will come in 25 annual installments.

"A state of shock," is how Despot described their reaction after finding out they held the winning ticket.

But both Despot and Woomer appeared

See WINNERS/Page 8A

TO SUBSCRIBE TO THE PRESS & SUN-BULLETIN, CALL 607-798-1161

October 20, 1987: On a day when billions evaporated in the stock market, a Pennsylvania pair took the first installment on what was the largest lottery winning ever. *Courtesy Rudy Bystrak*

Thursday
June 2, 1988
FINAL EDITION
Partly sunny
High: 67. Low: 45
Details on Page 2A

Consumer Thursday

Tasters are sweet on strawberry-filled cereal/1D

- Gas water heaters save money
- All-wheel drive cars find a niche

Pistons beat Boston /1C

Vestal teen wins school post/3B

Press & Sun-Bulletin

4 SECTIONS — BINGHAMTON, N.Y. — 35c NEWSSTAND

Mall gets early support from city council

Thomas C. Wilmot
President of Wilmorite

By STEVEN N. LEVINE
Staff Writer

The $87.5 million mall proposed for downtown Binghamton appears likely to receive a better reception from city council than did Binghamton Mayor Juanita M. Crabb's plan for a baseball stadium.

Interviews with seven of the nine council members show general support for the proposal, which needs formal approval by council this month to meet a deadline to apply for federal financial assistance.

The nine council members were briefed this week by Crabb, who yesterday made public tentative plans for a four-department-store mall that would feature 150 smaller retail stores, a convention center and an office tower.

The announcement — which did not spell out in detail financial plans or times for construction — came at city hall during an almost festive ceremony, complete with pink lemonade and iced tea.

The shopping district's developer, Wilmorite Inc. of Rochester, will bring Dey Brothers department store to downtown to anchor the south end of the mall, said Thomas C. Wilmot, Wilmorite president. The Rochester development firm is confident the proposed retail center, with a planned 1990 opening, will be successful. It will be the first time the firm has built in an urban setting, he said.

Wilmorite is required to contribute $60 million to the project under an agreement signed with the city last month. The same contract obli-

See MALL/Page 10A

City shops for shopping mall

- Funding may prove to be the sticking point for the proposed city mall — 4B.
- Dey Brothers is described as a "moderate to better" department store — 1B.
- Reactions from downtown merchants range from wildly enthusiastic to skeptical — 4B.
- Owners of buildings that may be demolished express anger and curiosity — Page 1B.
- Holiday-Inn Arena not yet committed to a conference center — 5B.
- Downtown proposals have city council members fighting one month, joining forces the next — 4B.
- Map shows the location of the proposed downtown mall — 1B.

Andy leaves powerful post, sets off political scrambling

NELL SEILER PHOTO

Sen. Warren M. Anderson sits back in his Albany office yesterday after surprising friends and colleagues with his decision to retire.

City councilman Libous sets sights on the job

By E.J. CONZOLA II
Staff Writer

Republican leaders in the Southern Tier barely waited for Senate Majority Leader Warren M. Anderson's retirement announcement yesterday to settle on a candidate to replace him.

And almost as fast, the list of potential Democratic challengers began to read like place markers at the head table of almost any Broome County Democratic Party function.

Less than two hours after the 72-year-old senator said he would not seek re-election to the seat he has held since 1953, GOP officials publicly rallied behind the candidacy of Binghamton City Councilman Thomas W. Libous.

Broome County Chairman Paul C. VanSavage and Tioga County Chairwoman Catherine T. Clement joined Libous at a press conference announcing his plans to seek the Republican nomination for Anderson's seat on the New York Legislature. Chenango County Chairman Thomas A. Morrone sent a letter proclaiming his endorsement of Libous.

Anderson also gave his blessing to Libous through a letter read by his Senate counsel, William E. Shamulka.

However, the anointing of Libous as Anderson's heir-apparent has not closed out others who are interested in the two-year seat, which will carry a base pay of $57,500 next January.

Robert J. Moppert, majority leader of the Broome County Legis-

See LIBOUS/Page 12A

JOHN BOHN PHOTO

Binghamton City Council member Thomas W. Libous is Anderson's choice to succeed him in the state Senate.

Senator's big secret kept the 'lame duck' at bay

By E.J. CONZOLA II
Staff Writer

Warren M. Anderson decided in January not to run a 20th time, but told only a few close friends and family members, he said yesterday.

A number of factors played into the timing of yesterday's announcement, Anderson said in an interview with the *Press & Sun-Bulletin*.

Had he announced earlier, his lame-duck status could have cost him influence during a particularly contentious legislative session, he said. Had he waited longer, his would-be successors would have found themselves face to face with political deadlines.

On a larger scale, the 1990 national census and the accompanying redrawing of legislative lines affected his decision. Forcing a new majority leader to face the pressures of drawing new district lines would have been unfair, and the alternative was to remain in office until 1992, Anderson said.

"I had some reservations about four (more) years," he said, calling his position "an all-encompassing job."

Anderson denied speculation that a difficult legislative year — including dissension within the Republican conference and a protracted budget battle with Gov. Mario M. Cuomo — contributed to his decision. "Nobody that really knows what's going on here would have told you that," he said.

Anderson also denied the timing of the announcement — one week before nominating petitions begin circulating — was an attempt to preclude serious opposition to his chosen successor, Binghamton City Councilman Thomas W. Libous. Any candidate interested in the seat has ample time to circulate pe-

See SENATOR/Page 13A

The inside story on Andy

- Thomas W. Libous, Senate contender, wasn't even born when Anderson was first elected to the Senate — Page 12A.
- Broome Democrats were floored by Anderson's decision to retire — 13A.
- I-88 is just one testament to Anderson's importance to this region. Jeff Davis column — 12A.
- Announcement solved a recent mystery — 13A.
- Eleanor Anderson says her husband's power lies in his ability to make things happen — 12A.
- At least four seek the Senate leadership position — 13A.
- Anyone interested in running for Anderson's post faces a July 14 deadline — 13A.

State lotteries

N.Y. Daily Number: 0-8-9
N.Y. Win 4: 4-5-3-0
N.Y. Keno: 5-7-11-29-32-36-44-45-46-52-54-55-56-58-60-72-74-77-78-79
N.Y. Lotto: 7-11-25-26-39-47 Supp.:22
Pa. Daily Lottery: 4-7-1
Pa. Big 4 Lottery: 1-2-6-5
Super 7: 10-14-16-31-35-46-54-56-75-76-77

Page index

Business	10B	Opinion	14-15A
Classified	10-16C	Sports	1C
Comics	8-9D	State	9C
Community	1-5B	Stocks	8-9B
Landers	6D	TV	2D
Living	1D	Washington	7A
Movies	3D	Weather	2A
Nation	3A	World	15A
Obituaries	9C		

Summit succeeds simply by altering attitudes

By JIM HOAGLAND
The Washington Post

ANALYSIS

MOSCOW — For diplomats and strategists, this was a summit that created only ripples on the lakes of arms control, regional wars and other matters of geopolitics. But for the politicians, this summit was a state-of-the-art gathering.

The diplomatic business conducted by the United States and the Soviet Union this week was routine. As described in press conferences and briefings yesterday by both sides, it could have been accomplished by a couple of assistant secretaries of state in Geneva before lunch.

But the business conducted by two of the most skilled political leaders in the world, President Reagan and Soviet leader Mikhail Gorbachev, involved an extraordinary exercise in changing the way the people of the two superpowers see each other.

The world has become accustomed to Reagan-Gorbachev meetings unleashing diplomatic tidal waves that take months to run their course.

Geneva, 1985, ended a six-year period of open hostility between the superpowers. Reykjavik, 1986, redefined the ultimate goals of arms control as both leaders promised to work for a nuclear-free world. Washington, 1987, marked the signing of the first treaty to eliminate an entire class of nuclear missiles.

But the meaning of Moscow this year lay in how normal and undramatic the Soviet-American political dialogue has become, as Gorbachev and Reagan explained in separate comments to the press yesterday. Both predicted the dialogue would continue under Reagan's successor.

Questioned yesterday, each leader held out a slim hope that they would meet a fifth time to sign a new arms-control treaty. But the extensive summations each of them offered of their joint dealings and accomplishments since the Geneva summit had the air of a political farewell.

As the host, and as a leader who intends to be in power for years to come, Gorbachev set a far more ambitious agenda for himself in this five-day meeting, which concludes ceremonially with Reagan's departure for London today.

Gorbachev sought diplomatic as well as political gains, springing a surprise proposal on conventional-arms control and a draft for a joint political statement renouncing

See SUMMIT/Page 10A

- Full coverage of the summit continues on Page 4A.

TO SUBSCRIBE TO THE PRESS & SUN-BULLETIN CALL: (607) 798-1161 OR 1-800-253-5343 (N.Y.). 1-800- 41- 2120 (PA.)

June 2, 1988: The baton is passed from state Senator Warren M. Anderson to Thomas Libous, who has been Binghamton's senator since Anderson's retirement. *Press & Sun-Bulletin archives*

Whalers are tied by Saints
SPORTS, Page 1C

• CLASS ACT • DAY TRIP • PROBLEM SOLVER • CUTTING EDGE

Blazers best attire for women
Page 1D

A little polish on shoes is step in right direction
SAVVY SATURDAY, Page 1D

Children may protest development
COMMUNITY, Page 1B

Press & Sun-Bulletin

4 SECTIONS | BINGHAMTON, N.Y. | 35¢ NEWSSTAND

Saturday
November 11, 1989
FINAL EDITION

Flurries
High: 44. Low: 30
Details on Page 2A

EAST GERMANY: Coverage continues inside on Pages 4A and 5A

German natives in S. Tier share in exhilaration Page 5A

Neighbors fear prospect of reunification Page 4A

Day-trippers make history with West visit Page 5A

Soviet Union will not tolerate one Germany Page 4A

Breakthrough

New passages cut into Berlin Wall

AP PHOTO

A Berliner sits atop the Berlin Wall Friday and uses a hammer and chisel to chip away at the wall that has divided the city for 28 years. A police officer said, "It will be a pretty hole that will make it possible for people and cars to come through."

By NESHA STARCEVIC
The Associated Press

BERLIN — East Germany ended all border restrictions Friday and cut a new passage in the Berlin Wall, where desperate people once leaped from windows and border guards shot down others trying to flee.

Work was reported on many more new openings in the wall that divided the city for 28 years.

More than 100,000 jubilant East Germans climbed over and rushed through borders Friday for the first time since 1961. They chatted amiably with stony-faced guards who no longer have orders to open fire.

Thousands crossed back and forth during the day. Some East German border guards helped East Berliners climb the wall to avoid congested crossing. Some guards were handed roses by beaming girls.

Communist leader Egon Krenz told 150,000 people at a rally in East Berlin that his new reforms "will not be turned back." The party's Central Committee approved a document calling for free elections, more restrictions on its security forces and greater separation of party and state.

Chancellor Helmut Kohl of West Germany flew to West Berlin hoping to speak with Krenz, who has stunned the world with rapid reforms — and a pledge of free elections — intended to appease pro-democracy protesters and end emigration to the West.

Work began late Friday on a new crossing at Bernauer Strasse. The new crossing was scheduled to be opened at 8 a.m. today.

East Germans used a hydraulic crane to dismantle the round top of the concrete wall. East German workers could be heard knocking on the wall.

On the Western side, dozens of firemen dismantled observation platforms from which West Berliners used to gaze across the wall. About 400 people watched, occasionally setting off fireworks.

"We are speechless," said Helmut Keuchel, 48. "This is a fabulous and overwhelming experience."

Several thousand people celebrated at the Brandenburg Gate, the great monument that, like the wall, was a symbol of Berlin's division. Many danced on the wall, drank champagne, waved sparklers, set off fireworks and chanted: "The wall must go! The wall must go!"

East German border guards watched impassively as some in the crowd used picks and hammers to chip away pieces of the hated barrier for souvenirs.

Thousands of East Berliners poured across

See NEW, Page 4A

Two killed by military jet crash

SMYRNA, Ga. (AP) — A pregnant mother died Friday of burns inflicted when a fighter jet smashed into a suburban apartment complex the day before. Earlier, searchers found a man's body in the wreckage of his incinerated apartment.

Navy investigators, meanwhile, continued hunting through the debris for clues to Thursday evening's crash, but said they did not know what caused the accident.

Margie Padovani, 28, died Friday evening at Grady Memorial Hospital, said John Hester, night administrator.

The woman's 5-year-old daughter remained in critical but stable condition at Grady, Hester said. The pilot, who ejected before the jet crashed, also was in critical condition.

New area code arrives today in Chicago suburbs

CHICAGO (AP) — Telephone callers in the Chicago suburbs should be touching some new numbers Saturday, as the suburbs leave the familiar 312 area code for a new number: 708.

"In the Chicago metropolitan area, about 90 percent of our customers have awareness of the change," said Pat Montgomery, a spokeswoman for Illinois Bell. "Outside the Chicago area that number is probably less.

"We're urging the Chicago-area people to make sure their out-of-town customers, relatives and friends know about the change," said Montgomery on Friday.

The phone company is running out of prefixes — the first three digits after the area code. The shortage is not due to population growth but to the increase in new services that require separate telephone numbers, such as Fax machines, said Bell officials.

The 312 area code will remain for the city, and 708 will be applied to surrounding towns.

Medical examiner rules baby's death a homicide

BOSTON (AP) — A medical examiner ruled Friday that the death of an infant, delivered by Caesarean section after its mother was shot to death, was a homicide, adding a second murder charge if a suspect is found.

Suffolk County Medical Examiner Gerald Feigin concluded after an autopsy that the 17-day-old boy died Thursday as a result of complications stemming from the gunshot wound his mother sustained last month. The infant was delivered eight weeks premature.

Carol Stuart, 30, a lawyer who was seven months pregnant, and her husband, Charles, 29, a furrier, were accosted in their car at a Boston stop light. A gunman forced them to drive a short distance where he robbed them and shot Carol Stuart in the head and her husband in the abdomen. Charles Stuart contacted rescuers using a cellular telephone.

Woman buried in back of her 1976 Cadillac

AURORA, Ind. (AP) — A woman was buried Friday in the back of her beloved red Cadillac convertible, said funeral home officials.

Aurora Schuck told her husband, Raymond, about 10 years ago she wanted to be buried with her 1976 Cadillac, so Schuck bought 14 plots at the Riverview Cemetery.

"The casket is going to be placed on the back of the car. The top's down, so it will just be placed on that, across the back," said a spokesman for Rullman Funeral Home who would not give his name.

State lotteries

N.Y. Daily Number: 1-1-4
N.Y. Win 4: 5-6-1-6
N.Y. Keno: 3-10-18-22-25-27-28-29-30-31-32-52-55-56-58-59-60-62-68-73
Pa. Daily Lottery: 1-0-0
Pa. Big 4 Lottery: 5-0-2-5
Pa. Wild Card: 7-12-18-26-30-38 Alt: 42

Page index

Questions or comments?

For matters regarding world, national and state news call News Editor Diana Bean at 798-1184, weekdays after 4 p.m.

SUNY-B ordered to cut $400,000 from budget

By GEORGE BASLER
Staff Writer

The state University Center at Binghamton plans to postpone renovation work and equipment purchases to comply with a $400,000 budget-cutting order from Gov. Mario M. Cuomo.

SUNY-Binghamton estimates the cut at $400,000, about 0.5 percent of its 1989-90 operating budget, Michael A. Scullard, SUNY-Binghamton's vice president for administration, said Friday. It could be as much as $500,000 or as little as $300,000, he said.

The university will put off renovation of some classrooms and laboratories and eliminate the purchase of some equipment and supplies, Scullard said. The cut will not affect employment, he said.

■ SUNY-B may get a new academic building and field house. Story, Page 1B.

"It's going to hurt the physical condition of the campus, some research and some instruction," said university President Clifford D. Clark.

"We'll be able to do some renovation work, but not as much as we should," Clark said.

The cut is part of a $22 million spending reduction that Cuomo ordered for the State University of New York system.

Cuomo's directive, issued Nov. 3, mandated a 2 percent across-the-board cut for all state agencies to help close the state's anticipated budget deficit. Cuomo said spending cuts are needed because of tax receipt shortfalls and overspending in Medicaid and foster-care programs.

The governor's directive was unexpected, Scullard said, adding: "We all got caught somewhat by surprise."

Postponing renovation and equipment purchases may not seem like a serious problem, but it will hurt because a university needs modern, up-to-date facilities for a quality research program, he said.

"If we defer the work year-in and year-out, it becomes a big deal. It hurts our recruitment of faculty and development of new programs," he said.

Scullard outlined the cuts at a Friday meeting of the SUNY-Binghamton Council, an advisory body at the university. The amount of the cut will not be finalized until the SUNY trustees, who govern the SUNY system, meet in Albany next week, he said.

In a related matter, Scullard discussed the budget request for 1990-91 submitted to the governor's office by the SUNY trustees. The trustees requested 7.8 percent more money.

As part of the overall budget request, SUNY-Binghamton's budget would increase to $74.7 million in 1990-91 from this year's $69.7 million, Scullard said.

Clifford D. Clark
Cuts will hurt some instruction

TO SUBSCRIBE TO THE PRESS & SUN-BULLETIN CALL: (607) 798-1161 OR 1-800-253-5343 (N.Y.), 1-800-241-2120 (PA.)

November 11, 1989: The Berlin Wall is finished and the Cold War is ending. *Courtesy David Silvanic*

Sports Tuesday

The pros and cons of artificial surfaces/4C
S. Tier coaches split on turf/4C
New coach puts life in Sabres/5C

George Brett no friend of artificial turf.

Vikings win Central title/1C
Holiday spirit on the job/1B
Deals change business/6B

Press & Sun-Bulletin

4 SECTIONS BINGHAMTON, N.Y. 35¢ NEWSSTAND

Tuesday
December 26, 1989
FINAL EDITION

Snow
High: 17. Low: Teens
Details on Page 2A

Billy Martin dies

Ex-Yank skipper killed in crash near Broome home

ADDITIONAL MARTIN STORIES, PAGES 3A, 1C, 6C

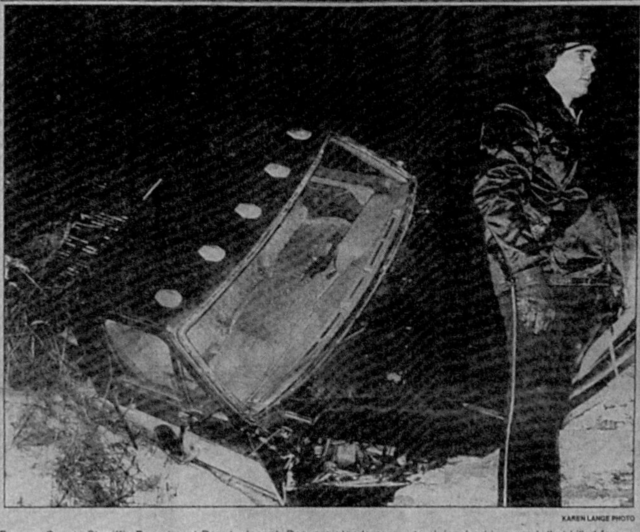
KAREN LANGE PHOTO

Broome County Sheriff's Department Deputy Joseph Danvers stands near a truck involved in a crash that killed former New York Yankees manager Billy Martin Monday night. Martin, a passenger, was pronounced dead at 6:56 p.m. at Wilson Memorial Hospital. The impact of the crash knocked Martin against the windshield and knocked the glass out.

By STEVEN LEVINE and KAREN LANGE
Staff Writers

Baseball's legendary New York Yankee Billy Martin died in a one-vehicle drunken driving accident at the foot of his driveway in rural Broome County about 5:45 p.m. Monday.

Sheriff's deputies charged the operator of the vehicle, a friend of Martin's, with driving while intoxicated. Neither man was wearing seat belts, deputies said.

"It's like losing a part of my own family," said Yankees majority owner George Steinbrenner. "I was just with him last Wednesday when he came down to entertain 2,000 underprivileged kids in Tampa. Billy said this meant so much to him because he never had anything like this when he was a kid."

Billy Martin

County Sheriff Anthony C. Ruffo said Martin, 61, was a passenger when the vehicle operated by William Reedy, 53, of Detroit, Mich., skidded out of control on the icy two-lane country road. Reedy was charged with driving while intoxicated, a misdemeanor, two hours after the crash. He is to appear in Town of Fenton Court on Jan. 4.

District Attorney Gerald S. Mollen Monday night was reviewing more serious charges against Reedy, deputies said.

Reedy sustained a fractured right hip and fractured rib in the crash on Potter Hill Road at Hunt Hill Road in the Town of Fenton. He was transferred about 11 p.m. to University Hospital of the Health Science Center at Syracuse for reconstructive surgery on his hip.

See MARTIN/Page 3A

Israeli Army orders trial of colonel

JERUSALEM (AP) — The army Monday ordered the court-martial of an Israeli colonel accused of telling troops to break the bones of 20 bound-and-gagged Palestinian prisoners.

Col. Yehuda Meir will be the highest ranking officer to face trial during the 2-year-old Palestinian uprising against Israeli occupation. The army announcement gave no date for the trial.

Meir was reprimanded by Lt. Gen. Dan Shomron, the armed forces chief of staff, for the January 1988 incident and given the choice of leaving the army or standing trial. Meir, the former military commander in the occupied West Bank city of Nablus, resigned.

Meir is accused of ordering troops to beat and break the legs of 20 Palestinians. Soldiers under his command left beaten Palestinians in a field until other Arabs arrived and rushed them to a hospital.

Mandela's Christmas is 28th in prison

CAPE TOWN, South Africa (AP) — Jailed black leader Nelson Mandela, whose 28th Christmas behind bars will almost certainly be his last in custody, opened presents and had a quiet dinner with his family Monday.

Mandela's wife, Winnie, their daughter, Zindzi, and her three young children spent most of the day at the comfortable three-bedroom home where Mandela is held at the Victor Verster Prison outside Cape Town.

Mandela, 71, is the country's best-known black leader and the world's most famous prisoner. He has been jailed since 1962 and is serving a life sentence for plotting an anti-government sabotage campaign. His release is widely expected within weeks.

Cuban arms shipments may use Mexican route

WASHINGTON (AP) — Cuba is believed to be sending weapons to leftist rebels in El Salvador through a remote land route that begins in Mexico's Yucatan Peninsula, according to U.S. officials.

Cuba has traditionally used Nicaragua as its primary transit point for weapons deliveries to its allies in El Salvador, but is believed to have started using the alternate route some time ago, officials said.

As described by officials, the Cubans ship weapons across the narrow channel that separates Cuba from the Yucatan Peninsula. From there, the equipment is sent by truck to El Salvador via Guatemala.

At Last: A white Christmas in Buffalo

BUFFALO (AP) — After struggling for three years to stage a Winterfest of snow sculpting and ice skating amid balmy January temperatures more suited to New Orleans than New York, organizers this year just gave up.

Then the snow began.

Buffalonians awoke Monday to their first white Christmas since 1985, in a December that figures to be one of the two coldest on record. Nearly 3 feet of snow have fallen.

Despite the wintry weather, however, the Greater Buffalo Chamber of Commerce is adamant: there will be no Winterfest this year.

The Chamber won't quite say that the lack of snow was the reason it decided in September to cancel the festival. But spokeswoman Karen Wodarczak said the Chamber did not believe it was getting its money's worth from the festival.

The situation has prompted a few jokes. "Someone just called me and said, 'Can't you bring it back? Then we won't have any snow,' " said Dottie Gallagher, spokeswoman for an organization that oversees the downtown shopping district.

Due to the holiday, there were no lotteries drawn Monday.

Page index

Questions or comments?

For matters regarding world, national and state news call News Editor Diana Bean at 798-1184, weekdays after 4 p.m.

Romania executes Ceausescus after trial

By MORT ROSENBLUM
The Associated Press

BUCHAREST, Romania — Ousted President Nicolae Ceausescu and his wife Elena were executed Monday after they were convicted of genocide and "grave crimes" against Romania at a secret military trial, the provisional government said.

Ceausescu, 71, the last hard-line Communist leader in the Warsaw Pact, was chased from power Friday after his dreaded security forces massacred thousands protesting his repressive 24-year rule and harsh economic policies.

He and his wife, who served as a virtual second-in-command, were executed by firing squad after a trial at an undisclosed location, Romanian televsision said.

> 'Oh, what wonderful news! The anti-Christ died' on Christmas Day.
> — Unidentified announcer on Bucharest Radio

Fighting in central Bucharest, which continued sporadically late into the night, had driven many people from the streets by the time the announcement of the executions was made around 8:30 p.m. (1:30 p.m. EST.) However, cheers rang out from the few people on the streets and from apartment balconies.

Film shown on Romanian television late Monday showed the Ceausescus before their execution, being brought to an undisclosed location in an armored car.

Ceausecu, dressed in a dark suit and a heavy black overcoat, looked gaunt and tired but smiled as a man in a white coat checked his blood pressure. His wife looked forlorn as she sat against a wall, dressed in a beige fur-lined coat with her head covered peasant-style in a scarf.

Romanian staff at the Hotel Intercontinental clustered cheering around a television set when the film appeared. Some even spat in the direction of the television in a gesture of contempt.

The film was the first of Ceausescu to be shown since the provisional government announced his capture Saturday.

Bucharest Radio blamed the

See CEAUSESCUS/Page 5A

Inside stories

- Years of repressed hatred caused Romania to explode into violence. **Story, Page 5A.**
- Romania's new leader has ties to Soviet leader Mikhail S. Gorbachev. **Story, Page 5A.**
- United States and 12 other nations establish diplomatic ties with Romania. **Story, Page 5A.**

FULL PAGE OF COVERAGE, PAGE 5A.

SUNSPOT

Dog returns home after painful detour

SAN FRANCISCO (AP) — Teddy Bear made it home for Christmas, a happy sight to his owners, who were almost fleeced out of reward money offered for the pet.

The 4-year-old Chinese Shih Tzu slipped its collar last Monday, leading Dean and Susan Rider to post reward offers. They got a call from a man who said he had the dog in San Diego. In exchange for wiring of the $300 reward money, the caller said he would ship Teddy Bear home.

But when Dean Rider checked the address, he learned it was a residential hotel that doesn't allow pets. And there was no one registered there under the name given to Rider. But then the Riders got another phone call, this one legitimate. An employee at the Mission District animal shelter recognized the dog pictured in a newspaper story as one at the center after being hit by a car.

"He's got a big fat lip, and a bruised hip, a gash in his paw and an eye infection, but he was wild with joy when he saw us," said Rider about his pet.

U.S. troops, Noriega at 'Mexican standoff'

By JOSEPH B. FRAZIER
The Associated Press

PANAMA CITY, Panama —U.S. troops kept a vigil Monday on the Vatican mission where Gen. Manuel Antonio Noriega sought asylum as U.S. officials demanded the former strongman be turned over for trial in the United States.

Fighting was reported Monday night in downtown Panama City, and diplomats reached at the Spanish Embassy said the nearby Chamber of Commerce was on fire. U.S. troops in the area said they were taking sniper fire about two hours after a 6 p.m. curfew.

Dozens of U.S. soldiers, armored vehicles and helicopters ringed the Vatican mission, where Noriega turned himself in Sunday five days after the U.S. invasion overthrew his government, blasted his headquarters and drove him into hiding.

In Washington, the administration demanded "in extraordinarily tough terms" that Vatican authorities turn Noriega over, a State Department source said.

Negotiations have brought "a Mexican standoff," the official said, with church authorities rebuffing the request and trying — unsuccessfully so far — to find a country to take Noriega.

Defense Secretary Dick Cheney, who arrived in Panama City to be with U.S. troops Christmas Eve, said at a news briefing Monday that Noriega had been "very skilful" in eluding capture and moving every night.

Cheney called the U.S. invasion "the most surgical operation of its size ever carried out, not only by our forces but by anybody else's forces."

After congratulating U.S. soldiers on their mission and touring Noriega's battered headquarters, Cheney met with leaders of the new U.S.-backed government. He reiterated Washington's desire to have Noriega brought for trial in the United States.

The area of Monday night's fighting includes the Cuban Embassy, which is surrounded by U.S. troops, as well as the Foreign Ministry, where the government of new President Guillermo Endara has set up shop.

The secretary of the Spanish Embassy, Javier Herrera, said his embassy's personnel lay on the floor during the firing, which slackened after 45 minutes. He said Spanish Ambassador Tomas Lozano called a U.S. colonel in charge of operations in the area and the colonel said, "I'm on the ground, too."

Endara, the U.S.-backed leader who took power minutes after the U.S. invasion, visited refugees during a Christmas Mass at a camp in a soccer stadium. He refused to comment on Noriega's status, saying, "It is a very delicate diplomatic matter with the papal

See NORIEGA/Page 7A

Manuel Antonio Noriega
Seeking political asylum

Inside stories

- Bush's options move from military front to diplomacy. **Analysis, Page 7A.**
- The Vatican says Manuel Noriega's legal status has not been determined. **Story, Page 7A.**
- Refugees celebrate Christmas. **Story, Page 7A.**

FULL PAGE OF COVERAGE, PAGE 7A.

December 26, 1989: Legendary Yankee skipper Billy Martin, who lived in Greater Binghamton, died in a Christmas Day accident. *Courtesy Dolly Escovar*

Merissa Kraham shows support for the troops during the first Gulf War, January 1991. Kraham is the daughter of County Executive Jeffrey P. Kraham. *Press & Sun-Bulletin archives*

The Pops on the River summer concert could draw thousands, even after a decade, June 1991. *Press & Sun-Bulletin archives*

1990 - 1999

Take me out to the ballgame

SEVEN FULL PAGES INSIDE

Thursday January 17, 1991 FINAL EDITION	82nd Airborne prepped for attack Story, Page 14A	Saddam takes control of Iraqi forces Story, Page 15A	Strike in gulf takes Saudis by surprise Story, Page 16A	Americans jolted by U.S.-led air strike Story, Page 17A	War news silences SUNY-B campus Story, Page 18A	Tokyo market rises after attack Story, Page 19A	World jolted from peaceful course Story, Page 20A	Also: The war affects Oil, banking, and sports Stories, Pages 8B, 1C Editorials, Page 10A
Flurries High: 35. Low: 25. Details on Page 2A.								

Press & Sun-Bulletin

4 SECTIONS — BINGHAMTON, N.Y. — 35¢ NEWSSTAND

WAR

Massive air strike starts 'Desert Storm'

Air-Strike Targets
Chemical, nuclear or biological warfare facilities
Conventional weapons plants
Air bases
Oil refineries
TURKEY
SYRIA
IRAN
IRAQ
SAUDI ARABIA
KUWAIT
Al Kindi
Mosul
Erbil
Tall Afar
Qayyarah
Kirkuk
Tigris R.
Bayji
Balad
Tikrit
Samarra
Al Qaim
Baghdad
Rashid
Tuwaitha
Salman Pak
Shaik Mazhur
Al Asad
Al Fallujah
Iskandariya
Ubaydah bin al Jarrah
Al Amarah
Euphrates R.
Shatt-al-Arab R.
Tallil
Jalibah
Basra
Rumaila
Bubiyan Island
Kuwait
100 miles
100 km.

Thirteen hundred sorties were launched against Iraqi targets this morning according to a Pentagon source. The attack put out a portion of Saddam Hussein's elite Republican Guard. Waves of cruise missiles hit Iraq.

Sources: *The New York Times*, AP research — AP/Martha P. Hernandez, Pat Lyons

The Associated Press

CENTRAL SAUDI ARABIA — The United States and its allies hurled a mighty air armada against Iraq early today to crush the Arab nation's military power and drive it from conquered Kuwait.

"The liberation of Kuwait has begun," President Bush declared in Washington.

Wave after wave of warplanes, in hundreds of sorties, streaked north from Saudi Arabian bases to punish Iraq for its five-month defiance of the rest of the world.

See WAR/Page 15A

Bush vows liberation of Kuwait 'will not fail'

By TOM RAUM
The Associated Press

WASHINGTON — President Bush summoned American and allied forces into war with Iraq on Wednesday night, declaring solemnly that "the battle has been joined" to free Kuwait.

Operation Desert Storm began with an aerial assault that met little resistence, military officials said.

"We will not fail," Bush vowed as F-15E fighter bombers were locking onto their strategic military targets across Iraq and Kuwait. Hostilities were well under way when the president spoke to the nation at 9 p.m. EST.

The president expressed hope "this fighting will not go on for long, and that casualties will be held to an absolute minimum."

Congressional leaders, informed in advance by the president, swiftly pledged backing for American troops. Sen. Sam Nunn, who led the opposition to war authority, said, "Our servicemen and women will be given all the resources to do the job. I believe we will prevail in a matter of days or weeks."

About 100 anti-war protesters maintained a vigil in the dark drizzle outside the White House.

The president marshalled a potent international alliance to challenge Iraq's occupation of the oil-rich kingdom of Kuwait and issued his war order less than 24 hours after the expiration of a United Nations deadline.

Within moments of Bush's comments, Defense Secretary Richard Cheney said the first foray was conducted by hundreds of American, British, Saudi Arabia and Kuwaiti aircraft. "So far, there has been no air resistance" from the Iraqis, Cheney said.

He provided no details on casualties, but said reports were "very encouraging," and said the battle plan was designed to "focus on military targets, to minimize U.S. casualties.

See BUSH/Page 17A

Winning numbers

N.Y. Daily Number: 7-5-0
N.Y. Win 4: 8-4-1-7
N.Y. Pick 10: 3-4-5-8-9-10-16-17-21-26-28-29-30-45-48-56-57-70-72-73
N.Y. Lotto: 4-5-16-17-40-49 Supp.:20
Pa. Daily Lottery: 7-9-8
Pa. Big 4 Lottery: 7-4-7-6
Super 7: 15-17-19-25-28-29-40-61-63-67-71

Index

Business	8B	Opinion	10-11A
Classified	6-12C	Sports	1C
Comics	6-7D	State	4B
Community	1-4B	Stocks	6-7B
Landers	6D	TV	2D
Living	1D	Washington	2A
Movies	3D	Weather	2A
Nation	3A	World	8A
Obituaries	4B		

Questions or comments?

For matters regarding world, national and state news call the news desk at 798-1184 between 4 and 11 p.m. weekdays. Leslie Spalding is the news editor.

News of war stops Tier residents in their tracks

By ERIC RESULTAN
Staff Writer

As the news of Operation Desert Storm made its way to American television, all one mother could picture was an infant, the one she gave birth to 28 years ago.

Carole J. Kunkle watched as news networks reported the U.S. bombing of Iraqi forces. With her chin in her hand, she stared at a wall of television sets at Montgomery Ward & Co. in the Oakdale Mall tuned to all three networks and the Cable News Network bringing the latest news about Operation Desert Storm.

Her son, Daniel W. Reeder, is stationed on the battleship *USS Missouri*, deployed in the Persian Gulf.

"When I first heard . . . the only thing that flashed through my mind was a blond-haired baby boy," Kunkle said while fighting back tears. "My son is 28 years old, but that's all I can see.

"I think it's very sad that we have to stand by and watch those young boys go through this. Instead of protesting, we should turn to prayer."

When the news of the attack hit the television screens, shoppers immediately congregated around the store's electronics department. CNN brought the sounds of the war within inches of shoppers.

Customers and workers 'were shocked and some started crying. We were all very shocked. It's a very sad feeling.' —Sears employee

"About 30 people gathered," Montgomery Ward salesman Edward F. O'Neil said. "There was no immediate reaction. . . . The store cleared out right afterwards."

At Sears Roebuck and Co.'s electronics department, some took the news hard, a saleswoman said.

"They were shocked and some started crying," the woman said. She declined to give her name. "We were all very shocked. It's a very sad feeling.

See TIER/Page 18A

NELL SEILER PHOTO

Carole J. Kunkle of Binghamton and Garry Flagg, an employee at Montgomery Ward & Co., watch television in the store's electronics department Wednesday night. Kunkle was particularly concerned about the news out of the gulf because her son serves on the battleship *USS Missouri* and she hadn't heard from him recently.

TO SUBSCRIBE TO THE PRESS & SUN-BULLETIN CALL: (607) 798-1161 or 1-800-253-5343 (N.Y.). 1-800-241-2120 (PA.)

January 17, 1991: The Press & Sun-Bulletin devoted seven pages to the outbreak of the war. *Courtesy David Silvanic*

The decade opened with war. The first President Bush promised to liberate Kuwait from Iraqi occupation, and the Armed Forces accomplished the mission quickly. Bush stopped the fighting, leaving Saddam Hussein in power.

In Binghamton, the big news was the return of baseball. The New York Yankees once had their top farm club in Johnson City, but years of dwindling attendance and the construction of Route 17 drove baseball away.

In 1992, after years of struggle, Binghamton Mayor Juanita Crabb presided over the construction of what is now NYSEG Stadium and the creation of the Binghamton Mets.

Nationally, William Jefferson Clinton took the nation through an amazing decade. The Arkansas governor was one of the few Democrats who dared to take on the first President Bush. And when the national economy slumped, Clinton won the presidency.

In Greater Binghamton, the big stories were weather related. We had a blizzard, a tornado and, of course, floods.

Thursday
February 28, 1991
FINAL EDITION
Snow
High: 38. Low: 16.
Details on Page 2A.

Consumer Thursday

Judges praise cleaner, not price/1D

- Times good for new car buys
- Hook-on baby chairs risky

State warns Broome on jail practices
Page 1B

Press & Sun-Bulletin

4 SECTIONS — BINGHAMTON, N.Y. — 35¢ NEWSSTAND

THREE FULL PAGES OF COVERAGE INSIDE

VICTORY

Bush says Iraq defeated

From wire service reports

WASHINGTON — President Bush said Wednesday night that U.S. and allied forces have won the Persian Gulf War and announced that coalition and U.S. forces would cease combat operations as of midnight EST.

Declaring that "Kuwait is liberated, Iraq's army is defeated," Bush announced that at midnight "all United States and coalition forces will suspend offensive combat operations."

"This is a victory for the United Nations, for all mankind, for the rule of law and for what is right," Bush told the nation in a dramatic televised address.

See VICTORY/Page 6A

AP PHOTO

Kuwaiti celebration

Kuwaiti soldiers, armed with Soviet-made AK-47s and rocket-propelled grenade launchers, wave their weapons and cheer Wednesday as they parade through the streets of Kuwait City. Kuwaitis were celebrating the liberation of their capital from the Iraqi army.

GULF WAR COVERAGE

Winning numbers

N.Y. Daily Number: 8-5-3
N.Y. Win 4: 3-1-0-4
N.Y. Pick 10: 6-11-19-20-31-33-36-41-45-48-52-58-61-62-71-73-74-77-79-80
N.Y. Lotto: 2-14-21-46-49-52 Supp.:30
Pa. Daily Lottery: 5-1-4
Pa. Big 4 Lottery: 2-1-0-9
Super 7: 1-9-15-19-20-38-40-54-62-66-78

Index

Questions or comments?

For matters regarding world, national and state news call the news desk at 798-1184 between 4 and 11 p.m. weekdays. Leslie Spalding is the news editor.

Tier family faces war three times over

By KAREN LANGE
Staff Writer

The fighting stopped at midnight, but the worry didn't end for a Binghamton family with three sons serving in the Army in the Persian Gulf.

"This is not a time of euphoria," President Bush said, as he announced the suspension of offensive combat operations in a 9 p.m. speech.

- The Hopkins wait for their sons, **Photo, Page 9A.**

Charles E. and Judith A. Hopkins, of 240 Robinson St., didn't think so, either.

Their oldest son, 23-year-old Specialist Four Daniel M. Hopkins, is probably in Iraq with the 82nd Airborne Division, his father said.

Their middle son, 21-year-old Specialist Four Michael J. Hopkins, is also probably in that country with the 101st Airborne.

Robert W. Hopkins — Daniel M. Hopkins — Michael J. Hopkins

Their youngest son, 18-year-old Pvt. Robert W. Hopkins, has been clearing minefields with the 82nd Airborne.

Bush finished his speech and Charles Hopkins looked at his watch, adjusting for the time difference between Washington, D.C., and the Persian Gulf, to come up with the time his sons would see the start of the cease-fire. "That would make it eight o'clock (in the morning)," he said.

"That's hard to believe," Judith Hopkins said. "It happened so quickly." But the Hopkinses are holding off on the celebration. "There's only one thing better than that to hear," Judith Hopkins said. "It's the knock on the door when the three boys walk in," her husband said.

"I'll take a phone call or anything to show they're all right," she said.

They last talked to Daniel several days before the ground war began. They received a letter dated Feb. 7 Saturday from Robert. They have had no contact with Michael since a telephone conversation Christmas Day and a letter received soon after.

"I'm still scared for them," Charles Hopkins said. "There's still many, many ways they could get hurt."

"You can't really relax, even though you know the thing is over," his wife said.

Nine yellow ribbons hang in a window of the Hopkins' house — one for each of their sons, one for a nephew who served until December on a ship in the Persian Gulf, and one each for five of their sons' Army friends. An Army flag hangs in another window. The family's two dogs wear yellow ribbons. Pictures of their sons hang on the front door.

TO SUBSCRIBE TO THE PRESS & SUN-BULLETIN CALL: (607) 798-1161 or 1-800-253-5343 (N.Y.). 1-800-241-2120 (PA.)

February 28, 1991: Victory in the first Persian Gulf War. *Courtesy David Silvanic*

BASEBALL: Binghamton Mets rout Hagerstown, 7-2 SPORTS 1C

HOCKEY PLAYOFFS: Binghamton Rangers nip Utica, take 3-0 lead SPORTS 1C

SCHOOL: Deposit plan cuts some teachers' hours COMMUNITY 1B

Chance of rain High: 50. Low: 40. Details 2A

Press & Sun-Bulletin

5 SECTIONS BINGHAMTON, N.Y. 35¢ NEWSSTAND

Thursday
April 16, 1992
FIRST EDITION

'Tax Freedom' days late this year

WASHINGTON (AP) — As millions of Americans settled their 1991 tax accounts with Uncle Sam on Wednesday, they learned they'll have to work a record 126 days to pay this year's federal taxes.

Tax Freedom Day 1992 is May 5, four days later than was necessary to pay 1991 taxes, the Washington, D.C.-based Tax Foundation announced in issuing its annual report. But for New Yorkers, Tax Freedom Day won't hit until May 23, the latest of any state and three days later than last year.

■ Residents in 14 states have to work extra this year to cover taxes. Chart, Page 12B.

N.Y. development plan links Thruway, canal

WATERFORD (AP) — A more powerful Thruway Authority would run the state's canal system and mount development projects along the Thruway and the waterways under a plan unveiled Wednesday.

Gov. Mario M. Cuomo said the proposed "Thruway 2000" legislation would create more than 6,000 jobs, improve roads and bridges and boost tourism.

The plan, subject to approval by the state Legislature, would shift responsibility of the canal system from the Department of Transportation to the Thruway Authority. Officials said it would provide for easier maintenance along the 524-mile Barge Canal system. Cuomo said $100 million worth of projects are waiting in the wings, including waterfront development in Syracuse and Buffalo.

Philadelphia commissioner to succeed LA's Gates

LOS ANGELES (AP) — Willie L. Williams, police commissioner of Philadelphia, will become Los Angeles' first black police chief, his current boss said Wednesday.

Williams, 48, one of six finalists to replace Chief Daryl F. Gates when he steps down in June, also will be the first [illegible] in more than 40 years to come from outside the department. The search for a new chief began after Gates disclosed he was leaving in the aftermath of the March 3, 1991, videotaped beating of motorist Rodney King, a clubbing that led to a nationwide examination of police brutality.

Spring Fun

A dramatization of "The Last Supper" is scheduled to start at 7:30 tonight at the Conklin Presbyterian Church, 1175 Conklin Road, Conklin. All are welcome.

Winning numbers

N.Y. Daily Number: 3-5-5
N.Y. Win 4: 6-3-0-9
N.Y. Pick 10: [illegible]
N.Y. Lotto: 13-15-40-41-47-49. Supp [illegible]
Pa. Daily Lottery: 3-5-5
Pa. Big 4 Lottery: 2-2-5-3
Super 7: [illegible]

Index

Business	12B	Obituaries	8B
Classified	6-7B, 8-14C	Opinion	6-7A
Comics	4D	Sports	1-8C
Community	1-4B	State	8B
Crossword	5D	Stocks	10-11B
Landers	3D	TV	2D
Living	1D	Washington	3A
Movies	3D	Weather	2A
Nation	3A	World	4A

Questions or comments?

Baseball scheduled to open today in Binghamton

Special Section: Home at last

Opening day weather: 80% chance of rain High 45-50

In today's *Press & Sun-Bulletin* you'll find a 24-page special section on the new stadium and the new Binghamton Mets

Extra

Barring a rainout, a 20-page EXTRA edition will be sold this evening to help celebrate opening day. Look for it right outside the ballpark, at selected stores, at the *Press & Sun-Bulletin* lobby and in some neighborhoods.

MAUREEN HUGHES/PRESS & SUN-BULLETIN

Rich Green of American Cleaning Services in Binghamton uses a high-pressure hose Wednesday to wash off some of the 6,000 seats at the Binghamton Mets' new downtown stadium. Green was sprucing the seats up for today's home opener against the Harrisburg Senators. The game is scheduled to start at 3 p.m. after pre-game ceremonies, starting at 2:30. Mayor Juanita M. Crabb, Gov. Mario M. Cuomo and New York Mets President Fred Wilpon are expected to be on hand.

Baseball is back in town

... Give me the thrill
Of the springtime chill
Of baseball's opening day
— Damon Runyon

By JOHN W. FOX
Sports Editor

This is it.

The scheduled opening day for professional baseball in Broome County after a 23-year dry spell is today. Now all that's needed is a dry spell this afternoon.

■ Someday has arrived. Editorial, Page 6A.
■ Fans need a plan. Gonzalez column, Page 1B.

The Binghamton Mets' scheduled 3 p.m. home opener against the Harrisburg Senators will go on if the weather

See METS/Page 7A

Line up comfort

Gear up for comfort at today's Binghamton Mets home opener:

■ A SWEATER or jacket or perhaps a raincoat will come in handy if there's soggy weather, in addition to your Mets' cap, of course.

■ SWEAT PANTS, loose-fitting jeans or any material that "gives" are ideal when sitting for three hours.

■ FOR THE FEET, wear a pair of broken-in shoes or sneakers.

DOWNTOWN BINGHAMTON PARADE

MAP AREA
Binghamton
Binghamton Municipal Stadium
Henry St.
Pine St.
Court St.
Main St.
Hawley St.
Fayette St.
Parade starts at noon at Court St./Fayette St.
Parade ends Court St./Hawley St.

Chenango charter option hits snag

By JIM WRIGHT
Staff Writer

NORWICH — Money — or lack of it — could mean that no commission will study whether Chenango County needs to change its form of government, county leaders said Wednesday.

The Charter Commission, a voluntary panel, was to study the merits of having a county manager or an administrative assistant to the chairman of the county Board of Supervisors. However, no money is available to pay the anticipated salary of either one, said members of the board's Safety and Rules Committee.

"The average salary of similar positions in counties of our size was the upper $40,000 to low $50,000. Nobody had any ideas of where we would get funding for such a position," said board Chairman Glenn R. Angell. Angell receives $20,085 as board chairman.

The committee, in a 4-0 vote, believed that it would be a waste of time to have a commission conduct a study if there's no intention of funding the position, Angell said. Because of the committee's action Wednesday, the full board will be asked next month to rescind a 4-month-old resolution proposing creation of the commission.

The new position was among [illegible] proposals another countywide group recommended for approval by the county. On Tuesday, a member of the Chenango 2020 Vision of the Future Plan recommended the county head in that direction.

Wednesday's action disappointed Commission Chairman [illegible] Mitchell. "I think their action shows a lack of foresight of the committee as to what the commission was really recommending," he said.

He hopes further study of county government is planned. "We really need to look at a reorganization of our government," Mitchell said.

Glenn R. Angell
Cites cost concerns

United Nations' sanctions clamp down on Libya

From wire service reports

TRIPOLI, Libya — Countries barred Libyan jets from their airspace Wednesday and ordered diplomats to go home, tightening a noose around the Arab country to pressure it to turn over suspects in the bombing of Pan Am Flight 103.

The punitive measures were sanctions approved by the United Nations, but a defiant Libya tried to flout them by sending jets and an airliner into the sky. Egyptian air controllers twice turned away Libyan jets as they tried to enter its airspace, and Italy's air force scrambled warplanes to intercept a Libyan airliner approaching Italian air space. "Libyan-Arab Airlines, if it continues to fly, in our opinion will have a great deal of difficulty finding places to land," said State Department spokesman Margaret Tutwiler.

■ The U.N. sanctions aren't likely to have any short-term effect on Libyans. Story, Page 4A.

Land and sea links remained.

Although there is Arab sentiment against the sanctions, nations in the region and around the world abided by a U.N. resolution passed March 31 banning arms sales to Libya and calling on countries to cut back Libyan diplomatic staffs.

The sanctions do not include a boycott of Libya's oil sales, which account for 90 percent of the country's earnings. But British Foreign Secretary Douglas Hurd said [illegible]

TO SUBSCRIBE TO THE PRESS & SUN-BULLETIN CALL: (607) 798-1161 or 1-800-253-5343 (N.Y.) 1-800-241-2120 (PA.)

April 16, 1992: Baseball's return merited an Extra edition. *Microfilm archives*

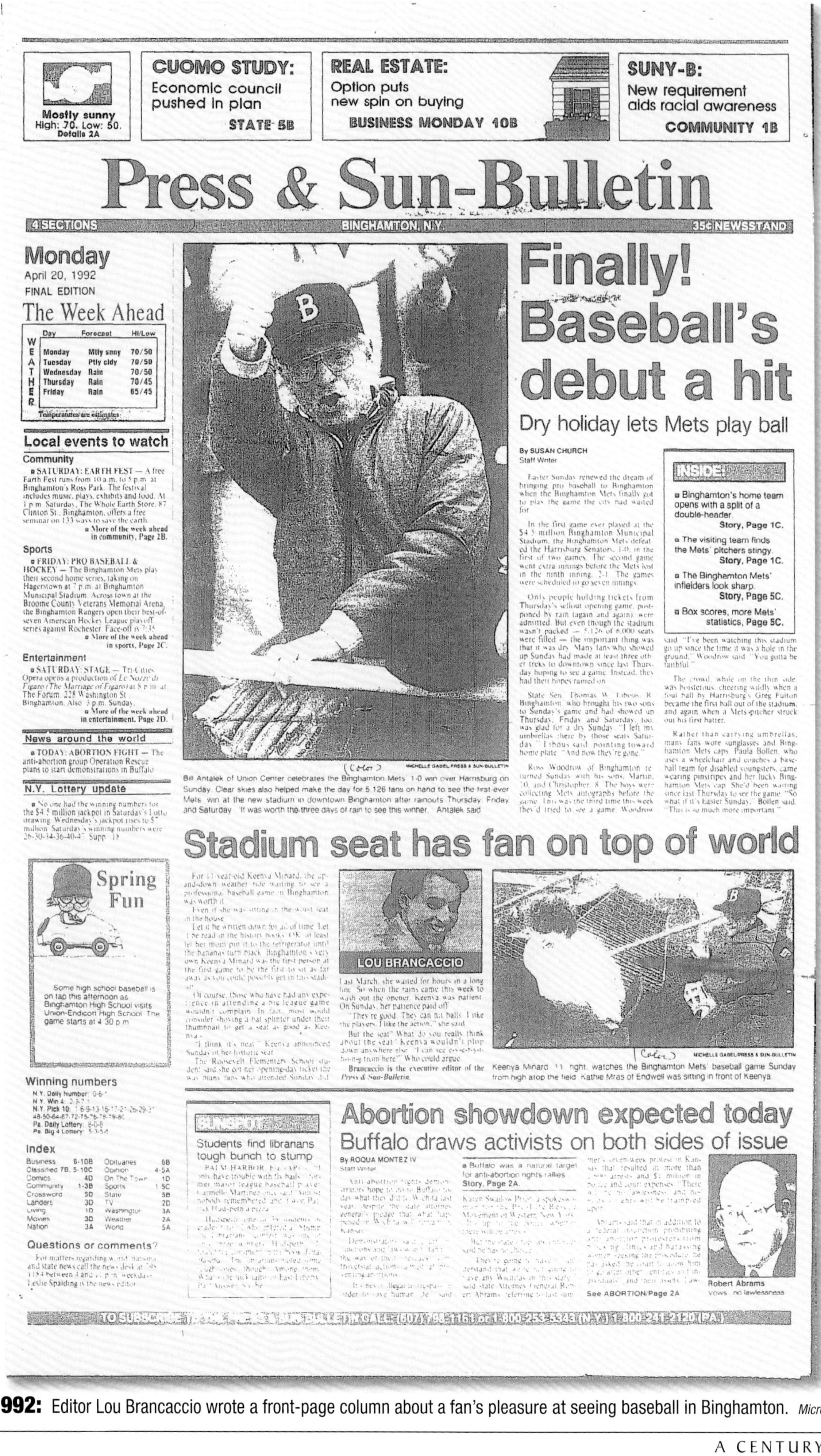

Mostly sunny High: 70. Low: 50. Details 2A

CUOMO STUDY: Economic council pushed in plan — STATE 5B

REAL ESTATE: Option puts new spin on buying — BUSINESS MONDAY 10B

SUNY-B: New requirement aids racial awareness — COMMUNITY 1B

Press & Sun-Bulletin

4 SECTIONS — BINGHAMTON, N.Y. — 35¢ NEWSSTAND

Monday
April 20, 1992
FINAL EDITION

The Week Ahead

WEATHER

Day	Forecast	Hi/Low
Monday	Mfly snny	70/50
Tuesday	Ptly cldy	70/50
Wednesday	Rain	70/50
Thursday	Rain	70/45
Friday	Rain	65/45

Temperatures are estimates.

Local events to watch

Community

SATURDAY: EARTH FEST — A free Earth Fest runs from 10 a.m. to 5 p.m. at Binghamton's Ross Park. The festival includes music, plays, exhibits and food. At 1 p.m. Saturday, The Whole Earth Store, 87 Clinton St., Binghamton, offers a free seminar on 133 ways to save the earth.

More of the week ahead in community, Page 2B.

Sports

FRIDAY: PRO BASEBALL & HOCKEY — The Binghamton Mets play their second home series, taking on Hagerstown at 7 p.m. at Binghamton Municipal Stadium. Across town at the Broome County Veterans Memorial Arena, the Binghamton Rangers open their best-of-seven American Hockey League playoff series against Rochester. Face-off is 7:35.

More of the week ahead in sports, Page 2C.

Entertainment

SATURDAY: STAGE — Tri-Cities Opera opens a production of *Le Nozze di Figaro (The Marriage of Figaro)* at 8 p.m. at The Forum, 228 Washington St., Binghamton. Also 3 p.m. Sunday.

More of the week ahead in entertainment, Page 2D.

News around the world

TODAY: ABORTION FIGHT — The anti-abortion group Operation Rescue plans to start demonstrations in Buffalo.

N.Y. Lottery update

No one had the winning numbers for the $4.5 million jackpot in Saturday's Lotto drawing. Wednesday's jackpot rises to $7 million. Saturday's winning numbers were 26-30-34-36-40-47. Supp. 18.

Spring Fun

Some high school baseball is on tap this afternoon as Binghamton High School visits Union-Endicott High School. The game starts at 4:30 p.m.

Winning numbers

N.Y. Daily Number: 0-6-1
N.Y. Win 4: 2-3-7-[illegible]
N.Y. Pick 10: 1-6-9-13-16-17-21-26-29-3[illegible]-48-50-64-67-72-75-76-78-79-80
Pa. Daily Lottery: 8-0-8
Pa. Big 4 Lottery: 5-3-5-4

Index

Business	8-10B	Obituaries	6B
Classified 7B, 5-10C		Opinion	4-5A
Comics	4D	On The Town	1D
Community	1-3B	Sports	1-5C
Crossword	5D	State	5B
Landers	3D	TV	2D
Living	1D	Washington	3A
Movies	3D	Weather	2A
Nation	3A	World	5A

Questions or comments?

For matters regarding world, national and state news call the news desk at 798-1184 between 4 and [illegible] p.m. weekdays. Leslie Spalding is the news editor.

Finally! Baseball's debut a hit

Dry holiday lets Mets play ball

By SUSAN CHURCH
Staff Writer

Easter Sunday renewed the dream of bringing pro baseball to Binghamton when the Binghamton Mets finally got to play the game the city had waited for.

In the first game ever played at the $4.5 million Binghamton Municipal Stadium, the Binghamton Mets defeated the Harrisburg Senators, 1-0, in the first of two games. The second game went extra innings before the Mets lost in the ninth inning, 2-1. The games were scheduled to go seven innings.

Only people holding tickets from Thursday's sellout opening game, postponed by rain (again and again), were admitted. But even though the stadium wasn't packed — 5,126 of 6,000 seats were filled — the important thing was that it was dry. Many fans who showed up Sunday had made at least three other treks to downtown since last Thursday hoping to see a game. Instead, they had their hopes rained on.

State Sen. Thomas W. Libous, R-Binghamton, who brought his two sons to Sunday's game and had showed up Thursday, Friday and Saturday, too, was glad for a dry Sunday. "I left my umbrellas there by those seats Saturday," Libous said, pointing toward home plate. "And now they're gone."

Ross Woodrow of Binghamton returned Sunday with his sons, Martin, 10, and Christopher, 8. The boys were collecting Mets autographs before the game. This was the third time this week they'd tried to see a game. Woodrow said. "I've been watching this stadium go up since the time it was a hole in the ground," Woodrow said. "You gotta be faithful."

The crowd, while on the thin side, was boisterous, cheering wildly when a foul ball by Harrisburg's Greg Fulton became the first ball out of the stadium, and again when a Mets pitcher struck out his first batter.

Rather than carrying umbrellas, many fans wore sunglasses and Binghamton Mets caps. Paula Bollen, who uses a wheelchair and coaches a baseball team for disabled youngsters, came wearing pinstripes and her lucky Binghamton Mets cap. She'd been waiting since last Thursday to see the game. "So what if it's Easter Sunday," Bollen said. "This is so much more important."

INSIDE:

- Binghamton's home team opens with a split of a double-header. Story, Page 1C.
- The visiting team finds the Mets' pitchers stingy. Story, Page 1C.
- The Binghamton Mets' infielders look sharp. Story, Page 5C.
- Box scores, more Mets' statistics, Page 5C.

(Color) MICHELLE GABEL/PRESS & SUN-BULLETIN

Bill Antalek of Union Center celebrates the Binghamton Mets' 1-0 win over Harrisburg on Sunday. Clear skies also helped make the day for 5,126 fans on hand to see the first-ever Mets win at the new stadium in downtown Binghamton after rainouts Thursday, Friday and Saturday. "It was worth the three days of rain to see this winner," Antalek said.

Stadium seat has fan on top of world

LOU BRANCACCIO

For 11-year-old Keenya Minard, the up-and-down weather ride waiting to see a professional baseball game in Binghamton was worth it.

Even if she was sitting in the worst seat in the house.

Let it be written down for all of time. Let it be read in the history books. OK, at least let her mom pin it to the refrigerator until the bananas turn black. Binghamton's very own Keenya Minard was the first person at the first game to be the first to sit as far away as you could possibly get in this stadium.

Of course, those who have had any experience in attending a big league game wouldn't complain. In fact, most would consider shoving a bat splinter under their thumbnail to get a seat as good as Keenya's.

"I think it's neat," Keenya announced Sunday of her historic seat.

The Roosevelt Elementary School student said she got her opening-day ticket the way many fans who attended Sunday did. Last March, she waited for hours in a long line. So when the rains came this week to wash out the opener, Keenya was patient. On Sunday, her patience paid off.

"They're good. They can hit balls. I like the players. I like the action," she said.

But the seat? What do you really think about the seat? Keenya wouldn't plop down anywhere else. "I can see e-v-e-r-y-t-h-i-n-g from here!" Who could argue.

Brancaccio is the executive editor of the *Press & Sun-Bulletin*.

(Color) MICHELLE GABEL/PRESS & SUN-BULLETIN

Keenya Minard, 11, right, watches the Binghamton Mets' baseball game Sunday from high atop the field. Kathie Mras of Endwell was sitting in front of Keenya.

SUNSPOT

Students find librarians tough bunch to stump

PALM HARBOR, Fla. (AP) — [illegible]

Abortion showdown expected today

Buffalo draws activists on both sides of issue

By ROQUA MONTEZ IV
Staff Writer

Buffalo was a natural target for anti-abortion rights rallies. Story, Page 2A.

[illegible]

See ABORTION/Page 2A

Robert Abrams
Vows no lawlessness

TO SUBSCRIBE TO THE PRESS & SUN-BULLETIN CALL: (607) 798-1161 or 1-800-253-5343 (N.Y.) 1-800-241-2120 (PA.)

April 20, 1992: Editor Lou Brancaccio wrote a front-page column about a fan's pleasure at seeing baseball in Binghamton. *Microfilm archives*

VAUGHN
27

Rangers' left wing Eric Flinton, wearing number 27, goes for the puck during a Rangers game as Baltimore Bandits' left wing Ryan Sittler follows close behind. On guard is Ranger goalie Dan Cloutier. *Press & Sun-Bulletin archives*

Binghamton Mets Inaugural Team, 1992. Front row: (standing) Reuteman (GM), Fordyce, Allison, Saunders, Niemann (pitching coach), Swisher (Manager), Gideon (Coach), Pride, Howard, Hoffner. Second row: Walker, Johnstone, Delli Carri, Wegmann, Dorn, Douma, Rogers, Katzaroff, Zinter, Hawkins (Trainer). Third row: Butterfield, Dzidkowiec, Hunter, Vitki, Vasquez, Jones, White, Langbehn. *Press & Sun-Bulletin archives*

Press & Sun-Bulletin

Wednesday November 4, 1992 FINAL EDITION

4 SECTIONS BINGHAMTON, N.Y. 35¢ NEWSSTAND

EIGHT PAGES OF COVERAGE INSIDE — PAGES 8-15A

U.S. SENATE: D'Amato wins barroom brawl Page 10A

N.Y. SENATE: Libous clobbers Porter for win Page 11A

U.S. HOUSE: Boehlert crushes four opponents Page 9A

UNION: Bertoni wins his 4th term Page 14A

BROOME: Split whittled down to 11-8 Page 12-13A

ELECTION '92 CHECKLIST

✓ Indicates winning candidate

PRESIDENT

- George Bush (Republican)
- ✓ Bill Clinton (Democrat)
- Ross Perot (Independent)

U.S. SENATE

New York
- Robert Abrams (D/Lib)
- ✓ Alfonse M. D'Amato (R/Con./R-to-L)

Pennsylvania
- ✓ Arlen Specter (R)
- Lynn Yeakel (D)

U.S. HOUSE

23rd District
- ✓ Sherwood L. Boehlert (R)
- Paula DiPerna (D)
- Geoffrey P. Grace (Con)
- Randall A. Terry (R-to-L)
- Ted F. Janowski (Ind)

25th District
- Rhea Jezer (D)
- ✓ James T. Walsh (R/Con)

26th District
- ✓ Maurice D. Hinchey (D/Lib)
- Robert J. Moppert (R/Con)
- Mary C. Dixon (R-to-L)

STATE SENATE

40th District
- Jack Kellner (D)
- ✓ Charles D. Cook (R)
- Richard I. Coombe (Con)
- Vincent F. Rush (R-to-L)

50th District
- ✓ James L. Seward (R/Con)
- Beverly E. Livesay (D)
- Sara J. Mendez (R-to-L)

51st District
- Steven Porter (D)
- ✓ Thomas W. Libous (R/Con)

STATE ASSEMBLY

111th District
- ✓ William Magee (D)
- Phyllis G. Lewis (R/Con)

123rd District
- Kevin M. McManus (D)
- ✓ Richard H. Miller (R/Con)

124th District
- ✓ James R. Tallon (D)
- James L. Evans (R/Con)

126th District
- ✓ Daniel J. Fessenden (R/Con)
- Michael E. O'Hora (D/R-to-L)

127th District
- Byron L. Grover (D)
- ✓ George H. Winner Jr. (R/Con)

BROOME COUNTY

County Executive
- ✓ Timothy M. Grippen (D)
- Emil J. Bielecki (R)

Winning numbers

N.Y. Daily Number: 8-4-7
N.Y. Win 4: 9-6-5-7
N.Y. Take Five: 3-6-11-19-21
N.Y. Pick 10: 1-5-12-14-15-16-17-28-33-34-39-47-50-52-59-61-62-64-73-80
Pa. Daily Lottery: 3-8-7
Pa. Big 4: 9-7-2-0
Wild Card: 8-10-17-27-37-44 Alt.: 13

Index

Questions or comments?

For matters regarding world, national and state news, call 798-1184 between 4 and 11 p.m.

N.Y. BOND ACT

$800 million 'jobs' proposal runs out of gas

From wire service reports

ALBANY — A proposal to revamp New York's economy by borrowing $800 million to fund sewer upgrades, road work and other construction projects statewide trailed at the polls early today.

The proposed "Jobs for the New, New York Bond Act" was the centerpiece of Gov. Mario M. Cuomo's plan to revive the state's sagging economy.

With 68 percent of precincts reporting, 54 percent of voters, or 1,193,080, disapproved, compared to 46 percent, or 1,012,582 approving. In the Southern Tier, the plan received the following votes: Broome County — 32,606 no, 17,001 yes; Tioga — 10,220 no, 2,950 yes; Chenango — 9,877 no, 2,530 yes; Delaware — 10,260 no, 2,287 yes; and Otsego — 12,054 no, 3,336 yes.

Cuomo had told New Yorkers that the sewer, road and other infrastructure improvements paid for by the new borrowing would create more than 35,000 immediate construction jobs. And those projects would attract businesses that would mean another 122,000 jobs, he said.

"It's all a plus. It's not giving money to people to pick up leaves from a park or to paint murals on public buildings. It's to create assets. It's to create wealth," Cuomo said.

But critics, ranging from the state's Conservative Party

See NEW YORK/Page 11A

PRESIDENT

A Clinton crusher

ASSOCIATED PRESS

Bill Clinton and his wife, Hillary, lock hands in a victory salute Tuesday night along with their daughter, Chelsea, left, and Vice President-elect Al Gore and Gore's wife, Tipper. Clinton said his win was a "call for our country to face" new challenges.

From wire service reports

Bill Clinton, the self-styled "new kind of Democrat" who promised immediate help for the nation's troubled economy, claimed a stunning victory over President Bush on Tuesday, taking states that Republicans called their own for more than a decade.

From coast to coast and in overwhelming numbers, voters rejected the 68-year-old Republican's bid for four more years and turned instead to the 46-year-old Democrat, who will be the first president born after World War II and one of the youngest ever to assume the office.

Ross Perot, a Texas tycoon with a jes'-folks persona, ran surprisingly strong for an independent candidate. Perot spent $60 million to finance his candidacy.

With 80 percent of the nation's precincts reporting: Clinton had 35,793,098 votes, or 43 percent. He won 29 states and the District of Columbia, totaling 349 electoral votes. He needed 270 to win.

Bush had 31,709,483 votes, or 38 percent. He won 14 states with 129 electorals. Perot received 15,159,457 votes, or 18 percent. He won no state's electorals.

Clinton swept much of the East and Midwest and other traditionally Republican states in the South that had been considered crucial to Bush's re-election chances.

Democrats started celebrating early in Little Rock, Ark., where Clinton watched returns with his family. Clinton said he felt "wonderful," wrapping up a campaign in which he cast himself as the candidate of new economic opportunity, appealing for voters to summon the "courage to change."

Clinton's running mate, Sen. Al Gore, ending the campaign in his home of Car-

See CLINTON/Page 8A

U.S. HOUSE

Hinchey holds off Moppert in close contest

By EDIE LAU
Staff Writer

Where there was once Matthew F. McHugh, there's now Maurice D. Hinchey.

Hinchey, 54, a Democrat from Saugerties, won a tight contest against Chenango Bridge Republican Robert J. Moppert, 50, for the 26th District seat in Congress.

With 99 percent of ballots counted, Hinchey had 50.5 percent of the vote, and Moppert, 46.6 percent. Right to Life candidate Mary C. Dixon of Endicott, who dropped out of the race last weekend to endorse Moppert, got 2.9 percent. The candidates were competing for the seat being vacated this year by McHugh, an Ithaca Democrat who had the job for 18 years. Hinchey has been an assemblyman for 18 years.

In a long campaign, Hinchey bested two Broome County residents for the seat in the U.S. House of Representatives. Before facing Moppert, Hinchey beat Binghamton Mayor Juanita M. Crabb in a Democratic primary.

As a congressman, Hinchey said, "I'll be spending a lot of time in Binghamton. You can be sure of that."

Moppert was stalwart and gracious in defeat. At a gathering at the Hotel de Ville in Binghamton, he urged supporters to be of good cheer. "This has been a great experience," he said. Moppert is co-owner of Mapes Moving and Storage Co.

Hinchey has won a two-year term, with a base yearly salary of $129,500. The 26th District encompasses all of Ulster County and parts of Broome, Delaware, Tioga, Tompkins, Dutchess, Orange and Sullivan counties.

BROOME COUNTY

Grippen turns back Bielecki to retain county reins

By DON SBARRA
Staff Writer

President-elect Bill Clinton laid claim to the handle "The Comeback Kid," but Broome County Executive Timothy M. Grippen could just as well claim the title.

After presiding over a budget with the largest property tax increase in county history, few would have predicted three years ago that Grippen would win a second term by beating Republican challenger Emil J. Bielecki, 54 percent to 46 percent. Elections officials Tuesday night put the complete, but unofficial count at 47,958 for Grippen to Bielecki's 40,873, with more than 6,000 absentee ballots outstanding.

"It was a very good night. The people of this county recognized my leadership," said Grippen, speaking at a celebration at the Binghamton Regency Hotel. "I think we were able to explain (1990's record 42 percent average tax rate increase). I wanted to see a sales tax, not a property tax. My opponent wanted a property tax."

Clearly surprised by the defeat, Bielecki said the Grippen campaign was apparently successful in creating doubt in the public's mind over the failed incinerator project. "That lingering non-issue continued to haunt me," Bielecki said, referring to the $80 million incinerator proposal rejected by the state. "He effectively exploited it and was able to turn an issue I did not create into a character issue."

Grippen, a former City of Binghamton public works commissioner, won his first-ever election in 1988, beating former two-term County Executive Carl S. Young with roughly 53 percent of the vote.

Promising to control taxes through better management, Grippen entered office in January 1989, and by November was proposing a 1990 budget with millions in new taxes and spending. After a prolonged squabble with legislators over a plan to raise the county sales tax rate, the budget was adopted with a record 42 percent increase in the average county property tax rate. The four-year post paid a salary of $63,500 this year.

CHUCK HAUPT/PRESS & SUN-BULLETIN

Timothy M. Grippen, with his wife, Sally, and daughter, Kara, 9, celebrate his re-election Tuesday at the Binghamton Regency.

TO SUBSCRIBE TO THE PRESS & SUN-BULLETIN CALL: (607) 798-1161 or 1-800-253-5343 (N.Y.) 1-800-241-2120 (PA.)

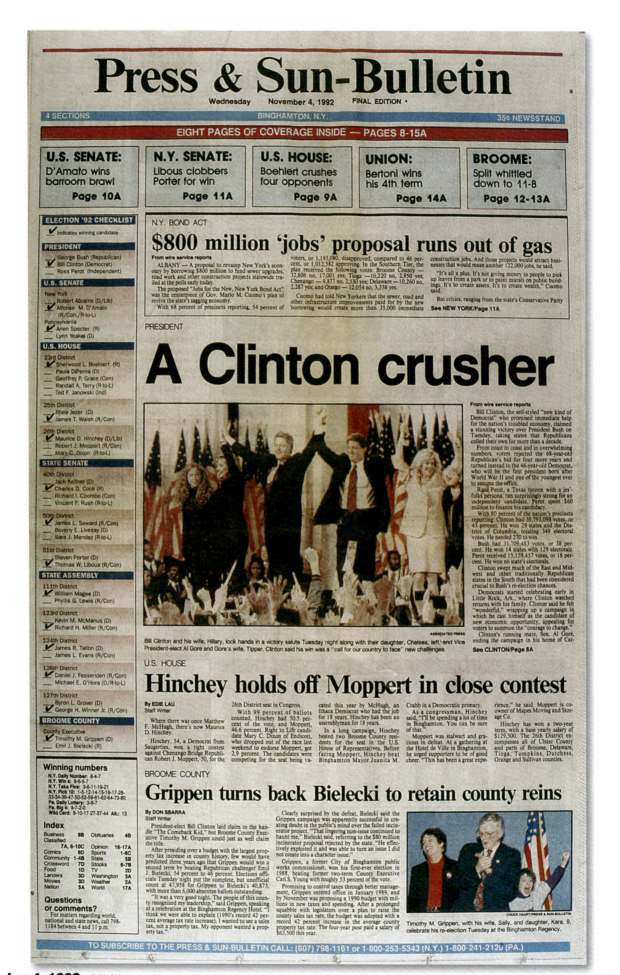

November 4, 1992: Bill Clinton whips the first President Bush, who was so popular after the Gulf War victory that few Democrats dared challenge him. *Courtesy Dolly Escovar*

HOCKEY: Binghamton Rangers play despite storm SPORTS 1C

GAELIC: Tier group struggles for Irish identity LIVING 1D

GAMBLING: State negotiates on Indian casinos NEW YORK 6B

Sunday
March 14, 1993
FINAL EDITION

Press & Sun-Bulletin

7 SECTIONS | BINGHAMTON, N.Y. | $1.50 NEWSSTAND

BLIZZARD

William Roque fends off the wind's sting Saturday afternoon on Main Street in Binghamton.

Saturday's storm emptied the usually bustling streets of downtown Johnson City. Broome County Transit ran until 5:30 p.m. to service the few who chose to brave the storm.

JON WILLIAMS PHOTOS

TURNS TIER INTO

GHOST TOWN

By ELIZABETH WOODS
Staff Writer

The jar of baking soda Fred Bogaczyk delivered to his daughter-in-law Saturday afternoon said it all — Blizzard of '93.

But the weekend blast is more than just the blizzard of the year. It's possibly the fiercest snowstorm since the National Weather Service began keeping records in Broome County in 1952.

The storm relentlessly pounded the area Saturday, dropping 17.4 inches of snow since midnight Friday and hurling 45 mph wind gusts. Up to three feet of snow is expected before the blizzard ends tonight, said meteorologist Joe Dellicarpini, reporting from Binghamton Regional Airport. The record snowfall for a 24-hour period recorded by the Broome County station is 23 inches, which fell Feb. 3 to Feb. 4, 1961.

The record for total snow on the ground — 33 inches — was set Dec. 28, 1969. Saturday night, there were 30 inches on the ground. The monthly record for March snowfall, 33.5 inches, was set in 1971.

A state of emergency announced at 2 p.m. Saturday kept cars off the roads. Instead of driving, Kelly Bogaczyk sheltered herself with a fuchsia umbrella and walked to the corner of Hooper Road and Pruyne Street in Endwell for the soda handoff.

"I couldn't make my oatmeal cookies without baking soda and my husband wouldn't let me drive," she said. She recently moved to her Brookcrest Drive home and didn't know the new neighbors well enough to borrow. That's when she called her father-in-law.

"I said if you need anything, give us a call," said Fred Bogaczyk. "Baking soda, that isn't exactly a blizzard call."

But he didn't walk away empty-handed. In exchange for the soda and four-block walk from his Verna Drive home, he was

See SNOW/Page 7A

Kelly Bogaczyk trades some quiche for a jar of baking soda from her father-in-law Frank Bogaczyk on Hooper Road in Endwell.

The forecast

Is the storm the big one? We still don't know. But if you had to bet, pick this as the Mother of All Storms. Late last night we were just a few inches away from the all-time 24-hour record of 23 inches at Binghamton Regional Airport. The snow and high winds are likely to continue through the day.

Snow schedule

TODAY: Snow accumulations to reach 2 to 3 feet.
Temperatures will be zero to 15.
Winds will be 30 to 50 mph.

MONDAY: Snow will taper off.
Temperatures will be 0 to 20.
Winds will be 20 to 30 mph.

TUESDAY: Small chance of flurries.
Temperatures will be 0 to 32.

Emergency

Gov. Cuomo, Pa. Gov. Casey, Deputy County Executive Tobin and Binghamton Mayor Crabb declared emergencies.

What does that mean?

Basically, don't drive.

When will they be lifted?

Maybe today, but the weather must ease and major roads cleared.

Winning numbers

N.Y. Daily Number: 5-4-0
N.Y. Win 4: 4-2-3-6
N.Y. Lotto: 13-17-27-37-40-54 **Supp:** 28
N.Y. Pick 10: 2-4-7-8-17-19-25-26-27-29-31-32-34-37-40-51-53-65-67-74
Pa. Daily Lottery: 3-3-4
Pa. Big 4: 2-2-6-5

Index

INSIDE

NOTE TO READERS: We're sorry if the paper was delivered to you late. But the weather has made our delivery schedules uncertain.

TO SUBSCRIBE TO THE PRESS & SUN-BULLETIN CALL: (607) 798-1161 or 1-800-253-5343 (N.Y.) 1-800-241-2120 (PA.)

March 14, 1993: The biggest storm in years all but shut down the Tier. *Courtesy David Silvanic*

Using his children's sled to get groceries home to his family through snow-clogged streets, Dick Velle walks along Route 26 in West Corners after making a one-mile trip to Reliable Market, one of the few stores open in the Tier after the blizzard of 1993. *Press & Sun-Bulletin archives*

NEXT

David Jackson spends a second day digging out his one-fifth-of-a-mile driveway off Route 38B in the Town of Newark Valley after the blizzard of 1993. Most of Jackson's driveway was buried under five-foot drifts from the blizzard that dumped about two feet of snow around the Southern Tier. *Press & Sun-Bulletin archives*

Rain
High: 45. Low: 35.
Details 2A

EMMY AWARDS: Nominations shine on 'Guiding Light' LIVING 1D

METS: Ex-football player goes to bat for Binghamton SPORTS 1C

WEATHER: March 'madness' one for record books COMMUNITY 1B

Press & Sun-Bulletin

4 SECTIONS | BINGHAMTON, N.Y. | 35¢ NEWSSTAND

Thursday
April 1, 1993
FINAL EDITION

RISING RIVERS

Rains may swamp Tier

River may be highest since floods of 1936

CHUCK HAUPT/PRESS & SUN-BULLETIN

From staff reports

Today's rain will bring rapidly rising water that threatens the entire Susquehanna River basin, authorities said Wednesday.

The City of Binghamton was bracing for a new round of flooding as about an inch of rain was forecast throughout the region, on top of waters already swollen by snow runoff.

Broome County is working with computer models that indicate the river could rise to 29 feet in Vestal, a level exceeded only by the 30.5 feet reached during the terrible floods of 1936.

"That's the worst-case scenario," said Edward Humphrey, deputy director of emergency services for Broome County. The computer models were provided by the National Weather Service, he

See FLOODING/Page 9A

- Binghamton maps out strategy.
- Anglers out for trout season today should be wary.

— Stories, Page 9A.

Dan Wdowiak, **ABOVE,** of Riverside Lane, Kirkwood, hauls out a load of his family's belongings from his flood-endangered home near the Susquehanna River on Wednesday. Wdowiak, said that by late morning, a laundry room had 3 inches of water in it and the water was 8 inches high in a storage building.

AT RIGHT, Clayton Misner and Dolora Williams unload supplies from a boat outside the home of their neighbor, Ella Shaver, Misner's mother, on Riverside Lane in Kirkwood. The homes were surrounded by Susquehanna River water Wednesday. "I wonder why we ever built a house in the middle of the Susquehanna River," Williams joked.

CHUCK HAUPT/PRESS & SUN-BULLETIN

What's next? Mudslides

First a blizzard, then a flood, now a . . . mudslide?

Sure enough, the oozing, sucking, sliding brown muck is next on the list of things to be on the lookout for this busy spring, a National Weather Service forecaster said Wednesday. "We've got to watch out for mud coming down, now that the snow is gone," said David Croft, a forecaster at Binghamton Regional Airport. "More mess." He said the Catskill areas and eastern Broome County, with their steep hills, are particularly prone.

Allen Street in Deposit has already had a minor mudslide, said Deposit Public Works Superintendent Robert L. Mills. He recommended that people be alert for mudslides and report those they see to local authorities.

— EDIE LAU

N.Y. lawmakers gain budget agreement

ALBANY (AP) — New York began a new fiscal year today the same way as the past eight, without a state budget in place. Shortly after midnight, Gov. Mario M. Cuomo and legislative leaders said they had a tentative deal. But even with that, aides said it may be days before budget bills are passed. Without a budget in place, legislators had to pass emergency legislation to cover a $305 million Medicaid bill.

- School aid was one hurdle. Stories, Page 6B.

German plan taxes Holocaust survivors

BONN, Germany (AP) — Chancellor Helmut Kohl's government said Wednesday that Holocaust survivors and their heirs must pay tax if they want to regain east German property they lost to the Nazis.

The proposal, which also affects people recovering property taken by the Communists, is intended in part to create a fund to compensate those who want money rather than lost property. The package was approved by Kohl's Cabinet and now goes to Parliament. People who choose compensation would receive 1.3 times the taxable value of their property in 1935. Those who want back property seized by the Communists would have to pay one-third of the 1990 taxable value of their old real estate. Nazi victims or their relatives would pay one-quarter of property value.

N.Y. cities to help test vaccines in AIDS battle

ROCHESTER (AP) — The first U.S. study of vaccines for children with HIV will be conducted in 12 cities — including Syracuse and Rochester — to see if the inoculations will boost immune systems against the virus, which causes AIDS.

Preliminary evidence from tests on adults has shown that some vaccines can boost the immune system's fight against HIV. Ninety children between 1 month and 12 years old, will be recruited for the study of three experimental vaccines at 12 sites, including Rochester's Strong Memorial Hospital. The other target cities are Syracuse; New York City; Durham, N.C.; Worcester, Mass.; San Francisco; Boston; Los Angeles; Houston; Denver; New Brunswick, N.J.; and Chicago.

SPRING FUN

A walk on the wild side

A wildlife expert will bring along some big cats, bear cubs, reptiles and birds of prey for his talk at 8 tonight in the Farrell Hall Theater at the State University of New York College of Technology at Delhi. There is no admission charge.

Winning numbers

N.Y. Daily Number: 8-5-2
N.Y. Win 4: 8-2-9-9
N.Y. Pick 10: 3-5-6-14-16-32-33-34-42-46-50-54-55-58-59-60-62-67-68-74
N.Y. Lotto: 3-10-11-18-21-40 Supp.: 46
Pa. Daily Lottery: 9-0-8
Pa. Big 4 Lottery: 9-4-0-0
Super 7: 8-16-38-51-55-57-61-63-64-69

Index

Questions or comments?

For matters regarding world, national and state news call the news desk at 798-1184 between 4 and 11 p.m. weekdays. Leslie Spalding is the news editor. To fax information: 798-1113.

BINGHAMTON PROPERTY FIGHT

Battle embroils city, councilman

By DON SBARRA
Staff Writer

A Binghamton city councilman is heading to court after failing to correct a list of code violations at rental property he owns downtown.

Councilman B.E. "Bob" Kashou, R-3rd District, on Wednesday acknowledged that violations still exist at the 48 Court St. building, but said many have been corrected since city code officials inspected the three-story structure Jan. 12.

A seven-page inspection report by the city's code enforcement office cited numerous problems at the building's second- and third-floor apartments, which at the time were both occupied. They included several mentions of bare electrical wires, lack of smoke detectors, poor ventilation, flaking paint, holes in walls, improper lighting, poor weatherproofing and a leaking roof. The inspector also noted the presence of bats and mice, and ordered extermination.

B.E. Kashou
Claims unfair treatment

Kashou, who received a

See COUNCILMAN/Page 9A

RENT DISPUTE

Playhouse gets reprieve

Court ruling holds off final curtain

By GENE GREY
Staff Writer

The show can go on — at least until Aug. 31.

The Cider Mill Playhouse Inc. was granted a stay of eviction by Town of Union Justice Woodruff A. Gaul Sr. after a three-hour hearing Wednesday. Orlando J. Ciotoli, owner of the 2 S. Nanticoke Ave., Endicott, building occupied by the non-profit theater group, is seeking back rent and possession of his property.

"It's like being granted a stay of execution and knowing at least you've got until Aug. 31 to live," said a relieved Ruth Foley Ahearn, president of the playhouse board of directors.

The stay will allow the theater, which has been on the site for 17 years, to complete its current season and a summer season. The next show, *Homeward Bound,* will open April 15 as scheduled.

Ciotoli said he'd obey the court's ruling, but didn't think the playhouse has much of a future. "It's a loser," he said. "I'm not in the position to finance community theater."

Edie Hungerford heard about the reprieve, but expressed no relief. The Binghamton resident, who's attended every play for the past few years, called the prospect of losing the theater "very sad. People love the Cider Mill."

Gaul gave the board and Ciotoli 10 days to find a third party to referee the lease differences and negotiate a reasonable rent increase. In making his decision, Gaul said a landlord may not be entitled to an eviction if it will cause unnecessary and significant harm to the tenant.

Attorney David Gouldin
Calls witnesses to cite Cider Mill Playhouse's importance in community

David M. Gouldin, playhouse attorney, called John W. Ellis, executive director of the Broome County Arts Council, and Leonard J. Jacobs Jr., president and executive director of the county Chamber of Commerce, to attest to the theater's importance to the community.

Ciotoli's attorney, James G. Collins, granted that, but said his client, as property owner, has the right to a fair and equitable rent. The rent has been $3,600 a month, and Ciotoli wants $4,500, testimony indicated.

— Staff Writer Mark Winheld contributed to this report.

TO SUBSCRIBE TO THE PRESS & SUN-BULLETIN CALL: (607) 798-1161 or 1-800-253-5343 (N.Y.) 1-800-241-2120 (PA.)

April 1, 1993: All that snow threatened flooding. *Courtesy Dolly Escovar*

Friday
April 2, 1993
FINAL EDITION

Rain
High: 48. Low: 30.
Details 2A

EJ STRIDES:
Dressing down pushes sales up
MONEY REPORT 12B

FAMILY FESTIVAL:
Children's Fair mixes fun & learning at BCC
GOOD TIMES!

Press & Sun-Bulletin

5 SECTIONS — BINGHAMTON, N.Y. — 35¢ NEWSSTAND

Swamped

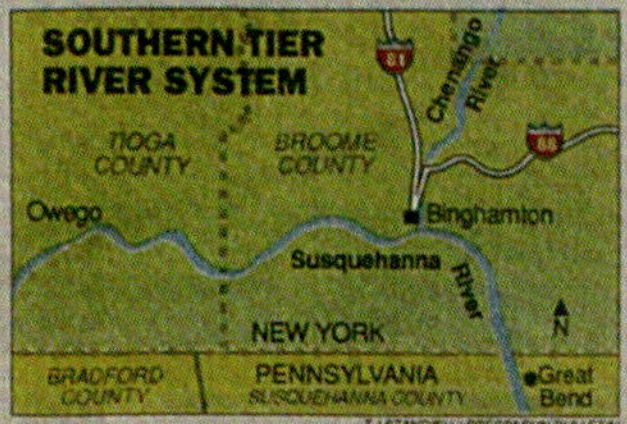
SOUTHERN TIER RIVER SYSTEM
TIOGA COUNTY
BROOME COUNTY
Chenango River
Owego
Binghamton
Susquehanna River
NEW YORK
N
BRADFORD COUNTY
PENNSYLVANIA
SUSQUEHANNA COUNTY
Great Bend

T.J. STANDISH / PRESS & SUN-BULLETIN

ERIC C. HEGEDUS/PRESS & SUN-BULLETIN

An aerial view of Route 7 in the Town of Conklin on Thursday shows buildings and trees in the midst of severe flooding from the Susquehanna River. The riverbed, located at the top of the photograph, rose to the fourth-highest level ever recorded in Conklin on Thursday. The 17.9-foot-high level hadn't been reached since waters hit 18.3 feet in Conklin on March 10, 1964. Most Tier rivers are expected to crest by this afternoon.

RAGING RIVERS

Southern Tier waters hit highest levels since 1964

By EDIE LAU
Staff Writer

Rainfall Thursday pushed Southern Tier rivers — already swollen from the melting snow of last month's blizzard — into more neighborhoods, forcing residents from their homes, turning roads into lakes and closing schools.

In some areas, the rising waters hadn't been this bad in almost 30 years. In Conklin, for example, the Susquehanna River rose to 17.9 feet, the fourth-highest level recorded there. The last time the river rose higher at that point was March 10, 1964, when it hit 18.3 feet.

On Stillwater Road in Conklin, Richard Kipp watched from the water's edge as the river inched toward the level of his house. Everything Kipp owned except his refrigerator was on the second floor. "I've lived here for 30 years and I never seen it this bad," he said.

Areas flooded Thursday should find relief coming slowly as today's forecast calls for more rain, which means water will recede slowly. It could have been worse. Forecasts for Thursday originally called for torrential rains. But only one-third of an inch had fallen at Binghamton Regional Airport by 7 p.m.

Even though the Binghamton region didn't get soaked from the sky, rain that fell upstream eventually will get here via the river, said National Weather Service forecaster David N. Martin. "There's a delayed effect," Martin said. That's why the Susquehanna River at Vestal, more than 7 feet above the flood stage Thursday, was expected to continue rising until early today. It should crest at 26 feet, said forecaster Scott White with the National Weather Service.

About a dozen major thoroughfares — including parts of Route 7 in Conklin, Route 17C in Endwell and Old Vestal Road in Vestal — were closed by flooding. The towns of Conklin, Kirkwood, Union and Vestal declared states of emergency, giving officials the power to compel evacuations and ticket sightseers, said Broome County Emergency Services Director Michael F. Aswad. No arrests had been made as of nightfall, he said.

High water forced more than 200 families from their homes in Conklin and Kirkwood by late Thursday afternoon, Aswad said. The Broome County Chapter of the American Red Cross was sheltering 10 persons in two locations Thursday evening, said William B. Epps, chapter manager. The Red Cross also fed dinner to 50, including emergency services workers and flood victims who had found refuge elsewhere.

Pupils in the Susquehanna Valley and Tioga Central school districts got a day off because of flooded roads around buildings, as did pupils in two schools in the Windsor Central School District.

— **Staff writers Steven N. Levine, Mary Margaret Earl and George Basler contributed to this report.**

CHUCK HAUPT/PRESS & SUN-BULLETIN

Mike Doolittle, Endwell Mobile Home Park owner, gets his dog, Misty, away from Susquehanna River flood waters on Thursday. The park was evacuated.

The forecast:

- **RAIN TODAY,** changing to light snow tonight, continuing Saturday. About one-quarter inch of rain is expected today.

The river:

- **WATER WILL RISE** throughout the region, with most crests expected to occur by today.
- **IN VESTAL,** the Susquehanna River should crest at 26 feet, more than 8 feet above the flood stage.

Winning numbers

Saturday's Lotto jackpot: $2.5 million
N.Y. Daily Number: 3-4-5
N.Y. Win 4: 0-5-1-7
N.Y. Pick 10: 4-14-17-19-20-23-30-31-32-40-54-55-57-59-62-63-65-66-70-78
Pa. Daily Lottery: 4-4-3
Pa. Big 4: 4-2-3-2
Pa. Cash 5: 1-9-13-28-30

Index

THREE FULL PAGES OF COVERAGE INSIDE

TO SUBSCRIBE TO THE PRESS & SUN-BULLETIN CALL: (607) 798-1161 or 1-800-253-5343 (N.Y.) 1-800-241-2120 (PA.)

April 2, 1993: The paper wasn't fooling with its day-earlier warning of floods. *Courtesy Dolly Escovar*

Snow
High: 36. Low: 20.
Details 2A

Happy New Year

Press & Sun-Bulletin

4 SECTIONS — BINGHAMTON, N.Y. — 35¢ NEWSSTAND

Saturday
January 1, 1994
HOLIDAY EDITION

Wynette fights bile duct infection

NASHVILLE, Tenn. (AP) — Country music queen Tammy Wynette, "the heroine of heartbreak," was said to be improving Friday but was still in critical condition with an infection of the bile duct.

"Doctors are quite impressed with Ms. Wynette's improvement, but caution that she is not out of the woods yet," said her spokeswoman, Evelyn Shriver. Wynette, 51, best known for her hits *Stand by Your Man* and *D-I-V-O-R-C-E*, spent her fourth day at Baptist Hospital, where she was in the intensive care section.

Doctors said the bile duct infection was apparently caused by scarring from previous surgery.

4 snowmobilers die in Montana avalanche

KALISPELL, Mont. (AP) — A group of snowmobilers was caught in an avalanche Friday on a mountain ridge and at least four were killed, authorities said.

Two others were rescued with minor injuries, authorities at the scene were trying to resucitate another, and an eighth person was missing, said Corky Derby, spokeswoman for the Flathead County sheriff's department.

Search efforts continued in the dark for the missing rider, Derby said.

Officials said the avalanche occurred on Peter's Ridge, about 6,000 feet up in the Swan Range some 15 miles east of Kalispell. It is a popular snowmobile riding area and had up to a foot of new, powdery snow over the previous 24 hours. Derby had no information on the people involved but said most of them were believed to be from the Kalispell area.

Oneidas pay off debt on Verona casino

VERONA (AP) — The Oneida Indian Nation has already paid for its $10 million Turning Stone gambling casino, which has been open only five months.

"It's dramatically exciting," casino spokeswoman Diane Stirling said this week of paying off the bill.

Turning Stone, which offers most traditional casino games except for slot machines, has attracted an average of about 7,000 people on weekdays and 11,000 on Saturdays and Sundays since it opened July 20. All told, about 850,000 people have attended the gambling hall about 35 miles east of Syracuse. The Oneidas already have plans to expand the casino.

WINTER FUN

Rockers in J.C.

The rock group Rival Suns will be unleashing songs from its debut album *Feel*, when appearing at The Amsterdam, 40 Willow St., Johnson City.

Music will be played from 10 a.m. to closing and admission is $3 at the door.

Winning numbers

N.Y. Daily Number: 5-4-9
N.Y. Win 4: 8-6-0-1
N.Y. Take Five: 5-20-24-35-38
N.Y. Pick 10: 4-8-20-22-26-30-31-37-38-40-46-55-56-59-60-68-70-75-77-80
Pa. Daily Lottery: 2-6-7
Pa. Big 4 Lottery: 7-6-4-1
Pa. Wild Card: 2-19-34-40-42-43 Alt: 44

Index

Business	8B	Obituaries	4B
Classified	5-8C	Opinion	6A
Comics	4D	Sports	1-5C
Community	1-3B	State	4B
Crossword	5D	Stocks	6-7B
Landers	3D	TV	2D
Living	1D	Washington	3A
Movies	5D	Weather	2A
Nation	3A	World	7A

Questions or comments?

For matters regarding world, national and state news call the news desk at 798-1184 between 4 and 11 p.m. weekdays. Leslie Spalding is the news editor. To fax information: 798-1113.

OBITUARY

IBM legend Watson dies

Tier leaders, employees remember a great man

By LAURIE A. LUEBBERT
Business Writer

■ The year in review at IBM. Story, Page 8B.

Whether walking in his father's footsteps or straying from that path to accomplish new feats, Thomas J. Watson Jr. will be remembered for enriching the Southern Tier personally and professionally.

Watson, 79, who was chief executive officer of IBM Corp. from 1956 to 1971, died Friday in Greenwich, Conn., of complications from a stroke.

"You talk about great people and great contributions to the community, and you're talking about Tom Watson," said Assemblyman Dick Miller, who worked closely with IBM when he served the Town of Union in various capacities from 1967 to 1984.

Watson was said to have followed in his father's footsteps, in terms of maintaining the principles set forth by the founder of IBM.

But he also blazed new trails, taking the reins of IBM when technology was turning typewriters and adding machines into the unexplored world of corporate computing.

"We all did, and still do, follow the traditions he set," said Thomas Ruane, who retired as site manager at IBM-Endicott in late 1993. "Respect for the individual was one of his guiding principals, and that always was instilled in management training as soon as you entered those ranks."

Watson led IBM through the longest and most spectacular growth in modern business history. The company grew from about $700 million in annual revenues to $7.5 billion during his tenure as chief executive, developing into a paternalistic organization that engendered hard work, pride, loyalty and lifelong employment.

But since the late 1980s, the company has gone through wrenching adjustments to align itself with customers who are interested in smaller computers, which sell at a lower profit margin, than the big mainframes that have been its dominant product.

Its payroll went from 302,000 to around 255,000 in 1993, the first time fewer people worked at IBM than in Watson's day.

"When you see something you love have great difficulties, you are very sad about it," Watson told *The Wall Street Journal* in December 1992.

"I have every confidence they'll prevail," he said. "But meanwhile it's a pretty hard pot of porridge

See WATSON/Page 4A

Thomas Watson Jr.
Former IBM CEO

Celebrating the new year

MAUREEN HUGHES/PRESS & SUN-BULLETIN

Rose Poss, right, of Endicott celebrates the New Year with her mother Agata Clara Gance, 93, during a New Year's Eve party Friday at the Susquehanna Nursing Home in Johnson City. Gance's hope for 1994: "I wish for good health, happiness and peace." Between 70 and 80 nursing home revelers attended the party, throwing confetti and tooting horns.

WEATHER

11 feet of snow:

It happened here in '93

By SERGIO G. NON
Staff Writer

According to legend, when Wenceslaus, Duke and patron saint of Bohemia, looked out from his castle one Dec. 26 evening, he was greeted by an exceedingly thick and level blanket of snow.

He should've seen the Southern Tier this year.

"We had a wonderful blizzard," said Conklin resident Ruth Hopkins. "I love snow. I just like to look at it."

Although the National Weather Service tracks snowfall totals by winter seasons, rather than calendar years, its statistics do show the Binghamton area was covered by 136.7 inches of snow in 1993 — the most recorded in the last 30 calendar years. Bill Davis, a meteorologist at the weather service's Binghamton Regional Airport bureau, said most of that came from East Coast storm systems picking up moisture from the Atlantic Ocean. "We get that east to west air flow," he said.

Snowfalls earlier this year at

See SNOW/Page 4A

NEW YORK TAXES

Cuomo, Legislature work on break for businesses

By MARC HUMBERT
The Associated Press

ALBANY — A substantial tax cut for New York's business community in 1994 is being examined by state government leaders, officials said Friday.

Gov. Mario M. Cuomo is considering proposals to reduce the state's 15 percent surcharge on corporate taxes, a policy thrust that could be unveiled Wednesday when he delivers his 12th annual State of the State address to the Legislature. The surcharge costs businesses about $800 million annually.

State Senate Majority Leader Ralph Marino, state government's most powerful Republican, has already come out in favor of phasing out the 15 percent surcharge.

With Democrat Cuomo and Republican Marino backing such a move, chances would increase dramatically that the state Assembly's Democratic majority would agree. Cuomo and Assembly Speaker Saul Weprin are close political allies, but a spokesman for Weprin said Friday that a possible corporate tax surcharge reduction has yet to be discussed by the Assembly hierarchy.

And Weprin spokesman Michael Moran said the Assembly Democrats would give a higher priority to advancing an earned income tax credit to help the working poor than to a corporate tax reduction. An earned income tax credit, already in place at the federal level, is being considered by Cuomo.

Mario M. Cuomo

Cuomo, eyeing a possible tough run for a fourth term in 1994, made it clear during an interview with Public Television's *Inside Albany* this week that a cut in the corporate surcharge may be in the cards.

"The corporate tax will probably go down. The hotel tax will probably go down," he said.

A surcharge on corporate profits was imposed by the state in 1990 to help balance an out-of-whack state budget. The surcharge was supposed to have dropped to 10 percent in 1992 and be eliminated completely in 1993. But Cuomo and the Legislature have twice delayed any reduction.

A reduction to 10 percent in the surcharge could save businesses about $275 million to $300 million annually, according to state officials. Cuomo and the Legislature may first opt for a reduction to 12.5 percent.

COLLEGE FOOTBALL

Holiday bowl blitz

National championship at stake today

The Associated Press

Don't call tonight's Orange Bowl matchup between No. 1 Florida State and No. 2 Nebraska a national championship game unless you're ready to argue the issue with No. 3 West Virginia and coach Don Nehlen.

Or, perhaps worse than that, No. 4 Notre Dame.

Both Nehlen, preparing for a Sugar Bowl date against No. 8 Florida, and Lou Holtz, whose Irish face No. 7 Texas A&M at the Cotton Bowl, figure they should be in the title picture, too.

West Virginia is 11-0 and suggests that with Nebraska as the only other undefeated team, it ought to be in a showdown with the Cornhuskers. Failing that, Nehlen insists that a victory over Florida should assure the Mountaineers at least a piece of the title.

Notre Dame is 10-1 and armed with a victory over Florida State. If both teams win Saturday, Holtz wonders why his team's head-to-head victory over the Seminoles shouldn't settle the issue.

Other games today:

■ The Rose Bowl offers No. 9 Wisconsin and No. 14 UCLA.

■ No. 10 Miami faces No. 16 Arizona in the Fiesta Bowl.

■ The Hall of Fame Bowl No. 23 Michigan against North Carolina State.

■ No. 13 Penn State plays No. 6 Tennessee in the Citrus Bowl.

■ No. 15 Boston College plays Virginia in the Carquest Bowl.

■ Southern plays South Carolina State in the Heritage Bowl.

■ Friday's bowl results; today's lineup, Pages 1, 4, 5C.

TO SUBSCRIBE TO THE PRESS & SUN-BULLETIN CALL: (607) 798-1161 or 1-800-253-5343 (N.Y.), 1-800-241-2120 (PA.)

January 1, 1994: The death of Thomas Watson Jr. marred the celebration of a New Year. *Courtesy Dolly Escovar*

Saturday
April 23, 1994
FINAL EDITION

Sunny
High: 63. Low 40.
Details 2A

PROTECTION FOR BABY:
Just a few preventive measures can 'childproof' your home
FAMILY & FRIENDS 1D

NEW CHAMPION:
Moorer upsets Holyfield in 12 rounds
SPORTS 1C

Press & Sun-Bulletin

4 SECTIONS · BINGHAMTON, N.Y. · 35¢ NEWSSTAND

37TH PRESIDENT

NIXON DIES

Tumultuous career shaped post-war America

Nixon persona made positive mark in Tier

Editor's note: People throughout the Tier had associations with Richard Nixon during his long political career. Here's what some of them told Staff Writer Mark Winheld:

Eugene C. Gerhart, 82, Binghamton. Lawyer.

To Lt. j.g. Eugene C. Gerhart, Lt. Richard Nixon was a deadly poker player, a straight-arrow family man and a "perfectly friendly, decent guy."

Gerhart, then 32, was Nixon's roommate for a few months early in 1945 when they were assigned to a Navy Air Corps office in Philadelphia.

They met when Gerhart's previous roommate at the Princeton Club moved out, and Nixon, fresh from wartime duty, was looking for a place to stay.

"He came in from the Pacific with $10,000 he won playing poker," said Gerhart, adding he didn't play cards with Nixon because "I knew I'd lose."

He recalled Nixon as a reserved young man with a Quaker background who didn't get drunk, didn't womanize and never gave Gerhart reason to doubt his word. "He said he wanted to get into politics because he wanted to make war a thing of the past," Gerhart recalls.

Nixon invited Gerhart and his wife, Mary, to his inaugurations — once as Eisenhower's vice president and twice as president — and sent him personally inscribed copies of his books.

Gerhart, an independent who voted for Nixon, praised his friend's foreign policy expertise. Nixon's role in the Watergate scandal, Gerhart said, consisted of "a few mistakes," notably "loyalty to friends and colleagues in the White House for what he thought was a minor thing, and it was used as a club to beat him with."

Marcia R. MacKellar, 35, Montrose, Pa. Lamaze instructor.

When MacKellar's father, James B. Rhoads, was administrator of the national archives in the late 1960s, the family attended a prayer brunch at the White House. It was "very exciting," MacKellar recalls, but involved a certain amount of property destruction.

On the way out the door of their home in Lanham, Md., a Washington suburb, her older brother, Jim, then 12, slipped on ice and ripped out the knee of his new suit, bought expressly for the occasion.

"Total family chaos," she recalls. Their mother repaired the pants, but they were late. Not too late to worship in the Gold Room with the late Rev. Norman Vincent Peale and hear the Vienna Boys Choir sing, but the ensuing brunch proved MacKellar's undoing.

"Being 10 years old, I was kind of nervous. I spilled a glass of orange juice in the Blue Room and it landed on the satin-covered chairs. I was very embarrassed. I just walked away."

Nixon, his wife and daughters stood in a receiv-

See NIXON'S/Page 6A

ASSOCIATED PRESS

President Richard M. Nixon died at 9:08 p.m. Friday at the New York Hospital-Cornell Medical Center.He was 81. Nixon died as a result of complications from a massive stroke he suffered on Monday at his home in Park Ridge, N.J. The former president fell into a deep coma Thursday. Experts said the coma greatly reduced his chances of survival and virtually guaranteed that he would never regain his powers of expression. President Clinton made the formal announcement of Nixon's death from the Rose Garden Friday night. "He experienced his fair share of adversity," Clinton said. "I was deeply grateful to President Nixon for his wise counsel on many occasions" over the past year. Clinton noted the contributions Nixon made in reaching out to adversary nations such as China and the Soviet Union. Services for the former president will be held at 7 p.m. EDT Wednesday at the Richard Nixon Library & Birthplace in Yorba Linda. His wife Patricia Ryan Nixon, who died last year, is buried there.

By RICK HAMPSON
The Associated Press

NEW YORK — Richard Milhous Nixon died Friday, four days after suffering a stroke that had left him in a deep coma. He was 81.

The former president died at 9:08 p.m. at New York Hospital, said spokeswoman Myrna Manners. "His family was with him," she said.

Reporters gathered outside the Manhattan hospital learned the news about 1½ hours after his death in a two-sentence news release. Soon after the news was announced, the flag was lowered to half-staff over the White House.

The body had been removed from the hospital and taken to an area funeral home by the time the death was made public. Nixon's body won't lie in state in the Capitol rotunda, according to the family's wishes. The former president was involved in planning the funeral arrangements, family spokeswoman Liz Johnston said.

A statement from the Richard M. Nixon Presidential Library and Birthplace in Yorba Linda, Calif., said the body will be flown to California on Tuesday and will lie in state in the library's lobby for public viewing beginning at 3 p.m. The viewing will continue through the night until 11 a.m. Wednesday.

All three networks interrupted regular programming to announce the death and present highlights of Nixon's career. The news drew expressions of sorrow from both political friends and foes.

President Clinton called a news conference in the Rose Garden to make the formal announcement.

"I was deeply grateful to President Nixon for his wise counsel on many occasions," Clinton said. "Our relationship continued to be warm and constructive ... He went out of his way to give me his best advice."

"To Nancy and I he was a cherished friend and brilliant counselor," former President Reagan said from Los Angeles. "Richard Nixon understood the world. He understood politics, power and the fragile yet undeniable force of history.

Services were scheduled for 7 p.m. EDT Wednesday at the Nixon Library with family friend, the Rev. Billy Graham, officiating. Graham also presided over the funeral last year of Nixon's wife, Pat. A private interment will follow at the library near Mrs. Nixon's grave.

Eulogies will be delivered by Clinton, Sen. Bob Dole, R-Kansas, and California Gov. Pete Wilson.

Nixon was brought to the hospital after suffering the stroke Monday night at his Park Ridge, N.J., home.

His daughters, Julie Eisenhower and Tricia Cox, were at his side as his condition deteriorated.

He was partly paralyzed on the right side and unable to speak even before he slipped into the coma Thursday.

In the hours after the stroke, doctors said Nixon was out of grave danger, alert and in good spirits. He was moved out of intensive care briefly Tuesday, but returned two hours later when doctors discovered a swelling of the brain.

Doctors sometimes try to reduce brain swelling after a stroke by using a respirator to speed up breathing. Nixon was not put on a respirator. He had left a living will, and several news organizations reported that it included instructions that he not be resuscitated.

Nixon's stroke apparently was the result of a blood clot that formed in his heart and moved to the brain's middle cerebral artery. The blockage deprived this crucial cranial region of oxygen, damaging some brain tissue and causing the swelling.

INSIDE:
Four pages of coverage

Winning numbers

N.Y. Daily Number: 7-1-6
N.Y. Win 4: 1-9-5-3
Take Five: 2-10-30-33-37
N.Y. Pick 10: 2-3-5-13-14-16-17-21-28-30 34-47-49-50-52-63-66-72-74-80
Pa. Daily Lottery: 3-6-1
Pa. Big 4: 6-1-3-6
Pa. Wild card: 8-24-27-36-44-45 Supp:17

Index

Questions or comments?

Call the News Desk at 798-1184 between 4 and 11 p.m. weekdays. Fax: 798-1113. Leslie Spalding is the news editor.

BALKANS CONFLICT

NATO ultimatum threatens massive strikes against Serbs

From wire service reports

BRUSSELS, Belgium — Reacting to mounting international outrage, the NATO alliance Friday delivered an ultimatum to Bosnian Serb forces to stop their attacks on the besieged city of Gorazde or face immediate air strikes against a range of military targets.

"The situation demands action," NATO Secretary-General Manfred Woerner told reporters.

Hundreds of civilians have died in recent days as the defenseless city — one of six areas in war-torn Bosnia that the United Nations declared so-called "safe havens" — has been subjected to relentless Serb artillery, mortar and tank bombardment.

That shelling continued Friday for hours beyond announcement of the NATO ultimatum, killing 99 people and wounding nearly 300, according to trapped city officials and relief workers communicating via ham radios.

Late Friday, U.N. specia' envoy to the former Yugoslavia Yasushi Akashi said the Serbs had agreed to cease-fire around Gorazde beginning at noon local time today. But dozens of such agreements have gone unfulfilled or lasted mere minutes.

In addition to the immediate cease-fire, ambassadors to the 16-nation Ne-th Atlantic Treaty Organization also demanded:

■ That all Bosnian Serb forces withdraw at least 1.9 miles from the Gorazde city center by one minute past midnight Sunday morning local time.

■ That a 12.5 miles military exclusion zone from the Gorazde city center be established by one minute past midnight Wednesday morning. Any heavy weapons remaining in this zone would be subject to air strikes. (A small section of Serbia proper that lies within the 12.5-mile zone was specifically excluded, however.)

■ That United Nations peacekeeping forces, humanitarian relief convoys and medical assistance teams be able to enter Gorazde unimpeded and that medical evacuations are permitted.

Calling the measures "some of the most far-reaching decisions in the history of our alliance," Woerner warned that "It is now up to the Bosnia Serbs to heed these demands or face the most serious consequences."

Wording of the ultimatum, which threatens air strikes against Bosnian Serb "heavy weapons and other military targets" within the 12.5-mile zone, constitutes both a significant broadening of NATO options for military action in Bosnia and, at least potentially, a deeper involvement in the war.

Coverage inside:

TO SUBSCRIBE TO THE PRESS & SUN-BULLETIN CALL: (607) 798-1161 or 1-800-253-5343 (N.Y.). 1-800-241-2120 (PA.)

April 23, 1994: The death of former President Richard Nixon merited four pages of coverage. *Courtesy Dolly Escovar*

Thursday
February 16, 1995

Partly cloudy
Hi: 40 Lo: 15
Details 2A

EXTRA EDITION

EXTRA

Press & Sun-Bulletin

4 SECTIONS | BINGHAMTON, N.Y. | 35¢ NEWSSTAND

1,500 jobs

Pataki says N.Y. will move workers to IBM-Glendale

By DON SBARRA
Staff Writer

As many as 1,500 state jobs will move to the vacant IBM-Glendale campus in the Town of Union this fall, Gov. George E. Pataki announced today.

As part of a huge agreement designed to keep the giant computer company based in New York, Pataki outlined plans to consolidate the state's back-office computer operations in Glendale and in the Hudson Valley.

G. Pataki

T. Libous

The deal calls for the state to buy about 325,000 square feet in the Glendale complex, including buildings Nos. 8, 9 and 16.

The campus, off Route 17C on Endicott's west-ern border, contains about 1 million square feet of space. It was once home to about 3,500 IBM workers, many of whom fell victim to layoffs or relocations under a company downsizing effort. Since 1988 the IBM work force in Broome and Tioga counties dropped from nearly 12,000 employees to fewer than 5,000 today. IBM employs about 25,000 statewide.

Pataki, IBM Chief Executive Officer Louis V. Gerstner Jr., and state Office of General Services Commissioner Peter Delaney made an initial announcement at 11 a.m. in New York City, then flew by helicopter directly to the Glendale facility for a 1:30 p.m. unveiling of the local plans.

The 1,500 jobs will cover such state functions as data processing, purchasing and other similar operations.

Under the agreement, the state will pay IBM about $13 million for the locations. But, consolidating about three dozen scattered state offices will save taxpayers about $50 million per year. The government has also agreed to pay a payment in lieu of taxes, or PILOT, to the host communities. The PILOT amount was not released.

State Sen. Thomas W. Libous, R-Binghamton, who has been working on the deal with the Pataki administration since January, earlier today said the agreement provides evidence of the governor's commitment to keep IBM in New York, as well as to helping the struggling Southern Tier.

"I just want to say 'thank you' to Gov. Pataki for helping out this community," Libous said. "I think it's indicative of his interest in our community."

PRESS & SUN-BULLETIN

The state is buying about a third of the IBM-Glendale campus in a $13 million deal with the computer giant that includes a Hudson Valley site. The plan will bring 1,500 jobs to the Town of Union plant.

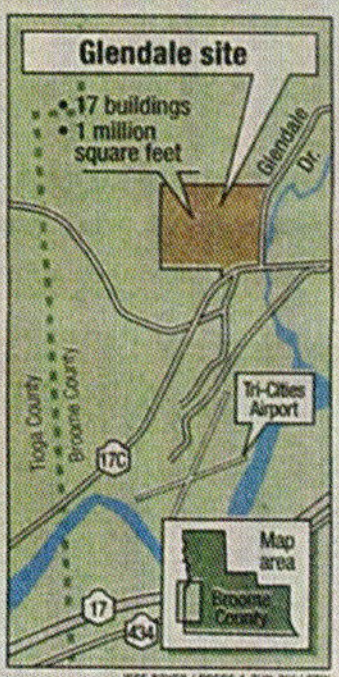
Glendale site
• 17 buildings
• 1 million square feet
Glendale Dr.
Tioga County
Broome County
17C
Tri-Cities Airport
Map area
17
434

JEFF BOYER / PRESS & SUN-BULLETIN

Job announcement reverses trend

By JEFF PLATSKY
Business Editor

Today's announcement is unexpected good news for Broome and Tioga counties, which have lost 15,000 manufacturing jobs since 1988.

Growth in the region's service sector has compensated for a small portion of those lost jobs, but often those jobs have paid workers lower wages than the lost manufacturing positions.

The loss of manufacturing and other jobs has dealt a blow to the region's once vibrant economy. Manufacturing employment in Broome and Tioga suffered from major cuts in the IBM work force and slashed defense budgets, both lynchpins in the local economy.

Here is list of major cutbacks in the past several years:

- **October 1992**: Endicott Johnson closes Ranger Rubber division in Johnson City with 300 workers losing their jobs.
- **June 1993**: Microflite, which employs 120 in the manufacturing of commercial simulation equipment for the airline industry, closes.
- **August 1993**: Martin Marietta closes a plant in the Conklin Corporate park, idling 350 people.
- **December 1993**: New York State Electric & Gas cuts 600 people through attrition and layoffs.
- **February 1994**: IBM lays off 320 workers at its Endicott facility. Another 200 layoffs followed later in the year in various divisions of the North Street operation and the relocation of at least 100 more people to other IBM sites.
- **April 1994**: CAE-Link announces that it will lay off as many as 400 people in the next year.
- **April 1994**: Loral Federal Systems in Owego trims its work force by 200, citing defense cuts.
- **June 1994**: AT&T cuts 80 operators in Binghamton as it consolidates operations.
- **June 1994**: SCI Systems closes plant in Owego, which once employed more than 200 people.

About this EXTRA

This special afternoon EXTRA of the *Press & Sun-Bulletin* is only the fourth such edition the *Press* has produced in 50 years. It contains an entirely new front page and **new editorial on Page 10A.** This EXTRA is a reflection of the *Press'* firm commitment to serving its readers.

Coming tomorrow: Complete coverage of the IBM-Glendale deal and its impact on the Southern Tier.

Winning numbers

N.Y. Daily Number: 2-9-2
N.Y. Win 4: 4-5-0-0
N.Y. Lotto: 9-18-23-43-46-53
Supp: 35
N.Y. Pick 10: 12-13-15-16-18-32-39-43-46-49-51-53-54-56-65-66-67-68-72-74
Pa. Daily Lottery: 0-6-1
Pa. Big 4: 8-6-9-7
Pa. Hearts: KH-3D-6D-9D-AD

0 40901 00701 2

Index

Questions or comments?

Call the News Desk at 798-1184 between 4 and 11 p.m. weekdays. Leslie Spalding is the news editor. Fax 798-1113. Subscription problems: Call 798-1161.

Site has been on market since November

By JEFF PLATSKY
Business Editor

The site selected for the state's centralized back-office operations, IBM Corp's Glendale Product Development Laboratory, once housed as many as 3,500 high-technology workers.

Late last year, the 1-million-square-foot site was put up for sale or lease by the Armonk-based computer giant. IBM is vacating the site as it consolidates its leaner work force — reduced in Endicott from about 12,000 in the mid-'80s to about 5,000 today — at the company's main manufacturing site at Endicott's North Street.

The state will take about one-third of the 17-building site, where IBM added some 200,000 square feet in a multi-million dollar construction project in 1986.

According to promotional material from real estate agents, many of the buildings on the 127-acre site were expanded and renovated in the '80s, and are well suited for back-office-type operations. The site's building sizes range from a 300-square-foot, one-story storage building to a 129,100-square-foot, four-story administrative and data center.

IBM Endicott spokeswoman Betty Casey said this morning that "a couple of hundred" people remain at Glendale, with all remaining workers expected to move to the North Street complex by mid-March.

Glendale Technology Park
754-5990
Robert A. Mead, Inc.

PRESS & SUN-BULLETIN

The IBM-Glendale site contains 1 million square feet of space.

The complex is located in a state Economic Development Zone, which provides tax incentives for private employers creating jobs within the zone. Local economic developers had hoped to use the zone designation to attract private employers to the site.

TO SUBSCRIBE TO THE PRESS & SUN-BULLETIN CALL: (607) 798-1161 or 1-800-253-5343 (N.Y.). 1-800-241-2120 (PA.)

February 16, 1995: The deal to bring 1,500 state jobs to Glendale prompted an extra. *Press & Sun-Bulletin archives*

Friday
February 17, 1995
Mostly sunny
Hi: 40 Lo: 30
Details 4A
FINAL EDITION

5 PAGES OF COVERAGE on IBM-Glendale deal

Press & Sun-Bulletin

5 SECTIONS | BINGHAMTON, N.Y. | 35¢ NEWSSTAND

1,500 jobs coming to Tier

A shot in the arm

Community soars with excitement

By CHRISTINE L. RIDARSKY
Staff Writer

After years of grim economic news, Broome County was ready for a gift.

It arrived Thursday, containing up to 1,500 jobs and a twinkling of renewal.

"It's exciting for the community," said John G. Spencer, executive director of the United Way of Broome County. "We sure need a lift. The community is getting into a cycle of doom and gloom and fear."

Even Kevin Babcock, who said he's "anti-government," was excited. He said business at his store, Babcock Bicycles, 501 W. Main St., Endicott, fell off after IBM started laying off workers. "It's going to help me," he said. "How can it hurt me when all these people are going to be buying houses and driving right past my store on their way to work?"

Although a few people said they're disappointed that more job openings would not be created — most of the state workers will move here from out of town — most said the influx of people will help the community.

"I'm thrilled," said Arlene L. Ryan, an associate broker with Herrick Realty in Binghamton. "I hope this will bring the real estate market up, too. There are 3,000 houses on the market."

Assemblyman Jay J. Dinga, R-Endicott, agreed the move would help the local housing market. "Everywhere we look, we have "For Sale" signs," Dinga said. "People are going to be coming into this town and buying these homes."

Best news in '15 or 20 years'

Sen. Thomas W. Libous, R-Binghamton, at a press conference with Gov. George E. Pataki, said the area waited a long time for an announcement such as the one that came Thursday. "This is probably the best news we've had in the Southern Tier in 15 or 20 years," he said.

Over the past few years, IBM Corp. and other major employers have laid off thousands of workers, several Southern Tier businesses have closed and charities have been unable to raise money they need to meet the rising demand. The effect, officials and individuals said, was a pervasive sense of despair.

Pataki's announcement gives a sense of hope back to the community, said Bernard M. Bass,

See EXCITEMENT/Page 4A

JULIA SCHMALZ/PRESS & SUN-BULLETIN

Gov. George E. Pataki announces Thursday that the state will buy portions of IBM Corp.'s Glendale Technology Park and relocate 1,500 workers to the complex. With Pataki at the Glendale plant were, from left, Sen. Thomas W. Libous, Office of General Services Commissioner Peter Delaney and Assemblyman Jay J. Dinga, R-Endicott. The computer-oriented jobs pay relatively high wages, officials said.

Tier begins 'a new era,' Pataki says

By DON SBARRA
Staff Writer

Broome County got a welcome dose of economic news Thursday when Gov. George E. Pataki announced plans to bring about 1,500 well-paying jobs to IBM Corp.'s Glendale Technology Park.

Declaring it the "beginning of a new era" for the economically struggling Southern Tier and for the entire state, Pataki said the Broome site was chosen as one of three new centralized data-processing centers, which will replace 49 offices scattered around the state. He said the move will not only provide a much-needed boost for Broome County, but save taxpayers about $50 million per year through consolidation.

Many factors influenced the decision to move state jobs to Broome County, Pataki said, including IBM's interest in the area, pressures to cut the state budget and state Sen. Thomas W. Libous' persistence in having the Glendale site considered. "Senator Libous was tenacious," Pataki said.

"It was something that was just meant to happen," Pataki said at a 1:30 p.m. press conference at the Glendale site in the Town of Union.

'Great-paying jobs' hailed

"This is great news. We needed a shot in the arm like this," said County Executive Timothy M. Grippen, a Democrat. "I couldn't even think of anything bad to say about it. Those are great-paying jobs and even if only half of those people bought homes, it's going to be a great boost for the local real estate market. It's going to be a great shot in the arm all the way around."

Under the agreement with IBM, the state will buy about 325,000 square feet of the roughly 1-million-square-foot Glendale complex. The state also is buying IBM's Hudson Valley facilities in Kingston and leasing space from IBM in East Fishkill, paying a total of $13 million for the three.

The first workers will start arriving this fall. There should be 300 workers within 12 to 18 months, with the remainder within four or five years, Pataki said. Libous, R-Binghamton, said most of the workers would transfer to the area, but that about 300 positions would become available for local residents. Other state officials said the number could be as high as 450 positions.

The state expects to spend up to

See JOB/Page 4A

JULIA SCHMALZ/PRESS & SUN-BULLETIN

Kevin Babcock, owner of Babcock Bikes, 501 W. Main St., just down the street from the Glendale plant, said the influx of the new state jobs is "gonna help me."

Libous brings jobs home

By DON SBARRA
Staff Writer

Sen. Thomas W. Libous had hinted that good things could come to the Southern Tier as a result of his early support for the man who went on to become governor, but even he didn't expect so much so soon.

"I've hardly slept the last few nights," Libous said Thursday, describing his excitement over Gov. George E. Pataki's decision to place up to 1,500 state jobs in a vacant IBM Corp. plant in Glendale. "It's tremendous. It's incredible news for this community."

At his announcement of the deal Thursday, Pataki gave Libous much of the credit for the Glendale selection, noting that negotiations had focused on IBM's Hudson Valley-area facilities until the Binghamton Republican began pushing the site in western Broome County.

The consolidation move will put large data-processing centers in Broome as well as East Fishkill and Kingston.

Libous said he heard of the state's consolidation plans almost by accident, when it turned up in a mid-January conversation with Peter Delaney, commissioner of the state Office of General Services. He said Delaney had never heard of the Glendale complex, but immediately agreed to have a look.

"I said, 'I have a million square feet at Glendale that fits everything you want to do, and it's a beautiful campus,'" Libous said, recalling the conversation.

After sending a packet of information about the site to Delaney, and several telephone calls back and forth, Libous said the commissioner called and indicated Glendale "was on the table." Finally, after a brief conversation with the governor Monday, Libous said a site visit was arranged for Tuesday.

Libous, who this past fall won a fifth two-year term with more than 80 percent of the vote, was among the first Senate members to support Pataki's candidacy. The move was considered risky because then-Senate Majority Leader Ralph Marino opposed Pataki. Marino was later replaced by Sen. Joseph Bruno, R-Brunswick, in what's been dubbed the Thanksgiving Day Coup, which Libous helped orchestrate. He has since been rewarded with one of the top six jobs in the Senate, heading the Program Committee.

Inside

- Community leaders now need to make the most of the jobs bonanza. **Page 2A.**
- The incoming workers should bring smiles to those selling homes. **Page 3A.**
- Many other businesses will benefit from the incoming jobs. **Page 5A.**
- The 1,500 jobs will inject much needed spending power into the community. **Editorials, Page 12A.**

New paychecks will average $39,000

By JEFF PLATSKY
Business Editor

The state data center will add $58.5 million annually to the Binghamton region's economy when it's fully staffed at 1,500 people.

The average wage for workers at the consolidated state center will be $39,000, said Peter Delaney, commissioner of the Office of General Services. Add to that another $8,000 average in fringe benefits, Delaney said, and the average compensation for the average worker at the site grows to $47,000.

"At $750 a week, these wages are higher than the average manufacturing wage," said Joseph J. Kozlowski, research analyst for the state Department of Labor in Binghamton. "It's a replacement for the jobs we lost." Broome and Tioga counties have lost up to 15,000 manufacturing jobs since 1988.

The average Binghamton resident receives an annual salary of $25,500, state statistics show. Manufacturing workers in the region are paid about $38,400, excluding fringe benefits. The area also should benefit from renovations at the Glendale site, expected to cost up to $7 million. Local contractors will get much of the work, Delaney said.

Traditionally, white-collar administrative jobs have a ripple effect, creating two to three times the amount in economic impact as money filters through the economy, said Manas K. Chatterji, professor at Binghamton University's School of Management.

The relocation of state workers and hiring of others could only begin to replace an estimated $550 million in wages lost in recent years at regional manufacturers, including IBM Corp. Though the wages are relatively high in comparison to elsewhere in the community, Kozlowski didn't think it would pressure other employers to raise wages. He said the supply of unemployed people outpaces the demand for workers, which will keep other wages in check.

Wages go to $55,000

Office of General Services Commissioner Peter Delaney said wages at Glendale will break down as follows:

- **$35,000 for computer operators.**
- **$25,000 for data-entry clerks.**
- **$55,000 for supervisors.**
- **$40,000 for technical support staff.**
- **$50,000 for administrative support staff.**

A proportional breakdown of staffing was unavailable Thursday.

Winning numbers

Saturday's Lotto jackpot: $4 million
N.Y. Daily Number: 7-7-8
N.Y. Win 4: 2-5-8-6
N.Y. Pick 10: 12-13-22-24-25-34-36-39-41-42-43-48-50-56-58-61-67-71-74-76

Pa. Daily Lottery: 8-2-1
Pa. Big 4: 4-1-8-4
Pa. Cash 5: 6-18-19-25-39

0 40901 00701 2

Index

Business	6B	Nation	6A
Classified	4C	Obituaries	3B
Community	1B	Opinion	12A
Crossword	7D	Sports	1-4C
Landers	3D	State	3B
Living	1D	TV	2D
Movies	Pullout	World	11A

Questions or comments?

Call the News Desk at 798-1184 between 4 and 11 p.m. weekdays. Leslie Spalding is the news editor. Fax 798-1113. Subscription problems: Call 798-1161.

TO SUBSCRIBE TO THE PRESS & SUN-BULLETIN CALL: (607) 798-1161 or 1-800-253-5343 (N.Y.). 1-800-241-2120 (PA.)

February 17, 1995: The paper came back with five pages of coverage inside. For a variety of reasons, the full 1,500 jobs never materialized. *Press & Sun-Bulletin archives*

Johnny Hart, creator of the BC comic strip, takes a minute to pose with Gene Perry, on the left, in 1995. *Courtesy Gene Perry*

CRIME SCENE DO NOT CROSS

Scene of the Barta shooting. August 2, 1995. *Press & Sun-Bulletin archives*

Waneta Hoyt wipes a tear as she is being sentenced, September 11, 1995, in Tioga County Court for the deaths of five of her childern. At her side is her husband, Tim. *Press & Sun-Bulletin archives*

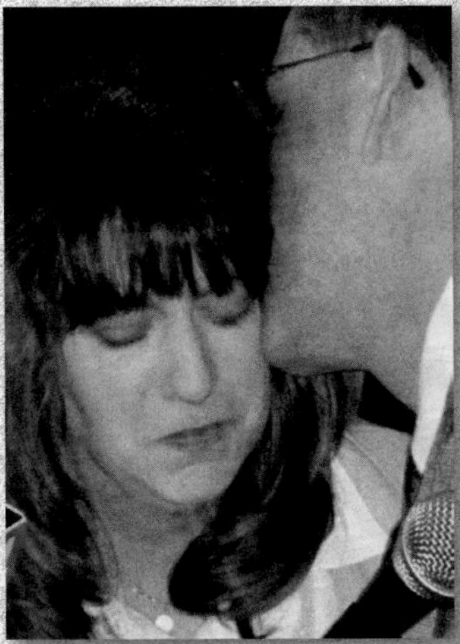

A tearful Mary Barta, widow of slain Binghamton Patrolman Lee Barta, receives a reassuring kiss from Assistant Police Chief Joseph Zikuski at the city's annual police awards ceremony, September 1996. Barta received a posthumous Medal of Honor. *Press & Sun-Bulletin archives*

KIRKWOOD FIRE DEPT.

Kirkwood Fire Co. assistant chiefs Tom Studer, left (in red), and Jerry Wheelock, right, guide a boat full of people who needed to be rescued from their Conklin home (Alta Road), which was surrounded by water during the flooding in 1996. Pictured are Tanya Miller, 13, left front, her mother, Sharon Miller, right front, and Stewart Miller, next to Sharon wearing a baseball cap. *Press & Sun-Bulletin archives*

Thursday
April 20, 1995

Mostly sunny
Hi: 60 Lo: 45
Details 2A

FINAL EDITION

Jewish treasures abound

Special event to benefit S. Tier school puts historical exhibits up for sale

Page 1C

Press & Sun-Bulletin

4 SECTIONS BINGHAMTON, N.Y. 35¢ NEWSSTAND

TWO PAGES OF COVERAGE OF OKLAHOMA TERROR, 4A & 5A

'It was like Beirut'

ASSOCIATED PRESS

Nothing remains of one side of the nine-story Alfred P. Murrah Federal Building in Oklahoma City after Wednesday's bombing.

ASSOCIATED PRESS

An emergency worker passes an injured child to a firefighter after Wednesday's explosion at the Oklahoma City federal building. Officials believe 40 children were at a day-care center in the building when the bomb went off.

Car blast kills 31; bombers hunted

By JUDY GIBBS
The Associated Press

OKLAHOMA CITY — A car bomb ripped deep into America's heartland Wednesday, killing at least 31 persons and leaving 300 missing in a blast that gouged a nine-story hole in a federal office building.

The dead included about a dozen children from a day-care center. Rescuers said Wednesday night that they were talking to a woman trapped in the basement, who said there were two others in the area.

"It was like Beirut; everything was burning and flattened," said Dr. Carl Spengler, who was one of the first doctors at the scene.

There was no claim of responsibility for the attack, the deadliest U.S. bombing in 75 years. At least 200 people were injured — 58 critically, according to Fire Chief Gary Marrs — and scores were feared trapped in the rubble of the Alfred P. Murrah Federal Building hours

See BOMB/Page 4A

City family relieved to learn son survives

By SERGIO G. NON
Staff Writer

Gloria Gordon feared her son was dead Wednesday when she heard about the explosion at Oklahoma City's federal building.

"I said, 'What? That's where my son works,'" said the Binghamton woman, who hurried home from work, fearing the worst as she saw her husband walking up their driveway. "I thought, 'Oh, my God, he's coming to tell me Steve's been blown away.'"

S. Gordon

Fortunately for the Gordons, Wednesday was one of the luckiest days of their son's life. Master Sgt. Steven Gordon, 42, was on an Arkansas road trip Tuesday and Wednesday, inspecting

See BINGHAMTON/Page 5A

At center of terror: 'Babies were crying and screaming'

By JULIA PRODIS
The Associated Press

OKLAHOMA CITY — The blast occurred at the start of the work day, as parents were dropping off their youngsters at the day-care center in the federal building. Before the smoke cleared, Heather Taylor, an emergency worker, had tagged the feet of a nearly a dozen children at the morgue.

Two were burned beyond recognition. The bodies of the rest, up to 7 years old, were mangled. Ten to 20 other children were unaccounted for late in the day. Taylor knew of only two who survived. One was in surgery, the other was in intensive care. "The day-care center is totally gone," said Dr. Carl Spengler, who helped Taylor with the victims.

It was on the second floor of the nine-story Albert Murrah Building, just above the spot where Wednesday's car bomb exploded. Toys and games were scattered amid broken glass and other debris on the street. A nearby YMCA also had a day-care center. "It was really terrible with the (YMCA) day-care center," said state Rep. Kevin Cox, who was a half-block away when the 9 a.m. blast occurred. "Babies were crying and screaming, with blood and plaster and insulation on their bodies."

TV stations broadcast a description of an injured red-headed toddler, asking for her parents to contact the hospital because she needed surgery.

Faith Wohl of the General Services Administration Office, said 41 children were enrolled in the day-care program in the federal building, with about 30 attending each day. "We don't know yet, and may never know, how many children were there ..." she said.

One woman stood outside the building, screaming for her child. Rescuers led her away just before they brought out a victim they believed to be her dead son.

Elsewhere, parents wearing masking tape name tags waited for word at Children's Hospital of Oklahoma. Wanda McNeely searched frantically for her 6-month-old grandson's name on a list. After checking with three hospitals, she went to the morgue at St. Anthony Hospital. "We've checked all the lists, now we're going to the other side," she said.

George Young, St. Anthony Hospital chaplain, sat on a bench holding a small blond girl with bandages on her face. "I've seen five or six children seriously injured," he said. A lot of them had been hurt by flying glass. One little boy was in shock."

Winning numbers

N.Y. Daily Number: 5-8-6
N.Y. Win 4: 3-6-1-9
N.Y. Pick 10: 8-10-13-14-18-20-28-33-35-36-45-46-50-55-64-65-70-71-76-80
N.Y. Lotto: 1-6-21-26-41-50 **Supp.:** 10
Pa. Daily Lottery: 2-1-5
Pa. Big 4: 4-4-1-3
Pa. Hearts: 10H-2D-3D-5D-AD

0 40901 00701 2

Index

Questions or comments

For matters regarding world, national and state news, call the News Desk at 798-1184 between 4 and 11 p.m. weekdays. Leslie Spalding is the news editor. Fax 798-1113.

Hoyt case expected to go to jury today

By MICHELLE YORK
Staff Writer

HOYT TRIAL

District Attorney Robert J. Simpson gave an electrifying speech to jurors Wednesday in his closing statement in Waneta E. Hoyt's trial.

Simpson said Erik, James, Julie, Molly, and Noah Hoyt endured "two minutes of agony," suffocated by someone supposed to care for and nurture them. Hoyt, 48, of Route 38, Newark Valley, is charged with killing her five children between 1965 and 1971. Doctors at the time attributed the deaths to sudden infant death syndrome.

"She's been lucky," he said of Waneta Hoyt, to enjoy life when her children did not.

"The events took place a long time ago," he said. "It would be easy to minimize the impact. But five young people are not here today because of her."

Defense attorney Robert L. Miller told jurors that Hoyt's confession to police was faulty and coerced because Hoyt is mentally unstable. Beyond the confession, which alone cannot be used to convict her, evidence of suffocation does not exist, he said.

Earlier in the day, Dr. David J. Barry, a forensic psychiatrist from Rochester, testified as an expert witness for the prosecution. Barry disagreed with defense testimony that Hoyt suffers from personality disorders that would make her susceptible to police intimidation.

Tioga County Judge Vincent Sgueglia this morning is expected to instruct the jury on deliberations.

Waneta Hoyt

■ Closing statements bring tears to the eyes of those in the courtroom. Page 1B.

April 20, 1995: The worst individual case of domestic terrorism brought shock to the Tier. *Microfilm archives*

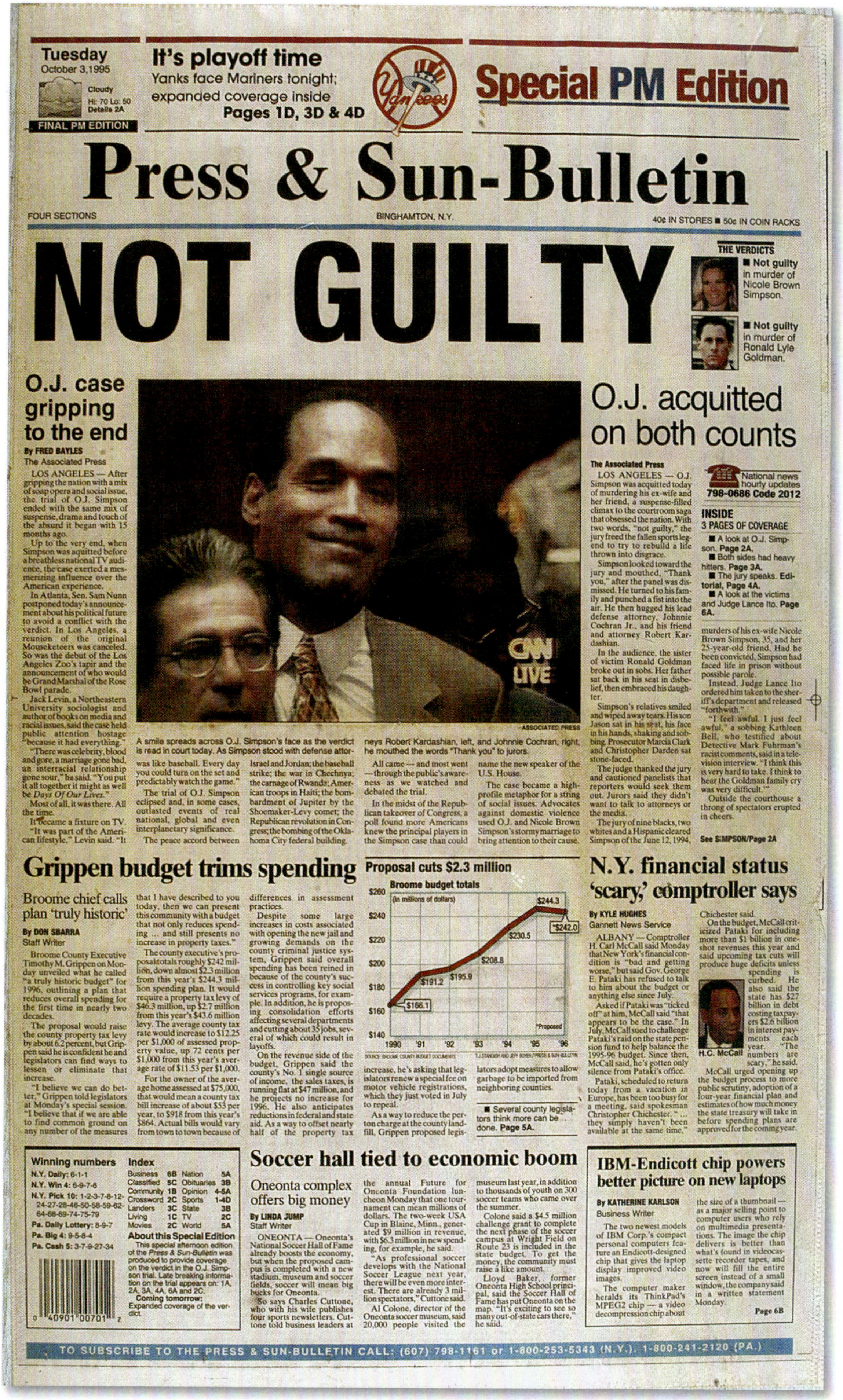

Tuesday
October 3,1995
Cloudy
Hi: 70 Lo: 50
Details 2A
FINAL PM EDITION

It's playoff time
Yanks face Mariners tonight; expanded coverage inside
Pages 1D, 3D & 4D

Special PM Edition

Press & Sun-Bulletin

FOUR SECTIONS — BINGHAMTON, N.Y. — 40¢ IN STORES ■ 50¢ IN COIN RACKS

NOT GUILTY

THE VERDICTS
■ **Not guilty** in murder of Nicole Brown Simpson.
■ **Not guilty** in murder of Ronald Lyle Goldman.

O.J. case gripping to the end

By FRED BAYLES
The Associated Press

LOS ANGELES — After gripping the nation with a mix of soap opera and social issue, the trial of O.J. Simpson ended with the same mix of suspense, drama and touch of the absurd it began with 15 months ago.

Up to the very end, when Simpson was aquitted before a breathless national TV audience, the case exerted a mesmerizing influence over the American experience.

In Atlanta, Sen. Sam Nunn postponed today's announcement about his political future to avoid a conflict with the verdict. In Los Angeles, a reunion of the original Mouseketeers was canceled. So was the debut of the Los Angeles Zoo's tapir and the announcement of who would be Grand Marshal of the Rose Bowl parade.

Jack Levin, a Northeastern University sociologist and author of books on media and racial issues, said the case held public attention hostage "because it had everything."

"There was celebrity, blood and gore, a marriage gone bad, an interracial relationship gone sour," he said. "You put it all together it might as well be *Days Of Our Lives*."

Most of all, it was there. All the time.

It became a fixture on TV.

"It was part of the American lifestyle," Levin said. "It was like baseball. Every day you could turn on the set and predictably watch the game."

The trial of O.J. Simpson eclipsed and, in some cases, outlasted events of real national, global and even interplanetary significance.

The peace accord between Israel and Jordan; the baseball strike; the war in Chechnya; the carnage of Rwanda; American troops in Haiti; the bombardment of Jupiter by the Shoemaker-Levy comet; the Republican revolution in Congress; the bombing of the Oklahoma City federal building.

All came — and most went — through the public's awareness as we watched and debated the trial.

In the midst of the Republican takeover of Congress, a poll found more Americans knew the principal players in the Simpson case than could name the new speaker of the U.S. House.

The case became a high-profile metaphor for a string of social issues. Advocates against domestic violence used O.J. and Nicole Brown Simpson's stormy marriage to bring attention to their cause.

ASSOCIATED PRESS

A smile spreads across O.J. Simpson's face as the verdict is read in court today. As Simpson stood with defense attorneys Robert Kardashian, left, and Johnnie Cochran, right, he mouthed the words "Thank you" to jurors.

CNN LIVE

O.J. acquitted on both counts

The Associated Press

LOS ANGELES — O.J. Simpson was acquitted today of murdering his ex-wife and her friend, a suspense-filled climax to the courtroom saga that obsessed the nation. With two words, "not guilty," the jury freed the fallen sports legend to try to rebuild a life thrown into disgrace.

Simpson looked toward the jury and mouthed, "Thank you," after the panel was dismissed. He turned to his family and punched a fist into the air. He then hugged his lead defense attorney, Johnnie Cochran Jr., and his friend and attorney Robert Kardashian.

In the audience, the sister of victim Ronald Goldman broke out in sobs. Her father sat back in his seat in disbelief, then embraced his daughter.

Simpson's relatives smiled and wiped away tears. His son Jason sat in his seat, his face in his hands, shaking and sobbing. Prosecutor Marcia Clark and Christopher Darden sat stone-faced.

The judge thanked the jury and cautioned panelists that reporters would seek them out. Jurors said they didn't want to talk to attorneys or the media.

The jury of nine blacks, two whites and a Hispanic cleared Simpson of the June 12, 1994, murders of his ex-wife Nicole Brown Simpson, 35, and her 25-year-old friend. Had he been convicted, Simpson had faced life in prison without possible parole.

Instead, Judge Lance Ito ordered him taken to the sheriff's department and released "forthwith."

"I feel awful. I just feel awful," a sobbing Kathleen Bell, who testified about Detective Mark Fuhrman's racist comments, said in a television interview. "I think this is very hard to take. I think to hear the Goldman family cry was very difficult.'"

Outside the courthouse a throng of spectators erupted in cheers.

See SIMPSON/Page 2A

National news hourly updates
798-0686 Code 2012

INSIDE
3 PAGES OF COVERAGE
■ A look at O.J. Simpson. **Page 2A.**
■ Both sides had heavy hitters. **Page 3A.**
■ The jury speaks. **Editorial, Page 4A.**
■ A look at the victims and Judge Lance Ito. **Page 6A.**

Grippen budget trims spending

Broome chief calls plan 'truly historic'

By DON SBARRA
Staff Writer

Broome County Executive Timothy M. Grippen on Monday unveiled what he called "a truly historic budget" for 1996, outlining a plan that reduces overall spending for the first time in nearly two decades.

The proposal would raise the county property tax levy by about 6.2 percent, but Grippen said he is confident he and legislators can find ways to lessen or eliminate that increase.

"I believe we can do better," Grippen told legislators at Monday's special session. "I believe that if we are able to find common ground on any number of the measures that I have described to you today, then we can present this community with a budget that not only reduces spending ... and still presents no increase in property taxes."

The county executive's proposal totals roughly $242 million, down almost $2.3 million from this year's $244.3 million spending plan. It would require a property tax levy of $46.3 million, up $2.7 million from this year's $43.6 million levy. The average county tax rate would increase to $12.25 per $1,000 of assessed property value, up 72 cents per $1,000 from this year's average rate of $11.53 per $1,000.

For the owner of the average home assessed at $75,000, that would mean a county tax bill increase of about $53 per year, to $918 from this year's $864. Actual bills would vary from town to town because of differences in assessment practices.

Despite some large increases in costs associated with opening the new jail and growing demands on the county criminal justice system, Grippen said overall spending has been reined in because of the county's success in controlling key social services programs, for example. In addition, he is proposing consolidation efforts affecting several departments and cutting about 35 jobs, several of which could result in layoffs.

On the revenue side of the budget, Grippen said the county's No. 1 single source of income, the sales taxes, is running flat at $47 million, and he projects no increase for 1996. He also anticipates reductions in federal and state aid. As a way to offset nearly half of the property tax increase, he's asking that legislators renew a special fee on motor vehicle registrations, which they just voted in July to repeal.

As a way to reduce the per-ton charge at the county landfill, Grippen proposed legislators adopt measures to allow garbage to be imported from neighboring counties.

Proposal cuts $2.3 million

Broome budget totals
(In millions of dollars)

1990	$166.1
'91	$191.2
'92	$195.9
'93	$208.8
'94	$230.5
'95	$244.3
'96	*$242.0

*Proposed

SOURCE: BROOME COUNTY BUDGET DOCUMENTS — T.J. STANDISH AND JEFF BOYEN / PRESS & SUN-BULLETIN

■ Several county legislators think more can be done. **Page 5A.**

N.Y. financial status 'scary,' comptroller says

By KYLE HUGHES
Gannett News Service

ALBANY — Comptroller H. Carl McCall said Monday that New York's financial condition is "bad and getting worse," but said Gov. George E. Pataki has refused to talk to him about the budget or anything else since July.

Asked if Pataki was "ticked off" at him, McCall said "that appears to be the case." In July, McCall sued to challenge Pataki's raid on the state pension fund to help balance the 1995-96 budget. Since then, McCall said, he's gotten only silence from Pataki's office.

Pataki, scheduled to return today from a vacation in Europe, has been too busy for a meeting, said spokesman Christopher Chichester. " ... they simply haven't been available at the same time," Chichester said.

On the budget, McCall criticized Pataki for including more than $1 billion in one-shot revenues this year and said upcoming tax cuts will produce huge deficits unless spending is curbed. He also said the state has $27 billion in debt costing taxpayers $2.6 billion in interest payments each year. "The numbers are scary," he said.

H.C. McCall

McCall urged opening up the budget process to more public scrutiny, adoption of a four-year financial plan and estimates of how much money the state treasury will take in before spending plans are approved for the coming year.

Winning numbers
N.Y. Daily: 6-1-1
N.Y. Win 4: 6-9-7-6
N.Y. Pick 10: 1-2-3-7-8-12-24-27-28-46-50-58-59-62-64-68-69-74-75-79
Pa. Daily Lottery: 8-9-7
Pa. Big 4: 9-5-8-4
Pa. Cash 5: 3-7-9-27-34

0 40901 00701 2

Index

Business	6B	Nation	5A
Classified	5C	Obituaries	3B
Community	1B	Opinion	4-5A
Crossword	2C	Sports	1-4D
Landers	3C	State	3B
Living	1C	TV	2C
Movies	2C	World	5A

About this Special Edition
This special afternoon edition of the *Press & Sun-Bulletin* was produced to provide coverage on the verdict in the O.J. Simpson trial. Late breaking information on the trial appears on: 1A, 2A, 3A, 4A, 6A and 2C.
Coming tomorrow: Expanded coverage of the verdict.

Soccer hall tied to economic boom

Oneonta complex offers big money

By LINDA JUMP
Staff Writer

ONEONTA — Oneonta's National Soccer Hall of Fame already boosts the economy, but when the proposed campus is completed with a new stadium, museum and soccer fields, soccer will mean big bucks for Oneonta.

So says Charles Cuttone, who with his wife publishes four sports newsletters. Cuttone told business leaders at the annual Future for Oneonta Foundation luncheon Monday that one tournament can mean millions of dollars. The two-week USA Cup in Blaine, Minn., generated $9 million in revenue, with $6.3 million in new spending, for example, he said.

"As professional soccer develops with the National Soccer League next year, there will be even more interest. There are already 3 million spectators," Cuttone said.

Al Colone, director of the Oneonta soccer museum, said 20,000 people visited the museum last year, in addition to thousands of youth on 300 soccer teams who came over the summer.

Colone said a $4.5 million challenge grant to complete the next phase of the soccer campus at Wright Field on Route 23 is included in the state budget. To get the money, the community must raise a like amount.

Lloyd Baker, former Oneonta High School principal, said the Soccer Hall of Fame has put Oneonta on the map. "It's exciting to see so many out-of-state cars there," he said.

IBM-Endicott chip powers better picture on new laptops

By KATHERINE KARLSON
Business Writer

The two newest models of IBM Corp.'s compact personal computers feature an Endicott-designed chip that gives the laptop display improved video images.

The computer maker heralds its ThinkPad's MPEG2 chip — a video decompression chip about the size of a thumbnail — as a major selling point to computer users who rely on multimedia presentations. The image the chip delivers is better than what's found in videocassette recorder tapes, and now will fill the entire screen instead of a small window, the company said in a written statement Monday.

Page 6B

TO SUBSCRIBE TO THE PRESS & SUN-BULLETIN CALL: (607) 798-1161 or 1-800-253-5343 (N.Y.). 1-800-241-2120 (PA.)

October 3, 1995: The Press put out an extra to announce the O.J. Simpson verdict. *Courtesy Jackie Deinhardt*

Monday
September 1, 1997
Partly sunny
Hi 83 Lo 60
Details 2B
HOLIDAY EDITION

NFL Opening Day
Giants top Eagles, 31-17
Jets crush Seahawks, 41-3
Vikings beat Bills, 34-13
Pages 1D, 4-5D

Kyle Brady of the Jets

Water woes plague Park Terrace 1B
Many try home-based businesses 8B
Seles, Williams, Agassi advance 1D

Press & Sun-Bulletin

FOUR SECTIONS © 1997 THE BINGHAMTON PRESS CO., BINGHAMTON, N.Y. Fifty cents

SPECIAL REPORT DEATH OF A PRINCESS

World mourns Diana

Tier Britons devastated

By ERIKA STUTZMAN
Staff Writer

Rhoda Schaeffer of Binghamton remembers getting a day off from school as a school girl in York, England, to watch the fairy-tale wedding of Lady Diana Spencer and Prince Charles on television.

On Saturday night, the English native watched the fairy tale's tragic end on CNN.

"I was in total shock. I broke down," she said.

Schaeffer, who married a Southern Tier native and moved to the area 11 years ago, lives with her family in Binghamton.

She said that she phoned her mother in England Sunday morning to talk about Princess Diana's death.

"She was totally, totally devastated and in total shock," she said. "They are waiting to find out when the day of mourning will be, and whether she will have a state burial."

Schaeffer, who last visited England in July, said Princess Diana "brought fun to the monarchy, because it was getting a bit dull."

In July, Schaeffer noticed "a lot of British people were already upset with the British press." That anger surfaced strongly Sunday — in Great Britain and abroad — as many blamed the paparazzi, who had been following the princess, for causing the deaths of Diana, her companion Dodi Fayed and their driver.

Ruth Ferrari, a clinical nurse specializing in psychiatry in Binghamton, said that blame and anger are natural.

"The first step is denial, and then there is a lot of anger," she said. "And hearing some of this is amazing, placing the blame on other people, and not on the speed of the car, or the accident itself."

The next step in the grieving process is bargaining. People who are grieving may try to think of ways the tragedy could have been avoided. After that, a situational depression sets in, and after that, finally, comes acceptance.

"At church this morning, there was a lot of anger," she said. "But anger can be a healthy and necessary part of the healing process" as long as it's not used to hurt someone, she said.

Paul Elliott of Binghamton, who moved to the United States from his native England in 1949, called the tragedy "shocking."

"It's shocking because she is a very public figure, a very prominent woman and of course, she was very young," he said.

ASSOCIATED PRESS

The coffin containing the body of Diana, princess of Wales, is carried by a Royal Air Force honor guard after arriving Sunday at Northholt Royal Air Force base. The princess, her companion, Dodi Fayed, and their driver were fatally injured when their car crashed in a Paris tunnel while they were being chased by photographers.

Prince Charles travels home with her remains

From wire service reports

LONDON — Prince Charles brought Princess Diana home for the last time Sunday, escorting the body of his "English rose" back to the land where their storybook romance ended in sorrow and scandal, a nation now plunged into grief and outrage over a stunning final tragedy.

A jet carrying the somber prince and the coffin bearing his ex-wife's remains landed outside London 16 hours after Diana died from injuries suffered when her automobile, chased by photographers, crashed in a Paris traffic tunnel.

Prince Charles

At St. Paul's Cathedral, where Diana was married 16 years ago, nearly 2,000 people, most in casual weekend dress, crowded into the vast nave for a special evening service.

Outside her London palace home, mourners heaped flowers in tribute to the much-admired Diana. But the sadness mixed with anger — outrage at a press that pursued the princess relentlessly in life, and may have contributed to her death.

"I always believed the press would kill her in the end," said her brother, Charles Spencer, who lives in South Africa.

French police were investigating the role seven pursuing paparazzi photographers may have played in the tragedy early Sunday morning. The crash also took the lives of the 36-year-old

SEVERAL PAGES OF COVERAGE

- Investigation continues into fatal crash in Paris.
- Britons grieve for their darling Diana.
- Many lash out at role of media.

Page 2A.

- House of Windsor reels from death.
- Diana had planned to drop out of public life.
- Death leaves many questions about fortune.

Page 3A.

- Doctors describe treatment of princess.

Page 4A.

- **Editorial:** An appreciation.

Page 6A.

Diana's companion, the millionaire Dodi Fayed, and their chauffeur.

The red-tailed jet from Paris landed at the Northholt air base, where a grim array of dignitaries, led by Prime Minister Tony Blair, had gathered under leaden skies. A Royal Air Force honor guard solemnly bore the coffin, draped in a flag signifying the presence of the monarch, from the aircraft to a waiting hearse.

After the brief airport ceremony, Charles flew back to Scotland to be with the couple's two sons, Princes William, 15, and Harry, 12.

Diana's body was examined by a coroner at a private mortuary before being taken early Monday to the Chapel Royal of St. James's Palace, the London home of her ex-husband, Prince Charles.

See DIANA/Page 4A

"I always believed the press would kill her in the end. But not even I could imagine that they would take such a direct hand in her death."

Charles Spencer
Princess Diana's brother

Americans embraced her, faults and all

By TED ANTHONY
The Associated Press

NEW YORK — She was a princess, yes — the perfectly wrapped package of British royalty complete with tiara, shining eyes and an all-too-photogenic smile.

But Americans found other, very American reasons to watch, if not adore, Diana. Here was a woman who battled an eating disorder, fended off suicide rumors, stole jet-set kisses and finally divorced her prince and became a single mother.

The things that so piqued British traditionalists made Diana's life resonate on this side of the Atlantic, where foible so often augments halo and fairy-tale lives melt into dysfunction.

"We knew in this country that the Cinderella story was no longer supposed to be true. Then we saw her. She was a princess for the post-feminist generation," said Shari Roberts, a Penn State University assistant professor who studies how Americans perceive celebrity.

In this nation that shed blood so long ago to purge royalty from its society, the "People's Princess" made a lasting impression. Disappointed by latter-day Kennedys, left without vicarious royal glitter since Princess Grace, many Americans looked to Diana as their princess by proxy.

"It's like we've lost one of our own political figures," said Joni Van Vliet, 18, of Bend, Ore.

From the early years when they imitated her hairdo by the thousands, Americans watched Diana closely as the shy, big-eyed 20-year-old married Prince Charles. They watched her grow into a poised socialite, then a willful activist who hugged AIDS patients and denounced land mines. When she visited the United States, they flocked around her.

"Not since Jackie O had someone come along who was accessible, had the common touch and married a prince," said Carol Wallace, managing editor of *People Magazine*.

"I think Americans are always captivated by how the other half lives," she said.

Diana had U.S. ties as well: A great-grandmother was born in New York City in 1857. Her distant cousins, according to Boston genealogist Gary Roberts, who has traced her ancestry, include Americans from John Adams and Franklin D. Roosevelt to Humphrey Bogart and Katharine Hepburn to Louisa May Alcott.

"A piece of her was definitely American," Roberts said. "It reinforced our special relationship with her."

ASSOCIATED PRESS

A note to Princess Diana sits among flowers placed Sunday in front of the British Consulate in New York.

Winning numbers
Wednesday's Lotto jackpot is $3 million.
N.Y. Daily: 0-0-3
N.Y. Win 4: 5-5-6-1
N.Y. Pick 10: 2-7-10-11-18-28-34-35-38-41-44-47-61-64-66-67-69-75-78-80
Pa. Daily Lottery: 4-1-2
Pa. Big 4: 7-2-4-5
Pa. Cash 5: 10-11-26-28-38

Index

0 40901 00701 2

Note to readers

Beginning today, the price of the daily *Press & Sun-Bulletin* at newsstands and stores will increase to 50 cents, the same price now charged at newspaper vending machines. The cost of home delivery and the price of the Sunday *Press & Sun-Bulletin* do not change. If you have a comment, please contact Circulation Director Barbara Gallo at 798-1365.

To reach us

Information	798-1234
Circulation	798-1161
Classified	798-1141
Retail ads	798-1131

For additional listings please turn to Page 2A.

Cubicles add privacy, encourage teamwork

But some workers only tolerate them

JOBS

By WYN HORNBUCKLE
Staff Writer

Life in a cubicle is so mundane
No walls or doors or windowpanes
Look overhead, there's nothing but air
I got no privacy, it's so unfair

Joy Owen
(posted on the World Wide Web)

Since Christopher Hill began working at Universal Instruments Corp. in Kirkwood in 1984, he has seen the cubicles come and go.

The "big cubes" of the early 1980's nearly reached the ceiling, and actually came with doors. The deconstructionist period of the early 1990s corralled workers into smaller "bull pens," before they became a little too close for comfort.

And now, for the turn of the century, the more individual-friendly "modular cubicles" have come into vogue with higher walls and adjustable furniture. Just right, Hill says.

"The work envelope is adjustable so you can set it up according to your needs."

The cubicle was supposed to transform the traditional office of closed-door compartments into an open-air bazaar, an incubator of ideas, innovation and productivity. But has the cubicle age been as good for workers as it has for work? Or are laborers this

See CUBICLES/Page 5A

BETH KAPLAN/PRESS & SUN-BULLETIN

Ellen Miller, a total quality manager at Universal Instruments, says cubicles encourage workers to interact.

U-E cancels staff meeting

In what the union president said could be seen as an insult, Union-Endicott Superintendent Dennis M. Sweeney has canceled an opening day meeting with staff because of an impasse in contract negotiations.

In an Aug. 25 letter to staff, Sweeney said he is canceling the general meeting Tuesday because it "does not hold prospects for being productive" in light of the current impasse in bargaining.

Union-Endicott's 370 teachers have been working without a new contract since July 1996.

Page 1B.

September 1, 1997: After the news of Princess Diana's death broke in Sunday's paper, the Press & Sun-Bulletin gave extensive coverage to the world's reaction. *Microfilm archives*

SPORTS FURYK AMONG 137 COMMITTED TO B.C. OPEN 1D

Press & Sun-Bulletin

SEPTEMBER 9, 1998 FINAL EDITION © 1998 THE BINGHAMTON PRESS CO., BINGHAMTON, N.Y. www.pressconnects.com FIFTY CENTS

62!! McGwire makes his mark

ASSOCIATED PRESS

ST. LOUIS — History wasn't made with one of his magical moonshots or majestic arcs.

Mark McGwire simply lined a laser to left Tuesday night — his shortest home run of the season at 341 feet — and the biggest, most glamorous record in sports was his.

Homer No. 62 barely cleared the wall. But no matter. His mighty swing won the race to break Roger Maris' 37-year-old record, without a doubt or an asterisk, and with plenty of games to spare.

"I tell you what, I was so shocked because I didn't think the ball had enough to get out," McGwire said. "It's an absolutely incredible feeling. I can honestly say I did it."

McGwire connected with two outs in the fourth inning off the Chicago Cubs' Steve Trachsel for the historic homer, punctuating the chase that reinvigorated the game and captivated the nation.

McGwire was so caught up in the moment that he missed first base as he rounded the bag and had to return to touch it, pulled back by coach Dave McKay.

From there, McGwire got handshakes from every Chicago infielder as he trotted home and then hugged catcher Scott Servais.

McGwire was mobbed by his teammates at home plate, where he hoisted his 10-year-old batboy son Matt high into the air. McGwire then ran into the seats to hug the family of Maris, whose record he had just broken.

As the ball cleared the left-field fence, there was no scramble to retrieve it. It landed in an area where no fan could get it.

Tim Forneris, a ground-crew worker, picked it up and later gave it to McGwire in a postgame party on the field. McGwire also got a '62 red Corvette from the Cardinals in the tribute and he and his son took a slow victory drive around the field as the crowd cheered. The homer triggered an 11-minute delay, baseball's biggest midgame celebration since Cal Ripken broke Lou Gehrig's consecutive games record in 1995.

After McGwire finished celebrating with his teammates and the Maris family, he grabbed a microphone to address the sellout crowd of 43,688, which was still standing and cheering.

"To all my family, my son, the Cubs, Sammy Sosa. It's unbelievable," he said. "Thank you, St. Louis."

The home run, despite its short distance, surely will rank as one of the biggest in history, up there with the ones hit by Bobby Thomson, Bill Mazeroski, Hank Aaron, Carlton Fisk, and Joe Carter.

McGWIRE'S GREATEST HIT
COVERAGE, 1D, 4D

ASSOCIATED PRESS
Mark McGwire swings his way into history.

Wednesday

LIVING

Make kids' lunch a healthy one

With a little ingenuity, lunches for school children easily can become an occasion to work more grains, such as bread, fruits and vegetables, into children's diets.

PAGE 1C

SPORTS

Eastern League playoffs begin

The Binghamton Mets will face an all-star-laden foe in the New Britain Rock Cats starting tonight in the first round of the best-of-five Eastern League baseball playoffs.

STORY, PAGE 1D
POSITION-BY-POSITION ANALYSIS, PAGE 3D

MONEY

Now, what are we paying for again?

You'd be glad to pay the phone company, if only you knew what those fees were for. The government wants phone bills translated into English. And, surprise, phone companies resent the intrusion.

PAGE 10B

TOMORROW

LIVING
Hate to go to the dentist? You're not alone. But there are things you can do to ease your fears.

WEATHER

RAIN POSSIBLE
63°/45°
DETAILS 2B

INDEX

4 sections 32 pages

TO SUBSCRIBE
798-1161
NY 1-800-253-5343
PA 1-800-241-2120
ONLINE
PressConnects
www.pressconnects.com
0 40901 00701 2

SCHOOL'S OPEN

Doing Our Part To Make
It A Great
YEAR!

CHUCK HAUPT staff photographer

Lisa Guinan, a special education teacher at Horace Mann Elementary School in Binghamton, gets ready for the first day of school. She is one of 60 new teachers hired this year by the Binghamton School District. Retirement incentives, tougher state testing and a need for more special education teachers have caused schools to hire more teachers than in previous years.

Students aren't the only new faces

Retirement, stricter standards create need for more teachers

BY GEORGE BASLER
Staff Writer

Fresh out of Marist College in Poughkeepsie, Jessica Goldstein had the choice of five job offers as a beginning teacher.

The 22-year-old New Jersey native chose the Binghamton City School District because she likes the area and the school system. She will teach special education at Horace Mann Elementary School, which, like most Southern Tier schools, starts classes today.

While Goldstein is happy to come here, city school district officials are happy she's coming. They had to fill 60 teaching positions over the summer, the largest number in recent memory. And they had to work hard to do it.

Binghamton wasn't alone. As schools open for classes today, many Southern Tier school districts are reporting their largest teacher turnovers and largest numbers of new teacher hires in recent years.

"Our numbers (of job openings) are about double that of a typical year," said W. Edward Ermlich, superintendent of Chenango Forks Central School District, which had to fill 17 positions in its 160-person teaching staff.

Filling all the openings hasn't been easy, Ermlich said. The Chenango Forks district began working before the end of the last school year and only made its final hire last Friday.

Goldstein said she took the job in Binghamton in part because it was the first offer

SEE NEW FACES 3A

MEMBERS OF THE CLASS

Name: Jane Hores
Age: 43
Hometown: Apalachin
College: Binghamton University
Her new job: Special education teacher at George W. Johnson School in Endicott.
Why she got into teaching: "I wanted to make a difference in the lives of children with special needs."

Name: Lisa Ricci
Age: 25
Hometown: Endwell
College: SUNY Geneseo
Her new job: Speech pathologist at George W. Johnson School.
Why she got into teaching: "I think being a teacher has the most positive effects on the student for their future."

Buying frenzy pushes Dow to record gain

Greenspan's suggestion of rate cuts thrills market

NEW YORK — The Dow industrials jumped 380 points Tuesday — the biggest single-day point gain in history — and vaulted back into positive territory for the year amid hopes the Federal Reserve will protect the economy from a spreading financial crisis abroad.

The Dow Jones industrial average surged 5 percent higher, rising 380.53 to 8,020.78, a gain that nearly wiped out last week's losses.

The buying frenzy followed a speech Friday evening by Alan Greenspan in which the Federal Reserve chairman signaled the central bank may cut interest rates to offset the drag from economic turmoil gripping Asia and Russia.

"Part of me says the forces of light and reason have returned and the market should be going up. But the other part of me says let's not get back to irrational exuberance," said Joe Battipaglia, chief investment strategist at Gruntal & Co.

The leap back above 8,000 came just a week after a steep selloff, including a 512-plunge Aug. 31, that pushed the Dow below this year's starting point, 7,908.25, and as low as 7,400.

But even with its sizable bounce, the barometer of 30 major companies is still about 1,300 points, or 14 percent below the record of 9,337.97 set less than two months ago on July 17.

Tuesday's rise eclipsed the Dow's record 337-point bounce on Oct. 28, a day after its record plunge.

Some analysts saw danger in the Dow's dizzying climb.

Bill Meehan, chief market analyst for Cantor Fitzgerald, warned that Tuesday's rebound could be a "bear market trap" for investors if they "believe that worst has been seen. It builds confidence again and gets them to put cash into the market and watch it disappear."

Federal Reserve Chairman Alan Greenspan flexed his muscle when a buying frenzy followed his hint at lower interest rates. PAGE 10B

LOCAL STOCKS

Company	Tue. Close	Chg.	YTD* % chg.
BSB	21[illegible]	-[illegible]	-21.3
Chase	47[illegible]	+1[illegible]	13.5
Dll Grp	14[illegible]	+1 1/16	-46.8
Dover	27 15/16	+1 11/16	-22.7
Energy East	46[illegible]	+[illegible]	+32
Hadco	21[illegible]	+2[illegible]	-51.9
IBM	125 15/16	+6 9/16	+20.4
Lock. Martin	95[illegible]	+1[illegible]	-2.8
P&G	79[illegible]	+4	-0.2

*Year-to-date change. Percentage change since Jan. 2

New turf would allow more uses for stadium

BY SEAN MAYER
Staff Writer

Binghamton Municipal Stadium next year may be home to an array of sporting and community events besides professional baseball.

Plans are in the works to replace the field at the stadium — home to the Eastern League's Binghamton Mets — with a more durable surface that would allow for other sports and community activities, state Sen. Thomas Libous, R-Binghamton, and Mets general manager R.C. Reuteman said Tuesday.

The surface is Grassmaster, a high-grade natural turf interspersed with artificial green fibers. It would be installed by Delhi-based Clark Companies Inc. and would be ready for April 1999 and the start of the baseball season.

Such sports as football, soccer and lacrosse could be played at the stadium, with no appreciable damage to the new turf.

LIBOUS

REUTEMAN

Binghamton Municipal Stadium would be the first facility in the country to feature Grassmaster, created by Holland-based Desso DLW — the largest sports surface company in the world, with about 50 facilities in Europe sporting its product, said Scott Clark, owner of Clark Companies.

All that is necessary is for the Binghamton City Council to accept a $1 million grant secured by Libous and earmarked for enhancement of the stadium. The City Council, in turn, would give the money to Clark Companies.

Libous said he hopes the

SEE STADIUM 5A

New York lobbying laws need teeth, reformers say

State is one of 7 with lax rules, report says

BY JAY GALLAGHER
Albany Bureau Chief

ALBANY — The state government should ban lobbyists from making campaign donations during the legislative session and also prohibit them from giving dinners and other gifts to lawmakers at any time, a group of reformers proposed Tuesday.

"Imagine if you allowed lawyers to take judges and members of the jury to dinner while they were trying cases," said Blair Horner of the New York Public Interest Research Group, one of the reform advocates. It's just absurd on its face, and yet we allow it in the legislative process."

NYPIRG, along with the League of Women Voters and Common Cause, sent letters Tuesday to Gov. George E. Pataki and other candidates for governor asking them to support the reforms.

Lawmakers now routinely hold fund-raisers near the Capitol during the legislative session — 201 of them this year, according to Horner, who said he's concerned that lawmakers who take money from someone the night before may tend to vote the way that lobbyist wants the next day.

"This is just an unbelievable nighttime activity," Horner said, "the blue-suited nomads of Albany wander ... from fund-raiser to fund-raiser ... some nights as many as 18."

There are also currently no limit on what gifts lobbyists can provide to lawmakers, and individuals can give up to $11,500 to Senate candidates, $5,600 to Assembly hopefuls and $41,400 to statewide office-seekers. The reformers want to reduce that limit to $250 per election cycle.

"Lobbying should be based on persuasive passion and ideas, not on the deep pockets of the clients," said Barbara Bartoletti of the League of Women Voters.

The groups also issued a report showing New York in a group of seven states with the most lax lobbying laws in the country. New Hampshire, Alabama, Louisiana, South Dakota, Wyoming and Idaho are the others.

The report found that 23 states limit lobbyists' ability to raise campaign donations for candidates, 25 limit lobbyists' gifts to lawmakers and six states ban all gifts.

September 9, 1998: Home-run history was the most important story this day. *Courtesy David Silvanic*

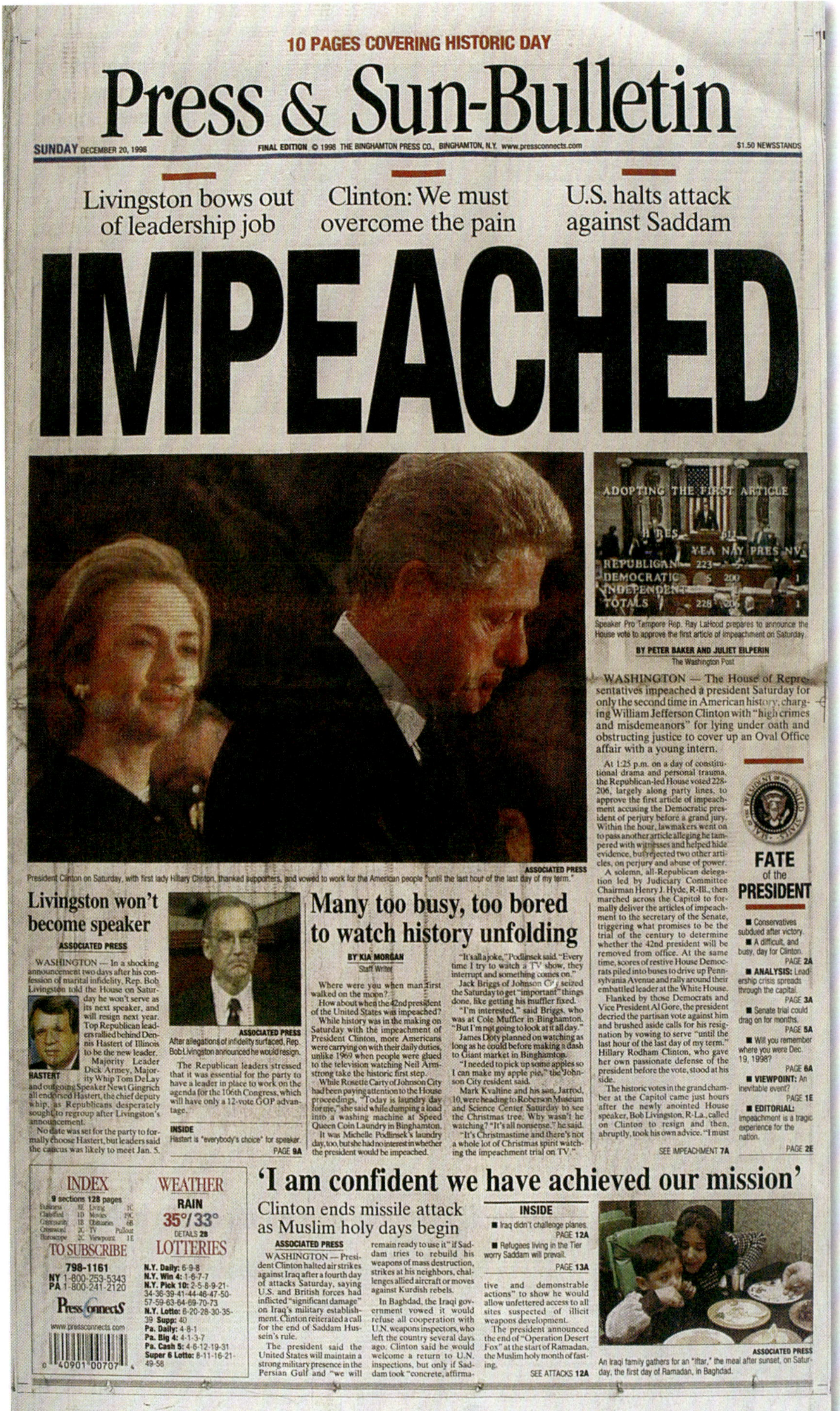

10 PAGES COVERING HISTORIC DAY

Press & Sun-Bulletin

SUNDAY DECEMBER 20, 1998 — FINAL EDITION © 1998 THE BINGHAMTON PRESS CO., BINGHAMTON, N.Y. www.pressconnects.com — $1.50 NEWSSTANDS

Livingston bows out of leadership job | Clinton: We must overcome the pain | U.S. halts attack against Saddam

IMPEACHED

ASSOCIATED PRESS
President Clinton on Saturday, with first lady Hillary Clinton, thanked supporters, and vowed to work for the American people "until the last hour of the last day of my term."

ADOPTING THE FIRST ARTICLE

Speaker Pro Tempore Rep. Ray LaHood prepares to announce the House vote to approve the first article of impeachment on Saturday.

BY PETER BAKER AND JULIET EILPERIN
The Washington Post

WASHINGTON — The House of Representatives impeached a president Saturday for only the second time in American history, charging William Jefferson Clinton with "high crimes and misdemeanors" for lying under oath and obstructing justice to cover up an Oval Office affair with a young intern.

At 1:25 p.m. on a day of constitutional drama and personal trauma, the Republican-led House voted 228-206, largely along party lines, to approve the first article of impeachment accusing the Democratic president of perjury before a grand jury. Within the hour, lawmakers went on to pass another article alleging he tampered with witnesses and helped hide evidence, but rejected two other articles, on perjury and abuse of power.

A solemn, all-Republican delegation led by Judiciary Committee Chairman Henry J. Hyde, R-Ill., then marched across the Capitol to formally deliver the articles of impeachment to the secretary of the Senate, triggering what promises to be the trial of the century to determine whether the 42nd president will be removed from office. At the same time, scores of restive House Democrats piled into buses to drive up Pennsylvania Avenue and rally around their embattled leader at the White House.

Flanked by those Democrats and Vice President Al Gore, the president decried the partisan vote against him and brushed aside calls for his resignation by vowing to serve "until the last hour of the last day of my term." Hillary Rodham Clinton, who gave her own passionate defense of the president before the vote, stood at his side.

The historic votes in the grand chamber at the Capitol came just hours after the newly anointed House speaker, Bob Livingston, R-La., called on Clinton to resign and then, abruptly, took his own advice. "I must

SEE IMPEACHMENT 7A

FATE of the PRESIDENT

- Conservatives subdued after victory.
- A difficult, and busy, day for Clinton. PAGE 2A
- **ANALYSIS:** Leadership crisis spreads through the capital. PAGE 3A
- Senate trial could drag on for months. PAGE 5A
- Will you remember where you were Dec. 19, 1998? PAGE 6A
- **VIEWPOINT:** An inevitable event? PAGE 1E
- **EDITORIAL:** Impeachment is a tragic experience for the nation. PAGE 2E

Livingston won't become speaker

ASSOCIATED PRESS

WASHINGTON — In a shocking announcement two days after his confession of marital infidelity, Rep. Bob Livingston told the House on Saturday he won't serve as its next speaker, and will resign next year. Top Republican leaders rallied behind Dennis Hastert of Illinois to be the new leader.

HASTERT

Majority Leader Dick Armey, Majority Whip Tom DeLay and outgoing Speaker Newt Gingrich all endorsed Hastert, the chief deputy whip, as Republicans desperately sought to regroup after Livingston's announcement.

No date was set for the party to formally choose Hastert, but leaders said the caucus was likely to meet Jan. 5.

ASSOCIATED PRESS
After allegations of infidelity surfaced, Rep. Bob Livingston announced he would resign.

The Republican leaders stressed that it was essential for the party to have a leader in place to work on the agenda for the 106th Congress, which will have only a 12-vote GOP advantage.

INSIDE
Hastert is "everybody's choice" for speaker. PAGE 9A

Many too busy, too bored to watch history unfolding

BY KIA MORGAN
Staff Writer

Where were you when man first walked on the moon?

How about when the 42nd president of the United States was impeached?

While history was in the making on Saturday with the impeachment of President Clinton, more Americans were carrying on with their daily duties, unlike 1969 when people were glued to the television watching Neil Armstrong take the historic first step.

While Rosette Carty of Johnson City had been paying attention to the House proceedings, "Today is laundry day for me," she said while dumping a load into a washing machine at Speed Queen Coin Laundry in Binghamton.

It was Michelle Podlinsek's laundry day, too, but she had no interest in whether the president would be impeached.

"It's all a joke," Podlinsek said. "Every time I try to watch a TV show, they interrupt and something comes on."

Jack Briggs of Johnson City seized the Saturday to get "important" things done, like getting his muffler fixed.

"I'm interested," said Briggs, who was at Cole Muffler in Binghamton. "But I'm not going to look at it all day."

James Doty planned on watching as long as he could before making a dash to Giant market in Binghamton.

"I needed to pick up some apples so I can make my apple pie," the Johnson City resident said.

Mark Kvaltine and his son, Jarrod, 10, were heading to Roberson Museum and Science Center Saturday to see the Christmas tree. Why wasn't he watching? "It's all nonsense," he said.

"It's Christmastime and there's not a whole lot of Christmas spirit watching the impeachment trial on TV."

INDEX
9 sections 128 pages

WEATHER
RAIN
35°/33°
DETAILS 2B

TO SUBSCRIBE
798-1161
NY 1-800-253-5343
PA 1-800-241-2120
PressConnects
www.pressconnects.com

LOTTERIES
N.Y. Daily: 6-9-8
N.Y. Win 4: 1-6-7-7
N.Y. Pick 10: 2-5-8-9-21-34-36-39-41-44-46-47-50-57-59-63-64-69-70-73
N.Y. Lotto: 6-20-28-30-35-39 Supp: 40
Pa. Daily: 4-8-1
Pa. Big 4: 4-1-3-7
Pa. Cash 5: 4-6-12-19-31
Super 6 Lotto: 8-11-16-21-49-58

'I am confident we have achieved our mission'

Clinton ends missile attack as Muslim holy days begin

ASSOCIATED PRESS

WASHINGTON — President Clinton halted air strikes against Iraq after a fourth day of attacks Saturday, saying U.S. and British forces had inflicted "significant damage" on Iraq's military establishment. Clinton reiterated a call for the end of Saddam Hussein's rule.

The president said the United States will maintain a strong military presence in the Persian Gulf and "we will remain ready to use it" if Saddam tries to rebuild his weapons of mass destruction, strikes at his neighbors, challenges allied aircraft or moves against Kurdish rebels.

In Baghdad, the Iraqi government vowed it would refuse all cooperation with U.N. weapons inspectors, who left the country several days ago. Clinton said he would welcome a return to U.N. inspections, but only if Saddam took "concrete, affirmative and demonstrable actions" to show he would allow unfettered access to all sites suspected of illicit weapons development.

The president announced the end of "Operation Desert Fox" at the start of Ramadan, the Muslim holy month of fasting.

SEE ATTACKS 12A

INSIDE
- Iraq didn't challenge planes. PAGE 12A
- Refugees living in the Tier worry Saddam will prevail. PAGE 13A

ASSOCIATED PRESS
An Iraqi family gathers for an "iftar," the meal after sunset, on Saturday, the first day of Ramadan, in Baghdad.

December 20, 1998: This page marking President Clinton's impeachment was saved by many of our readers. *Courtesy Carolyn Fitzgerald*

SPORTS STARS TOP SABRES 4-2 IN GAME 2 1D

Press & Sun-Bulletin

JUNE 11, 1999 — FINAL EDITION © 1999 THE BINGHAMTON PRESS CO., BINGHAMTON, N.Y. www.pressconnects.com — FIFTY CENTS

Friday

SPORTS

Knight in trouble

Indiana basketball coach Bob Knight could be charged with battery for allegedly choking a man Monday night.
PAGE 1D

RACING EXTRA

Gibbs gets going

Former NFL coach Joe Gibbs might want to clear some space next to his Super Bowl trophies. His racing team has a legitimate shot at winning the NASCAR title.
PAGE 6D

GIBBS

OUT & ABOUT

Meals and more

The sights will make you want to visit Pennsylvania Dutch country. The meals will make you want to stay.
PAGE 1C

COMMUNITY

Get festive!

Here's your guide to making the most of a weekend packed with summer festivals.
PAGE 1B

WEATHER

PARTLY CLOUDY
79°/60°
DETAILS 2B

INDEX

4 sections 44 pages

Business	10B	Movies	5C
Classified	6C	Obituaries	6B
Crossword	2C	Opinion	12-13A
Horoscope	2C	TV	2C
Landers	5C	World	2A

LOTTERIES

N.Y. Daily: 9-3-7
N.Y. Win 4: 8-0-8-8
N.Y. Take 5: 1-3-6-11-39
N.Y. Pick 10: 5-12-19-24-29-36-39-43-48-49-51-54-55-57-63-64-70-73-77-80
Pa. Daily: 7-4-9
Pa. Big 4: 0-7-7-3
Pa. Cash 5: 4-9-25-30-33

TO SUBSCRIBE

798-1161
NY 1-800-253-5343
PA 1-800-241-2120

ONLINE

Press Connects
www.pressconnects.com

INSIDE TODAY: SPECIAL SECTION

1999 GRADUATES

Celebrate the season with your favorite high school graduates. Find out all you need to know about local ceremonies in today's special section, which includes lists of graduates, graduation times and places and profiles of valedictorians and salutatorians.

Boy is guest star during first lady's visit

BY DON SBARRA
Staff Writer

The meetings were brief, sometimes only a handshake or a nod of acknowledgment. But for some of the hundreds who came in contact with Hillary Rodham Clinton during her three-hour visit to Binghamton on Wednesday, the memories will last a lifetime.

And those who had special encounters with Clinton had fun Thursday replaying their experiences.

Take 7-year-old Marty Beloch and his mom, Denise Dean, of Binghamton's East Side. Hanging out in the lobby of the Holiday Inn Arena and hoping to catch a glimpse of the first lady, the mother and son got more than they ever expected. Dean said Thursday that she would have been satisfied with simply snapping a photograph of Clinton waving to onlookers as she headed toward the reception hall. But when Clinton turned and headed back toward a small group of gawkers, Dean said she was stunned by what happened next. Marty took off on a run and was scooped into the arms of the first lady.

MARTY

"I was just in shock," Dean said.

Marty, a first-grader at Calvin Coolidge Elementary, brought pictures of the encounter with him to school Thursday. "He was the talk of the whole school," Dean said. "He was so proud."

Clinton arrived at Binghamton Regional Airport aboard an Air Force jet about 3 p.m. The first person to greet her as she stepped from the plane was Binghamton Mayor Richard A. Bucci, a conservative Republican who was determined not to let political differences tarnish the liberal first lady's view of the city. After the initial how-do-you-dos, Bucci said Clinton appeared genuinely pleased

SEE CLINTON 3A

PHOTO PROVIDED
Marty Beloch hoped for a glimpse of the first lady on Wednesday. He ended up with a terrific memory.

BUILDING PEACE IN THE BALKANS

Yugoslav withdrawal begins

Clinton lashes out at Milosevic

ASSOCIATED PRESS

WASHINGTON — President Clinton told Americans Thursday night "we have achieved victory for a safer world" in Kosovo. He warned Serbs that the United States will not help them rebuild from bombing "as long as your nation is ruled by an indicted war criminal."

CLINTON

In an address from the Oval Office, Clinton all but called for an uprising against Slobodan Milosevic, telling Serbs they had needlessly suffered airstrikes because he was determined "to eliminate Kosovar Albanians from Kosovo, dead or alive."

"But we are ready to provide humanitarian aid now and to help to build a better future for Serbia, too, when its government represents tolerance and freedom, not repression and terror," Clinton added.

A wave of euphoria swept through the White House on the day the bombing stopped and Serb troops began withdrawing from Kosovo. But Clinton was somber as he warned of the dangers still facing 50,000 peacekeeping troops — including 7,000 American forces — in escorting refugees home and clearing mines.

"This next phase also will be dangerous," Clinton said. "Bitter memories will still be fresh and there may well be casualties."

ASSOCIATED PRESS
Yugoslav army soldiers leaving the province of Kosovo flash traditional Serb nationalist salutes from their vehicles Thursday. The withdrawal of Yugoslav troops led NATO to suspend its 78-day air war.

NATO suspends Kosovo airstrikes

ASSOCIATED PRESS

PRISTINA, Yugoslavia — Yugoslav troops rumbled out of Kosovo in trucks, armored cars and buses Thursday, prompting NATO to suspend its punishing 78-day air war and the United Nations to authorize a heavily armed security force to restore peace and begin reconstruction.

NATO troops massed in neighboring Macedonia to begin the peacekeeping mission, with the first soldiers ready to enter Kosovo as early as today.

"We shall be off quite soon," Lt. Gen. Michael Jackson, commander of NATO forces in Macedonia, said Thursday night.

Jackson also warned the rebel Kosovo Liberation Army not to try to take advantage of the withdrawal to pursue its fight with Serb forces.

He said U.N. Secretary-General Kofi Annan and other senior political leaders made it "quite clear that it would be foolish in the extreme to interfere with or create incidents" connected with the pullout.

"I would endorse that and say it would indeed be very stupid," Jackson said.

Despite the death and destruction wreaked by the bombing campaign and the imminent arrival of a huge foreign force on Yugoslav soil, President Slobodan Milosevic proclaimed victory.

"The people are the heroes," Milosevic said on national television at the same time that NATO Secretary-General Javier Solana announced the bombing campaign had been suspended.

In Washington, President Clinton praised NATO's unity and warned Milosevic that airstrikes would resume if he reneges on a peace deal to allow more than 860,000

SEE WITHDRAWAL 2A

LATEST DEVELOPMENTS

ASSOCIATED PRESS
Refugees Marigona Nerecau, 8, and Sahide Dulovi, 14, laugh Thursday at a camp in Macedonia.

- President Clinton proclaims victory in the 11-week conflict against Yugoslavia.
- The U.N. Security Council approves a resolution authorizing a peacekeeping force of as many as 50,000 troops, including 7,000 Americans. Clinton could not say how long the peacekeepers would stay.
- NATO says the first peacekeepers could enter Kosovo today.
- The Security Council resolution also authorizes an interim civilian administration for Kosovo.

INSIDE

- Milosevic declares victory, too.
- U.S. troops are ready for dangerous work.
- Refugees prepare to head home.

PAGE 2A

U-E residents talk turf but not tough

BY BRYAN CHAMBALA
Staff Writer

If a large group of Union-Endicott residents opposes an artificial turf field at the high school, it must be holding secret meetings.

While about 25 residents made the trip to U-E High School Thursday night for a public hearing on the proposed $6.3 to $6.8 million upgrade, they questioned only minor details, not the overall validity of the project.

On June 16, Union-Endicott voters will decide whether to pass a $6.3 million undertaking that includes renovations to the district's athletic facilities, the high school auditorium and a few minor improvements throughout the high school. A second proposition will give voters the option of installing a $500,000 artificial turf surface on the football field.

Steven Stanko said he agreed with both propositions but questioned the need for a $110,000 expenditure to renovate existing soccer fields at Ann McGuinness Elementary School.

"I don't see why they can't use the new football field for soccer, especially if it has the artificial turf on it," Stanko said. "They (soccer teams) used to use the outfield of the baseball field."

Dennis Sweeney, superintendent of U-E schools, said the proposed football field could be used by a number of varsity and junior varsity teams, in addition to band, intramural sports and community members, because of the increased durability of an artificial turf surface. The grass surface can be used only for sanctioned games because of its limited durability.

Terry Hogan, a lifelong resident of Endicott, questioned whether an artificial turf field would be able to withstand the flooding that often occurs on the property.

Sweeney explained that the turf being proposed had undergone and withstood a series of flood tests that simulated much more rigorous conditions than are usually present at the U-E facility.

Sweeney also explained the state would reimburse the district for 71 percent of the expense of the project, making it an opportune time for voters to approve the project.

"This is as good a rate as we're going to get," he said. "We've taken the time to put together a proposal that efficiently addresses some very pressing needs in the district."

Chris Damigos said he felt the voters should act in the interest of the district's children and not their own pocketbooks. "If the tax money doesn't go to projects like this for the schools, it's going to go somewhere else," he said.

THE VOTE

U-E voters will will decide on the athletic facilities plan June 16.

Wild police chase has unusual end

Suspects in drug case try to hide at nursing home, Bible college

BY WYN HORNBUCKLE
Staff Writer

Two Binghamton men were in custody and facing drug charges Thursday after fleeing police and hiding out in a nursing home and a Bible college in Johnson City.

About 11:30 a.m., Special Investigative Units from the Binghamton Police Bureau and state police, armed with a search warrant, attempted to stop a Nissan Ultima near West End Avenue. The vehicle, occupied by Jermaine D. Cooper, 26, of 160 West End Ave., Apt. 1, and Gerald J. Graven, 39, of 102 Liberty St., stopped initially and then took off, said State Police Senior Investigator Patrick J. Brady.

Graven, the driver, led several police vehicles on a short, high-speed chase through residential streets in the West End area. During their flight, police say the men threw more than three ounces of crack cocaine out the car window and headed west on Riverside Drive.

SEE SUSPECTS 10A

CHUCK HAUPT staff photographer
A state police officer and a Binghamton K-9 officer guard a doorway on the campus of Practical Bible College during a search for a suspect Thursday.

June 11, 1999: A young boy met the first lady, and his proud mother saved the page. *Courtesy Denise Dean*

Fireworks light up the sky over Binghamton, bringing in the new millennium at the third-annual First Night Binghamton. *Press & Sun-Bulletin archives*

GOV. BUSH
PLEASE SHAKE MY
HAND Love
LINDSEY

Texas Governor, George W. Bush, at the St. Patrick's Day Parade in 2000, poses with Lindsey Tamblyn and her stepfather, Jim Foley. *Courtesy Jim Foley*

Amanda King, 11, of Wilkes-Barre, Pa., celebrates 2000 and her birthday at First Night's Mega Mini Countdown at the Broome County Veterans Memorial Arena. *Press & Sun-Bulletin archives*

2000 - 2004

Into a new millennium

Happy 21st Century

Press & Sun-Bulletin

JANUARY 1, 2000 — HOLIDAY EDITION © 2000 THE BINGHAMTON PRESS CO., BINGHAMTON, N.Y. www.pressconnects.com — FIFTY CENTS

Saturday

OUR CENTURY

These photos tell the Tier's tale

It's everybody's century. Take a look at the Tier's history as told by photographs of your friends and family. PAGES 9-11A

SPORTS

Bowl game update

Friday's games brought the usual bowl celebration and anguish, and today offers another full slate of games. PAGES 1D, 4D

BU to face ACC teams next season

The Binghamton University men's basketball team will play Virginia and Florida State in the 2000-2001 season. PAGE 1D

NATION

Elliot Richardson dies Friday at 79

Elliot Lee Richardson, who resigned as attorney general in 1973, died Friday of a cerebral hemorrhage. PAGE 3A

RICHARDSON

COMING UP

SUNDAY

Get complete information on how stocks performed for the year.

WEATHER

PARTLY CLOUDY 43°/32° DETAILS 2B

INDEX

4 sections 44 pages

Business 5B Movies 5C Classified 6C Obituaries 4B Horoscope 5C Opinion 16-17A

LOTTERIES

N.Y. Daily: 7-8-0
N.Y. Win 4: 2-4-4-5
N.Y. Take 5: 4-14-15-29-34
N.Y. Pick 10: 6-8-11-13-16-17-19-24-32-49-52-53-58-59-64-70-71-73-77-78
Millennium Lotto: 8-23-38-39-46 Bonus: 14
Pa. Daily: 6-3-1
Pa. Big 4: 3-3-6-5
Pa. Cash 5: 14-26-32-35-39

TO SUBSCRIBE

798-1161
NY 1-800-253-5343
PA 1-800-241-2120

ONLINE

Press Connects www.pressconnects.com

It's finally here ...

WELCOME TO 2000

Tier, world fight off Y2K bug

BY JEFF PLATSKY
Business Editor

Good morning.

Surprised?

Power stayed on. Computers didn't crash. Nobody saw the Four Horsemen of the Apocalypse trotting down Vestal Parkway.

And if all is not yet right with the world, at least for most people it's not significantly worse than it was yesterday.

Welcome to 2000.

The billions of dollars pumped into computer systems to prepare critical systems for the date rollover apparently achieved the desired result. The power grid functioned normally. Automated teller machines belched out money to the cash deprived. And the telephone lines were still carrying conversations.

Not that people weren't anxious going into last night. At Kmart on Binghamton's North Side, clerks were telling shoppers searching the shelves for lamp oil that they had sold out on Thursday morning, and bottled water sold briskly at groceries across the region as people prepared for the unexpected.

No drastic measures were necessary at midnight. Across the world and in the United States, there were few reports of computer glitches. Those that were reported were minor.

"Everything went as dull as possible," said George Bonner, vice president of gas operations for New York State Electric & Gas Corp. "No problem whatsoever."

Todd McAdam and Tom Wilber contributed to this report.

DAVE KENNEDY staff photographer

Fireworks light up the sky over Binghamton, ushering in the year 2000 with a festive bang. More than 13,000 people attended festivities during downtown Binghamton's First Night celebration.

Worries give way to First Night fun

BY ELIZABETH COHEN
Staff Writer

There were no terrorist attacks. The power grid did not collapse. Despite a two-alarm fire, most of the drama of New Year's Eve 2000 in Binghamton took place on stages, and the only things that exploded were the fireworks at midnight, over the Chenango and Susquehanna rivers.

Binghamton's First Night went "smoothly, with no glitches" said Broome County sheriff's Detective Jason Ellis, who spent Friday evening stationed on Court Street in a high-tech community-policing command vehicle.

That appeared to be the consensus of the 13,000-plus attendees, wearing glitter-spattered hats and hats made of tied balloons, tooting horns and twirling noisemakers. Beneath star-swirled skies and in not-too-low temperatures — 31 degrees downtown — the crowd, which seemed mostly composed of families with children, attended an eclectic banquet of cultural events.

A fire at The Royal lounge at 138 Washington St. that began at 7:30 p.m. proved a minor distraction from music, dance, puppetry, theater and other cultural fare early in the evening, but the desire to stay warm and keep kiddies content kept people moving.

"You would never know that New Year's 2000 was different from any other New Year's," said Ellis, who added that police had no special Y2K plan except to "react to any emergency as we normally would."

Event coordinator Naima Kradjian said two of the First Night venues were shut down because of the fire, the Art Mission Gallery and the Salvation Army. Acoustic blues guitarist David Sliwinski was moved from the Salvation Army to the Forum's rehearsal hall for his performance.

"The fire was a distraction," Kradjian said, but the only

SEE VENUES 5A

INSIDE

■ Binghamton firefighters, above, battle a blaze that destroyed The Royal lounge downtown. PAGE 18A

■ Broome County Emergency Services workers enjoy a nice, quiet night. PAGE 4A

■ More than 2 million ring in the new year at Times Square. Page 7A

NEW YEAR'S BABY

At 1:39 a.m. today, Broome County saw a brand new bouncing baby boy. Lourdes Hospital spokesman Jeffery K. Davis, however, had no further details on the hospital's first birth of the year.

As 19th century book predicted, maybe 20th was worth napping through

DAVID ROSSIE
Commentary

Edward Bellamy (1850-98) was a Massachusetts lawyer who went straight and became a journalist and book author. In 1888 he published a novel titled *Looking Backward 2000-1887*, a copy of which was made available to me by Charles Rosenthal.

Looking Backward is the story of Julian West, a 37-year-old Bostonian who falls into a deep hypnotic sleep on the night of May 30, 1887, and is awakened on the morning of Sept. 10, 2000.

West has managed to sleep through the 20th century, which means he has a lot of catching up to do. He is assisted in this endeavor by the man who roused him, a Dr. Leete, who is described as a retired physician.

The historian Isaiah Berlin called the 20th century "the most terrible in Western history," and he may have been right. Certainly it was not the century Bellamy hoped for. He was a Romantic and a Utopian Socialist. He did not live to see the 20th century, and it is probably just as well. Following are some examples of the century Bellamy envisioned in his book, interspersed with a few reality checks:

Dr. Leete: "Early in the last century (the 20th) the evolution was completed by the final consolidation of the entire capital of the nation. The industry and commerce of the country, ceasing to be conducted by a set of irresponsible corporations and syndicates of private persons at their caprice and for their profit, were entrusted to a single syndicate representing the people, to be conducted in the common interest for the common profit."

Microsoft, Time Warner, Mobil/Exxon, General Motors, Archer Daniels Midland, Lockheed Martin.

■ ■ ■

West: "When you want a doctor, do you simply apply to the proper bureau and take any that can be sent?"

Dr. Leete: "That rule would not work well in the case of a physician. The good a physician can do a patient depends largely on his acquaintance with his constitutional tendencies and condition. The patient must be able, therefore, to call a particular doctor, and he does so, just as the patient did in your day. The only difference is that instead of collecting his fee for himself, the doctor collects it for the nation by pricking off the amount according to a regular scale for medical attendance from the patient's credit card."

HMOs, managed care.

■ ■ ■

Dr. Leete: "In your day governments were accustomed on the slightest international misunderstanding, to seize upon the bodies of citizens and deliver them over by the

SEE BOOK 6A

Hostage drama ends; India frees 3 militants

BY KATHY GANNON
Associated Press

INSIDE

Hijacking victims describe their terror and misery. PAGE 2A

KANDAHAR, Afghanistan — Waving pistols in the air, five hijackers sped off in waiting cars Friday with three prisoners released from Indian jails and escaped the country — ending a tense eight-day standoff.

All 155 hostages on the Indian Airlines plane were freed unharmed, but the crisis — the longest hijacking drama in more than a decade — highlighted the explosive nature of the long-running dispute over the Himalayan territory of Kashmir.

Under the agreement made between India, the hijackers and the Taliban militia who rule most of Afghanistan, the hijackers agreed to end the eight-day crisis and free the hostages in exchange for the three imprisoned militants.

The hijackers and their three associates sped away at sunset in four-wheel drive vehicles from the Kandahar airport, where they had kept the hostages in an Indian Airlines plane parked on the tarmac.

This morning, a Taliban official said the hijackers had crossed the border. He did not say where they escaped to, but most likely it was into Pakistan, which shares a long border with Afghanistan.

ASSOCIATED PRESS

Captain D. Sharan, left, of the hijacked Indian Airlines plane is hugged by Minister of Civil Aviation Sharad Yadav on Friday in New Delhi.

Repentant Yeltsin resigns, names Putin as successor

BY DAVID HOFFMAN
The Washington Post

INSIDE

How did the Tier and the world react to Yeltsin's resignation? PAGES 14-15A

YELTSIN

MOSCOW — President Boris Yeltsin, asking Russians for "forgiveness" for the difficulties of recent years, unexpectedly resigned Friday, saying he wanted Russia to enter the new millennium "with new politicians, new faces, new intelligent, strong and energetic people."

Yeltsin named Prime Minister Vladimir Putin, who has been in office only since August, as acting president. Under the 1993 Constitution, Russia will have presidential elections in three months. Putin earlier had said he will campaign for the presidency, and he is far and away the front-runner for the post.

Acting President Putin later signed a decree giving "legal, social and other" guarantees for Yeltsin and his family, including immunity against prosecution.

"Many times I have heard it said, Yeltsin will try to hold onto power by any means, he won't hand it over to anyone," Yeltsin said. "That is all lies. That is not the case."

January 1, 2000: The Press marked the new millennium with several pages of pictures contributed by our readers. *Courtesy David Silvanic*

The Press & Sun-Bulletin greeted the year 2000 with news of the night's big party. The Y2K bug never struck, and the party went on into the wee hours.

These four years brought some of the biggest stories in years through the newsroom. Editors and reporters stayed with the election results through four editions as the results changed throughout the night.

On September 11, 2001, we published two Extras about the devastating attack on New York and Washington. Old-timers at the paper cannot recall publishing two Extras in one day, although it happened frequently in World War II.

Local economic news continued to dominate front pages, much as it has since the first Binghamton Press appeared. That paper promised we stood for "Home, Patriotism and Prosperity."

For 100 years we've tried to live up to that promise. We will continue on that path for the next 100 years.

8–PAGES OF ELECTION COVERAGE INSIDE

Press & Sun-Bulletin

ELECTION EDITION
WEDNESDAY, NOVEMBER 8, 2000 — pressconnects.com — FIFTY CENTS

KEY LOCAL RACES

Congressional: 26th District

Maurice Hinchey (D)	115,835
Bob Moppert (R)	69,658
Paul Laux (Rtl.)	1,938

Story, Page 4A

Congressional: 23rd District

Sherwood Boehlert (R)	85,957
Richard Englebrecht (D)	26,754
David Vickers (C)	27,052

Story, Page 4A

Congressional: 25th District

James Walsh (R)	139,632
Francis Gavin (D)	59,458
Howie Hawkins (G)	3,475

Story, Page 4A

Transportation Bond

Yes	1,161,265
No	1,368,158

Story, Page 6A

Broome County Executive

Jeffrey Kraham (R)	44,824
John Kowalchyk (D)	24,241
Tom Gillespie (G)	945

Story, Page 6A

Town of Union Supervisor

John Chevers (D)	11,939
Gary Lesnow (R)	8,130

Story, Page 7A

Endicott Village Trustees
(Top three chosen)

Alberta Ford-Gazda (D)	1,706
Frank Palmisano (D)	1,792
Cheryl Chapman (D)	1,871
Bonnie Cornick (R)	2,052
Timothy Burns (R)	2,088
Clarence "Rocky" Helmer (R)	1,391

Story, Page 7A

Broome County Surrogate Judge

Eugene Peckham (R)	38,758
Peter Charnetsky (D)	28,385

Story, Page 6A

ELECTION COVERAGE

■ Look for results and complete coverage of local, state and national races online at our Web site – pressconnects.com

WEATHER
MOSTLY CLOUDY
60°/45°
DETAILS 2B

INDEX
4 sections 44 pages

Classified	5C	Movies	2D
Horoscope	5D	Obituaries	4B
Money	12B	Opinion	12-13A

LOTTERIES
N.Y. Daily: 6-0-8
N.Y. Win 4: 5-7-8-8
N.Y. Take 5: 1-3-9-23-38
N.Y. Pick 10: 2-12-14-16-21-24-27-29-30-37-41-45-46-49-62-64-66-68-70-77
Pa. Daily: 4-1-1
Pa. Big 4: 1-8-2-4
Pa. Cash 5: 13-16-19-29-37

© THE BINGHAMTON PRESS CO., BINGHAMTON, N.Y.

Bush-Gore cliffhanger; Clinton outruns Lazio

U.S. SENATE

ASSOCIATED PRESS
First lady Hillary Rodham Clinton celebrates her Senate victory with her daughter Chelsea in New York City.

First lady: 'I will work my heart out'

BY JAY GALLAGHER AND DOUG SCHNEIDER
Press & Sun-Bulletin

N.Y. SENATOR
HILLARY CLINTON 3,356,303 — 55%
RICK LAZIO 2,630,410 — 43%
97% of precincts reported

Hillary Rodham Clinton became the only first lady ever to win elective office Tuesday, defeating Republican Rick Lazio to become the first woman ever to represent New York in the Senate.

Democrat Clinton, 53, overcame a "carpetbagger" label and intense animosity from her conservative opponents to succeed four-term Democrat Daniel Patrick Moynihan, who is retiring at the end of the year.

She promised to work in the Senate "for all New Yorkers" and offered her gratitude to supporters. "I will work my heart out for you in the next six years," she told joyous supporters at a Manhattan hotel.

"I feel like the Mets," Lazio, 42, a four-term congressman from Suffolk County, told his supporters after conceding the race. "We came in second."

"The huge voter turnout is an indication of such strong support for Hillary," said Linda Biemer, co-chairperson of Clinton's Broome County campaign.

"The support for Lazio was really against her — people said she's never held office, but she knows politics and that's what really matters," said Binghamton resident Trystran Spiro-Sostello.

But Tier Republicans didn't see it that way.

Ann Hutchings, a Republican from Chenango Bridge, said she's "very disappointed" in the result.

"The first time I saw Lazio was in Chenango Commons, and I was very impressed," she said. "I didn't know who he was, but I just think he had the experience, the class and is the kind of person I would trust."

The level of animosity against Clinton helped Lazio raise $30 million — which Clinton came close to matching — and also brought the little known congressman even in the polls just a few weeks after he entered the race even though New York has 2 million more Democrats than Republicans.

"She worked very hard and focused on the issues. That made a difference," said state Comptroller H. Carl McCall, a key supporter.

PRESIDENT OF THE UNITED STATES

ASSOCIATED PRESS
Texas Gov. George W. Bush and his father, former president George Bush, watch election results Tuesday night in Austin, Texas.

Presidential race results too close to call

BY JON FRANDSEN AND JOHN YAUKEY
Gannett News Service

ELECTORAL VOTE
AL GORE 225
GEORGE W. BUSH 242
Results as of 1 a.m. EST. 270 votes are needed to win.

WASHINGTON — In a wildly unpredictable and close election that reflected a sharply divided nation, Texas Gov. George Bush rolled up impressive victories in the heartland, the South and a handful of Democratic states and Vice President Al Gore won California, the Northeast and key industrial states.

As of 1 a.m. today, Bush was holding a narrow lead over Gore nationwide — with 72 percent of the vote counted, Bush had 49 percent, or 37,318,933 votes, to Gore's 48 percent, or 36,623,145.

As polls in all the states but Alaska closed, the outcome appeared to hinge on a handful of states that were too close to call: Florida, Wisconsin, Washington, Oregon and Iowa. However, it was clear Gore could not win without capturing Florida.

It was unclear whether Green Party candidate Ralph Nader might throw some key states to Bush, but he was expected to do better in the Pacific Northwest states that had not been decided. But nationwide he was pulling only 2 percent.

"It's going to be a long night," Bush said, watching returns from the private living quarters of the governor's mansion. "But this is exciting. Evidently, the turnouts are big, and that's good for America. A lot of people spoke."

"Florida is the key. ... It is white-knuckle time here," said Mark Fabiani, deputy campaign manager of the Gore campaign.

Some history was made early in the evening: Hillary Clinton became the first first lady to go to the Senate from the White House — winning in New York even though she and President Clinton bought a house there just last year so she could make the race.

SEE PRESIDENTIAL 2A

ANALYSIS

Voters hand nation a split decision

BY CHUCK RAASCH
Gannett News Service

WASHINGTON — It ended as tightly as it was fought, with the verdict of the 2000 election still hanging in the balance late into one of America's longest political days.

The vote Tuesday hardly developed into a crushing mandate for anyone, or any issue. If anything, the new Congress may wind up in an even tighter partisan clinch than before due to likely Democratic gains in the Senate.

And in the first draft of Bill Clinton's legacy, the president got no great confirmation, nor any overwhelming rebuke.

His wife, Hillary Rodham Clinton, was triumphant in New York's Senate race, but Vice President Al Gore struggled to hold onto the presidency, and prolong the Clinton-Gore reign, despite unprecedented prosperity of the past eight years.

Many Americans left the voting booth unfulfilled with their choices. An exit poll by Voter News Service found that 43 percent had "reservations" about the man they voted for. Independents split right down the middle between Texas Gov. George W. Bush and Gore.

Whoever finally won the presidency could also be the third straight president not receiving a majority of the popular vote.

A nation divided - big states vs. small states, the coasts vs. the heartland, states with heavy union presence vs. those

SEE ANALYSIS 2A

ASSOCIATED PRESS
Vice President Al Gore hugs his wife Tipper as they emerge from voting booths at Forks River Elementary school in Elmwood, Tenn.

November 8, 2000: The Press kept on top of the shifting election returns. The paper kept printing editions until Florida decided it was going to recount ballots. *Press & Sun-Bulletin archives*

8—PAGES OF ELECTION COVERAGE INSIDE

Press & Sun-Bulletin

ELECTION EDITION
WEDNESDAY, NOVEMBER 8, 2000

pressconnects.com

FIFTY CENTS

Bush wins cliffhanger; Clinton outruns Lazio

KEY LOCAL RACES

Congressional: 26th District	
Maurice Hinchey (D)	115,835
Bob Moppert (R)	69,658
Paul Laux (RtoL)	1,938
	Story, Page 4A
Congressional: 23rd District	
Sherwood Boehlert (R)	85,857
Richard Englebrecht (D)	28,754
David Vickers (C)	27,052
	Story, Page 4A
Congressional: 25th District	
James Walsh (R)	139,632
Francis Gavin (D)	59,456
Howie Hawkins (G)	3,475
	Story, Page 4A
Transportation Bond	
Yes	1,161,265
No	1,368,158
	Story, Page 5A
Broome County Executive	
Jeffrey Kraham (R)	44,824
John Kowalchyk (D)	24,241
Tom Gillespie (G)	945
	Story, Page 6A
Town of Union Supervisor	
John Cheevers (D)	11,939
Gary Lesnow (R)	9,130
	Story, Page 7A
Endicott Village Trustees (Top three chosen)	
Alberta Ford-Gaza (D)	1,766
Frank Palmisano (D)	1,792
Cheryl Chapman (D)	1,871
Bonnie Cornick (R)	2,052
Timothy Burns (R)	2,093
Clarence "Rocky" Holmes (R)	1,391
	Story, Page 7A
Broome County Surrogate Judge	
Eugene Peckham (R)	33,758
Peter Charnetsky (D)	28,305
	Story, Page 6A

ELECTION COVERAGE

■ Look for results and complete coverage of local, state and national races online at our Web site – pressconnects.com

WEATHER
MOSTLY CLOUDY
60°/45°
DETAILS 2B

INDEX
4 sections 44 pages

Classified	5C	Movies	2D
Horoscope	5D	Obituaries	4B
Money	12B	Opinion	12-13A

LOTTERIES
N.Y. Daily: 6-0-8
N.Y. Win 4: 5-7-8-8
N.Y.Take 5: 1-3-9-23-38
N.Y. Pick 10: 2-12-14-18-21-24-27-29-30-37-41-45-48-49-62-64-66-68-70-77
Pa. Daily: 4-1-1
Pa. Big 4: 1-8-2-4
Pa. Cash 5: 13-18-19-29-37

© THE BINGHAMTON PRESS CO., BINGHAMTON, N.Y.

0 40901 00701 2

U.S. SENATE

ASSOCIATED PRESS

First lady Hillary Rodham Clinton celebrates her Senate victory with her daughter Chelsea in New York City.

First lady: 'I will work my heart out'

BY JAY GALLAGHER AND DOUG SCHNEIDER
Press & Sun-Bulletin

N.Y. SENATOR
HILLARY **CLINTON**
3,356,303 — 55%
RICK **LAZIO**
2,630,410 — 43%
97% of precincts reported

Hillary Rodham Clinton became the only first lady ever to win elective office Tuesday, defeating Republican Rick Lazio to become the first woman ever to represent New York in the Senate.

Democrat Clinton, 53, overcame a "carpetbagger" label and intense animosity from her conservative opponents to succeed four-term Democrat Daniel Patrick Moynihan, who is retiring at the end of the year.

She promised to work in the Senate "for all New Yorkers" and offered her gratitude to supporters. "I will work my heart out for you in the next six years," she told joyous supporters at a Manhattan hotel.

"I feel like the Mets," Lazio, 42, a four-term congressman from Suffolk County, told his supporters after conceding the race. "We came in second."

"The huge voter turnout is an indication of such strong support for Hillary," said Linda Biemer, co-chairperson of Clinton's Broome County campaign.

"The support for Lazio was really against her — people said she's never held office, but she knows politics and that's what really matters," said Binghamton resident Trystran Spiro-Sostello.

But Tier Republicans didn't see it that way.

Ann Hutchings, a Republican from Chenango Bridge, said she's "very disappointed" in the result.

"The first time I saw Lazio was in Chenango Commons, and I was very impressed," she said. "I didn't know who he was, but I just think he had the experience, the class and is the kind of person I would trust."

The level of animosity against Clinton helped Lazio raise $30 million — which Clinton came close to matching — and also brought the little known congressman even in the polls just a few weeks after he entered the race even though New York has 2 million more Democrats than Republicans.

"She worked very hard and focused on the issues. That made a difference," said state Comptroller H. Carl McCall, a key supporter.

PRESIDENT OF THE UNITED STATES

ASSOCIATED PRESS

Texas Gov. George W. Bush and his father, former president George Bush, watch election results Tuesday night in Austin, Texas.

Florida ballots put governor over the top

BY JON FRANDSEN AND JOHN YAUKEY
Gannett News Service

ELECTORAL VOTE
AL **GORE**
249
GEORGE W. **BUSH**
271
Results as of 2:15 a.m. EST. 270 votes are needed to win.

WASHINGTON — Self-proclaimed "compassionate conservative" George W. Bush apparently was elected the 43rd president of the United States early today by narrowly defeating Al Gore — gaining sweet retribution against the Democrat who had helped sweep his father out of the White House eight years ago.

All major television networks declared Bush the winner shortly after 2:15 a.m.

In a battle so close that it came down to close races being counted in Florida and a handful of other states hours after the polls closed, Bush overcame questions about whether six years as governor of Texas was enough experience to run the country.

Bush now has the opportunity to prove that his conservative approach — cutting taxes, giving greater power to states and asking churches and charities to play a greater role in helping the poor — can keep the prosperity that was established under the Democrats rolling and extend it to those still struggling.

But Bush will be working with a sharply divided Congress — probably with the GOP in charge of both houses, but with margins so narrow that the chambers will be difficult to govern. And he doesn't have a huge mandate — winning what appears to be second-closest election in a century, surpassed only by the Kennedy-Nixon nail-biter of 1960.

Bush made the history books by making his family only the second to have a father-son team serve in the White House. John Adams (1797-1801) and John Quincy Adams (1825-1829) were the first.

But the Clintons made history of their own and will not be leaving Washington when they leave the White House in January — New York made Hillary Clinton the first first lady elected to the Senate.

ANALYSIS

Race hard fought from beginning to end

BY CHUCK RAASCH
Gannett News Service

WASHINGTON — It ended as tightly as it was fought.

The vote Tuesday hardly developed into a crushing mandate for anyone, or any issue. If anything, the new Congress may wind up in an even tighter partisan clinch than before due to likely Democratic gains in the Senate.

And in the first draft of Bill Clinton's legacy, the president got no great confirmation, nor any overwhelming rebuke.

His wife, Hillary Rodham Clinton, was triumphant in New York's Senate race, but Vice President Al Gore couldn't hold onto the presidency, and prolong the Clinton-Gore reign, despite unprecedented prosperity of the past eight years.

Many Americans left the voting booth unfulfilled with their choices. An exit poll by Voter News Service found that 43 percent had "reservations" about the man they voted for. Independents split right down the middle between Texas Gov. George W. Bush and Gore.

Bush could be the third straight president not receiving a majority of the popular vote.

A nation divided — big states vs. small states, the coasts vs. the heartland, states with heavy union presence vs. those

SEE ANALYSIS 2A

ASSOCIATED PRESS

Vice President Al Gore hugs his wife Tipper as they emerge from voting booths at Forks River Elementary school in Elmwood, Tenn.

8—Pages of Election Coverage Inside

Press & Sun-Bulletin

Election Edition
WEDNESDAY, NOVEMBER 8, 2000

presscconnects.com

FIFTY CENTS

Key Local Races

Congressional: 26th District	
Maurice Hinchey (D)	32,968
Bob Moppert (R)	24,388
Paul Laux (RtL)	107
Story, Page 4A	

Congressional: 23rd District	
Sherwood Boehlert (R)	48,171
Richard Englebrecht (D)	16,022
David Vickers (C)	NA
Story, Page 4A	

Congressional: 25th District	
James Walsh (R)	63,517
Francis Gavin (D)	25,573
Howie Hawkins (G)	NA
Story, Page 4A	

Transportation Bond	
Yes	369,771
No	414,649
Story, Page 5A	

Broome County Executive	
Jeffrey Kraham (R)	44,824
John Kowalczyk (D)	24,241
Tom Gillespie (G)	945
Story, Page 6A	

Town of Union Supervisor	
John Chevres (D)	11,939
Gary Ledzow (R)	9,130
Story, Page 7A	

Endicott Village Trustees (Top three chosen)	
Alberta Fiori-Gazda (D)	1,766
Frank Palmisano (D)	1,782
Cheryl Chapman (D)	1,871
Bonnie Cossick (R)	2,052
Timothy Bordo (R)	2,083
Clarence "Rocky" Helmer (R)	1,391
Story, Page 7A	

Broome County Surrogate Judge	
Eugene Peckham (R)	38,758
Peter Charnetsky (D)	23,385
Story, Page 6A	

Election Coverage

■ Look for results and complete coverage of local, state and national races online at our Web site – presscconnects.com

Weather

MOSTLY CLOUDY
60°/45°
DETAILS 2B

Index

4 sections 44 pages

Lotteries

N.Y. Daily: 6-0-8
N.Y. Win 4: 5-7-6-8
N.Y. Take 5: 1-3-9-23-38
N.Y. Pick 10: 2-12-14-16-21-24-27-29-30-37-41-45-46-49-62-64-66-68-70-77
Pa. Daily: 4-1-1
Pa. Big 4: 1-8-2-4
Pa. Cash 5: 13-18-19-29-37

0 40901 00701 2

Bush-Gore too close to call; Clinton wins

President Of The United States

ASSOCIATED PRESS

Presidential candidates Vice President Al Gore and Texas Gov. George W. Bush campaign in the final minutes of the election.

Election goes down to photo finish

BY JON FRANDSEN AND JOHN YAUKEY
Gannett News Service

WASHINGTON — In a wildly unpredictable election, Vice President Al Gore used a massive turnout by labor and minority voters to win California and key industrial states, but Texas Gov. George Bush rolled up impressive victories in the heartland and a handful of Democratic states to keep the race close.

As of 11:10 p.m. EST, Bush was holding a narrow lead over Gore nationwide: Bush had 49 percent, or 26,348,826 votes, to Gore's 48 percent, or 25,724,039, with 49 percent of the vote counted.

Florida, with the fourth largest treasure trove of electoral votes, was too close to call, pulled from the Gore column because of suspect voting data.

Bush tilted the electoral map to his favor as he continued to collect small and midsize states across the Midwest and mountains Tuesday night, including Missouri, West Virginia, and Gore's home state of Tennessee — all states that voted for President Clinton in 1996.

Gore, meanwhile collected wins in New Mexico and Minnesota — leaving the outcome up to Florida and the West.

In Michigan, some 400,000 autoworkers had the day off because of a recently negotiated contract that gave them Tuesday as a paid holiday. In North Philadelphia, Jesse Jackson was herding voters to the polls late in the day in a state Gore had to win.

Gore picked up solidly Democratic states of New York, Connecticut, New Jersey, Delaware, Maryland and Illinois, as well as Washington, D.C. Bush pocketed Georgia, Virginia, Kansas, Oklahoma, North Carolina, Idaho, Utah, Mississippi, Missouri, and his home state of Texas.

The election perhaps was the closest in four decades and the most important in years. Each party savored the opportunity to capture not just the White House — and the right to name possibly three Supreme Court justices — but also the House and Senate.

The closeness of the race raised the possibility of what would be a hugely controversial result — a candidate winning the Electoral College vote and the presidency while losing the popular vote.

It was unclear whether Green Party candidate Ralph Nader might throw some key states to Bush, but in national returns he was pulling only 2 percent. He issued a concession statement shortly after 9 p.m. EST.

In the vote that really mattered, the race for 270 Electoral College votes, Bush had won 23 states worth 213 electoral votes and Gore had won 14 states and the District of Columbia, worth 222 electoral votes.

The Democrats appeared to be making at least modest gains in the Senate although they would have to win most of 10 competitive races to take control. The Democrats' most vulnerable incumbent, Sen. Chuck

SEE RACE 2A

U.S. Senate

ASSOCIATED PRESS

President Clinton joins his wife Hillary Rodham Clinton at the celebration party for the first lady's Senate win.

'I will work my heart out'

NEWSDAY

NEW YORK — Hillary Rodham Clinton soared to a historic victory in New York's Senate race Tuesday, overcoming a "carpetbagger" label and intense animosity from her conservative opponents to become the only first lady ever elected to public office.

Boosted by unusually heavy turnout in Democratic areas of New York City, Clinton handily defeated Republican Rep. Rick Lazio, whose campaign never seemed to take hold after he stepped in for the ailing Mayor Rudolph Giuliani.

The mayor's withdrawal to seek treatment for prostate cancer may well have assured Clinton's victory in one of the most expensive and closely watched Senate races in history.

Clinton's decisive win was apparent as soon as the polls closed at 9 p.m., and two hours later an ebullient Clinton thanked supporters at Manhattan's Grand Hyatt Hotel with President Clinton and their daughter, Chelsea.

Noting that she had started her campaign in July 1999 on Sen. Daniel Patrick Moynihan's farm in Pindars Corners, Clinton poked fun at her trademark wardrobe, saying that "62 counties, 16 months, three debates, two opponents, and six black pantsuits later, because of you, here we are."

She promised to work in the Senate "for all New Yorkers" and offered her gratitude to supporters. "I will work my heart out for you for the next six years," she promised.

Acting in a supporting political role for the first time in the couple's 25-year marriage, President Clinton stood smiling silently as his wife delivered her acceptance speech.

Clinton, 53, delivered her victory speech just after Lazio conceded before a cheering group of Republicans at Manhattan's Roosevelt Hotel, three blocks from the Democrat's victory party.

Hillary

SUZIE O'ROURKE staff photographer

Pat Giglio of Binghamton, left, and Edna Boone of Endicott, right, waves her sign frantically upon hearing the First Lady's results over the television at the Binghamton Regency.

Analysis

Election results tied up in tight battles

BY CHUCK RAASCH
Gannett News Service

WASHINGTON — It ended as tightly as it was fought, with the verdict of the 2000 election still hanging in the balance late into one of America's longest political days.

It was hardly shaping up as a crushing mandate. If anything, the new Congress may wind up in an even tighter partisan clinch than before Tuesday.

Whoever finally wins the presidency — Vice President Al Gore or Texas Gov. George W. Bush — could also be the third straight president not receiving a majority of the popular vote.

A nation divided — big states vs. small states, the coasts vs. the heartland, states with heavy union presence vs. those without — was slowly rendering its results as polls closed from East to West.

By late evening, Gore was winning enough big states and traditional Democratic states that would ordinarily put him on the cusp of the presidency.

But Bush was piling up victories in enough smaller states, including some that have gone Democrat in recent years, to keep hope alive for the GOP.

Tuesday was a day that flouted conventional wisdom — and long-held political axioms.

A combination of factors, including Gore's choice of Connecticut Sen. Joe Lieberman as his running mate, made Florida a tight battleground between Bush and Gore, despite the fact that Bush's brother, Jeb, is governor there.

SEE ANALYSIS 2A

ELECTION EXTRA!

Press & Sun-Bulletin

WEDNESDAY, NOVEMBER 8, 2000 pressconnects.com FIFTY CENTS

KEY LOCAL RACES

Congressional: 26th District	
Maurice Hinchey (D)	115,835
Bob Moppert (R)	69,658
Paul Laux (RtL)	1,838
Story, Page 4A	

Congressional: 23rd District	
Sherwood Boehlert (R)	85,957
Richard Englebrecht (D)	28,754
David Vickers (C)	27,052
Story, Page 4A	

Congressional: 25th District	
James Walsh (R)	139,632
Francis Gavin (D)	58,458
Howie Hawkins (G)	3,475
Story, Page 4A	

Transportation Bond	
Yes	1,161,265
No	1,368,158
Story, Page 5A	

Broome County Executive	
Jeffrey Kraham (R)	44,824
John Kowalchyk (D)	24,241
Tom Gillespie (G)	945
Story, Page 6A	

Town of Union Supervisor	
John Cheevers (D)	11,539
Gary Ledzian (R)	9,130
Story, Page 7A	

Endicott Village Trustees (Top three chosen)	
Alberta Fusco-Gazda (D)	1,766
Frank Palmisano (D)	1,792
Cheryl Chapman (D)	1,871
Bonnie Cornick (R)	2,052
Timothy Burns (R)	2,083
Clarence "Bucky" Helmer (R)	1,391
Story, Page 7A	

Broome County Surrogate Judge	
Eugene Peckham (R)	38,758
Peter Charnetsky (D)	28,385
Story, Page 6A	

ELECTION COVERAGE

■ Look for results and complete coverage of local, state and national races online at our Web site – pressconnects.com

WEATHER

MOSTLY CLOUDY
60°/45°
DETAILS 2B

INDEX

4 sections 44 pages

Classified	5C	Movies	2D
Horoscope	5D	Obituaries	4B
Money	12B	Opinion	12-13A

LOTTERIES

N.Y. Daily: 6-0-8
N.Y. Win 4: 5-7-8-8
N.Y.Take 5: 1-3-9-23-38
N.Y. Pick 10: 2-12-14-16-21-24-27-29-30-37-41-45-46-49-62-64-66-68-70-77
Pa. Daily: 4-1-1
Pa. Big 4: 1-8-2-4
Pa. Cash 5: 13-18-19-29-37

RECOUNT!

Florida dead heat puts presidential race in limbo

ASSOCIATED PRESS
Vice President Al Gore hugs his wife Tipper as they emerge from voting booths at Forks River Elementary school in Elmwood, Tenn.

ASSOCIATED PRESS
Texas Gov. George W. Bush and his father, former president George Bush, watch election results Tuesday night in Austin, Texas.

Bush prematurely projected as winner; cliffhanger race stretches into second day

BY RON FOURNIER
Associated Press

Texas Gov. George W. Bush fought Al Gore in an agonizingly close presidential election Tuesday that came down to one state and a few thousand votes. Gore called Bush with congratulations, then called back to say he wasn't ready to concede.

There was no argument from the Bush campaign, just disbelief at the turn of events. It all came down to Florida.

"Unbelievable," sighed Bush adviser Karen Hughes. Bush aide Ari Fleischer met the historic outcome with gallows humor: "Does President Clinton get to stay?"

It was an incredible political spectacle by any standard. "There's never been a night like this one," said Gore campaign chairman William Daley, after his boss retired for the night — unsure whether he had won or not.

ELECTORAL VOTE
AL GORE 243
GEORGE W. BUSH 246
Results as of 5:30 a.m. EST. 270 votes are needed to win.

"Until the results in Florida become official," Daley told cheering supporters, "our campaign continues."

And it was so. After months of campaigning and $3 billion in political spending, Election Day passed without the country knowing who would be president.

Not that it mattered in the Electoral College, but with votes tallied from 96 percent of the precincts, Gore had 47,242,846 and Bush had 47,101,968 votes. Green Party candidate Ralph Nader was at 3 percent and Pat Buchanan barely registered.

Nader did well enough in to potentially tip several states to Bush. "You can't spoil a system spoiled to the core," he said.

TV networks projected Bush the winner, igniting GOP celebrations in Austin. The Associated Press — partners with the networks in Voter News Service — did not declare a presidential winner, citing the ongoing tally. Later the networks rolled back and declared the election too close to call, as did the *New York Times*.

Florida had been the epicenter of the campaign all along and Tuesday night was beyond chaotic. At mide-vening news organizations said Gore was the winner, but they backtracked as more votes were counted and Bush eased ahead. Hours later, the TV outlets did it again, this time for Bush.

Republicans maintained precarious control of Congress as the GOP bid to hold the House, Senate and presidency for the first time in 46 years.

Republicans held 50 seats to the Democrats' 48 with races in Michigan and

SEE RECOUNT 2A

ASSOCIATED PRESS
Chad Thompson, of Kingsport, Tenn. reacts to an announcement by William Daley, campaign chairman for Vice President Al Gore, that Gore had not lost and that a recount would be conducted.

Clinton outruns Lazio for Senate seat

First lady: 'I will work my heart out'

ASSOCIATED PRESS
First lady Hillary Rodham Clinton celebrates her Senate victory with her daughter Chelsea in New York City.

BY JAY GALLAGHER AND DOUG SCHNEIDER
Press & Sun-Bulletin

Hillary Rodham Clinton became the only first lady ever to win elective office Tuesday, defeating Republican Rick Lazio to become the first woman ever to represent New York in the Senate.

Democrat Clinton, 53, overcame a "carpetbagger" label and intense animosity from her conservative opponents to succeed four-term Democrat Daniel Patrick Moynihan, who is retiring at the end of the year.

She promised to work in the Senate "for all New Yorkers" and offered her gratitude to supporters. "I will work my heart out for you in the next six years," she told joyous supporters at a Manhattan hotel.

N.Y. SENATOR
HILLARY CLINTON 3,356,303 — 55%
RICK LAZIO 2,630,410 — 43%
97% of precincts reported

"I feel like the Mets," Lazio, 42, a four-term congressman from Suffolk County, told his supporters after conceding the race. "We came in second."

"The huge voter turnout is an indication of such strong support for Hillary," said Linda Biemer, co-chairperson of Clinton's Broome County campaign.

"The support for Lazio was really against her — people said she's never held office, but she knows politics and that's what really matters," said Binghamton resident Trystran Spiro-Sostello.

But Tier Republicans didn't see it that way.

Ann Hutchings, a Republican from Chenango Bridge, said she's "very disappointed" in the result.

"The first time I saw Lazio was in Chenango Commons, and I was very impressed," she said. "I didn't know who he was, but I just think he had the experience, the class and is the kind of person I would trust."

The level of animosity against Clinton helped Lazio raise $30 million — which Clinton came close to matching— and also brought the little known congressman even in the polls just a few weeks after he entered the race even though New York has 2 million more Democrats than Republicans.

"She worked very hard and focused on the issues. That made a difference," said state Comptroller H. Carl McCall, a key supporter.

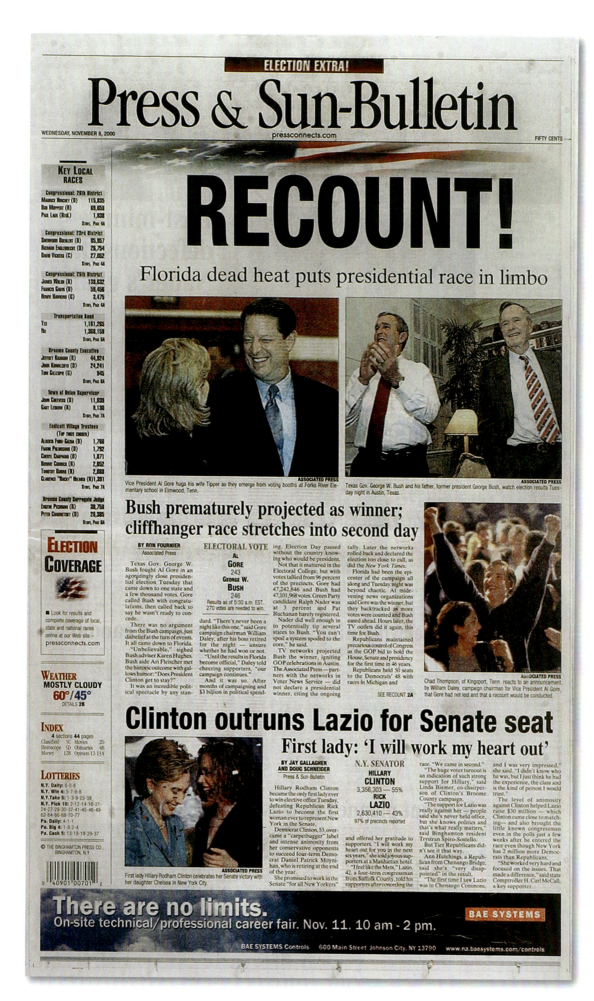

EXTRA!

Press & Sun-Bulletin

SEPTEMBER 11, 2001 | pressconnects.com | FIFTY CENTS

U.S. attacked

World Trade Center destroyed by terrorist plane attacks; Plane explodes at Pentagon; car bomb hits State Dept.

CHOPPER 4

Associated Press

Smoke and fire surround the upper floors of the World Trade Center in New York City after a second jet crashed into the buildings. Both towers were hit minutes apart, taking an unknown human toll and causing both towers to collapse.

Associated Press

Moments after the first plane crashed into one of the two World Trade Center towers, a second plane, shown here, heads for the other tower. The explosions destroyed both towers.

By JERRY SCHWARTZ
AP National Writer

NEW YORK — In a horrific sequence of destruction, terrorists crashed two planes into the World Trade Center and knocked down both of the 110-story towers Tuesday morning. Explosions also rocked the Pentagon and the State Department and spread fear across the nation.

The fate of those in the twin skyscrapers was not immediately known. Authorities had been trying to evacuate the 50,000 people who work in the twin towers, but many were thought to be trapped.

A witness said he saw bodies falling from the twin towers and people jumping out.

President Bush ordered a full-scale investigation to "hunt down the folks who committed this act."

Within the hour of the World Trade Center attack, an aircraft crashed on a helicopter landing pad near the Pentagon, a car bomb exploded outside the State Department, and the West Wing of the White House was evacuated amid threats of terrorism. And another explosion rocked New York about an hour after the crash.

"Today we've had a national tragedy," Bush said in Sarasota, Fla. "Two airplanes have crashed into the World Trade Center in an apparent terrorist attack on our country." He said he would be returning immediately to Washington.

Near Pittsburgh, a large plane crashed just north of the Somerset County Airport, airport officials said. The plane, believed to be a Boeing 767, crashed about 10 a.m. about 8 miles east of Jennerstown, according to county 911 dispatchers, WPXI-TV in Pittsburgh reported.

There were no other immediate details on the Pennsylvania crash and it was not clear whether the crash was related to the others.

One of the planes that crashed into the Trade Center was American Airlines Flight 11, hijacked after takeoff from Boston en route to Los Angeles, American Airlines said.

The planes blasted fiery, gaping holes in the upper floors of the twin towers. The southern tower collapsed with a roar about an hour later. The north tower collapsed shortly before 10:30 a.m.

"This is perhaps the most audacious terrorist attack that's ever taken place in the world," said Chris Yates, an aviation expert at *Jane's Transport* in London. "It takes a logistics operation from the terror group involved that is second to none. Only a very small handful of terror groups is on that list. ... I would name at the top of the list Osama Bin Laden."

All planes were grounded across the country by the Federal Aviation Administration. All bridges and tunnels into Manhattan were closed down.

The twin disaster at the World Trade Center happened shortly before 9 a.m. and then right around 9 a.m.

Heavy black smoke billowed into the sky above the gaping holes in the side of the twin towers, one of New York City's most famous landmarks, and debris rained down upon the street, one of the city's busiest work areas. When the second plane hit, a fireball of flame and smoke erupted, leaving a huge hole in the glass and steel tower.

John Axisa, who was getting off a PATH train to the World Trade Center, said he saw "bodies falling out" of the building. He said he ran outside, and watched people jump out of the first building, and then there was a second explosion, and he felt heat on the back of neck.

WCBS-TV, citing an FBI agent, said five or six people jumped out of the windows. People screamed every time another person leaped.

0 40901 00701 2

MORE ON THE ATTACK, PAGE 6A

September 11, 2001: We put out an extra soon after word hit about the attacks. *Courtesy David Silvanic*

EXTRA!

Press & Sun-Bulletin

SEPTEMBER 11, 2001 | pressconnects.com | FIFTY CENTS

DARKEST DAY

World Trade Center destroyed by terrorist attacks; Pentagon, State Dept. hit; death toll 'horrendous'; Bush: We'll hunt down and punish perpetrators

Associated Press

Workers in Manhattan flee as the World Trade Center explodes in the background.

Associated Press

Both towers of the World Trade Center were destroyed today when terrorists, directing hijacked jets, flew into the buildings around 9 a.m.

Associated Press

In the worst terrorist attack ever on U.S. soil, the World Trade Center in New York City was destroyed and the Pentagon was heavily damaged today, resulting in a death toll officials could only describe as "horrendous."

In a coordinated series of attacks, two hijacked planes slammed into the twin, 110-story Trade Center towers just before and shortly after 9 a.m. Both towers eventually collapsed.

Another plane slammed into the Pentagon, and a car bomb exploded outside the State Department, raising fears that the seat of government was under attack.

President Bush, who was in Florida at the time of the attacks, planned to return to Washington immediately, but Air Force One was later diverted to an undisclosed location.

"Terrorism against our nation will not stand," Bush vowed. "Freedom itself was attacked this morning and I assure you freedom will be defended. Make no mistake. The United States will hunt down and pursue those responsible for these cowardly actions."

New York City Mayor Rudolph Giuliani said: "I have a sense it's a horrendous number of lives lost."

About 50,000 people work at the Trade Center. American Airlines said the two aircraft that struck the towers were carrying a total of 156 people.

■ The Pentagon took a direct, devastating hit from an aircraft less than an hour after the attack on the World Trade Center. The nerve center of the nation's military burst into flames and a portion of one side of the five-sided structure collapsed when the plane struck in mid-morning.

■ A car bomb exploded outside the State Department.

■ In Pennsylvania, United Airlines Flight 93, a Boeing 757 en route from Newark, N.J., to San Francisco, crashed about 80 miles southeast of Pittsburgh. It was not clear if the crash was related to the disasters elsewhere.

■ A second plane, United 175, a Boeing 767, carrying 56 passengers, two pilots and seven flight attendants, also crashed, the airline confirmed. The airline would not say where that plane crashed.

■ The White House and the Capitol were evacuated.

Associated Press

Flames and smoke pour from a building after a jet was crashed into the Pentagon.

Tier reacts: Polls closed, flights halted

Effects of the terrorist attacks on the Pentagon and World Trade Center rumbled through the Southern Tier today. The latest developments:

■ Polls closed in Broome, Tioga and Chenanago counties, as Gov. George E. Pataki postponed primary elections throughout the state. Primaries have not been rescheduled.

■ Armed guards stopped people and searched packages outside the state and county office buildings in Binghamton and at city hall.

■ Blood centers mobilized. Donors can give blood until 10 p.m. today at the American Red Cross, 26 Court St., Binghamton. It will be open from 8 a.m. to 10 p.m. Wednesday. Special blood drives are scheduled for noon to 6 p.m. Wednesday at Broome Developmental Center, and 1 to 6 p.m. Wednesday at Binghamton University's East Lounge.

■ Activity at Binghamton Regional Airport screeched to a halt as flights were canceled across the United States.

■ Public schools in Broome and Tioga counties remained open today.

■ Binghamton University and other State University of New York campuses sent students home. Many stunned BU students have family or friends who work in lower Manhattan.

■ Broome Community College canceled classes scheduled for 3 p.m. or later, and Broome-Tioga BOCES canceled evening classes.

■ Binghamton, Harpursville, Montrose, Pa., Susquehanna Valley, Sidney, Susquehanna, Pa., Unatego, Chenango Valley, Candor, Maine-Endwell and some other school districts canceled after-school activities.

■ Armed guards patrolled outside the federal building on Henry Street in Binghamton. The facility closed just before 11 a.m.

■ Binghamton Police Bureau moved patrol cars onto the street around city hall to help respond quickly to emergencies.

■ Broome County Security called in off-duty workers to bolster security at the Broome County Health Department and other buildings, and closed the county's Department of Motor Vehicles offices.

0 40901 00701 2

MORE ON THE ATTACK, PAGES 2A-6A

September 11, 2001: We added four pages for more news of the attacks and put out a second extra. *Courtesy David Silvanic*

Press & Sun-Bulletin

WEDNESDAY, SEPTEMBER 12, 2001 pressconnects.com FIFTY CENTS

THOUSANDS DIE IN DAY OF TERROR

'Today, our nation saw evil' — President Bush

Associated Press

Two unidentified women console each other as they watch the World Trade Center burn. At left, firefighters and rescue workers comb through the remains of the towers.

Terrorists crash hijacked planes into World Trade Center and Pentagon

Associated Press

In the most devastating terrorist onslaught ever waged against the United States, knife-wielding hijackers crashed two airliners into the World Trade Center on Tuesday, toppling its twin 110-story towers.

Another plane slammed into the Pentagon, collapsing part of the structure. A fourth plane crashed into a field outside Pittsburgh.

A grim-faced President Bush mourned the deaths of thousands of Americans and vowed to avenge their killings.

"Today, our nation saw evil," he said.

Establishing the U.S. death toll could take weeks. The four airliners alone had 266 people aboard and there were no known survivors. At the Pentagon, about 100 people were believed dead, and a firefighters union official said he feared an estimated 200 New York City firefighters had died in rescue efforts.

"The number of casualties will be more than most of us can bear," a visibly distraught Mayor Rudolph Giuliani said.

No one took responsibility for the attacks, but federal authorities identified Osama bin Laden, who has been given asylum by Afghanistan's Taliban rulers, as the prime suspect.

The people aboard planes who managed to make cell phone calls each described similar circumstances: They indicated the hijackers were armed with knives, in some cases stabbing flight attendants.

At the World Trade Center, the dead and the doomed plummeted from the skyscrapers, among them a man and woman holding hands.

"Freedom itself was attacked this morning, and I assure you freedom will be defended," said Bush, who was in Florida at the time of the catastrophe.

FULL COVERAGE ■ PAGES 2A-14A

■ Editorial — Acts devoid of humanity PAGE 18A

■ Sports — Sports world shuts down PAGE 1C

■ Living — Helping kids cope PAGE 1D

September 12, 2001: We devoted 13 pages inside to news of the attacks, among the most space we've devoted to one news event.

Courtesy David Silvanic

Press & Sun-Bulletin

THURSDAY, SEPTEMBER 13, 2001 | pressconnects.com | FIFTY CENTS

TERROR IN THE U.S.

GRIM REALITY

City asks federal officials for 6,000 body bags

■ Ashcroft: White House, Air Force One were intended targets, 2A

■ FBI finds clues in Boston, Florida, 3A

■ Mortuary experts from Tier called to the scene, 4A

■ Binghamton University community starts counting its dead, 5A

■ Hopes dim for survivors at Pentagon, 7A

■ The view from ground zero, 8A

■ Young Americans line up to enlist, 9A

■ List of victims, 11A

Associated Press

Firefighters take a break Wednesday in the middle of an exhausting day's work. As many as 200 firefighters are feared to have lost their lives in response to the most catastrophic incident on U.S. soil.

'We're going to try and recapture the plane and overpower the terrorists.'

PASSENGER JEREMY GLICK, IN A CALL TO HIS WIFE

In calls from plane, passengers revealed plan to stop hijackers

From wire service reports

They called families in the final minutes of United Airlines Flight 93. One was confident that he and fellow passengers could overpower the terrorists; another calmly told her husband she loved him as others cried in the background. Others made calls for help.

As the Boeing 757 approached Cleveland, the plane unexpectedly made a 180-degree turn and headed back toward Pennsylvania. Cleveland Mayor Michael White said air traffic controllers reported they could hear screaming over the cockpit radio.

Then came a distress call to a 911 dispatcher. "We're being hijacked!" an unidentified man said.

Jeremy Glick, 30, of Greenwood Lake, N.J., spoke to his wife and family for about 15 minutes, plotting how to fight three terrorists who took over the cockpit, said his father-in-law, Richard Makely, 61, of Jewett, N.Y. Then the plane crashed into a field in western Pennsylvania.

"We're going to try and recapture the plane and overpower the terrorists," Glick told his wife.

"He and several others, about three or four men, were considering whether they should rush the three terrorists in the cockpit," Makely said.

The new details corroborate other phone calls made from the doomed plane, the last of four hijacked planes to crash Tuesday. It appears that several passengers were devising a brave attack minutes before the crash, which killed all 45 on the plane.

"A group of us are going to do something," passenger Thomas E. Burnett Jr., 38, told his wife, Deena, in a call.

SEE PASSENGERS 10A

Associated Press

With portions of World Trade Center buildings still falling onto the mountain of rubble already on the ground, rescue workers continued the grim and painstaking work of searching for survivors. Five people were pulled out of the debris alive Wednesday.

Death toll rises; FBI pursues leads in Boston, Florida

The Washington Post

Its transportation network snarled, financial markets shuttered, and military on high alert, an anxious nation struggled Wednesday with the unprecedented consequences of Tuesday's terrorist attacks in New York and Washington.

The death toll from the three jetliners that terrorists crashed into the World Trade Center and the Pentagon remained obscured by mountains of rubble, but authorities continued to suggest the carnage will number in the thousands and may exceed the nation's losses at Pearl Harbor.

New York City Mayor Rudolph Giuliani said Wednesday night that 82 people are confirmed dead and 1,700 injured in his city — but much, much worse is to come. Giuliani confirmed he has asked the federal government for 6,000 body bags.

Defense Secretary Donald Rumsfeld said he has reason to hope the death toll at the Pentagon will be lower than originally feared — somewhere between 100 and 200 people. Already accounted for are 266 passengers and crew on the four jets.

In other developments:

■ Two men who went to Florida for flight training school a year ago emerged as suspects Wednesday in the FBI investigation into the terror attacks. A former employee at Huffman Aviation in Venice said FBI agents told him the two were involved in Tuesday's attack of the World Trade Center.

■ The FBI said it is investigating terrorist mastermind Osama bin Laden's strong family ties and other links to Boston, where the two hijacked airliners that demolished the World Trade Center took off.

■ NATO allies took the extraordinary step of agreeing to offer military assistance to the United States if requested.

■ Air traffic, entirely frozen for the first time in American history, remained severely and indefinitely limited. Planes could stay grounded until Friday or beyond.

■ Wall Street remained closed and does not plan to reopen at least until Friday.

FULL COVERAGE ■ PAGES 2A-11A

■ For the latest news
The *Press & Sun-Bulletin's* Web site
pressconnects.com

■ Living
Tier residents reach out to help.
PAGE 1D

September 13, 2001: The intense coverage continued. *Courtesy David Silvanic*

Keith Hayes of Johnson City drops off bottled water at the collection point in the Town Square Mall, Vestal, September 12, 2001. Catholic Charities of Broome County, radio station 105.7 and Roger's Service Group assisted the Red Cross in collecting supplies for victims of the September 11 terrorist attack. *Press & Sun-Bulletin archives*

National Guardsmen gather under an American Flag in the Binghamton Armory as they prepare to mobilize, September 11, 2001. *Press & Sun-Bulletin archives*

Blood donors stood in a line extending around the corner onto Court Street to donate blood at the Red Cross on State Street, September 11, 2001. *Press & Sun-Bulletin archives*

Press & Sun-Bulletin

pressconnects.com

July 1, 2002 | Binghamton, N.Y. | Fifty cents

Final Edition

Monday

Money

Plasma propels Tier business

Starting today, the Money page returns to Mondays.

This week: A Binghamton man finds his niche with plasma televisions. PAGE 6D

Sports

Andy dandy, blanks Mets

Pitcher Andy Pettitte, above, fires a three-hit shutout to lead the New York Yankees to an 8-0 victory over the New York Mets. It was Pettitte's first shutout at Yankee Stadium. PAGE 1D

Lifestyle

This is not your dad's yearbook

High school yearbooks have evolved over the years. PAGE 1C

Weather

WARM AND HUMID

87°/69°

DETAILS 2B

Index

4 sections 36 pages

Horoscope	5C	Movies	2C
Marketplace	6C	Obituaries	4B
Money	6D	Opinion	8-9A

For a subscription or customer service call 231-PRESS

Printed on recycled paper

© The Binghamton Press Co., Binghamton, N.Y.

IBM-Endicott site sold; 2,000 jobs appear safe

IBM's sprawling campus along North Street in Endicott has been sold to investors, who will lease portions of the site back to IBM.

CHUCK HAUPT / Press & Sun-Bulletin

Officials to announce deal today

© 2002 Press & Sun-Bulletin

By DOM YANCHUNAS and JEFF PLATSKY
Press & Sun-Bulletin

ENDICOTT — IBM Corp. has agreed to sell its local microelectronics manufacturing operations to an investor group that includes Southern Tier businessmen, state and county officials said Sunday.

The agreement likely preserves — at least for now — about 2,000 of the approximately 4,000 local jobs at the unit, said Assemblyman Jay J. Dinga, R-Chenango Bridge. Civic leaders had feared IBM was planning to close the facility.

Investors include the local Maines and Matthews families, plus outside stakeholders, said Dinga and Broome County Executive Jeffrey P. Kraham. The Maines family operates Conklin-based Maines Paper & Food Service, a $1 billion food distribution company. The Matthews family owns a collection of companies, including electronics subcontractors.

State economic development aid is expected to finance as much as 84 percent of the estimated $63 million purchase, which includes IBM's Endicott real-estate assets.

"This is the best scenario we could have hoped for," Dinga said. "It's a continued presence of manufacturing with local investors at a time when IBM corporate interests aren't necessarily looking out for the Endicott site."

The deal calls for the building to be sold to investors who would then lease portions of it back to IBM for 10 years. IBM will also give the new owners a four-year agreement to buy material produced by the manufacturing plant.

Terms of the purchase were still being feverishly discussed as late as Sunday, as IBM sought to account for the transaction in its quarter that ended at midnight Sunday.

The buyers are expected to:

- Purchase all of the about 4 million square-feet IBM owns in Endicott.
- Operate the microelectronics manufacturing division.
- Lease back buildings housing other IBM units to the company.

IBM officials did not return telephone messages Sunday night.

Several elected officials, including Dinga and Kraham, would not outline the terms of the agreement

SEE IBM 6A

Pragmatic deal allows IBM to cut expenses by several million dollars

© 2002 Press & Sun-Bulletin

Analysis

By JEFF PLATSKY
Press & Sun-Bulletin

It might not be the perfect scenario, but the deal to sell the manufacturing arm of IBM-Endicott to a team of investors at least preserves about 2,000 local jobs that could have headed offshore in another plan under serious consideration.

Most would have preferred IBM Corp. to remain what it once was, the employer that provided secure, high-paying jobs in a community forever indebted to its founder, Thomas J. Watson. Emotional ties don't count any longer.

Even though IBM was founded in Binghamton and Endicott, this deal is more pragmatic for the computer giant's executives.

In a world with global competition, IBM is following the path of so many other brand-name manufacturers — letting others produce the guts of the machine, while it concentrates on technology, innovation, marketing and software.

IBM Corp. came within a hairsbreadth of selling the Endicott manufacturing operations to California-based Sanmina Corp. The deal would have meant certain closure of all manufacturing operations in Endicott and would have jeopardized other IBM jobs at the site. Sanmina likely would have shipped the work to one of its many factories overseas.

Instead, the community will have 2,000 IBM jobs — at least for now — and about 2,000 production jobs in a new company that is expecting to expand the business with top-notch technology inherited from IBM.

This deal, no doubt, will be described at today's announcement as a "win-win" for IBM and the local community.

While it preserves jobs, it also rids IBM of several million dollars in expenses, a major consideration for a company under severe pressure to improve results under the helm of new Chief Executive Officer Samuel Palmisano. IBM's stock price is down 40 percent since January.

Today's announcement is sure to send shock waves through this "Valley of Opportunity," where IBM buildings stand as landmarks and the company's rich tradition is steeped throughout its legacy.

But the fact remains that local and other interested investors, aided by the state, are coming in to give the site a larger degree of permanence than it would have had under IBM's umbrella.

The Deal

- **Who is affected:** About 2,000 of the roughly 4,000 IBM Corp. Endicott employees would become employees of a new investment group. That group includes representatives of the Maines and Matthews families, as well as other investors.
- **Terms of the sale:** The buyers would pay about $63 million for the approximately 4 million square feet IBM owns in Endicott. State economic development aid would fund up to 84 percent of the purchase price.
- **What happens next:** Some of the buildings involved in the sale would be leased back to IBM. IBM would also agree to buy material produced by the plant over the next four years. Details of the sale are expected to be announced at an 11 a.m. press conference featuring Gov. George E. Pataki.
- **More coverage inside:** A chronology of IBM-Endicott and photos from throughout its history, PAGES 6A & 7A.
- **Latest news online:** Go to www.pressconnects.com

— Compiled by Doug Schneider

Part-time firefighter accused of setting Arizona wildfire

Associated Press

SHOW LOW, Ariz. — A part-time firefighter looking for work was charged Sunday with using matches to set dry grass aflame, starting a blaze that turned into the worst wildfire in Arizona history.

Leonard Gregg, 29, worked part time as a firefighter for the Bureau of Indian Affairs and was one of the first people called to fight the blaze. Gregg admitted setting the fire so he could get work on a fire crew, according to a statement filed in federal court by a BIA investigator.

"This fire was started with a profit motive behind it," U.S. Attorney Paul Charlton said Sunday.

GREGG

Gregg is the second person employed to fend off wildfires who is accused of setting the blazes during one of the country's most destructive fire seasons. Terry Barton, a U.S. Forest Service employee, was charged earlier in June with setting Colorado's largest-ever wildfire.

At a hearing in Flagstaff federal court Sunday, a tired-looking Gregg said, "I'm sorry for what I did."

But U.S. Magistrate Stephen Verkamp cut him off, saying he shouldn't make any admission of guilt at the hearing.

Gregg was arrested Saturday in connection with two fires set June 18 near the Fort Apache Indian Reservation town of Cibecue. One fire was put out, but the other exploded up steep terrain and quickly spread, threatening the town of Show Low and overrunning two smaller communities just to the west.

The wildfire merged with another, started by a lost hiker signaling a helicopter, and became the largest in Arizona history.

By Sunday, the 452,000-acre combined blaze had destroyed at least 423 homes. It was about 35 percent contained by fire lines near Show Low but continued to burn out of control to the west.

According to the criminal complaint, Gregg said he had set the fires near Cibecue by using matches to set dry grass aflame. Before the fire was reported, he told a woman he had to get home because there was going to be a fire call, the complaint said.

If convicted of both counts of willfully setting fire to timber or underbrush, Gregg could face 10 years in prison and be fined $500,000.

INSIDE

Another wildfire forces thousands to evacuate in South Dakota.

PAGE 2A

Associated Press

A plane drops slurry onto the burning forest Sunday in the Fort Apache Indian Reservation near Cibecue, Ariz. The dump was part of a burnout operation, in which a fire is purposely set to reduce fuel for the main fire.

July 1, 2002: The ancestral home of IBM is sold, ending an era in Greater Binghamton. *Courtesy William Nash*

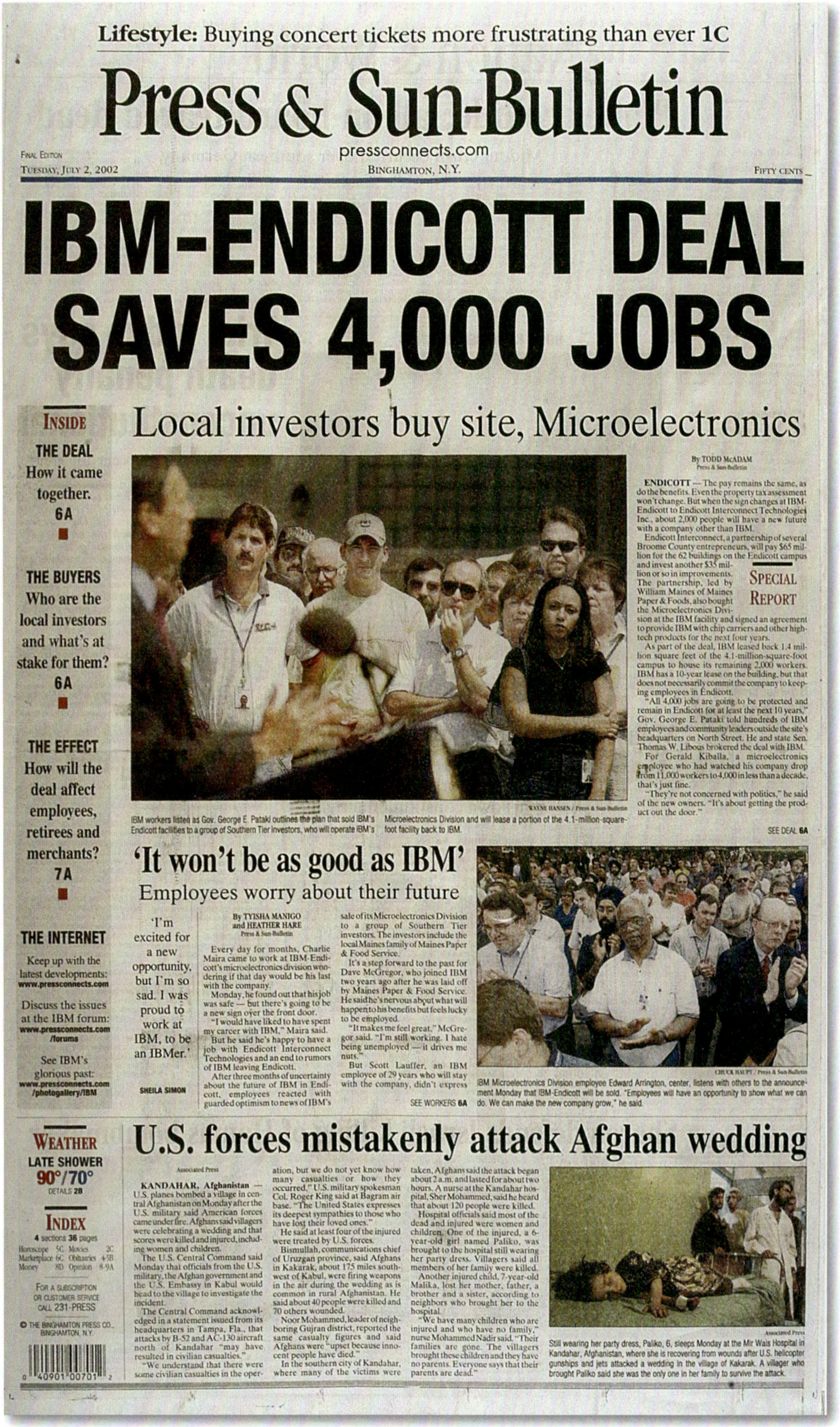

Lifestyle: Buying concert tickets more frustrating than ever 1C

Press & Sun-Bulletin

pressconnects.com

Final Edition
Tuesday, July 2, 2002 — Binghamton, N.Y. — Fifty cents

IBM-ENDICOTT DEAL SAVES 4,000 JOBS

Local investors buy site, Microelectronics

Inside

THE DEAL How it came together. 6A

THE BUYERS Who are the local investors and what's at stake for them? 6A

THE EFFECT How will the deal affect employees, retirees and merchants? 7A

THE INTERNET Keep up with the latest developments: www.pressconnects.com

Discuss the issues at the IBM forum: www.pressconnects.com/forums

See IBM's glorious past: www.pressconnects.com/photogallery/IBM

WAYNE HANSEN / Press & Sun-Bulletin

IBM workers listen as Gov. George E. Pataki outlines the plan that sold IBM's Endicott facilities to a group of Southern Tier investors, who will operate IBM's Microelectronics Division and will lease a portion of the 4.1-million-square-foot facility back to IBM.

By TODD McADAM
Press & Sun-Bulletin

SPECIAL REPORT

ENDICOTT — The pay remains the same, as do the benefits. Even the property tax assessment won't change. But when the sign changes at IBM-Endicott to Endicott Interconnect Technologies Inc., about 2,000 people will have a new future with a company other than IBM.

Endicott Interconnect, a partnership of several Broome County entrepreneurs, will pay $65 million for the 62 buildings on the Endicott campus and invest another $35 million or so in improvements. The partnership, led by William Maines of Maines Paper & Foods, also bought the Microelectronics Division at the IBM facility and signed an agreement to provide IBM with chip carriers and other high-tech products for the next four years.

As part of the deal, IBM leased back 1.4 million square feet of the 4.1-million-square-foot campus to house its remaining 2,000 workers. IBM has a 10-year lease on the building, but that does not necessarily commit the company to keeping employees in Endicott.

"All 4,000 jobs are going to be protected and remain in Endicott for at least the next 10 years," Gov. George E. Pataki told hundreds of IBM employees and community leaders outside the site's headquarters on North Street. He and state Sen. Thomas W. Libous brokered the deal with IBM.

For Gerald Kiballa, a microelectronics employee who had watched his company drop from 11,000 workers to 4,000 in less than a decade, that's just fine.

"They're not concerned with politics," he said of the new owners. "It's about getting the product out the door."

SEE DEAL 6A

'It won't be as good as IBM'

Employees worry about their future

'I'm excited for a new opportunity, but I'm so sad. I was proud to work at IBM, to be an IBMer.'

SHEILA SIMON

By TYISHA MANIGO and HEATHER HARE
Press & Sun-Bulletin

Every day for months, Charlie Maira came to work at IBM-Endicott's microelectronics division wondering if that day would be his last with the company.

Monday, he found out that his job was safe — but there's going to be a new sign over the front door.

"I would have liked to have spent my career with IBM," Maira said.

But he said he's happy to have a job with Endicott Interconnect Technologies and an end to rumors of IBM leaving Endicott.

After three months of uncertainty about the future of IBM in Endicott, employees reacted with guarded optimism to news of IBM's sale of its Microelectronics Division to a group of Southern Tier investors. The investors include the local Maines family of Maines Paper & Food Service.

It's a step forward to the past for Dave McGregor, who joined IBM two years ago after he was laid off by Maines Paper & Food Service. He said he's nervous about what will happen to his benefits but feels lucky to be employed.

"It makes me feel great," McGregor said. "I'm still working. I hate being unemployed — it drives me nuts."

But Scott Lauffer, an IBM employee of 29 years who will stay with the company, didn't express

SEE WORKERS 6A

CHUCK HAUPT / Press & Sun-Bulletin

IBM Microelectronics Division employee Edward Arrington, center, listens with others to the announcement Monday that IBM-Endicott will be sold. "Employees will have an opportunity to show what we can do. We can make the new company grow," he said.

Weather
LATE SHOWER
90°/70°
DETAILS 2B

Index
4 sections 36 pages

Horoscope	5C	Movies	2C
Marketplace	6C	Obituaries	4-5B
Money	8D	Opinion	8-9A

For a subscription or customer service call 231-PRESS

© The Binghamton Press Co., Binghamton, N.Y.

U.S. forces mistakenly attack Afghan wedding

Associated Press

KANDAHAR, Afghanistan — U.S. planes bombed a village in central Afghanistan on Monday after the U.S. military said American forces came under fire. Afghans said villagers were celebrating a wedding and that scores were killed and injured, including women and children.

The U.S. Central Command said Monday that officials from the U.S. military, the Afghan government and the U.S. Embassy in Kabul would head to the village to investigate the incident.

The Central Command acknowledged in a statement issued from its headquarters in Tampa, Fla., that attacks by B-52 and AC-130 aircraft north of Kandahar "may have resulted in civilian casualties."

"We understand that there were some civilian casualties in the operation, but we do not yet know how many casualties or how they occurred," U.S. military spokesman Col. Roger King said at Bagram air base. "The United States expresses its deepest sympathies to those who have lost their loved ones."

He said at least four of the injured were treated by U.S. forces.

Bismullah, communications chief of Uruzgan province, said Afghans in Kakarak, about 175 miles southwest of Kabul, were firing weapons in the air during the wedding as is common in rural Afghanistan. He said about 40 people were killed and 70 others wounded.

Noor Mohammed, leader of neighboring Gujran district, reported the same casualty figures and said Afghans were "upset because innocent people have died."

In the southern city of Kandahar, where many of the victims were taken, Afghans said the attack began about 2 a.m. and lasted for about two hours. A nurse at the Kandahar hospital, Sher Mohammed, said he heard that about 120 people were killed.

Hospital officials said most of the dead and injured were women and children. One of the injured, a 6-year-old girl named Paliko, was brought to the hospital still wearing her party dress. Villagers said all members of her family were killed.

Another injured child, 7-year-old Malika, lost her mother, father, a brother and a sister, according to neighbors who brought her to the hospital.

"We have many children who are injured and who have no family," nurse Mohammed Nadir said. "Their families are gone. The villagers brought these children and they have no parents. Everyone says that their parents are dead."

Associated Press

Still wearing her party dress, Paliko, 6, sleeps Monday at the Mir Wais Hospital in Kandahar, Afghanistan, where she is recovering from wounds after U.S. helicopter gunships and jets attacked a wedding in the village of Kakarak. A villager who brought Paliko said she was the only one in her family to survive the attack.

July 2, 2002: Employees fretted about their futures. *Courtesy William Nash*

USA
EXCELS

IBM workers listen as New York Governor George E. Pataki outlines the plan that sold IBM's Endicott facilities to a group of Southern Tier investors, who will continue IBM's Microelectronics division and will lease a portion of the 4 million-square-foot facility back to IBM, July 1, 2002.
Press & Sun-Bulletin archives

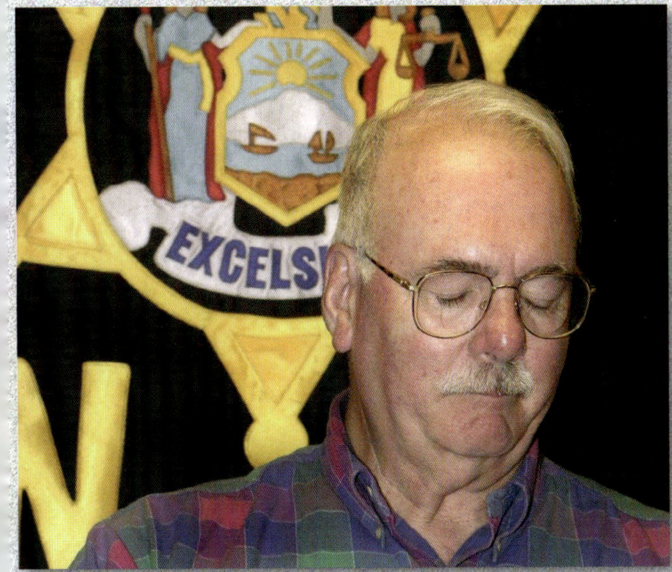

Broome County Sheriff Dave Harder fights back tears during a 2002 press conference regarding sheriff deputy Kevin Tarsia, 36, who died in the line of duty after coming across possible robbery suspects near Grange Hall Park near the New York-Pennsylvania state line. *Press & Sun-Bulletin archives*

Tammie Simmons-Parker, daughter of Valerie Spears, touches her mother's casket after the graveside service at Vestal Hills Memorial Park Cemetery, July 2002. Her husband, Vernon E. Parker Jr., 32, faced a second-degree murder charge in the death of her 14-year-old sister, Devin Spears. *Press & Sun-Bulletin archives*

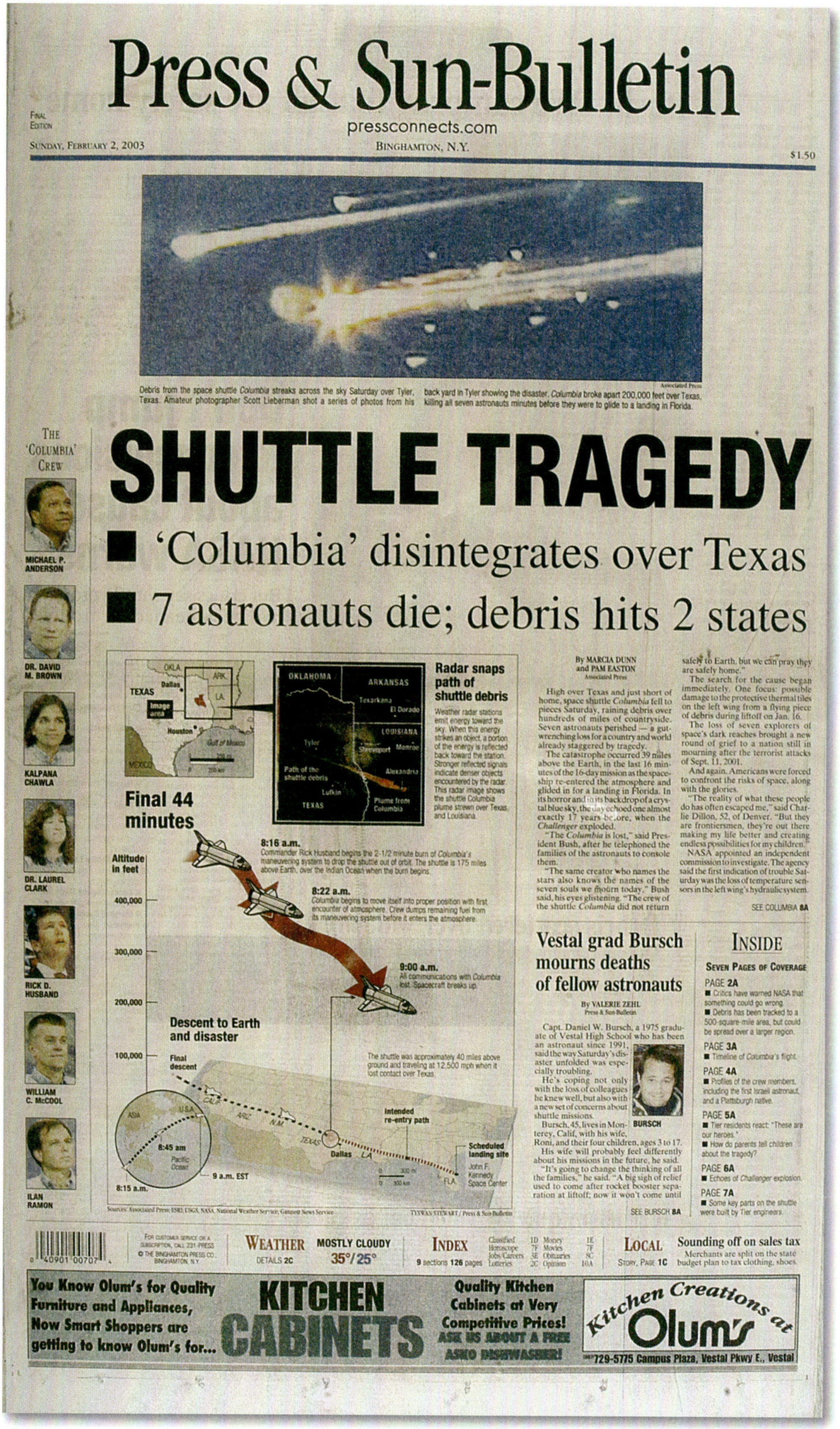

Press & Sun-Bulletin

Final Edition

pressconnects.com

Sunday, February 2, 2003 | Binghamton, N.Y. | $1.50

Associated Press

Debris from the space shuttle *Columbia* streaks across the sky Saturday over Tyler, Texas. Amateur photographer Scott Lieberman shot a series of photos from his back yard in Tyler showing the disaster. *Columbia* broke apart 200,000 feet over Texas, killing all seven astronauts minutes before they were to glide to a landing in Florida.

The 'Columbia' Crew

Michael P. Anderson
Dr. David M. Brown
Kalpana Chawla
Dr. Laurel Clark
Rick D. Husband
William C. McCool
Ilan Ramon

SHUTTLE TRAGEDY

■ 'Columbia' disintegrates over Texas

■ 7 astronauts die; debris hits 2 states

OKLA
ARK.
TEXAS
Dallas
LA
Image area
Houston
Gulf of Mexico
MEXICO

OKLAHOMA
ARKANSAS
Texarkana
El Dorado
LOUISIANA
Tyler
Shreveport
Monroe
Path of the shuttle debris
Alexandria
Lufkin
TEXAS
Plume from Columbia

Radar snaps path of shuttle debris

Weather radar stations emit energy toward the sky. When this energy strikes an object, a portion of the energy is reflected back toward the station. Stronger reflected signals indicate denser objects encountered by the radar. This radar image shows the shuttle Columbia plume strewn over Texas and Louisiana.

Final 44 minutes

Altitude in feet
400,000
300,000
200,000
100,000

8:16 a.m.
Commander Rick Husband begins the 2-1/2 minute burn of *Columbia's* maneuvering system to drop the shuttle out of orbit. The shuttle is 175 miles above Earth, over the Indian Ocean when the burn begins.

8:22 a.m.
Columbia begins to move itself into proper position with first encounter of atmosphere. Crew dumps remaining fuel from its maneuvering system before it enters the atmosphere.

9:00 a.m.
All communications with *Columbia* lost. Spacecraft breaks up.

Descent to Earth and disaster

Final descent

The shuttle was approximately 40 miles above ground and traveling at 12,500 mph when it lost contact over Texas.

ASIA
U.S.A.
8:45 am
Pacific Ocean
8:15 a.m.
9 a.m. EST
CALIF.
ARIZ.
N.M.
TEXAS
Dallas
LA
Intended re-entry path
Scheduled landing site
John F. Kennedy Space Center
FLA.

Sources: Associated Press; ESRI; USGS; NASA; National Weather Service; Gannett News Service

TYSWAS STEWART / Press & Sun-Bulletin

By MARCIA DUNN and PAM EASTON
Associated Press

High over Texas and just short of home, space shuttle *Columbia* fell to pieces Saturday, raining debris over hundreds of miles of countryside. Seven astronauts perished — a gut-wrenching loss for a country and world already staggered by tragedy.

The catastrophe occurred 39 miles above the Earth, in the last 16 minutes of the 16-day mission as the spaceship re-entered the atmosphere and glided in for a landing in Florida. In its horror and in its backdrop of a crystal blue sky, the day echoed one almost exactly 17 years before, when the *Challenger* exploded.

"The *Columbia* is lost," said President Bush, after he telephoned the families of the astronauts to console them.

"The same creator who names the stars also knows the names of the seven souls we mourn today," Bush said, his eyes glistening. "The crew of the shuttle *Columbia* did not return safely to Earth, but we can pray they are safely home."

The search for the cause began immediately. One focus: possible damage to the protective thermal tiles on the left wing from a flying piece of debris during liftoff on Jan. 16.

The loss of seven explorers of space's dark reaches brought a new round of grief to a nation still in mourning after the terrorist attacks of Sept. 11, 2001.

And again, Americans were forced to confront the risks of space, along with the glories.

"The reality of what these people do has often escaped me," said Charlie Dillon, 52, of Denver. "But they are frontiersmen, they're out there making my life better and creating endless possibilities for my children."

NASA appointed an independent commission to investigate. The agency said the first indication of trouble Saturday was the loss of temperature sensors in the left wing's hydraulic system.

SEE COLUMBIA 8A

Vestal grad Bursch mourns deaths of fellow astronauts

By VALERIE ZEHL
Press & Sun-Bulletin

Capt. Daniel W. Bursch, a 1975 graduate of Vestal High School who has been an astronaut since 1991, said the way Saturday's disaster unfolded was especially troubling.

He's coping not only with the loss of colleagues he knew well, but also with a new set of concerns about shuttle missions.

BURSCH

Bursch, 45, lives in Monterey, Calif., with his wife, Roni, and their four children, ages 3 to 17.

His wife will probably feel differently about his missions in the future, he said.

"It's going to change the thinking of all the families," he said. "A big sigh of relief used to come after rocket booster separation at liftoff; now it won't come until

SEE BURSCH 8A

Inside

Seven Pages of Coverage

PAGE **2A**
■ Critics have warned NASA that something could go wrong.
■ Debris has been tracked to a 500-square-mile area, but could be spread over a larger region.

PAGE **3A**
■ Timeline of *Columbia's* flight.

PAGE **4A**
■ Profiles of the crew members, including the first Israeli astronaut, and a Plattsburgh native.

PAGE **5A**
■ Tier residents react: "These are our heroes."
■ How do parents tell children about the tragedy?

PAGE **6A**
■ Echoes of *Challenger* explosion.

PAGE **7A**
■ Some key parts on the shuttle were built by Tier engineers.

For customer service or a subscription, call 231-PRESS
© The Binghamton Press Co. Binghamton, N.Y.

Weather Details 2C — Mostly cloudy 35°/25°

Index 9 sections 126 pages

Classified	1D	Money	1E
Horoscope	7F	Movies	7F
Jobs/Careers	3E	Obituaries	8C
Lotteries	2C	Opinion	10A

Local Story, Page 1C — **Sounding off on sales tax**
Merchants are split on the state budget plan to tax clothing, shoes.

February 2, 2003: The second shuttle tragedy. *Courtesy William Nash*

Press & Sun-Bulletin

pressconnects.com

Thursday March 20, 2003 — Binghamton, N.Y. — Final Edition — Fifty cents

WAR!

U.S. forces bomb Baghdad

'Now that the conflict has come, the only way to limit its duration is to apply decisive force. This will not be a campaign of half-measures, and we will accept no outcome but victory.'
PRESIDENT BUSH

Associated Press

Members of the Royal Irish Rangers walk Wednesday in the Kuwaiti desert as they head toward Iraq. Columns of tanks, fighting vehicles and fuel trucks also made their way through the Kuwaiti desert.

✔ Missiles target Iraqi leadership

✔ 300,000 troops near Iraq border

By DAVID ESPO
Associated Press

The United States launched the opening salvo Wednesday night of a war to topple Saddam Hussein, firing cruise missiles and precision-guided bombs into Baghdad. U.S. officials said the Iraqi leader himself was among the targets.

"This will not be a campaign of half-measures and we will accept no outcome but victory," President Bush said in an Oval Office address shortly after explosions ricocheted through the pre-dawn light of the Iraqi capital.

Anti-aircraft tracer fire arced across the Baghdad sky as the American munitions bore in on their targets. A ball of fire shot skyward after one explosion.

Saddam appeared on state-run television a few hours after the attack. He said the United States had committed a "shameful crime" by attacking Iraq, and urged his country to "draw your sword" against the enemy. He appeared unhurt, and wore a military uniform.

The missiles struck less than two hours after the expiration of Bush's deadline for Saddam to surrender power or face war.

Bush described the targets as being of "military importance," and one White House official said the attack was the result of fresh intelligence that prompted an earlier-than-planned opening strike.

Two officials knowledgeable about the operation said the Iraqi dictator was among the "leadership targets" that the strikes were aimed at.

It was clear from Bush's words — he called it the opening stages of a "broad and concerted campaign" — that the war to topple the Iraqi dictator and eliminate his weapons of mass destruction had begun.

SEE ATTACK 10A

Associated Press

U.S. Marines with the 15th Marine Expeditionary Unit take position Wednesday in the Kuwait desert, near the Iraqi border.

Inside

STATE TO SCHOOLS: BE ON GUARD
Local school districts increase surveillance efforts.
Page 2A

OPENING WITH LESS OF A BANG
A surprising first attack from U.S.-led forces.
Page 3A

TAKING THE FIGHT TO THE STREETS
Urban warfare would prolong the fight.
Page 5A

THE MAKING OF A MENACE
Saddam's rise to power.
Page 6A

N.Y. BULKS UP BORDER SECURITY
Pataki sends troopers to Canadian border.
Page 9A

INDEX
5 sections 64 pages

Classified	6C	Movies	2C
Horoscope	5C	Obituaries	4-5B
Money	8D	Opinion	12-13A

0 40901 00701 2

Tier still conflicted even as military action begins

From staff reports

Southern Tier residents greeted the war with a mixture of determination and regret Wednesday night.

And some spent the evening preparing to take up posts in support of the military action, after they were called to duty mere hours before the bombing began.

"My main thought is that we get in, do what we have to do and get our military people out of there," Binghamton resident Connie Legos said.

Her son Nicholas, 21, is a Marine lance corporal. The last she knew, he was stationed in a tent city 45 miles north of Kuwait City.

Connie Legos said her son's unit has been trained to handle itself during war.

"They know each other inside and out," she said. "They're ready."

While the Rev. Timothy Taugher anticipated President Bush's address announcing military action, he said he remained saddened by the news.

"As Pope John Paul II said, 'War is always a defeat for humanity,'" said Taugher, director of social action ministry for the Diocese of Syracuse.

He said a pre-emptive attack on Iraq may lead to "bad consequences" for the United States and the world.

"The war can have consequences we don't know," he said.

But Binghamton University senior Brian Smollett sees a troubling certainty as the country goes to war.

"I think that this is a very sad day because whatever the result may be, it will certainly result in the countless loss of lives, both American and Iraqi," he said.

"I think there's such a thing as a just war, but it's vital not to go at this alone and that's what we are doing," Smollett added.

Still, BU students' sentiments about the conflict are divided.

"I support the war," sophomore Beth Orrico said.

She said Saddam Hussein has been making weapons of mass destruction and needs to be stopped.

"We could wait and let him attack us first or go at him now, which is the right thing to do," Orrico said.

And while they won't be headed overseas, 150 local National Guard members will be supporting that effort as they take up stations throughout the state.

Members of Company B of the 204th Engineering Battalion,

SEE REACTION 10A

March 20, 2003: The second war with Iraq begins. *Courtesy David Silvanic*

Press & Sun-Bulletin

MONDAY
DECEMBER 15, 2003
pressconnects.com
BINGHAMTON, N.Y.
50 CENTS
FINAL EDITION

WAYNE HANSEN / Press & Sun-Bulletin

"My toes are cold," says Andre Lassiter, 11, left, as he and James Levene, 11, walk along Schiller Street in Binghamton in search of sidewalks to shovel Sunday.

Nor'easter deals region a snowy hand

Total accumulation may exceed a foot

By RION A. SCOTT
Press & Sun-Bulletin

A week before winter's arrival, the season sent a message to Southern Tier residents in the form of a nor'easter that had dumped 9½ inches of snow at Binghamton Regional Airport/Edwin A. Link Field by Sunday night.

The airport is where the National Weather Service measures for its official records. Meterologists said snowfall totals would vary widely around the region.

The storm delivered a warning from winter that it would be arriving soon and promised more snow today and later this week.

The falling snow left canceled events in its wake and made driving throughout the Southern Tier difficult.

The weather service predicts that Sunday's steady snows will taper off to snow showers early this morning. All in all, the weather service expects 10 to 15 inches to blanket the Southern Tier over two days.

"We're looking for over a foot of snow in parts of the Binghamton area," said Mitch Gilt, a weather service meteorologist.

The weather service issued steady winter storm warnings for the area, cautioning residents about slippery snow-covered roads. Local police reported fender-benders throughout the area.

Tuesday's partly cloudy skies are expected to give way to rain and snow Tuesday night through Wednesday. Solid snow is expected to resume Thursday.

The snow also sent residents scrambling to reschedule their plans as events large and small were shut down because of the snow. A women's basketball game at Binghamton University was canceled Sunday.

SEE STORM 12A

INSIDE
Scenes from a day of winter weather in the Southern Tier.
LOCAL & STATE 6B

ON THE NET
For the latest on the nor'easter and other weather information, go to **pressconnects.com/weather**

SADDAM 'CAUGHT LIKE A RAT'

'GOT HIM'

- Former dictator found hiding in hole near hometown
- Low-level aides helped U.S. troops discover hideout

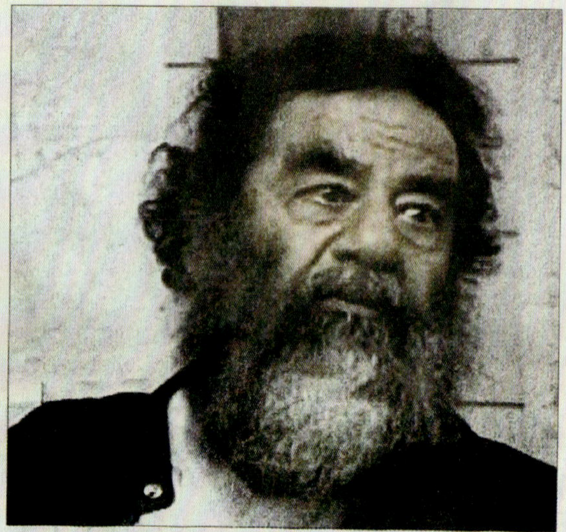

Associated Press

A disheveled Saddam Hussein is seen in Baghdad after being captured Sunday in a cramped "spider hole" by U.S. troops.

By BILL NICHOLS, TOM SQUITIERI and DAVE MONIZ
Gannett News Service

The end for the dictator who fought two wars with the United States and bedeviled three presidents began with interrogations of low-level aides and family members — cousins, drivers, bodyguards, secretaries and other insiders who might know his whereabouts.

Months of questioning of high-level Iraqi officials had produced few useful leads. So CIA and military interrogators shifted gears and began asking for names of relative nobodies — the trusted junior aides and functionaries who might have better information about Saddam Hussein's hiding place.

Then, on Saturday, a former Saddam bodyguard finally gave interrogators what they were after: the location of a farm outside Tikrit where he said Saddam might be hiding.

'Now the former dictator of Iraq will face the justice he denied to millions.'
PRESIDENT BUSH

The end for Saddam came no more than eight hours later, in a filthy 6-foot dirt hole near a farmhouse outside Saddam's hometown of Tikrit.

Saddam was captured by about 600 4th Infantry Division soldiers and special operations forces at 8:26 p.m. Iraqi time Saturday in a specially constructed "spider hole" designed with an air vent to allow long periods of hiding. A "spider hole" is a very tight camouflaged hiding place. The name comes from World War II when the Japanese used the holes to launch ambushes. U.S. officials said Saddam might have had 20 to 30 such holes and moved around every three to four hours.

U.S. military and political officials were jubilant and relieved.

"Ladies and gentlemen, we got him," U.S. administrator L. Paul Bremer told a news conference. "The tyrant is a prisoner."

"He was just caught like a rat," Maj. Gen. Raymond Odierno said in Tikrit. "When you're in the bottom of a hole, you can't fight back. ... Many will rest much better tonight knowing Iraq is moving forward."

Here's how it happened:

■ The tip: Military officials said they were surprised only by the timing of the capture. Tips about Saddam's whereabouts had increased dramatically in recent weeks, and many top commanders had become newly confident that he would be caught.

SEE CAPTURE 5A

INSIDE

Iraqis celebrate in Baghdad. STORY 4A

For some Tier families, joy tinged with reality

Soldiers' kin know danger isn't over

By GEORGE BASLER
Press & Sun-Bulletin

At 8 a.m. Sunday, Diane Croop answered a telephone call from her son. A few minutes later, she was close to tears — tears of joy.

Her son, Pfc. Michael Bidwell, was calling from northern Iraq, where he is stationed with the U.S. Army, to tell her of the capture of Saddam Hussein.

"He just said, 'we definitely got him.' I was ecstatic," said Croop, who lives in the Town of Nanticoke. Then the emotion took over. She almost cried.

She believes capturing Saddam is important and hopes it will make the Iraqi people feel more secure.

She also hopes it will reduce attacks against U.S. troops. But she's realistic. She doesn't think the attacks will end because other insurgents are out there, she said.

Croop's reaction mirrored that of other family members of American servicemen and women who were stationed, or are stationed, in Iraq and Afghanistan.

In interviews Sunday, they expressed excitement over Saddam's capture, pride in the troops

SEE FAMILIES 5A

FOR A SUBSCRIPTION OR CUSTOMER SERVICE CALL 231-PRESS

0 40901 00701 2

WEATHER
28°/22°
WINDY WITH SNOW SHOWERS. TEMPS SHOULD WARM UP BY TUESDAY. MORE SNOW SHOWERS THIS WEEK.
DETAILS 2B

NFL Week 15

Martin powers Jets to victory

Curtis Martin, left, rushes for 174 yards in the snow to lead the New York Jets over the lowly Pittsburgh Steelers. Martin becomes the second NFL player to run for 1,000 yards in nine straight seasons to start a career.
NFL COVERAGE, PAGES 1D, 4-5D

Jets 6
Steelers 0

Titans 28
Bills 26

Retro toys for the holidays

Toys from the 1980s such as Strawberry Shortcake dolls, He-Man action figures and the Care Bears, left, are filling toy aisles and toy boxes.
LIFESTYLE 1C

INDEX

December 15, 2003: Saddam's capture doesn't stop worry. *Courtesy David Silvanic*

Dear U.S. soldier,
This is Inna
I live in New
I watch

Students at Woodrow Wilson Elementary School write letters, like this one, to soldiers in Iraq, March 2003. *Press & Sun-Bulletin archives*

John Vanco of Binghamton displays a photograph of his son, Spc. 4 Patrick Allen, on his helmet as he took part in a demonstration in support of United States troops, in front of the Federal Building on Henry Street in Binghamton, March 2003. Vanco is a veteran of Vietnam, while Allen is with the U.S. Army's 101st Airborne Division in Iraq. *Press & Sun-Bulletin archives*